Enabling Real–Time Mobile Cloud Computing through Emerging Technologies

Tolga Soyata
University of Rochester, USA

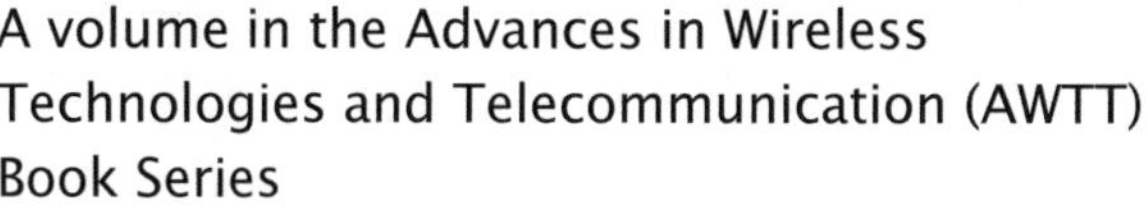
A volume in the Advances in Wireless Technologies and Telecommunication (AWTT) Book Series

Managing Director: Lindsay Johnston
Managing Editor: Austin DeMarco
Director of Intellectual Property & Contracts: Jan Travers
Acquisitions Editor: Kayla Wolfe
Production Editor: Christina Henning
Development Editor: Brandon Carbaugh
Cover Design: Jason Mull

Published in the United States of America by
Information Science Reference (an imprint of IGI Global)
701 E. Chocolate Avenue
Hershey PA, USA 17033
Tel: 717-533-8845
Fax: 717-533-8661
E-mail: cust@igi-global.com
Web site: http://www.igi-global.com

Library of Congress Cataloging-in-Publication Data

Enabling real-time mobile cloud computing through emerging technologies / Tolga Soyata, editor.
pages cm
Includes bibliographical references and index.
ISBN 978-1-4666-8662-5 (hc) -- ISBN 978-1-4666-8663-2 (eISBN) 1. Cloud computing. 2. Mobile computing. I. Soyata, Tolga, 1967-
QA76.585.E55 2015
004.67'82--dc23

2015015533

This book is published in the IGI Global book series Advances in Wireless Technologies and Telecommunication (AWTT) (ISSN: 2327-3305; eISSN: 2327-3313)

British Cataloguing in Publication Data
A Cataloguing in Publication record for this book is available from the British Library.

All work contributed to this book is new, previously-unpublished material. The views expressed in this book are those of the authors, but not necessarily of the publisher.

For electronic access to this publication, please contact: eresources@igi-global.com.

Advances in Wireless Technologies and Telecommunication (AWTT) Book Series

Xiaoge Xu
The University of Nottingham Ningbo China

ISSN: 2327-3305
EISSN: 2327-3313

Mission

The wireless computing industry is constantly evolving, redesigning the ways in which individuals share information. Wireless technology and telecommunication remain one of the most important technologies in business organizations. The utilization of these technologies has enhanced business efficiency by enabling dynamic resources in all aspects of society.

The **Advances in Wireless Technologies and Telecommunication Book Series** aims to provide researchers and academic communities with quality research on the concepts and developments in the wireless technology fields. Developers, engineers, students, research strategists, and IT managers will find this series useful to gain insight into next generation wireless technologies and telecommunication.

Coverage

- Wireless Technologies
- Radio Communication
- Mobile Technology
- Telecommunications
- Wireless Sensor Networks
- Virtual Network Operations
- Global Telecommunications
- Mobile Web Services
- Mobile Communications
- Grid Communications

IGI Global is currently accepting manuscripts for publication within this series. To submit a proposal for a volume in this series, please contact our Acquisition Editors at Acquisitions@igi-global.com or visit: http://www.igi-global.com/publish/.

The Advances in Wireless Technologies and Telecommunication (AWTT) Book Series (ISSN 2327-3305) is published by IGI Global, 701 E. Chocolate Avenue, Hershey, PA 17033-1240, USA, www.igi-global.com. This series is composed of titles available for purchase individually; each title is edited to be contextually exclusive from any other title within the series. For pricing and ordering information please visit http://www.igi-global.com/book-series/advances-wireless-technologies-telecommunication-awtt/73684. Postmaster: Send all address changes to above address.

Titles in this Series

For a list of additional titles in this series, please visit: www.igi-global.com

Technological Breakthroughs in Modern Wireless Sensor Applications
Hamid Sharif (University of Nebraska – Lincoln, USA) and Yousef S. Kavian (Shahid Chamran University of Ahvaz, Iran)
Information Science Reference • copyright 2015 • 417pp • H/C (ISBN: 9781466682511) • US $200.00 (our price)

Handbook of Research on Software-Defined and Cognitive Radio Technologies for Dynamic Spectrum Management
Naima Kaabouch (University of North Dakota, USA) and Wen-Chen Hu (University of North Dakota, USA)
Information Science Reference • copyright 2015 • 927pp • H/C (ISBN: 9781466665712) • US $505.00 (our price)

Interdisciplinary Mobile Media and Communications Social, Political, and Economic Implications
Xiaoge Xu (The University of Nottingham Ningbo China, China)
Information Science Reference • copyright 2014 • 409pp • H/C (ISBN: 9781466661660) • US $205.00 (our price)

Cognitive Radio Sensor Networks Applications, Architectures, and Challenges
Mubashir Husain Rehmani (Department of Electrical Engineering, COMSATS Institute of Information Technology, Pakistan) and Yasir Faheem (Department of Computer Science, COMSATS Institute of Information Technology, Pakistan)
Information Science Reference • copyright 2014 • 313pp • H/C (ISBN: 9781466662124) • US $235.00 (our price)

Game Theory Applications in Network Design
Sungwook Kim (Sogang University, South Korea)
Information Science Reference • copyright 2014 • 500pp • H/C (ISBN: 9781466660502) • US $225.00 (our price)

Convergence of Broadband, Broadcast, and Cellular Network Technologies
Ramona Trestian (Middlesex University, UK) and Gabriel-Miro Muntean (Dublin City University, Ireland)
Information Science Reference • copyright 2014 • 333pp • H/C (ISBN: 9781466659780) • US $235.00 (our price)

Handbook of Research on Progressive Trends in Wireless Communications and Networking
M.A. Matin (Institut Teknologi Brunei, Brunei Darussalam)
Information Science Reference • copyright 2014 • 592pp • H/C (ISBN: 9781466651708) • US $380.00 (our price)

Broadband Wireless Access Networks for 4G Theory, Application, and Experimentation
Raul Aquino Santos (University of Colima, Mexico) Victor Rangel Licea (National Autonomous University of Mexico, Mexico) and Arthur Edwards-Block (University of Colima, Mexico)
Information Science Reference • copyright 2014 • 452pp • H/C (ISBN: 9781466648883) • US $235.00 (our price)

www.igi-global.com

701 E. Chocolate Ave., Hershey, PA 17033
Order online at www.igi-global.com or call 717-533-8845 x100
To place a standing order for titles released in this series, contact: cust@igi-global.com
Mon-Fri 8:00 am - 5:00 pm (est) or fax 24 hours a day 717-533-8661

Editorial Advisory Board

Table of Contents

Preface xiv

Acknowledgment xx

Chapter 1
Conceptualizing a Real-Time Remote Cardiac Health Monitoring System 1
Alex Page, University of Rochester, USA
Moeen Hassanalieragh, University of Rochester, USA
Tolga Soyata, University of Rochester, USA
Mehmet K. Aktas, University of Rochester, USA
Burak Kantarci, Clarkson University, USA
Silvana Andreescu, Clarkson University, USA

Chapter 2
Energy Efficient Real-Time Distributed Communication Architectures for Military Tactical Communication Systems 35
Bora Karaoglu, The Samraksh Company, USA
Tolga Numanoglu, ASELSAN Inc., Turkey
Bulent Tavli, TOBB University of Economics and Technology, Turkey
Wendi Heinzelman, University of Rochester, USA

Chapter 3
Sensing as a Service in Cloud-Centric Internet of Things Architecture 83
Burak Kantarci, Clarkson University, USA
Hussein T. Mouftah, University of Ottawa, Canada

Chapter 4
Secure Health Monitoring in the Cloud Using Homomorphic Encryption: A Branching-Program Formulation 116
Scott Ames, University of Rochester, USA
Muthuramakrishnan Venkitasubramaniam, University of Rochester, USA
Alex Page, University of Rochester, USA
Ovunc Kocabas, University of Rochester, USA
Tolga Soyata, University of Rochester, USA

Chapter 5
Volunteer Computing on Mobile Devices: State of the Art and Future Research Directions 153
Cristiano Tapparello, University of Rochester, USA
Colin Funai, University of Rochester, USA
Shurouq Hijazi, University of Rochester, USA
Abner Aquino, University of Rochester, USA
Bora Karaoglu, The Samraksh Company, USA
He Ba, University of Rochester, USA
Jiye Shi, UCB Pharma, UK
Wendi Heinzelman, University of Rochester, USA

Chapter 6
Selling FLOPs: Telecom Service Providers Can Rent a Cloudlet via Acceleration as a Service (AXaaS) 182
Nathaniel Powers, University of Rochester, USA
Tolga Soyata, University of Rochester, USA

Chapter 7
Towards Privacy-Preserving Medical Cloud Computing Using Homomorphic Encryption 213
Ovunc Kocabas, University of Rochester, USA
Tolga Soyata, University of Rochester, USA

Chapter 8
Hardware and Software Aspects of VM-Based Mobile-Cloud Offloading 247
Yang Song, University of Rochester, USA
Haoliang Wang, George Mason University, USA
Tolga Soyata, University of Rochester, USA

Chapter 9
A Tutorial on Network Latency and Its Measurements 272
Minseok Kwon, Rochester Institute of Technology, USA

Chapter 10
Operational Cost of Running Real-Time Mobile Cloud Applications 294
Ovunc Kocabas, University of Rochester, USA
Regina Gyampoh-Vidogah, Independent Researcher, UK
Tolga Soyata, University of Rochester, USA

Chapter 11
Theoretical Foundation and GPU Implementation of Face Recognition 322
William Dixon, University of Rochester, USA
Nathaniel Powers, University of Rochester, USA
Yang Song, University of Rochester, USA
Tolga Soyata, University of Rochester, USA

Chapter 12
Reach to Mobile Platforms and Availability: A Planning Tutorial 342
Rex A Buddenberg, Naval Postgraduate School, USA

Compilation of References 358

About the Contributors 390

Index 396

Detailed Table of Contents

Preface...xiv

Acknowledgment...xx

Chapter 1
Conceptualizing a Real-Time Remote Cardiac Health Monitoring System 1
Alex Page, University of Rochester, USA
Moeen Hassanalieragh, University of Rochester, USA
Tolga Soyata, University of Rochester, USA
Mehmet K. Aktas, University of Rochester, USA
Burak Kantarci, Clarkson University, USA
Silvana Andreescu, Clarkson University, USA

In today's technology, even leading medical institutions diagnose their cardiac patients through ECG recordings obtained at healthcare organizations (HCO), which are costly to obtain and may miss significant clinically-relevant information. Existing long-term patient monitoring systems (e.g., Holter monitors) provide limited information about the evolution of deadly cardiac conditions and lack interactivity in case there is a sudden degradation in the patient's health condition. A standardized and scalable system does not currently exist to monitor an expanding set of patient vitals that a doctor can prescribe to monitor. The design of such a system will translate to significant healthcare savings as well as drastic improvements in diagnostic accuracy. In this chapter, we will propose a concept system for real-time remote cardiac health monitoring, based on available and emerging technologies today. We will analyze the details of such a system from acquisition to visualization of medical data.

Chapter 2
Energy Efficient Real-Time Distributed Communication Architectures for Military Tactical Communication Systems 35
Bora Karaoglu, The Samraksh Company, USA
Tolga Numanoglu, ASELSAN Inc., Turkey
Bulent Tavli, TOBB University of Economics and Technology, Turkey
Wendi Heinzelman, University of Rochester, USA

For military communication systems, it is important to achieve robust and energy efficient real-time communication among a group of mobile users without the support of a pre-existing infrastructure. Furthermore, these communication systems must support multiple communication modes, such as unicast, multicast, and network-wide broadcast, to serve the varied needs in military communication systems. One use for these military communication systems is in support of real-time mobile cloud computing, where the response time is of utmost importance; therefore, satisfying real-time communication requirements is crucial. In this chapter, we present a brief overview of military tactical communications and networking (MTCAN). As an important example of MTCAN, we present the evolution of the TRACE family of protocols, describing the design of the TRACE protocols according to the tactical communications and networking requirements. We conclude the chapter by identifying how the TRACE protocols can enable mobile cloud computing within military communication systems.

Chapter 3
Sensing as a Service in Cloud-Centric Internet of Things Architecture 83
Burak Kantarci, Clarkson University, USA
Hussein T. Mouftah, University of Ottawa, Canada

Sensing-as-a-Service (S2aaS) is a cloud-inspired service model which enables access to the Internet of Things (IoT) architecture. The IoT denotes virtually interconnected objects that are uniquely identifiable, and are capable of sensing, computing and communicating. Built-in sensors in mobile devices can leverage the performance of IoT applications in terms of energy and communication overhead savings by sending their data to the cloud servers. Sensed data from mobile devices can be accessed by IoT applications on a pay-as-you-go fashion. Efficient sensing service provider search techniques are emerging components of this architecture, and they should be accompanied with effective sensing provider recruitment algorithms. Furthermore, reliability and trustworthiness of participatory sensed data appears as a big challenge. This chapter provides an overview of the state of the art in S2aaS systems, and reports recent proposals to address the most crucial challenges. Furthermore, the chapter points out the open issues and future directions for the researchers in this field.

Chapter 4
Secure Health Monitoring in the Cloud Using Homomorphic Encryption: A Branching-Program Formulation 116
Scott Ames, University of Rochester, USA
Muthuramakrishnan Venkitasubramaniam, University of Rochester, USA
Alex Page, University of Rochester, USA
Ovunc Kocabas, University of Rochester, USA
Tolga Soyata, University of Rochester, USA

Extending cloud computing to medical software, where the hospitals rent the software from the provider sounds like a natural evolution for cloud computing. One problem with cloud computing, though, is ensuring the medical data privacy in applications such as long term health monitoring. Previously proposed solutions based on Fully Homomorphic Encryption (FHE) completely eliminate privacy concerns, but are extremely slow to be practical. Our key proposition in this paper is a new approach to applying FHE into the data that is stored in the cloud. Instead of using the existing circuit-based programming models, we propose a solution based on Branching Programs. While this restricts the type of data elements that FHE can be applied to, it achieves dramatic speed-up as compared to traditional circuit-based methods. Our claims are proven with simulations applied to real ECG data.

Chapter 5
Volunteer Computing on Mobile Devices: State of the Art and Future Research Directions 153
Cristiano Tapparello, University of Rochester, USA
Colin Funai, University of Rochester, USA
Shurouq Hijazi, University of Rochester, USA
Abner Aquino, University of Rochester, USA
Bora Karaoglu, The Samraksh Company, USA
He Ba, University of Rochester, USA
Jiye Shi, UCB Pharma, UK
Wendi Heinzelman, University of Rochester, USA

Different forms of parallel computing have been proposed to address the high computational requirements of many applications. Building on advances in parallel computing, volunteer computing has been shown to be an efficient way to exploit the computational resources of under utilized devices that are available around the world. The idea of including mobile devices, such as smartphones and tablets, in existing volunteer computing systems has recently been investigated. In this chapter, we present the current state of the art in the mobile volunteer computing research field, where personal mobile devices are the elements that perform the computation. Starting from the motivations and challenges behind the adoption of personal mobile devices as computational resources, we then provide a literature review of the different architectures that have been proposed to support parallel computing on mobile devices. Finally, we present some open issues that need to be investigated in order to extend user participation and improve the overall system performance for mobile volunteer computing.

Chapter 6
Selling FLOPs: Telecom Service Providers Can Rent a Cloudlet via Acceleration as a Service (AXaaS) 182
Nathaniel Powers, University of Rochester, USA
Tolga Soyata, University of Rochester, USA

To meet the user demand for an ever-increasing mobile-cloud computing performance for resource-intensive mobile applications, we propose a new service architecture called Acceleration as a Service (AXaaS). We formulate AXaaS based on the observation that most resource-intensive applications, such as real-time face-recognition and augmented reality, have similar resource-demand characteristics: a vast majority of the program execution time is spent on a limited set of library calls, such as Generalized Matrix-Multiply operations (GEMM), or FFT. Our AXaaS model suggests accelerating only these operations by the Telecom Service Providers (TSP). We envision the TSP offering this service through a monthly computational service charge, much like their existing monthly bandwidth charge. We demonstrate the technological and business feasibility of AXaaS on a proof-of-concept real-time face recognition application. We elaborate on the consumer, developer, and the TSP view of this model. Our results confirm AXaaS as a novel and viable business model.

Chapter 7
Towards Privacy-Preserving Medical Cloud Computing Using Homomorphic Encryption 213
Ovunc Kocabas, University of Rochester, USA
Tolga Soyata, University of Rochester, USA

Personal health monitoring tools, such as commercially available wireless ECG patches, can significantly reduce healthcare costs by allowing patient monitoring outside the healthcare organizations. These tools transmit the acquired medical data into the cloud, which could provide an invaluable diagnosis tool for healthcare professionals. Despite the potential of such systems to revolutionize the medical field, the adoption of medical cloud computing in general has been slow due to the strict privacy regulations on patient health information. We present a novel medical cloud computing approach that eliminates privacy concerns associated with the cloud provider. Our approach capitalizes on Fully Homomorphic Encryption (FHE), which enables computations on private health information without actually observing the underlying data. For a feasibility study, we present a working implementation of a long-term cardiac health monitoring application using a well-established open source FHE library.

Chapter 8
Hardware and Software Aspects of VM-Based Mobile-Cloud Offloading 247
Yang Song, University of Rochester, USA
Haoliang Wang, George Mason University, USA
Tolga Soyata, University of Rochester, USA

To allow mobile devices to support resource intensive applications beyond their capabilities, mobile-cloud offloading is introduced to extend the resources of mobile devices by leveraging cloud resources. In this chapter, we will survey the state-of-the-art in VM-based mobile-cloud offloading techniques including their software and architectural aspects in detail. For the software aspects, we will provide the current improvements to different layers of various virtualization systems, particularly focusing on mobile-cloud offloading. Approaches at different offloading granularities will be reviewed and their advantages and disadvantages will be discussed. For the architectural support aspects of the virtualization, three platforms including Intel x86, ARM and NVidia GPUs will be reviewed in terms of their special architectural designs to accommodate virtualization and VM-based offloading.

Chapter 9
A Tutorial on Network Latency and Its Measurements 272
Minseok Kwon, Rochester Institute of Technology, USA

Internet latency is crucial in providing reliable and efficient networked services when servers are placed in geographically diverse locations. The trend of mobile, cloud, and distributed computing accelerates the importance of accurate latency measurement due to its nature of rapidly changing locations and interactivity. Accurately measuring latency, however, is not easy due to lack of testing resources, the sheer volume of collected data points, the tedious and repetitive aspect of measurement practice, clock synchronization, and network dynamics. This chapter discusses the techniques that use PlanetLab to measure latency in the Internet, its underlying infrastructure, representative latency results obtained from experiments, and how to use these measure latencies. The chapter covers 1) details of using PlanetLab, 2) the Internet infrastructure that causes the discrepancy between local and global latencies, and 3) measured latency results from our own experiments and analysis on the distributions, averages, and their implications.

Chapter 10
Operational Cost of Running Real-Time Mobile Cloud Applications 294
Ovunc Kocabas, University of Rochester, USA
Regina Gyampoh-Vidogah, Independent Researcher, UK
Tolga Soyata, University of Rochester, USA

This chapter describes the concepts and cost models used for determining the cost of providing cloud services to mobile applications using different pricing models. Two recently implemented mobile-cloud applications are studied in terms of both the cost of providing such services by the cloud operator, and the cost of operating them by the cloud user. Computing resource requirements of both applications are identified and worksheets are presented to demonstrate how businesses can estimate the operational cost of implementing such real-time mobile cloud applications at a large scale, as well as how much cloud operators can profit from providing resources for these applications. In addition, the nature of available service level agreements (SLA) and the importance of quality of service (QoS) specifications within these SLAs are emphasized and explained for mobile cloud application deployment.

Chapter 11
Theoretical Foundation and GPU Implementation of Face Recognition 322
William Dixon, University of Rochester, USA
Nathaniel Powers, University of Rochester, USA
Yang Song, University of Rochester, USA
Tolga Soyata, University of Rochester, USA

Enabling a machine to detect and recognize faces requires significant computational power. This particular system of face recognition makes use of OpenCV (Computer Vision) libraries while leveraging Graphics Processing Units (GPUs) to accelerate the process towards real-time. The processing and recognition algorithms are best sorted into three distinct steps: detection, projection, and search. Each of these steps has unique computational characteristics and requirements driving performance. In particular, the detection and projection processes can be accelerated significantly with GPU usage due to the data types and arithmetic types associated with the algorithms, such as matrix manipulation. This chapter provides a survey of the three main processes and how they contribute to the overarching recognition process.

Chapter 12
Reach to Mobile Platforms and Availability: A Planning Tutorial 342
Rex A Buddenberg, Naval Postgraduate School, USA

This chapter is practical system planning tutorial for internetworks that include radio-WANs. Author is retired USCG officer with both operational and program planning experience. In second career, author taught 'plowshares into swords internetworking' at the graduate level. The coaching herein reflects operational, planning, and academic experiences. Considering mobile communications requires adjusting some assumptions and working knowledge from a wholly wired internetwork. The advent of radio – the necessary means to mobile – entails changes in topology, capacity and nature of the media (shared). Further, the extension of the internetwork to mobile usually means rather overt embracing of mission critical applications.

Compilation of References 358

About the Contributors 390

Index 396

Preface

This book contains a collection of tutorial and research articles related to real-time Mobile-Cloud Computing, which is the state-of-the-art computational infrastructure for running advanced mobile applications. When the *real-time* constraint is placed on mobile applications, every possible resource surrounding these devices is stretched to its limits: Even to merely offload the application to the cloud, mobile devices have to meet certain computational, storage, and memory requirements. The communication network must be fast enough to handle reasonable data rates during this offloading process. Additionally, even the definition of the term *offloading* is a topic of research. This book is meant for graduate-level students who are pursuing research directions in advanced mobile-cloud computing. Faculty members who are interested in this research field will also benefit significantly from this book. To understand the motivation behind this book in a lot more detail, let's look at the evolution of mobile cloud computing.

Using an analog mobile phone two decades ago that weighed more than a kilogram (probably half of which was the battery), I welcomed every generation's improvement on mobile phones that made them lighter. It also was equally important that I could use the phone for two, three, or four hours without having to charge it. If a mobile phone's battery lasts for two hours, it hardly qualifies to be called *mobile*, whereas, being able to use it for a full day without charging it makes it a useful mobile device that can be enjoyed throughout one's entire day. An average user had his/her priorities in weight and battery life two decades ago, since these two were the limiting features within that time frame.

All of this started changing a decade ago when things started shifting from these big bulky analog phones to digital ones that you could carry inside your pocket throughout the day. In my mother language Turkish, a cell phone is still called a *pocket phone*, having its origins in this era. I wouldn't be surprised if similar terms are associated with cell phones in other languages. Digital phones owed their success to more sophisticated digital data encoding techniques as well as the progress of VLSI technology that afforded IC (chip) designers to cram more transistors into these chips. More transistors meant more processing, allowing increasingly more sophisticated digital encoding, which in turn yielded higher communication rates. Once you could put a sufficient number of transistors into a device, the device could do much more than just phone calls. I specifically remember Blackberry introducing a device that is capable of receiving and sending emails a decade ago. Right after this, my wife and I purchased a Palm Treo device that could also have *Calendar* and *Contacts*. This is the time frame when *Personal Digital Assistants* (PDAs) were separate handheld devices, not associated with *phones*. I remember a company selling a GPS attachment for our Palm Treo units. I bought one, and was ready to use it despite its messy connection cables and bulkiness. I could just never get it to work stably. I guess this technology was *too* soon. I returned it. This shows how receptive I was - as an average user - to new functionality that could be built-into my phone and could improve my life.

Despite such unsuccessful attempts as the external GPS functionality I just mentioned, the introduction of the PDAs and added functionality inside the phones sparked an avalanche of interest within tech enthusiasts and business folks that wanted to use these devices for business functions: as a calculator, email device, storing contacts, or whatever else you could introduce at a reasonable price. To be able to perform these functions, Palm and Blackberry had to incorporate a *Radio Processor* (or B*aseband Processor*) and an *Application Processor* into these devices. The Radio Processor was responsible for the *phone call* functionality, implementing the previously mentioned sophisticated data encoding and communication. Application Processor, on the other hand, was responsible for turning the phone into a computer (almost). It was only a matter of time when the Application Processor became sophisticated enough to turn this device into a full-blown computer, and was eventually accompanied with his sister: *Media Processor*, which was responsible for heavy-duty signal or image processing. For this to materialize, a lot of simultaneous progress was needed in different fields: VLSI technology had to advance to a point where hundreds of millions of transistors could be built into the Application and Media Processor chips, and, major advances in Computer Architecture were needed to make sure that, this device could operate at a very low (1W or 2W) power budget, while delivering the computation that these applications needed. Battery technology didn't advance as fast as the previous two, but a deeper understanding of the Lithium Ion rechargeable batteries a allowed more intelligent usage of them, which in turn increased battery life.

The term *smart phone* originates in this era, when mobile devices could perform so many different functions that, they even started communicating with their user to improve Human-Computer Interaction (e.g., the Siri on the iPhone and many similar implementations in other brands).We are now in an era where these smart phone devices are an indispensible part of human life, connecting us to the internet and social networks. The breakneck speed in application development put almost every imaginable application in the market which can be inexpensively purchased and run on smart phones and the next natural question is: what do we go from here ? The previous half decade has seen an explosion of research interest in answering this question. With very stable and fast connections to the internet backbone, smart phones' capabilities were no longer limited to their own hardware. One parallel development effort aimed to take advantage of an emerging concept: *the cloud.*

When the internet connection speeds of smart phones reached a threshold and became increasingly more affordable through the introduction of faster data connection standards such as 3G, 4G, and LTE, it became possible to augment the capabilities of smart phones with the vast resources residing in large scale datacenters (the cloud). This synergistic coupling, *Mobile-cloud computing*, marked a new era in the development for smart phone applications. Using Mobile-Cloud Computing allowed using less capable smart phones to perform highly sophisticated functions, partly making the capabilities of the smart phone itself less relevant. Additionally, offloading parts (or all) of a mobile application to the cloud could save precious battery life. More excitingly, Mobile-Cloud Computing could allow smart phones to run applications that they could never run themselves in the foreseeable future, due to the limitation of their resident hardware.

Mobile Cloud Computing is in its infancy, much like the smart phone itself was a decade ago. Much research effort will be devoted to making it a usable computational and resource sharing model in the following decade. There will be missteps and major success stories. One thing that is for sure: its continuous progress will never stop. Using Mobile-Cloud Computing, combined with the future communication standards such as LTE Advanced and 5G that aim much higher data rates than what is available today, it will be possible to run applications that will never be possible to run on mobile devices alone. Such applications are extremely resource intensive (computation, memory, and storage-wise) and may require access to real-time data that is only resident in the cloud. One such family of applications, ones that utilize Real-time Mobile Cloud Computing, is the focus of this book. A good representative example of this application family is *Real-time Mobile-Cloud Face Recognition*, which initially motivated the authoring of this book. The family of resource-hungry mobile applications are not designed to extend mobile applications to the cloud, but rather, they are designed as mobile-cloud applications right from the start, since it is not possible to run them solely on mobile devices.

This book contains a total of 12 tutorial and research chapters which describe new and innovative mobile applications and provide supporting surveys to understand the operating characteristics of these applications. The applications described in this book are resource-hungry in different ways: Some of them require an extensive amount of processing power, RAM (short-term memory) or flash/hard disk storage (long-term memory). Some require access to an enormous amount of data that is updated in real-time. Such a quantity of data (e.g., Peta bytes) is far beyond the capability of any single device to process or handle, including smart phones (*i.e., Big Data*). All of these challenges introduce many research directions to make these exciting applications a reality. Solutions to these challenges span multiple disciplines in Electrical Engineering and Computer Science, and is the primary focus of this book. The chapters of this book are organized as follows:

Chapter 1 describes a concept system for remote health monitoring of cardiac patients outside a healthcare organization. Four separate components of this system are described in detail: The bio-sensor component of the system involves the design of custom advanced sensors that are capable of detecting proteins such as Troponin, Myoglobin and CRP, that are essential for advanced cardiac patient monitoring. The custom circuit interface for these sensors is detailed and the operational characteristics are described. Communication interface of the system uses standardized communication components found in mobile cloud computing (e.g., cloudlet), while an integration to the emerging Internet-of-Things (IoT) infrastructure is also described in terms of the concentrator-cloudlet co-operation. Finally, the authors aim at formulating a new visualization mechanism for cardiac data that can provide summarized information over the duration of the long-term health monitoring. This is aimed at remedying the shortcomings of the short-term, in-hospital ECG recordings that only provide limited information about the evolution of the patients' health condition.

Chapter 2 provides an extensive survey of Military Tactical Communications and Networking (MTCAN). To summarize, MTCAN algorithms and protocols are similar to Mobile Ad Hoc networks (MANETs), however, they are distributed to introduce robustness and scalability and to eliminate single points of failure. Authors provide a survey of the TRACE (Time Reservations using Adaptive Control for Energy efficiency) family of protocols that have been developed at the University of Rochester, through the financial support of Harris Corporation, RF Communications Division, which is a leader in MTCAN. The protocols that are surveyed in the chapter include SH-TRACE (Single-Hop Time Reservation using Adaptive Control for Energy efficiency), MH-TRACE (Multi Hop Time Reservation using Adaptive Control for Energy efficiency), NB-TRACE (Network-wide Broadcasting through Time Reservation using Adaptive Control for Energy efficiency), MC-TRACE (Multi Casting through Time Reservation using Adaptive Control for Energy efficiency), MMC-TRACE (multi-rate multicasting), AR-TRACE (adaptive redundancy), CDCA-TRACE (Cooperative node balancing and dynamic channel allocation with Time Reservation using Adaptive Control for Energy efficiency) and U-TRACE (Unified TRACE). the authors conclude by providing future research directions.

Chapter 3 provides a survey of the technologies, infrastructure components, and research leading to the formation of an emerging cloud-based service: Sensing as a Service (S^2aaS). In this new service offering, any mobile device that is connected to the internet can be a part of the *sensing network*. Wireless Sensor Networks (WSNs), mobile phones, and other emerging Internet-of-Things (IoT) devices can contribute their local data to an application that aggregates this information with the intent to provide a much more comprehensive version of this data (i.e., a globalized or much more expanded version). This data can be used to provide statistics or sensing results to all (or some) of the contributing nodes. Since the only limitation for the mobile devices is a form of connection to the sensing network, and, clearly, the willingness of a node to contribute all of part of the data, the sensing network could be extremely flexible. Finally, the global authority for the application is in the cloud with almost no resource constraints, especially as compared to the contributing small nodes. This could be used to perform resource-intensive analytics on the received data, thereby opening the door to a set of exciting applications and service offerings. However, this form of a sensing network introduces significant challenges such as privacy concerns and reliability of the acquired data. This chapter provides a survey of the techniques to deal with such challenges.

Chapter 4 introduces a remote health monitoring system where a patient's vitals are being monitored in his/her house and the results are being transmitted to the cloud. An algorithm running in the cloud detects potential hazardous health conditions, such as abnormal cardiac function and warns the doctor in real-time. During the execution of this algorithm, the acquired patient medical data is transmitted from the patient's house into the cloud and it is processed in the cloud. The results are transmitted into the doctor's tablet. This chapter primarily focuses on the privacy of the data during the transmission. An emerging encryption technique, called Fully Homomorphic Encryption (FHE), is used to encrypt the data that is being transmitted. However, this type of encryption causes significant expansion of the data and is highly computationally-intensive to process. Traditionally, circuit-based solutions are used in conjunction with FHE by turning each *computation* into a *circuit*. This circuit is implemented using FHE building blocks to yield the final result. A different approach is introduced in this chapter which uses a *Branching Program*. In their approach, each Yes/No decision (such as a patient has a health hazard vs. does not have a health hazard) is formulated as a Branching Program, which has a True/False answer. This Branching Program can be solved using FHE building blocks. While this limits the applicability of FHE to a restricted set of medical computations, authors report a 20x speed-up in the overall execution time for certain useful medical applications.

Chapter 5 introduces a computational infrastructure where multiple smart phones contribute their computational power to an application. This concept, termed *Volunteer Computing,* allows computationally-intensive applications to be run by a set of distributed mobile devices that are owned by volunteers that *opt-in* to the computational network. Authors break down the approaches into major categories that are defined by the volunteering entity: 1) Server-driven mobile-distributed computing approaches surveyed in this chapter are a) prime-number research, b) text search; π value estimation, c) distributed hash-cracking, d) distributed multimedia search, e) dynamic life-cycle assessment of a building, and f) DNA sequence matching. 2) User-driven approaches are a) speech-to-text, b) face detection and collaborative photography, c) collaborative file download, and d) testing of the cloudlet formation algorithm. 3) Mobile Volunteer Computing approaches include a) scientific research projects, b) protein structure predictions and multiple other ones. The authors conclude with a summary and provide pointers to future research directions.

Chapter 6 details a new cloud-based service model called Acceleration as a Service (AXaaS). Authors base the conceptualization of this new aaS model on the acceleration capability of a cloudlet. To speed-up mobile-cloud applications, such as real-time face recognition, it is known that, a cloudlet can be placed locally within the WiFi reach of a mobile device, providing a fast and dedicated link to the cloud. The significant difference between a traditional cloudlet and what is prescribed in this chapter is *where* the cloudlet is placed. Rather than the standard model where a user owns a cloudlet, *renting the cloudlet* is suggested. The best entity for renting the cloudlet is determined to be the Telecom Service Provider (TSP). The TSP can rent a cloudlet through a monthly fee, which eliminates the need for the user to own or upgrade such a device. Since it is very expensive to shuttle data back and forth between mobile devices and the TSP, one important research challenge is to determine which parts of the code require computational speed-up (i.e., *acceleration*). The significant research challenge in such an infrastructure is *what to accelerate* using the TSP. This is analyzed by the authors through code profiling. It is determined that, a very limited library of functions, such as Fast Fourier Transform (FFT) and Basic Linear Algebra Subroutines (BLAS) are sufficient as acceleration points. Merely accelerating these two API functions provides drastic overall application speed-up, thereby creating a TSP service that the users are willing to pay for. A business ROI analysis is also provided from the standpoint of the TSP and the user.

Chapter 7 provides a framework for generalized privacy-preserving medical cloud computing. Running medical applications in the cloud offers a healthcare organization significant cost savings by being able to outsource the storage and computation of medical data to a cloud operator. However, this implies that, the breach of the medical data during cloud computing could result in a violation of Health Information Portability and Accountability Act (HIPAA) and is not acceptable. Authors propose to use Fully Homomorphic Encryption (FHE) to operate on the medical data that is stored in the cloud. While the storage of data can preserve privacy by using traditional encryption algorithms such as Advanced Encryption Standard (AES), no computation can be done on AES-encrypted data. On the other hand, FHE-based encryption allows both storage and computation in a privacy-preserving fashion, since the cloud cannot observe the data that it is computing. However, FHE-based computation and storage are substantially more costly than their AES-counterpart. Authors formulate a mechanism where some non-computationally-expensive medical computations can be performed in the cloud, such as minimum/maximum/average heart rate computations during remote patient monitoring, as well as the detection of certain cardiac health hazards such as Long-QT syndrome (LQTS). A detailed analysis is provided for each step of these computations.

Chapter 8 provides a survey of hardware and software support for Virtual-Machine (VM) based mobile-cloud application offloading. Mobile offloading concepts are briefly surveyed and the areas where VMs can help are determined. Advantages and disadvantages of virtualization are explained in detail. This is followed by a survey of software support including virtualization approaches, hypervisor types, Operating System support, as well as existing VM types. A survey of hardware assisted virtualization is also provided which details the Instruction Set support that is resident in three popular manufacturers' CPUs: Intel, AMD and ARM. Hardware assisted virtualization allows the virtualization of memory, I/O, and the CPU cores. Challenges in virtualization are listed such as the security and overhead of virtualization. A summarized discussion of GPU virtualization is also provided.

Chapter 9 is a practical and theoretical tutorial on network latency measurement. The author provides an extensive set of latency measurements provided by his research team. These measurements are done in a PlanetLab environment which is a network of volunteering academic institutions. A detailed discussion of how to repeat these experiments is also provided through a brief introduction to PlanetLab. Based on the measured data, author draws conclusions about what the distributions of the global latency values are. Latency is an important performance-limiting factor for mobile-cloud applications as it determines the speed at which a mobile device can access the cloud. The intuitions and practical measurements provided in this chapter are, therefore, an important guide to designing real-time mobile-cloud applications.

Chapter 10 focuses on the business aspects of running highly resource-intensive applications in the cloud and the cost of outsourcing such applications into the cloud. A list of the operating costs for the three popular cloud operators (Amazon, Google, and Microsoft Azure) are provided. These operators charge fees based on a) storage, b) computation, and c) network traffic. The analysis provided in this chapter breaks the application costs into these three categories and associates metrics for each one of these parameters. This analysis is not trivial in that, cloud operators provide a vast array of options based on commitment levels (in terms of time duration). Authors suggest the best choices for these options based on the characteristics of two resource-intensive applications: 1) a remote health monitoring application using Fully Homomorphic Encryption to perform privacy-preserving medical cloud computing, and 2) real-time mobile-cloud face recognition. Both of these applications are analyzed in terms of their functional characteristics and their resource demands are determined. These results are converted to a monthly operating cost in the cloud for three different cloud operators.

Chapter 11 provides a technical and practical tutorial for understanding and running face recognition, which is a good representative case for resource-intensive mobile-cloud applications. The theory behind this application is described by breaking the application into three of its distinct execution phases: Face Detection, Projection, and Search. The theory behind these three different phases is detailed and the steps required to run this application on commodity computers using the OpenCV library are provided in a tutorial format. By following the steps that are provided in this chapter, other researchers in resource-intensive mobile-cloud computing can easily run face recognition using freely available open source tools.

Chapter 12 provides a practical view to the expected characteristics of mobile platforms. The author is a retired USG officer who brings a practical view to the importance of these parameters in generalized radio communication and draws conclusions from his practical experience. Availability (Ao) is explained as one of the most important parameters and the details are provided in regard to Ao and its effect on radio communication.

Tolga Soyata
University of Rochester, USA

Acknowledgment

This book project was supported in part by the National Science Foundation grant CNS-1239423 and a gift from Nvidia corporation.

Chapter 1
Conceptualizing a Real-Time Remote Cardiac Health Monitoring System

Alex Page
University of Rochester, USA

Mehmet K. Aktas
University of Rochester, USA

Moeen Hassanalieragh
University of Rochester, USA

Burak Kantarci
Clarkson University, USA

Tolga Soyata
University of Rochester, USA

Silvana Andreescu
Clarkson University, USA

ABSTRACT

In today's technology, even leading medical institutions diagnose their cardiac patients through ECG recordings obtained at healthcare organizations (HCO), which are costly to obtain and may miss significant clinically-relevant information. Existing long-term patient monitoring systems (e.g., Holter monitors) provide limited information about the evolution of deadly cardiac conditions and lack interactivity in case there is a sudden degradation in the patient's health condition. A standardized and scalable system does not currently exist to monitor an expanding set of patient vitals that a doctor can prescribe to monitor. The design of such a system will translate to significant healthcare savings as well as drastic improvements in diagnostic accuracy. In this chapter, we will propose a concept system for real-time remote cardiac health monitoring, based on available and emerging technologies today. We will analyze the details of such a system from acquisition to visualization of medical data.

INTRODUCTION

Conventional tests to assess the risk of cardiovascular diseases (CVD) involve clinical history, physical examination and electrocardiogram (ECG), which are highly observational and relatively insensitive (Petr, et al., 2014; Prasad, et al., 2013; Saul, Schwartz, Ackerman, & Triedman, 2014; Vatta, 2009). Although the pathology of CVD starts at earlier stages than it is observable by conventional methodologies, there

DOI: 10.4018/978-1-4666-8662-5.ch001

are no clinical tests that can detect the onset and progression of CVD. Continuous disease monitoring at a healthcare organization (HCO) is difficult as most tests rely on extensive hospital based procedures, and results can vary (Ndumele, Baer, Shaykevich, Lipsitz, & Hicks, 2012; Loon, et al., 2011; Kobza, et al., 2014; Juntilla, et al., 2014). Long-term real-time monitoring of clinically-relevant cardiac biomarkers remotely (e.g. at the patient's house) could provide invaluable diagnostic information, while eliminating the need to administer such tests at the HCO could translate to substantial cost savings.

Currently, there are no suitable methods to assess and predict the risk of CVD and chronic heart failure in real time to enable effective therapeutic intervention (Lin, Zhang, & Zhang, 2013; Jiao, et al., 2014; Gonzales, White, & Safranek, 2014). Mechanisms that are involved in the development of CVD are complex and involve a variety of interrelated processes including changes in blood cholesterol, lipid metabolism, inflammation and oxidative stress. Pathological role of reactive oxygen species (ROS) in the development of CVD, especially in conditions related to cardiac ischemia and chronic heart failure is well studied (Nojiri, et al., 2006; Otani, 2004; Searles, 2002; Singh, 1995; Tsutsui, 2001). Among ROS species, superoxide radicals and nitric oxide (NO) have both been identified as important parameters in the pathophysiological alterations in myocardial and vascular function (Kundu, 2012; Salamifar & Lai, 2013). Other studies have related cardiac proteins including cardiac troponins (cTn), myoglobin (MYO), b-type natriuretic peptide (BNP) and C-reactive protein (CRP) with the onset of cardiac infarction (Wojciechowska, et al., 2014).

The proposed system in Figure 1 will enable physicians to monitor patients and have automatic alarm providing feedback on patient long-term health status. This monitoring can be continuous in patients with high risk for life-threatening events, or periodic with a recording frequency depending on disease severity. This system is capable of monitoring ECG-related parameters using commercially available ECG patches, as well as multiple other aforementioned bio-markers of a patient via custom bio-sensors in real-time. Sensory recordings of the patient will be transmitted from the patient's house (or any remote location) to the datacenter of the HCO in real-time in a secure fashion using well established encryption mechanisms (NIST:FIPS-197, 2001). Combining ECG monitoring parameters with such biomarkers improves the utility of the monitoring system to far beyond what is currently achievale with ECG-only monitoring or single-biomarker monitoring (e.g., Glucose (Sensys Medical)). This technology will be disruptive because it has the potential to shift the paradigm of patient management in the US healthcare system.

While the comprehensive nature of this system substantially improves its diagnostic value, it introduces research challenges which this chapter aims to address. Visualization of such multi-dimensional data, encompassing ECG parameters and multiple bio-markers is not straightforward. Well known ECG-based visualization of a patient's cardiac operation has been in use for over a century (Fridericia, 1920), but provides limited information for a short operational interval. In this chapter, visualization mechanisms will be presented that allow the doctor to visualize ECG recording parameters over 24 hours.

The chapter will detail the design of a concept real-time remote health monitoring system as follows. Next section presents the state of the art in bio-medical sensing, particularly focusing on nanoparticle-based detection of biomarkers, use of electrochemical sensors for the detection of oxidative stress, label-free aptasensors for the detection of bio-molecular recognition process and the integration of field portable biosensors with wireless communication devices. This first section, which focuses mainly on the chemical aspects of the system in Figure 1, will be followed by design considerations for bio-sensor circuit interface. A tamper-resistant sensing mechanism will be introduced along with the circuit interface which takes advantage of the chemical properties of the sensors. Third section will present an Internet-

Figure 1. Proposed cardiac monitoring system: I) sensory acquisition, II) sensor interface, III) secure data transmission, IV) visualization and analytics.

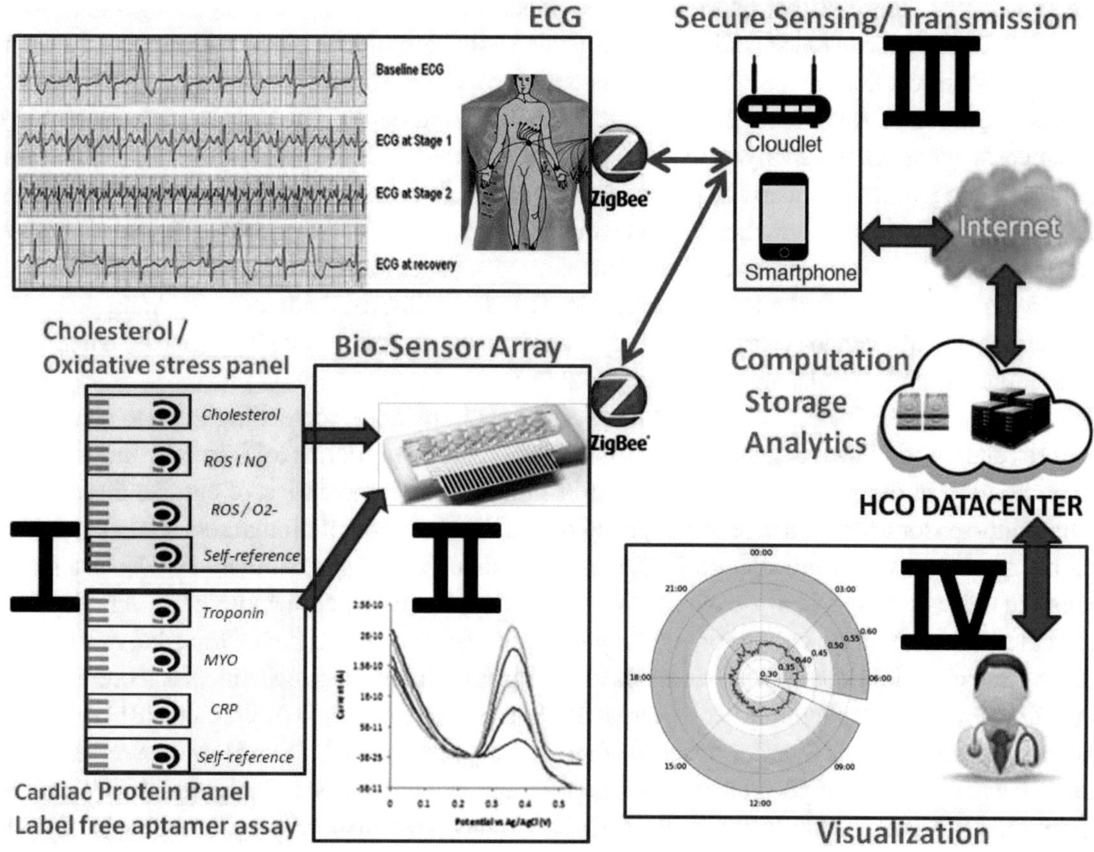

of-Things (IoT)-based sensory architecture, focusing on concentrator and cloudlet designs, as well as reliable and trustworthy sensing schemes. Communications standards, as well as inter-operability issues for the presented architecture will be elaborated on in the fourth section, followed by the last section presenting visualization components. Concluding remarks as well as a discussion of the open issues and future directions will be provided at the end of the chapter.

BIO-MEDICAL SENSOR DESIGN

A comprehensive cardiac monitoring system requires the real-time detection of oxidative stress as well as the aforementioned cardiac proteins such as Troponin, MYO, and CRP as shown in Figure 1 (denoted as "I"). For the nanoparticle based detection of clinically relevant biomarkers, Andreescu's laboratory has pioneered an inexpensive sensing technology based on redox active nanoparticle of cerium oxide (nanoceria) used as catalytic amplifiers (Ornatska, Sharpe, Andreescu, & Andreescu, 2011). This technology is based on probing biomolecular interactions to determine clinically relevant biomarkers with high sensitivity and selectivity, enabling the detection of NO, superoxide radicals, H_2O_2, glucose, dopamine, glutamate and antioxidants (Sharpe, Frasco, Andreescu, & Andreescu, 2013) in biological fluids including plasma, cerebrospinal fluid, tissues and animals (Cortina-Puig, et al., 2010; Njagi, Ball, Best, Wallace, & Andreescu, 2010; Ozel, Ispas, Ganesana, Leiter, & Andreescu, 2014; Ganesana, Erlichman, & Andreescu, 2012). These designs take advantage of redox and surface functionality changes of nanoceria particles in the presence of redox compounds associated with biomolecular recognition events, including catalytic enzyme reactions and biomolecular recognition events (Hayat & Andreescu, 2013; Hayat A., Andreescu, Bulbul, & Andreescu, 2014; Hayat, Bulbul, & Andreescu, 2014). In the presence of H_2O_2, the nanoceria enhances the catalytic oxidation of H_2O_2 (Ornatska, Sharpe, Andreescu, & Andreescu, 2011) leading to increased sensitivity for the detection of H_2O_2 as a model of ROS, and of substrates of oxidase enzymes that are enzymatically producing H_2O_2 (Babko & Volkova, 1954; Hayes, Yu, OKeefe, & Stoffer, 2002). These sensors have detected physiological levels of glucose, dopamine, glutamate and lactate in clinical samples using both colorimetric (Ornatska, Sharpe, Andreescu, & Andreescu, 2011) and electrochemical methods (Ornatska, Sharpe, Andreescu, & Andreescu, 2011; Ispas, Njagi, Cates, & Andreescu, 2008; Njagi, Ispas, & Andreescu, 2008).

We hypothesize that by measuring various biomarkers in parallel, correlating them to conventional ECG tests, and tracking their evolution, it is possible to quantitatively define a clinical cardiac risk profile that can be used in the prevention and personalized therapeutic intervention of cardiac diseases. Two custom multi-sensor arrays must be developed to assess the evolution of biomarkers related to different CVD mechanisms as shown in Figure 1. Cholesterol/oxidative stress panel includes Cholesterol(Ch), superoxide radicals ($O2^-$) and nitric oxide (NO), while the protein panel includes cTn, MYO and CRP, which have been associated with the onset of myocardial infarction. In (Alkasir, Ornatska, & Andreescu, 2012), Alkasir et al. developed portable sensors with colorimetric and electrochemical detection for monitoring clinical analytes including glucose (Ornatska, Sharpe, Andreescu, & Andreescu, 2011) glutamate, dopamine and antioxidants (Sharpe, Frasco, Andreescu, & Andreescu, 2013), and low-cost screen-printed sensors that are the basis of portable glucose monitoring devices (Alkasir, Ganesana, Won, Stanciu, & Andreescu, 2010; Istamboulie, Andreescu, Marty, & Noguer, 2007; Andreescu, Barthelmebs, & Marty, 2002; Andreescu, Magearu, Lougarre, Fournier, & Marty, 2001) and a multi-sensor array that allows field detection of multiple compounds (Sharpe, et al., 2014), where each sensor in the array contains a different signal responsive material that reacts with a target analyte (Hayat & Andreescu, 2013), as exemplified in Figure 2. Proposed system should expand on (Hayat & Andreescu, 2013) to monitor conformational changes of surface-confined aptamers towards biomarkers including MYO, CRP and BNP.

The proposed system in this chapter is based on the sensors developed in (Ornatska, Sharpe, Andreescu, & Andreescu, 2011; Hayat, Bulbul, & Andreescu, 2014; Ozel, Ispas, Ganesana, Leiter, & Andreescu, 2014). Figure 3 depicts a NO sensor voltammogram, in which the sensor responds to different voltage excitations (x axis) with a resulting current (y axis) at varying NO concentrations (different colors). Figure 3 could be thought of as being a 3D plot, with voltage (x), current (y), and concentration (z) axes. For sensing, voltage axis (x) is omitted by plotting concentration–current curves at a fixed voltage yielding the highest current (e.g., 0.35V for the NO sensor in Figure 3). The resulting 2D calibration curve contains all necessary information for optimum sensitivity.

To enable early detection and prevention, there is a need for a methodology that could quantify clinical changes related to the evolution of disease and transmit the information in real time to the health care provider for early intervention. In this aim, we suggest that, cardiac biomarkers, combined with ECG parameters will provide a comprehensive set of diagnosis data. The proposed sensor will consist of a series of electrodes, each designed to detect one specific biomarker. The probe can be multiplexed in order to quantify multiple cardiac biomarkers simultaneously. To draw fundamental biomedical information

Figure 2. Label free detection of OTA based on conformational changes of surface confined aptamer-PEG macromolecular adducts showing sequential electrochemical detection steps.

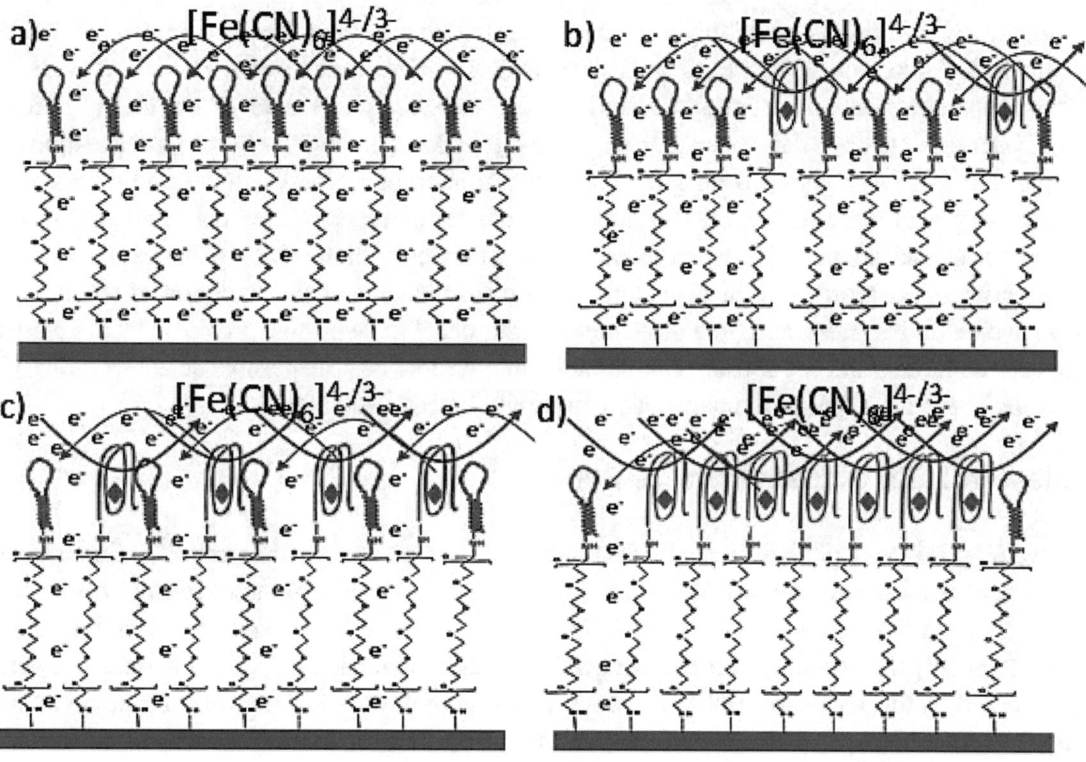

Figure 3. Electrochemical responses to various concentrations of NO using differential pulse voltammetry.

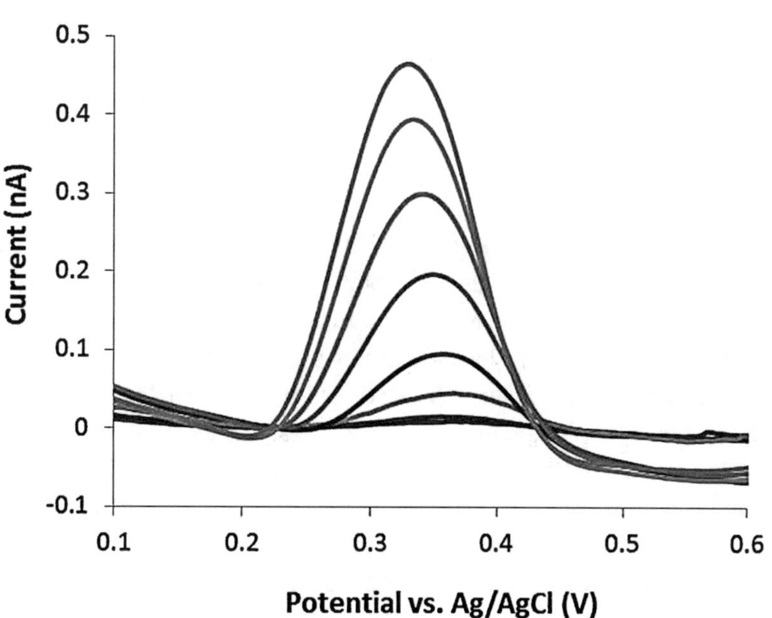

regarding the evolution of these biomarkers, this sensor data must be correlated with ECG recording from cardiac patients. This will allow individual profiling of a cardiac risk for monitoring the progression of cardiac disease and assess an individualized risk factor. The development of electrochemical micro-sensors, which have been successfully used in vitro and in vivo settings are documented in (Ganesana, Erlichman, & Andreescu, 2012; Njagi, Ball, Best, Wallace, & Andreescu, 2010).

This chapter proposes to integrate these sensors to measure comprehensively the oxidative/nitrosative profile, and correlate these data with cardiac protein biomarkers, and ECG. Our proposed testing of this technology is to study samples from cardiac patients in microliter blood samples and the assessment of the selectivity of these sensors for measurements in other matrices that are collected non-invasively including urine and saliva. This chapter focuses on two classes of biomarker signatures: (a) cholesterol and oxidative stress profile that involves time point measurements of the evolution of the cholesterol system and oxidative stress, and (b) a protein biomarker panel to determine proteins that are predictive of myocardic infarction. The sensors can be fabricated on low cost disposable screen-printing (SPE) platforms. These two types of biomarker signatures will be detailed below.

Cholesterol and Oxidative Stress Panel

First, we propose to integrate the recently developed sensor with nanoparticle amplification (Ornatska, Sharpe, Andreescu, & Andreescu, 2011) into an array system. The cholesterol sensor will utilize the enzyme cholesterol oxidase that will be stabilized on the SPE working electrode which will measure electrochemically the enzyme generated H_2O_2 at its oxidation potential of 0.5 V. Previously developed sensors based on this technology allow sensitive detection of physiological levels of glucose in human serum (Ornatska, Sharpe, Andreescu, & Andreescu, 2011). The superoxide sensor will use surface attached cytochrome c and will measure the reduction of cytochrome c by $O2^-$ as was reported in (Ganesana, Erlichman, & Andreescu, 2012). Cytochrome c must be immobilized on self-assembled monolayers of mixed thiols to facilitate direct electron transfer upon interaction with $O2^-$ (Winterbourn, 2008; Ge & Lisdat, 2002)· For NO, we propose to use permselective membranes and electrodeposited Meldola Blue catalysts which we found to selectively interact with NO, thus enhancing sensitivity (Njagi, Ball, Best, Wallace, & Andreescu, 2010). NO must be quantified electrochemically at 0.9 V vs. Ag/AgCl. Readings will be repeated over time at different periods to provide a longitudinal monitoring profile of these species.

Protein Biomarker Sensors

We propose to design a sensor array with biomolecular recognition using aptamers which consists of four sensors: three to analyze a cardiac biomarker: cTn, MYO and CRP; and a control sensor for use in the tamper-resistance scheme as will be explained later in this chapter. Aptamers for cardiac cTn, MYO and CRP are commercially available and will be used in our sensor design. Figure 4 highlights the general fabrication procedure and detection mechanism based on redox nanoparticles and aptamer chemistry as an example of sensor for Troponin (cTn). Aptamer functionalized screen-printed electrodes with both recognition and sensing functions must be used as active sensing components. As previously discovered, nanoceria particles can act as redox amplifiers in biorecognition assays and enhance catalytic and electrochemical signals allowing us to measure nM concentration of target analytes (Hayat & Andreescu, 2013). Binding of target functionalized nanoceria to aptamer modified electrodes after exposure to the target analyte will induce specific binding and conformational changes of the aptamer through a competitive mechanism, which will change the electrochemical properties of the bioelectrode in a concentration dependent manner.

Figure 4. Aptamer biosensor fabrication using affinity recognition and redox active nanoceria particles as catalytic amplifiers.

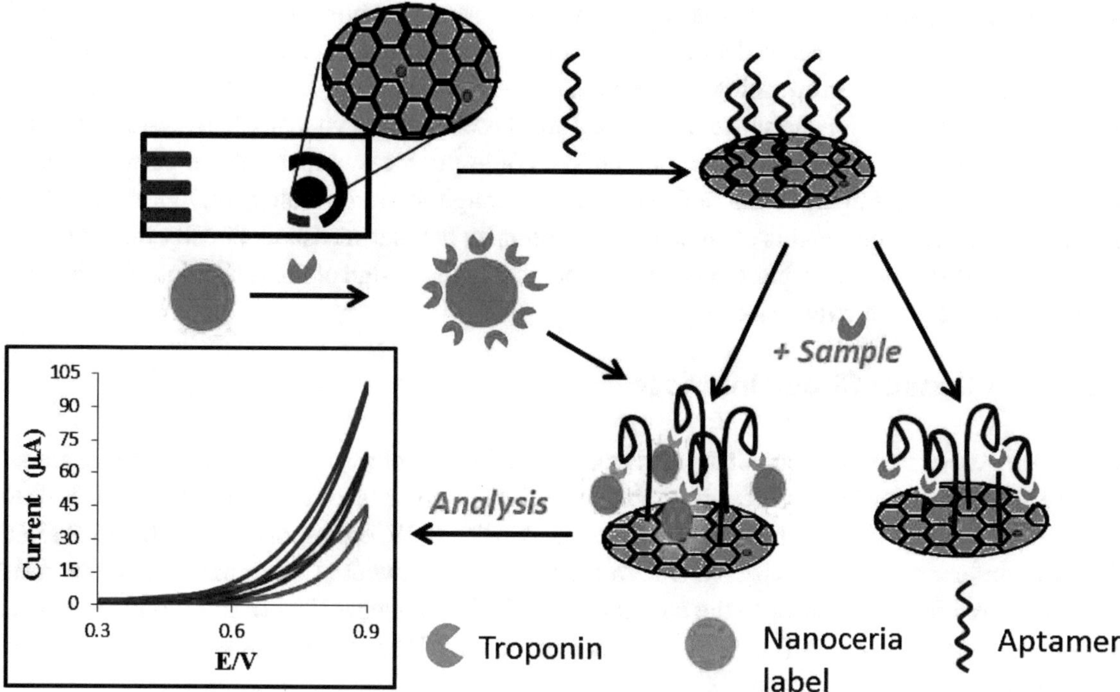

We propose to evaluate the Redox behavior of aptamer binding by measuring the spectral and electrochemical properties of unmodified and modified bioelectrodes in the presence and absence of cardiac biomarkers using electrochemistry. Redox reactivity studies and the effect of surface coverage will be evaluated by electrochemical methods, cyclic voltammetry (CV) and electrochemical impedance spectroscopy (EIS). Biomodification of the nanoceria particles with cardiac specific aptamers is expected to increase the electron transfer resistance and induce a decrease in the voltammetric response of an electrode covered with biofunctionalized nanoceria, in a concentration-dependent manner. The effect of the amount of immobilized bioreceptors and biofunctionalized particles, the incubation time and specificity of binding, and the electrochemical parameters (e.g. electrolyte, potential) must be established and optimized. Higher concentration of biomolecules and particle bioconjugates can potentially increase the signal, but they can also reduce the sensitivity and increase non-specific recognition. Long incubation time will enhance the signal but it will also increase analysis time and decrease sensitivity. Operational parameters including concentration of nanoparticles, incubation time and linearity range must be optimized. Tests for long-term stability upon storage of the biofunctionalized must also be performed using similar procedures. Conventional biochemical ELISA assays must be used for validation of the proposed sensor array. Protocols for optimum bioassay design that provides the highest biorecognition ability, stability and sensitivity must be determined. At the end of this task, we expect to have bioactive sensors with high affinity recognition and detection capability for cardiac biomarkers, and identifying the best sensor design for uses in real clinical samples.

BIO-SENSOR CIRCUIT INTERFACE

The circuit interface to the sensor array design that we proposed in the previous section is denoted as "II" in Figure 1 and will be explained in detail in this section. Figure 3 shows the response of an example NO sensor which has an optimum operating voltage of 0.35V. A calibration curve (i.e., concentration–current curve) is created such as the one shown in Figure 5 for these optimum voltages. Therefore, the voltage axis is eliminated in the resulting calibration curve. While the measurement of the current response involves applying 0.35V to the sensor and performing a straightforward Analog-to-Digital (ADC) conversion on the current, our goal is to embed built-in security counter-measures directly into the sensor operation against sensor tampering. So, we will be proposing the design of the sensor interface circuitry with tamper-resistance as a top priority.

Low Power Sensor Circuit Interface

The primary goal of the sensor circuit design is measuring the sensor response by using the least amount of energy. We envision an inexpensive disposable sensor which operates from a standard CR2032 Lithium coin battery (CR2032) CR2032 has a 225mAh energy density @3V, corresponding to a 0.225x3x3,600 = 2,790 Joules energy storage capacity. Due to the very low bandwidth of the information that needs to be transmitted from the sensor to the concentrator, which aggregates data from multiple sensors, if we assume a duty cycle of 1% (i.e., 99% no transmission, and 1% burst transmission), average power consumption of the sensing circuitry is

$$\begin{aligned} P_{avg} &= P_{sensor} + P_{uC} + P_{Zigbee} \\ &= (10\mu A \times 0.35V \times 8) + (150\mu A \times 3V) + (60mW \times 0.01) \approx 1.06mW \end{aligned} \quad (1)$$

Figure 5. 2D Calibration curve of an NO sensor.

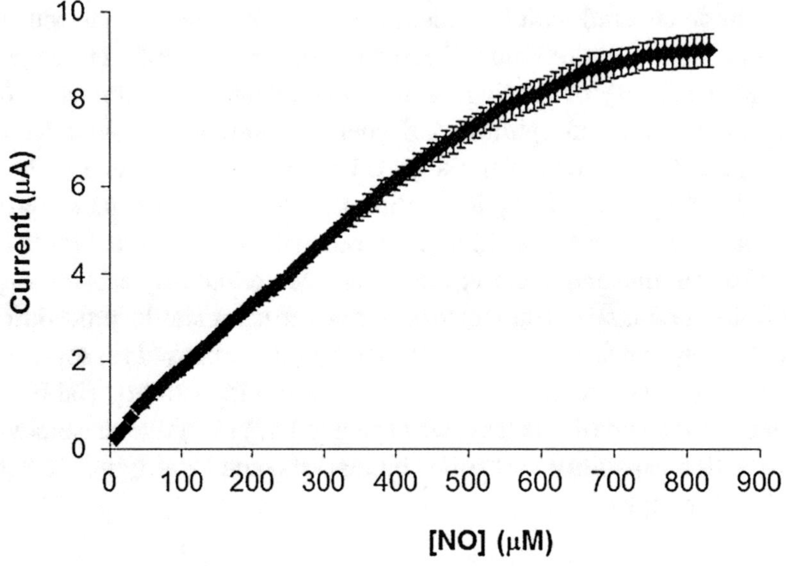

where P_{sensor} is the power consumption of each sensor circuit (total 8 sensors), P_{uC} is the power consumption of an 8 bit microcontroller which is sufficient for this operation with a built-in ADC, and P_{Zigbee} is the power consumption of Zigbee communication at the activity rate of 1%. This simple back-of-the-envelope calculation shows that, a CR2032 battery can sustain the sensor circuitry for 2,790/(1.06 x 10^{-3} x 3,600) = 731 hours which corresponds to almost a month. We do not envision the remote patient monitoring to be longer than this, so, this design with a CR2032 battery is sufficient. However, other techniques to reduce the power consumption via more sophisticated communication techniques, which can in turn be used for implementing higher security measures, are feasible and is left for future research.

Current going through the sensor can be measured by measuring the voltage drop on a sense resistor placed in series with the sensor (Hassanalieragh, Soyata, Nadeau, & Sharma, 2014). Sense resistor voltage drop can either be directly fed into a an ADC or it has to be amplified prior to conversion, by using a *current sense amplifier*. If the voltage drop is too small, a sense amplifier must be used to bring the voltage drop within the range of the ADC. Figure 6 shows a simple circuit for sensing/amplifying the sensor current. The circuit portion encompassed in the dashed lines can be eliminated if signal amplification is not needed. This is the case when a high-valued sense resistor is used, resulting in a large voltage drop such as ~1V, which can be directly converted by the ADC within the microcontroller without loss of conversion accuracy.

A high valued sense resistor implies a high power consumption incurred by the sense resistor, thereby increasing the power burden of the sensing operation. On the contrary, a small sense resistor eliminates excessive power consumption due to the low voltage drop across it (e.g., 20-100 mV), albeit at a reduced accuracy of conversion (Gekakis, et al., 2015). For example, if only a 100 mV voltage drop

Figure 6. A simple sense and amplifying circuit for the NO sensor current readout. The circuit part included in dashed line can be eliminated when using an adjustable excitation voltage and highly enough sense resistor for direct measurement of the voltage drop.

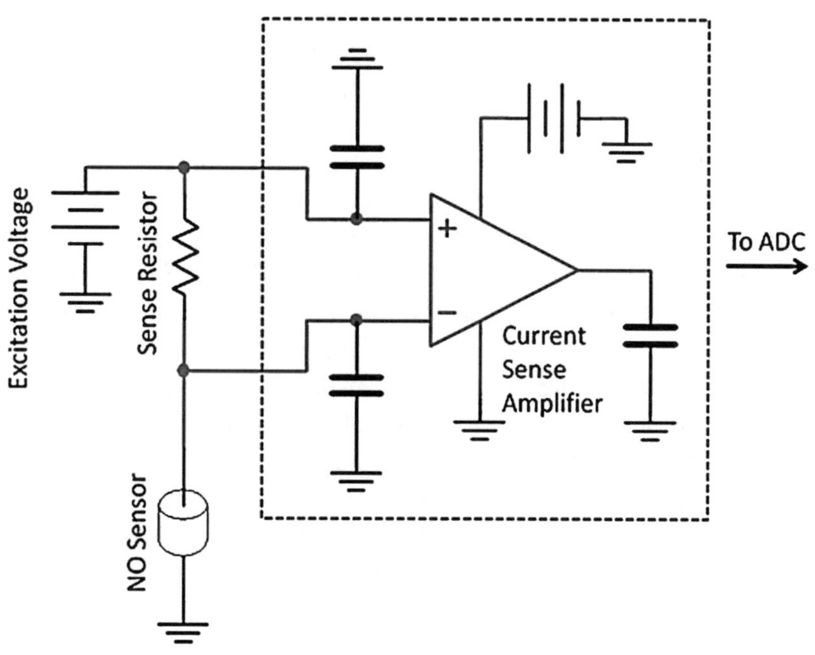

is allowed across the sense resistor which is applied to a 12b ADC operating from a voltage references of V_{ref} = 1.024 V, full range of 1.024 V means 12 bits of accuracy, while only an 7 or 8 bit accuracy can be achieved with a 100 mV sense voltage due to the 10x range reduction. Considering the 1 to 2 bit of built-in inaccuracy that is inherent in the design of the ADC itself, this only equates ton effective 6 bit overall conversion accuracy. The accuracy problem is exacerbated when even a lower voltage drop is allowed in the sense resistor, thereby making the use of a current sense amplifier necessary. However, this also introduces a power consumption that is incurred by the sense amplifier itself. From a practical standpoint, the measurement accuracy is always a much more important consideration than the small amount of incremental power consumption incurred by the sense amplifier. A vast array of commercially-available ultra-low power consumption sense amplifiers (e.g., (MAX4372)) make the use of an amplifier the most meaningful choice in such a system.

As we can see in Figure 3, for the best sensitivity of sensor current to NO concentration, the excitation voltage applied to the sensor must be approximately 350 mV. According to Figure 6, sensor voltage is the excitation voltage subtracted by the voltage drop on the sense resistor. For precise measurements, we would like to keep the sensor voltage fixed. As the sensor current changes, so does the voltage drop on the sense resistor. We can achieve fixed sensor voltage goal by two means: 1) Using a small enough sense resistor so the variation of sense voltage is negligible compared to the applied excitation voltage, and 2) dynamically adjust the excitation voltage based on the measured voltage drop to keep the sensor voltage constant. In case of a fixed excitation voltage reference of 350 mV, in order to keep the sensor voltage within 5% of the desired 350 mV voltage, a maximum voltage drop of 18 mV is allowed on the sense resistor in full scale. In order to use off-the-shelf ADCs with high resolution data conversion, a current sense amplifier with a gain of order of 100 is required to amplify the voltage drop. Choosing an appropriate amplifier in data conversion applications which meets the circuit voltage range, noise, and bandwidth specifications is a key factor. A complete guide for amplifying circuit design for interfacing to data converters can be found in (ADI-ReportADC, 2015). Since in our proposed battery based system, low power consumption and operation longevity are key parameters, excessive care must be taken when adding an extra component which increases the overall system power consumption. For example, MAX4372H (MAX4372) is a low cost, but reasonable precision current sense amplifier, demanding a supply current of 30 μA. If operated at 3 volts, it consumes 90 μW which almost adds 10% to the pre calculated average power consumption.

In our proposed system, a programmable excitation voltage is a more desirable choice, as it provides the system with the flexibility of interrogating the sensors within an extended range of excitation voltages, which will increase the system's security against possible sensor tampering, as will be explained shortly in our *Challenge-based Sensing* section. PIC16F1783 (PIC16F1783) which is an 8-bit low power microcontroller with an integrated ADC (Analog-to-Digital Converter) and DAC (Digital-to-Analog Converter), which completely suits our application. An internal 12 bit differential ADC with a programmable reference voltage can be used for direct measurement of the sense voltage. The integrated DAC in the microcontroller can be used to generate the variable excitation voltage.

Sense resistor value can easily be calculated according to the ADC full scale voltage and the NO sensor current. As we can see in Figure 3, at the excitation voltage 350 mV, maximum sensor current is approximately 0.45 nA. So if the ADC full scale voltage is 1024 mV, a sense resistor smaller than 2.28 $M\Omega$ should be used. However in order to keep sensor voltage at 360 mV, the applied excitation voltage has to vary in the range 350 mV - 1384 mV.

Incorporating Tamper-Resistance into the Sensor and Sensing Circuitry

To ensure tamper-resistance within the sensor array against different tampering scenarios, we propose two ideas during the sensing operation: 1) Through the addition of a fourth *blank* sensor, and 2) by interrogating the sensors at different multiple redundant voltages. Both of these scenarios imply redundant work to achieve sensing privacy. In the proposed medical data acquisition system, the benefits of privacy are clear and the additional power consumption incurred by these techniques through redundant sensing and redundant computations are more than justifiable. We will now explain our tamper-resistance ideas in detail below.

Control Sensor to Detect Relocation Tampering

The first idea is the addition of a fourth sensor (control sensor) to each sensor array, in addition to the three other sensors, each sensing a specific biomarker. We hypothesize that, the addition of this fourth sensor can facilitate the bio-identification of the patient that is being monitored. This will allow the detection of a simple placement of the sensor to *another person*. We define this as *relocation tampering*. Although this is the simplest form of tampering, its ability to fool the system is surprisingly high. This is a highly likely scenario when an involuntary (or even voluntary) placement of a sensor to another person happens during the remote monitoring period.

Tamper-resistance will be ensured by challenging and interrogating the sensor with a key value obtained from the bioprint which is derived from the combination of three biosensors and control sensors (for each panel in Figure 1), which is specific to the monitored patient. Furthermore, since the biosensors provide a comprehensive multimodal panel that will monitor the evolution of cardiac markers over time against the initial time (e.g. time zero stored in the doctor's office); we hypothesize that each individual will be characterized by a unique cardiac fingerprint much like a biometric fingerprint that is person-specific. The self-reference sensor will act as a blank electrode that will provide an individualized value -as a unique background current– characteristic to the biofluid sample of each individual (e.g. blood). Variability in these values among different individuals will be established experimentally.

Challenge Based Sensing to Avoid Replacement Tampering

The second tamper resistance approach we propose deals with breaches through the replacement of the healthy sensors with fake ones. We define this as *replacement tampering*. Our proposed challenge-based sensing to detect sensor-tampering is inspired by the following concepts: i) US Department of Homeland Security reports trusted cyber future as a visionary goal for the next few decades (DHS-Goals, 2015), where security is built directly into non-invasive screening devices. ii) Non-invasive tampering on anti-lock braking systems (ABS) in a car could cause the car to crash by making the ABS system think that the car is travelling slower than it actually is (Shoukry, Martin, Tabuada, & Srivastava, 2013). This can be achieved by a surprisingly simple tampering, where a thin electromagnetic actuator is placed near the ABS wheel sensors and the resulting electro-magnetic interference alters speed measurements.

As reported by the authors (Shoukry, Martin, Tabuada, & Srivastava, 2013), operating knowledge of the sensors is required against such an attack, which is used to challenge the sensory data. In our proposed remote health monitoring system, each sensor will have an electronically stored calibration curve at the potential characteristic of the electrochemical process of the electrode surface; purposely, a second calibration curve (or a few more), at a different potential range will also be recorded and stored to allow *replacement-tamper-resistance*. The purpose of these additional calibration curves is to create multiple other operating points, even if not efficient, with the intention to use them for challenging the sensor.

Although additional challenges for the sensor correspond to additional measurements, from Equation 1 we observe that, this introduces a negligible additional system power consumption. Especially since the results are being transmitted in a burst, additional challenges (i.e., redundant measurements at multiple sub-optimum operating points) do not create a noticeable communication overhead either. For example, assuming 10 redundant measurements for each actual measurement, the increase in P_{sensor} and P_{uC} is negligible, since we already assumed 100% activity for these two components. Assuming that the increase in the Zigbee activity (P_{Zigbee}) is 50% (not more, since the amount of data is very low), this only reduces the battery life to 570 hours (23 days) from the original 30 days. Different challenge scenarios and optimum challenge vs. energy consumption trade-offs are possible and they are left for future research topics.

Robust Sensing

Validity of a patient's sensed biomedical information is highly dependent on two major factors: First, the precision of the sensor measurement which is limited by the ADC quantization noise and the amplification/sensing circuitry noise. Second, the robustness of the mapping of the measured sensor response to the patient's biomedical information in the presence of general noise and variations in conditions such as temperature and the excitation voltage. Limited storage capacity on the sensing/mapping device requires applying robust methods to extract a patient's biomedical information with a minimum amount of stored data.

On the circuit side, apart from using low noise elements, efficient techniques can be applied to reduce noise levels based on the low frequency nature of measurements. Commercial off-the-shelf ADCs are able to achieve a sampling rate of the order kilo samples per second. Since measuring patient's biomedical information is carried out at a much lower frequency, over-sampling based techniques can be employed to improve the signal-to-noise ratio while keeping the number of bits in the ADC samples constant. According to Figure 3, there is a one-to-one mapping between the sensor current and the biomarker concentration at a given applied excitation voltage. However, due to the presence of noise and limited accuracy of stored data, a single measurement may not be sufficient to describe the sensor response accurately. Measuring the sensor response at different excitation voltage levels and using a systematic approach such as Kalman filtering (Sorenson, 1970) to combine measurement results can lead to more robust and accurate mappings. Kalman filtering has been extensively used for robust estimations of unobservable variables in a variety of fields (Nadeau, Sharma, & Soyata, 2014) including medical science. For example in (Li, Mark, & Clifford, 2008), a Kalman filtering approach has been introduced for robust heart beat estimations from multiple asynchronous noisy sources.

INTERNET-OF-THINGS BASED SENSORY ARCHITECTURE

Development of cloudlet and concentrator design are two key components in Internet of Things (IoT)-based sensory architecture. This section overviews these two key enablers towards IoT-integration of the proposed system, which is indicated as "III" in Figure 1.

Cloudlet Design

Cloudlet is a limited-resource local computing and storage platform that eliminates outsourcing certain resource-intensive tasks to the enterprise cloud (Hoang, Niyato, & Wang, 2012; Jararweh, Tabalweh, Ababneh, & Dosari, 2013; Li & Wang, 2013; Soyata T., et al., 2012). Cloudlet computing is a strong candidate for health monitoring applications via body area networks as it reduces the delay of accessing the enterprise cloud (Quwaider & Jararweh, 2013). Furthermore, user privacy can be substantially improved by Map-Reduce based watermarking running on a cloudlet system.

Our proposed cloudlet design adopts the Kimberly architecture which delivers VM overlays to the mobile clients in order to utilize a dedicated VM in the cloudlet (Satyanarayanan, Bahl, Caceres, & Davies, 2009). In order to perform virtualization, Oracle VM VirtualBox must be installed in the cloudlet server. VM overlay sizes must be determined empirically, however, given that the full VM image can go up to a few gigabytes, VM overlay sizes must be configured to be some hundred megabytes. On the cloudlet server, we propose to implement a pseudo-distributed single node Hadoop cluster in order to run time critical analysis of sensed data. The reason behind adopting Kimberly architecture is that the cloudlet is self-manageable and flexible for the developer. On the other hand, the downside is the overlong VM synthesis (60-90 seconds). VM overlay prefetching mechanism must be applied along with parallel compression/decompression in order to reduce the VM synthesis delay. Nevertheless, we propose a holistic and interoperable cardiac monitoring system. Therefore once it is validated, this conceptual model can be implemented on other cloudlet architectures as well such as the Clonecloud (Chun, Ihm, Maniatis, Naik, & Patti, 2011) or Mobile Assistance Using Infrastructure (MAUI) (Cuervo, et al., 2010).

Concentrator Design

With the advent of sensing based applications, billions of uniquely-identifiable embedded devices are expected to be interconnected in the Internet of Things (IoT) architecture (Aggarwal, Ashish, & Sheth, 2013), in which a concentrator acts as a communication gateway for the sensors and connects each sensor to the Internet (Vazquez & Ipina, 2008). Connecting sensors to the internet involves collecting sensed data, as well as interpretation of the data locally or at a remote host. These steps can be achieved in a cost efficient and scalable manner if cloud computing is integrated into the IoT architecture (Gubbi, Buyya, Marusic, & Palaniswami, 2013). Remote healthcare monitoring is reported to be an application domain that can benefit from cloud-IoT integration (Doukas & Maglogiannis, 2012). The sensory network infrastructure that we propose departs from this vision as shown in Figure 1 by treating the bio-sensor array as a form of an IoT infrastructure, where the HCO datacenter is a private cloud, and the cloudlet in the patient's house is a concentrator (either the patient's smartphone, or a dedicated cloudlet as in (Soyata T., Muraleedharan, Funai, Kwon, & Heinzelman, 2012)).

Smartphones of the patient and/or the attendants can offer ideal platforms to replace the concentrators in the Internet of Things (IoT) infrastructure as current smart phones can use both LTE and WiFi as the backhaul network. Aggregation tasks can be handled either in a local cloudlet or in the HCO's datacenter. We propose context-aware concentration of the data in the cloudlet (i.e., via WiFi connectivity) or in the HCO datacenter (i.e., via LTE connectivity). The former leads to one tenth of the latter's access delay, half the power of the latter's power consumption and ten times the latter's throughput (Jararweh, Tabalweh, Ababneh, & Dosari, 2013; Wang, Liu, & Soyata, 2014). The tasks on the aggregated data will be partitioned between the cloudlet and the data center, however this research proposes context-aware partitioning of the data between these two entities. Context must be defined as a function of the current and expected status of the patient, whereas this decision making system will be implemented as an integrated component of the concentrator. Learning automata-based concentration is expected to address (i.e., adapt) the trade-off between computation and performance subject to the context, i.e., environmental dynamics (Soyata, Friedman, & Mulligan, 1997). In order to ensure fast convergence and efficiency, the concentrator will adopt the estimator algorithms applied to learning automata (Oommen, 2010).

Concentrator can be implemented as a mobile application in the mobile sensing environment. Android Software Development Kit (SDK) can be used to build the mobile application. The mobile application will be communicating with the sensory circuit through WiFi module of the mobile device and temporarily store and aggregate the sensed data based on context-aware burstification. The application will transmit the burstification through either cellular or WiFi module of the mobile device based on the time criticality metric which is denoted by the context. Communication via WiFi module will enable starting VM synthesis function in the cloudlet.

Reliable and Secure Sensing Algorithms

Sensing is proposed as a cloud-based service (Lauro, Lucarelli, & Montella, 2012; Rao, Saluia, Sharma, Mittal, & Sharma, 2012; Sheng, Tang, Xiao, & Xue, 2013), while trustworthy sensing has been studied in the context of sensor reputation-awareness and accurate sensing (Kazemi, Shahabi, & Chen, 2013; Shahabi, 2013), user privacy and data integrity (Gilbert, Cox, Jung, & Wetherall, 2010). Kantarci and Mouftah have proposed a trustworthy sensing-as-a-service architecture (Kantarci & Mouftah, 2014; Kantarci & Mouftah, 2014) for a public safety application, presenting a framework to ensure trustworthiness of the sensed data. In their proposal, sensors are recruited based on their reputation, which is defined as the percentage of correct readings after eliminating the outliers through the algorithm in (Zhang, Meratnia, & Havinga, 2010) and adopting a Wilson score to increase the confidence of reputation calculation (Carullo, et al., 2013). Most of these ideas will be applied to the proposed system.

Trust-based data aggregation methods for wireless sensor networks (WSNs) have been studied in the literature however, most of these studies address sensing data accuracy (Sun, Luo, & Das, 2012) or detect threats on individually compromised nodes (Zhang, Das, & Liu, 2006). In our proposed system, multiple sensors are deployed in the same region and mostly in the same transmission range. This introduces resiliency issues to the sensory system where the entire sensor network can fail requiring prompt intervention. As the collected data from the sensory system is expected to be correlated with any other indicator of cardiac status, this research aims at integrating off-the-shelf heart monitoring systems (Agu, et al., 2013) into the proposed sensory system, and detect anomalies in the biosensor signals through correlation analysis.

COMMUNICATIONS ARCHITECTURE

As shown in Figure 1, our proposed system which consists of the data acquisition, data aggregation, and application layers. The data acquisition layer consists of the sensory circuit, the concentrator and the cloudlet. The concentrator can be implemented within a smart phone in the vicinity of the patient and the cloudlet can be implemented by a computer accessible via WiFi or a smartphone. Sensory circuit communicates with the concentrator via a IEEE 802.15.4 (Zigbee) interface as Zigbee provides low power, low cost communication in a short range. Concentrator should also use Zigbee to avoid depleting the battery power due to WiFi or LTE access (Olteanu, Oprina, Tapus, & Zeisberg, 2013; Kwon M., 2015). The concentrator is also equipped with a WiFi interface to communicate with the cloudlet and an LTE interface to communicate with the Cloud via a mobile backhaul (Kwon, et al., 2014). Visualized data represented to the Application layer via WAN over the Internet backbone and the mobile backhaul as the doctor will be able to access the visualized data via his/her smart phone anytime and anywhere. The challenges and novel solutions for the communication infrastructure of the proposed architecture are as follows:

Urgent data aggregation tasks are handled in the cloudlet (Powers, Alling, Gyampoh-Vidogah, & Soyata, 2014). Besides designing specific cloudlet functions, this research aims at generalizing and standardizing cloudlet operation for medical data acquisition. Building blocks for cloudlet design are virtualization, standardized signaling mechanisms for admission control, resource allocation, quality of service provisioning for associated mobile devices, and resiliency of the cloudlet including security and privacy concerns. Virtualization is the most straightforward block as it will be achieved by a hypervisor implementation. The novelty of the proposed system lies on the blocks above virtualization, all of which will be designed with abstract interfaces so that any application (e.g., telemedicine, military, traffic) can request admission to the cloudlet by implementing the appropriate interface. Based on the requirements of the application, resources will be allocated by considering QoS metrics and encapsulated with security and privacy services.

Contemporary sensing systems offer integrated solutions that incorporate individual sensor design with the aggregation system. However, near-commodity acquisition system is only software, whereas the intellectual property of the telecommunication companies is embedded into the sensor design. In this chapter, we propose to decouple the acquisition software from the sensor design via a novel interoperable sensor data transmission mechanism. The interoperability mechanism will enable each party to be interfaced through the proposed wireless sensing platform by adopting existing IEEE 1451 and ISO IEEE 11073 standards. IEEE 1451 standardizes the communication interface between sensors and micro-controllers and/or control networks whereas ISO IEEE 11073 defines communication standards between the healthcare devices and external computing resources. Our proposed system will adopt these standards and extend them towards a tamper-resistant interoperable wireless sensing platform.

Although personally-identifiable information will be removed before communicating sensed data, aggregate disclosure attacks aim at deducing information through pattern recognition methods (Abbas & Khan, 2014; Gkoulalas-Divannis, Loukides, & Sun, 2014; Alling, Powers, & Soyata, 2015). Novel algorithms must be developed to hide sensitive sequential patterns in the aggregated cardiac data. We envision the overall sensory system to be tamper-resistant, however, context-awareness may introduce privacy vulnerabilities under aggregate disclosure attacks by allowing the intruder to infer information regarding the health condition of the monitored patient based on concentrator-to-mobile-backhaul network traffic patterns even if the patient identity is not revealed. Random linear network coding along with lightweight homomorphic encryption has been shown to be efficient to overcome malicious adversities via network analysis in multi-hop wireless networks (Fan, Zhu, Chen, & Shen, 2011), although fully homomorphic encryption is too slow for practical use (Kocabas & Soyata, 2014; Kocabas, et al., 2013; Page, Kocabas, Soyata, Aktas, & Couderc, 2014; Page, Kocabas, Ames, Venkitasubramaniam, & Soyata, 2014). We propose to adopt existing approaches (Fan, Zhu, Chen, & Shen, 2011), but to unwrap network coding from lightweight homomorphic encryption. The concentrator will be designed to employ a network coding-inspired approach to assign data aggregation tasks to the cloudlet and the HCO datacenter, thereby achieving resistance to aggregated disclosure attacks.

VISUALIZATION OF THE ACQUIRED SENSORY DATA

The previous section discussed secure methods for uploading medical sensor data to the healthcare provider. We will now explain a procedure for cleaning up the raw data and presenting it to the doctor. This is the part of our proposed system in Figure 1, which is denoted as "IV." Currently, doctors will review snapshots of results that may overly-simplify the true situation, or otherwise miss vital pieces of the full picture. For example, with ECG, a cardiologist may never see what happens to your heart rate during sleep, because he only checks it while you're present during clinic hours. With 24-hour monitoring data, we can look at these periods. However, we still need to greatly compress the information so that the doctor can read a summary in a few seconds; we cannot give him a list of the patient's heart rate for all of yesterday's 100,000 heart beats, for example, nor should we simply average them to produce a single number. Visualization techniques must be developed that can quickly present long-term data while preserving all important information and revealing problems that conventional techniques would have missed. This will require massive computation and filtering in the cloud, and experimentation to determine the most useful way to display the results. We now present a case study to illuminate this process.

Background/Case Study

One application that can greatly benefit from long-term monitoring is diagnosis of the Long QT Syndrome (LQTS). This is a disorder that may be drug induced or genetic, and is easy to detect from an ECG signal. Figure **7** illustrates the relevant intervals on an ECG. As the QT interval becomes more prolonged relative to the RR interval, risk of potentially-fatal arrhythmias such as torsades de pointes (TdP) is greatly increased (Shah, 2004). To evaluate this risk, the QT and RR intervals are typically merged into a single variable, QTc, which is the *corrected* QT based on RR. Two typical correction equations are:

$$QTcB = \frac{QT}{\sqrt{RR\,/\,\sec}}$$

and

$$QTcF = \frac{QT}{\sqrt[3]{RR\,/\,\sec}}$$

where the 'B' and 'F' indicate that these are the Bazett (Bazett, 1920) and Fridericia (Fridericia, 1920) corrections, and the division by 1 second is to preserve the units of QT. There are gender-dependent thresholds above which a patient's QTc is considered dangerous. While there is no universal standard for these thresholds, they are generally around 450ms-470ms. When evaluating a patient's QTc, a cardiologist will usually review a 10-second ECG snapshot, or possibly a single daily average.

The genetic mutations that can cause LQTS are denoted LQT1, LQT2, … LQT13 (Hedley, et al., 2009). LQT2 and LQT3 tend to cause more problems at night (Stramba-Badiale, et al., 2000), when the heart rate is low (i.e. when RR is high), meaning that the single average QTc value reviewed by the doctor is unlikely to show the full scope of a patient's LQTS. When a subject has periods of prolonged QT that are not always present, we say that they have *concealed* LQTS. Additionally, certain prescription drugs can prolong QT in ways that may not be fully characterized during clinical tests, resulting in more prolongation when the patient goes home than the doctor was able to predict from in-hospital monitoring. To better detect and treat patients in these situations, we envision a long-term remote-monitoring system that can upload ECG signals to the healthcare provider for automated analysis of QTc. Ideally, this system will provide a 24-hour picture to the doctor in a simple form containing all key information; i.e. we want to summarize, while avoiding under-sampling or over-averaging of the data.

Components

The process we have just introduced requires several stages. First, sensor data must be collected and stored in a standardized way. Existing standards may be very different across technologies, so another standardization layer may be necessary to simplify access to heterogeneous sensor data. Once the data is organized for easy access, we need to know what features a doctor will be interested in. Heart rate, for example, is very likely to be of interest. Some ECG sensors may output this directly, but they may simply annotate where each beat occurred, or give RR rather than heart rate. Or, in the worst case, they may only give us amplitude (voltage) vs. time. In all of the latter cases, calculations are required to get the heart rate, and the cloud and/or cloudlet should therefore immediately start computing and storing it for rapid retrieval. Other features (such as the PR interval) may not be as useful, so we may choose only to compute them on demand rather than wasting time and storage up front.

To collect ECG data over 24 hours or more, the standard method is a Holter monitor (Holter, 1961). A Holter monitor is a portable ECG device that records data for later retrieval and review, usually on 2-3 separate sensors (which are typically referred to as *leads*). Many other portable ECG devices are now available, such as the AliveCor Heart Monitor (AliveCor, 2014) and the Clearbridge VitalSigns CardioLeaf (CardioLeaf, 2013). These devices take care of the data collection and upload portions of our system. However, for this proof of concept, we will simply download Holter recordings from the

Figure 7. Typical ECG trace, with QT and RR intervals labeled. (Image based on SinusRhythmLabels.png by Anthony Atkielski.)

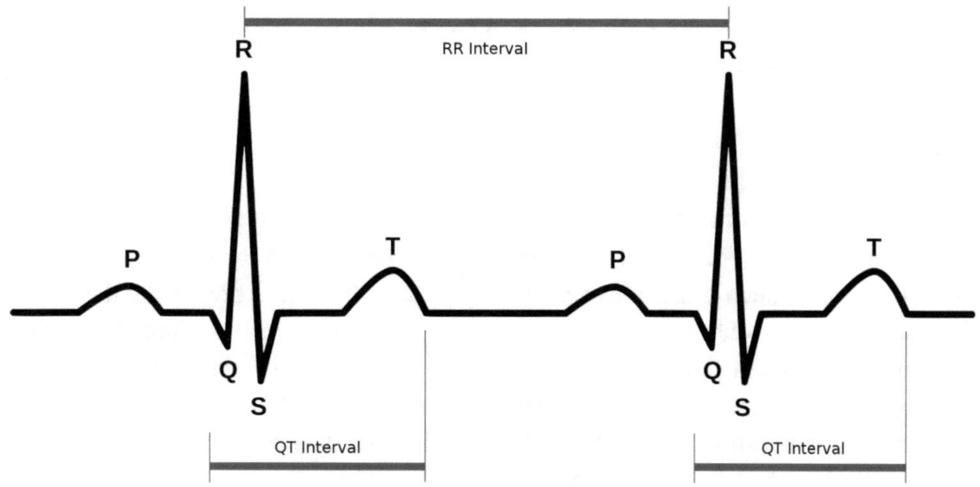

THEW database (Couderc, 2010). One of the main advantages to this approach is the availability of ECG recordings from known LQTS patients, which allows us to test our analysis and visualization processes on relevant data.

From the raw ECG data (in ISHNE format (Badilini, 1998)), we must build a hierarchical database that has the original data at its lowest layer, commonly-requested features such as heart rate at the highest layer, and primitives such as "R peak locations" in between. This structure allows us to generate results more quickly than building them from the raw data on every request, and it also allows us to standardize the interface to clinically-relevant features at the highest layers when dealing with different types of sensors. We construct the database for our LQTS application in two major steps:

1. ISHNE-formatted ECG recordings are converted to annotations of every feature in the recording; these annotations include the lead, location, and amplitude for features such as Q, R, and S in every heartbeat. These are the 'primitives' mentioned above; from them, we should be able to calculate almost any result without returning to the original data. This annotation is performed by an open-source C++ library (Chesnokov, Nerukh, & Glen, 2006). The results for each recording are then stored in a SQLite (SQLite, 2015) database corresponding to that recording. In the long term, a different database system such as MySQL (MySQL, 2015) or MariaDB (MariaDB, 2015) will likely be a better solution, but for now, SQLite simplifies portability across our test systems.
2. From the primitives computed in step 1, we can now compute the values of interest such as QT and heart rate. Although these computations are relatively simple – e.g. subtracting Q from T – there are ~100,000 heart beats per patient per day, detected on 3 separate leads. This begins to add up to a lot of computation if we wait until the doctor asks for it. Further, if we want to aggregate results, perhaps to see the average heart rate for a group of 1000 people, we are much better off having pre-computed it across each recording. So this step will save a lot of time for future queries. These results are stored in a separate table in the SQLite database associated with each recording.

While building this database, we can take advantage of redundant ECG sensors to clean things up a bit. If 'R' was detected on 3 different leads in the original recording, for example, we may use the *median* R value to calculate RR. Or, we may choose to average each value across all leads, weighed by their signal quality. In this way, we can keep the higher layers of the database leaner and more accurate.

The final component in the overall system is the "frontend" part, which will use the database to generate tables and plots. We perform the computation and plotting for this final stage mainly using NumPy (NumPy, 2015) and matplotlib (matplotlib, 2015). The details are discussed in the following section.

Output/Filtering

One useful result that can be drawn from the database we've constructed is a view of the typical range for a given feature over 24 hours – either for a single patient, or the average for a population. For example, we may want to see how much heart rate decreases at night compared to during the day, and also how its variability changes. One way to visualize this is with a plot of heart rate vs. time, as seen in Figure 8.

While this format is instructive, we have found that conventional Cartesian plots are somewhat cumbersome to interpret due to the discontinuities at the endpoints and the inconsistent or inconvenient placement of the origin in terms of time-of-day. Plots of 24-hour data are much more intuitive on polar axes, once the viewer becomes accustomed to this style. In polar coordinates, we use the angle to indicate

Figure 8. Median heart rate (beats per minute) in healthy subjects, male vs. female. Error bars indicate standard deviation, and are drawn in only one direction to avoid overlap. RR is in beats per minute, and hours are indexed from midnight. Results generated from THEW E-HOL-03-0202-003 database.

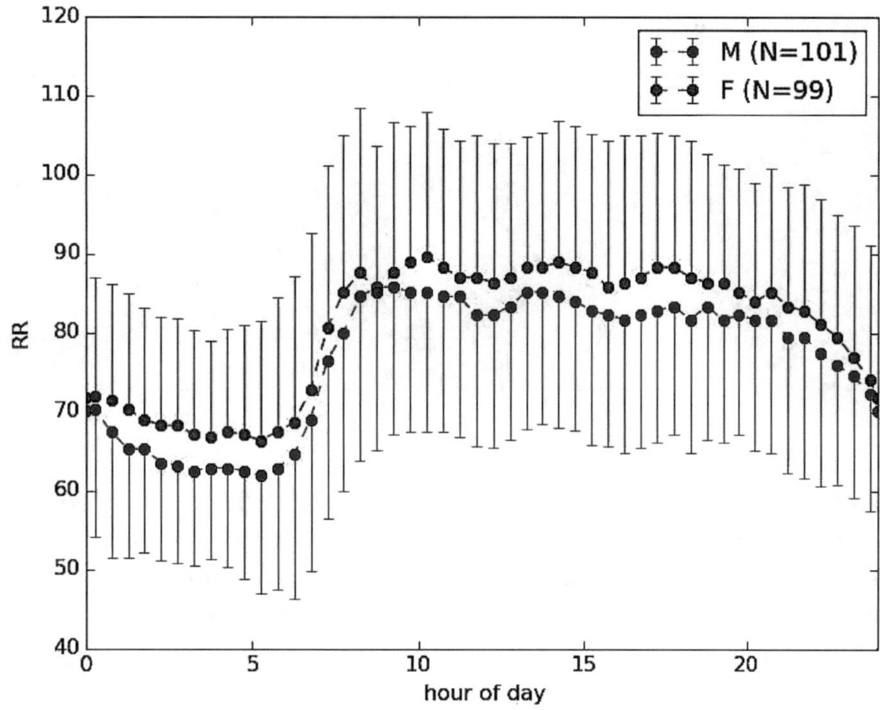

time of day and the radius to indicate the value of a feature (such as QTc). We have also found that it is best to maintain fixed axes ranges for any particular feature, e.g. 300ms-600ms for QTc, so that the viewer doesn't need to adjust to a new scale for each plot. Some examples of this technique are given in Figure 9, Figure 10, and Figure 11.

In the histogram in Figure 9, we have plotted QTcB for every heartbeat from 94 24-hour recordings –approximately 10 million data points in total. We then produce a similar plot showing points within 1 standard deviation of the median as a solid color. Median is used rather than mean because we expect to have a non-negligible number of erroneous values in our data set due to the noisy environment and imperfect annotation algorithm, and we want to avoid giving weight to these bad values. However, these outliers still affect the standard deviation; the width of the band in the center plot is a result of this. Further, the standard deviation across multiple patients gives a false sense of how much variability is really normal for a single patient. To get a more representative view of QTcB, we produce the same plot using median absolute deviation (MAD) instead of standard deviation. This results in the final plot in Figure 9.

Next, we would like to look at a single patient's QTc, and compare it to their peers (or to a healthy population). The first plot in Figure 10 illustrates the effects of noise when we attempt to simply view QTcB vs. time on one of our "clock" plots. Noise is not washed out like it was in the histogram; a line is being drawn to every outlier, and even relatively small error rates can produce a few thousand outliers over the course of a day (which consists of ~100,000 heart beats). This is amplified by the fact that a single faulty detection can result in two incorrect values; with heart rate, for example, wrongly detecting

Figure 9. Visualizing the typical range of values for a feature. These 3 plots are for QTcB in LQT1 female subjects who are not on beta blockers. Left: histogram of QTcB for all heart beats, with white circles at radii of 470ms and 500ms ("warning" and "danger" for females). Center: median QTcB +/- 1 standard deviation. Right: median QTcB +/- median absolute deviation. Results generated from THEW E-HOL-03-0480-013 database.

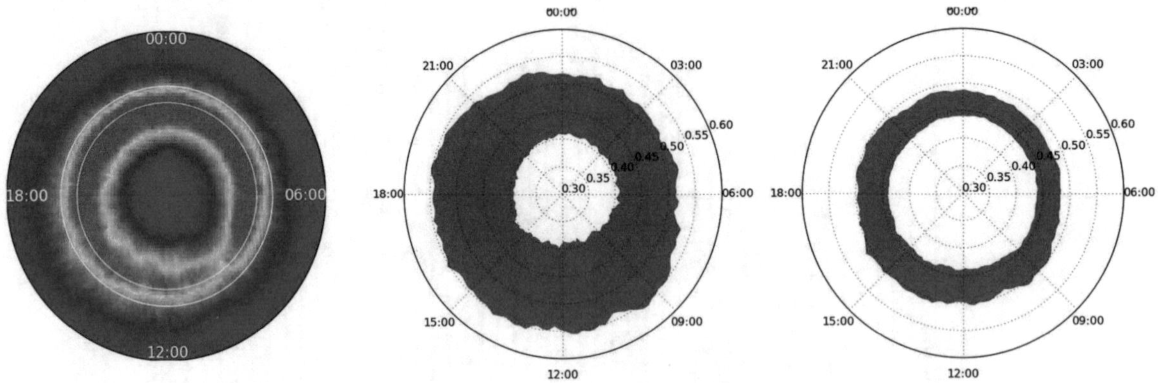

Figure 10. QTcB extracted from Holter recording of a 32yo female LQT1 patient. Left: unfiltered. Center: sliding window median filter, width = 2 minutes. Right: sliding window median filter, width = 20 minutes. Green background: typical range for healthy female subjects. Turquoise background: typical range for female LQT1 subjects. The 'notch' around 4-5PM was not recorded.

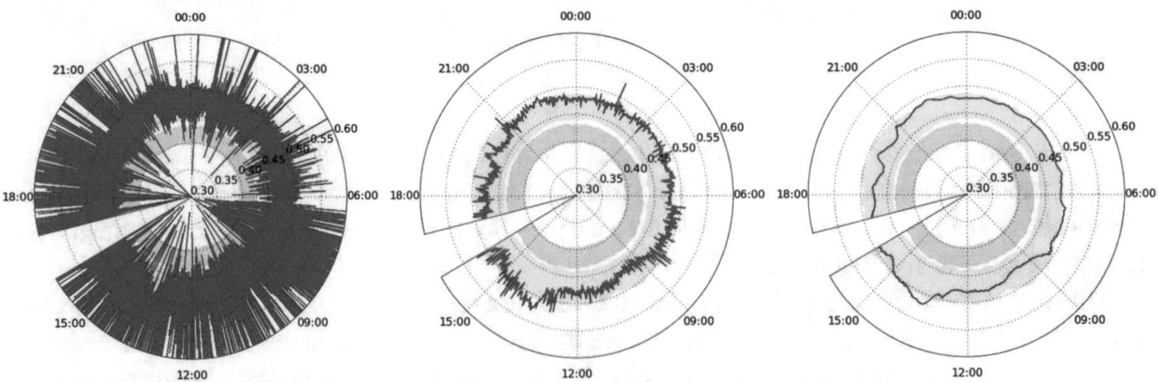

an extra heart beat would make the heart rate appear to jump up for 2 beats and then return to normal. Further, QTc is somewhat dynamic; much of its variation isn't "noise," it's real. To smooth the plot, we apply a median filter to the list of QTc values, replacing each point with the median of the points around it. The impact of this filtering process is shown in the remaining plots in Figure 10. This approach will cause problems, though, if the doctor is interested in short-duration events; events that occur for less than ~5 minutes, for example, are likely to be removed by the filter. The best solution for this is to collect a cleaner signal (e.g. using better sensors) and to apply more advanced annotation techniques. It is also important to eliminate errors at each stage in the database construction. Because there are so many data points to work with, it is generally safe to discard all questionable values. Relatively wide filters do not cause a problem for the QTc case study, but physicians will need to select filtering windows that make sense for their application.

Figure 11. QTc in LQT2 patients exhibiting LQTS concealment during the day. Left: 1yo female, not on beta blockers. Right: 38yo male on beta blockers. Green background: typical range for healthy individuals of same gender. Turquoise background: typical range for patients with same gender and LQT genotype. Note that the nocturnal QTc of these patients would not be seen during clinic hours. Further note that some nighttime QTc prolongation in these populations is normal, as shown by the asymmetry of the turquoise bands.

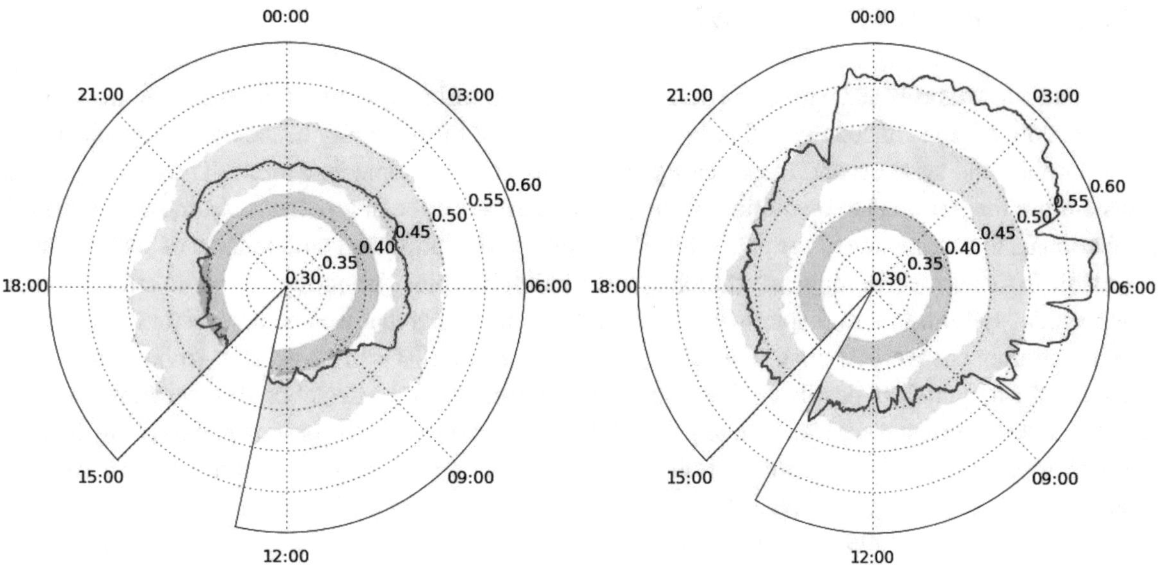

At this point, we have accomplished the main goal of our case study: to present 24 hours of QTc information to the doctor in a concise and useful form. One of the intended applications for this tool was detection of concealed LQTS. As we mentioned earlier, doctors normally only check a patient's QTc for a few seconds during the day, or as an average value over a longer period of time. Figure 11 shows two cases where current methods would fail to reveal the full extent of a patient's QT prolongation, but our "QTc clock" reveals it immediately. The plots in this figure only take a few seconds for the doctor to review, which is important for a physician who may have 20 or more patients to check on each day, and who will likely want to review other features (e.g. heart rate) as well.

IMPLICATIONS AND FUTURE RESEARCH DIRECTIONS

We have shown that doctors can use the QTc clocks to detect concealed LQTS, but these plots have many other uses as well. They can reveal whether a patient is taking certain prescriptions correctly or not, if a prescription should be adjusted, or even what dose is likely to be safe for someone being started on a new drug. Further, the database we've developed can be used for purposes other than visualization, such as decision support. The increased availability of sensor data from a wide variety of patients will yield very refined characterizations of specific groups, differentiated by genetic mutation types, drug use, age, etc., allowing software to make diagnosis recommendations and even to predict the effects a prescription would have on a certain patient. Finally, we remind the reader that long-term QTc monitoring is only one example of a medical data visualization problem. The same techniques we've presented can immediately be extended to other features (such as heart rate) and other sensors (such as glucose monitors). Without these tools, the increasing volume of sensor data will become overwhelming to the clinicians who need to process it.

CONCLUSION AND FUTURE WORK

In this chapter, we proposed a real-time remote patient monitoring system for cardiac conditions. Such a system does not exist in today's technology both in terms of the difficulty in standardizing data acquisition formats and systems, and the strict regulations governing the medical arena. The design of such a system has the potential to revolutionize the patient care since it can provide real-time data to health professionals in a summarized format. While the design of the individual components of such a system is feasible in today's technology, integration of these individual pieces requires a lot more effort to result in a practical system. In this chapter we described the components that we deem necessary in detail.

First component we described is a set of novel biosensors that can detect non-trivial biomarkers related to the diagnosis of deadly cardiac conditions. We analyzed the detection of these biomarkers in two distinct categories: the i) Protein and ii) Oxidative Stress panels. In the protein panel (i), we detailed the design of a biosensor array for detecting such biomarkers as Cardiac Troponin (cTn), C-reactive protein (CRP), and Myoglobin (MYO). In the Oxidative Stress panel (ii), we described the design of a second biosensor array capable of measuring Cholesterol(Ch), superoxide radicals ($O2^-$) and nitric oxide (NO) levels.

The second component we described is a custom sensor-interface circuitry which interfaces with these two biosensor arrays and reports the measurement results to the communication infrastructure using the low-power Zigbee communication protocol. As a crucial part of the circuit design, we described how to take advantage of the knowledge of the electrochemical properties of the six biosensors to achieve tamper-resistance. We introduced two separate methods for achieving tamper-resistance: i) by adding a blank control electrode to each panel in both sensor arrays, thereby increasing the total number of sensors to eight in the entire system. The addition of the control sensors can facilitate the establishment of individualized bioprints for each patient, thereby enabling the identification of our first conceptualized tamper scenario which we defined as *relocation tampering*. ii) by performing redundant measurements during the sensing process for the purpose of identifying the validity of the results to these additional measurements. This will enable the detection of the second kind of tampering which we defined as *replacement tampering*, in which a sensor is placed with a fake one by an adversary. Since the adversary will not be able to answer the additional measurements (which we called *challenges*) correctly, we can detect the breach and ignore even the correct results.

The third component we described is the communication architecture which is composed of an Internet-of-Things (IoT)-like sensor array, followed by a concentrator to collect and accumulate the results from multiple sensors. Within this communication infrastructure we described the functionality of a cloudlet, which is a device that is capable of performing non-trivial computations at the site of data acquisition. We proposed to utilize the cloudlet to perform sensor interrogations controlled by the algorithms that are stored in the cloud. The final destination of the acquired data, after being aggregated by the concentrator and verified by the cloudlet is the HCO's datacenter, which can be considered to be a private cloud. This proposed communication architecture places the *application intelligence* inside the cloud, based on our conceptualization that, the most privacy-vulnerable of this system is the least computationally-capable portion of it, which is the sensory acquisition IoT network. Therefore, our proposed system can achieve arbitrarily high levels of privacy, constrained only by the capabilities of the sensory network. In other words, the development of an ever-increasing set of sophisticated cloud-cloudlet-concentrator algorithms is possible with an increasing number of *software-knobs* provided by the sensory network.

The final components of our system is the visualization of the acquired data once it is stored in the private cloud. We proposed novel methodologies for visualizing long-term monitoring results which permits a doctor to visualize data for multiple patients within seconds. An example of QTc (corrected QT) monitoring over a 24 hour period is described where, by using intuitive colored bands, a doctor can immediately see abnormal cardiac functionality. Future research includes the visualization using the same scheme, albeit with an increased number of co-plotted biomarkers. While the visualization of a single biomarker (QTc) provided a very intuitive way to monitor patient health, adding an increasing number of biomarkers to the same plot (e.g., Cholesterol, Troponin) will require further investigation. We believe that, the proposed system in this chapter has the potential to revolutionize the healthcare of the 21st century.

ACKNOWLEDGMENT

This work was supported in part by the National Science Foundation grant CNS-1239423 and a gift from Nvidia corporation.

REFERENCES

Abbas, A., & Khan, S. (2014). A review on the state-of-the-art privacy-preserving approaches in the e-health clouds. *IEEE Journal of Biomedical and Health Informatics*, 1431-1441.

ADI-ReportADC. (2015). *Analog-digital conversion.* Analog Devices, Inc. Retrieved from http://www.analog.com/library/analogDialogue/archives/39-06/Chapter%202%20Sampled%20Data%20Systems%20F.pdf

Aggarwal, C., Ashish, N., & Sheth, A. (2013). *The internet of things: A survey from the data-centric perspective*. Managing and Mining Sensor Data.

Agu, E., Pedersen, P., Strong, D., Tulu, B., He, Q., Wang, L., & Li, Y. (2013). The smartphone as a medical device. *10th Annual IEEE Communications Society Conference on Sensor, Mesh and Ad Hoc Communications and Networks (SECON)*, (pp. 76-80).

AliveCor. (2014). *AliveCor Heart Monitor*. Retrieved from http://www.alivecor.com/home

Alkasir, R. S., Ganesana, M., Won, Y. H., Stanciu, L., & Andreescu, S. (2010). Enzyme functionalized nanoparticles for electrochemical biosensors: A comparative study with applications for the detection of bisphenol a. *Biosensors & Bioelectronics*, *26*(1), 43–49. doi:10.1016/j.bios.2010.05.001 PMID:20605712

Alkasir, R. S., Ornatska, M., & Andreescu, S. (2012). Colorimetric paper bioassay for the detection of phenolic compounds. *Analytical Chemistry*, 972909737. PMID:23113670

Alling, A., Powers, N., & Soyata, T. (2015). Face Recognition: A Tutorial on Computational Aspects. In *Emerging Research Surrounding Power Consumption and Performance Issues in Utility Computing*. Hershey, Pennsylvania: IGI Global.

Andreescu, S., Barthelmebs, L., & Marty, J. L. (2002). Immobilization of acetylcholinesterase on screen-printed electrodes: Comparative study between three immobilization methods and applications to the detection of organophosphorus insecticides. *Analytica Chimica Acta*, *464*(2), 171–180. doi:10.1016/S0003-2670(02)00518-4

Andreescu, S., Magearu, V., Lougarre, A., Fournier, D., & Marty, J. L. (2001). Immobilization of enzymes on screen-printed sensors via an histidine tail. application to the detection of pesticides using modified cholinesterase. *Analytical Letters*, *34*(4), 529–540. doi:10.1081/AL-100002593

Babko, A., & Volkova, A. (1954). The colored peroxide complex of cerium. *Ukrains' kii Khemichnii Zhurna*, 211-215.

Badilini, F. (1998). The ISHNE holter standard output file format. *Annals of Noninvasive Electrocardiology*, *3*(3), 263–266. doi:10.1111/j.1542-474X.1998.tb00353.x

Bazett, H. C. (1920). An Analysis of Time Relations of the Electrocardiogram. *Heart (British Cardiac Society)*, 353–370.

CR2032. (n.d.). Retrieved from http://en.wikipedia.org/wiki/CR2032_battery

CardioLeaf. (2013). *Clearbridge VitalSigns CardioLeaf PRO*. Retrieved from http://www.clearbridgevitalsigns.com/pro.html

Carullo, G., Castiglione, A., Cattaneo, G., Santis, A., Fiore, U., & Palmieri, F. (2013). Feeltrust: Providing trustworthy communications in ubiquitous mobile environment. *IEEE 27th International Conference on Advanced Information Networking and Applications (AINA)*, (pp. 1113-1120).

Chesnokov, Y., Nerukh, D., & Glen, R. (2006). Individually adaptable automatic QT detector. *Computers in Cardiology*, 337–340.

Chun, B. G., Ihm, S., Maniatis, P., Naik, M., & Patti, A. (2011). Clonecloud: Elastic execution between mobile device and cloud. *Proceedings of the Sixth Conference on Computer Systems*, (pp. 301-314). doi:10.1145/1966445.1966473

Cortina-Puig, M., Scangas, A. C., Marchese, Z. S., Andreescu, S., Marty, J. L., & Calas-Blanchard, C. (2010). Development of a xanthine oxidase modified amperometric electrode for the determination of the antioxidant capacity. *Electroanalysis*, *22*(20), 2429–2433. doi:10.1002/elan.201000248

Couderc, J. (2010). The telemetric and holter ECG warehouse initiative (THEW). A data repository for the design, implementation and validation of ECG-related technologies. *Annual International Conference of the IEEE Engineering in Medicine and Biology Society (EMBC)*, 6252-6255. doi:10.1109/IEMBS.2010.5628067

Cuervo, E., Balasubramaniam, A., Cho, D., Wolman, A., Saroiu, S., Chandra, R., & Bahl, P. (2010). MAUI: Making Smartphones last longer with code offload. *Proceedings of the 8th International Conference on Mobile Systems, Applications, and Services*, (pp. 49-62). doi:10.1145/1814433.1814441

DHS-Goals. (2015). *US Department of Homeland Security. Visionary Goals.* Retrieved from http://www.dhs.gov/science-and-technology/visionary-goals

Doukas, C., & Maglogiannis, I. (2012). Bringing IoT and cloud computing towards pervasive healthcare. *Sixth International Conference on Innovative Mobile and Internet Services in Ubiquitous Computing (IMIS)*, (pp. 922-926). doi:10.1109/IMIS.2012.26

Fan, Y., Zhu, H., Chen, J., & Shen, X. (2011). Network coding based privacy preservation against traffic analysis in multi-hop wireless networks. *IEEE Transactions on Wireless Communications*, *10*(3), 834–843. doi:10.1109/TWC.2011.122010.100087

Fridericia, L. S. (1920). Die Systolendauer im Elektrokardiogramm bei normalen Menschen und bei Herzkranken. *Acta Medica Scandinavica*, 469–486.

Ganesana, M., Erlichman, J. S., & Andreescu, S. (2012). Real-time monitoring of superoxide accumulation and antioxidant activity in a brain slice model using an electrochemical cytochrome c biosensor. *Free Radical Biology & Medicine*, *53*(12), 2240–2249. doi:10.1016/j.freeradbiomed.2012.10.540 PMID:23085519

Ge, B., & Lisdat, F. (2002). Superoxide sensor based on cytochrome c immobilized on mixed-thiol SAM with a new calibration method. *Analytica Chimica Acta*, *454*(1), 53–64. doi:10.1016/S0003-2670(01)01545-8

Gekakis, N., Nadeau, A., Hassanalieragh, M., Chen, Y., Liu, Z., Honan, G., & Soyata, T. (2015). Modeling of Supercapacitors as an Energy Buffer for Cyber-Physical Systems. In *Cyber Physical Systems - A Computational Perspective*. Boca Raton, Florida: CRC.

Gilbert, P., Cox, L. P., Jung, J., & Wetherall, D. (2010). Toward trustworthy mobile sensing. *ACM Proceedings of the Eleventh Workshop on Mobile Computing Systems and Applications,* (pp. 31-36).

Gkoulalas-Divannis, A., Loukides, G., & Sun, J. (2014). Toward smarter healthcare: Anonymizing medical data to support research studies. *IBM Journal of Research and Development*, 1–11.

Gonzales, S., White, G., & Safranek, T. (2014). Near-realtime assessment of cardiovascular disease risk factors in nebraska by using essence. *Online Journal of Public Health Informatics*, 103–104.

Gubbi, J., Buyya, R., Marusic, S., & Palaniswami, M. (2013). Internet of things (iot): A vision, architectural elements. *Future Generation Computer Systems*, *29*(7), 1645–1660. doi:10.1016/j.future.2013.01.010

Hassanalieragh, M., Soyata, T., Nadeau, A., & Sharma, G. (2014). Solar-Supercapacitor Harvesting System Design for Energy-Aware Applications. *Proceedings of the 27th IEEE International System-on-Chip Conference (IEEE SOCC).* Las Vegas, NV. doi:10.1109/SOCC.2014.6948941

Hayat, A., Andreescu, D., Bulbul, G., & Andreescu, S. (2014). Redox reactivity of cerium oxide nanoparticles against dopamine. *Journal of Colloid and Interface Science*, *418*, 240–245. doi:10.1016/j.jcis.2013.12.007 PMID:24461841

Hayat, A., & Andreescu, S. (2013). Nanoceria particles as catalytic amplifiers for alkaline phosphatase assays. *Analytical Chemistry*, *85*(21), 10028–10032. doi:10.1021/ac4020963 PMID:24053108

Hayat, A., Bulbul, G., & Andreescu, S. (2014). novel colorimetric approach for the detection of enzyme activity. *Biosensors & Bioelectronics*, *56*, 334–339. doi:10.1016/j.bios.2014.01.003 PMID:24531308

Hayes, S. A., Yu, P., O'Keefe, T. J., O'Keefe, M. J., & Stoffer, J. O. (2002). The phase stability of cerium species in aqueous systems i. e-ph diagram for the ce hclo 4 h 2 o system. *Journal of the Electrochemical Society*, *149*(12), C623–C630. doi:10.1149/1.1516775

Hedley, P. L., Jrgensen, P., Schlamowitz, S., Wangari, R., Moolman-Smook, J., Brink, P. A., & Christiansen, M. et al. (2009). The genetic basis of long qt and short qt syndromes: A mutation update. *Human Mutation*, *30*(11), 1486–1511. doi:10.1002/humu.21106 PMID:19862833

Hoang, D. T., Niyato, D., & Wang, P. (2012). *Optimal admission control policy for mobile cloud computing hotspot with cloudlet. IEEE Wireless Communications and Networking Conference (WCNC)* (pp. 3145–3149). IEEE.

Holter, N. (1961). New Method for Heart Studies: Continuous electrocardiography of active subjects over long periods is now practical. *Science*, *134*(3486), 1214–1220. doi:10.1126/science.134.3486.1214 PMID:13908591

Ispas, C., Njagi, J., Cates, M., & Andreescu, S. (2008). Electrochemical studies of ceria as electrode material for sensing and biosensing applications. *Journal of the Electrochemical Society*, *155*(8), F169–F176. doi:10.1149/1.2936178

Istamboulie, G., Andreescu, S., Marty, J. L., & Noguer, T. (2007). Highly sensitive detection of organophosphorus insecticides using magnetic microbeads and genetically engineered acetylcholinesterase. *Biosensors & Bioelectronics*, *23*(4), 506–512. doi:10.1016/j.bios.2007.06.022 PMID:17826976

Jararweh, Y., Tabalweh, L., Ababneh, F., & Dosari, F. (2013). Resource efficient mobile computing using cloudlet infrastructure. *IEEE Ninth International Conference on Mobile Ad-hoc and Sensor Networks (MSN)* (pp. 373-377). IEEE. doi:10.1109/MSN.2013.75

Jiao, F. F., Fung, C. S., Wong, C. K., Wan, Y. F., Dai, D., Kwok, R., & Lam, C. L. (2014). Effects of the multidisciplinary risk assessment and management program for patients with diabetes mellitus (rampdm) on biomedical outcomes, observed cardiovascular events and cardiovascular risks in primary care: A longitudinal comparative study. *Cardiovascular Diabetology*, 1–10. PMID:25142791

Juntilla, M. J., Tikkanen, J. T., Kentta, T., Anttonen, O., Aro, A. L., Porthan, K., . . . Huikuri, H. (2014). Early repolarization as a predictor of arrhythmic and nonarrhythmic cardiac events in middle-aged subjects. *Heart rhythm: the official journal of the Heart Rhythm Society*, 1701-1706.

Kantarci, B., & Mouftah, H. (2014). Trustworthy crowdsourcing via mobile social networks. *IEEE Global Communications Conference (GLOBECOM)*, (pp. 1-6).

Kantarci, B., & Mouftah, H. (2014). Trustworthy sensing for public safety in cloud-centric internet of things. *IEEE Internet of Things Journal*, 360-368.

Kazemi, L., Shahabi, C., & Chen, L. (2013). Trustworthy query answering with spatial crowdsourcing. *Proceedings of the 21st ACM SIGSPATIAL International Conference on Advances in Geographic Information Systems*, (pp. 314-323).

Kobza, R., Cuculi, F., Abacherli, R., Toggweiler, S., Suter, Y., Frey, F., . . . Erne, P. (2014). Twelve-lead electrocardiography in the young. *Heart rhythm: the official journal of the Heart Rhythm Society*, 2018-2022.

Kocabas, O., & Soyata, T. (2014). Medical Data Analytics in the cloud using Homomorphic Encryption. In *Handbook of Research on Cloud Infrastructures for Big Data Analytics* (pp. 471–488). Hershey, Pennsylvania, US: IGI Global. doi:10.4018/978-1-4666-5864-6.ch019

Kocabas, O., Soyata, T., Couderc, J.-P., Aktas, M., Xia, J., & Huang, M. (2013). Assessment of Cloud-based Health Monitoring using Homomorphic Encryption. *Proceedings of the 31st IEEE International Conference on Computer Design (ICCD)*, (pp. 443-446). Ashville, VA, USA. doi:10.1109/ICCD.2013.6657078

Kundu, E. A., Ghosh, P., Datta, S., Ghosh, A., Chattopadhyay, S., & Chatterjee, M. (2012). Oxidative stress as a potential biomarker for determining disease activity in patients with rheumatoid arthritis. *Free Radical Research*, *46*(12), 1482–1489. doi:10.3109/10715762.2012.727991 PMID:22998065

Kwon, M. (2015). *A Tutorial on Network Latency and its Measurements*. Hershey, Pennsylvania: IGI Global.

Kwon, M., Dou, Z., Heinzelman, W., Soyata, T., Ba, H., & Shi, J. (2014). Use of Network Latency Profiling and Redundancy for Cloud Server Selection. *Proceedings of the 7th IEEE International Conference on Cloud Computing (IEEE CLOUD 2014)*, (pp. 826-832). Alaska. doi:10.1109/CLOUD.2014.114

Lauro, R., Lucarelli, F., & Montella, R. (2012). Siaas - sensing instrument as a service using cloud computing to turn physical instrument into ubiquitous service. *IEEE 10th International Symposium on Parallel and Distributed Processing with Applications (ISPA)*, (pp. 861-862).

Li, Q., Mark, R. G., & Clifford, G. D. (2008). Robust heart rate estimation from multiple asynchronous noisy sources using signal quality indices and a Kalman filter. *Physiological Measurement*, *29*(1), 15–32. doi:10.1088/0967-3334/29/1/002 PMID:18175857

Li, Y., & Wang, W. (2013). *The unheralded power of cloudlet computing in the vicinity of mobile devices. IEEE Globecom Workshops* (pp. 4994–4999). GC Wkshps.

Lin, W. H., Zhang, H., & Zhang, Y. T. (2013). Investigation on cardiovascular risk prediction using physiological parameters. *Computational and Mathematical Methods in Medicine*, 1–21. PMID:24489599

Loon, M. S., Eurlings, J. G., Winkens, B., Elwyn, G., Grol, R., Steenkiste, B., & Weijden, T. (2011). Small but important errors in cardiovascular risk calculation by practice nurses: A cross-sectional study in randomised trial setting. *International Journal of Nursing Studies*, *48*(3), 285–291. doi:10.1016/j.ijnurstu.2010.03.016 PMID:20439105

MAX4372. (n.d.). *Low-Cost, UCSP/SOT23, Micropower, High-Side Current-Sense Amplifier with Voltage Output*. Retrieved from http://datasheets.maximintegrated.com/en/ds/MAX4372-MAX4372T.pdf

Maria, D. B. (2015). Retrieved from https://mariadb.org/

matplotlib. (2015). Retrieved from http://matplotlib.org/

MySQL. (2015). Retrieved from http://www.mysql.com/

Nadeau, A., Sharma, G., & Soyata, T. (2014). State-of-charge Estimation for Supercapacitors: A Kalman Filtering Formulation. *Proceedings of the 2014 IEEE International Conference on Acoustics, Speech and Signal Processing (ICASSP 2013)*, (pp. 2213-2217). Florence, Italy. doi:10.1109/ICASSP.2014.6853988

Ndumele, C. D., Baer, H. J., Shaykevich, S., Lipsitz, S. R., & Hicks, L. S. (2012). Cardiovascular disease and risk in primary care settings in the united states. *The American Journal of Cardiology*, *109*(4), 521–526. doi:10.1016/j.amjcard.2011.09.047 PMID:22112741

NIST. FIPS-197. (2001). Advanced encryption standard (AES). National Institute of Standards and Technology.

Njagi, J., Ball, M., Best, M., Wallace, K. N., & Andreescu, S. (2010). Electrochemical quantification of serotonin in the live embryonic zebrafish intestine. *Analytical Chemistry*, *82*(5), 1822–1830. doi:10.1021/ac902465v PMID:20148518

Njagi, J., Ispas, C., & Andreescu, S. (2008). Mixed ceria-based metal oxides biosensor for operation in oxygen restrictive environments. *Analytical Chemistry*, *80*(19), 7266–7274. doi:10.1021/ac800808a PMID:18720950

Nojiri, H., Shimizu, T., Funakoshi, M., Yamaguchi, O., Zhou, H., Kawakami, S., & Ishikawa, H. et al. (2006). Oxidative stress causes heart failure with impaired mitochondrial respiration. *The Journal of Biological Chemistry*, *281*(44), 33789–33801. doi:10.1074/jbc.M602118200 PMID:16959785

NumPy. (2015). Retrieved from http://www.numpy.org/

Olteanu, A. C., Oprina, G. D., Tapus, N., & Zeisberg, S. (2013). Enabling mobile devices for home automation using Zigbee. *19th International Conference on Control Systems and Computer Science (CSCS)*, (pp. 189-195). doi:10.1109/CSCS.2013.63

Oommen, B. (2010). Recent advances in learning automata systems. *2nd International Conference on Computer Engineering and Technology (ICCET)*, (pp. 724-735).

Ornatska, M., Sharpe, E., Andreescu, D., & Andreescu, S. (2011). Paper bioassay based on ceria nanoparticles as colorimetric probes. *Analytical Chemistry*, *83*(11), 4273–4280. doi:10.1021/ac200697y PMID:21524141

Otani, H. (2004). Reactive oxygen species as mediators of signal transduction in ischemic preconditioning. *Antioxidants and Redox Signaling*, 449-469.

Ozel, R. E., Ispas, C., Ganesana, M., Leiter, J., & Andreescu, S. (2014). Glutamate oxidase biosensor based on mixed ceria and titania nanoparticles for the detection of glutamate in hypoxic environments. *Biosensors & Bioelectronics*, *52*, 397–402. doi:10.1016/j.bios.2013.08.054 PMID:24090755

Page, A., Kocabas, O., Ames, S., Venkitasubramaniam, M., & Soyata, T. (2014). Cloud-based Secure Health Monitoring: Optimizing Fully-Homomorphic Encryption for Streaming Algorithms. *IEEE Globecom 2014 Workshop on Cloud Computing Systems, Networks, and Applications (CCSNA)*. Austin, TX.

Page, A., Kocabas, O., Soyata, T., Aktas, M., & Couderc, J.-P. (2014). Cloud-Based Privacy-Preserving Remote ECG Monitoring and Surveillance. *Annals of Noninvasive Electrocardiology*, n/a. doi:10.1111/anec.12204 PMID:25510621

Petr, E. J., Ayers, C. R., Pandey, A., Lemos, J. A., Powell-Wiley, T., Khera, A., & Berry, J. D. et al. (2014). Perceived lifetime risk for cardiovascular disease (from the dallas heart study). *The American Journal of Cardiology*, *114*(1), 53–58. doi:10.1016/j.amjcard.2014.04.006 PMID:24834788

PIC16F1783. (n.d.). *PIC16F1783 28-Pin 8-Bit Advanced Analog Flash Microcontroller*. Retrieved from http://ww1.microchip.com/downloads/en/DeviceDoc/40001579E.pdf

Powers, N., Alling, A., Gyampoh-Vidogah, R., & Soyata, T. (2014). AXaaS: Case for Acceleration as a Service. *IEEE Globecom 2014 Workshop on Cloud Computing Systems, Networks, and Applications.*

Prasad, K., Sharma, V., Lackore, S. M., Jenkins, K., Prasad, A., & Sood, A. (2013). Use of Complementary Therapies in Cardiovascular Disease. *The American Journal of Cardiology*, *111*(3), 339–345. doi:10.1016/j.amjcard.2012.10.010 PMID:23186602

Quwaider, M., & Jararweh, Y. (2013). Cloudlet-based for big data collection in body area networks. *International Conference for Internet Technology and Secured Transactions (ICITST)*, (pp. 137-141). doi:10.1109/ICITST.2013.6750178

Rao, B., Saluia, P., Sharma, N., Mittal, A., & Sharma, S. (2012). Cloud computing for internet of things sensing based applications. *Sixth International Conference on Sensing Technology (ICST)*, (pp. 374-380). doi:10.1109/ICSensT.2012.6461705

Salamifar, S. E., & Lai, R. Y. (2013). Use of combined scanning electrochemical and fluorescence microscopy for detection of reactive oxygen species in prostate cancer cells. *Analytical Chemistry*, *85*(20), 9417–9421. doi:10.1021/ac402367f PMID:24044675

Satyanarayanan, M., Bahl, P., Caceres, R., & Davies, N. (2009). The case for vm-based cloudlets in mobile computing. *Pervasive Computing*, 14-23.

Saul, J., Schwartz, P. J., Ackerman, P. J., & Triedman, J. K. (2014). Rationale and objectives for ECG screening in infancy. *Heart rhythm: the official journal of the Heart Rhythm Society*, 2316-2321.

Searles, C. D. (2002). The nitric oxide pathway and oxidative stress in heart failure. *Congestive Heart Failure (Greenwich, Conn.)*, *8*(3), 142–155. doi:10.1111/j.1527-5299.2002.00715.x PMID:12045382

Sensys Medical, I. (n.d.). *Near-Infrared Spectroscopy*. Retrieved from http://www.diabetesnet.com/diabetes-technology/meters-monitors/future-meters-monitors/sensys-medical

Shah, R. (2004). Drug-induced QT interval prolongation: Regulatory perspectives and drug development. *Annals of Medicine*, *36*(s1), 47–52. doi:10.1080/17431380410032445 PMID:15176424

Shahabi, C. (2013). Towards a generic framework for trustworthy spatial crowdsourcing. *12th International ACM Workshop on Data Engineering for Wireless and Mobile Access (MobiDE)*, (pp. 1-4). doi:10.1145/2486084.2486085

Sharpe, E., Bradley, R., Frasco, T., Jayathilaka, D., Marsh, A., & Andreescu, S. (2014). Metal oxide based multisensor array and portable database for field analysis of antioxidants. *Sensors and Actuators. B, Chemical*, *193*, 552–562. doi:10.1016/j.snb.2013.11.088 PMID:24610993

Sharpe, E., Frasco, T., Andreescu, D., & Andreescu, S. (2013). Portable ceria nanoparticle-based assay for rapid detection of food antioxidants (nanocerac). *Analyst (London)*, *138*(1), 249–262. doi:10.1039/C2AN36205H PMID:23139929

Sheng, X., Tang, J., Xiao, X., & Xue, G. (2013). Sensing as a service: Challenges, solutions and future directions. *IEEE Sensors Journal*, *13*(10), 3733–3741. doi:10.1109/JSEN.2013.2262677

Shoukry, Y., Martin, P., Tabuada, P., & Srivastava, M. (2013). Non-invasive spoofing attacks for anti-lock braking systems. In G. Bertoni & J. S. Coron (Eds.), *Cryptographic Hardware and Embedded Systems* (pp. 55–72). Heidelberg, Germany: Springer. doi:10.1007/978-3-642-40349-1_4

Singh, N. (1995). Oxidative stress and heart failure. 77-81.

Sorenson, H. W. (1970, July). Least-squares estimation: From Gauss to Kalman. *IEEE Spectrum*, *7*(7), 63–68. doi:10.1109/MSPEC.1970.5213471

Soyata, T., Ba, H., Heinzelman, W., Kwon, M., & Shi, J. (2013). Accelerating mobile cloud computing: A survey. In *Communication Infrastructures for Cloud Computing* (pp. 175–197). Hershey, Pennsylvania: IGI Global.

Soyata, T., Friedman, E. G., & Mulligan, J. H. (1997, January). Incorporating Interconnect, Register, and Clock Distribution Delays into the Retiming Process. *IEEE Transactions on Computer-Aided Design of Integrated Circuits and Systems*, *16*(1), 105–120. doi:10.1109/43.559335

Soyata, T., Muraleedharan, R., Ames, S., Langdon, J., Funai, C., Kwon, M., & Heinzelman, W. (2012). COMBAT: Mobile Cloud-based cOmpute/coMmunications infrastructure for BATtlefield applications. [Baltimore, MD.]. *Proceedings of the Society for Photo-Instrumentation Engineers*, *8403*, 84030K–84030K, 84030K-13. doi:10.1117/12.919146

Soyata, T., Muraleedharan, R., Funai, C., Kwon, M., & Heinzelman, W. (2012). Cloud-Vision: Real-time face recognition using a mobile-cloudlet-cloud acceleration architecture. *Computers and Communications (ISCC), 2012 IEEE Symposium on*, 59-66.

SQLite. (2015). Retrieved from https://www.sqlite.org/

Stramba-Badiale, M., Priori, S. G., Napolitano, C., Locati, E. H., Vinolas, X., Haverkamp, W., & Schwartz, P. J. et al. (2000). Gene-specific differences in the circadian variation of ventricular repolarization in the long QT syndrome: A key to sudden death during sleep? *Italian Heart Journal*, 323–328. PMID:10832806

Sun, Y., Luo, H., & Das, S. (2012). A trust-based framework for fault-tolerant data aggregation in wireless multimedia sensor networks. *IEEE Transactions on Dependable and Secure Computing*, *9*(6), 785–797. doi:10.1109/TDSC.2012.68

Tsutsui, H. (2001). Oxidative stress in heart failure: The role of mitochondria. *Internal Medicine (Tokyo, Japan)*, *40*(12), 1177–1182. doi:10.2169/internalmedicine.40.1177 PMID:11813840

Vatta, M. (2009). Intronic variants and splicing errors in cardiovascular diseases. *Heart rhythm: the official journal of the Heart Rhythm Society*, 219-220.

Vazquez, J., & Ipina, D. L. (2008). Social devices: Autonomous artifacts that communicate on the internet. In *The Internet of Things* (pp. 308–324). Berlin, Germany: Springer-Verlag. doi:10.1007/978-3-540-78731-0_20

Wang, H., Liu, W., & Soyata, T. (2014). Accessing Big Data in the Cloud Using Mobile Devices. In P. R. Dek (Ed.), *Handbook of Research on Cloud Infrastructures for Big Data Analytics* (pp. 444–470). Hershey, PA: IGI Global; doi:10.4018/978-1-4666-5864-6.ch018

Winterbourn, C. C. (2008). Reconciling the chemistry and biology of reactive oxygen species. *Nature Chemical Biology*, *4*(5), 278–286. doi:10.1038/nchembio.85 PMID:18421291

Wojciechowska, C., Romuk, E., Tomasik, A., Skrzep-Poloczek, B., Nowalany-Kozielska, E., Birkner, E., & Jachec, W. (2014). Oxidative stress markers and c-reactive protein are related to severity of heart failure in patients with dilated cardiomyopathy. *Mediators of Inflammation*, *2014*, 1–10. doi:10.1155/2014/147040 PMID:25400332

Zhang, W., Das, S., & Liu, Y. (2006). A trust based framework for secure data aggregation in wireless sensor networks. 3rd Annual IEEE Communications Society on Sensor and Ad Hoc Communications and Networks, (pp. 60-69).

Zhang, Y., Meratnia, N., & Havinga, P. (2010). Outlier detection techniques for wireless sensor networks: A Survey. *IEEE Communications Surveys and Tutorials*, *12*(2), 159–170. doi:10.1109/SURV.2010.021510.00088

KEY TERMS AND DEFINITIONS

AES (Advanced Encryption Standard): An encryption specification for digital data. It is built on Rijandel cipher which facilitates ciphers with different key and block sizes. AES based on symmetric cryptography which utilizes the same key for encryption and decryption of digital data.

Analog-to-Digital Converter (ADC): A device used to turn an analog voltage into a digital number represented in bits. If the reference voltage of the converter is Vref and the ADC sample is n bits, quantization step which is the distance between two successive binary represented samples is $V_{ref}/(2^n - 1)$. Input to an ADC can either be differential or single ended. Differential input is useful when signal of interest is not referenced to ground.

Analyte: A chemical substance that is of interest to be analyzed.

Aptamer: Oligonucleotide sequences that can bind to a specific target molecule.

Aptasensor: A sensor based on aptamer recognition.

Bioelectrode: An electrode that contains a biological reagent.

Biomarker: An indicator of change in biological systems.

Bioprint: A biological pattern that can be used to define characteristics of a system.

Biorecognition: A biological interaction used for recognition of molecules.

Biosensor: A sensing device that incorporates a biomolecule.

CloneCloud: A task partitioning system which clones and offloads a part of a mobile application onto a cloud infrastructure to meet computing, storage and/or communication requirements. CloneCloud was proposed by Byung-Gon Chun et al. (2011) for the first time in order to accelerate execution speeds of some applications while saving significant amount of computing power on mobile devices.

Cloudlet: Computing and storage resources that are available in a nearby infrastructure which is accessible via wireless LAN. Cloudlet has limited computing capability compared to the enterprise cloud. However it is beneficial for delay-sensitive and less compute intensive tasks as it enables bypassing the wireless backbone latency.

Concentrator: A communication gateway for the sensors in the IoT architecture, and it and connects each sensor to the Internet. Concentrator can be implemented within a smart phone in the vicinity of a sensory system. The difference between concentrator and cloudlet is that the former acts as a tiny-scale cloud infrastructure whereas the latter acts as a burst assembly mechanism for the sensed data.

CRP (C-Reactive Protein): A protein produced by the liver and found in blood that has been often used as a market for inflammation, heart disease and stroke.

cTn (Cardiac Troponin): A complex of proteins commonly used as a marker of hearth disorders.

Current Sense Amplifier: Special class of precision amplifiers primarily intended to amplify the small voltage drop on a current sense resistor. Based on which side of the circuit the sense resistor is placed, these amplifiers fall into two broad categories: High side and low side current sense amplifiers. If the sense resistor is placed right beside the circuit supply, most of the time it experiences a high common mode voltage. In this case, high side current sense amplifiers must be used. In the other case where we intend to measure the load current, common mode voltage on the sense resistor is low and a low side current sense amplifier is primarily used.

Digital-to-Analog Converter (DAC): A device whose output voltage varies according to the input binary number. Similar to ADC, if the reference voltage is Vref and the samples are n bits, DAC resolution is $V_{ref}/(2^n - 1)$.

Electrocardiogram (ECG or EKG): A measurement of the electrical activity of the heart - i.e. polarization/depolarization - taken by sensors on the skin. Separate sensors are referred to as *leads*, and typical ECG systems use up to 12 leads. The waveform produced by plotting amplitude (voltage) vs. time has been instrumental in diagnosing cardiac illnesses for approximately 100 years.

ELISA (Enzyme-Linked Immunosorbent Assay): A procedure based on the use of enzyme labeled immunoreagents that is commonly used to determine various disease biomarkers.

Holter Monitor: A portable ECG recorder that is typically used to capture ECG data over 24 hours or more. The patient wears the monitor during normal activities, and returns it to the healthcare provider for the data to be analyzed.

IaaS (Infrastructure as a Service): A service model in cloud computing. The service providers offer compute servers, data storage, load balancers and security firewalls as a service via a virtual infrastructure manager. The virtual machines are allocated on physical machines by hypervisors. A hypervisor is reponsible for parititioning the hardware among several guest virtual machines. The most popular hypervisors are Xen, Oracle VirtualBox, KVM, VMware, ESXi and Hyper-V.

Internet-of-Things (IoT): Virtually interconnected objects that are identifiable and equipped with sensing, computing and communication capabilities. Sensors, RFID tags, smart phones, and various other devices are interconnected in a scalable manner in the IoT architecture. Application areas of the IoT are various such as healthcare, smart environments, transportation, social networking, personal safety, environmental sensing and urban planning.

Kalman Filter: A systematic approach to estimate an unknown state based on noisy observations and an imprecise model iteratively. Original Kalman filter was based on linear dynamic systems. Other extensions such as Extended Kalman Filter (EKF) has been introduced to work with nonlinear systems. Typically, an asymptotic model based on physics of the system is constructed for prediction of the hidden state in Kalman filter. Results from the measurements are also collaboratively used in a systematic manner to modify the prediction towards more precise estimates.

Lightweight Homomorphic Encryption: Digital encryption technique utilizes homomorphic encryption which inherits the homomorphism principle on plain text and reflects the same operations on the encrypted text. For real time and delay sensitive applications, homomorphic encryption is not efficient in terms of encryption/decryption latency. Use of homomorphic encryption functions on Global Encoding vectors can address efficiency in privacy preservation while addressing the malicious adversaries via network traffic analysis.

Long Term Evolution (LTE) Standard: Wireless communications standard which builds on the 2nd generation networking technology, GSM, pre-3rd generation networking technology EDGE, 3rd generation networking technology Universal Mobile Telecommunciations Standard (UMTS) and post-3rd generation network technology High Speed Packet Access (HSPA). The capacity and bitrate are improved by LTE by improving network backbone. The operating frequency bands of LTE differ between various geographic regions.

LQTS (Long QT Syndrome): Condition that occurs when QTc is prolonged, i.e. when QT is longer than normal relative to RR. This prolongation greatly increases the risk of entering a potentially-fatal arrhythmia. LQTS may be genetic or drug-induced.

Map Reduce: A programming model to process large data set in parallel and distributed manner. MapReduce conssits of two primary procedures, namely the Map() procedure which takes care of filtering and sorting subtasks, and the Reduce() procedure which takes the inputs and generates a single output.Apache Hadoop is a widely adopted open source implementation of MapReduce. An important property of Hadoop is its resiliency as Hadoop modules are designed with the assumption that hardware failures may occur rapidly, and those failures should be handled in software.

MYO (Myoglobin): An iron or oxygen binding protein; along with troponin it has been used as a maker of cardiac injury.

Nanoceria: Nanoparticles (less than 100 nm) of cerium oxide.

Oversampling: Oversampling is primarily sampling an analog signal at a rate order of magnitude higher than the Nyquist rate. Oversampling introduces the benefits of lowering the complexity of analog anti-aliasing filters commonly used in data converters and also spreading the quantization noise power over a wide spectrum. Proper low pass filtering and decimation followed by over sampling can improve the signal to noise ratio in analog to digital conversion applications.

Oxidative Stress: A stress condition generated by an imbalance in the production of reactive oxygen species and the antioxidant system.

PaaS (Platform as a Service): A service model in cloud computing which enables delivering a computing platform. The service content can be programming languages, frameworks, mashup editors or structured data. PaaS is accessed and managed through a cloud development environment. The most popular PaaS solutions are Microsoft Azure and Google App Engine.

QRS Complex: The most distinguishable feature on an ECG waveform, comprised of the Q, R, and S waves. The is a measure of the ventricular depolarization time.

QT Interval: Time between the start of the Q wave and the end of the T wave for one heart beat on an ECG. This interval is a measure of the ventricular depolarization time (QRS) plus the repolarization time.

QTc (Corrected QT) Interval: QT interval, adjusted for heart rate. Common correction equations are QTc = QT/(RR/sec)^(1/2) and QTc = QT/(RR/sec)^(1/3). This value is used in diagnosing LQTS.

Reactive Oxygen Species (ROS): Chemically reactive molecules containing oxygen.

Redox: A process involving an oxidation or reduction reaction.

RR Interval: Time between two consecutive R wave peaks on an ECG. Heart rate in beats per minute is calculated directly from RR as: 60/(RR in seconds).

SaaS (Software as a Service): A service model in cloud computing where application software and databases are provided as services. SaaS solutions are generally offered and managed through web browsers. Users are charged by monthly or annually flat rates rather than a pay-per-use fashion. To improve security of SaaS content, third party key management systems are being adopted by the SaaS customers.

Voltammogram: A plot which shows the voltage (Volt) and Current (Am) relationship of a sensor based on different concentration of a biomarker.

WiFi: A networking technology for wireless local area which is standardized in IEEE 802.11. WiFi utilizes 2.4 GHz Ultra-high frequency and 5 GHz industrial, scientific and medical radio bands. The range of WiFi access points is around 20 meters whereas outdoor coverage is higher. If 802.11b/g is adopted in the access point, the range can be extended up to 100 meters. Security is an important concern in WiFi access points, and it is aimed to be addressed by WiFi Protected Access (WPA/WPA2) encryption.

Zigbee: A protocol specification suite which is based on IEEE 802.15.4 standard. Zigbee is used to build personal area networks via low power digital radios. Range of Zigbee network interfaces varies between 10-100 meters line of sight coverage, and operate at 250 kbit/s. For long-range transmission, Zigbee device serve as the front end as the data has to be relayed through wireless mesh networks with extended ranges. Security in Zigbee devices is ensured through 128-bit symmetric key encryption.

Chapter 2
Energy Efficient Real-Time Distributed Communication Architectures for Military Tactical Communication Systems

Bora Karaoglu
The Samraksh Company, USA

Bulent Tavli
TOBB University of Economics and Technology, Turkey

Tolga Numanoglu
ASELSAN Inc., Turkey

Wendi Heinzelman
University of Rochester, USA

ABSTRACT

For military communication systems, it is important to achieve robust and energy efficient real-time communication among a group of mobile users without the support of a pre-existing infrastructure. Furthermore, these communication systems must support multiple communication modes, such as unicast, multicast, and network-wide broadcast, to serve the varied needs in military communication systems. One use for these military communication systems is in support of real-time mobile cloud computing, where the response time is of utmost importance; therefore, satisfying real-time communication requirements is crucial. In this chapter, we present a brief overview of military tactical communications and networking (MTCAN). As an important example of MTCAN, we present the evolution of the TRACE family of protocols, describing the design of the TRACE protocols according to the tactical communications and networking requirements. We conclude the chapter by identifying how the TRACE protocols can enable mobile cloud computing within military communication systems.

DOI: 10.4018/978-1-4666-8662-5.ch002

MILITARY TACTICAL COMMUNICATIONS AND NETWORKING: OVERVİEW

Military tactical communications and networking (MTCAN) has been evolving from push-to-talk radios (Sass, 1999) to complex computer networks with the help of software defined radio (SDR) technology (Dillinger, Madani, & Alonistioti, 2005; Sterling, 2008). SDRs make use of flexible hardware coupled with high computational capability, which facilitate the use of complex signal processing, modulation, and coding techniques. As a result of these advances in communication technology, the network built on top of this advanced communications backbone has constantly evolved to provide never before available applications for its users.

Currently, most of the military applications utilizing MTCAN employ IP-based infrastructure and platforms. These applications range from a simple file transfer protocol (ftp) that allows sharing data across the military IP cloud to voice over IP calling between the command control and civilian cellular/landline networks (Morris, 2011).

Enabled by the use of SDRs, military networks can host applications that interact with each other over the network to accomplish computing intensive tasks that cannot be performed by a single node. One can call this military cloud computing (*i.e.*, the military cloud), which can be considered as a private cloud built on top of the IP infrastructure provided by interconnected military networks. Even though the military cloud can access or interface to any civilian cloud, military cloud applications are restricted to utilize only military infrastructures and platforms (Burbank, Chimento, Haberman, & Kasch, 2006; Lund, Eggen, Hadzic, Hafsoe, & Johnsen, 2007).

In this chapter, we describe how the available collective computing power of SDRs can be utilized by the protocols and algorithms designed for MTCAN. We also explain the requirements and priorities of MTCAN, which have been shaping the solutions offered by the research community, and we discuss how these solutions differ from that of civilian communication networks. We start by introducing the motivation behind MTCAN. In other words, we briefly explain why there is a need for a distinction between military and civilian communications and networking. Then we summarize the design principles, priorities and requirements of MTCAN. The rest of this chapter details the evolution of a specific family of MTCAN protocols, which have been shaped by the requirements of military applications.

Motivation behind MTCAN

MTCAN can be classified as Mobile Ad hoc Networks (MANETs) where the network management is carried out in a distributed fashion. This is due to the fact that central controllers (*i.e.*, base stations) are easy targets for the enemy and constitute single points of failure. This fact alone introduces challenges that are specific to MTCAN and limit the use of most civilian solutions.

Military applications require support from a robust, secure, and fast communication network. Although civilian networks do have the same set of goals, the level of robustness, degree of security, and speed of the response required from MTCAN is more constrained than that of a civilian network. One could accept a cellular network to be unreachable if the base station is far away or there is a source of interference in between, however, military networks are expected to cover large distances and offer ways to overcome service outages due to interference at all times (Yang, Luo, Ye, Lu, & Zhang, 2004).

Security in MTCAN is indispensable. Requiring advanced solutions for providing communication and transmission security, MTCAN is assumed to be under constant threat. A civilian network, on the other hand, most often is required to provide only a certain level of transmission security, and communication security is omitted, only to be fulfilled by the application itself if it is required (Perrig, Stankovic, & Wagner, 2004).

It is not a straight forward task to compare speed requirements of military and civilian applications from their networks. This is due to the fact that most civilian networks need to make sure their users can wirelessly reach a base station as fast as possible. Speed is determined by this single hop communication, and beyond this single hop, everything is done over an ultra-fast wired backbone. On the other hand, MTCAN takes place in a scenario where there are no base stations, and networking in the field can only utilize multihop communication over the wireless medium, which has to be shared by many other MTCAN applications, including, potentially, that of the enemy (Prehofer & Bettstetter, 2005).

In addition to these differences between civilian and military communications, there is also the fact that civilian networks are planned before deployment, and the backbone of the network is stationary. Network planning in military applications need to be adaptive and should consider the fact that there is no fixed infrastructure to support the network (Numanoglu, Karadeniz, Onat, & Kolagasioglu, 2012).

Design Principles and Requirements of MTCAN

Military applications introduce a unique set of challenges for MTCAN, which are usually overlooked, ignored, and/or not required for civilian applications. Although the smart phone era facilitated an extreme leap of technology in civilian wireless communication and networking, most of the solutions (if not all) fueling this leap cannot be employed or need considerable revisions before they can be utilized in MTCAN.

The driving force behind the civilian communications industry is simply increasing the communication speed experienced by the end user (*i.e.*, bps per user). The speed experienced by the end user has made cloud computing possible, and increasing this speed has allowed cloud computing to strive. Because of the increasing speed of communication, more and more applications have switched from being offline to online, and new applications emerge continuously. In order to continue this trend, there are three main approaches that can be employed individually or together as a combination. These three approaches have also been utilized by military communication systems.

The first approach is to increase the bandwidth allocation. However, there is a limit to the bandwidth that can be allocated for specific use in civilian communication systems. That limit seems to be near, if not already reached, and the only way to allocate more bandwidth requires sharing, which has been the focus of new initiatives such as cognitive radios and spectrum sharing. On the other hand, when we consider bandwidth allocation in MTCAN, there has always been bandwidth sharing between many co-located military applications, which utilize the same frequency band via different tactical waveforms.

The second approach is to develop new technologies that allow transmitting more information using the same amount of bandwidth. As the digital hardware technology continues to provide ever increasing processing power and speed, there has been and will continue to be speed gains brought by new techniques utilizing this increased processing power and speed. MTCAN used to have a leading role in introducing new technologies, which were utilized by civilian communications.

The third approach is to increase frequency re-use by employing low powered base stations (*e.g.*, picocells, femtocells) that provide service for fewer nodes while causing less interference to the rest of the network. Reduced interference results in increased ability to re-use the frequencies. In MTCAN, interference management has been and will be one of the key communication requirements. Without interference management, due to the lack of infrastructure (*i.e.*, base stations) to coordinate the communication, MTCAN cannot sustain the required performance as the load on the network starts to increase. Therefore, civilian communication systems are still behind their military counterparts in terms of the re-use of the resources.

When we look at MTCAN protocols and algorithms, they have specific and detailed requirements that stem from different priorities. The rules of thumb of MTCAN protocol and algorithm design can be summarized as follows:

- Carefully test every protocol and algorithm so that the resulting performance stays within the required limits at all times.
    - Design according to the worst case scenario, then try to improve the usual scenario performance.
    - Failure due to a certain design decision is unacceptable, even if the decision improves the network at other times.
- MTCAN algorithms and protocols have to be distributed because centralized solutions constitute:
    - Single point of failure: If the central decision making node (*i.e.*, base station) is compromised, the system collapses. MTCAN has to survive and keep functioning in a combat situation, where attacks can come from any direction.
    - Slow response: Having to relay information to and from a central node causes delays. Moreover, this wastes resources during the collection and distribution of data. MTCAN decision making mechanisms have to be as time accurate and resource efficient as possible to allow as much actual communication as possible take place (*i.e.*, accurate decisions will require some overhead but this should not exceed certain limits).
    - Poor Quality of Service (QoS): In the tactical field, environmental factors vary greatly due to both the size and mobility of the network. Centralized protocols and algorithms cannot fine tune their performance based on the conditions at each locality, therefore, causing unfair and far from optimal solutions for many parts of the network. MTCAN has to provide a sustainable level of QoS throughout the network (*i.e.*, performance at the worst node is a more important metric that the average performance of the network).
    - Limited scalability: MTCAN can hardly be considered as a stable network where nodes are switched on at the beginning of a scenario and stay that way until the end. The number of nodes entering and leaving a network can vary continuously during a scenario, and due to tactical decisions made on the fly, the network size and topology may change drastically, rendering centralized optimization useless and/or impossible. MTCAN solutions have to be scalable and adaptive in order to accommodate varying network size and topology.
- Every bit transmitted over the network has to be well utilized.
    - Underutilizing the occupied channel increases the overhead and reduces the network throughput (*e.g.*, make ways to combine data and control traffic to make sure each slot is efficiently utilized).
    - Inspect and refine each algorithm and protocol so that their overhead vs. performance tradeoff is optimized (*e.g.*, allow just enough overhead, which ensures the protocol/algorithm can function properly).

- Use cross layer design to optimize collective performance of the protocols/algorithms that have overlapping/sequential functionalities.
    - Transmitting different versions of the same information coming from two different layers does not make sense and contradicts the channel utilization principle.
    - If the performance of a higher layer protocol will benefit from knowing lower layer information, allow cross-layer design.
- Tradeoffs are important to provide balanced performance under varying channel and network conditions. Design adaptive protocols/algorithms that allow various tradeoffs between performance metrics such as, delay, throughput, data rate, and error protection.

TRACE FAMILY OF PROTOCOLS

History

The TRACE (Time Reservations using Adaptive Control for Energy efficiency) family of protocols is the culmination of a twelve year (2002-2014) research project at the University of Rochester, Department of Electrical and Computer Engineering, supported with financial and technical support of Harris Corporation, RF Communications Division, a leader in MTCAN. During these twelve years of research, the authors of this chapter have extended and perfected the TRACE architecture by building, from the ground up, protocols and algorithms that can support the goals of MTCAN as described in the previous section. We present the TRACE family of protocols in the chronological order.

SH-TRACE

Single-Hop Time Reservation using Adaptive Control for Energy efficiency (SH-TRACE) (Tavli & Heinzelman, 2003, 2006; Tavli, 2005) is a MAC protocol that combines different features of centralized and distributed MAC protocols to achieve high performance for peer-to-peer single-hop, infrastructureless wireless networks (see Figure1). SH-TRACE establishes one node in the network as a controller. To balance the coordinator energy load, SH-TRACE employs dynamic controller switching.

SH-TRACE is organized around time frames with duration matched to the periodic rate of voice packets. The frame format is presented in Figure 2. Each frame consists of two subframes: a control subframe and a data subframe. The control subframe consists of a beacon slot, a contention slot, a header slot, and an IS slot. At the beginning of every frame, the controller node transmits a beacon message. This is used to synchronize all the nodes and to signal the start of a new frame. The contention slot, which immediately follows the beacon message, consists of *NC* sub-slots. Upon hearing the beacon, nodes that have data to send but did not reserve data slots in the previous frame, randomly choose sub-slots to transmit their requests. If the contention is successful (*i.e.*, no collisions), the controller grants a data slot to the contending node. The controller then sends the header, which includes the data transmission schedule of the current frame. The transmission schedule is a list of nodes that have been granted data slots in the current frame along with their data slot numbers. A contending node that does not hear its ID in the schedule understands that its contention was unsuccessful (*i.e.*, a collision occurred or all the

Figure 1. Overview of SH-TRACE operation.

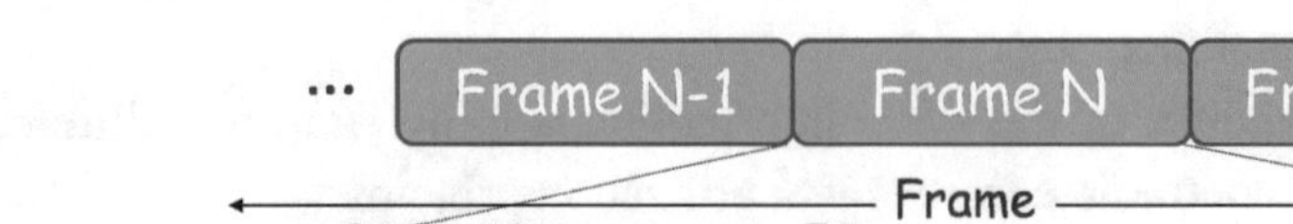

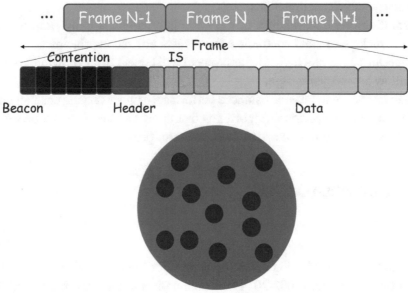

data slots are already in use) and contends again in the following frame. If the waiting time for a voice packet during contention for channel access exceeds the threshold, *Tdrop*, it is dropped. The header also includes the ID of the controller for the next frame, which is determined by the current controller according to the node energy levels.

The IS slot begins just after the header slot and consists of *ND* sub-slots. Nodes that are scheduled to transmit in the data subframe transmit a short IS message exactly in the same order as specified by the data transmission schedule. An IS message includes the energy level of the transmitting node, enabling the controller node to monitor the energy level of the entire network, and an end-of-stream bit, which is set to one if the node has no data to send. Each receiving node records the received power level of the transmitting node and inserts this information into its IS table. The information in the IS table is used as a proximity metric for the nodes (*i.e.*, the higher the received power the shorter the distance between transmitter and receiver nodes). If the number of transmissions in a particular frame is higher than a predetermined number transmissions, *NMAX*, each node schedules itself to wake up for the top *NMAX* transmissions that are the closest transmitters to the node.

The data subframe is broken into constant length data slots. Nodes listed in the schedule in the header transmit their data packets at their reserved data slots. Each node listens to at most *NMAX* data transmissions in a single frame; therefore each node is on for at most *NMAX* data slots. All nodes are in the sleep mode after the last reserved data slot until the beginning of the next frame.

Figure 2. SH-TRACE frame format.

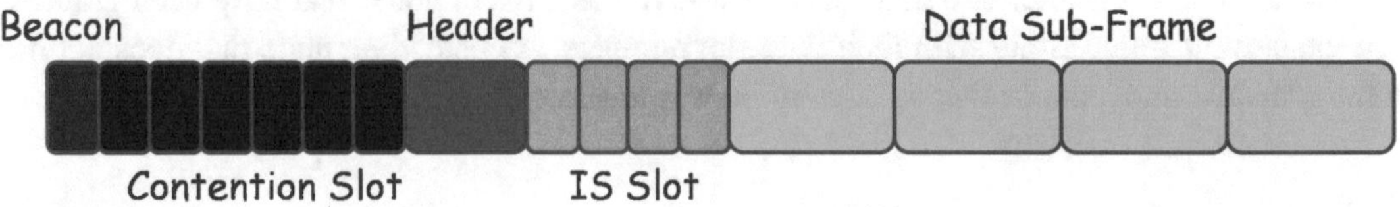

If the power level of the controller node is lower than any other node by a predetermined threshold, then in the next frame controller handover takes place. The controller node assigns another node (any other node in the network with energy level higher than that of the controller) as the controller, effective with the reception of the header packet. Upon receiving the header packet, the node assigned to be the controller assumes the controller duties.

A node keeps a data slot once it is scheduled for transmission as long as it has data to send. A node that sets its end-of-stream bit to one because it has no more data to send will not be granted channel access in the next frame (*i.e.*, it should contend to get a data slot once it has new data to send). Automatic renewal of data slot reservation enables real-time data streams to be uninterrupted (Goodman, Valenzuela, Gayliard, & Ramamurthi, 1989).

At the initial startup stage, a node listens to the medium to detect any ongoing transmissions for one frame time, *TF*, because it is possible that there might already be an operational network. If no transmission is detected, then the node picks a random time, smaller than the contention slot duration, *TCS*, at which to transmit its own beacon signal, and the node listens to the channel until its contention timer expires. If a beacon is heard in this period, then the node stops its timer and starts normal operation. Otherwise, when the timer expires, the node sends a beacon and assumes the controller position. In case there is a beacon collision, none of the colliding nodes will know it, but the other nodes hear the collision, so the initial startup continues. All the previously collided nodes, and the nodes that could not detect the collision(s) because of capture, will learn of the collisions with the first successful beacon transmission.

SH-TRACE is an energy-efficient QoS supporting reliable MAC protocol for fully connected ad hoc networks. However, due to limited radio range, barriers, and interference, it is not possible to restrict a communication network to a fully-connected topology. Although for certain application scenarios, users need to communicate with their immediate (*i.e.*, single-hop) neighbors, a multihop extension of the SH-TRACE protocol to support single-hop communications within a multihop (*i.e.*, not fully connected) network topology is necessary. Furthermore, this is the logical next step to pave the way for energy-efficient, QoS supporting, multihop, real-time data broadcast, multicast, and unicast routing.

MH-TRACE

MultiHop Time Reservation using Adaptive Control for Energy efficiency (MH-TRACE) (Tavli & Heinzelman, 2004, 2006) is a protocol architecture for energy efficient single-hop voice broadcasting in a multihop network. Figure 3 shows a snapshot of MH-TRACE clustering and medium access for a portion of an actual distribution of mobile nodes. In MH-TRACE, the network is organized into overlapping clusters through a distributed algorithm. Time is organized around superframes with duration, *TSF*, matched to the periodic rate of voice packets, where each superframe consists of *NF* frames. The frame format is presented in Figure 4. Each frame consists of two subframes: a control subframe and a data subframe. The control subframe consists of a beacon slot, a clusterhead announcement (CA) slot, a contention slot, a header slot, and an information summarization (IS) slot.

At the beginning of each occupied frame, the clusterhead transmits a beacon message. This is used to announce the existence and continuation of the cluster to the cluster members and the other nodes in the transmit range of the clusterhead. By listening to the beacon and CA packets, all the nodes in the carrier sense range of this clusterhead update their interference level table. Each clusterhead chooses the least noisy frame to operate within and dynamically changes its frame according to the interference level of the dynamic network. Collisions with the members of other clusters are minimized by the clusterhead's selection of the minimal interference frame.

Figure 3. A snapshot of MH-TRACE clustering and medium access for a portion of an actual distribution of mobile nodes. Nodes CH1 through CH6 are clusterhead nodes.

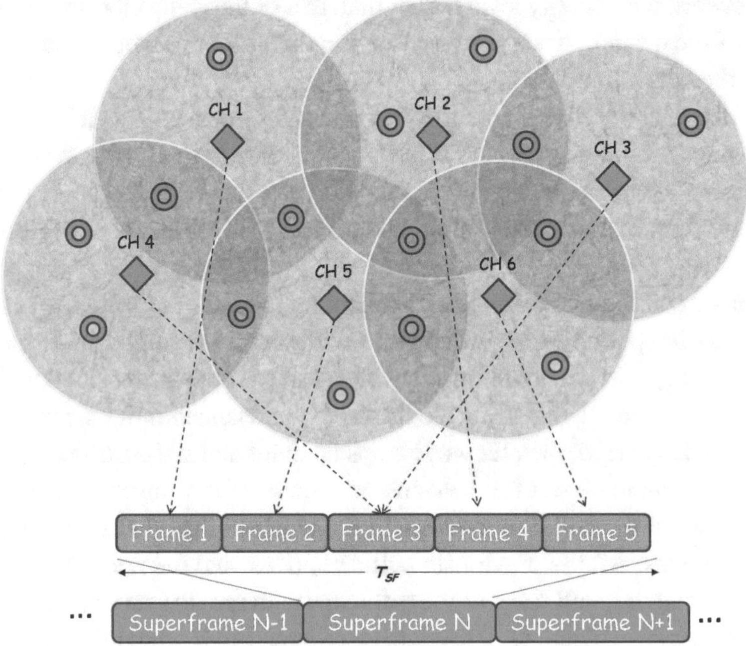

The contention slot, which immediately follows the CA slot, consists of *NC* sub-slots. Upon hearing the beacon, each node that has data to send but did not reserve a data slot in the previous cyclic superframe, randomly chooses a subslot to transmit its request. If the contention is successful (*i.e.*, no collisions), the clusterhead grants a data slot to the contending node.

Following the contention subslot, the clusterhead sends the header, which includes the data transmission schedule of the current frame. The transmission schedule is a list of nodes that have been granted data slots in the current frame, along with their data slot numbers. A contending node that does not hear its ID in the schedule understands that its contention was not successful (*i.e.*, a collision occurred or all the data slots are already in use) and contends again in the following superframe. If the waiting time for a voice packet during contention for channel access exceeds the threshold, *Tdrop*, the packet is dropped.

The information summarization (IS) slot begins just after the header slot and consists of *ND* sub-slots. Each node that is scheduled to transmit data sends a short IS packet prior to actual data transmission exactly in the same order as specified by the data transmission schedule. Based on these IS packets, neighbor nodes decide whether to stay awake and receive the data packets or enter the sleep mode for

Figure 4. MH-TRACE frame format.

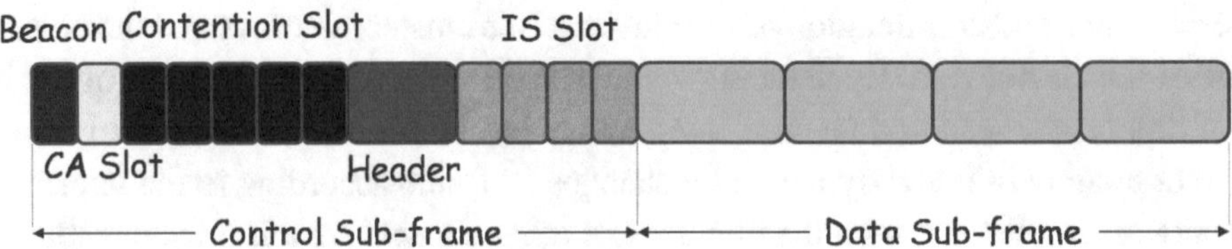

the duration of the data packet and avoid reception of irrelevant or collided data packets. An IS packet includes the ID of the transmitting node and an end-of-stream bit, which is set to one if the node has no data to send. Each receiving node records the received power level of the transmitting node and inserts this information into its IS table. The IS table is used as a proximity metric for the nodes. Nodes that are not members of this cluster also listen to the IS slot and record the received power level. Each node creates its own listening cluster by selecting the top *NMAX* transmissions that are the closest transmitters to the node. Note that other methods of deciding which nodes to listen to can be used within the MH-TRACE framework by changing what data nodes send in the IS slot. Hence the network is softly partitioned into many virtual clusters (called listening clusters) based on the receivers.

The data subframe is broken into constant length data slots. Nodes listed in the schedule in the header transmit their data packets at their reserved data slots. A node keeps a data slot once it is scheduled for transmission as long as it has data to send, which enables real-time data streams to be uninterrupted. A node that sets its end-of-stream bit (in the IS packet) to one because it has no more data to send will not be granted channel access in the next superframe.

Any node in the startup mode cannot enter the sleep mode until it reaches the steady-state mode. If a node either transmitted (clusterhead node) or received (non-clusterhead node) a header packet within 2*TSF* time, it is in steady-state mode. Otherwise, it is in startup mode. Similarly, all nodes are required to be awake for all beacon, CA and IS slots for all the frames within the superframe to gather the control information to run MH-TRACE seamlessly. Ordinary nodes also stay awake to receive the header slot of their own clusterhead. In addition, clusterheads stay awake in their own frames through the contention slot to receive any contention requests.

At the initial startup stage, a node listens to the medium to detect any ongoing transmissions for the duration of one superframe time, *TSF*, to create its interference table for each frame within the superframe. If there is already a clusterhead in its receive range, the node starts its normal operation. If more than one beacon is heard, the node that sent the beacon with higher received power is chosen as the clusterhead (*i.e.*, the closest clusterhead is chosen). If no beacon is detected, then the node chooses the least noisy frame, picks a random time within that frame to transmit its own beacon signal, and begins to listen to the channel until its contention timer expires. If a beacon is heard in this period, then the node just stops its timer and starts normal operation. Otherwise, when the timer expires, the node sends a beacon and assumes the clusterhead position. In case there is a beacon collision, none of the colliding nodes will know it, but the other nodes hear the collision, so the initial startup continues. All the previously collided nodes, and the nodes that could not detect the collision(s) because of capture, will learn of the collisions with the first successful header transmission.

Each clusterhead continuously records the interference level of each frame by listening to the beacon transmission and CA transmission slots, which are at the beginning of each frame. Since only the clusterheads are allowed to transmit in these slots, it is possible for each clusterhead to measure the received power level from other clusterheads and know the approximate distances to other clusterheads in the carrier sense range. A clusterhead can record the interference level of each frame by listening to the beacon slot, but the beacon slot becomes useless for a clusterhead's own frame, because it is transmitting its own beacon. A CA packet, which is transmitted with a probability *pCA*, is used to determine the interference level of the co-frame clusters. If this probability is set to 0.5, then each clusterhead records the interference level in its frame, on the average, at 4*TSF* time.

A clusterhead keeps its frame and continues to operate in its steady state mode unless another clusterhead enters in its receive range. When two clusterheads enter in each other's receive range, the one who receives the other's beacon first resigns directly. A clusterhead leaves a frame with high interference (*e.g.*, two clusterheads enter each other's interference range but not receive range) and moves to a low interference frame with probability *pCF*. The reason for adding such randomness is to avoid the simultaneous and unstable frame switching of co-frame clusters, which are the interference source for each other. If *pCF* is set to 0.5, then the probability that only one of the two co-frame clusterheads switches to a new frame becomes 0.67. If a node does not receive a beacon packet from its clusterhead for *2TSF* time, either because of mobility of the node or the clusterhead or the failure of the clusterhead, then it enters the initial startup procedure.

Many nodes in the network are in the transmit range of more than one clusterhead, and the default action for these nodes is to choose to request channel access from the closest clusterhead. For these nodes, if all the data slots in the closest cluster are in use and another cluster in range has available data slots, they can contend for channel access from the further clusterhead with unused data slots rather than the one that is closer but does not have available data slots. Note that the available data slot information of the previous superframe is included in the beacon packet. Figure 5 shows a snapshot of a portion of the network structure, where nodes A-G are clusterheads with transmission ranges represented by the circles around them and node X is an ordinary node with its receive range represented by the shaded disk. Node X has three clusterheads (E, F, and G) in its receive range. The closest clusterhead is G, but if G does not have available data slots, then node X can choose to request channel access from E or F depending on the availability of the data slots in these clusters. By incorporating this dynamic channel allocation scheme into MH-TRACE, one more degree of freedom is added to the network dynamics, which enables efficient utilization of the bandwidth and reduces the adverse affects of clustering.

Figure 5. Network partitioning into clusters. Nodes A-G are clusterhead nodes and node X is an ordinary node.

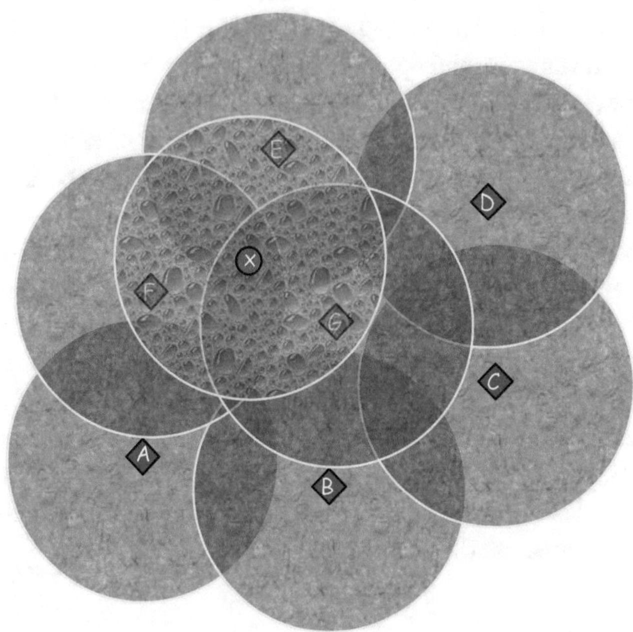

MH-TRACE was investigated through extensive simulations and theoretical analysis. It was shown that MH-TRACE outperforms existing distributed MAC protocols like IEEE 802.11 and Sensor MAC (SMAC) (Ye, Heidemann, & Estrin, 2002), in terms of energy efficiency and throughput, approaching the theoretical maximum throughput and theoretical minimum energy dissipation. Furthermore, resilience of MH-TRACE against channel errors was investigated through extensive simulations (Numanoglu, Tavli, & Heinzelman, 2006) which reveal that it is possible to achieve satisfactory system performance with coordinated MAC protocols, such as MH-TRACE, even in lossy channels, provided that the BER (Bit Error Rate) level is not extremely high.

Although single-hop real-time data broadcasting has many applications through MH-TRACE, due to the limited radio range, single-hop broadcasting to all the nodes in the network is not possible in many ad hoc network scenarios, and thus multihop broadcasting is necessary. Characterizing the effects of medium access control on the behavior of network-wide broadcasting is essential for designing high performance broadcasting architectures (network layer and MAC layer). QoS and energy dissipation characteristics of flooding, when it is used for real-time data broadcasting, for three different MAC protocols (MH-TRACE, SMAC, and IEEE 802.11) were investigated and quantified through extensive simulations and in-depth analysis (Tavli & Heinzelman, 2007). Flooding was utilized as the network layer broadcast algorithm due to its simplicity, which makes the role of the MAC layer more transparent and observable than more complicated broadcast algorithms. It was shown that MH-TRACE energy dissipation is significantly lower than the other schemes for the entire parameter space due to its schedule based channel access and data discrimination mechanisms. Although MH-TRACE-based flooding is an energy efficient broadcasting scheme, all of the flooding architectures (including MH-TRACE-based flooding) have low spatial reuse efficiency due to the redundancy of flooding as a network layer broadcast technique. Thus, the need for a network layer broadcast architecture, which inherits the energy efficiency of MH-TRACE and combines it with spatial reuse efficiency, is obvious.

NB-TRACE

Since in the design of Network-wide Broadcasting through Time Reservation using Adaptive Control for Energy efficiency (NB-TRACE) (Tavli & Heinzelman, 2006) we wanted to keep the MH-TRACE structure intact, we followed a bottom up approach to design the network layer architecture, rather than a top down approach (*i.e.*, the network layer is tailored according to the MAC layer). In NB-TRACE, the network is organized into overlapping clusters, each managed by a CH. Channel access is granted by the CHs through a dynamic, distributed Time Division Multiple Access (TDMA) scheme, which is organized into periodic superframes. Initial channel access is though contention; however, a node that utilizes the granted channel access automatically reserves a data slot in the subsequent superframes. The superframe length, *TSF*, is matched to the periodic rate of voice generation, *TPG*.

Data packets are broadcast to the entire network through flooding at the beginning of each data session. Each rebroadcasting (relay) node explicitly acknowledges (ACKs) the upstream node as part of its data transmission. Relay nodes that do not receive any ACK in *TACK* time cease to rebroadcast. As an exception, the CHs continue to rebroadcast regardless of any ACK, which prevents the eventual collapse of the broadcast tree. Due to node mobility, the initial tree will be broken in time, so NB-TRACE is equipped with several mechanisms to maintain the broadcast tree over time. In NB-TRACE, a broadcast tree is formed by the initiation of a source node, however, once a tree is formed (*i.e.*, once nodes determine their roles), then other sources do not need to create another tree; instead, they use the existing organization to broadcast their packets.

Figure 6. Illustration of NB-TRACE broadcasting. The hexagon represents the source node; diamonds are clusterheads; the large circles centered at the disks represents the transmit range of the clusterheads, squares are gateways, and the arrows represent the data transmissions.

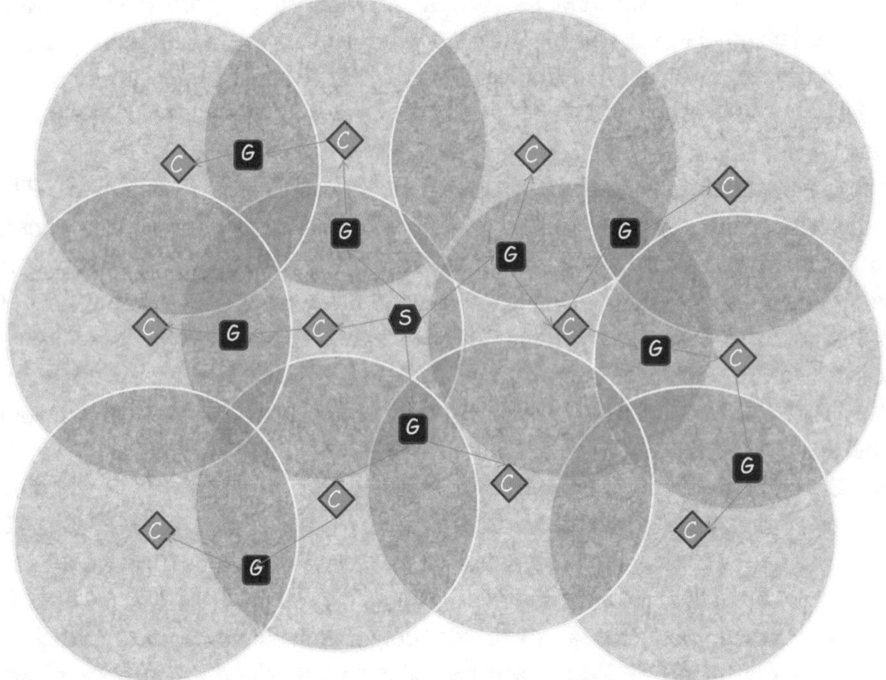

NB-TRACE broadcasting and packet flow is illustrated in Figure 6. NB-TRACE is composed of five basic building blocks: (*i*) Initial Flooding (IFL), (*ii*) Pruning (PRN), (*iii*) Repair Branch (RPB), (*iv*) Create Branch (CRB), and (*v*) Activate Branch (ACB). Actually, all of these building blocks are functioning simultaneously; however, we described them as sequential mechanisms to make them easier to understand.

A source node initiates a session by broadcasting packets to its one-hop neighbors. Nodes that receive a data packet contend for channel access, and the ones that obtain channel access retransmit the data they received. Eventually, the data packets are received by all the nodes in the network, possibly multiple times. Each rebroadcasting node ACKs its upstream node by announcing the ID of its upstream node in its IS packet, which precedes its data packet transmission (see Figure 4). A source node announces its own ID as its upstream node. Source node ID, Flow ID, Packet ID, CH Status, and IFL ID are also announced in the IS packet (see Figure 7). At the beginning of a broadcast session IFL ID is set to one for *TIFL* time to force the nodes to switch to active mode. At this point, some of the nodes have multiple upstream nodes. A node with multiple upstream nodes chooses the upstream node that has the least packet delay as its upstream node to be announced in its IS packet in order to minimize the delay.

Whenever a source node stops its broadcast, it sets the Packet ID field to null ID. Nodes that receive an IS packet with a null Packet ID mark the corresponding source and flow IDs as inactive for future reference. Furthermore, all the nodes record the time instants that they last received an IS packet with the Upstream Node ID set as their own ID from any other node (*i.e.*, ACK reception).

Figure 7. Illustration of IFL and IS contents. Diamonds and hexagons represent CHs and ordinary nodes, respectively. Node-0 is the source node. The entries below the nodes represent the contents of ([Source Node ID] [Flow ID] [Packet ID] [Upstream Node ID] [(CH Status)] [IFL ID]) fields of their IS packets (t_i's represent time instants).

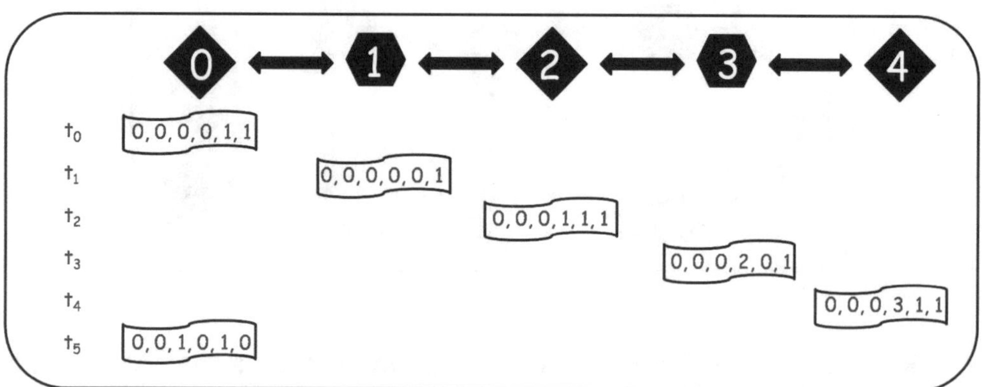

During the initial flooding, the broadcast relays are determined in a distributed fashion. Actually, a node can be in only three states: (*i*) passive, (*ii*) active, and (*iii*) ACB (activate branch). Nodes in passive mode do not relay packets, they just receive them. Nodes in the active state act as relays, because they are the only nodes that participate in broadcast data forwarding, excluding the transients where some nodes temporarily stay in the active mode. During Initial Flooding all nodes that obtained channel access switch to the active state (*i.e.*, they rebroadcast data packets). Active nodes that do not receive an ACK for *TACK* time cease rebroadcasting and return to passive mode. Nodes need to wait for *TACK* time to cease relaying because network dynamics may temporarily prevent a downstream node from ACKing an upstream node (*e.g.*, mobility, cluster maintenance). However, this algorithm has a vital shortcoming, which will eventually lead to the silencing of all relays. The outermost (leaf) nodes will not receive any ACKs, thus they will cease relaying, which also means that they cease ACKing the upstream nodes. As such, sequentially all nodes will cease relaying and ACKing, which will limit the traffic to the source, only.

To solve this problem, we introduced another feature to the algorithm, which is that the CHs always retransmit, regardless of whether or not they receive an ACK. Thus, the broadcast tree formed by IFL and PRN always ends at CHs. Note that the CHs create a non-connected dominating set. Thus, if we ensure that all the CHs relay broadcast packets, then the whole network is guaranteed to be completely covered. However, this is not the optimal solution, because in some topologies some CHs have only one neighbor, which is their upstream node (*e.g.*, node-4 in Figure 7). Such redundant rebroadcasts deteriorate the spatial reuse efficiency of NB-TRACE. Nevertheless, comparative evaluations of NB-TRACE with other broadcast architectures show that overall the spatial reuse efficiency of NB-TRACE is better than other architectures.

The IFL and PRN mechanisms are illustrated in Figure 8. After the IFL all the nodes in the network receive the data packets and they determine whether they are receiving ACKs or not. Eventually, nodes 1, 3, 5, and 7 cease retransmitting and switch to the passive mode and nodes 0, 2, 4, and 6 stay in the active mode (*i.e.*, the broadcast tree consists of nodes 0, 2, 4, and 6 and all the other nodes are in the one-hop neighborhood of at least one tree member). Node-5 ceases rebroadcasting *TACK* time after its first data transmission because it does not receive any ACK from any of its neighbors; however, until that time,

Figure 8. Illustration of IFL and PRN. Diamonds and hexagons represent CHs and ordinary nodes, respectively. Node-0 is the source node. Dotted lines represent the links between the nodes. Solid and dash-dotted lines represent the data and IS flows, respectively.

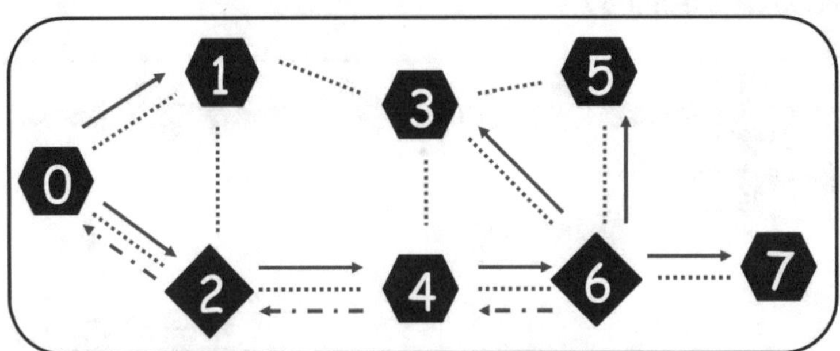

node-5 is ACKing node-3. Node-3 ceases rebroadcasting 2*TACK* time after its first data transmission, because for the first *TACK* time, node-3 was being ACKed by node-5. With the same token, node-1 ceases rebroadcasting 3*TACK* time after its first data transmission. Although the pruning of redundant rebroadcasts takes some time, this does not introduce any additional delay in data traffic (*i.e.*, all of the members of the broadcast tree start to relay packets as soon as they get channel access).

The first two blocks of the algorithm (IFL and PRN) are sufficient to create a broadcast tree for a static network. However, for a dynamic (mobile) network, we needed extra blocks in the algorithm, because due to mobility the broadcast tree will be broken in time. The simplest solution would be to repeat the IF block periodically, so that the broken links will be repaired (actually recreated) periodically. Although this algorithm is simple, it would deteriorate the overall bandwidth efficiency of the network. The quest for more efficient compensation mechanisms leads us to design three maintenance procedures.

One of the major effects of node mobility on NB-TRACE is the resignation of existing CHs and the appearance of new CHs (*i.e.*, when two CHs enter each others' receive range, one of them resigns, and if there are no CHs in the receive range of a node, it contends to become a CH). At the beginning of its operation as a CH, the CH stays in startup mode until it sends its header packet and announces its status with a bit included in the beacon packet. The appearance of a new CH generally is associated with the resignation of an existing CH. Whatever the actual situation, the nodes that receive a beacon packet from a CH in startup mode switch to active mode and rebroadcast the data packets they receive from their upstream neighbors until they cease to relay due to pruning. Figure 9 illustrates the RPB mechanism in a simple scenario. In the upper panel only node-1 is a CH and the broadcast tree consists of nodes 0 and 1. Nodes 2 and 3 receive data packets through node-1. However, due to the movement of node-3 (center panel), node-1 is out of the reach of node-3, thus, node-3 becomes a CH. Upon receiving the beacon of node-3, which indicates that it is in the startup mode, node-2, which was in the passive mode, switches to the active mode, thus, node-3 starts to receive data packets from node-2 (lower panel).

Although RPB significantly improves the system performance in combating node mobility, it cannot completely fix the broken tree problem. For example, a CH could just move away from its only upstream neighbor, which creates a broken tree. This problem (and other similar situations) cannot be handled by RPB. Thus, we introduced CRB, which, in conjunction with RPB, almost completely alleviates the tree breakage problem.

Figure 9. Illustration of the RPB mechanism.

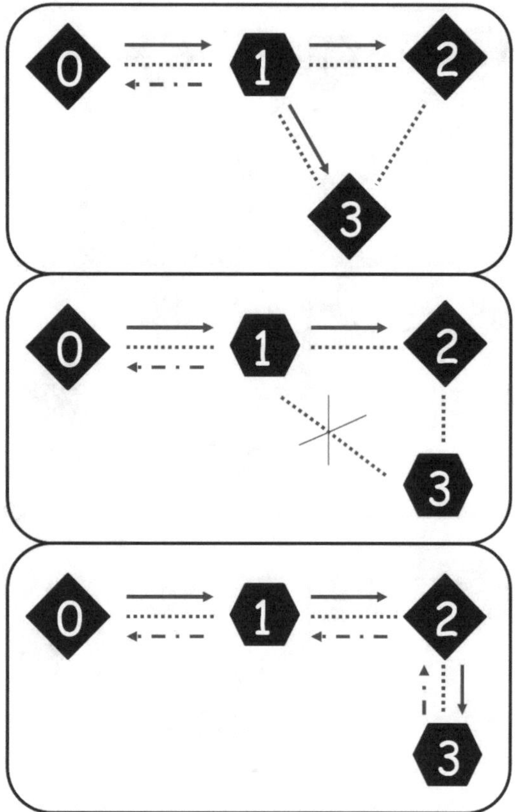

One of the basic principles of the NB-TRACE algorithm is that all the CHs should be rebroadcasting. If an ordinary node detects any of the CHs in its receive range is inactive for *TCRB* time, then it switches to active mode and starts to rebroadcast data. As in the RPB case, redundant relays will be pruned in *TACK* time. The CRB mechanism is illustrated in an example scenario in Figure 10. Node-4, which is a CH, receives data through node-3 (upper panel). Due to mobility node-4 moves away from node-3 and the link between node-3 and node-4 is broken. However, node-4 enters into the receive range of node-2 (center panel). Upon detecting an inactive CH (node-4) in its receive range for *TCRB* time, node-2 switches to the active mode and node-4 starts to receive data from its new upstream node, which is node-2 (lower panel).

The first four building blocks (IFL, PRN, RPB, and CRB) create an almost complete broadcasting algorithm capable of handling mobility. However, in some scenarios none of the aforementioned blocks can repair broken links. The upper panel of Figure 11 illustrates a network with a complete broadcast tree, where all the nodes can receive the broadcast packets. After some time, due to the mobility of nodes 3 and 5, node- 3 gives up being a CH and node-5 becomes a CH (center panel). However, the potential upstream node of node-5, which is node-4, cannot relay data packets to node-5 by using the CRB mechanism, because the potential upstream node of node-4, which is node-2, is in the passive mode and does not supply node-4 with data packets. The ACB block comes into play at this point to fix this problem.

Figure 10. Illustration of the CRB mechanism.

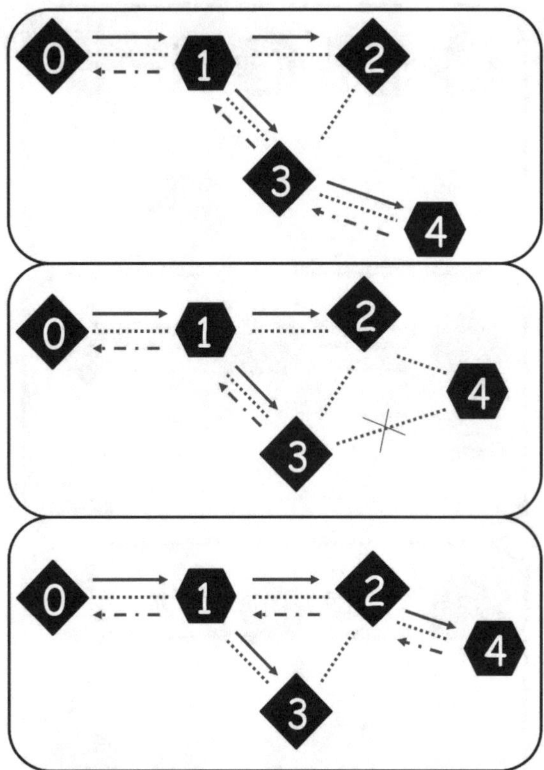

Figure 11. Illustration of the ACB mechanism.

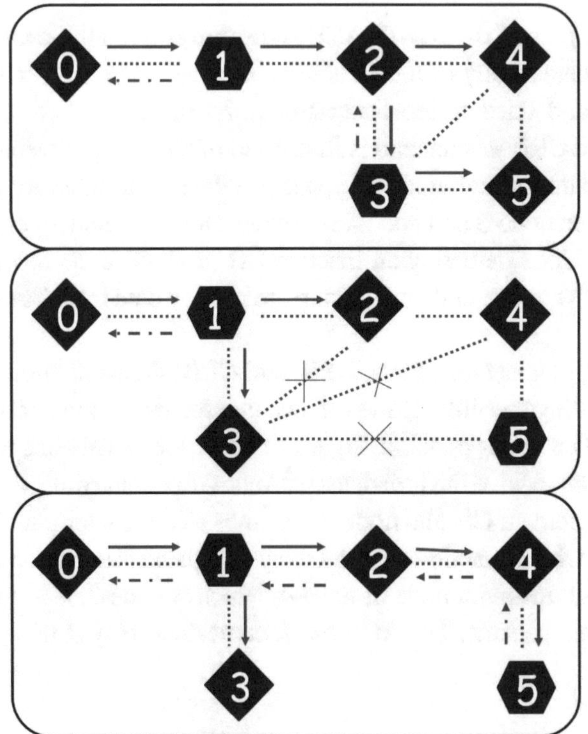

An ordinary node that does not receive any data packets for *TACB* time switches to ACB mode, and sends an ACB packet with probability *pACB*. The underlying MH-TRACEMAC does not have a structure that can be used for this purpose, thus we modified MH-TRACE to be able to send ACB packets without actually affecting any major building blocks of MH-TRACE. ACB packets are transmitted by using the IS slots, because all the nodes will be listening to the IS slots regardless of their energy saving mode. Upon reception of an ACB packet, the receiving nodes switch to active mode, and start to relay data. If the nodes that receive ACB packets do not have data to send, they are either in ACB mode or they will switch to ACB mode. Upon receiving the first data packet, the nodes in ACB mode will switch to active mode.

The lower panel of Figure 11 illustrates the ACB mechanism. Upon detecting the inactivity of the CH in its receive range (node-5), node-4 switches to active mode in *TCRB* time, which does not help to fix the broken link in this situation. After *TACB* time node-4 switches to ACB mode and sends its ACB packet to node-2. Upon receiving and ACB packet from node-4, node-2switches to active mode and starts to relay the data packets it receives from its upstream node (node-1) to node-4, and then node-4 switches to active mode and relays the packets to node-5.

The main functionality of ACB is to activate an inactive distributed gateway formed by two ordinary nodes (*i.e.*, nodes 2 and 4 in Figure 11). Once the distributed gateway is activated, then the flow of data packets, possibly from multiple flows and/or from multiple sources, can reach the leaf CH (*i.e.*, node-5), hence the nodes in the CH's one-hop neighborhood. Thus, ACB is not for actually searching for any particular broadcast flow from any particular source node, rather it is for connecting the disconnected section of the broadcast tree to the rest of the broadcast tree.

Detailed simulation-based comparative evaluations of NB-TRACE revealed the relative impact of the different building blocks and design tradeoffs of the NB-TRACE architecture. Furthermore, the performance gains of NB-TRACE over MH-TRACE-based flooding in terms of spatial reuse and energy efficiency were quantified. Comparisons with other broadcast architectures showed that NB-TRACE performance in terms of energy efficiency, jitter, PDR, and ARN is better than the other architectures and delay performance is worse than several other architectures at low node density and low data rate networks. However, with increasing node density and/or data rate networks, the relative delay performance of NB-TRACE becomes better than the other architectures due to the deterioration of the performance of these architectures and the relative stability of NB-TRACE with harsher network conditions.

Although NB-TRACE was shown to posses high spatial reuse efficiency, it is incapable of providing a selective group communication service. In other words, NB-TRACE always constructs a broadcast tree rather than a multicast tree, which does not necessarily span all of the nodes in a network. Furthermore, scalability of multicasting is better than broadcasting, provided that the multicast group size is finite and small when compared to the total number of nodes in the network. Thus, there is a need for another group communication architecture within the TRACE framework that supports multicasting.

MC-TRACE

MultiCasting through Time Reservation using Adaptive Control for Energy efficiency (MC-TRACE) is a cross-layer network architecture designed for energy-efficient voice multicasting that incorporates network layer and medium access control (MAC) layer functionality into a single layer; thus, it is a monolithic design (Tavli & Heinzelman, 2011). While preserving the energy efficiency provided by the MAC layer (*i.e.*, MH-TRACE) in idle listening or unnecessary carrier sensing, MC-TRACE also improves the energy efficiency by minimizing the number of retransmissions as well as ensuring that nodes to not receive unnecessary data packets.

MC-TRACE is built on the MH-TRACE architecture and is fully integrated with MH-TRACE, which makes MC-TRACE highly energy efficient. Although, MH-TRACE provides many advantageous features to MC-TRACE (*e.g.*, availability of controlled channel access, organization of the network into clusters) it also restricts the design of MC-TRACE in many ways.

There are five basic building blocks in MC-TRACE: (*i*) Initial Flooding (IFL), (*ii*) Pruning (PRN), (*iii*) Maintain Branch (MNB), (*iv*) Repair Branch (RPB), and (*v*) Create Branch (CRB). MC-TRACE creates a broadcast tree through flooding (IFL) and then prunes redundant branches of the tree using receiver based (or multicast leaf node-based) feedback (PRN). It ensures every multicast node remains connected to the tree while minimizing redundancy and uses IS slots so nodes can keep track of their role in the tree (*e.g.*, multicast relay node) as well as the roles of their neighbors. Finally, MC-TRACE contains mechanisms for allowing broken branches of the tree to be repaired locally (MNB and RBP) and globally (CRB). The MC-TRACE architecture is designed for multiple multicast groups and it can support multiple flows within each multicast group. However, for the sake of clarity we will describe the architecture for a single multicast group with a single source and a single data flow.

The source node initiates a session by broadcasting packets to its one-hop neighbors. Nodes that receive a data packet contend for channel access, and the ones that obtain channel access retransmit the data they received. Eventually, the data packets are received by all the nodes in the network, possibly multiple times. Each retransmitting node acknowledges its upstream node by announcing the ID of its upstream node in its IS packet, which precedes its data packet transmission (see Figure 4 and Figure 12). The source node announces its own ID as its upstream node ID. Initially all retransmitting nodes announce a null ID as their downstream node ID. However, when an upstream node is acknowledged by a downstream node, the node updates its downstream node ID by the ID of this node. The leaf nodes (*i.e.*, nodes that do not have any downstream nodes that are acknowledging them as upstream nodes) continue to announce the null ID as their downstream node ID.

Figure 12. Illustration of initial flooding. Triangles, squares, diamonds, and circles represent sources, multicast group members, multicast relays, and non-relays, respectively. The entries below the nodes represent the contents of([Upstream Node ID], [Downstream Node ID], [Multicast Group ID], [Multicast Relay Status]) fields of their IS packets (f represent null IDs and t_i's represent time instants).

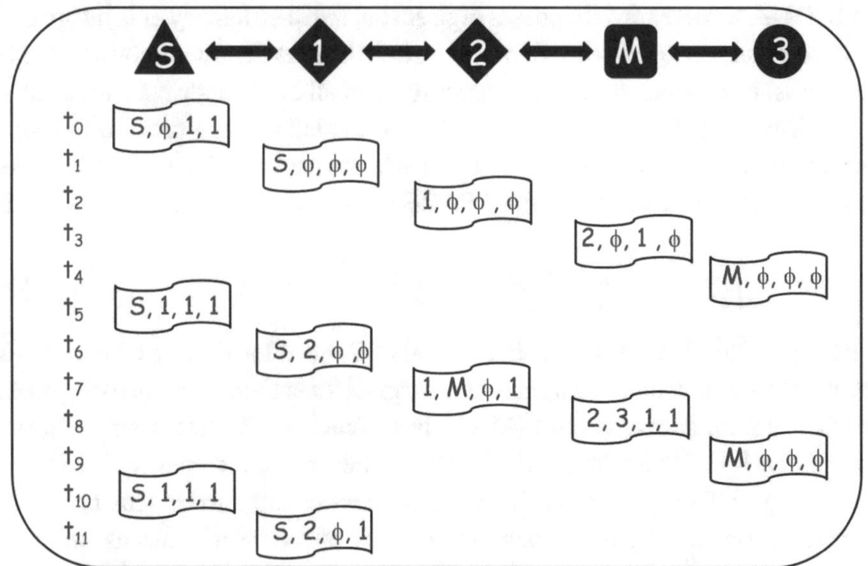

At this point, some of the nodes have multiple upstream nodes (*i.e.*, multiple nodes that have lower hop distance to the source than the current node) and downstream nodes (*i.e.*, multiple downstream nodes acknowledging the some upstream node as their upstream node). A node with multiple upstream nodes chooses the upstream node that has the least packet delay as its upstream node to be announced in its IS slot. Since a retransmitting node indicates its hop distance to the source (HDTS) in its IS packet, it is possible to choose the node with the least HDTS as the upstream node; however, our primary objective is minimizing delay rather than minimizing the multicast tree size. Anode updates its own HDTS by incrementing the least HDTS it hears within *THDTS*1 time. The initial HDTS value is set to HDTS*MAX*, and the HDTS value is again set to HDTS*MAX* if a node does not receive any IS or data packet for more than *THDTS*2 time, where *THDTS*2 is larger than *THDTS*1.

Multicast group member nodes indicate their status by announcing their multicast group ID in the IS packet (see Figure 12). Nodes that are not members of the multicast group set their multicast group ID to the null multicast group ID. If an upstream node receives an acknowledgment (ACK) from a downstream multicast group member, it marks itself as a multicast relay and announces its multicast relay status by setting the corresponding status (*i.e.*, multicast relay bit) in the IS packet. The same mechanism continues in the same way up to the source node. In other words, an upstream node that gets an ACK from a downstream multicast relay marks itself as a multicast relay. Furthermore, a multicast group member that receives an ACK from an upstream multicast relay marks itself as a multicast relay also. Multicast relay status expires if no ACK is received from any downstream (for both members and nonmembers of the multicast group) or upstream (only for members of the multicast group) multicast relay or multicast group member for *TRLY* time. For the sake of simplicity, we assumed a link between any node pair is bidirectional at this point; however, this is not necessary for MC-TRACE to operate successfully. Initial flooding results in a highly redundant multicast tree, where most of the nodes receive the same data packet multiple times. Thus, a pruning mechanism is needed to eliminate the redundancies of the multicast tree created by the initial flooding.

Actually initial flooding and pruning are two mechanisms working simultaneously; however, we described these as sequential mechanisms to make them easier to understand. During the initial flooding, the multicast relays are determined in a distributed fashion. Pruning uses the multicast relays to create an efficient multicast tree. As described previously, a multicast relay node that does not receive any upstream or downstream ACK for *TRLY* time ceases to be a multicast relay (for the sake of simplicity, we assumed the multicast group members are always the leaf nodes). Furthermore, a node, which is not a multicast relay also ceases to retransmit the multicast data if it does not receive an ACK from any downstream node.

Figure 13 illustrates the operation of the pruning mechanism. After the initial flooding all the nodes receive the data packets and they determine their upstream and downstream nodes. Multicast relays are also determined. Nodes 4, 5, and M along with S are multicast relays. However, nodes 1, 2, and 3 are not multicast relays, because there is not a multicast group member connected to that branch of the network. Node-3 will cease retransmitting the packets that it received from its upstream node-2 *TRLY* time after its first retransmission of data, because no node is acknowledging its data transmissions. However, until that time node-3 acknowledges its upstream node, which is node-2. Node-2 ceases retransmitting packets 2*TRLY* times after its first data transmission. Note that node-2 acknowledges its upstream node (node-1) for 2*TRLY* time.Node-1 ceases retransmitting 3*TRLY* time after its first data transmission. Thus, the redundant upper branch, where no multicast group members are present, is pruned.

Figure 13. Illustration of pruning and multicast tree creation.

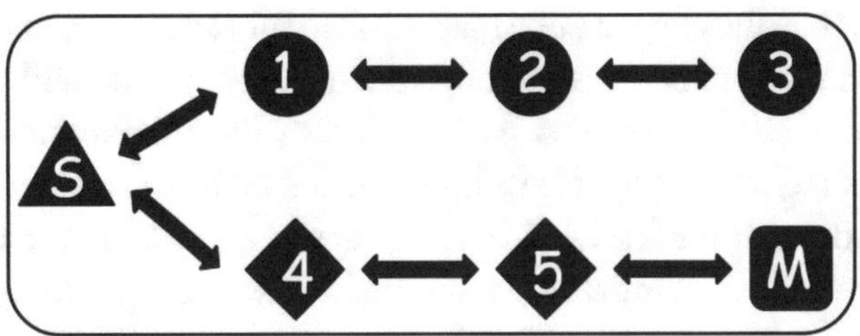

Unlike the upper branch, the lower branch is not pruned due to the fact that the lower branch has a multicast node as the leaf node. Node-M acknowledges the upstream node (node-5) upon receiving the first data packet. Since node-5 receives an ACK form its downstream node (node-M) and also node-M indicates its multicast group membership in its IS packet, node-5 marks itself as a multicast relay and announces its status in its following IS transmission. Upon receiving that IS packet from its downstream node (node-5), node-4 marks itself as a multicast relay also. Thus, the branch of the multicast tree consisting of node-4, node-5, and node-M is created in a distributed fashion. When compared to completion of the pruning of the upper branch the completion of the creation of the lower branch is realized in much shorter time.

Although in most cases initial flooding and pruning are capable of creating an initial efficient multicast tree, they are not always capable of maintaining the multicast tree in a mobile network. Thus, the need for additional mechanisms to repair broken branches is obvious. Maintain Branch, Repair Branch, and Create Branch mechanisms are utilized to maintain the multicast tree.

Some of the multicast group members are not multicast relays. The upper panel of Figure 14 illustrates such a situation. Multicast node (node-M1) is a multicast relay, which is indicated by the two-way arrows; whereas node-M2 is not a multicast relay it just receives the packets from the upstream node (node- 2). Hence, node-M2 does not acknowledge node-2 (node-2 is acknowledged by node-M1. Note that any node can acknowledge only one upstream and one downstream node with a single IS packet. When node-M1 moves away from node-2's transmit range and enters node-1's transmit range, it either begins to acknowledge node-1 as its upstream node if the transition happens in less than *TRLY* time (*i.e.*, node-M1's multicast relay status does not expire before *TRLY* time) or just receives the data packets from node-1 without acknowledging node-1 if node-M1's transition takes more than *TRLY* time. In any case, node-2 does not receive any ACK from node-M1, and starts to set its downstream node ID as the null ID. However, node-2 does not cease retransmitting data packets that it receives from its upstream node (node-1) instantly, because, a multicast relay does not resets its status for *TRLY* time and continues to retransmit data packets.

Although node-M2 does not acknowledge any node, it monitors its upstream node through IS and data packets. When the upstream node of a multicast group member node (*i.e.*, node-M2) announces null ID as its downstream node ID, the multicast node (M2) starts to acknowledge the upstream node by announcing the ID of the upstream node (node-2) as its upstream node in its IS packet. Thus, node-2 continues to be a multicast relay and node-M2 becomes a multicast relay after receiving a downstream ACK from its upstream node (node-2). Actually, the situation illustrated in Figure 14 is just one example for MNB mechanism. There are several other situations that can be fixed by the MNB mechanism.

Figure 14. Illustration of the Maintain Branch Mechanism.

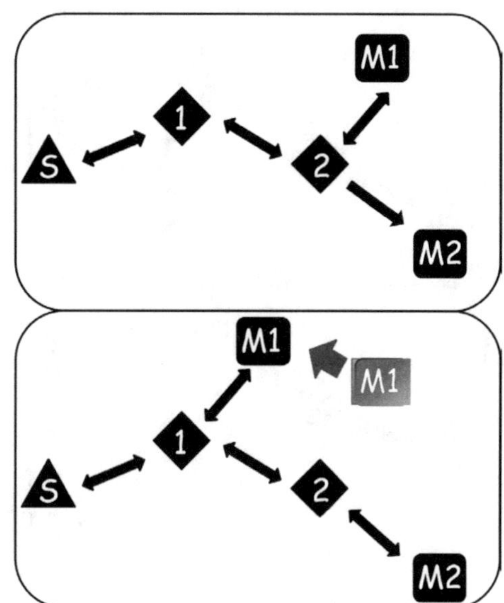

The MNB mechanism does not necessarily create a new branch, yet it prevents an existing operational branch from collapse. However, just maintaining the existing multicast relays is not enough in every situation. There are situations where new relays should be incorporated to the tree.

After a node marks itself as a multicast relay, it continuously monitors its upstream node to detect a possible link break between itself and its upstream multicast relay node, which manifests itself as the interruption of the data flow without any prior notification. If such a link break is detected, the downstream node uses the RPB mechanism to fix the broken link. Figure 15 illustrates an example of a network topology where a branch of the multicast tree is broken due to the mobility of a multicast relay and fixed later by the RPB mechanism. The upper panel of Figure 15 shows a multicast tree formed by the source node, node-S, multicast relay nodes, node-1 and node-2, and the multicast group node, node-M, which is a multicast relay as well. Node-3 is neither a multicast relay node nor a multicast group member; however, it receives the IS packets from node-1, node-2, and node-M (*i.e.*, node-3 is in the receive range of all three nodes). After some time, as illustrated in the lower panel of Figure 15, node-2 moves away from its original position and node-1 and node-2 cannot hear each other; thus, the multicast tree is broken. At this point node-2 realizes that the link is broken (*i.e.*, it does not receive data packets from its upstream node anymore) and the RPB mechanism is used to fix the broken tree. Node-2sets its RPB bit to one in the IS packets that it sends. Upon receiving an RPB indicator, all the nodes in the receive range start to retransmit data packets as they do in the initial flooding stage. One of these nodes, which is node-3 in this scenario, replaces node-2 as a multicast relay node and the multicast tree branch is repaired.

We assumed node-3 remains in the transmit range of node-1, node-2, and node-M even after node-2 moved away from node-1's transmit range. However, even if node-3 was not in the transmit range of node-2, the tree can again be fixed. Since node-M does not receive any data packets from its upstream node (node-2), it sets its RPB bit to one and announces this in its IS packet. Upon receiving the RPB of node-M, node-3 starts to relay data packets, and upon receiving an upstream ACK from node-M, marks itself as a multicast relay.

Figure 15. Illustration of the Repair Branch Mechanism.

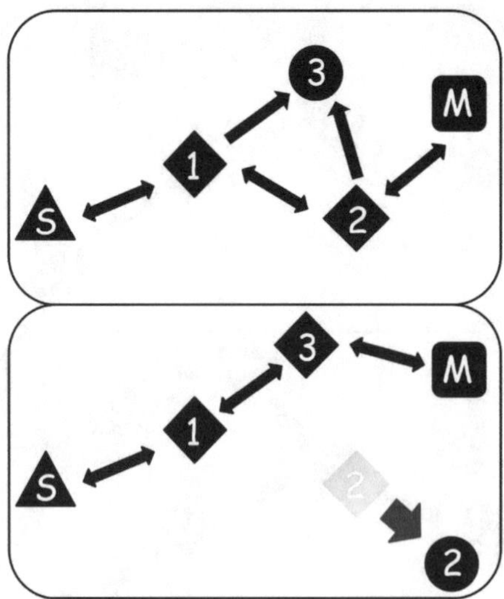

Both MNB and RPB are limited scope maintenance algorithms (*i.e.*, they can fix mostly one-hop tree breaks). However, in a dynamic network, limited scope algorithms are not capable of completely eliminating multicast tree breaks or, in some cases, the total collapse of the multicast tree. Thus, the create branch (CRB) mechanism is needed.

It is possible that due to the dynamics of the network (*e.g.*, mobility, unequal interference) a complete branch of a multicast tree can become inactive, and the leaf multicast group member node cannot receive the data packets form the source node. Figure 16 illustrates a network with one active branch, composed of the nodes S, 1, 2 and M1, and one inactive branch, composed of nodes 3, 4, 5, and M2.

Figure 16. Illustration of the Create Branch Mechanism.

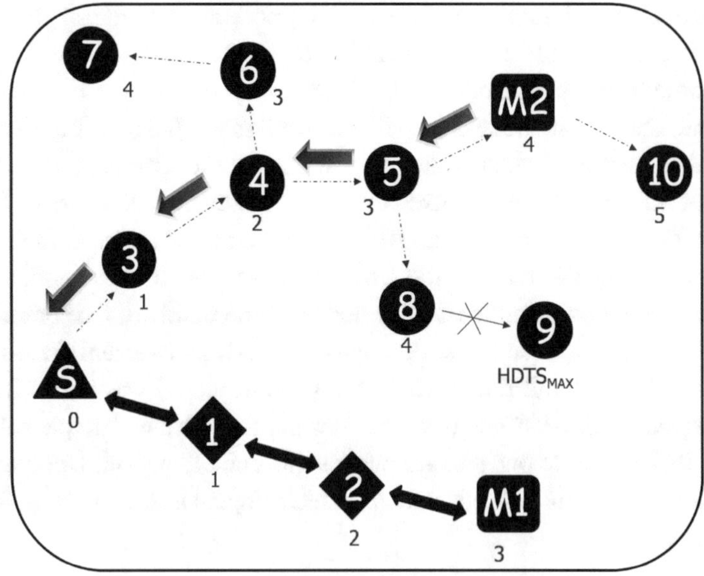

The double arrows indicate an active link with upstream and downstream ACKs. Dash-dotted arrows indicate an inactive link. The numbers below the nodes show their HDTS, which they acquired during previous data transmissions. One situation that can create such inactivity is that the upstream ACKs of nodes 8 and M1 are colliding and node-5 cannot receive any downstream ACK. Thus, node-5 ceases to relay packets, which eventually results in silencing all the upstream nodes up to the source (*i.e.*, if node-5 does not get any downstream ACKs it ceases acknowledging its upstream node, node-4, after *TRLY* time, which results in silencing of node-4 in 2*TRLY* time and node-3 in 3*TRLY* time).

If a multicast group member, which is node-M2 in this scenario, detects an interruption in the data flow for *TCRB* time, it switches to Create Branch status and announces this information via a CRB packet. A CRB packet is transmitted by using one of the IS slots, which is chosen randomly. Upon receiving a CRB packet, all the nodes in the receive range of the transmitting node switch to CRB status if their own HDTS is lower than or equal to the HDTS of the sender (*e.g.*, node-5, which has an HDTS of 4, switches to CRB status; however, node-10, which has an HDTS of 5, does not). When a node switches to CRB mode, it starts to relay the data packets if it has data packets for the desired multicast group. If it does not have the desired data packets, it propagates the CRB request by broadcasting a CRB packet to its one-hop neighbors. This procedure continues until a node with the desired data packets is found, which is illustrated by the block arrows in Figure 16. After this point, the establishment of the link is similar to the initial flooding followed by pruning mechanisms. However, in this case only the nodes in CRB mode participate in data relaying. Looking at the initial collapse of the branch, we saw that node-8 does not participate in CRB due to its HDTS and it does not create interference for node-M2 in this case.

The performance of MC-TRACE was compared with ODMRP-I and ODMRP-S in terms of packet delivery ratio, delay, jitter, spatial reuse efficiency, and energy dissipation through simulations and it was shown that MC-TRACE outperforms both of the ODMRP variants (Lee, Su, & Gerla, 2002).

MMC-TRACE

MTCAN solutions need to offer different ways to provide tradeoffs between wireless communication and networking performance metrics (*e.g.*, throughput, energy efficiency, channel access delay, end-to-end packet delay, congestion avoidance, etc.). One of the most important tradeoffs is between the throughput and end-to-end packet delay. In this section, we described our further extension of this TRACE framework to allow users to select the appropriate tradeoff among energy dissipation, end-to-end packet delay and data quality (*i.e.*, throughput), enabling TRACE to be much more responsive to end-user requirements and adaptive as these requirements change over time. Coupled with scalable video or audio coding, multi-rate multicasting (MMC-TRACE) enables users to receive high quality video/audio with a potential delay increase.

Motivation

In MANETs, the communication medium is often called the broadcast channel, where transmissions occur from one user to many others simultaneously. Although broadcasting makes it easier to reach many receivers through a single transmission, it is difficult to satisfy the individual needs of different receivers simultaneously. In a broadcast channel, the capacities of the communication links from the source to the intended recipients vary greatly due to differences in communication range, fading, and interference on these links. By varying the modulation and coding scheme (MCS) TRACE protocol family can offer different levels of robustness against the varying link qualities in a MTCAN environment. In order to provide different levels of robustness (*i.e.*, different rates of information) without having to adjust the MCS and retransmit, we have utilized the idea of Cover and Bergmanns, who showed ways to provide multiple rates to different receivers through a single transmission while causing little degradation for the receiver with the worst channel capacity (Bergmans, 1973; Cover, 1972). The technique utilized in multi-rate broadcasting is called the *superposition coding*.

The idea of superposition coding is to add additional coding on top of the first coding in such a way that already separated codewords are displaced again according to new information. The second displacement is smaller than the first one, and it is unlikely to be detected by any receiver with a poor channel. However, any receiver with a good channel will be able to detect both the first and the second displacements of the codewords. Therefore, nodes with poor channels decode only the lower rate information (*i.e.*, the first displacement of the codewords) while nodes with good channels decode both the lower rate and the additional information.

The Protocol

We take the idea of multi-rate broadcasting one step further than the original goal of single-hop broadcasting, and we utilize multi-rate broadcasting to provide a flexible throughput-delay tradeoff. This tradeoff between throughput and delay can be exploited within the network according to the different requirements of the different members of a multicast group. Multi-rate availability through a single transmission can be used to facilitate the co-existence of streams with different importance. Using Cover's idea of superimposing information, an additional (probably less important) stream can be transmitted simultaneously with the essential stream, which carries crucial information needed by all of the members of a multicast group (*i.e.*, with a single transmission, the nodes with "high quality" links receive "high rate" information whereas the nodes with "low quality" links receive "low rate" information). Figure 17 illustrates the idea of multi-rate transmission. When node S broadcasts a packet, the received energy per bit at node A is higher than that at node B because of the decrease in the received signal strength due to the extended propagation distance. Therefore, node A has the "high quality" link in this case.

Figure 17. Illustration of different link qualities in broadcasting mode.

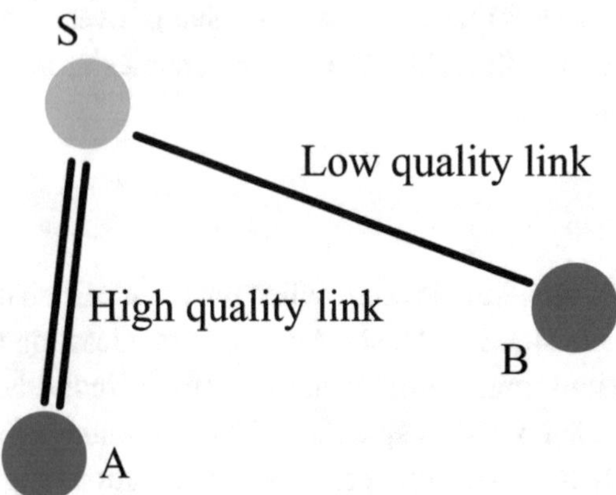

Figure 18. Non-uniform Quadrature Amplitude Modulation (QAM).

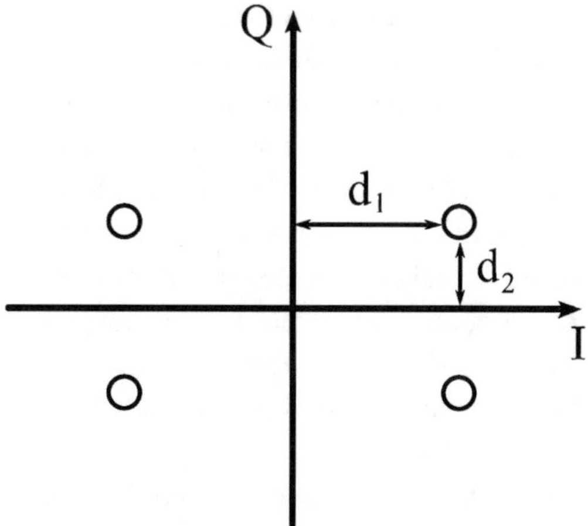

Figure 18 shows the non-uniform Quadrature Amplitude Modulation (QAM) constellation which is obtained by assigning a smaller displacement to the quadrature component than the in-phase component in the BPAM constellation. This can be thought of as both non-uniform QAM and non-uniform QPSK.

We can further use this idea to introduce many levels of noise margins. Figure 19 shows a nonuniform16-ary QAM constellation, which provides four different noise margins for the encoded four bits of information per symbol. If we assume again that the propagation loss mainly depends on distance, we have four different penetration distances for these bits. In other words, there are four regions in which the transmitted symbol can be decoded at four different rates. Sun et al. (2004) utilize a special case of the non-uniform 16-ary QAM constellation in achieving a flexible unequal error protection.

Figure 19. 16 point non-uniform Quadrature Amplitude Modulation (QAM).

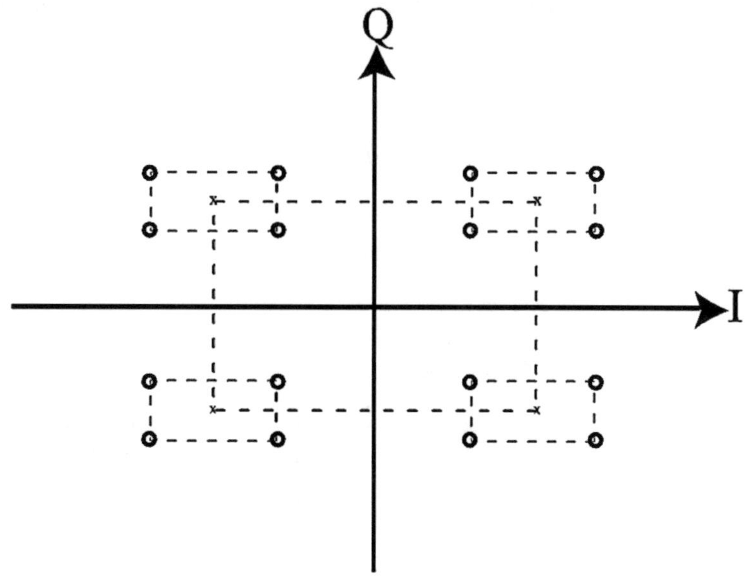

We propose the new idea of multi-rate multicast routing, and we incorporate this idea into an existing multicasting protocol, MC-TRACE. We name this new version of MC-TRACE as Multi-rate MC-TRACE (MMC-TRACE). We combine the idea of multi-rate coding with scalable source coding (Dong & Gibson, 2006) to provide multi-level resolution of conversational voice or video. Scalable source coding is basically a hierarchical coding scheme, where coarser representations are embedded into finer ones, thereby allowing access to the source at a variety of resolutions. Rimoldi (1994) generalized the scalable source coding problem and discovered necessary and sufficient conditions for the achievability of any sequence of rates and distortions. Scalable source coding is often used in wireless communication applications where the available communication rate is time-varying. When we combine multi-rate transmission with scalable coding in a MTCAN, nodes with different link qualities will have different rates available to them instead of a single rate that varies according to a predetermined source coding (Numanoglu, Heinzelman, & Tavli, 2007).

In Figure 20, we demonstrate two possible scenarios where the multicast member has two different priorities, low-delay and high-rate, respectively. The low-delay priority is often the goal for many routing protocols, and this might be achieved by using different priorities such as minimum number of hops routing and shortest distance routing (if location information is available). We demonstrate two examples of multicast branches that can be formed between the source (S) and the multicast member (M) after the initial flooding and pruning. Branch I is a regular branch that could have been formed by MC-TRACE. However, branch II includes a high-rate link between the source (the triangle) and the rebroadcasting node (the diamond) and can only be formed if there is multi-rate availability. Although this high-rate connectivity is not utilized by the next hop of branch II, both branches are two hops long and multicast branch candidates for the multicast member (M). In such a case where M has more than one upstream node (*i.e.*, nodes with lower hop distance to the source than M), the node that has the least packet delay is chosen as the upstream node and announced in M's IS slot.

In Figure 20-b, the branches are formed according to high-rate requirement imposed by the multicast member. The reason for the difference between the different branch formations obtained by utilizing MMC-TRACE is the fact that the multicast group members have two different priorities, namely high-rate and low-delay. For these two different requests, different multicast branches are formed between the members. MMCTRACE can support all these requests without having to send two different trans-

Figure 20. a) Low-delay priority forwarding. b) High-rate priority forwarding.

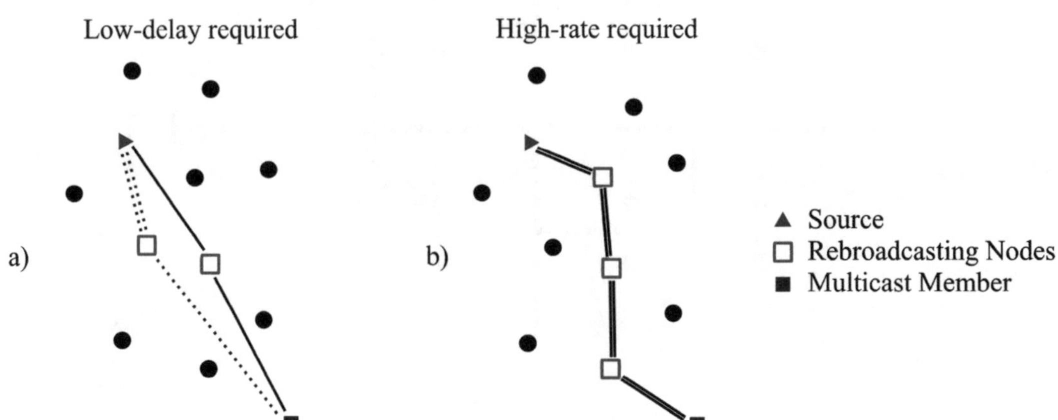

missions. This is the main advantage of MMC-TRACE over single-rate multicasting. The performance of multi-rate multicasting can be calibrated according to the specific needs of different scenarios by modifying the multi-rate broadcast parameters such as the number of rates available, type of modulation, and power allocation between the rates.

MMC-TRACE provides an important tradeoff between throughput and end-to-end packet delay, which can be exploited within a MTCAN according to the different requirements of the different members of a multicast group (Numanoglu, 2009).

AR-TRACE

The objective of a multicast routing protocol for MANETs is to support the dissemination of information from a sender to all multicast group members while trying to use the available bandwidth efficiently in the presence of frequent topology and channel condition changes. In a MTCAN, node mobility due to tactical operations and the fact that wireless links are more prone to transmission errors due to harsh environments result in higher packet drop probability when compared to civilian MANETs. Therefore, multicast routing protocols that provide route redundancy (*i.e.*, routing packets along multiple paths from source to receivers), typically outperform multicast routing mechanisms that offer no redundancy. However, increased redundancy can cause significant overhead in a resource-constrained MTCAN, even though it provides higher packet delivery ratios.

When channel conditions are good (*i.e.*, link reliability is high), having larger redundancy in the network does not significantly increase packet delivery ratio (PDR). However, when channel conditions get worse, having greater redundancy does have a considerable impact on the packet delivery ratio. Our proposed multicasting mechanism with adaptive redundancy varies the redundancy in the network according to the local packet reception history. Redundancy is managed locally and adaptive behavior is controlled by the multicast members (*i.e.*, receivers). A multicast member node controls the amount of redundancy depending on the stability of its upstream node and incoming traffic. If the upstream node is volatile and data packets do not arrive in order, the number of upstream nodes is increased. If a consistent upstream node exists and data packets continue to arrive in order, the number of upstream nodes is decreased. This process is repeated by each relay to provide a greater number of non-overlapping redundant branches between the source and the multicast member (Numanoglu & Heinzelman, 2008).

We aim to achieve adaptive redundancy (AR-TRACE) through varying the number of upstream nodes. When channel conditions are bad, more upstream nodes are needed to create a mesh-like routing that delivers data packets multiple times using different routes. When conditions are good, fewer upstream nodes are needed to create a tree-like routing that reduces the number of unnecessary routes between the source and destination pairs. The minimum amount of redundancy is achieved when there is a single route between each source-destination pair. The maximum level of redundancy can be considered as flooding where all routes between the source-destination pair are utilized. However, as we increase the number of upstream nodes (*i.e.*, transition from tree-based to mesh-based routing), we will reach to a point where increasing the redundancy in the network is either not possible or not worth the price we pay in terms of bandwidth and energy efficiency (Numanoglu & Heinzelman, 2009).

We can demonstrate the need for an upper limit to the number of routes with the help of an example given in Figure 21. For a given bit error rate BER, if we assume that a single bit error is enough to corrupt a data packet and cause it to be dropped, the probability of having at least one bit in error in a data packet of size LD bits becomes

$P_{drop} = 1 - (1 - BER)^{LD}$.

In a real-time traffic scenario, where retransmissions are not utilized, the packet delivery ratio (PDR) of branch I in Figure 21 can be written in terms of the number of hops in the branch (N_{hop}) as

$PDR_1 = [(1 - BER)^{LD}]N_{hop}$.

Following the same idea, we can rewrite the effective PDR of having k non-overlapping branches between the source-multicast member pair as

$PDR_k = 1 - (1 - PDR_1)^k$.

For k = 3 and assuming the number of hops in all three branches is the same, we can calculate the effective PDR of the scenario illustrated in Figure 21. The existence of the interconnections between the nodes (*i.e.*, the dashed lines in Figure 21) does not contribute to the effective PDR since each node rebroadcasts the same data packet only once. Moreover, non-overlapping branches always will outperform partially overlapping routes. As *k* increases, one can see that the increase in the effective PDR saturates. On the other hand, the amount of traffic generated and the energy consumption are linearly related with k. Therefore, it is necessary and wise to limit the number of non-overlapping branches in order to strike a well-balanced tradeoff between the amount of redundancy and energy consumption.

It is possible to further investigate these results to determine an optimum number of branches for a given set of constraints on bandwidth, energy consumption and PDR. However, our approach, as dictated by the need of distributed solutions for MTCANs, locally increases the number of upstream nodes, and therefore, resulting branches will be sub-optimal and may be overlapping depending on the node distribution and density of the network.

Figure 21. Illustration of multiple branches between a source-multicast member pair. Solid lines represent possible non-overlapping routes between the source and member. Dashed lines represent possible interconnections between the branches.

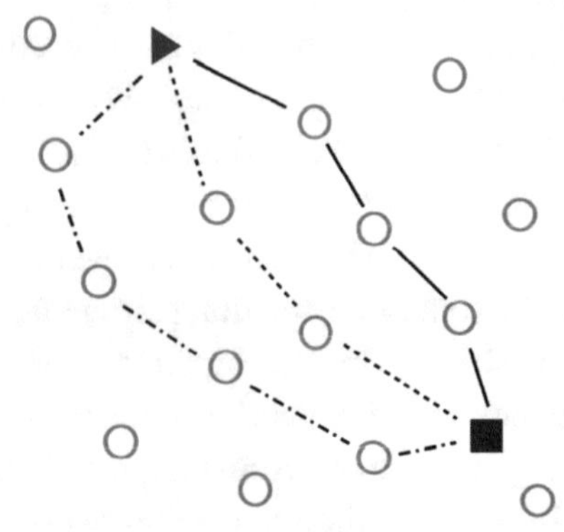

We also design this distributed redundancy solution to be adaptive in order to react to changing conditions at a rate fast enough to sustain a desired level of performance. In particular, we aim to achieve a better QoS for time sensitive or real-time applications under increasing channel errors while keeping the unnecessary redundancy and energy consumption as low as possible.

In order to keep our approach as an adaptive, distributed, and lightweight addition to a multicasting protocol, we locally vary the redundancy in the multicast tree according to the data packet reception history (*i.e.*, history of link quality between the two nodes). Each node in a multicast tree monitors data packet receptions and the corresponding upstream nodes to make sure that data packets are arriving regularly from the same upstream node (*i.e.*, the link is stable). If there is a disruption of data packet flow, the adaptive redundancy mechanism will increase the number of upstream nodes until a maximum number of allowed upstream nodes is reached.

Under perfect channel conditions and in the presence of a well maintained broadcast tree, multicast members periodically receive data packets broadcasted by the source node through the branches formed between themselves and the source node. However, when a data packet is not received (*i.e.*, dropped or never routed to a certain node A), node A reduces its link quality metric associated with the upstream node and depending on the decision boundaries (pre-determined or adaptively adjusted according to packet reception history), if it is necessary, starts the process to increase its number of upstream nodes. Node A switches to Increase Redundancy status and announces this information via an Increase Redundancy (INR) packet. Upon receiving an INR packet, all the nodes in the receive range of the transmitting node switch to INR status if their own hop distance to source (HDTS) is less than or equal to the HDTS of the sender (e.g., if node A's HDTS is equal to 4, nodes with an HDTS less than or equal to 4 switch to INR status; however, nodes with an HDTS larger than 4 do not). When a node switches to INR mode, it starts to relay the data packets if it has data packets for the desired multicast group. Moreover, it propagates the INR request by broadcasting an INR packet to its one-hop neighbors and starts ACKing an additional upstream node (a node with a lower HDTS) in order to sustain the required redundancy level. This procedure is repeated by all the nodes until the source node is reached. After this point, newly established links are maintained by ACK and pruning mechanisms.

Upon receiving the first sequential set of data packets from the same upstream node, node A will increase the link quality metric and depending on the decision boundaries may start the procedure to reduce the number of its upstream nodes by sending out a DEcrease Redundancy (DER) packet. Therefore, the data packet reception history plays the main role in determining the level of redundancy in the network.

Note that increased redundancy causes more energy consumption, and the improvement in the performance of slows down after a certain level of redundancy. Therefore, there should be a limit to the level of redundancy that can be introduced in order to avoid unnecessary energy consumption and traffic.

Figure 22 shows a simple flow chart for our adaptive redundancy mechanism, where only last two packets are utilized for decision making purposes. After each decision period nodes check whether or not consecutive data packets have been received from the same upstream node. The level of redundancy is updated periodically after each decision period according to two conditions; (i) a node must receive two packets in a row from the same upstream node to be able to transmit a DER packet, and (ii) failure to receive any consecutive data packets is enough to increase the level of redundancy (send INR).

Figure 22. Simple flow chart of the adaptive redundancy algorithm.

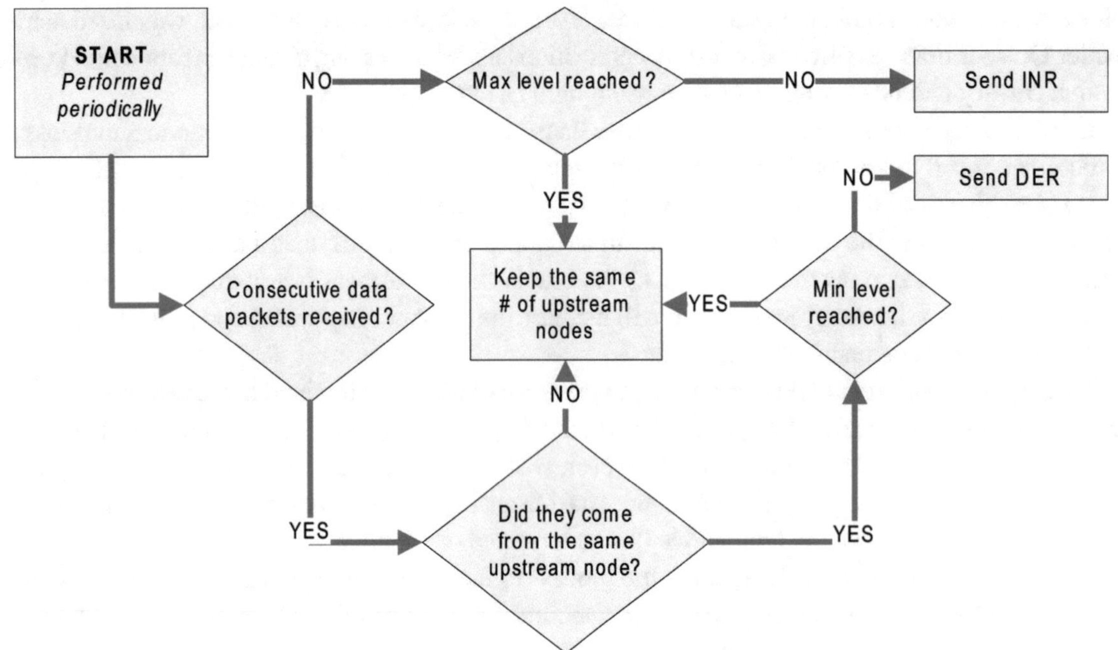

CDCA-TRACE

Cooperative node balancing and dynamic channel allocation with Time Reservation using Adaptive Control for Energy efficiency (CDCA-TRACE) (Karaoglu & Heinzelman, 2014) is a protocol architecture for energy efficient and bandwidth aware single-hop voice broadcasting in a multihop network.

Integrating spatial reuse into a MAC protocol drastically increases bandwidth efficiency (Leiner, Nielson, & Tobagi, 1987). Reusing the channels more frequently in the network increases the transmission opportunities for nodes but also increases the interference and collisions. It has been shown that both throughput and the energy efficiency of MANET protocols can be improved by adjusting the frequency of reusing the channels (Karaoglu, Numanoglu, & Heinzelman, 2011). At the same time, in a MANET, the traffic load may be highly non-uniform over both the network area and time. Thus, it is also crucial that the MAC protocol be able to not only dynamically change the amount of spatial reuse incorporated but also efficiently handle spatially non-uniform traffic loads. Uncoordinated protocols intrinsically incorporate spatial reuse and adapt to the changes in load distribution through the carrier sensing mechanism. However, coordinated protocols, such as TRACE family of protocols, require careful design at the MAC layer, allowing the channel controllers to utilize spatial reuse and adapt to any changes in the traffic distribution.

Since the early development stages of wireless communication, efficient channel utilization has been the center of attention (Leiner, Nielson, & Tobagi, 1987). Cidon & Sidi (1989) present a distributed dynamic channel allocation algorithm with no optimality guarantees for a network with a fixed a-priori control channel assignment. Alternatively, there are various game-theoretic approaches to the channel allocation problem in ad hoc wireless networks (Gao & Wang, 2008; Felegyhazi, Cagalj, Bidokhti, & Hubaux, 2007). Gao & Wang (2008) model the channel allocation problem in multihop ad hoc wireless networks as a static cooperative game, in which some players collaborate to achieve a high data rate. However, these approaches are not scalable, as the complexity of the optimal dynamic channel allocation problem has been shown to be NP-hard (Ramaswami & Parhi, 1989; Ephremides & Truong, 1990; Sen & Huson, 1996; Raniwala & Chiueh, 2005).

In multihop wireless networks, CSMA (Kleinrock & Tobagi, 1975) techniques enable the same radio resources to be used in distinct locations, leading to increased bandwidth efficiencies at the cost of possible collisions due to the hidden terminal problem (Tobagi & Kleinrock, 1975). Different channel reservation techniques are used to tackle the hidden terminal problem. Karn (1990) use an RTS/CTS packet exchange mechanism before the transmission of the data packet. 802.11 distributed coordination function (DCF) uses a similar mechanism. Although this handshake reduces the hidden node problem, it is inefficient under heavy network loads due to the exposed terminal problem. Several modifications to the RTS/CTS mechanisms have been proposed to increase the bandwidth efficiency (Toumpis & Goldsmith, 2006; Shukla, Chandran-Wadia, & Iyer, 2003) including use of multiple channels such as (Nasipuri & Das, 2000; Jain, Das, & Nasipuri, 2001).

However, these approaches do not cover group communication and only attempt to solve the problem of channel assignment when there is a single intended destination of each transmission. Using link layer multicasting/broadcasting increases the efficient use of network resources in many cases (Kappes, 2006). Indeed, many MANET applications such as military field communications (Tang & Gerla, 2000) and inter vehicle communication systems (Zhu & Roy, 2003) make use of broadcast services. In this section, we particularly focus on link layer broadcasting and consider MANET scenarios where the destination of the generated packet is not a specific node in the local neighborhood but all the nodes in the immediate neighborhood of the transmitter. The IEEE 802.11 standard defines and allows link layer broadcasting services for both infrastructure and ad hoc modes. In ad hoc broadcast communication mode, the IEEE 802.11 MAC DCF specification disables the RTS/CTS mechanism as well as acknowledgments (ACKs). There is no MAC-level recovery or re-transmission for broadcast frames. The broadcast performance of IEEE 802.11 has been studied through simulations (Xie, Das, Nandi, & Gupta, 2005) as well as analytically (Ma & Chen, 2008). In coordinated MAC protocols, channel assignment is performed by channel coordinators. Channel reuse is incorporated into the system through use of the same channel by coordinators that are spatially separated. The cellular concept (MacDonald, 1979) that regulates channel access through fixed infrastructure called base stations also forms the basis of the widely deployed GSM systems.

In cellular systems, there are two types of strategies for on-demand dynamic channel allocation: centralized and distributed schemes. In centralized dynamic channel allocation schemes (Katzela & Naghshineh, 1996), the available channels are kept in a pool and distributed to various cells by a central coordinator. Although quite effective in maximizing channel usage, these systems have a high overhead and cannot be applied to MANETs due to the lack of high bandwidth and low latency links between the cluster heads for coordination.

Distributed dynamic channel allocation for cellular networks has also been studied extensively (I & Chao, 1993; I & Chao, 1994; Jiang, 2002). In distributed dynamic channel allocation, each cell is assigned a number of channels. These channels can be exchanged among adjacent cells through message exchange mechanisms between the channel regulators (cell towers) in an on demand basis. This approach, too, is not directly applicable to MANETs. Unlike in the cellular case, in MANETs, the message exchanges between the channel regulators also consume network resources. Due to node mobility and the dynamic behavior of the network, the large overhead associated with the frequent message exchanges may overwhelm the network and decrease the bandwidth efficiency.

Load balancing has also been studied within the context of heterogeneous networks. In the case of excess demand, part of the network load can be offloaded to other networks using heterogeneous gateway nodes. Song et al. (2007) present a policy framework for such resource management in a loosely coupled cellular/WLAN integrated network. Although dynamic channel allocation and channel handoff are studied extensively within the context of cellular networks, they have not been studied much in the context of MANETs, where the bandwidth efficiency and load balancing are mostly studied at the network layer (Wu, Kumekawa, & Kato, 2009; Adya, Bahl, Padhye, Wolman, & Zhou, 2004; Raniwala & Chiueh, 2005). Wu et al. (2009) extend the AODV protocol to include a distributed system to infer the network status and to optimize routes considering bandwidth efficiency and stability. A centralized load aware joint channel assignment and routing algorithm is proposed in Raniwala & Chiueh (2005).

At the MAC layer, Sheu (2002) propose a location aware dynamic channel allocation scheme for MANETs. However, their protocol mandates that location information be provided to each node. Namboothiri & Sivalingam (2010) study the capacity of the IEEE 802.15.4 protocol for linear and grid topologies and calculate the optimal channel assignment yielding the maximum possible channel reuse. However, the results are not generalizable to the complex and dynamic topologies of typical MANETs. Primary Collision Avoidance type channel allocation algorithms (Bonuccelli, 1995; Battiti, Bertossi, & Bonuccelli, 1999; Hu, 1993; Schurgers, Kulkarni, & Srivastava, 2002) assign channels to the nodes one by one, mitigating the conflict relationships in a connection graph at each iteration. Finally, Chowdhury (2005) propose a dynamic channel allocation scheme for IEEE 802.15.4 systems using a single hop overlay weight-based clustering structure. Although the proposed system reduces the message exchanges over previously built Primary Collision Avoidance algorithms, the proposed system is entirely message driven and requires the construction of clusters. Also this system is susceptible to topology changes during the channel allocation phase. To the best of our knowledge, CDCA-TRACE protocol was the first attempt to solve the dynamic channel allocation problem solely based on carrier sense measurements (i.e., spectrum sensing), greatly reducing the overhead.

CDCA-TRACE is a combination of two protocols, DCA-TRACE and CMH-TRACE, which introduce the following algorithms each into the TRACE family to address this problem:

- DCA-TRACE (Karaoglu & Heinzelman, 2012) adds a light weight distributed dynamic channel allocation algorithm based on spectrum sensing on top of MH-TRACE, and
- CMH-TRACE (Karaoglu B., 2014) adds a cooperative load balancing algorithm in which nodes select their channel access providers based on the availability of the resources.

Dynamic Channel Allocation

In CDCA-TRACE, similar to MH-TRACE, each CH selects one of the frames in the superframe and use that frame to distribute channel access to its neighbors. Since the number of data slots is fixed, the CH can only provide channel access to a limited number of nodes. Due to the dynamic structure of MANETs, one CH may be overloaded while others may not be using their data slots. In that case, although there are unused data slots in the superframe, the overloaded CH would provide channel access only to a limited number of nodes, which is equal to the number of data slots per frame, and the CH would deny the channel access requests of the others. Distributed dynamic channel allocation algorithm lets CHs operate in more than one frame per superframe, if they are overloaded. Figure 23 depicts a snapshot of CDCA-TRACE with the medium access pattern.

Figure 23. A snapshot of CDCA-TRACE algorithm and medium access. Dynamic channel allocation algorithm enables CHs operate in multiple frames, when they are overloaded.

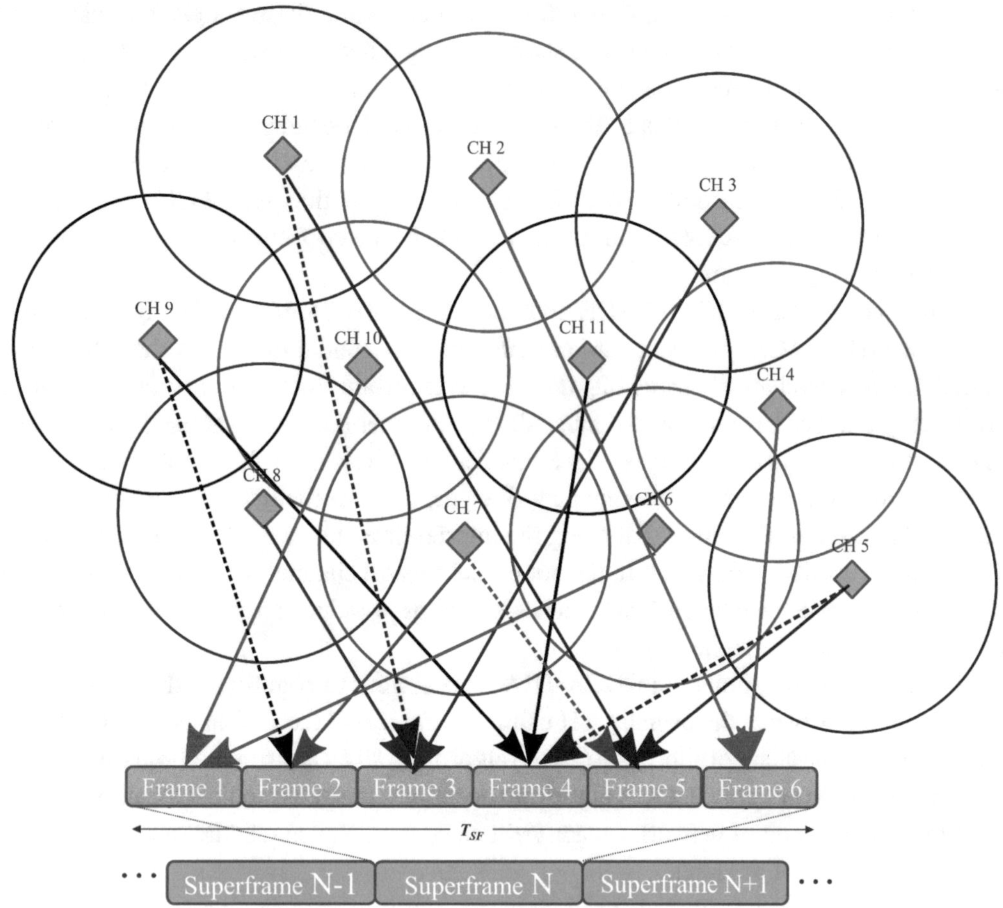

Instead of choosing and operating in the least noisy frame as in MH-TRACE, in CDCA-TRACE, CHs decide on the number of frames they require and opportunistically choose that many frames from the least noisy frames, based on the local load level. For example, in Figure 23, CH1, which is located on the left upper corner is operating using both Frame 5 and Frame 3 due to the high channel access demand of its neighbors at that time instant. On the other hand, the CH2, which is located right next to it is operating using only Frame 6 at the same time instant.

The MH-TRACE structure provides CHs the ability to measure the interference from other CHs in their own frame and in other frames through listening to the medium in the CA slot of their own frame and the beacon slots of other frames. CDCA-TRACE makes use of the same structure. However, in order to accommodate temporary changes in the interference levels that may occur due to CH resignation or unexpected packet drops, an exponential moving average update mechanism is used to determine the current interference levels in each frame. At the end of each frame, the interference level of the beacon and CA slots are updated with the measured values in that frame.

In CDCA-TRACE, CHs mark a frame as unavailable if there is another cluster that uses the frame and resides closer than a certain threshold, Tr_{intf}, measured through the high interference value of that frame. Even under high local demand, CHs refrain from accessing these frames that have high interference measurements, in order to protect the stability of the clustering structure and the existing data transmissions. At the end of each superframe, each CH determine the number of frames that it needs to access, m, based on the reservations in the previous frame. Depending on the interference level of each frame, each CH chooses the least noisy $k \leq m$ frames that have an interference value also below a common threshold, Th_{intf}. If the number of available frames is less than m, the CHs operate only in the available frames. Th_{int} prevents excessive interference in between co-frame clusters that can potentially destabilize the clustering structure.

Another mechanism that CDCA-TRACE adds on top of MH-TRACE is the dynamic assignment of data slots. In MH-TRACE, data slots are assigned in a sequential order. On the other hand, since DCA-TRACE introduces channel borrowing, the CH has to refrain from reallocating a data slot that has been borrowed by another CH and instead must allocate another data slot that has a lower interference value. In order to do this, CHs keep track of the interference levels of each IS slot of each frame in the superframe. In order to accommodate temporary changes, the exponential moving average smoothing mechanism is also used for IS frames. Knowing the interference values of all IS slots, the CH opportunistically assigns the available data slots to the nodes that request channel access beginning with the slot that has the lowest interference value. This mechanism helps to reduce any possible collisions between the transmissions sharing the same data slot.

Channel sensing and assignment in CDCA-TRACE is similar to cognitive radio systems. However, there is no distinction between the primary CH using the frame and the CH that starts using it based on the load level. In dynamic channel allocation (DCA) algorithm, all CHs are treated equally in accessing to the available data slots in any frame. DCA algorithm decouples the geographical location of the channel coordinator from the amount of network capacity allocated to it. Hence it addresses the non-uniformity in the spatial distribution of the load.

In addition to this, DCA algorithm also addresses non-uniformity in the time distribution of the load, since all CHs dynamically increase or decrease the number of slots based on the local load level. When the network load level is low, each CH uses a single frame and in turn channel reuse rate is kept at a minimum. On the other extreme, when the network load is very high, CHs use as many frames as they can that effectively increasing channel reuse.

Cooperative Load Balancing

Cooperative load balancing complements the dynamic channel allocation algorithm by approaching the problem of non-uniform load distribution from the perspective of member nodes instead of CHs. A significant portion of the nodes in a TRACE network are in the vicinity of more than one CH (Karaoglu, Numanoglu, & Heinzelman, 2011). The nodes that are in the vicinity of more than one CH can ask for channel access from any of these CHs. Using a cooperative approach and a clever CH selection algorithm on the nodes, CDCA-TRACE allows transferring the load from heavily loaded CHs to the CHs with more available resources.

Figure 24. Demonstration of a scenario for the collaborative load balancing algorithm.

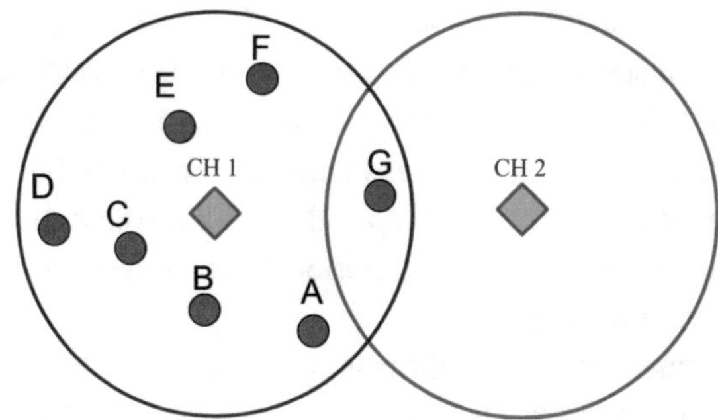

In order to further elaborate this, consider Figure 24. Nodes A-G are source nodes and need to contend for data slots from one of the CHs. Each CH has 6 available data slots. In MH-TRACE, if their contentions go through in alphabetical order, node G would mark *CH1* as full and would ask for channel access from *CH2*. However, if node G secures a data slot from *CH1* before any of the nodes A-F, one of the source nodes would not be able to access to the channel.

With dynamic channel allocation, once *CH1* allocates all of its available slots, it triggers the algorithm to select an additional frame. However, accessing one additional frame might not always be possible, if the interference levels on all the other frames are too high. Moreover, accessing additional frames increases the interference in the beacon and header slots of these frames and may trigger CH resignations and reselections in the rest of the network that temporarily disturbs ongoing data streams on the resigned CHs. Finally, accessing additional frames increases interference on the IS and data slots of the new frame and decreases the potential extent these packets can reach.

In order to overcome these difficulties, CDCA-TRACE adds cooperative CH monitoring and reselection. In CDCA-TRACE, nodes continuously monitor the available data slots at the CHs around themselves announced by the beacon messages. When all the available data slots for a CH are allocated, with a probability *p*, the active nodes attempt to trigger the cooperative load balancing algorithm. When the cooperative load balancing is triggered, the node that is currently using a data slot from the heavily loaded CH contends for data slots from other nearby CHs while keeping and using its reserved data slot until it secures a new data slot from another CH.

Cooperative load balancing does not alter the clustering structure, and it is desirable over selecting an additional frame at the CH. However, cooperative balancing does not completely solve the problem. The source nodes may not be in the vicinity of another CH, and hence their load cannot be transferred to another CH. In that case, triggering the DCA algorithm is required. Thus, CDCA-TRACE also includes the additional frame selection algorithm of DCA-TRACE with some delay. A fully loaded CH resets a counter, $N_{DCA} = 0$, and starts incrementing it at the beginning of each superframe while it remains fully loaded. The CH attempts to (subject to the interference levels in the frames) access an additional frame when $N_{DCA} \geq T_{DCA}$. This provides time for the active member nodes to trigger the cooperative load balancing algorithm and transfer their load to nearby CHs.

The parameters for *p* and T_{DCA} determine the response time of the algorithms. A small *p*value leads to a slower response time for the cooperative load balancing algorithm, while a large *p* value potentially increases the contention overhead on the neighboring CHs. On the other hand, a small T_{DCA} value leads to CHs triggering dynamic channel allocation before cooperative load balancing has a chance to free up resources in the CH's current frame, while a large T_{DCA} value decreases the system response time. In the initial implementation, these parameters were selected as $T_{DCA} = 3$ and $p = 0.5$. These parameters can be further optimized for a given scenario and a desired optimal performance metric.

The proposed a light weight dynamic channel allocation algorithm and a cooperative load balancing algorithms are investigated through simulations and theoretical analysis. They have been shown to be very effective in increasing the service levels as well as the throughput in the system with minimal effect on energy consumption and packet delay variation. Two algorithms can be used simultaneously, maximizing the improvements in the system.

CDCA-TRACE, that combines these algorithms is compared with the existing distributed MAC protocols both employing coordinated approach such as beacon enabled IEEE 802.15.4 and uncoordinated approach such as IEEE 802.11 as well as earlier versions of the TRACE family. The carrier sensing mechanism enables CDCA-TRACE to select the channel coordinators more effectively compared to IEEE 802.15.4. Through extensive simulation studies, it has been shown that CDCA-TRACE outperforms these algorithms for non-uniform distributions in terms of throughput, energy consumption, and inter-packet delay variation for a variety of scenarios involving both uniform and non-uniform load distributions.

Furthermore, (Karaoglu, 2014) verified the feasibility of the CDCA-TRACE protocol in real life scenarios with a working prototype on Microsoft SORA (Tan, Liu, Zhang, Zhang, Fang, & Voelker, 2011) software defined radio systems communicating on the 2.4GHz ISM band. Even with high interference from WiFi operating devices in an office environment, CDCA-TRACE is shown to successfully maintain the stability of a multihop system and run an application providing real-time voice communication.

U-TRACE

Unified TRACE (U-TRACE) (Karaoglu & Heinzelman, 2010) is a protocol architecture that unifies the TRACE communication services described previously, providing them simultaneously, and adjusts the dissemination scheme for highest efficiency.

In multihop communications, nodes in the network are used not only as sources and sinks but also as relays helping end-to-end communication. Oftentimes, there are multiple sets of nodes that can support a given stream in a network. Each relay increases the bandwidth usage and consumes extra energy for both receiving and retransmitting the information. Hence, the selection of relays in a network is tightly linked to both energy and bandwidth efficiency for multihop communications. This selection is even more critical for MANETs given the characteristic of dynamic topology changes.

The data generated in a MANET is oftentimes intended to be sent to more than one destination. One-to-many group communications are generally classified into two types: network-wide broadcasting and multicasting. In network-wide broadcasting the objective is to distribute the generated data to all the nodes in the network. On the other hand, the objective of multicasting is to deliver the data to a subset of the nodes in the network, namely a multicasting group. Multicasting protocols prevent redundant transmissions on the parts of the network in which no multicast member resides. However, the overhead added to the packets in multicasting protocols is more than the overhead in network-wide broadcasting protocols. The driving idea behind U-TRACE is to use utilize this tradeoff between multicasting and broadcasting use the preferable scheme based on the network conditions. When network-wide broadcasting is used for a data stream that is intended to be sent to a multicast group, it is relayed following network-wide broadcasting scheme and dropped at the destinations that do not belong to the multicast group.

Both network-wide broadcasting and multicasting have been implemented in the TRACE framework. NB-TRACE (Tavli & Heinzelman, 2006) implements network-wide broadcasting, and MC-TRACE (Tavli & Heinzelman, 2011) implements multicasting. MC-TRACE and NB-TRACE utilize link layer broadcasting. It has been shown that supporting broadcasting at the link layer is essential for the efficient use of the network resources, since this approach eliminates the need for multiple transmissions of an identical payload while sending it to different destinations (Kappes, 2006). Link layer broadcasting combined with the underlying MAC protocol eliminating energy consumption due to overhearing maximize their efficiency. In fact, these protocols have been shown to outperform many other protocols in their class. Moreover, these protocols are built on top of the same MAC structure, and their sensitivity to MAC layer issues such as mobility and link errors are similar. Finally, the data maintained by the protocols are very similar to each other, and any additional burden of multicasting can directly be observed. Consequently, with minimal modifications, NB-TRACE and MC-TRACE protocols can be combined into a unique framework and coexist simultaneously. U-TRACE unifies these two protocols utilizing these properties and increases the performance further by selecting better approach (broadcasting or multicasting) depending on the situation.

MC-TRACE eliminates redundant retransmissions by confining the data dissemination to a limited area. However, this comes with the additional cost of overhead to keep the data distribution tree alive. Hence, while MC-TRACE offers a more efficient data distribution method for small group sizes, NB-TRACE is more efficient for large group sizes. Karaoglu & Heinzelman (2010) investigate the tradeoffs between multicasting and broadcasting and determine the conditions that make one of them preferable over the other from the perspective of both bandwidth and energy efficiency. In particular, the number of multicast group members beyond which NB-TRACE becomes more efficient for data dissemination, called the cross-over point, is determined for various scenarios. For large multicast groups, it has been shown that using broadcasting instead of multicasting leads to 75% saving in the number of transmitted packets and 21% savings in energy consumption. Similarly, for small multicast groups it has been shown that multicasting reduces the number of data transmission and the average energy consumption by 50% and 13%, respectively.

The cross over point is shown to vary based on the network size, transmission power, and the number of nodes in a network as well as the primary goals of the application such as bandwidth or energy efficiency. An increase in the total number of nodes in a region decreases the relative efficiency of broadcasting compared to multicasting from both energy efficiency and bandwidth efficiency perspectives, and hence the cross-over occurs at a larger number of multicast members. On the other hand, the increase in the size of the area does not affect the cross-over point significantly for the energy efficiency metric while increasing the cross-over point for the bandwidth efficiency metric.

As depicted in Figure 25, for each stream, U-TRACE determines and compares the size of the destination multicast group with the cross-over point and selects the dissemination method for the data stream. This selection is on a per stream basis. Other streams that select a different method can coexist in the network. The relay nodes decide on the appropriate response based on the dissemination type information added to the packet headers. Also, the dissemination method can be changed on the fly throughout the duration of a data stream. This feature makes it suitable to be combined with a feedback algorithm and allows the dynamic adjustment of the cross over point.

Figure 25. Block diagram depicting the decisions of the data dissemination steps of U-TRACE.

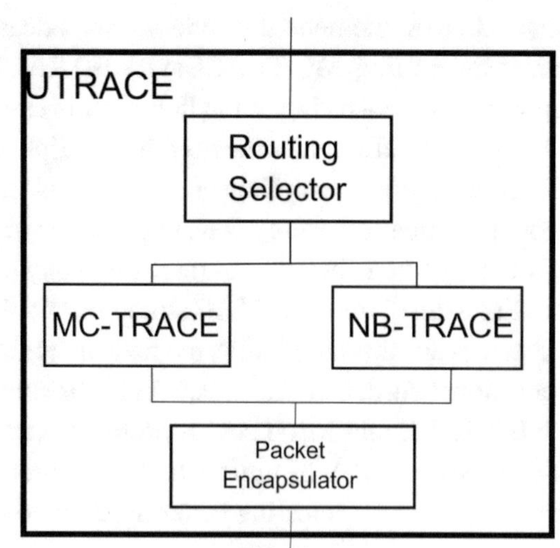

Finally, U-TRACE being a member of the TRACE family, shares the same MAC layer architecture. Although, it is originally built on top of MH-TRACE, it can be adopted to work with DCA-TRACE and CDCA-TRACE, combining with the efficient data dissemination strategies with the adaptable MAC layer features offered by the CDCA-TRACE. The TRACE prototype (Karaoglu, 2014) on Microsoft SORA radios, implement CDCA-TRACE together with a routing module that implements U-TRACE routing procedures.

FUTURE RESEARCH DIRECTIONS

Typically mobile devices have limited energy, storage, and computing resources, therefore, operations requiring rich resources cannot be handled by the mobile devices themselves. Offloading data from the mobile device to a resource rich platform to perform necessary computing tasks and returning to the mobile device the outputs (*e.g.*, information extracted from the raw data) would be an invaluable service. Mobile cloud computing is the abstraction for achieving such a service. For such a service to work, the mobile device should be able to establish efficient means of communication to the cloud. Especially for applications with real-time QoS requirements, the communication infrastructure should be able to provide real-time communication guarantees. Furthermore, energy efficiency of the communication should be maintained for mobile devices, even under real-time operation requirements. Keeping the communication links functional under mobility is also another desirable feature that should be satisfied by the underlying communication architecture.

The TRACE architecture is capable of performing as the communication infrastructure for mobile cloud computing because: (i) it can satisfy the real-time QoS requirements of the applications, (ii) the energy efficiency of the TRACE architecture is very high, and (iii) TRACE is designed to operate under extreme mobility scenarios. However, the TRACE architecture is not designed specifically as a solution to the communication requirements of mobile cloud computing. Therefore, it is necessary to adapt and extend TRACE for efficient and effective operation.

TRACE is designed to operate as a standalone communication system; however, for mobile cloud computing, the network should be able to connect to a larger, possibly tethered network (*e.g.*, the Internet). There are many alternatives to connect mobile devices networked by the TRACE architecture to the Internet (*e.g.*, one or more of the mobile nodes has/have access to the Internet and the remaining nodes can use TRACE to reach these gateway nodes). However, an efficient design should preserve the best features of the TRACE architecture (*i.e.*, energy efficiency, real-time QoS provisioning, mobility support, and robustness).

Distributed computing is another application of increasing importance for mobile ad hoc networks. CPU intensive computing jobs are split into multiple independent tasks and are distributed to multiple clients. The cooperation among the nodes is crucial for distributing the tasks among the nodes. The TRACE communication infrastructure can be used to distribute the tasks efficiently. Depending on the requirements of the job, the clusterheads can take the responsibility for distributing the tasks to the nodes within their clusters and requesting support from other clusters. Furthermore, employing mobile cloud computing options for accomplishing computation intensive tasks is also an interesting future research topic. For example, if the energy cost of communicating data to a remote cloud is higher than performing the computation locally by distributing the computation load to TRACE nodes, then the cloud option is not beneficial and the TRACE architecture can be used to distribute the load.

ACKNOWLEDGMENT

The work described in this book chapter was supported in part by Harris Corporation, RF Communications Division, and in part by the Center for Emerging and Innovative Sciences (CEIS), an Empire State Development designated Center for Advanced Technology.

REFERENCES

C2DMF. (2012). Retrieved from https://developers.google.com/android/c2dm/

Adya, A., Bahl, P., Padhye, J., Wolman, A., & Zhou, L. (2004). A multi-radio unification protocol for IEEE 802.11 wireless networks. *BroadNets*, (s. 344-354).

AES. (2012). Retrieved from http://en.wikipedia.org/wiki/Advanced_Encryption_Standard

Ali, M. (2009). Green Cloud on the Horizon. *Cloud Computing*, 451-459.

Anderson, D. P. (2004). BOINC: A system for public-resource computing and storage. *Grid Computing, 2004. Proceedings. Fifth IEEE/ACM International Workshop on* (s. 4-10). IEEE.

Android. (2012). Retrieved from http://www.android.com/

Apple. (2012). Retrieved from http://developer.apple.com/library/mac/#documentation/NetworkingInternet/Conceptual/RemoteNotificationsPG/ApplePushService/ApplePushService.html

AWS. (2012). Retrieved from http://aws.amazon.com

Ba, H., Heinzelman, W., Janssen, C., & Shi, J. (2013). Mobile computing - a green computing resource. *Wireless Communications and Networking Conference*. IEEE.

Battiti, R., Bertossi, A., & Bonuccelli, M. (1999). Assigning Codes in Wireless Networks: Bounds and Scaling Properties. *Wireless Networks*, *5*(3), 195–209. doi:10.1023/A:1019146910724

BBN. (2005). Retrieved from http://tools.ietf.org/pdf/rfc4301.pdf

Bergmans, P. (1973). Random coding theorem for broadcast channels with degraded components. *IEEE Transactions on Information Theory*, *19*(2), 197–207. doi:10.1109/TIT.1973.1054980

BOINC. (2012). Retrieved from http://nativeboinc.org/site/uncat/start

Bonuccelli, A. A. (1995). Code assignment for hidden terminal interference avoidance in multihop packet radio networks. *IEEE/ACM Transactions on Networking*, 441–449.

Burbank, J. L., Chimento, P. F., Haberman, B. K., & Kasch, W. (2006). Key challenges of military tactical networking and the elusive promise of MANET technology. *IEEE Communications Magazine*, *44*(11), 39–45. doi:10.1109/COM-M.2006.248156

Chen, E., Ogata, S., & Horikawa, K. (2012). Offloading Android applications to the cloud without customizing Android. *Pervasive Computing and Communications Workshops (PERCOM Workshops), 2012 IEEE International Conference on* (s. 788-793). IEEE.

Chen, E. Y., & Itoh, M. (2010). Virtual smartphone over IP. *World of Wireless Mobile and Multimedia Networks (WoWMoM), 2010 IEEE International Symposium on a* (s. 1-6). IEEE.

Chowdhury, K., Chanda, P., Agrawal, D., & Zeng, Q.-A. (2005). DCA-a distributed channel allocation scheme for wireless sensor networks. *IEEE PIMRC, 2*, s. 1297-1301.

Chun, B. G., Ihm, S., Maniatis, P., Naik, M., & Patti, A. (2011). Clonecloud: elastic execution between mobile device and cloud. *Proceedings of the sixth conference on Computer systems*, (s. 301-314). doi:10.1145/1966445.1966473

Chun, B. G., & Maniatis, P. (2009). Augmented smartphone applications through clone cloud execution. *Proceedings of the 8th Workshop on Hot Topics in Operating Systems (HotOS).*

Cidon, I., & Sidi, M. (1989). Distributed assignment algorithms for multi-hop packet-radio networks. *IEEE Transactions on Computers*, *38*(10), 1353–1361. doi:10.1109/12.35830

Corson, M. S., Laroia, R., Li, J., Park, V., Richardson, T., & Tsirtsis, G. (2010). Toward proximity-aware internetworking. *IEEE Wireless Communications, 17*(6), 26-33.

Cover, T. (1972). Broadcast channels. *IEEE Transactions on Information Theory*, *18*(1), 2–14. doi:10.1109/TIT.1972.1054727

Cuervo, E., Balasubramanian, A., Cho, D., Wolman, A., Saroiu, S., Chandra, R., & Bahl, P. (2010). Maui: making smartphones last longer with code offload. *Proceedings of the 8th international conference on Mobile systems, applications, and services* (s. 49--62). ACM. doi:10.1145/1814433.1814441

Dillinger, M., Madani, K., & Alonistioti, N. (2005). *Software defined radio: Architectures, systems and functions*. John Wiley & Sons.

Dinh, H. T., Lee, C., Niyato, D., & Wang, P. (2011). *A survey of mobile cloud computing: architecture, applications, and approaches*. Wireless Communications and Mobile Computing.

DOCSIS. (2012). Retrieved from http://en.wikipedia.org/wiki/DOCSIS

Dong, H., & Gibson, J. (2006). Structures for SNR scalable speech coding. *IEEE Transactions on Audio. Speech and Language Processing*, *14*(2), 545–557. doi:10.1109/TSA.2005.857804

Eastlack, J. R. (2011). *Extending volunteer computing to mobile devices.* (Master's thesis). New Mexico State University.

Ephremides, A., & Truong, T. (1990). Scheduling broadcasts in multihop radio networks. *IEEE Transactions on Communications*, *38*(4), 456–460. doi:10.1109/26.52656

Felegyhazi, M., Cagalj, M., Bidokhti, S., & Hubaux, J.-P. (2007). Non-Cooperative Multi-Radio Channel Allocation in Wireless Networks. *IEEE INFOCOM, 1*, s. 1442 -1450.

Fernando, N., Loke, S. W., & Rahayu, W. (2013). Mobile cloud computing: A survey. *Future Generation Computer Systems*, *29*(1), 84–106. doi:10.1016/j.future.2012.05.023

Fesehaye, D., Gao, Y., Nahrstedt, K., & Wang, G. (2012). Impact of Cloudlets on Interactive Mobile Cloud Applications. *Enterprise Distributed Object Computing Conference (EDOC)* (s. 123-132). IEEE. doi:10.1109/EDOC.2012.23

Flores, H., Srirama, S. N., & Paniagua, C. (2011). A generic middleware framework for handling process intensive hybrid cloud services from mobiles. *Proceedings of the 9th International Conference on Advances in Mobile Computing and Multimedia* (s. 87-94). ACM. doi:10.1145/2095697.2095715

Gao, L., & Wang, X. (2008). A game approach for multi-channel allocation in multi-hop wireless networks. *ACM MOBIHOC*, (s. 303-312).

GeForce500. (2011). Retrieved from http://en.wikipedia.org/wiki/GeForce_500_Series

GeForce600. (2012). Retrieved from http://en.wikipedia.org/wiki/GeForce_600_Series

Goodman, D. J., Valenzuela, R., Gayliard, K. T., & Ramamurthi, B. (1989). Packet reservation multiple access for local wireless communications. *IEEE Transactions on Communications*, *37*(8), 885–890. doi:10.1109/26.31190

Google. (2012). Retrieved from http://code.google.com/appengine

Guo, X., Ipek, E., & Soyata, T. (2010). Resistive computation: avoiding the power wall with low-leakage, STT-MRAM based computing. ACM SIGARCH Computer Architecture News (s. 371-382). ACM.

Ha, K., Pillai, P., Lewis, G., Simanta, S., Clinch, S., Davies, N., & Satyanarayanan, M. (2012). *The impact of multimedia applications on data center consolidation*. Carnegie Mellon University, School of Computer Seience.

HIPAA. (1996). Retrieved from http://www.hhs.gov/ocr/privacy/index.html

Hoang, D. B., & Chen, L. (2010). Mobile cloud for assistive healthcare (MoCAsH). *Asia-Pacific Services Computing Conference (APSCC)* (s. 325-332). IEEE.

Hoang, D. T., Niyato, D., & Wang, P. (2012). Optimal admission control policy for mobile cloud computing hotspot with cloudlet. *Wireless Communications and Networking Conference (WCNC)* (s. 3145-3149). IEEE. doi:10.1109/WCNC.2012.6214347

Hu, L. (1993). Distributed code assignments for CDMA packet radio networks. *IEEE/ACM Transactions on Networking*, *1*(6), 668–677. doi:10.1109/90.266055

I, C.-L., & Chao, P.-H. (1993). Local packing-distributed dynamic channel allocation at cellular base station. *IEEE GLOBECOM*, (s. 293 -301).

I, C.-L., & Chao, P.-H. (1994). Distributed dynamic channel allocation algorithms with adjacent channel constraints. *IEEE PIMRC, 1*, s. 169 -177.

Intel. (2012). Retrieved from http://en.wikipedia.org/wiki/Intel_Tick-Tock

IOT. (2012). Retrieved from http://en.wikipedia.org/wiki/Internet_of_Things

Jain, N., Das, S., & Nasipuri, A. (2001). A multichannel CSMA MAC protocol with receiver-based channel selection for multihop wireless networks. *IEEE ICCCN, 1*, s. 432 -439.

Jiang, J. H. (2002). On Distributed Dynamic Channel Allocation in Mobile Cellular Networks. *IEEE Transactions on Parallel and Distributed Systems*, *13*(10), 1024–1037. doi:10.1109/TPDS.2002.1041879

Kappes, M. (2006). An experimental performance analysis of (MAC) multicast in 802.11b networks for VoIP traffic. *Computer Communications*, *29*(8), 938–948. doi:10.1016/j.comcom.2005.06.014

Karaoglu, B. (2014). *Efficient Use of Resources in Mobile Ad Hoc Networks.* (Ph.D. dissertation). University of Rochester, Rochester, NY.

Karaoglu, B., & Heinzelman, W. (2010). Multicasting vs. Broadcasting: What Are the Trade-Offs? *IEEE GLOBECOM*, (s. 1-5).

Karaoglu, B., & Heinzelman, W. (2012). A Dynamic Channel Allocation Scheme Using Spectrum Sensing for Mobile Ad Hoc Networks. *IEEE GLOBECOM*, (s. 397-402).

Karaoglu, B., & Heinzelman, W. (2014). Cooperative Load Balancing and Dynamic Channel Allocation for Cluster-based Mobile Ad Hoc Networks. *IEEE Transactions on Mobile Computing, PP* (99), 1-1.

Karaoglu, B., Numanoglu, T., & Heinzelman, W. (2011). Analytical performance of soft clustering protocols. *Ad Hoc Networks*, *9*(4), 635–651. doi:10.1016/j.adhoc.2010.08.008

Karn, P. (1990). MACA-a new channel access method for packet radio. *ARRL/CRRL Amateur radio 9th computer networking conference*, (s. 134-140).

Katzela, I., & Naghshineh, M. (1996). Channel assignment schemes for cellular mobile telecommunication systems: A comprehensive survey. *IEEE Personal Communications*, *3*(3), 10–31. doi:10.1109/98.511762

Kleinrock, L., & Tobagi, F. (1975). Packet Switching in Radio Channels: Part I--Carrier Sense Multiple-Access Modes and Their Throughput-Delay Characteristics. *IEEE Transactions on Communications*, *23*(12), 1400–1416. doi:10.1109/TCOM.1975.1092768

Kovachev, D., Cao, Y., & Klamma, R. (2011). Mobile cloud computing: a comparison of application models. *arXiv preprint arXiv:1107.4940.*

Kumar, K., Liu, J., Lu, Y.-H., & Bhargava, B. (2013). A Survey of Computation Offloading for Mobile Systems. *Mobile Networks and Applications*, *18*(1), 129–140. doi:10.1007/s11036-012-0368-0

Lee, S. J., Su, W., & Gerla, M. (2002). On-Demand Multicast Routing Protocol in Multihop Wireless Mobile Networks. *Mobile Networks and Applications*, *7*(6), 441–453. doi:10.1023/A:1020756600187

Leiner, B., Nielson, D., & Tobagi, F. (1987). Issues in packet radio network design. *Proceedings of the IEEE*, *75*(1), 6–20. doi:10.1109/PROC.1987.13701

Leiner, B., Nielson, D., & Tobagi, F. (1987). Issues in packet radio network design. *Proceedings of the IEEE*, *75*(1), 6–20. doi:10.1109/PROC.1987.13701

Lund, K., Eggen, A., Hadzic, D., Hafsoe, T., & Johnsen, F. T. (2007). Using web services to realize service oriented architecture in military communication networks. *IEEE Communications Magazine*, *45*(10), 47–53. doi:10.1109/MCOM.2007.4342822

Ma, X., & Chen, X. (2008). Performance Analysis of IEEE 802.11 Broadcast Scheme in Ad Hoc Wireless LANs. *IEEE Transactions on Vehicular Technology*, *57*(6), 3757–3768. doi:10.1109/TVT.2008.918731

MacDonald, V. H. (1979). Advanced mobile phone service: The cellular concept. *The Bell System Technical Journal*, 15–41.

Marinelli, E. (2009). *Hyrax: Cloud computing on mobile devices using mapreduce.* (Master's thesis). Carnegie-Mellon University.

Microsoft. (2012). Retrieved from http://www.microsoft.com/windowazure

Morris, E. (2011). A new approach for handheld devices in the military. *SEI Blog*. Retrieved from http:// blog. sei. cmu. edu/post. cfm/a-new-approach-for-handheld-devices-in-the-military

Namboothiri, P., & Sivalingam, K. (2010). Capacity analysis of multi-hop wireless sensor networks using multiple transmission channels: A case study using IEEE 802.15.4 based networks. *IEEE LCN*, (s. 168-171).

Nasipuri, A., & Das, S. (2000). Multichannel CSMA with signal power-based channel selection for multihop wireless networks. *IEEE VTS Fall, 1*, s. 211 -218.

NIST. (2001). Retrieved from http://csrc.nist.gov/publications/fips/fips197/fips-197.pdf

Numanoglu, T. (2009). *Improving the reliability and performance of real-time communications in mobile ad hoc networks.* (Ph.D. dissertation). University of Rochester, Rochester, NY.

Numanoglu, T., & Heinzelman, W. (2008). Improving QoS under lossy channels through adaptive redundancy. *IEEE MASS*, 509-510.

Numanoglu, T., & Heinzelman, W. (2009). Improving QoS in multicasting through adaptive redundancy. *IEEE WCNC*, 1-6.

Numanoglu, T., Heinzelman, W., & Tavli, B. (2007). Multi-rate support for network-wide broadcasting in MANETs. *Networking*, 1140-1144.

Numanoglu, T., Karadeniz, B., Onat, F. A., & Kolagasioglu, A. E. (2012). An embedded radio software emulation platform using OPNET and VxWorks to develop distributed algorithms for military ad-hoc networks. *IEEE MILCOM*, 1-6.

Numanoglu, T., Tavli, B., & Heinzelman, W. B. (2006). Energy efficiency and error resilience in coordinated and non-coordinated medium access control protocols. *Computer Communications*, *29*(17), 3493–3506. doi:10.1016/j.comcom.2006.01.023

OSGi. (2012). Retrieved from http://www.osgi.org/

Pattichis, C. S., Kyriacou, E., Voskarides, S., Pattichis, M. S., Istepanian, R., & Schizas, C. N. (2002). Wireless telemedicine systems: An overview. *Antennas and Propagation Magazine*, *44*(2), 143–153. doi:10.1109/MAP.2002.1003651

Perrig, A., Stankovic, J., & Wagner, D. (2004). Security in wireless sensor networks. *Communications of the ACM*, *47*(6), 53–57. doi:10.1145/990680.990707

PIC32. (2012). Retrieved from http://www.microchip.com/pagehandler/en-us/family/32bit/

Prehofer, C., & Bettstetter, C. (2005). Self-organization in communication networks: Principles and design paradigms. *IEEE Communications Magazine*, *43*(7), 78–85. doi:10.1109/MCOM.2005.1470824

Qualcomm. (2012). Retrieved from http://www.qualcomm.com/snapdragon

Ramaswami, R., & Parhi, K. (1989). Distributed scheduling of broadcasts in a radio network. *IEEE INFOCOM*, (s. 497 -504).

Raniwala, A., & Chiueh, T.-c. (2005). Architecture and algorithms for an IEEE 802.11-based multi-channel wireless mesh network. *IEEE INFOCOM, 3*, s. 2223-2234.

Rellermeyer, J. S., Alonso, G., & Roscoe, T. (2007). R-OSGi: distributed applications through software modularization. *Proceedings of the ACM/IFIP/USENIX 2007 International Conference on Middleware* (s. 1-20). Springer-Verlag New York, Inc.

Richter, J. (2010). *CLR via c*. Microsoft Press.

Rimoldi, B. (1994). Successive refinement of information: Characterization of the achievable rates. *IEEE Transactions on Information Theory*, *40*(1), 253–259. doi:10.1109/18.272493

Sass, P. (1999). Communications networks for the force XXI digitized battlefield. *Mobile Networks and Applications*, *4*(3), 139–155. doi:10.1023/A:1019194714609

Satyanarayanan, M., Bahl, P., Caceres, R., & Davies, N. (2009). The case for vm-based cloudlets in mobile computing. *IEEE Pervasive Computing / IEEE Computer Society [and] IEEE Communications Society*, *8*(4), 14–23. doi:10.1109/MPRV.2009.82

Schurgers, C., Kulkarni, G., & Srivastava, M. (2002). Distributed on-demand address assignment in wireless sensor networks. *IEEE Transactions on Parallel and Distributed Systems*, *13*(10), 1056–1065. doi:10.1109/TPDS.2002.1041881

Sen, A., & Huson, M. (1996). A new model for scheduling packet radio networks. *IEEE INFOCOM, 3*, s. 1116 -1124.

Sheu, Y.-C. T.-M.-L.-P. (2002). Dynamic channel allocation with location awareness for multi-hop mobile ad hoc networks. *Computer Communications*, 676–688.

Shi, C., Ammar, M. H., Zegura, E. W., & Naik, M. (2012). Computing in cirrus clouds: the challenge of intermittent connectivity. *Proceedings of the first edition of the MCC workshop on Mobile cloud computing* (s. 23-28). ACM. doi:10.1145/2342509.2342515

Shukla, D., Chandran-Wadia, L., & Iyer, S. (2003). Mitigating the exposed node problem in IEEE 802.11 ad hoc networks. *IEEE ICCCN, 1*, s. 157 - 162.

Song, W., Zhuang, W., & Cheng, Y. (2007). Load balancing for cellular/WLAN integrated networks. *IEEE Network*, *21*(1), 27–33. doi:10.1109/MNET.2007.314535

Soyata, T. (1999). *Incorporating Circuit Level Information into the Retiming Process.* (Ph.D. thesis). University of Rochester.

Soyata, T., & Friedman, E. G. (1994). Synchronous performance and reliability improvement in pipelined ASICs. *ASIC Conference and Exhibit, 1994. Proceedings., Seventh Annual IEEE International. 3*, s. 383-390. IEEE. doi:10.1109/ASIC.1994.404536

Soyata, T., Friedman, E. G., & Mulligan, J. H., Jr. (1993). Integration of clock skew and register delays into a retiming algorithm. *Circuits and Systems, 1993., ISCAS'93, 1993 IEEE International Symposium on* (s. 1483-1486). IEEE.

Soyata, T., Friedman, E. G., & Mulligan, J. H., Jr. (1995). Monotonicity constraints on path delays for efficient retiming with localized clock skew and variable register delay. *Circuits and Systems, 1995. ISCAS'95., 1995 IEEE International Symposium on* (s. 1748--1751). IEEE.

Soyata, T., & Liobe, J. (2012). pbCAM: probabilistically-banked content addressable memory. *IEEE International System-On-Chip Conference* (s. 27-32). Niagara Falls, NY: IEEE.

Soyata, T., Muraleedharan, R., Funai, C., Kwon, M., & Heinzelman, W. (2012). Cloud-Vision: Real-time face recognition using a mobile-cloudlet-cloud acceleration architecture. *Symposium on Computers and Communications (ISCC)* (s. 59-66). IEEE. doi:10.1109/ISCC.2012.6249269

Soyata, T., Muraleedharan, R., Langdon, J., Funai, C., Ames, S., Kwon, M., & Heinzelman, W. (2012). *COMBAT: mobile-Cloud-based cOmpute/coMmunications infrastructure for BATtlefield applications. SPIE Defense, Security, and Sensing (s. 84030K-84030K).* International Society for Optics and Photonics.

Sterling, C. H. (2008). *Military communications: from ancient times to the 21st century*. Abc-clio.

Sun, T. W., Wesel, R. D., Shane, M. R., & Jarett, K. (2004). Superposition turbo TCM for multirate broadcast. *IEEE Transactions on Communications*, *3*(3), 368–371. doi:10.1109/TCOMM.2004.823646

Tan, K., Liu, H., Zhang, J., Zhang, Y., Fang, J., & Voelker, G. M. (2011). Sora: High-performance software radio using general-purpose multi-core processors. *Communications of the ACM*, *54*(1), 99–107. doi:10.1145/1866739.1866760

Tang, K., & Gerla, M. (2000). MAC layer broadcast support in 802.11 wireless networks. *IEEE MILCOM, 1*, s. 544-548.

Tavli, B. (2005). *Protocol architectures for energy efficient real-time data communications in mobile ad hoc networks.* (Ph.D. dissertation). University of Rochester, Rochester, NY.

Tavli, B., & Heinzelman, W. B. (2003). TRACE: Time reservation using adaptive control for energy efficiency. *IEEE Journal on Selected Areas in Communications*, *21*(10), 1506–1515. doi:10.1109/JSAC.2003.814897

Tavli, B., & Heinzelman, W. B. (2004). MH-TRACE: Multihop time reservation using adaptive control for energy efficiency. *IEEE Journal on Selected Areas in Communications*, *21*(10), 942–953. doi:10.1109/JSAC.2004.826932

Tavli, B., & Heinzelman, W. B. (2006). Energy and spatial reuse efficient network wide real-time data broadcasting in mobile ad hoc networking. *IEEE Transactions on Mobile Computing*, *5*(10), 1297–1312. doi:10.1109/TMC.2006.151

Tavli, B., & Heinzelman, W. B. (2006). *Mobile ad hoc networks: energy-efficient real-time group communications*. Dordrecht: Springer. doi:10.1007/1-4020-4633-2

Tavli, B., & Heinzelman, W. B. (2007). QoS and energy efficiency in network-wide broadcasting: A MAC layer perspective. *Computer Communications*, *30*(18), 3705–3720. doi:10.1016/j.comcom.2007.07.005

Tavli, B., & Heinzelman, W. B. (2011). Energy-efficient real-time multicast routing in mobile ad hoc networks. *IEEE Transactions on Computers*, *60*(5), 707–722. doi:10.1109/TC.2010.118

Tegra3. (2012). Retrieved from http://www.nvidia.com/object/tegra-3-processor.html

Tegra. (2012). Retrieved from http://en.wikipedia.org/wiki/Tegra

Tobagi, F., & Kleinrock, L. (1975). Packet Switching in Radio Channels: Part II--The Hidden Terminal Problem in Carrier Sense Multiple-Access and the Busy-Tone Solution. *IEEE Transactions on Communications*, *23*(12), 1417–1433. doi:10.1109/TCOM.1975.1092767

Toumpis, S., & Goldsmith, A. (2006). New media access protocols for wireless ad hoc networks based on cross-layer principles. *IEEE Transactions on Wireless Communications*, *5*(8), 2228–2241. doi:10.1109/TWC.2006.1687739

Varshney, U. (2007). Pervasive healthcare and wireless health monitoring. *Mobile Networks and Applications*, *12*(2-3), 113–127. doi:10.1007/s11036-007-0017-1

Verbelen, T., Simoens, P., De Turck, F., & Dhoedt, B. (2012). Cloudlets: Bringing the cloud to the mobile user. *Proceedings of the third ACM workshop on Mobile cloud computing and services* (s. 29-36). ACM. doi:10.1145/2307849.2307858

WiFiAlliance. (2012). Retrieved from http://www.wi-fi.org/knowledge-center/glossary/wpa2%E2%84%A2

Wood, A., Stankovic, J., Virone, G., Selavo, L., He, Z., Cao, Q., & Stoleru, R. et al. (2008). Context-aware wireless sensor networks for assisted living and residential monitoring. *IEEE Network*, *22*(4), 26–33. doi:10.1109/MNET.2008.4579768

Wu, C., Kumekawa, K., & Kato, T. (2009). A MANET protocol considering link stability and bandwidth efficiency. *ICUMT, 1*, s. 1 -8.

Xie, J., Das, A., Nandi, S., & Gupta, A. (2005). Improving the reliability of IEEE 802.11 broadcast scheme for multicasting in mobile ad hoc networks. *IEEE WCNC, 1*, s. 126-131.

Yang, H., Luo, H., Ye, F., Lu, S., & Zhang, L. (2004). Security in mobile ad hoc networks: Challenges and solutions. *IEEE Wireless Communications*, *11*(1), 38–47. doi:10.1109/MWC.2004.1269716

Ye, W., Heidemann, J., & Estrin, D. (2002). An energy-efficient MAC protocol for wireless sensor networks. *IEEE INFOCOM*, (s. 1567-1576).

Zhang, X., Kunjithapatham, A., Jeong, S., & Gibbs, S. (2011). Towards an elastic application model for augmenting the computing capabilities of mobile devices with cloud computing. *Mobile Networks and Applications*, *16*(3), 270–284. doi:10.1007/s11036-011-0305-7

Zhu, J., & Roy, S. (2003). MAC for dedicated short range communications in intelligent transport system. *IEEE Communications Magazine*, *41*(12), 60–67. doi:10.1109/MCOM.2003.1252800

KEY TERMS AND DEFINITIONS

Cluster: A group of nodes within a network (static or dynamic membership is possible) that are generally orchestrated by a clusterhead node for easing network management. Clustering can be static or dynamic. In mobile ad hoc networks, dynamic clustering is necessary to maintain network structure.

Distributed Networking: Network functionality is achieved by the local decisions made by individual nodes or groups of nodes. Three significant characteristics of distributed networks are: concurrency of protocols, lack of a central node, and independent failure of nodes. Scalability is also among the reasons for distributed decision making as opposed to centralized network management.

Mobile Ad Hoc Networks: A group of mobile devices that can communicate through wireless links and form a possibly multi hop network. Network formation, maintenance, reorganization, self-healing are among the properties of mobile ad hoc networks.

Multicast: A group communication type where information is addressed to a group of destination computers simultaneously. The members of a multicast group can be defined statically or dynamically. Unlike broadcasting where all nodes in a domain receive all traffic, only the members of a multicast group receive the traffic in multicasting.

Network Load: The total amount of data traffic pending to be transmitted at a given time in a network.

Network Protocol: A set of rules with well-defined syntax and semantics to enable certain functions for data communications. Network protocols are necessary for enabling inter operability among the devices and software from different sources.

Quality-of-Service (QoS): The performance level of a service offered by the network to the user. QoS requirements for different applications and scenarios vary. For example, in voice communications, delay, jitter, and packet delivery ratio are performance metrics.

Spatial Channel Reuse: Simultaneous use of the same channel by multiple transmitters targeting geographically separated receivers. Due to the wireless signal attenuation, provided that the receivers are geographically separated enough, communication is possible over non-orthogonal channels.

Superposition Coding: Adding additional coding on top of the first coding in such a way that already separated codewords are displaced again according to new information. Superposition coding is helpful in disseminating information at different rates to receivers with varying channel conditions.

Wireless Channel: The medium over which information signals are carried over geographic locations. Channels are defined by the characteristics of the carriers that have dimensions of time, frequency and code.

Chapter 3
Sensing as a Service in Cloud-Centric Internet of Things Architecture

Burak Kantarci
Clarkson University, USA

Hussein T. Mouftah
University of Ottawa, Canada

ABSTRACT

Sensing-as-a-Service (S2aaS) is a cloud-inspired service model which enables access to the Internet of Things (IoT) architecture. The IoT denotes virtually interconnected objects that are uniquely identifiable, and are capable of sensing, computing and communicating. Built-in sensors in mobile devices can leverage the performance of IoT applications in terms of energy and communication overhead savings by sending their data to the cloud servers. Sensed data from mobile devices can be accessed by IoT applications on a pay-as-you-go fashion. Efficient sensing service provider search techniques are emerging components of this architecture, and they should be accompanied with effective sensing provider recruitment algorithms. Furthermore, reliability and trustworthiness of participatory sensed data appears as a big challenge. This chapter provides an overview of the state of the art in S2aaS systems, and reports recent proposals to address the most crucial challenges. Furthermore, the chapter points out the open issues and future directions for the researchers in this field.

INTRODUCTION

The Internet of Things (IoT) paradigm denotes the pervasive and ubiquitous interconnection of billions of embedded devices that can be uniquely identified, localized and communicated (Aggarwal, C., Ashish, N. & Sheth, A., 2013). Sensors, RFID tags, smart phones, and various other devices are interconnected in a scalable manner in the IoT architecture. Application areas of IoT are various such as healthcare, smart environments, transportation, social networking, personal safety and several futuristic applications such as robot taxi (Atzori, A., Andlera, L. & Morabito, G., 2010; Miorandi, D., Sicari, S., De Pellegrini, F.

DOI: 10.4018/978-1-4666-8662-5.ch003

& Chlamtac, I., 2012). IoT architecture can be implemented as either Internet centric or object-centric. Internet centric architecture of IoT aims at provisioning services within the Internet where data are contributed by the objects. On the other hand, object-centric architecture aims at provisioning services via network of smart objects. Scalability and cost-efficient service provisioning of IoT services can be achieved by the integration of cloud-computing into the IoT architecture, i.e., cloud-centric IoT (Gubbi, J., Buyya, R., Marusic, S. & Palaniswami, M., 2013) as illustrated in Figure 1.

Figure 1. Minimalist illustration of cloud-centric IoT architecture

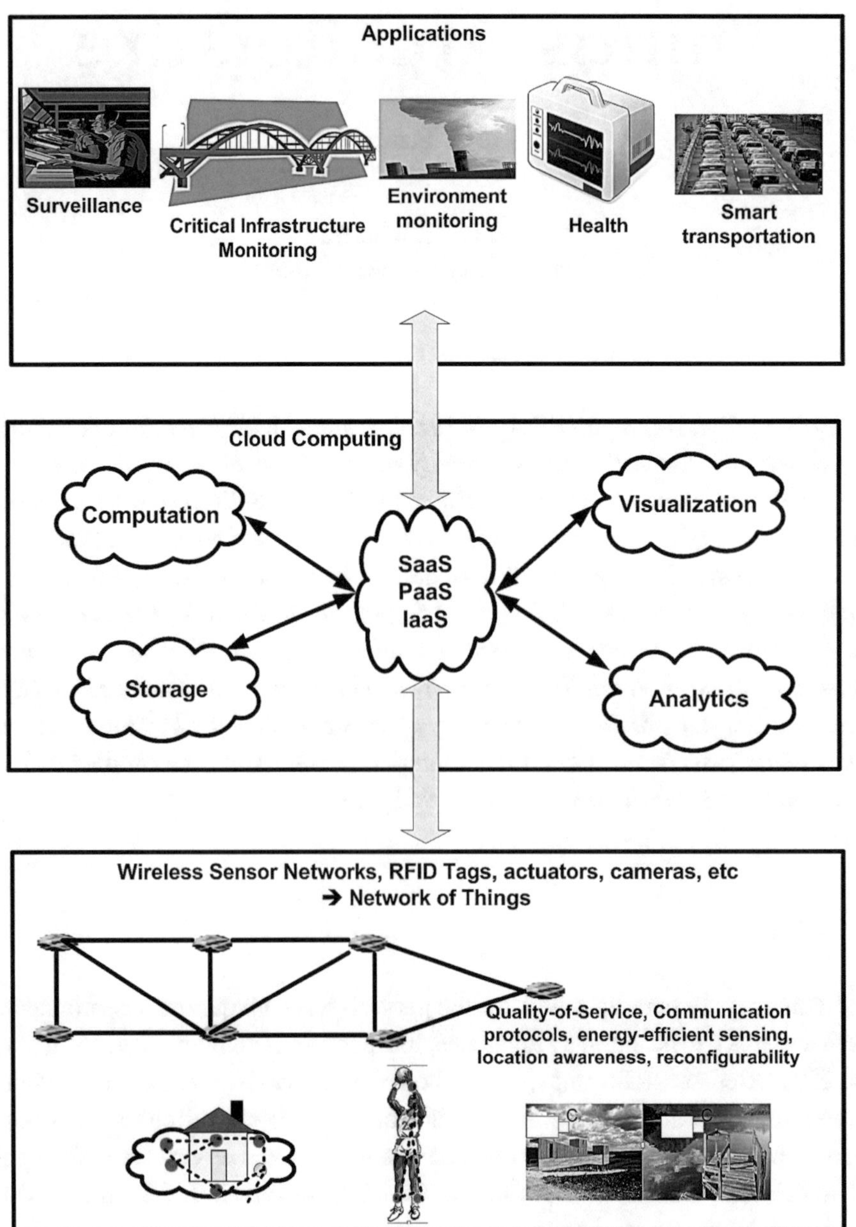

As future Internet is expected to offer everything-as-a-service (XaaS) such as CPU, network, memory and so on (Moreno-Vozmediano, R., Montero, R. S. & Llorent, I. M., 2013), sensing, as well, can be offered as a service within the cloud. Furthermore, cloud computing enables on demand access to the information and/or knowledge obtained from sensor data providers based on the pay-as-you-go fashion and providing software/platform/infrastructure as a service (SaaS/PaaS/IaaS).

The requirements of sensing objects driving the integration of cloud computing and IoT are summarized as huge computing and storage capacity, web-based interfaces for data exchange and integration, real-time processing of big data, web-based programming platforms, inter-operability between the sensing objects, cost-efficient and scalable on-demand access to the information technology (IT) resources, and security and privacy assurance. Therefore, Zhou et al. (Zhou, J., Leppanen, T., Harjula, E., Ylianttila, M., Ojala, T., Yu, C., Jin, H. & Yang, L. T., 2013) propose deployment, development and management of the IoT applications over the cloud, namely the CloudThings architecture.

Applications that can be improved by the integration of IoT with cloud computing are various; such as pervasive healthcare (Doukas, C. & Maglogiannis, I., 2012) where cloud platform enables efficient management of mobile and wearable body sensors; smart homes where appliance recognition via sensor data and energy usage profile of the household owners are performed within the cloud (Chen, S-Y., Lai, C-F., Huang, Y-M. & Jeng, Y-L., 2013); smart cities where distributed cloud services are deployed to manage and control the IoT devices (Suciu, G., Vulpe, A., Halunga, S., Fratu, O., Todoran, G. & Suciu, V., 2013), future transportation systems where in-vehicle smart phones, roadside sensors and/or cameras are connected to a cloud-based IoT platform for monitoring road condition and alert generation and so on (Ghose, A., Biswas, P., Bhaumik, C., Sharma, M., Pal, A. & Jha, A., 2012; Yu, X., Sun, F. & Cheng, X., 2012). Furthermore, public safety in smart city management can be efficiently addressed by taking advantage of cloud and IoT integration (Li, W., Chao, J. & Ping, Z., 2012). A travel recommendation system is proposed by Yerva et al. (Yerva, S. R., Saltarin, J., Hoyoung, J.& Aberer, K., 2012) where mood information of a particular user is extracted from the tweets of the corresponding user on Twitter, and it is associated with the weather information for a travel destination on a given date, which is obtained via sensors in that particular region. In the corresponding study, sensor data are not collected through smart phones but via sensors that are already deployed for an online weather report service.

In a cloud-centric IoT framework, sensors provide their sensed data to a storage cloud as a service, and the sensor data undergoes data analytics and data mining procedures for information retrieval and knowledge discovery. Visualization of the knowledge discovered from the sensing service is presented to the corresponding applications (Gubbi, J., Buyya, R., Marusic, S. & Palaniswami, M., 2013).

Built-in sensors in mobile devices can leverage the performance of IoT applications when sensors on mobile devices send their data to cloud servers leading to significant energy and communication overhead savings (Pereira, P. P., Eliasson, J., Kyusakov, R., Delsing, J., Raayetinezhad, A. & Johansson, M., 2013; Al-Fagih, A. E., Al-Turjman, F. M., Alsalih, W. M., Hassanein, H. S., 2013). Distefano et al. (2014) define this framework as a device-centric exploitation and management of the IoT resources as opposed to the conventional data centric approach in which the only focus is on the data provided by the IoT objects. The data-centric approach does not allow the users to participate in sensing and presentation of the data. The advantage of this approach is reported as decentralized control of resources and transmission of sensor data, pre-processing of sensor data prior to arrival at the sensing servers in the cloud platform, reduced bandwidth consumption in the wireless front-end due to reduced amount of data (i.e., filtered) to be transmitted, flexibility to repurpose the sensors, delegating the complex security algorithms on sensor data to mobile devices as long as there is sufficient computing capability, enabling information dissemination locally through topology discovery by the mobile devices. (Distefano, S., Merlino, G. & Puliafito, A., 2014). Therefore, Sensing-as-a-Service (S^2aaS) appears as a strong candidate for front-end access to the cloud-centric IoT where mobile devices provide their sensed data to the cloud platform based on the pay-as-you-go fashion (Sheng, X., Xiao, X., Tang, J. & Xue, G., 2012a, 2012b).

Figure 1 illustrates a minimalist view of the cloud-centric IoT architecture. The cloud-centric IoT architecture is presented as a three-layer system where the lowest layer corresponds to the sensing activities by the built-in sensors, wireless sensor network nodes or Radio Frequency Identification (RFID) tags. The sensing layer provides service (i.e., sensor data) to the processing and storage layer which corresponds to the cloud computing platform. The cloud platform provides service to the upmost layer which is the application layer. As mentioned earlier, application may denote surveillance, critical infrastructure monitoring, environment monitoring, health and smart transportation.

Besides benefits of S^2aaS, there are several barriers and challenges which are being addressed by ongoing research. Xiao et al. (2013) report these barriers under the following items: Heterogeneity of mobile platforms and sensing equipment, variety of mobile applications that the users must install on their mobile smart devices, and the increasing bandwidth demand of crowdsensing applications on wireless links. Given these challenges, S^2aaS calls for solutions that decouple application-centric design of data collection, and decentralized sensor data processing and aggregation methods. Data processing consists of outlier detection, noise filtering and sensing provider reputation maintenance. Aggregated crowdsensed data can be handled either in a local cloudlet or in the enterprise cloud. The former leads to one tenth of the latter's access delay, half the power of the latter's power consumption and ten times the latter's throughput (Jararweh, Y., Tawalbeh, L., Ababneh, F. & Dosari F., 2013; Soyata, T., Ba, H., Heinzelman, W., Kwon, M. & Shi, J., 2013). On the other hand, a cloudlet has limited computing capability compared to an enterprise cloud. The tasks on the aggregated data will be partitioned between the cloudlet and the enterprise cloud.

Sensory acquisition-based S^2aaS services can be implemented as mobile applications by using off-the shelf mobile application development platforms such as Android Software Development Kit (Developers). The mobile application utilizes the built-in sensors of smart mobile devices. Data analysis and aggregation algorithms complement the crowdsensing component. Criterion of success of a crowdsensing application is reliable and efficient communication between the end users and cloud platform, as well as improved accuracy of the analyzed sensor data.

This chapter presents the state of the art in Cloud-centric IoT and Sensing-as-a-Service focusing on challenges existing solutions and open issues. The chapter starts with a definition of the S^2aaS concept and two different S^2aaS approaches, namely the cloud-based WSN services and mobile phone sensing as a service. Then the S^2aaS section defines an aggregation framework for Wireless Sensor Networks to provide sensing and actuation clouds as a service. An extension of the S^2aaS, namely Sensing Instrument as a Service is also presented where sensors are virtualized in order to be shared among the end users over the cloud. Service Oriented Architecture (SOA)-based sensor data exchange in a cloud-centric IoT environment is also briefly presented along with the architectural discussion. Cloud-based crowdsensing applications form the most significant survey content of the chapter. At the end of the chapter a brief summary of the studied schemes are complemented by a comprehensive comparison in terms of various aspects. A thorough discussion on the challenges and opportunities are also presented in the last section of the chapter.

SENSING AS A SERVICE (S^2aaS)

Sensing as a Service S^2aaS has been studied in the context of cloud-based Wireless Sensor Network (WSN) services and device-centric mobile phone sensing as a service. The first initiative that can be considered under this category is to integrate sensor data into cloud services has been the sensor cloud concept which has been introduced by several researchers (Misra, S., Chatterjee, S. & Obaidat, M., 2014; Madria, S., Kumar, V. & Dalvi, R., 2014; Alamri, A., Ansari, W. S., Hassan, M. M., Hossain, M. S., Alelaiwi, A. & Hossain, M. A., 2013) whereas device-centric mobile phone-based participatory sensing has appeared as an advantageous solution that offers decentralized resource control, cloud-based security, and partitioned computing tasks between mobile devices and the cloud platform (Distefano, S., Merlino, G. & Puliafito, A., 2014).

Cloud-Based Wireless Sensor Networks (WSN) Services

As mentioned by Madria et al. (2014), sensor cloud concept denotes decoupling Wireless Sensor Network (WSN) owner and the user by allowing the user to access sensors, deploy sensing applications through programmable interfaces, and store sensor data in a cloud platform for analysis and further usage. As the formal 'cloud computing' definition denotes virtualization of computing, storage and communication resources in a shared pool, sensor cloud stands for virtualization of the sensing resources, namely the sensors. Virtualized sensors enable multiple WSNs cooperate for multiple applications while the users who access and program the sensors are isolated from each other (Madria, S., Kumar, V. & Dalvi, R., 2014). This principle also complies with the formal definition of a sensor cloud by MicroStrain which aims at storage, visualization and scalability of sensor data management (MicroStrain). A virtualization model has been presented by Misra et al. (2014), which studies virtual sensor-application mapping, physical sensor-virtual sensor-mapping and computational complexity analysis mapping an application onto a virtual sensor, and the corresponding virtual sensor to physical sensor. Based on the virtualization model, performance comparison between WSN and sensor cloud has been presented, and it is reported that in most cases sensor cloud deployment outperforms the conventional WSN deployment in terms of lifetime, fault tolerance, cost, profit and energy consumption. Although in a few cases the traditional WSN deployment has been shown to perform better, switching from the conventional WSN deployment to the sensor cloud deployment is advantageous because of the following reasons: Sensor cloud deployment enhances management of sensor nodes. Furthermore data collection cost can be reduced by sharing the sensor data among multiple users. Moreover, system-level details of the sensor nodes are hidden from the end-user so the user is only responsible for programming the sensors in order to fulfill the requirements of the requested application (Madria, S., Kumar, V. & Dalvi, R., 2014).

Phan et al. (2013) propose a three-layer architecture for WSN-cloud integration, and introduce it as Sensor-Cloud Integration Platform as a Service (SC-iPaaS). The three layers are sensor, edge and cloud layers. The sensor layer denotes the physical sensors whereas the edge layer denotes the sink nodes that collect and aggregate data from the sensor layer. The cloud layer hosts virtual sensors which are implemented as the software complements of the physical sensor hardware. The physical sensors collect data from the sinks in the edge layer, process and store those data for future use. As stated in (Phan, D. H., Suzuki, J., Omura, S. & Oba, Katsuya, 2013), this framework requires optimization of communication specifications such as data transmission rate at sensor and edge layers in order to meet the objectives of sensor data availability for the service in cloud layer, bandwidth utilization between the cloud and edge layers, and energy consumption in the sensor layer.

WSN-cloud integration is reported to address storage, accessibility, reliability and real time processing challenges in WSNs whereas the same setting will call for emergent solutions for the challenges regarding data format and event processing, event querying, latency due to network bandwidth limitations, online migration of WSN data across data centers and service charges (Liu, R. & Wassel, I. J., 2011).

Mobile Phone Sensing as a Service

Mobile devices can be deployed in a cloud inspired business model in order to enable access to the IoT applications by providing their sensor data based on pay-as-you-go fashion, and this paradigm is called mobile phone sensing as a service (Sheng, X., Xiao, X., Tang, J. & Xue, G., 2012a, 2012b). Figure 2 illustrates a minimalist presentation of the S^2aaS infrastructure. In such an infrastructure, crowdsensed data traverses the following four layers, sensing service providers, sensor data publishing layer (e.g., online social networks), the cloud platform which collects, processes and presents sensor data, and the end user requesting/receiving sensing as a service (Perera, C., Jayaraman, P., Zaslavsky, A., Christen, P. & Georgapoulos, D., 2014a). Applications that interact with the sensing service providers require massive processing power, tremendous storage capacity and huge network bandwidth in order to handle big data obtained through sensing services provided by large crowds. Therefore Rao et al. (2012) presume that big data will be the main driver in cloud-based real-time processing and storage, and define the cloud as the front-end of the IoT architecture. Since sensing in the IoT architecture mainly utilizes IEEE802.15.4, mobility of billions of sensors within the IoT appears as a challenge. Furthermore, IoT sensors are not necessarily to be stand-alone forming Wireless Sensor Network (WSN) clouds but are mostly built-in sensors in mobile devices providing crowdsourcing-based sensor data. Besides, IPv6 over Low power Wireless Personal Area Networks (6LoWPAN) has defined encapsulation and header compression solutions to transmit IEEE IPv6 data over 802.15.4 networks which will empower smart devices to participate in sensing activities (Montenegro, G., Kushalnagar, N., Hui, J. & Culler, D., 2007). More importantly, resource constrained nature of WSN nodes raises serious security concerns for both symmetric and asymmetric cryptography solutions. Due to limited computing capability of WSN nodes, asymmetric cryptography algorithms cannot be employed efficiently whereas storage limitation in the WSN nodes introduces challenges regarding centralized keying mechanisms (Kavitha, T. & Sridharan, D., 2010). Recent research reports that migration towards S^2aaS is inevitable for the following three reasons: *1)* WSNs run on limited battery power, and maintaining a certain energy level requires intervention or energy harvesting solutions which are still in infancy, *2)* WSNs are still not massively deployed to obtain contextual data whereas mobile smart devices are widely used with built-in sensors mostly being underutilized, *3)* Computing and storage limitations of stand-alone sensor nodes lead to severe challenges including security and privacy preservation. Hence, mobile smart devices appear as strong candidates to complement the convenience of WSNs through offering their built-in sensors as on-demand services (Mizouni, R. & El Barachi, M., 2013).

In order to exchange sensor and actuator data over the Internet, a Service Oriented Architecture (SOA) which utilizes Constrained Application Protocol (CoAP) has been proposed (Pereira, P. P., Eliasson, J., Kyusakov, R., Delsing, J., Raayetinezhad, A. & Johansson, M., 2013). CoAP is an application layer software protocol that has been developed for communication between resource-constrained environments, and it is intended for Machine-To-Machine communication applications in the IoT (Shelby, Z., Hartke, K. & Bormann, C., 2012). CoAP mainly runs on the UDP layer in the communication stack. The SOA consists of a web interface for the applications that monitor, configure and visualize the sensor

Figure 2. Minimalist overview of the S²aaS architecture

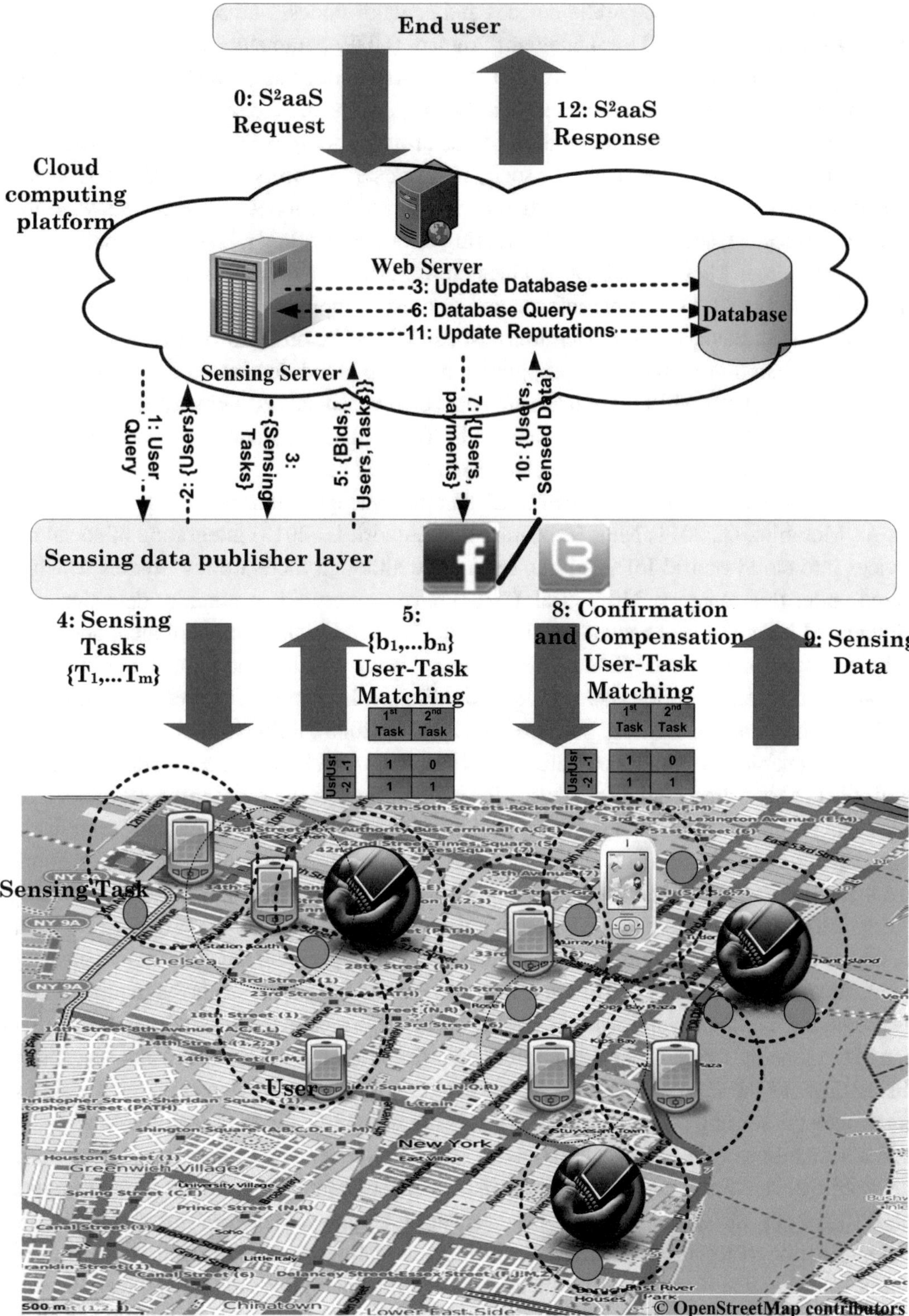

Created with Microsoft Visio drawing and diagramming software

and actuator data. Furthermore, the SOA enables collaboration between services running on wireless sensor nodes, built-in sensors in mobile devices and actuator nodes. The sensor node software in the proposed SOA reconfigures the User Datagram Protocol (UDP) parameters so that incoming/outgoing CoAP messages are managed. Pereira et al. (2013) have shown that use of SOA and CoAP can support up to several kHz data rates in real time between the IoT sensors and the servers.

Sheng et al. (2012b) state that integration of social networks into S^{2}aaS would introduce several benefits to both S^{2}aaS customers, as well as social network service users. Therefore, interconnection of sensors and social networks has been pointed as an important direction where social network platforms can be utilized to collect, analyze and publish sensing information (Baqer, 2011). Sensor data may refer to health data (Rahman, M., El-Saddik, A. & Gueaieb, W., 2011), environmental data (Rita, T. S. T., Liu, D., Fen, H. & Pau, G., 2011), weather information or noise mapping in a region (Yilmaz, Y. S., Bulut, M. F., Akcora, C. G., Bayir, M. A. & Demirbas, M., 2013) and so on. Knowingly, social networks and big data have appeared to be the leading applications in the cloud-dominated era (Han, X., Tian, L., Yoon, M & Lee, M., 2012). Millions of users are connected via social networks based on several criteria such as interests, relations or features. As stated in by Tan et al. (2013), social networks are expected to connect services and applications over the cloud in the close future.

As social networks in the IoT have been studied in the concept of Internet of Social Things (Atzori, L., Iera, A., Morabito, G., 2011; Nitti, M., Girau, R. & Atzori, L., 2013) integration of social networking services into cloud-centric IoT is still an open issue although there are few studies which may be considered under this category. Misra et al. (2012) have proposed a community detection algorithm for an integrated IoT and social network environment. CenceMe is an example of an application which uses built-in sensors in the smart phones to sense users' body position and publish the information on their social networks on Facebook and/or MySpace (Miluzzo, E., Lane, N. D., Peterson, K. F. R, Lu, H., Musolesi, M., Eiseman, S. B., Zheng, X. & Campbell, A. T., 2008). Rahman et al. (2011) have proposed a framework to enable sharing sensed data of one's Body Area Network over his/her social network. Rita et al. (2011) have presented a framework for integration of vehicular sensor networks and social networks. The proposed application is mainly designed for environmental monitoring with the purpose of energy saving and reducing CO2 emissions, and envisioned to be implemented with Foursquare. Besides, weather information and noise mapping via S^{2}aaS have been implemented over Twitter.

Sensing scheduling is handled based on a five-way handshake mechanism proposed by Sheng et al (2014), and as illustrated in Figure 3. The first step consists of periodic location update messages sent by the sensing provider. Upon arrival of a sensing task, the sensing server sends the requested task to the sensing provider. Once the sensing tasks are confirmed by the provider, the provider sends a confirmation message to the sensing server. Upon receipt of the confirmation message, the sensing server schedules the sensing times of the sensing events for the corresponding sensing service provider. Sensing service completes once the sensing service provider uploads the sensed data to the sensing server.

Besides scheduling between server and sensing service provider, scheduling of mobile application to manage mobile device workload is also crucial in presence of contending mobile sensing applications. Ju et al. (2012) have introduced a sensing flow execution engine called *SymPhoney* which aims at effective coordination of resources of different sensing applications in case of contention. The objective of resource coordination is maximizing the utilities of the contending sensing applications subject to resource constraints. SymPhoney facilitates a new concept called frame externalization which denotes

Figure 3. Sensing scheduling protocol between sensing server and sensing provider
(Sheng, X., Xiao, X., Tang, J. & Xue, G., 2014)

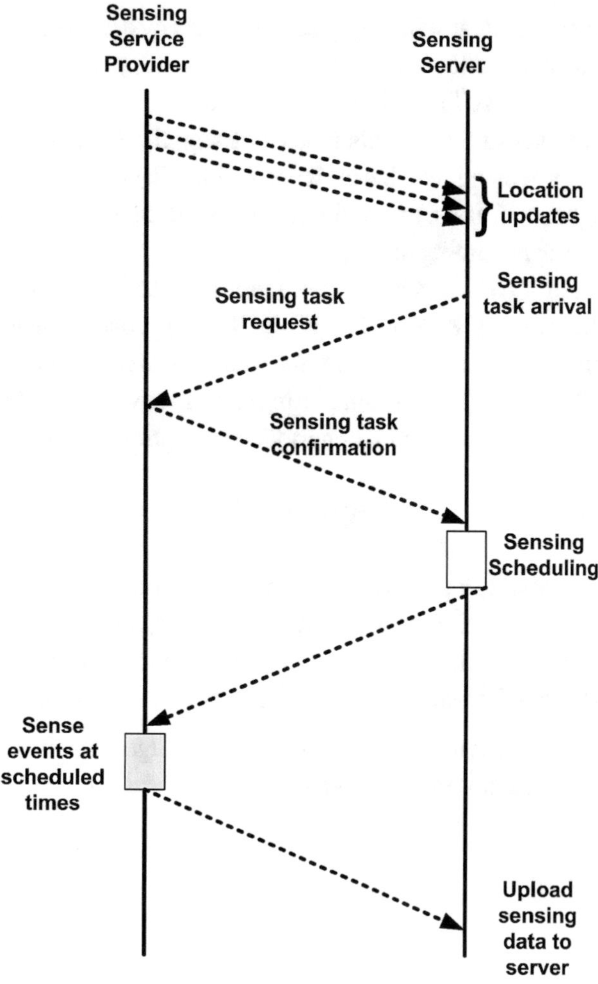

searching and identifying semantic information in the applications so that resource usage patterns of specific sensing applications can be recognized for future resource allocation. In a semantic structure embedded to the application, two types of frames are considered, namely a feature frame (f-frame) and a context frame (c-frame). The f-frame denotes a stream of sensor data which represents a context whereas an f-frame is a sequence of feature extraction processes. The c-frames handle flow coordination in case of contending flows for limited resources. The f-frame runs a pipeline in which complicated procedures of sensing and processing take place. The first step is called c-frame-based flow coordination whereas the second step is called f-frame-based flow execution.

Sheng et al. (2012b) summarize emergent issues that need to be addressed in S^{2}aaS infrastructure as follows: Global Positioning System (GPS)-less mobile phone scheduling, sensing task scheduling on a mobile phone, privacy preserving incentive mechanisms, development of new reputation systems for mobile users and mobile phone sensing-based social networking.

GPS-Less Mobile Phone Sensing and Energy Efficiency

GPS-less mobile phone sensing aims at scheduling sensing tasks by deactivating the GPS. The motivation of GPS-less sensing is significant amount of battery power consumption of the GPS. Besides, location information obtained by WiFi or cellular signalling introduces precision problems. Once the GPS is deactivated, the participatory sensing mechanism has to assign time and location to the sensing devices that will join the participatory sensing. Furthermore, probabilistic coverage models, as well as enhanced mobility prediction techniques will assist improving GPS-less mobile phone sensing. Moreover, efficient sensing scheduling algorithms are emergent.

Sheng et al have proposed a GPS-less sensing scheduling mechanism in order to address this challenge (Sheng, X., Xiao, X., Tang, J. & Xue, G., 2014). Two approaches have been presented, namely Energy-constrained Maximum Coverage Sensing Scheduling (EMCSS) and Fair Maximum Coverage Sensing Scheduling (FMCSS). The former aims at maximum coverage under limitations whereas the latter aims at addressing fairness on individual energy consumption of sensing service providers.

Energy-Constrained Maximum Coverage Sensing Scheduling (EMCSS)

EMCSS is defined by the following optimization model in (1) and (2). The objective function aims at maximizing the number of sensors selected out of the sensors set, *S* that will lead to maximum coverage of the destination regions. Thus, in the equation, s_i denotes sensor-*i* out of the available sensors set, S whereas $P_{err_i^j}$ is the probability of sensor-*i*'s covering region-j with location errors. As shown in (2), the size of the sensors set is constrained to the available sensing budget which is basically the sensing cost (i.e., battery drain) introduced to the sensing devices.

$$\max \sum_{j} \left(1 - \prod_{s_i \in S} \left(1 - P_{err_i^j} \right) \right) \tag{1}$$

Subject to $|S| \leq |B|$ (2)

Sheng et al. (2014) modeled this problem as the server placement problem with budget constraint (Yang, D., Fang, X. & Xue, G., 2011). The proposed greedy heuristic for EMCSS starts with an empty set and adds sensing service providers (i.e., virtual sensors) incrementally based on their contribution to the improvement of the objective function. Thus, the sensing provider leading to the highest contribution is added before the provider leading to lesser contribution. Addition of the sensing service providers goes on until the sensing budget is reached.

Fair Maximum Coverage Sensing Scheduling (FMCSS)

FMCSS is modeled as a discrete mathematics problem which aims at maximizing the submodular set cover on a matroid (Gargano, L, & Hammar, M., 2009). Performance evaluation of FMCSS has been shown to be promising in addressing the trade-off between coverage and fairness among sensing service providers. Sheng et al have re-formulated the objective function in (3) by aiming at finding the largest set covering a matroid where Ω is the set of subsets of the ground set. In order to obtain fast solution, Sheng et al. have proposed a greedy heuristic for FMCSS, as well. Thus, the heuristic adopts the same approach in EMCSS, and adds sensors incrementally to the set of sensing service providers based on their incremental contribution to the coverage over the matroid. For details of this work and the proof of matroids, the reader is referred to the related reference (Sheng, X., Xiao, X., Tang, J. & Xue, G., 2014).

$$\max_{S \in \Omega} \sum_{j} \left(1 - \prod_{s_i \in S} \left(1 - P_{err_i^j} \right) \right) \tag{3}$$

As reported by the previous work, in S²aaS, scheduling of sensing tasks has to introduce efficient utilization of the battery power. To this end, the S²aaS system has to determine how the sensing tasks are correlated, and based on the correlation mobile device-sensing task matching has to be built in addition to the GPSless sensing solutions..

Besides, Wang et al. (2013) have studied energy efficient data uploading problem in crowdsensing environments by classifying sensing tasks as delay tolerant and delay intolerant. Lane et al. (2013) have proposed piggyback crowdsensing in order to exploit the times when smart phone users place phone calls or use smart phone apps so that energy required for sensing is reduced.

Effective Sensor Search Techniques for S²aaS

Recruitment of the most appropriate sensing service providers is a challenging issue in S2aaS as the set of sensors directly impacts the performance of sensing services. Furthermore due to the large set of sensing devices participating in collaborative sensing and the variety of selection criteria makes the problem further challenging. The criteria for sensing service provider selection are reliability, sensing accuracy, residual battery, battery usage efficiency, current location and so on. Perera et al (2014b) have proposed the Context-Aware Sensor Search and Selection and Ranking Model (CASSARAM) in order to address this challenge. A minimalist overview of CASSARAM is illustrated in Figure 4 which basically consists of four steps as follows: Selecting the requirements; searching eligible sensing service providers; indexing the devices based on proximity-based user requirements, and ranking the providers based on the likelihood scores obtained through weighted user priorities and proximity-based user requirements.

CASSARAM receives the number of sensing service providers requested (*n*) and the end user's requirements as the input, and forms a query based on the user requirements. The query runs on a previously built ontology which has all sensor descriptions, as well as context definitions. The ontology is used to run the query and to retrieve a list of sensing devices that could meet the point-based requirements of the user. It is worthwhile mentioning that the point-based requirements of the user are defined to be non-negotiable, and they have to be met by the sensing service providers precisely, e.g., temperature, humidity, motion and so on. Once the list of sensing service providers that could meet the point-based requirements of the end user are obtained, user priorities are assigned appropriate weights, and for each sensing device a likelihood index is obtained in the multi-dimensional space. Here, proximity-based user requirements are used to prioritize user requests. Proximity-based user requirements are defined as negotiable sensing requirements such as motion sensor data within 2% proximity of the accurate value. Finally, the sensors are sorted based on their ranking values, and the first *n* sensing providers are assigned the sensing tasks.

Figure 4. Context-Aware Sensor Search and Selection and Ranking Model
(Perera, C., Zaslavsky, A., Liu, C.H, Compton, M., Christen, P. & Georgapoulos, D., 2014b)

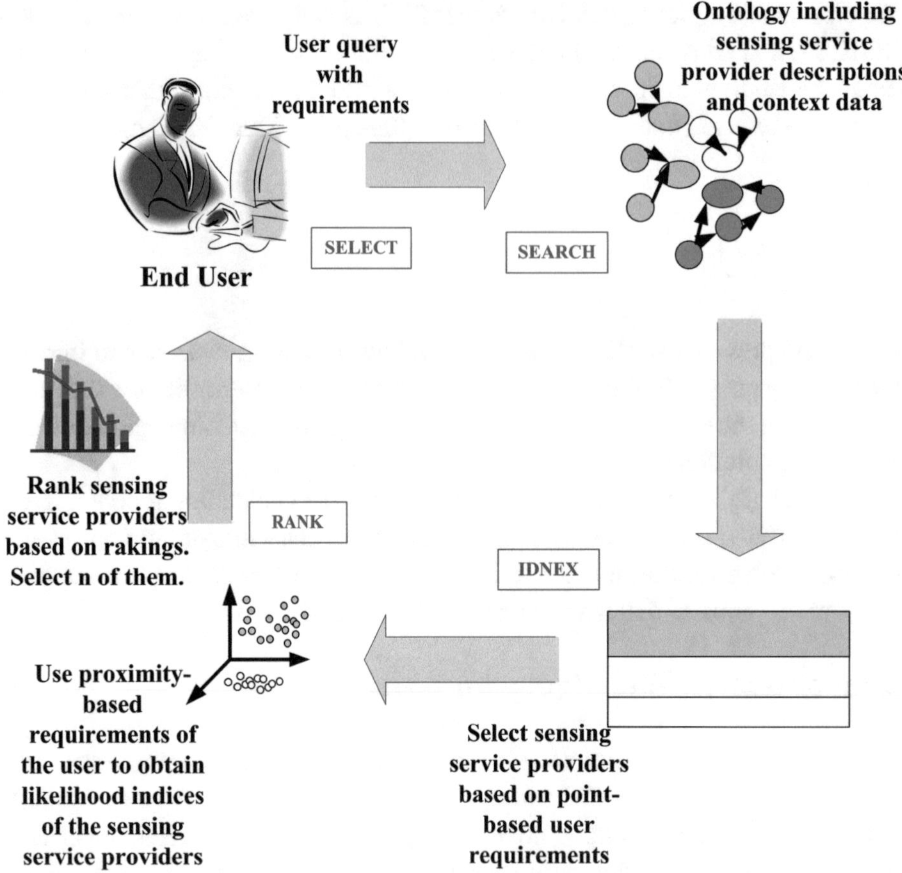

Effective User Incentives for S²aaS

Effective data collection via S²aaS also calls for effective incentive mechanisms ensuring user privacy and trustworthiness of the crowdsensed data. In this chapter, a reputation-based sensing as a service scheme is also introduced where crowdsensed data trustworthiness is ensured along with effective compensation of the S²aaS providers. Besides trustworthiness, reliability of S²aaS is another challenging concern. Sensor data quality assurance can also be overcome by maintaining a robust mobile user reputation system. For various types of tasks, performance and efficiency of users can provide user reputation scores for future task assignments. Fairness and robustness should be considered when establishing a mobile user reputation system.

Incentives can be either user-centric or platform centric as proposed by Yang et al. (2012). The former is based on the assumption that users enthusiastically participate in the crowdsourcing activity by joining an auction to be selected for a particular sensing task whereas the latter selects the users for a particular sensing task and allows them to make their own sensing plans for the corresponding assignments in a game theoretical way. The authors have shown that both approaches are efficient in several aspects. It is worthwhile mentioning that as crowdsourcing through smart devices is a new concept for the users, not every user is comfortable to share his/her sensor data even though providing sensing service will be paid back.

MSensing

Yang et al. (2012) have proposed two user-centric incentives for participatory mobile phone sensing systems. The first scheme runs a local-search based auction which maximizes the platform's utility, i.e., S^2aaS requester. On the other hand, local-search based auction has been shown to be vulnerable to untruthful bidding of the users who aim at increasing their income by participating in the auction with higher bids. This vulnerability has been addressed by MSensing auction. In the same study, MSensing has been shown to introduce high platform and user utility along with truthfulness in mobile phone-based crowdsourcing. Therefore, it can be adopted by a cloud-centric IoT framework where S^2aaS forms the front-end. When such a framework is used for public safety applications, users aiming at disinformation can cause more severe problems in public when compared to the users aiming at increasing their incomes by higher bids. Thus, malicious users participate in the auction with lower bids, guarantee to be selected in an auction, and when selected, send altered data to the sensor data publisher layer of the IoT. In such a scenario, public safety authority may request several types of sensor data such as temperature, noise, motion, image and so on; and sensing services are provided by the crowd which consists of people who have gathered for a particular event. Therefore addressing this vulnerability by a reputation-aware crowd management scheme for a truthful and trustworthy S^2aaS in a cloud-centric IoT architecture remains as a significant challenge, and it has formed the main motivation of the trustworthy crowdsensing algorithms that will be presented in the next section.

Trustworthy crowdsensing has also been studied in the context of user reputation-awareness and accurate sensing (Shahabi, C., 2013; Kazemi, L. Shahabi, C., Chen, L., 2013), user privacy and data integrity (Gilbert, P., Cox, L. P., Jung, J. & Wetherall, D., 2010).

CrowdRecruiter

Piggyback crowdsensing (Lane, N. D., Chon, Y., Zhou, L., Zhang, Y., i, F., Kim, D., Ding, G., Zhao, F. & Cha, H., 2013) has been used as a basis for an incentive framework, called *CrowdRecruiter* which aims at minimizing the number of recruiter sensing service providers while meeting the coverage requirements for the sensing tasks (Zhang, D., Xiong, H., Wang, L. & Chen G., 2014). The proposed recruitment scheme consists of two steps. The first step runs a prediction algorithm which uses the previous locations and call history of the mobile device users (i.e., sensing service providers). The output of the prediction function gives information about the location and the GPS status of the mobile device users during the sensing cycles of the next piggyback crowdsensing task. Once this information is obtained, the platform aims at selecting minimum number of mobile device users as the sensing providers by fulfilling coverage constraints of the sensing tasks while maximizing the number of users who are forecasted to have placed calls (i.e., turned GPS services on) during the corresponding sensing cycle. Thus, by minimizing the numbers of recruited users, S^2aaS cost is aimed to be minimized whereas maximizing the number of users with active calls aims at minimizing the energy consumption overhead of the S^2aaS cycle.

Steered Crowdsensing

Kavajiri et al (2014) have proposed Steered Crowdsensing, which is a quality-oriented S^2aaS solution. Steered crowdsensing uses gamification to increase user participation however differs from conventional crowdsensing as gamification in crowdsensing is primarily used to increase the quantity of crowdsensed data whereas steered crowdsensing aims at increasing the quality of crowdsensed data by introducing quality indicators. Steered crowdsensing defines user-centric incentives as mobile device users determine to participate in S^{2}aaS activities based on coupon points introduced by the platform. In order to increase user engagement, the platform introduces coupon points to compensate sensing services. The platform calculates the values of the coupons through service quality indicators that are obtained by running online machine learning algorithms.

Crowdsensing over Social Networks

Crowdsensing over social networks is still in its infancy although there are a few proposals bridging two paradigms. Akbas et al. (2011a/b) have proposed an application called, fAPEbook for animal social life monitoring. Hu et al. (2014) presented social network architecture for mobile crowdsensing to ease context-aware mobile applications. Besaleva and Weaver (2013) have demonstrated a system named Crowd bridging social networks and crowdsensing whereas Wozniak et al. (2013) have presented another application of disaster management via crowdsensed data through social networks. Cooperative crowdsensing via social networks has been proposed by Chang and Wu (2014a).

Mobile Social Network-Aware Crowdsourcing (MSNAC)

As crowdsensing via mobile social networks has an emerging application with the advent of S^{2}aaS in the cloud-centric Internet of Things (IoT) architecture, Kantarci and Mouftah (2014d) have proposed two mobile social network-aware frameworks for a cloud centric IoT architecture. The first scheme is called Mobile Social Network-Aware Crowdsourcing (MSNAC) whereas the second scheme is called Trustworthy and Mobile Social Network-Aware Crowdsourcing (T-MSNAC). A set of sensing tasks and sensing service providers (i.e., mobile device users) in a terrain are considered; and the cloud platform is not granted access to the online interaction values of the mobile device users over social network services (e.g., Facebook, Twitter, FourSquare) in order to respect users privacy. However, the cloud platform is informed about the social network topology in the region and the location updates of the users. As the cloud platform does not have access to online interactions of the mobile device users, it aims at predicting the interaction values between them based on co-location, proximity and connectedness over the social network topology. Through estimated interactions between mobile device users, the platform aims at forecasting future locations of the sensing service providers so that they can be assigned appropriate sensing tasks in order to maximize the utility of the platform, and consequently the utility of the S^{2}aaS customer. As illustrated in Figure 5, mobile social network-aware S^{2}aaS runs over the cloud-centric IoT architecture presented in Figure 2. Apart from the scenario in Figure 2, here, mobile device users are considered non-stationary. Furthermore, the mobile device users move in communities towards socially attractive destinations.

MSN-aware S^{2}aaS uses user-centric recruitment mechanism for the sensing service providers which is based on an (Akbas, M. I., Brust, M. R., Riberio, C.H. C. & Turgut, D., 2011a) auction between the sensing service providers and the cloud platform which negotiates with the providers, assigns sensing tasks, compensates service providers, analyzes participatory sensed data and presents it to the S^{2}aaS customer. MSN-aware S^{2}aaS auction extends the MSensing auction proposed by Sheng et al. (2012). MSN-Aware Crowdsensing runs as follows: The participants of the auction are marked as winners as long as they introduce positive marginal contribution to the platform utility. It is worthwhile noting that

Figure 5. Mobile Social Network (MSN)-Aware S2aaS
(Kantarci & Mouftah., 2014d)

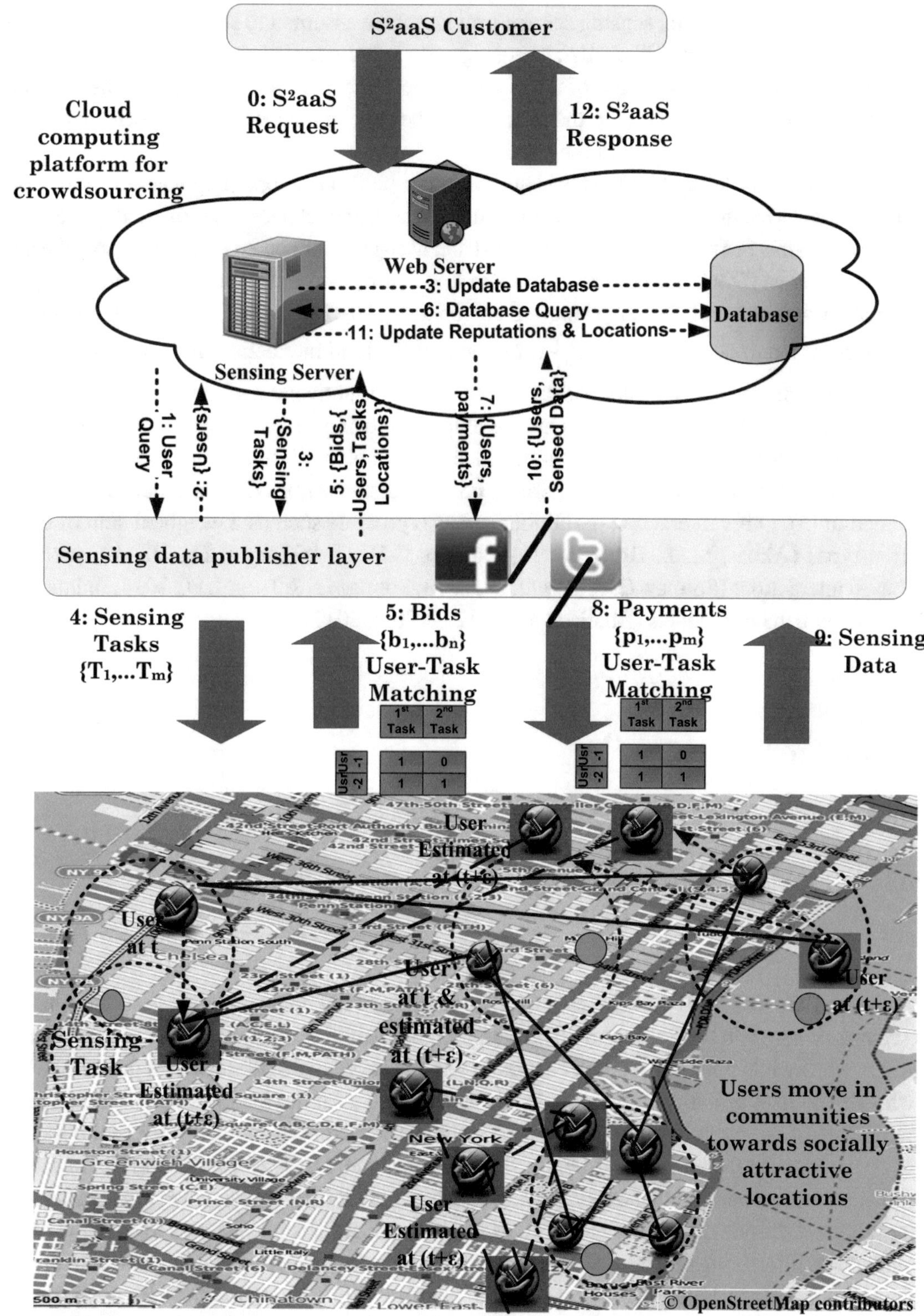

Created with Microsoft Visio drawing and diagramming software

marginal contribution stands for the difference between the marginal value introduced by the collaboratively sensed tasks that are also contributed by the corresponding user; and payment made to him/her. As mobile device users (i.e., sensing service providers) are assumed to select destinations based on social attractiveness criteria, it is likely that a sensing service provider is forecasted to be out of range of a particular task before the completion of the auction. Therefore, a sensing task is forecasted to be out of range of a mobile device user due to the mobility of the mobile device user, the corresponding user is not selected as one of the winners of the auction.

Social attractiveness defined by Musolesi and Mascolo (2007) is adopted by Kantarci and Mouftah (2014d), and adapted to the S^2aaS environment so that the user trajectories are estimated. Given *I* as the interaction rate matrix in a region, $0 < I_{ij} < 1$ if user-I and user-j are connected in the same social network. The terrain of interest ($D_1 \times D_2$) is partitioned into an $X \times Y$ grid, then each sub-grid-*xy* into $x' \times y'$ cells. Social attractiveness is a probabilistic value and can be formulated as in (4). Thus, social attractiveness of sub-grid-*xy* for smart device user-*i* $\left(A^i_{xy}\right)$ is the ratio of the total interaction of the smart device user-*i* with other smart device users in sub-grid-*xy* to total social attractiveness of the other sub-grids. Interaction can be formulated by different ways. One possible way is using the co-location and distance between the users on an $M \times N$ sub-grid. Since shorter distance denotes higher interaction, inverse of the ratio of the distance between user-*i* and user-*j* to maximum possible distance is used to formulate user interaction s formulated in (5). Other interaction definitions are also possible such as a weighted sum of different interaction types (Akbas, M. I., Brust, M. R., Riberio, C.H. C. & Turgut, D., 2011b), social force model-based interactions (Solmaz, G. & Turgut, D., 2013; Solmaz G. & Turgut, D., 2014) or interactions based on human behavior models (Bhatia et al., 2012; Bölöni, 2012).

$$A^i_{xy}\left(t\right) = \frac{\sum_{j \in xy} I_{ij}}{\sum_{x'y'} A^i_{x'y'}\left(t\right)} \tag{4}$$

$$I_{ij} = \alpha . I^{-}_{ij} + \left(1 - \alpha\right) \frac{\sqrt{M^2 + N^2}}{\sqrt{\left(y^t_i - y^t_j\right)^2 + \left(x^t_i - x^t_j\right)^2}} \tag{5}$$

Kantarci and Mouftah (2014d) have evaluated the mobile social network-aware S^2aaS in a heterogeneous scenario where 950 reputable and 50 non-reputable sensing service providers co-exist on a 1 km^2 terrain. It is worthwhile noting that a non-reputable sensing service provider denotes the mobile device users who aim at disinformation at the cloud platform, as well as at the S^2aaS customer. It has been assumed that 50% of the users have up to 15 connections in the terrain of interest, 35% of the users have up to 25 connections in the terrain, and 15% of the users have more than 25 connections in the terrain of interest. Under the assumption that every sensing task has a predefined value and every sensing service provider reports a sensing cost to the platform, MSN-aware S^2aaS has been shown to increase platform utility under heavily arriving sensing task requests. On the other hand, reputation-awareness incorporated with mobile social network-awareness enhances the platform utility by up to the order of 55% whereas disinformation probability is degraded by 70% if reputation-awareness is incorporated. Next section discusses incorporation of reputation-awareness for reliable crowdsensed data through S^2aaS.

TripleS

TripleS is an S2aaS architecture which utilizes cloud-based social networking services and incorporates open source principles (Hu, X., Liu, Q., Zhu, C., Leung, V. C. M., Chu, T. H. S. & Chan, H. C. B., 2013). TripleS consists of internetworking and opportunistic networking components. The former denotes cloud-based services whereas the latter denotes opportunistic networking services. The cloud platform consists of *management interface, storage service, deployment environment* and *process runtime environment. Management interface* provides application programming interfaces development platforms to allow integration of various mobile applications and services into TripleS. *Storage service* provides automated backup of crowdsensed data including analyzed data and the raw sensor data. *Deployment environment* is an enabler for dynamic implementation of mobile platforms and web services to mobile smart devices. Mobile smart device users, namely the sensing service providers will be able to participate in crowdsensing activities through these platforms and web services. *Process runtime environment* of the cloud platform hosts open souce procedures which enable collection, aggregation and analysis of crowdsensed data from various sensing service providers (i.e., smart mobile devices).

The opportunistic networking components of TripleS are the mobile service-oriented architecture (SOA) framework and an agent-based application programming framework. The mobile SOA framework offers application and service instances to enable users to join crowdsensing activities and provide their sensor data to the end users through cloud platform. The agent-based application programming framework builds on a previous framework, called *Aframe* (Hu, X., Du W., Spencer, B., 2011), and it enables collection, aggregation and processing the data in mobile agents locally. The benefits of TripleS are its offering flexible and open source cloud platform, and its facilitating agent-based aggregation and processing of crowdsensed data in conjunction with online social network services.

VeDi

The concept of mobile social networks-based crowdsourcing can be extended to Vehicular Social Network (VSN)-based crowdsourcing. VSNs consolidate social links between the vehicles of a vehicular ad hoc network (Mezghani, F., Daou, R., Nogueira, M. & Beylot, A –L., 2014). Alam et al (2014) have proposed a vehicular social network application, namely VeDi, to support crowdsourced video. One of the biggest challenges in vehicular networks is the distribution of video content since the nodes move faster than the conventional mobile ad hoc network nodes, and contention occurs rapidly in the communication medium. To cope with this challenge, VeDi (Alam, K. M., Saini, M., Ahmet, D. T., El-Saddik, A., 2014) proposes an application consisting of vehicular on-board units, road side units, home-based units, IEEE 802.11p communication links/messages and the VeDi cloud platform. The VeDi cloud hosts all vehicular interactions including inter-on-board unit, on-board unit-to-home-board unit, and on-board unit-to-road side unit communications and the Dedicated Shor Range Communications (DRSC) messages. According to VeDi, a vehicle shares the metadata of the video with the surrounding vehicles along with metadata scores. The video metadata scores include blur and shakiness analysis of the corresponding video. The passengers in the surrounding vehicles can select to download the videos based of their preferences, and the downloaded video is stored in the on-board unit. Upon arrival at the home board unit, the content is synchronized with the VeDi cloud. Furthermore, social interactions among VSN users are also stored and processed within the VeDi cloud through RSUs.

RELIABLE S²aaS AND TRUSTWORTHINESS OF CROWDSENSED DATA

Trustworthiness of crowdsensed data focuses on reputation of sensing devices and their corresponding sensing accuracy (Kazemi, L. Shahabi, C., Chen, L., 2013; Shahabi, C., 2013). In a reputation-based crowdsensing system, when the trustworthiness of a malicious and a non-malicious user are compared as time elapses, the following observation can be made: The user who continuously sends altered sensor data is not recruited anymore whereas the other user who aims at recovering his/her reputation by sending accurate sensor readings in order to be recruited in the next sensor data requests is recruited once his/her reputation exceeds a certain value (Kantarci, B. & Mouftah, H. T., 2014b).

Trustworthy Sensing for Crowd Management (TSCM)

In order to address the reliability of S²aaS and ensure trustworthiness of crowdsensed data, Kantarci and Mouftah have proposed reputation-aware sensing as a service (Kantarci, B. & Mouftah, H. T., 2014a, 2014b). The authors adopt the MSensing auction and extend it by incorporating reputation-awareness. The proposed framework is called Trustworthy Sensing for Crowd Management (TSCM), and its contribution is two-fold: i) A crowdsensing framework is proposed for management of a crowd gathered in a certain terrain; ii) user-centric incentives have been proposed to ensure trustworthiness. TSCM recruits the users based on their reputation. User reputation is defined as the running average ratio of the positive sensing readings to total sensing readings. Once all sensor data are collected for a set of tasks, for each task, an outlier detection algorithm (Zhang, Y., Meratnia, N. & Havinga, P., 2010) is run on the set of sensor readings, and the outliers are marked as negative readings whereas the rest are marked as positive readings.

Every task, t is considered to have a pre-defined value, ϑ_t, set by the end user and reported to the cloud platform. The cloud platform keeps track of the user reputation and recruits the users based on their reputable contributions to the set of sensed task. The difference between the reputable values of the set, W is defined as the reputable contribution of user-i as formulated in (6). Reputable value of a set is the total value of the sensing tasks handled by the user in W while the total is normalized by the average reputation of the user in W as shown in (7).

$$\vartheta_i^{\Re}\left(W\right) = \vartheta_i^{\Re}\left(W \cup \left\{i\right\}\right) - \vartheta^{\Re}\left(W\right) \tag{6}$$

$$\vartheta^{\Re}\left(W\right) = \sum_{t\in T_w}\sum_{j\in\Gamma_t}\vartheta_t.\Re_j \,/\, \left|\Gamma_t\right| \tag{7}$$

Every sensing service provider has a sensing cost, which is also called the bid of the user, which sets a lower bound to the payments to be made to the sensing service provider. TSCM adopts the MSensing auction proposed by Yang et al. (2012), and enhances it by introducing reputation-awareness. Instantaneous reputation of a sensing service provider is defined as the ratio of the positive sensor readings to all readings. As a provider can participate several sensing activities, overall reputation (i,e, trustworthiness) of a user is updated via weighted sum of past and current reputation values. The sensing service providers are selected based on a two-step auction. The bids of the providers are scaled by their reputation so that a provider with high reputation is trusted and it is considered that his/her actual bid/sensing cost is close to the reported bid whereas in case of a provider with low reputation, it is considered that the user aims at bidding lower than his/her actual sensing cost in order to guarantee being selected so that he/she can mislead the end user by sending maliciously altered sensor data. In the first step, winners are selected based on the following criterion: The providers whose modified bids are less than their reputable marginal values are selected as the winners of the auction, and they are added to the winners list, W in descending order. In the payment determination phase, for each selected sensing service provider, w¸ the algorithm seeks maximum possible bid which would still make the corresponding provider w preferable over the other providers whose payments have not been decided yet (i.e., every user w_v). To this end, the providers whose reputable marginal values are greater than their modified bids are sorted based on their reputable contributions as shown in (8) where $\vartheta_{w_v}^{\Re}$ denotes the reputable marginal value of user w_v on the set of users who have not been paid so far.

$$(\vartheta_{w_v}^{\Re} - b_{w_v} / \Re_{w_v}) > (\vartheta_{w_v+1}^{\Re} - b_{w_v+1} / \Re_{w_v+1}) \tag{8}$$

For the assessment of the framework, the following metrics are used:

- **Utility of the End User (Platform Utility):** As shown in (9), utility of the end user is the difference between the total reputable value of the sensing tasks and the total payments made to the winners in the auction $\left(\rho_i^{\tau}\right)$ where τ stands for the period in which the cloud platform requests a new set of sensing tasks from the sensing service providers.

$$U_{platform} = \sum_{\tau}\left(\sum_{t \epsilon T_{W_t}} \vartheta^{\Re}\left(W_{\tau}\right) - \sum_{i} \rho_i^{\tau}\right) \tag{9}$$

$$U_{prov} = \left(\sum_{\tau}((\sum_{i}\rho_i^{\tau} - \sum_{i} c_i^{\tau}\right) / \left|W_{\tau}\right|)) / \tau_{end} \tag{10}$$

- **Utility of the Sensing Service Provider:** Equation (10) formulates the average utility of a provider (i.e., mobile device user) as the difference between total payments made to the winners and the total sensing cost of the winners. The resulting value is averaged by τ_{end} which is the end time of the sensing task arrivals.
- **Disinformation Ratio:** The disinformation probability is formulated as the ratio of the tasks for which at least one malicious user has been paid, to the total number of tasks.

Based on the compensation paid to the sensing service providers, TSCM runs in two modes, namely the aggressive mode and non-aggressive mode. The aggressive mode uses the reputable value of the participatory sensor data $\left(\vartheta_{w_v}^{\Re}\right)$ whereas the non-aggressive mode takes the raw value of participatory

Figure 6. (a) Platform utility vs. task arrival rate under Aggressive and Non-Aggressive payment modes of TSCM (b) Average utility of a sensing service provider under Aggressive and Non-Aggressive payment modes of TSCM.

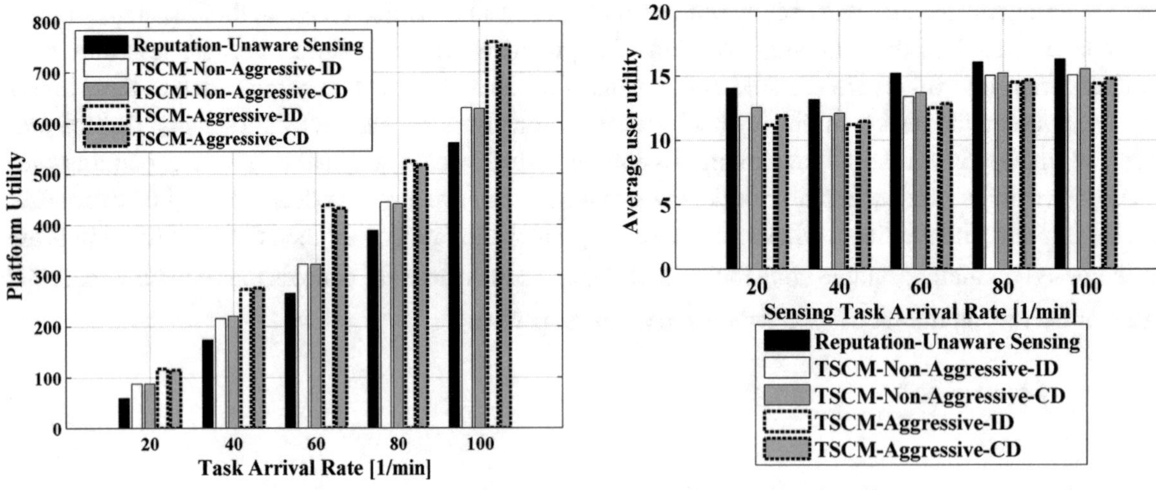

sensing tasks. A malicious service provider may adopt either continuous disinformation (CD) or intermittent disinformation (ID) policy. In case of ID, the provider sends accurate sensor data in order to increase his/her reputation before sending altered sensor data. As seen in Figure 6.a, reputation-awareness introduced by TSCM improves the utility of the end user by 12% under lightly arriving sensing task and by 85% under heavily arriving sensing tasks under the aggressive mode of TSCM. Due to the cuts introduced to the sensing service provider compensations, aggressive mode improves the end user utility by 15% compared to the end user utility under non-aggressive mode. As illustrated in Figure 6.b, non-aggressive mode can reduce cuts in compensations of non-malicious sensing service providers, and the end user and/or the cloud platform may end up paying to some malicious service providers for misleading sensor data.

Mobility-Aware Crowdsensing (MACS)

A big challenge in this framework is the mobility of the sensor data providers. The most naïve approach would be assuming that users follow the random waypoint mobility model (Kantarci, B. & Mouftah, H. T., 2014c). TSCM has also been modified to predict the location of the sensing service provider at the time of data collection. As the mobile device user who is providing sensing service might wander off the sensing range of a particular task although he/she has been recruited and paid to provide sensor data for the corresponding task. In order to prevent the cloud platform and the end user from making payments for non-received data, provider location is estimated by using the triangulation method as formulated in (11) and (12) where $\vec{V}_i$ denotes the velocity of the service provider-*i*.

$$x_i^{t+\tau} = \begin{cases} x_i^{\tau} + \dfrac{x_i.\left|\vec{V}_i\right|.\tau}{\sqrt{\left(y_i^t - y_i^{t-}\right)^2 + \left(x_i^t - x_i^{t-}\right)^2}} & x_i^t - x_i^{t-} \geq 0 \\ x_i^{\tau} - \dfrac{x_i.\left|\vec{V}_i\right|.\tau}{\sqrt{\left(y_i^t - y_i^{t-}\right)^2 + \left(x_i^t - x_i^{t-}\right)^2}} & else \end{cases} \tag{11}$$

$$y_i^{t+\tau} = \begin{cases} x_i^{\tau} + \dfrac{y_i.\left|\vec{V}_i\right|.\tau}{\sqrt{\left(y_i^t - y_i^{t-}\right)^2 + \left(x_i^t - x_i^{t-}\right)^2}} & y_i^t - y_i^{t-} \geq 0 \\ x_i^{\tau} - \dfrac{y_i.\left|\vec{V}_i\right|.\tau}{\sqrt{\left(y_i^t - y_i^{t-}\right)^2 + \left(x_i^t - x_i^{t-}\right)^2}} & else \end{cases} \tag{12}$$

The cloud platform keeps track of previous locations and velocities of the sensing service providers. For each sensing service provider, MACS re-computes the set of sensing tasks that are expected to be still within his/her range based on his/her estimated location by the end of the data collection process. It is worthwhile noting that the data collection process is based on an auction procedure as in MSensing which has been proposed for truthful data crowdsensing (Yang, D., Xue, G., Fan, X. & Tang, J., 2012).

Mobility-Aware Trustworthy Crowdsensing (MATCS)

Maliciously altered sensor data can lead to severe consequences while mobility-unaware crowdsensing results in unnecessary payments to sensing providers. Therefore, Mobility-Aware Trustworthy Crowdsensing (MATCS) has been proposed in order to jointly address these two issues. MATCS recruits the sensing service providers based on their future locations. Furthermore, it uses the reputable value of the set of users ((6) and (7)) while selecting the winners of the auction. MATCS also adopts the non-aggressive payment mode of TSCM.

As illustrated in Figure 7.a, under heavily arriving sensing tasks, mobility-awareness can improve the platform utility by 70% whereas by incorporation of trustworthiness, MATCS introduces 20% increase in the platform utility of MACS. As seen in Figure 7.b, improvement in platform utility is at the expense of providers' utility. However, under heavily arriving sensing tasks, the degradation in provider's utility under MATCS is significantly low.

It is worthwhile noting that the triangulation method is not a strong predictor for real-world user mobility as human mobility demonstrates regularity to some extent (Bayir, M. A., & Demirbas, M., 2014). Therefore incorporating more sophisticated clustering solutions such as Density-Based Spatial Clustering of Applications with Noise (DBSCAN) (Shi, J., Mamoulis, N., Wu, D.& Cheung, D. W., 2014) could improve the accuracy and provide a better fit for real-time mappings. Kantarci and Mouftah (2014d) used social attractiveness (Musolesi, M. & Mascolo, C., 2007) of the destinations to estimate the user trajectories as described in the previous section.

Figure 7. (a) Platform utility versus task arrival rate under MACS and MATCS (b) Average sensing service provider utility under MACS and MATCS

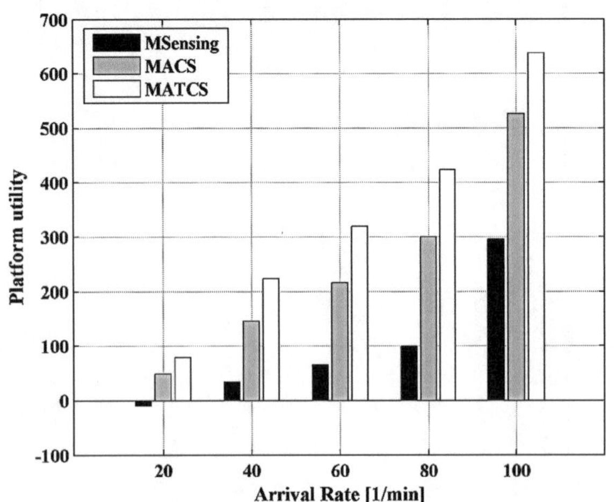

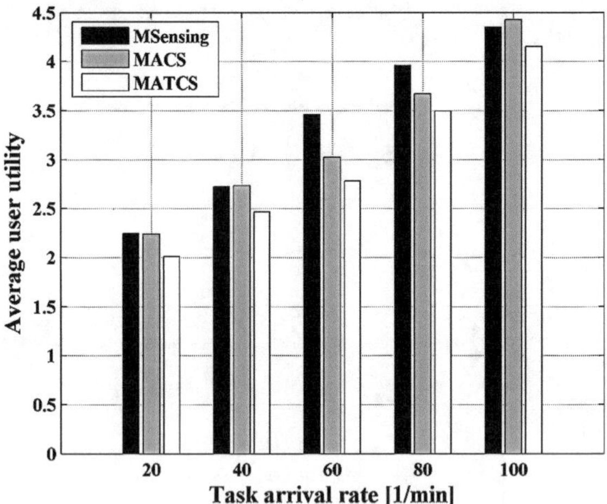

SUMMARY AND FUTURE DIRECTIONS

In the Internet of Things (IoT) era, mobile phones, tablet computers and other smart handheld devices offer advanced sensing and navigation capabilities which may promote cloud-inspired provisioning of sensing services, namely Sensing-as-a-Service (S^2aaS). S^2aaS is referred as the front-end access to the cloud-centric IoT framework. This chapter has provided a brief overview of the state of the art, current proposals and challenges in S^2aaS systems. Searching and recruitment of sensing service providers is a major challenge in this field. The chapter has presented a previously proposed context-aware sensor search framework which has been shown to be effective and efficient in providing sensing services in a cloud inspired environment. Besides, as mobile devices utilize GPS for localization, mobile crowd-sensing appears to be a power-hungry service. To this end, sensing by turning off the GPS as much as possible can introduce energy savings. Furthermore, energy-aware sensing activity scheduling is another crucial issue which can also incentivize the mobile device users to offer sensing services. Having said that mobile device users need to be incentivized, effective incentives are required to improve accuracy of the crowdsensed data. The chapter has introduced user-centric and platform-centric incentives that have recently been proposed. Although having more mobile device users participating in theS^2aaS activities is expected to increase the accuracy of the crowdsensed data, reliability is subject to the trustworthiness of the users participating in the crowdsensing activity. It is very likely that adversaries can take advantage of the user incentives and report altered sensor data to the cloud platform. Introducing reputation-aware mechanisms can improve reliability of the crowdsensed data. The chapter has introduced trustworthiness-based S^2aaS mechanisms that are particularly tailored for public safety and smart city applications. Addressing user mobility rises another challenge which could degrade the utility of the end user. Therefore S^2aaS calls for user mobility-aware approaches. User mobility is a function of several factors; thus, the users can move based on random basis, random Gauss-Markov mobility or social mobility. The chapter has also introduced reliable S^2aaS solutions considering random waypoint mobility and social mobility of the sensing service providers.

Table 1 summarizes the schemes that have been visited and studied in detail in the chapter. All schemes are compared in terms of their foci and direct/indirect objectives. Energy-efficiency and reliability are considered as direct objectives whereas context-awareness and mobility-awareness are considered as the indirect objectives. It is worthwhile noting that MSNAC and T-MSNAC aim at forecasting future locations of the sensing service providers based on the interactions with their social networks; hence they can also be considered as context-aware as the context denotes mobile device user interactions and locations. As seen in the table, all schemes need improvement and to be complemented by one of the direct/indirect objectives. For instance, T-MSNAC is aware of the context as it maintains a user interaction map accompanied with the sensing service providers' trajectories. Furthermore, it aims at reliable S^2aaS, and adopts the reputation-based sensing service provider recruitment principle in TSCM. On the other hand, battery drain of the sensing service providers is not a major concern for T-MSNAC. Similarly, EMCSS and FMCSS introduce promising results in terms of energy savings through GPS-less sensing however they need improvement by a reputation-based approach so that sensor data reliability is improved. Therefore, holistic schemes addressing all direct/indirect objectives and having multiple foci are emergent. Moreover, social networks can play a key role in handling the big sensor data.

S^2aaS has several open issues to be addressed by researchers pursuing study in this field, as well as challenges. Future research is expected to address technical, business, and economic issues that are necessary to accelerate the expansion of emerging crowdsensing applications Firstly, eliminating GPS usage in sensing service utilization still remains as a big challenge. As mentioned by the previous work, precision of the participatory sensed data is closely related to the detection and/or estimation of sensing service provider locations. Therefore relying on cellular signalling cannot guarantee quality of the crowdsensed data as it is likely that some mobile users are assigned sensing tasks at some locations that will not be within their sensing ranges at the time of sensing. On the other hand, when GPS is always enabled for S^2aaS, quick battery drain is inevitable for the sensing service providers.

One of the major challenges in trustworthiness models for S^2aaS is slow convergence due to use of heterogeneous metrics. Future research may consolidate collaborative trustworthiness metrics into the positive readings to total readings ratio in order to help the user reputation converge faster. Collaborative trustworthiness metrics will utilize the trust score of the sensing service provider based on the ratings of previous end users that are in the same social network with the user who is receiving sensing as a service. Ongoing research is investigating the impact of using Wilson score together with the advanced trustworthiness metrics to improve ratio-based reputation calculation techniques. Using positive readings to total readings ratio as the reputation may introduce problems especially under lightly arriving sensing task requests (Kantarci, B. & Mouftah, H. T., 2014a; 2014b). Recommendation-based trust scores have been used in several studies and they have been shown to be reliable (Chang, C., Ling, S. & Srirama, S., 2014b). Furthermore, Wilson score has been shown to increase the confidence of user reputation calculation (Xue, J., Yang, Z., Yang, X., Wang, X, Chen, L. & Dai, Y., 2013). Therefore, introducing compound metrics for trustworthiness evaluation in mobile social networks is emergent to improve system's reliability in reputation calculation.

Research pursued by industrial initiatives report that majority of the big data will be contributed by the sensing devices. Therefore, efficient data analytics algorithms and platforms are emergent to handle participatory sensor data. This introduces an inevitable combination of S^2aaS and Data Analytics As a Service (DaaS) which is also offered by the cloud platform. Researchers pursuing research in this area should also address integrated architectures for S^2aaS and DAaaS.

Table 1. Summary of the schemes that have been studied in detail in the chapter

Scheme	Focus	Energy-Efficiency	Context-Awareness	Reliability/ Trustworthiness	Mobility-Awareness
CASSARAM (Perera, C., Zaslavsky, A., Liu, C.H, Compton, M., Christen, P. & Georgapoulos, D., 2014b)	Sensing provider search	NO	YES	NO	NO
CrowdRecruiter (Zhang, D., Xiong, H., Wang, L. & Chen G., 2014)	User incentives and GPS-less sensing scheduling	YES	YES	NO	YES
EMCSS (Sheng, X., Xiao, X., Tang, J. & Xue, G., 2014)	GPS-less sensing scheduling	YES	NO	NO	NO
FMCSS (Sheng, X., Xiao, X., Tang, J. & Xue, G., 2014)	GPS-less sensing scheduling	YES	NO	NO	NO
TSCM (Kantarci, B. & Mouftah, H. T., 2014a, 2014b)	User incentives and S^2aaS provider recruitment	NO	NO	YES	NO
MACS (Kantarci, B. & Mouftah, H. T., 2014c)	User incentives and S^2aaS provider recruitment	NO	NO	NO	YES
MATCS (Kantarci, B. & Mouftah, H. T., 2014c)	User incentives, and S^2aaS provider recruitment	NO	NO	YES	YES
MSNAC (Kantarci, B. & Mouftah, H. T., 2014d)	User incentives, and S^2aaS provider recruitment via mobile social networks	NO	YES	NO	YES
Steered Crowdsensing (Kavajiri, R., Shimosaka, M. & Kashima, H., 2014)	User incentives and quality of S^2aaS data	NO	NO	NO	NO
T-MSNAC (Kantarci, B. & Mouftah, H. T., 2014d)	User incentives and S^2aaS provider recruitment via mobile social networks	NO	YES	YES	YES
TripleS (Hu, X., Liu, Q., Zhu, C., Leung, V. C. M., Chu, T. H. S. & Chan, H. C. B., 2013)	Flexible, open source S^2aaS platform	NO	YES	NO	NO
VeDi (Alam, K. M., Saini, M., Ahmet, D. T., El-Saddik, A., 2014)	Crowdsensing multimedia data in vehicular social networks	NO	YES	NO	YES

Mobile device users have to be incentivized to share their built-in sensor resources, and they have to be compensated due to their resource usage. However, major user concern in allowing access to the built-in sensing hardware is more related to privacy preservation. Besides compensation due to resource utilization, privacy assuring mechanisms are emergent in sensing service provider recruitment.

The ultimate societal impacts of the S[2]aaS can be listed as new crowdsensing applications in the areas of public safety, disaster management and community engagement that will be enabled by improved energy-efficient data collection, increased crowdsending trustworthiness through context aware sensing, and new crowdsensing business models that will incentivize more users to offer their mobile device built-in sensors as a service.

REFERENCES

Aggarwal, C., Ashish, N., & Sheth, A. (2013). The Internet of Things: A Survey from the Data-Centric Perspective. In C. Aggarwal, & C. Charu (Eds.), Managing and Mining Sensor Data (pp. 383--428). Springer. doi:10.1007/978-1-4614-6309-2_12

Akbas, M. I., Brust, M. R., Riberio, C. H. C., & Turgut, D. (2011a). fAPEbook - Animal Social life Monitoring with Wireless Sensor and Actor Networks. *IEEE Global Communications Conference (GLOBECOM)*, (pp. 1-5). doi:10.1109/GLOCOM.2011.6134364

Akbas, M. I., Brust, M. R., Riberio, C. H. C., & Turgut, D. (2011b). *Deployment and Mobility for Animal Social Life Monitoring Based on Preferential Attachment* (pp. 488–495). IEEE Local Computer Networks. doi:10.1109/LCN.2011.6115510

Al-Fagih, A. E., Al-Turjman, F. M., Alsalih, W. M., & Hassanein, H. S. (2013). A priced public sensing framework for heterogeneous IoT architectures. *IEEE Transactions on Emerging Topics in Computing, 1*(1), 133–147. doi:10.1109/TETC.2013.2278698

Alam, K. M., Saini, M., Ahmet, D. T., & El-Saddik, A. (2014). *VeDi: A vehicular crowd-sourced video social network for VANETs. IEEE Local Computer Networks (LCN)* (pp. 738–745). Conference Workshops.

Alamri, A., Ansari, W. S., Hassan, M. M., Hossain, M. S., Alelaiwi, A. & Hossain, M. A. (2013). A Survey on Sensor-Cloud: Architecture, Applications, and Approaches. *International Journal of Distributed Sensor Networks*, 917923.1—917923.18.

Atzori, A., Andlera, L., & Morabito, G. (2010). The Internet of Things: A survey. *Computer Networks, 54*(15), 2787–2805. doi:10.1016/j.comnet.2010.05.010

Atzori, L., Iera, A., & Morabito, G. (2011). SIoT: Giving a social structure to the Internet of Things. *IEEE Communications Letters, 15*(11), 1193–1195. doi:10.1109/LCOMM.2011.090911.111340

Baqer, M. (2011). Enabling collaboration and coordination of wireless sensor networks via social networks. *Proc. IEEE International Conference on Distributed Computing in Sensor Systems Workshops (DCOSSW)*, (pp. 1--2).

Basaleva, L. I., & Weaver, A. C. (2013). Applications of Social Networks and Crowdsourcing for Disaster Management Improvement. *Proc. Int. Conference on Social Computing (SocialCom)*, (pp. 213--219). doi:10.1109/SocialCom.2013.38

Bayir, M. A., & Demirbas, M. (2014). On the fly learning of mobility profiles for routing in pocket switched networks. *Elsevier Ad Hoc Network*, *16*, 13–27. doi:10.1016/j.adhoc.2013.11.011

Bhatia, T. S., Khan, S. A., & Bölöni, L. (2013). A modeling framework for inter-cultural social interactions. *Proc. 2nd International Workshop on Human-Agent Interaction Design and Models (HAIDM-13)*, (pp. 16--31).

Bölöni, L. (2012). The Spanish Steps flower scam - agent-based modeling of a complex social interaction. *Proc. 11th Int. Conf. on Autonomous Agents and Multiagent Systems (AAMAS)*, (pp. 1345--1346).

Chang, C., Ling, S., & Srirama, S. (2014b). Trustworthy Service Discovery for Mobile Social Network in Proximity. *Proc. IEEE Intl Conference on Pervasive Computing and Communications (PERCOM) Workshops*, (pp. 478--483). doi:10.1109/PerComW.2014.6815253

Chang, W., & Wu, J. (2014a). Progressive or Conservative: Rationally Allocate Cooperative Work in Mobile Social Networks. *IEEE Transactions on Parallel and Distributed Systems*. doi:10.1109/TPDS.2014.2330298

Chen, S.-Y., Lai, C.-F., Huang, Y.-M., & Jeng, Y.-L. (2013). Intelligent home appliance recognition over IoT cloud network. *Proc. Ninth International Wireless Communications and Mobile Computing Conference (IWCMC)*, (pp. 639--643). doi:10.1109/IWCMC.2013.6583632

Developers, A. (n.d.). *Tools Help*. Retrieved 2 6, 2015, from Android Developers: http://developer.android.com/tools/help/index.html

Distefano, S., Merlino, G., & Puliafito, A. (2014). A utility paradigm for IoT: The sensing Cloud. *Pervasive and Mobile Computing*. doi:10.1016/j.pmcj.2014.09.006

Doukas, C., & Maglogiannis, I. (2012). Bringing IoT and cloud computing towards pervasive healthcare. *Proc. Sixth International Conference on Innovative Mobile and Internet Services in Ubiquitous Computing (IMIS)*, (pp. 922—926). doi:10.1109/IMIS.2012.26

Gargano, L., & Hammar, M. (2009). A note on submodular set cover on matroids. *Discrete Mathematics*, *309*(18), 5739–5744. doi:10.1016/j.disc.2008.05.019

Ghose, A., Biswas, P., Bhaumik, C., Sharma, M., Pal, A., & Jha, A. (2012). Road condition monitoring and alert application: Using in-vehicle smartphone as Internet-connected sensor. *Proc. IEEE Intl. Conf. on Pervasive Computing and Communications Workshops (PERCOM Workshops)*, (pp. 489—491). doi:10.1109/PerComW.2012.6197543

Gilbert, P., Cox, L. P., Jung, J., & Wetherall, D. (2010). Toward Trustworthy Mobile Sensing. *Proc. 11th International Workshop on Mobile Computing Systems and Applicatons (HotMobile)*, (pp. 31--36).

Gubbi, J., Buyya, R., Marusic, S., & Palaniswami, M. (2013). Internet of Things (IoT): A vision, architectural elements, and future directions. *Future Generation Computer Systems*, *29*(7), 1645–1660. doi:10.1016/j.future.2013.01.010

Han, X., Tian, L., Yoon, M., & Lee, M. (2012). A big data model supporting information recommendation in social networks. *Proc. Second International Conference on Cloud and Green Computing (CGC)*, (pp. 810-813). doi:10.1109/CGC.2012.125

Hu, X., Du, W., & Spencer, B. (2011). A multi-agent framework for ambient systems development. *Procedia Computer Science*, *5*(1), 82–89. doi:10.1016/j.procs.2011.07.013

Hu, X., Li, X., Ngai, E.-C.-H., Leung, V., & Kruchten, P. (2014). Multidimensional Context-Aware Social Network Architecture for Mobile Crowdsensing. *IEEE Communications Magazine*, *52*(6), 78–87. doi:10.1109/MCOM.2014.6829948

Hu, X., Liu, Q., Zhu, C., Leung, V. C. M., Chu, T. H. S., & Chan, H. C. B. (2013). A Mobile Crowdsensing System Enhanced by Cloud-based Social Networking Services. *Proc. First International Workshop on Middleware for Cloud-enabled Sensing*, (pp. 3.1--3.6). doi:10.1145/2541603.2541604

Jararweh, Y., Tawalbeh, L., Ababneh, F., & Dosari, F. (2013). Resource efficient mobile computing using cloudlet infrastructure. *Proc. IEEE Ninth International Conference on Mobile Ad-hoc and Sensor Networks*, (pp. 373--377). doi:10.1109/MSN.2013.75

Ju, Y., Lee, Y., Yu, J., Min, C., Shin, I., & Song, J. (2012). SymPhoney: A Coordinated Sensing Flow Execution Engine for Concurrent Mobile Sensing Applications. *Proc. 10th ACM Conference on Embedded Networked Sensor Systems (SenSys)*. doi:10.1145/2426656.2426678

Kantarci, B., & Mouftah, H. T. (2014a). Reputation-based Sensing-as-a-Service for Crowd Management Over the Cloud. *Proc. IEEE International Conference on Communications (ICC)*, (pp. 3614--3619). doi:10.1109/ICC.2014.6883882

Kantarci, B., & Mouftah, H. T. (2014b). Trustworthy Sensing for Public Safety in Cloud-Centric Internet of Things. *IEEE Internet of Things Journal*, *1*(4), 360–368. doi:10.1109/JIOT.2014.2337886

Kantarci, B., & Mouftah, H. T. (2014c). Mobility-aware Trustworthy Crowdsourcing in Cloud-Centric Internet of Things. *Proc. IEEE International Symposium on Computers and Communications (ISCC)*. doi:10.1109/ISCC.2014.6912581

Kantarci, B., & Mouftah, H. T. (2014d). Trustworthy Crowdsourcing via Mobile Social Networks. *Proc. IEEE Global Communications Conference (GLOBECOM)*, (pp. 2905--2910).

Kavajiri, R., Shimosaka, M., & Kashima, H. (2014). Steered Crowdsensing: Incentive Design towards Quality-Oriented Place-Centric Crowdsensing. *ACM International Joint Conference on Pervasive and Ubiquitous Computing*, (pp. 691--701).

Kavitha, T., & Sridharan, D. (2010). Security vulnerabilities in wireless sensor networks: A survey. *Journal of Information Assurance and Security*, *5*, 31–44.

Kazemi, L., Shahabi, C., & Chen, L. (2013). Geotrucrowd: trustworthy query answering with spatial crowdsourcing. *Proc. 21st ACM SIGSPATIAL International Conference on Advances in Geographic Information Systems*, (pp. 304--313). doi:10.1145/2525314.2525346

Kim, M., Kotz, D., & Kim, S. (2006). Extracting a Mobility Model from Real User Traces. *Proc. 25th IEEE Intl. Conf. on Computer Communications (INFOCOM)*, (pp. 1--13). doi:10.1109/INFOCOM.2006.173

Lane, N. D., Chon, Y., Zhou, L., & Zhang, Y., i, F., Kim, D., Ding, G., Zhao, F. & Cha, H. (2013). Piggyback CrowdSensing (PCS): energy efficient crowdsourcing of mobile sensor data by exploiting smartphone app opportunities. *Proc. 11th ACM Conference on Embedded Networked Sensor Systems*, (pp. 7.1--7.14). doi:10.1145/2517351.2517372

Li, W., Chao, J., & Ping, Z. (2012). Security structure study of city management platform based on cloud computing under the conception of smart city. *In Proc. Fourth International Conference on Multimedia Information Networking and Security (MINES)*, (pp. 91--94). doi:10.1109/MINES.2012.255

Liu, R., & Wassel, I. J. (2011). Opportunities and Challenges of Wireless Sensor Networks Using Cloud Services. *Proc. Workshop on Internet of Things and Service Platforms*, (pp. 4.1--4.7). doi:10.1145/2079353.2079357

Madria, S., Kumar, V., & Dalvi, R. (2014). Sensor Cloud: A Cloud of Virtual Sensors. *IEEE Software*, *31*(2), 70–77. doi:10.1109/MS.2013.141

Mezghani, F., Daou, R., Nogueira, M., & Beylot, A.-L. (2014). Content dissemination in vehicular social networks: Taxonomy and user satisfaction. *IEEE Communications Magazine*, *52*(12), 34–40. doi:10.1109/MCOM.2014.6979949

MicroStrain. (n.d.). *Sensorcloud*. Retrieved Feb 2, 2015, from http://www.sensorcloud.com

Miluzzo, E., Lane, N. D., Peterson, K. F. R., Lu, H., Musolesi, M., Eiseman, S. B., & Campbell, A. T. et al. (2008). Sensing meets mobile social networks: The design, implementation and evaluation of the CenceMe application. *Proc. ACM Conf. on Embedded Network Sensor Systems*, (pp. 337--350). doi:10.1145/1460412.1460445

Miorandi, D., Sicari, S., De Pellegrini, F., & Chlamtac, I. (2012). Internet of things: Vision, applications and research challenges. *Ad Hoc Networks*, *10*(7), 1497–1516. doi:10.1016/j.adhoc.2012.02.016

Misra, S., Barthwal, R., & Obaidat, M. S. (2012). Community detection in an integrated Internet of Things and social network architecture. *Proc. IEEE Global Communications Conference (GLOBECOM)*, (pp. 1647--1652). doi:10.1109/GLOCOM.2012.6503350

Misra, S., Chatterjee, S., & Obaidat, M. (2014). *On Theoretical Modeling of Sensor Cloud: A Paradigm Shift From Wireless Sensor Network*. IEEE Systems Journal; doi:10.1109/JSYST.2014.2362617

Mizouni, R., & El Barachi, M. (2013). Mobile Phone Sensing as a Service: Business Model and Use Cases. *Proc. Sevent International Conference on Next Generation Mobile Apps, Services and Technologies (NGMAST)*, (pp. 116--121).

Montenegro, G., Kushalnagar, N., Hui, J., & Culler, D. (2007). *Transmission of IPv6 Packets over IEEE 802.15.4 Networks*. Internet Engineering Task Force.

Moreno-Vozmediano, R., Montero, R. S., & Llorent, I. M. (2013). Key challenges in cloud computing: Enabling the future internet of services. *IEEE Internet Computing*, *17*(4), 18–25. doi:10.1109/MIC.2012.69

Musolesi, M., & Mascolo, C. (2007). Designing mobility models based on social network theory. *Mobile Computing and Communications Review*, *11*(3), 59–80. doi:10.1145/1317425.1317433

Nitti, M., Girau, R., & Atzori, L. (2013). Trustworthiness management in the social internet of things. *IEEE Transactions on Knowledge and Data Engineering*, *26*(5), 1253–1266. doi:10.1109/TKDE.2013.105

Pereira, P. P., Eliasson, J., Kyusakov, R., Delsing, J., Raayetinezhad, A., & Johansson, M. (2013). Enabling Cloud Connectivity for Mobile Internet of Things Applications. *IEEE Seventh International Symposium on Service Oriented System Engineering (SOSE)*, (pp. 518--526). doi:10.1109/SOSE.2013.33

Perera, C., Jayaraman, P., Zaslavsky, A., Christen, P., & Georgapoulos, D. (2013). Dynamic configuration of sensors using mobile sensor hub in Internet of Things paradigm. *Proc. IEEE Eighth Intl. Conf. on Intelligent Sensors, Sensor Networks and Information Processing*, 473--478. doi:10.1109/ISSNIP.2013.6529836

Perera, C., Jayaraman, P., Zaslavsky, A., Christen, P., & Georgapoulos, D. (2014a). Sensing as a service model for smart cities supported by Internet of Things. *Transactions on Emerging Telecommunications Technologies*, *25*(1), 81–93. doi:10.1002/ett.2704

Perera, C., Zaslavsky, A., Liu, C. H., Compton, M., Christen, P., & Georgapoulos, D. (2014b). Sensor Search Techniques for Sensing as a Service Architecture for the Internet of Things. *IEEE Sensors Journal*, *14*(2), 406–420. doi:10.1109/JSEN.2013.2282292

Phan, D. H., Suzuki, J., & Omura, S. & Oba, Katsuya. (2013). Toward Sensor-Cloud Integration as a Service: Optimizing Three-tier Communication in Cloud-integrated Sensor Networks. *Proc. 8th International Conference on Body Area Networks*, (pp. 355-362). doi:10.4108/icst.bodynets.2013.253639

Rahman, M., El-Saddik, A., & Gueaieb, W. (2011). Augmenting context awareness by combining body sensor networks and social networks. *IEEE Transactions on Instrumentation and Measurement*, *60*(2), 345–353. doi:10.1109/TIM.2010.2084190

Rao, P., Saluia, P., Sharma, N., Mittal, A., & Sharma, S. V. (2012). Cloud computing for Internet of Things and sensing based applications. *Proc. Sixth International Conference on Sensing Technology (ICST)*, (pp. 374--380). doi:10.1109/ICSensT.2012.6461705

Rita, T. S. T., Liu, D., Fen, H., & Pau, G. (2011). Bridging vehicle sensor networks with social networks: Applications and challenges. *Proc. IET Intl. Conf. on Communication Technology and Application (ICCTA)*, (pp. 684--688).

Shahabi, C. (2013). Towards a Generic Framework for Trustworthy Spatial Crowdsourcing. *International ACM Workshop on Data Engineering for Wireless and Mobile Access (MobiDE)*, (pp. 1--4). doi:10.1145/2486084.2486085

Shelby, Z., Hartke, K., & Bormann, C. (2012). *Constrained Application Protocol (CoAP)*. IETF Draft.

Sheng, X., Xiao, X., Tang, J., & Xue, G. (2012a). Sensing as a service: A cloud computing system for mobile phone sensing. *Proc. IEEE Sensors Conference*, (pp. 1--4). doi:10.1109/ICSENS.2012.6411516

Sheng, X., Xiao, X., Tang, J., & Xue, G. (2012b). Sensing as a service: Challenges, solutions and future directions. *IEEE Sensors Journal*, *13*(10), 3733–3741. doi:10.1109/JSEN.2013.2262677

Sheng, X., Xiao, X., Tang, J., & Xue, G. (2014). Leveraging GPS-Less Sensing Scheduling for Green Mobile Crowd Sensing. *IEEE Internet of Things Journal*, *1*(4), 328–336. doi:10.1109/JIOT.2014.2334271

Shi, J., Mamoulis, N., Wu, D., & Cheung, D. W. (2014). Density-based place clustering in geo-social networks. *Proc. ACM SIGMOD International Conference on Management of Data*, (pp. 99--110).

Solmaz, G., & Turgut, D. (2013). Theme Park Mobility in Disaster Scenarios. *Proc. IEEE Global Communications Conference (GLOBECOM)*, (pp. 399-404).

Solmaz, G., & Turgut, D. (2014). Optimizing Event Coverage in Theme Parks. *Wireless Networks (WINET). Journal*, *20*(6), 1445–1459.

Soyata, T., Ba, H., Heinzelman, W., Kwon, M., & Shi, J. (2013). Accelerating mobile cloud computing: A survey. In H. T. Mouftah (Ed.), *Communication Infrastructures for Cloud Computing* (pp. 175–197). Hershey, PS: IGI Global.

Suciu, G., Vulpe, A., Halunga, S., Fratu, O., Todoran, G., & Suciu, V. (2013). Smart cities built on resilient cloud computing and secure Internet of Things. *Proc. 19th International Conference on Control Systems and Computer Science*, (pp. 513--518). doi:10.1109/CSCS.2013.58

Tan, W., Blake, M. B., Saleh, I., & Dutdar, S. (2013). Social-network-sourced big data analytics. *IEEE Internet Computing*, *17*(5), 62–69. doi:10.1109/MIC.2013.100

Wang, L., Xiong, H., & Zhang, D. (2013). effSense: Energy-Efficient and Cost-Effective Data Uploading in Mobile Crowdsensing. *Proc. International Workshop on Pervasive Urban Crowdsensing Architecture and Applications (PUCCA)*, (pp. 1075--1086). doi:10.1145/2494091.2499575

Wozniak, S., Rossberg, M., & Schaefer, G. (2013). *Towards trustworthy mobile social networking services for disaster response* (pp. 528–533). IEEE Pervasive Computing and Communications Workshops. doi:10.1109/PerComW.2013.6529553

Xiao, Y., Simoens, P., Pillai, P., Ha, K., & Satyanarayanan, M. (2013). Lowering the barriers to large-scale mobile crowdsensing. *Proc. 14th Workshop on Mobile Computing Systems and Applications*, (pp. 9.1--9.6). doi:10.1145/2444776.2444789

Xue, J., Yang, Z., Yang, X., Wang, X., Chen, L., & Dai, Y. (2013). VoteTrust: Leveraging friend invitation graph to defend against social network Sybils. *Proceedings - IEEE INFOCOM*, 2400–2408.

Yang, D., Fang, X., & Xue, G. (2011). ESPN: Efficientt server placement in probabilistic networks with budget constraint. *Proc. IEEE Int. Conference on Computer Communications (INFOCOM)*, (pp. 1269--1277). doi:10.1109/INFCOM.2011.5934908

Yang, D., Xue, G., Fan, X., & Tang, J. (2012). Crowdsourcing to smartphones: Incentive mechanism design for mobile phone sensing. *Proc. 18th International Conference on Mobile Computing and Networking (Mobicom)*, (pp. 173--184). doi:10.1145/2348543.2348567

Yerva, S. R., Saltarin, J., Hoyoung, J., & Aberer, K. (2012). Social and sensor data fusion in the cloud. *Proc. 13th Intl. Conf. on Mobile Data Management (MDM)*, (pp. 276--277). doi:10.1109/MDM.2012.52

Yilmaz, Y. S., Bulut, M. F., Akcora, C. G., Bayir, M. A., & Demirbas, M. (2013). Trend sensing via twitter. *International Journal of Ad Hoc and Ubiquitous Computing*, *14*(1), 16–26. doi:10.1504/IJAHUC.2013.056271

Yu, X., Sun, F., & Cheng, X. (2012). Intelligent urban traffic management system based on cloud computing and Internet of Things. *Proc. International Conference on Computer Science Service System (CSSS)*, (pp. 2169--2172). doi:10.1109/CSSS.2012.539

Zhang, D., Xiong, H., Wang, L., & Chen, G. (2014). CrowdRecruiter: Selecting Participants for Piggyback Crowdsensing under Probabilistic Coverage Constraint. *Proc. ACM International Joint Conference on Pervasive and Ubiquitous Computing*, (pp. 703--714). doi:10.1145/2632048.2632059

Zhang, Y., Meratnia, N., & Havinga, P. (2010). Outlier Detection Techniques for Wireless Sensor Networks: A Survey. *IEEE Communications Surveys and Tutorials*, *12*(2), 159–170. doi:10.1109/SURV.2010.021510.00088

Zhou, J., Leppanen, T., Harjula, E., Ylianttila, M., Ojala, T., Yu, C., & Yang, L. T. et al. (2013). CloudThings: A common architecture for integrating the Internet of Things with cloud computing. *Proc. IEEE 17th Intl. Conference on Computer Supported Cooperative Work in Design*, (pp. 651--657). doi:10.1109/CSCWD.2013.6581037

ADDITIONAL READING

Cardone, G., Foschini, L., Bellavista, P., Corradi, A., Borcea, C., Talasila, M., & Curtmola, R. (2013). Fostering participaction in smart cities: A geo-social crowdsensing platform. *IEEE Communications Magazine*, *51*(6), 112–119. doi:10.1109/MCOM.2013.6525603

Carullo, G., Castiglione, A., Cattaneo, G., & De Santis, A., Fiore, U., Palmieri, F. (2013). *FeelTrust: Providing Trustworthy Communications in Ubiquitous Mobile Environment*. Proc. IEEE 27th Int. Conference on Advanced Information Networking and Applications (AINA), 1113—1120.

Corradi, A., Fanelli, M., Foschini, L., & Cinque, M. (2013). Context data distribution with quality guarantees for Android-based mobile systems. *Journal of Security and Communciation Networks*, *6*(4), 450–460. doi:10.1002/sec.633

He, Y., & Li, Y. (2013). Physical activity recognition utilizing the built-in kinematic sensors of a smartphone. *International Journal of Distributed Sensor Networks*, 2013.

Li, W., Chao, J., & Ping, Z. (2012). *Security structure study of city management platform based on cloud computing under the conception of smart city. Proc. Fourth Intl. Conf. on Multimedia Information Networking and Security (MINES)*, 91—94. doi:10.1109/MINES.2012.255

Pan, B., Zheng, Y., Wilkie, D., & Shahabi, C. (2013). *Crowd sensing of traffic anomalies based on human mobility and social media. Proc. 21st ACM SIGSPATIAL International Conference on Advances in Geographic Information Systems*, 344—353. doi:10.1145/2525314.2525343

Sarma, S., Venkatasasubramanian, N., & Dutt, N. (2014). *Sense-making from distributed and mobile sensor data: A middleware perspective. Proc. 51st ACM/EDAC/IEEE Design Automation Conference*, 1—6. doi:10.1145/2593069.2596688

Yerva, S. R., Saltarin, J., Hoyoung, J., & Aberer, K. (2012). *Social and sensor data fusion in the cloud.* In Proc. IEEE 17th Intl. Conference on Mobile data Management (MDM), 276—277. doi:10.1109/MDM.2012.52

KEY TERMS AND DEFINITIONS

Cloud-Centric IoT: Integration of cloud-computing into the IoT architecture in order to enable scalability and cost-efficient service provisioning of IoT services. This is analogous to shifting the data-centric IoT to device-centric IoT concept in which users actively participate in sensing and computing tasks in collaboration with the cloud platform where compute intensive tasks are handled and analyzed data are stored.

Context-Awareness: The cloud platform aims at sensing the context by keeping track of and estimating user interactions, as well as future locations. Context information may denote the location of the sensing service provider at a particular time, the interactions of the sensing service provider with other proviedrs at a certain time, and/or the trustworthiness of the community with whom the sensing service provider is co-located.

Crowdsensing: A derivation of crowdsourcing where the crowdsourced data is collected through massively deployed distributed sensors. The sensors do not have to be a part of mission-centric network, and the sensor data regarding a particular phenomenon can be received from various mobile devices each of which is equipped with multiple built-in sensors.

Disinformation Probability: The ratio of the sensing tasks for which at least one outlier has been recruited to the total number of sensing tasks. High disinformation probability in an S^2aaS system introduces the risk of adversaries' manipulating the phenomenon to cause deception at the end user side.

Internet of Things (IoT): Virtually interconnected objects that are identifiable and equipped with sensing, computing and communication capabilities. The objects denote wireless/wired stand-alone sensors, RFID tags and/or built-in sensors in smart mobile devices. IoT is expected to accelerate several application areas including healthcare, smart environments, transportation, social networking, personal safety, environmental sensing and urban planning.

Mobile Social Network: Set of users that are connected to each other via their smart mobile devices. Users can be related to each other for having the same interest, living in the same area or, being co-workers.

Participatory Sensing: Collaborative sensing of a task; however in the context of S^2aaS, the sensors are not necessarily aware of each other. In most cases, participatory sensing and crowdsensing are used interchangeably.

Platform Utility: The difference between the total value of the sensing tasks received by the cloud platform and total compensation paid to the sensing service providers. In presence of adversaries who aim at disinformation, the value of the aggregated sensor data may be degraded.

Sensing Scheduling: Assigning timeslots to a sensing service provider for sensing each assigned task. In case of user-centric S^2aaS, the sensing service providers make their own sensing plans for the tasks that they are interested in, and they report their plans to the cloud platform. On the other hand, in case of platform-centric S^2aaS model, the platform recruits the mobile devices and assigns sensing plans for each task.

Sensing Service Provider Utility: The difference between compensation received by mobile device users for participating in S^2aaS activities and their sensing costs. Compensation can be by means of various types such as additional data package, additional voice package, cash and so on.

Sensing-as-a-Service (S²aaS): A cloud inspired architecture where mobile device users provide sensor data through the built-in sensors in their mobile devices. Besides, sensing services can also be provided through virtualized sensors that are deployed in a cloud platform as the software complements of Wireless Sensor Network nodes. However, the advantage of former is decentralized resource control, task partitioning between mobile devices and the cloud servers, and enhanced security.

Social Attractiveness: The probability of selecting a sub-region as the next destination based on the fact that the user has more interaction with the users in the corresponding region compared to other regions in a particular terrain.

Trustworthiness: A reputation score assigned to sensing service providers based on the accuracy of their current and past sensor readings. Accuracy can be calculated centrally based on the truthfulness analysis of data via outlier or anomaly detection techniques.

Chapter 4
Secure Health Monitoring in the Cloud Using Homomorphic Encryption:
A Branching-Program Formulation

Scott Ames
University of Rochester, USA

Alex Page
University of Rochester, USA

Muthuramakrishnan Venkitasubramaniam
University of Rochester, USA

Ovunc Kocabas
University of Rochester, USA

Tolga Soyata
University of Rochester, USA

ABSTRACT

Extending cloud computing to medical software, where the hospitals rent the software from the provider sounds like a natural evolution for cloud computing. One problem with cloud computing, though, is ensuring the medical data privacy in applications such as long term health monitoring. Previously proposed solutions based on Fully Homomorphic Encryption (FHE) completely eliminate privacy concerns, but are extremely slow to be practical. Our key proposition in this paper is a new approach to applying FHE into the data that is stored in the cloud. Instead of using the existing circuit-based programming models, we propose a solution based on Branching Programs. While this restricts the type of data elements that FHE can be applied to, it achieves dramatic speed-up as compared to traditional circuit-based methods. Our claims are proven with simulations applied to real ECG data.

INTRODUCTION

Software as a Service (SaaS) provides an excellent alternative to any corporation looking to simplify their IT infrastructure. By renting Software as a Service (SaaS), rather than purchasing, the responsibility of software upgrades, as well as the infrastructure to run the software are transferred to the provider of the software. Upgrades on the software could be done instantly, since new patches and code improvements

DOI: 10.4018/978-1-4666-8662-5.ch004

could be contained at the source, which resides within the servers of the provider of the software. While SaaS has been very successful in certain categories of applications, such as Salesforce.com (SalesForce.com, 2014), its adoption in the medical application arena has been very slow due to the strict rules and regulations introduced by Health Insurance Portability and Accountability Act - HIPAA (HIPAA, 2014). According to HIPAA regulations, private medical information should be treated with utmost care, and the penalties associated with the breach of HIPAA are steep and unacceptable. Despite the fact that a hospital can confidently switch its application hosting and file storage to cloud operators, save money, and simplify its IT infrastructure (Reichman, 2011; Good, 2013), this transition has been very slow.

A novel application introduced in (Kocabas, et al., 2013; Kocabas & Soyata, 2014)guarantees privacy of patient medical information during cloud computing. This technique owes its capability to using Fully Homomorphic Encryption (FHE) during its computations. FHE allows generalized operations on encrypted data (Gentry, 2009), without actually observing the underlying medical data, thereby completely eliminating privacy concerns due to processing sensitive medical information. While novel in theory, this technique is plagued by performance bottlenecks: FHE-based computations are orders of magnitude slower than their unencrypted counterparts, which confine the application space of FHE-based implementations to a very restricted set. Additionally, FHE-encrypted data takes up orders of magnitude larger storage space (Page, Kocabas, Soyata, Aktas, & Couderc, 2014). With this significant expansion in storage space, and extremely prolonged execution time, the cost-saving advantage of cloud outsourcing becomes questionable for FHE-based implementations.

This performance disadvantage of FHE motivated the launch of the large-scale DARPA PROCEED program (DARPA-PROCEED, n.d.) to improve FHE performance. While the privacy advantages of FHE-based implementations are clear, substantial work has to be done before FHE can be practical. In this chapter, a reformulation of the idea introduced in (Kocabas, et al., 2013) is discussed, where FHE is not applied to the problem in a generalized way. Instead, a meaningful trade-off is presented between performance and range of input data. It is shown through simulations that, when a medical application is performing operations on data elements that lie within a well-defined range (e.g., 0.4 and 0.6 in the case of the QT_c value extracted from an ECG as will be described shortly in this chapter), comparisons can be made drastically faster. While most of the existing FHE implementations treat the arithmetic operations within a computer application as a set of operations that can be represented as a *circuit*, the formulation in (Page, Kocabas, Ames, Venkitasubramaniam, & Soyata, 2014) takes a radically different approach and is described in detail in this chapter.

In (Page, Kocabas, Ames, Venkitasubramaniam, & Soyata, 2014), a study is provided on a set of arithmetic (and logical) operations required for the execution of a medical application. These operations primarily consist of integer comparisons to determine the health state of a patient. These comparisons are performed on the vitals of a patient, such as the heart rate, or certain other metrics extracted from an Electrocardiogram (ECG). Rather than using the usual circuit-based representation of the operations, a *branching program* approach is taken, where each comparison is represented as a set of decisions applied to the bits of the compared values. Allowing the medical application to be represented as a branching program opens the door to borrowing from a rich body of research that exists for this computational model (Barrington, 1989; Sander, Young, & Yung, 1999; Ishai & Paskin, 2007). While the branching program approach restricts the applicability of FHE due to the limited values that the input data can have, the performance advantage of this approach which will be demonstrated in the Evaluation section far outweighs this disadvantage. Especially for medical applications that will be described in the next section, since the values are indeed in a restricted range, the disadvantages that the Branching Program formulation introduces can be mostly eliminated by a careful selection of the branching program that is used to replace the equivalent circuit.

This rest of this chapter is organized as follows: In the next section, background information is provided on FHE and medical applications of interest, followed by a specific case study medical application. For this case study, a detailed description of the medical condition that is being detected by the application is provided along with a functional infrastructure. Mapping of this functional infrastructure to an FHE-based implementation is the key contribution of this chapter, which is based on the Branching Program. A theoretical background is provided for this implementation, followed by an evaluation based on a simulated program and ECG data. Conclusions and future research directions are provided after this evaluation.

MOTIVATING APPLICATION

Due to the complexity of Fully Homomorphic Encryption (FHE), attempting to formulate a generalized framework for running a wide variety of cloud-based medical applications is not realistic at this point. While a mainstream adoption for FHE might take years or decades, the goal of this chapter is to investigate a set of applications that can be executed in a privacy-preserving setting through the use of open source FHE libraries such as HElib (HElib, 2014), based on the Brakerski-Gentry-Vaikuntanathan (BGV) encryption scheme (Brakerski, Gentry, & Vaikuntanathan, 2012). Target applications that can be adapted to HElib possess similar characteristics and we will identify them in this section. To determine what type of applications can be formulated to run on FHE-encrypted data, we first need to understand the limitations of FHE, which manifests itself on multiple fronts:

1. Each arithmetic operation (e.g., addition) that would normally take one cycle on regular numbers (e.g., integers) takes hundreds of thousands, and in some cases millions of cycles,
2. Representing each bit in FHE-encrypted format occupies hundreds of thousands, and in some cases millions of times larger storage area,
3. Usual data formats, such as integer and floating point types are not necessarily native to the FHE-style formulation, thereby making the application of any function non-trivial,
4. Due to the improvements made in the state-of-the-art BGV scheme (Brakerski, Gentry, & Vaikuntanathan, 2012), operations are performed SIMD-like, i.e., Single Instruction Multiple Data. This requires re-thinking how data elements should be represented/packed for native application to these SIMD operations.

While a broad set of applications might be suitable to work in an environment with such constraints, we specifically focus on long term patient health monitoring applications in this chapter. Figure 1 depicts the conceptualized long term cardiac health monitoring for patients outside the healthcare organization. In this application scenario, patients are given a sensor that is capable of acquiring and transmitting ECG signals, which is called an ECG patch (CardioLeaf-Pro, n.d.). Since energy consumption is a top priority for the longevity of the device, a powerful processor cannot be incorporated into such an ECG patch. An example microcontroller that is suitable for such a device is a 16-bit Texas Instruments MSP430 (TI-MSP430, n.d.). MSP430 consumes only 600μW during operation and including the peripheral acquisition

Figure 1. A system for monitoring cardiac-related health vitals of a patient at home. An ECG patch is given to the patient (CardioLeaf-Pro, n.d.) which transmits its data to a nearby smart-phone or cloudlet.

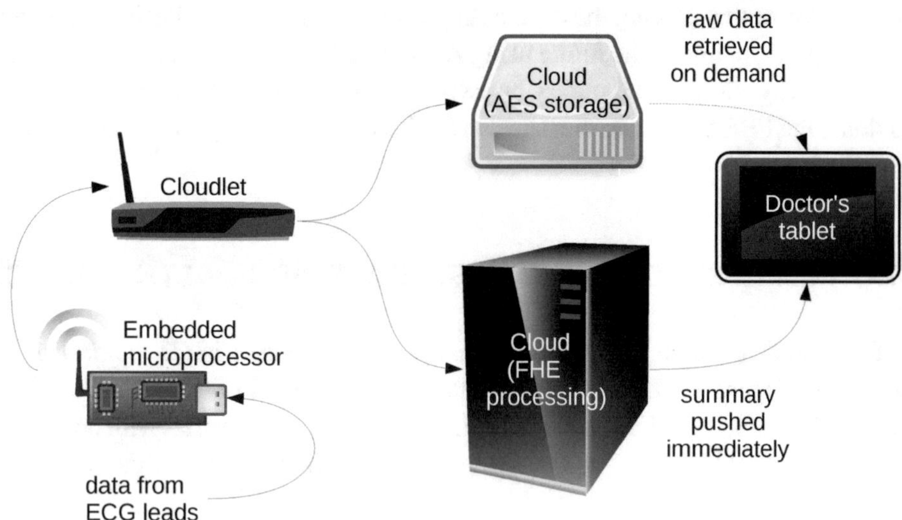

circuitry, an ECG patch that is architected around MSP430 could be expected to consume around 1mW during continuous operation. Additionally, communicating the acquired samples over a WiFi or Zigbee link can consume an average of 1mW, resulting in a total of 2mW power drain. A typical coin battery has 675 mWh energy stored in it (CR2032, n.d.), and can sustain this patch for almost two weeks, which is sufficient for long term cardiac monitoring. This patch has the capability to perform Digital Signal Processing (DSP) operations, which will allow it to compute preliminary metrics on the acquired ECG data, such as the QT and RR values, as we will describe later in this chapter.

While pre-calculating the QT and RR values from the ECG signals might make sense for the patch, it doesn't make sense when the *bigger picture* is concerned, which involves privacy-preserving transfer of these values into the cloud. To ensure privacy of the acquired ECG samples, this chapter proposes to apply FHE into these samples. To run the long-term health monitoring application in an FHE-based environment, the first step, *encryption*, must be performed at the source. This encryption operation is extremely computationally-intensive and the ECG patch has no way of performing it. Therefore, the data has to be transferred to a nearby computationally capable device. We conceptualize this device to be either a smart-phone, with approximately 5 GFLOPS computational capability (iPhone5s, n.d.) or a cloudlet with close to 100 GFLOPS capability (Soyata, Ba, Heinzelman, Kwon, & Shi, 2013; Soyata T., et al., 2012; Soyata T., Muraleedharan, Funai, Kwon, & Heinzelman, 2012; Wang, Liu, & Soyata, 2014; Alling, Powers, & Soyata, 2015; Powers, Alling, Gyampoh-Vidogah, & Soyata, 2014). Encrypted signals should include two different flavors: a traditional encryption, such as PGP or AES (NIST-AES, 2001), or FHE. While the traditionally-encrypted data occupies significantly lower amount of space in the cloud (and, therefore, during transmission through the internet), the FHE path is both computationally and communication-wise intensive. However, FHE-based data allows computations in the encrypted format. Our idea in this chapter is to use the AES or PGP based storage for permanent archiving, and the FHE version of the data for computation (i.e., health monitoring). Communication time of the FHE-based data is less of a concern when the cloudlet is transferring the data, rather than a 3G or 4G telecom network (Kwon, et al., 2014; Kwon M., 2015).

Medical records must be stored for a period of time to comply with regulations pertaining to Electronic Medical Records (EMRs). In the redundant storage mechanism described above, this obligation is complied with. Also note that, storing the data in AES format permanently allows the conversion of this data to FHE at any point in time in the future using AES to FHE conversion techniques (Gentry, Halevi, & Smart, 2012), thereby allowing temporary processing on the data until it is no longer needed. When processing is done, the FHE version of the data can be discarded, since the AES version is permanently stored for future reference.

APPLICATION CASE STUDY: LONG-TERM CARDIAC HEALTH MONITORING

One specific function that can be performed by the system in Figure 1 is *QT monitoring*. The QT interval – illustrated in Figure 2 – is an important marker for the onset of Torsades de Pointes (TdP), a potentially-fatal arrhythmia (Priori, Bloise, & Crotti, 2001). Because QT varies with heart rate, clinicians prefer to look at *corrected* QT, known as QT_c. Many QT correction formulas exist; the most popular is Fridericia's (Fridericia, 1920):

$$QT_{cF} = \frac{QT}{\sqrt[3]{RR / \sec}} \tag{1}$$

where 'F' denotes that this is the Fridericia correction, and QT and RR are the durations of the intervals illustrated in Figure 2. *Prolongation* of QT_{cF} is a warning sign for TdP. This prolongation may occur as a result of genetic mutations, or as a reaction to certain medications (Shah, 2004). Patients who are at risk due to any of these factors are frequently monitored via ECG, particularly when adjusting prescriptions. Based on a patient's gender, medications, and history, a cardiologist will assign some threshold for QT_c. If the patient's QT_c goes above this threshold, the doctor should be notified immediately. Thresholds are typically around 470ms.

While monitoring of QT_c is incredibly important for at-risk patients, it is usually only conducted in hospitals. This occurs in real-time, but does not provide a good picture of a patient's QT_c throughout a typical day/week. One solution is to discharge the patient with a *Holter monitor*. This device can record

Figure 2. QT and RR intervals in an ECG recording. Prolongation of the QT interval points to potentially hazardous cardiac events (known as Long QT syndrome). Image based on "SinusRhythmLabels" by Anthony Atkielski.

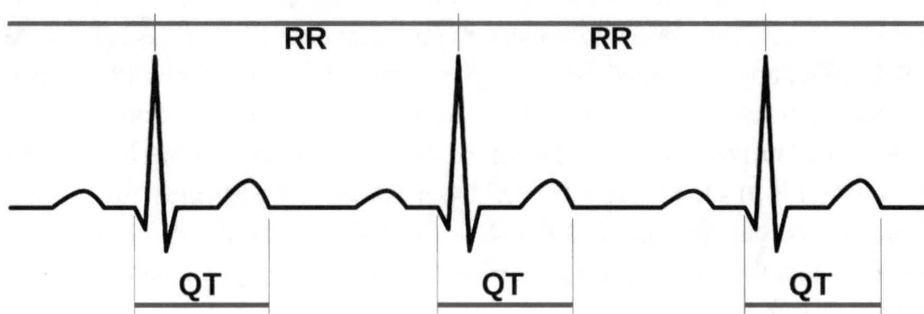

the patient's ECG for several days. It is then returned to the hospital for analysis. This provides a good long-term view of the patient's cardiac health, but does not allow for instant notifications of potential problems. Ideally, monitoring should be both long-term *and* real-time. Such a monitoring system would involve the patient's ECG data being continuously uploaded to a server for immediate analysis, which poses many challenges to hospitals in terms of privacy and administration (Patel & Shah, 2005).

The application (and problem) we've just described has a few features that make it ideal for FHE: (1) It involves only simple calculations, (2) privacy of the data is paramount, and (3) the algorithm cannot be released. (In this case, the algorithm isn't secret; by 'cannot be released' we really mean that it cannot be remotely updated on the patient's hardware, for security reasons.) We therefore envision a system where FHE-encrypted ECG data is uploaded to a cloud-based server for QT_c analysis. The server then pushes the encrypted results to the doctors' phones, which will decrypt them and raise an alarm if necessary. We will now look at some of the details of how data will be passed around in such a system.

ECG samples are generally taken with 16-bit resolution, on three or more leads, at 200-1000Hz. The resulting data stream is on the order of 10KB/sec. However, this stream can be preprocessed by a microprocessor on the patient to output only the QT and RR value associated with each heartbeat. This limits the upload stream to under 20 bytes per second, depending on the chosen data type for QT and RR, and on the patient's heart rate. For example, if we choose to represent QT and RR as 32-bit floating-point numbers, and heart rate is 60bpm, we will only need to upload and process two 4-byte values per second. On the download side of the system, we really only need to convey 1 bit of information to the doctor for each heartbeat: 'sick' or 'not sick'.

Because we intend to use HElib for processing (HElib, 2014), all values must be stored as integers. We could, for example, store the time durations in 'samples' or 'milliseconds' rather than 'seconds', or use a fixed-point notation to accomplish this. Also, because processing speed can be greatly increased by reducing the number of bits per value, it would be reasonable to store QT and RR as short ints, i.e. 16-bit values. And while the unencrypted QT and RR values are only generated at a rate of a few bytes per second, homomorphic encryption will explode them to several megabits per second. One way to avoid transferring QT and RR to the cloud at this exploded data rate is to use AES encryption for the upload, and an AES→FHE circuit in the cloud (Gentry, Halevi, & Smart, 2012). The consequences of using the AES→FHE technique will be extra computation in the cloud, and the need to distribute or generate the AES key without revealing it to the server.

We have described the input and output data rates and types, and now need to define the cloud-based function that will be reading and generating this data. The function to compute is given by Equation (1), which can be rewritten as:

$$QT^3 > t^3 \times (RR/\text{sec}) \qquad (2)$$

where t is the threshold QTc value above which a warning should be raised. Note that t^3/sec can be pre-computed, rather than actually performing the cube and division operations under FHE. Or, in the case where t=500 ms, we see that multiplication by t^3 will become a right shift operation. These types of simplifications will be useful when translating the equation to the FHE domain. Later sections will explain how to rewrite this function as a matrix of FHE-encrypted values.

Figure 3. Sample patient ECG data obtained from the THEW library (Couderc, 2010).

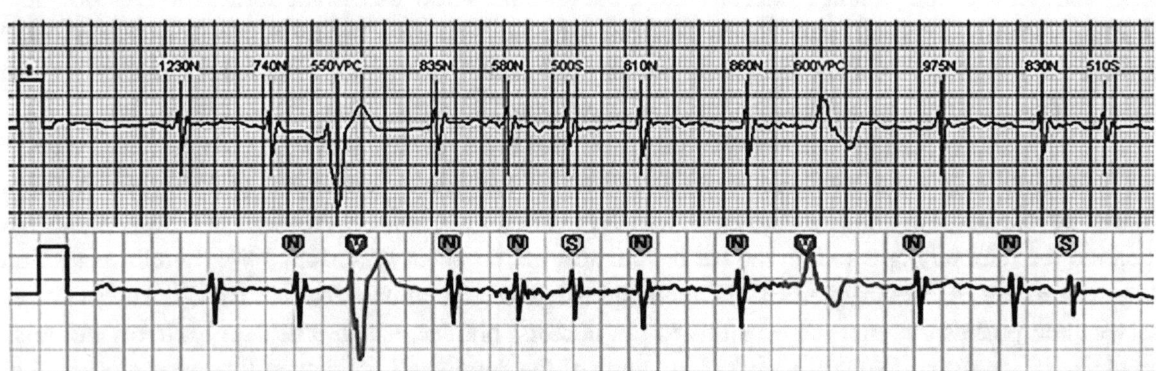

THEW ECG DATA REPOSITORY

The telemetric and holter ECG warehouse initiative (THEW) is a worldwide repository hosted by the University of Rochester (Couderc, 2010). This library contains patient-identification-removed ECG recordings for healthy and unhealthy patients with certain known cardiac problems (e.g., LQTS). Figure 3 shows an example ECG recording from the THEW library, which contains multiple Normal (N) heart beats, and multiple abnormal beats denoted as V and S types. To determine the correctness of the algorithms proposed in this chapter, simulations can be performed based on the data obtained from the THEW library. The storage of the recordings in the THEW library follows the ISHNE format (Badilini, 1998). In this format, there is a standard header that contains information such as the sampling rate and the number of samples between two beats.

Each beat is recorded as a 16-bit voltage value and the number of samples between two beats can be used to determine the temporal distance between two beats. This allows us to work with a summarized yet realistic ECG database, since in our concept system shown in Figure 1, we assume that the QT and RR values and the distance between two consecutive QT and RR values are being transferred to the cloud in FHE-encrypted format. Therefore, the knowledge of every single sample within the ~100 to 1000 samples between two heartbeats contains no additional useful information for our algorithm. Knowing the QT and RR values, the QT_{cF} value mentioned in the previous section can be computed in the cloud and compared against a known "hazard" value, such as 500 ms as previously described. As in some of our previous work (Kocabas & Soyata, 2014), we will use a long-term ECG recording data set, spanning approximately 24 hours. This dataset contains 87,896 heart beats (i.e., QT and RR values). Therefore, 87,896 comparisons will be necessary to determine any existing cardiac hazard conditions.

FULLY HOMOMORPHIC ENCRYPTION (FHE)

Homomorphic Encryption schemes provide a mechanism to compute over encrypted data. The first homomorphic encryption schemes supported adding or multiplying of the values encrypted but not both operations at the same time. The Goldwasser-Micali scheme (Goldwasser & Micali, 1982) and Paillier (Paillier, 1999) schemes supported Modulo N addition operations, making them *additively homomor-*

phic; while the ElGamal scheme (El Gamal, 1985) was *multiplicatively homomorphic*. None of these techniques could support simultaneous addition and multiplication operations. Boneh, Goh, and Nissim (Boneh, Goh, & Nissim, 2005) was the first scheme to support multiple operations, allowing arbitrary homomorphic additions operations along with a single homomorphic multiplication operation. As an example, a vector dot product operation could be performed homomorphically using the (Boneh, Goh, & Nissim, 2005) scheme. Sander, Young, Yung (Sander, Young, & Yung, 1999) showed how to compute any shallow-depth circuit (NC^1) but their construction required a significant blow-up in the ciphertext size. The Dåmgard-Jurik scheme (Damgard, Jurik, & Nielsen, 2010) was additively homomorphic and could offer an efficiency guarantee: For a fixed public key, it can encrypt plaintexts of any size, and the ciphertext associated with a plaintext is only additively larger than the plaintext. Ishai and Paskin (Ishai & Paskin, 2007) showed how to use this property to construct a homomorphic encryption scheme that could evaluate a branching program over encrypted data. Constructing a homomorphic encryption scheme that could perform arbitrary computations over encrypted data was a long-standing open problem.

Constructed on lattice-based cryptography, Craig Gentry (Gentry, 2009) achieved a major breakthrough by introducing the first provably secure fully-homomorphic encryption scheme in 2009. Much like other public-key cryptosystems (Rivest, Adleman, & Shamir, 1978; Diffie & Hellman, 1976), lattice-based cryptography is based on an intractable Closest Vector Problem (CVP): a lattice could have an infinite number of base vectors and it is computationally hard to find the closest vector unless a proper set of basis vectors are known associated with the lattice. Based on this Closest Vector Problem (CVP), Gentry scheme can support arbitrary number of addition and multiplication operations on encrypted ciphertexts. Since his work, there has been tremendous progress in Gentry's work by reducing the necessary hardness assumptions to just the Learning with Errors problem on lattices (LWE) and improving the efficiency of the construction (Brakerski & Vaikuntanathan, 2011; Brakerski, Gentry, & Vaikuntanathan, 2012; Dijk, Gentry, Halevi, & Vaikuntanathan, 2010). HElib (HElib, 2014) is an open source library implementing the best known (leveled) fully-homomorphic encryption system due to Brakerski, Gentry and Vaikuntanathan, which we will refer to as BGV in the rest of the chapter.

HElib LIBRARY

The HElib library that we will use in our analysis relies on the BGV FHE encryption scheme (Brakerski, Gentry, & Vaikuntanathan, 2012) and is an open source implementation (HElib, 2014) by Halevi and Shoup (Halevi & Shoup, 2014). To gain insight into the internal operation of this library, certain implementation concepts must be understood. For example, since HElib uses a *leveled* FHE scheme, this concept of the computation level will be explained in detail shortly.

- **The "Level" Concept:** One of the major improvements in the FHE schemes that were introduced after Gentry's original scheme is the concept of *computation level*. All FHE schemes introduced up to date rely on a small noise that is incorporated into the ciphertext during encryption. When the decryption key is not known, this noise makes decryption intractable, since it makes the decryption problem substantially harder than the case where there is no noise. While this intentional noise helps the security of the FHE scheme, it comes at a steep price: Each FHE operation performed on this *noisy* ciphertext makes this ciphertext noisier after each operation. While the effect of this growing noise is much smaller for addition operations, multiplication makes the noise grow exponentially. While evaluating a function homomorphically, a chain of addition and multiplication operations are performed, each contributing to the noise partially.

At some point during these chains of operations, the noise reaches a threshold, where decryption of the ciphertext no longer yields the correct plaintext. This threshold of the noise must never be exceeded to ensure correct decryption. *Noise Management*, i.e., guessing and controlling the amount of noise is, therefore, one of the most important aspects of any lattice-based FHE scheme. For example, for a threshold parameter of 40, a maximum of 40 multiplications can be performed, which can be intermixed with a much higher number of additions. Once this point has been reached (i.e., 40 multiplications), a decryption must be performed to reset the noise. Clearly, this implies switching to the unencrypted domain. Therefore, only 40 multiplications can be done in encrypted domain, after which the results must be transferred to the "friendly" source and decrypted. An important contribution by Gentry was to provide a special bootstrapping procedure that allows re-encrypting and resetting the noise without explicitly decrypting. Thereafter, 40 more multiplications can be performed before invoking the bootstrapping procedure again.

More recent FHE schemes are leveled-FHE schemes where there is a control parameter known as the *level*. In most constructions, this level is the maximum number of cascading multiplication operations that can be performed in a sequence of computations. If for a particular application this level can be estimated *a priori*, then the leveled-FHE scheme can be instantiated at the right level.

- **Plaintext and Ciphertext Spaces:** A "message" is defined as a string of bits to communicate between two parties. In the case of conventional cryptography, a message is encrypted with a public key and can only be decrypted when a private key is known. Therefore, in a communication system, the *transmitter* encrypts a message of M-bit length, and the *receiver* decrypts this message to obtain the original M-bits consisting of the message. In the case of the BGV scheme, the goal of the receiver is not to observe the message, but, rather, to perform computations on it. Therefore, the encryption operation should simply convert the message into a form, which can be later used for computation. In the case of BGV, messages are encoded as polynomial rings in the GF(p^d), where p is a prime number, and d is the degree of the polynomial that is representing the message. With this definition, homomorphic addition of a plaintext corresponds to the addition of the ciphertext. Furthermore, homomorphic multiplication of the plaintext polynomial ring corresponds to the multiplication of its ciphertext.

In the simplest case, where p=2 and d=1, each message is in GF(2) and the multiplication operation reduces to logical AND. Alternatively, addition operation reduces to XOR. These two operations are a functionally complete set, i.e., any operation can be represented as a combination of these two operations. An extension of the BGV scheme pursued by Smart and Vercauteren (Smart & Vercauteren, 2014) allows "packing" of multiple messages into a plaintext. Each packed message occupies a "slot" of the plaintext and corresponding ciphertext using their terminology. Any homomorphic operation performed on a packed ciphertext has the effect of applying the same operation on every slot. In essence, packed ciphertexts allow SIMD-like operations to be performed on an encrypted vector of data. The HElib implementation, in fact, considers this extension. For example, in our experiments, we were able to pack 682 bits into plaintext slot, which can hold floor(682/16)=42 messages (i.e., ECG values). If we take the homomorphic addition operation, then each operation is applied to the previously mentioned 42 messages in a bitwise manner. Unfortunately, this leaves 10 message slots wasted, however, this is the artifact of the BGV scheme.

Each packed plaintext will be encrypted into a single ciphertext, on which the aforementioned XOR and AND (i.e., homomorphic addition and multiplication, respectively) operations can be performed. To store the 87,896 ECG recordings that we previously mentioned, we would need ceil(87896/42)=2093 ciphertexts. Our goal is to perform the comparison operation on these ciphertexts, where each QTc value stored in a message can be compared against the "danger threshold" of 500 ms. that we previously described. This will allow us to detect the Long-QT syndrome (LQTS) on a beat-by-beat basis.

- **Available Operations in HElib:** In the BGV library, a rich set of operations exists. Within this set, we picked a functionally-orthogonal set to perform the LQTS comparison function. As mentioned above the extended BGV scheme allows operations to be applied to a set of messages packed in a ciphertext. While this results in significant performance improvements, it requires careful formulation of the functions that are being evaluated. Furthermore, it makes certain operations, such as, rotation and selection necessary to cope with the complexities arising from the "packing" concept. Details of the operations are as follows:
- **Encryption:** This operation converts a plaintext into a ciphertext. Since each plaintext contains multiple "slots," the encrypted ciphertext is the representation of every slot in the plaintext, stored in encrypted form. Let *Enc()* denote the encryption operation. Also, let *A* and *B* denote two plaintexts with 682 slots in GF(2) each. We will denote the encrypted ciphertexts *Enc(A)* and *Enc(B)*. Indeed, the size of the ciphertexts *Enc(A)* and *Enc(B)* are significantly larger then the corresponding plaintext sizes, *A* and *B*. Furthermore, the ciphertext sizes for *Enc(A)* and *Enc(B)* depend on the level at which A and B are being stored.

The dependence of the ciphertext sizes on the "BGV level" is an extremely important concept, which is the dominating factor in determining the speed and storage requirements of FHE. For example, take a plaintext ***A*** containing 682 slots in GF(2). Based on our experiments, storing the corresponding ciphertext, i.e., ***Enc (A)***, requires 1MB at Level=10. In other words, to store 682 bits worth of data, 1MB must be used in the encrypted domain, translating to a storage expansion of 1024*1024*8/682=12,000x. This four-order-of-magnitude storage expansion might not sound incredibly bad when we take a look at what happens when the BGV level goes up to 20. At this Level=20, the same plaintext requires 10MB of storage, corresponding to a 120,000x expansion. This explosive growth eventually makes the ciphertext size go up to 100MB at Level=100, corresponding to a 1,200,000x expansion at level 100.

- **Homomorphic Evaluation:** The primary reason for the storage expansion is the fact that, a lot more information has to be stored to represent the same encrypted number at higher levels. The intuition behind this is as follows: As we described before, the "level" indicates the "multiplicative depth," i.e., the maximum number of multiplications that can be performed using a ciphertext before the noise becomes too high. Assume a plaintext ***A***, whose Level=1 representation is a ciphertext *Enc(A)* of size 200KB. This means that, 682 slots (bits in GF(2)) require 200KB of storage, i.e., 300B for each bit at Level=1 (i.e., a 2,400x storage expansion). This size goes up to 300KB for the ciphertext, translating to 450B for each bit when the Level=2 (i.e., 3,600x storage expansion). The intriguing questions are: 1) what is being stored in 300B ? and, 2) why is the storage growing so fast when the level increases.

To answer the first question, we need to understand what is needed for *evaluating* a ciphertext. While addition operations are not as computationally-intensive, multiplication operations increase the noise exponentially, and requires a noise-reduction procedure. This procedure is computationally expensive and dominates the runtime of homomorphic evaluation. Performing evaluation on ciphertexts involves a massive amount of bitwise multiplications of the ciphertext bits with the appropriate public key bits. In FHE, a public key is composed of many parts (thousands or millions). Each part is needed to be stored within the public-key array for runtime evaluation, which increases the storage required.

- **Decryption:** Homomorphic Decryption operation, denoted as ***Dec()***, that on input a ciphertext and the private key, turns a ciphertext back to its corresponding plaintext. Note that, both for the ***Enc()*** and ***Dec()*** operations, the level is known a priori.
- **Homomorphic Addition:** While the GF(p^d) implementation of homomorphic addition is capable of adding packed integers in the corresponding ring, we prefer GF(2) due to the nature of the problems we are applying FHE to. In GF(2), homomorphic addition operation simply turns into the bitwise XOR operation. Assume that, two plaintexts *A* and *B* contain 682 slots each in GF(2). Also assume that, our messages are 16 bits each. As previously mentioned, this will allow us to store floor(682/16)=42 messages in each plaintext. The corresponding ciphertexts are *Enc(A)* and *Enc(B)*, which will be 100's of KB, or even MB depending on the BGV level. Now assume that, we are interested in performing a homomorphic addition on *Enc(A)* and *Enc(B)*. The result is *Enc(C)=Enc(A)+Enc(B)*. This assumes that, the result is being stored in a ciphertext whose decrypted version is *C* which also contains 682 slots, just like *A* and *B*. Since we performed a GF(2) addition (i.e., XOR) operation on *A* and *B*, what we did corresponds to performing *C =A XOR B* in the un-encrypted domain, which is bitwise *XOR* or every plaintext slot (bit) individually. More specifically, we performed *C[n]=A[n] XOR B[n]*, where *A[n]*, *B[n]*, and *C[n]* are the nth individual slot (i.e., n^{th} bit in GF(2)) of *A*, *B*, and *C* plaintexts.

As previously discussed, our messages are 16 bits each, which occupy 16 slots of plaintext space. Since we have 682 slots in each plaintext in the example described earlier, only 42*16=672 slots are meaningful to us, leaving 10 slots unused (wasted). Regardless of this waste, the homomorphic operation still performs bitwise XOR operations on all 682 slots of the plaintext, 10 results of which will be ignored as an artifact of the "packing" concept. This highlights some important points: 1) Continuous additions on the same plaintext will eventually cause carry on 16-bit messages, which is something that our algorithm has to deal with by manually accounting with the carry results of the messages, 2) clearly, this can be prevented if a string of additions will never cause the message to exceed 16 bits, 3) more importantly, even the carry from one bit to the other has to be accounted for, since bitwise-XOR works only on individual bits.

- **Homomorphic Multiplication:** Homomorphic multiplication performs bitwise AND operations on every plaintext slot. Following the same example as before, assume that, *A* and *B* are plaintexts with 682 slots each, and *Enc(A)* and *Enc(B)* are their corresponding ciphertexts. Therefore, *Enc(C)=Enc(A)*Enc(B)* operation on ciphertexts corresponds to the *C =A AND B* in the un-encrypted domain, which is bitwise *AND* or every plaintext slot (bit) individually. More specifically, we performed *C[n]=A[n] AND B[n]*, where *A[n]*, *B[n]*, and *C[n]* are the nth individual slot (i.e., n^{th} bit in GF(2)) of *A*, *B*, and *C* plaintexts. Exactly like the homomorphic addition operation, this operation will perform 10 multiplications that we will ignore. By properly choosing BGV parameters, the number of plaintext slots can be somehow manipulated to partially (or completely) avoid this waste.

- **Rotation:** As can be observed from the description of the homomorphic addition and multiplication operations, it is very difficult to define the evaluation function in terms of just these two operations. Since these two operations work in GF(2), the carry functionality must be taken care of by using other operations: Both the Rotation or Shift operations can be used to take care of carry propagation and are both available in HElib. Out of these two operations, we found the Rotation to be slightly less computationally intensive and will be using it in our implementation.

The Rotation operation, when applied to a ciphertext, rotates all of the messages in the plaintext slots. More specifically, assume that *A* is a plaintext and *Enc(A)* is its encrypted version. *RotL(Enc(A))* operation on the ciphertext *Enc(A)* is equivalent to *RotL(A)* in the unencrypted domain. This has the effect of converting the original 682 bit plaintext *A[681 680 679 ... 2 1 0]* to *A[680 679 678 ... 2 1 681]*, where 681, 680, ... 0 indicate the slot number of the plaintext. A few important notes to make about this operation are: 1) An "undesired" data element from slot 681 "diffuses" into slot 0 in the example above, which must be eliminated later, after the Rotation operation, 2) Since the value of the diffused undesired bit is not known, the only way to eliminate it involves setting it to a known value, 3) while a Left Rotation is described above, a Right rotation also available.

- **Bit Selection:** Let *A*, and *B* be two plaintexts and *S* be a selection mask. This operation chooses specific slots from *A* and *B* according to the selection masks. For example, assume that, *S=[*0 1 0 0 0 1 *...]*. In the selection operation *C=Select*(*A*, *B*, *S*), where A and B are 682 slot plaintexts as described before, C would end up including a *C=[A*[681] *B*[680] *A*[679] *A*[678] *A*[677] *B*[676] *...]*, which is a masked selection of bits from either plaintext *A* or *B*. While applicable to many useful functions, one immediate use of this is in eliminating the undesired diffused message bits after a rotation. For this, if a fixed value (i.e., all ones) is stored in plaintext B, selecting bits from B by using *C=Select*(*A*, *B*, *S*) will guarantee a known value in C in every slot that is specific as "1" in the selection mask.
- **Performance Characteristics of the Available HElib Operations:** Figure 4 shows the runtime of the homomorphic multiplication, addition, and rotation operations, denoted as HMul, HAdd, and HRotate. As can be clearly observed from this plot, homomorphic addition operations require a negligible runtime as compared to multiplication and rotation operations. Therefore, the goal of an evaluation function is to avoid the homomorphic multiplication operations as much as possible. Additionally, since rotation is performed in terms of computationally-expensive operations, they should be avoided too. Also note that, only multiplications are considered when determining the level, whereas rotation and addition operations do not affect the level. This is the reason behind the "multiplicative depth" terminology, which implies that, any number of select, add, and rotate operations can be performed on ciphertexts without worrying about the BGV level, however, multiplications take away from the maximum-available-level which was determined at the very beginning of a sequence of homomorphic operations.

Figure 4. Available operations in HElib and their runtimes. HAdd, HMul, and HRotate are the addition, multiplication, and rotation operations

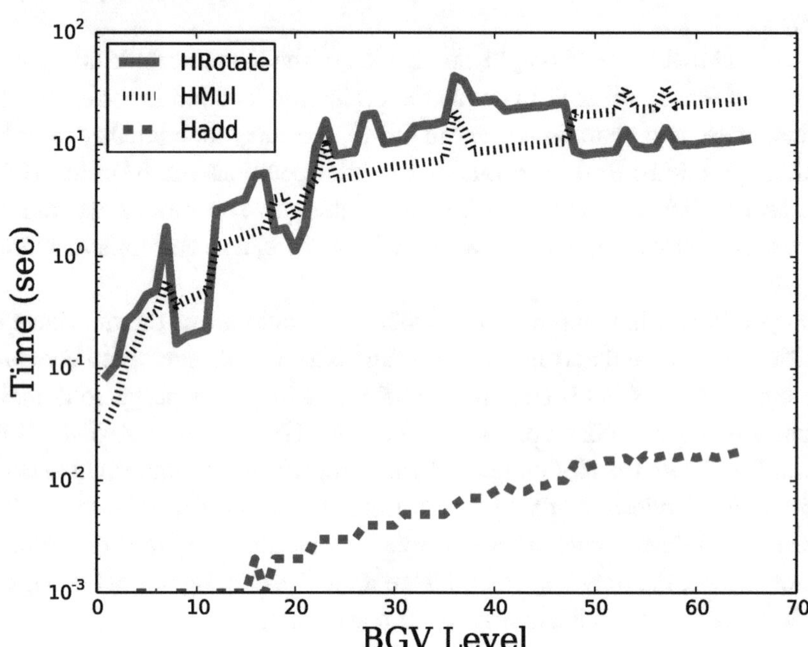

PROPOSED SOLUTION: OVERVIEW

In our motivating case study, we are interested in performing a simple computational task on encrypted data. More generally, in the context of cloud computing, our mechanism will be useful for securely implementing a streaming algorithm in the cloud. Informally, streaming algorithms involve performing the same simple operation on a stream of data arriving at a processing center, and then somehow aggregating the results. Examples include searching a database, indexing or collecting statistics.

More formally, in a streaming algorithm, we have a stream of data $x_1, x_2, x_3 \ldots$ arriving at the processing center and the goal is to compute a function of the stream. In our motivating case study, we want to detect if there exists an element x_i such that $f(x_i) = 1$ for the simple function f described in Equation (1), where $x_i = f(QT_i, RR_i)$. Concisely, we wish to compute

$$\vee f\left(QT_i, RR_i\right)$$

Since FHE allows for computing over encrypted data, the obvious approach is to send encryptions of the data elements to the cloud, homomorphically evaluate f on each element in the incoming stream, and then compute the "OR" of the result of the computations (again, homomorphically). As we show in our experimental results, this solution is computationally costly. This is because homomorphic operations are inherently expensive. As pointed out earlier, the BGV scheme or for that matter most known FHE schemes have a different cost model where performing a multiplication operation homomorphically is typically far more expensive than an addition operation and the cost of multiplication grows significantly (Goldreich, 2008) with the multiplication depth (i.e., a cascaded set of multiplications). A simple calculation will show that in order to do this following the naïve approach we need a depth $d = depth_f + logn$ to process n data elements (each∨requires 1-depth), where $depth_f$ is the multiplication depth of f. The main contribution of our work is to show how we can significantly improve the computational efficiency by relying on an alternative representation of the computation that will significantly reduce the depth of the overall computation, i.e. function evaluation and aggregation. In addition, our method will be easily parallelizable and have small input locality, i.e. our sequence of homomorphic operations can be broken down to smaller sets each only dependent on a few ciphertexts. Most FHE implementations show how to compute any circuit C over encrypted data. Our starting point deviates from this by first representing the function f as a branching program instead of a circuit. A branching program is a directed acyclic graph with a special start node s and final node t where each edge is labeled with either an input bit or its negation, in a sense, a form of combinatorial optimization (Soyata, Friedman, & Mulligan, 1997; Soyata & Friedman, 1994). The result of the computation is true if there is a path from the start to the final node traversing only edges for which the assignment sets the value on the edge true. Next, we show how to use an FHE scheme to evaluate a branching program and aggregate the results of the computation over streaming data. Using elementary linear algebra we first show that evaluating a branching program is equivalent to evaluating the determinant of a particular matrix. More precisely, the determinant will be $f(x)$ for the matrix corresponding to input x. Given the matrix representation of two inputs x_1 and x_2, computing the "AND" of $f(x_1)$ and $f(x_2)$ now reduces to simply multiplying the matrices corresponding to the inputs, since

$$det(AB) = det(A)det(B)$$

On a high level, our idea is to obtain encryption of the elements in the matrix from encrypted inputs via homomorphic evaluation and then multiply the matrices corresponding to all elements in the data stream. We can already see the benefit of our approach from observing that matrix multiplication is easily parallelizable. The main benefit, however, will result from the low multiplicative depth of our computation. In fact, the depth of our computation will be *logn*. An overview of the process we've just described is shown in Figure **5**. We will now explain our approach in detail.

Figure 5. Converting a circuit (representing a function, which is a part of an algorithm) into matrix form.

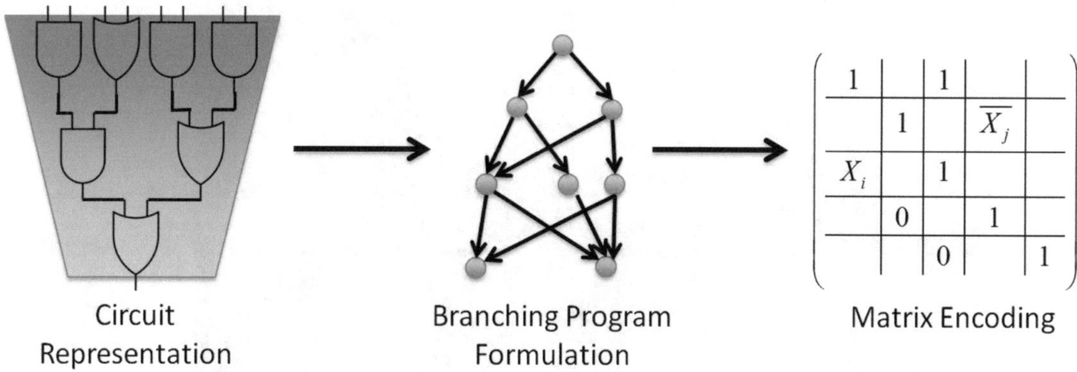

COMPUTATIONAL MODELS

Oded Goldreich (Goldreich, 2008) defines computation as "a process that modifies an environment via repeated applications of a predetermined rule". In the context of computers, this refers to defining artificial rules in an artificial environment towards achieving a precise and specific side effect. In order to formally model computation, we need to mathematically model the environment and the "transition" rules. Such a model will additionally provide a platform to understand the intrinsic complexity of computing any task in that environment. Turing machine is the simplest and most powerful model of computation that allows us to study this complexity as it can simulate most physical environments. While the goal of complexity theory is to understand the limits of computation, our focus is to identify the best computational model that can *represent* our computational task and the best environment to *securely* evaluate it. Towards this, we first discuss the computational models relevant to our discussion. We assume familiarity with Turing Machines and polynomial-time computation.

Circuit Model

The circuit model is the most popular model of computation to represent processes in electronic circuits and is more commonly referred to as "digital logic". It is a generalization of Boolean formulas and can be defined via directed acyclic graphs where each vertex has the effect of applying a certain Boolean operator on the values from incoming vertices and delivering the result of the computation to an output vertex. Now, we turn our focus on providing a formal framework for our circuit model.

Figure 6. The circuit for the comparison of two 4-bit numbers, denoted as X and Y.

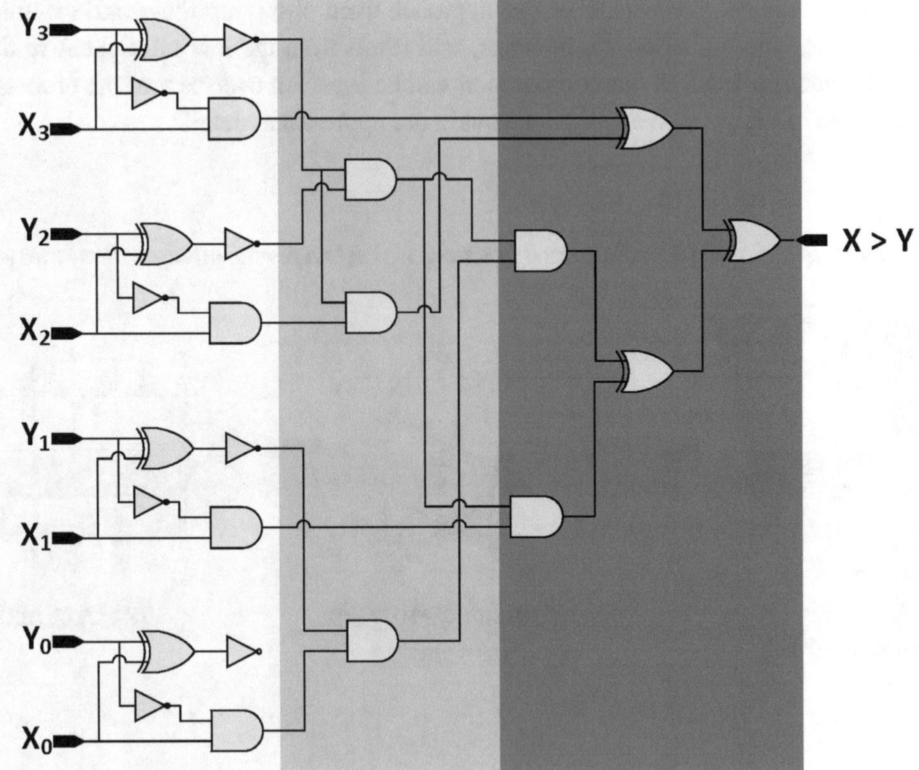

Definition 1: A circuit C is a 6-tuple (n, G, S, φ, θ, v^*) where $n \in N$, $G=(V,E)$ is a directed acyclic graph where each vertex has in-degree zero or two, $S, S \subseteq V$ is the set of vertices with in degree zero, $\varphi : S \rightarrow \{i\}_{1 \leq i \leq n}$ labels vertices in S with an input bit, $\theta : V \setminus S \rightarrow \{\vee, \oplus\}$ labels the rest of the vertices with a Boolean operation, and $v^* \in V$ is the output vertex. In the context of circuits, we use the terms "vertex" and "gate" interchangeably. The gates in S are input gates, and the rest of the gates are work gates. For any string $x \in \{0,1\}^n$, the output of any input gate is equal to $x_{\theta_{(s)}}$, and the output of any work gate $v \in V \setminus S$ is the result of the Boolean operation θ(v) when applied to the output of the two parent gates of v. The output of the circuit on input $x \in \{0,1\}^n$ is the output of v^* on input x. The input size of the circuit is n.

An important parameter of the circuit that will be of particular interest in this work will be the depth of the circuit. The depth of any input gate $s \in S$ is zero, and the depth of any work gate $v \in V \setminus S$ is one plus the larger of the depths of its two parent gates. The depth of a circuit is the depth of its output gate v^*. We denote this number by *Depth*(C). We define $Depth_{\vee}(C)$ similarly, except that $\oplus$ gates do not increase $\vee$-depth: the $\vee$-depth of a $\oplus$ work gate is defined as the maximum of the $\vee$-depth of its two parent gates.

Definition 2: A family of circuits $\{C_i\}_{i \in N}$ is a sequence of circuits such that for all $i \in N$, circuit C_i has input size i. The family is uniform if and only if there is a polynomial time Turing Machine such that for any $n \in N$, $M(1^n)$ outputs the description of C_i. The family is polynomial-sized if there exists a polynomial p such that for all $n \in N$, the number of gates in C_n is at most $p(n)$. We note that uniform families are always polynomial-sized because polynomial time Turing machines can only output polynomially many bits.

NC or Nick's Class is family of circuits that are polynomial-size and have poly-logarithmic depth. The motivation of considering this particular subclass is that these circuits can be evaluated in poly-logarithmic time on parallel computer with polynomially many processors.

Definition 3: NC^i is the set of languages accepted by a uniform, polynomial-sized family of circuits $\{C_j\}_{j \in N}$ such that $Depth(C_n) \leq O(\log^i n)$. We call any such family an NC^i circuit family.

The class of NC^i circuits is already a rich class which can compute basic arithmetic operations such as addition, multiplication and division on n-bit integers. In particular, we this model will allow computation of our function *f* Equation.

Branching Programs Model

Another natural model of computation that can represent Boolean formulas are Boolean branching programs. These are represented via directed acyclic graphs but have a different mode of operation compared to circuits.

Definition 4: A branching program is a tuple (*V, E,* φ*, s, t, n*), where (*V,E*) is a directed acyclic graph, $\varphi : E \rightarrow \{T\} \cup \{x_i, \overline{x_i}\}_{i \in V}$ maps edges to labels, *s*∈*V* is the start vertex, *t*∈*V* is the end vertex, and *n* is the input length. The size of the program is the number of vertices in *V*. For a string *x*∈{0,1}^{n}, we define the graph G_x as (V,E_0) where $E_0 \subseteq E$ is the set of edges which are labeled with *T*, or x_1 such that x_i=1 or $\overline{x_i}$ such that x_i=0. In other words, E_0 is the set of edges labeled as always present or are labeled with a corresponding input bit. The branching program accepts input *x* if and only if there is a path from *s* to *t* in G_x, and we say it outputs 1 if it accepts, and outputs 0 otherwise. A branching program has width *k*∈*N* if and only if for all *i*∈*N*, the set of vertices reachable from *s* in *G* in exactly *i* steps has cardinality at most *k*. The labels of the edges in *E* do not affect the width: any outgoing edge of a vertex can be traversed, regardless of label.

We show below a branching program for the comparison operator on 2-bit inputs *X* and *Y*. In order to compare two numbers, first, we compare the most significant bits in *X* and *Y* and then work down to the least significant digit. If the most significant bit of *X* is larger than the most significant bit of *Y*, then *X*>*Y*. If the most significant bit of *X* is smaller than we know *X*>*Y* is false. If they are equal then we move onto the next significant bit. Once we find a position where the bits in *X*>*Y* are, we don't have to look further. We implement this idea as a simple directed (acyclic) graph as shown in Figure 7.

The problem of determining whether *X*>*Y* is equivalent to determining whether there exists a path from the vertex *s* to the vertex *t* in the incident graph. In Figure **8**, the example on the left considers *X*>*Y* and the incident graph has a path from *s* and *t*. The other example considers *X*<*Y* which results in no path from *s* to *t*.

A branching program can compute any function with one bit of output by completely branching on all *n* input bits in sequence so that each of the 2*n* inputs *x* results in a unique path from *s* in G_x. The paths associated with strings such that *f*(*x*)=1 are attached to the terminal vertex *t*. This sort of method

Figure 7. A Branching Program for Comparison.

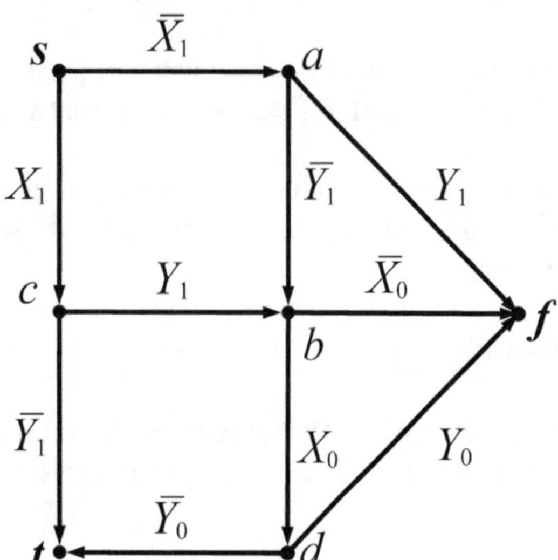

is impractical, since for large n it would require too much space to store the branching program itself. We are primarily interested in what branching programs with a small number of vertices can do. By Barrington's theorem, any circuit can be converted into an equivalent branching program.

Theorem 1 (Barrington's Theorem): For any circuit of depth d, there is an equivalent branching program with width 5 and at most 5×4^d vertices.

This means that branching program families of polynomial size and constant width can compute anything that can be computed by circuit families of logarithmic depth. We state without proof that NC^1 circuits can simulate branching programs with constant width. However, with polynomial width, branching programs can also do any computation that a logspace Turing machine can do.

Definition 5: A logspace Turing machine is a deterministic Turing machine that has a read only input tape and a small work tape. For all $n \in N$, and for any string of length n, the machine must use at most $O(\log n)$ cells of its work tape.

Lemma 1: Any logspace Turing machine can be uniformly converted into an equivalent branching program family of polynomial size.

Proof: We present a polynomial time algorithm to produce the branching program with input size n. First, we form the graph of the branching program as rows of vertices representing possible configurations of the machine. There are polynomially-many configurations of the logspace machine, and it can only take a polynomial maximum number of steps. Except in the last row, we give each vertex the appropriately-labeled outgoing edge to two others in the next row, one for each possible value of the current cell of the simulated input tape. Vertices in the final row connect to a terminal vertex t if and only if the vertex represents an accepting configuration. This program can be outputted in polynomial time, it has polynomial size, and it is equivalent to the logspace machine on inputs of the desired length.

Figure 8. Evaluation of a Branching Program.

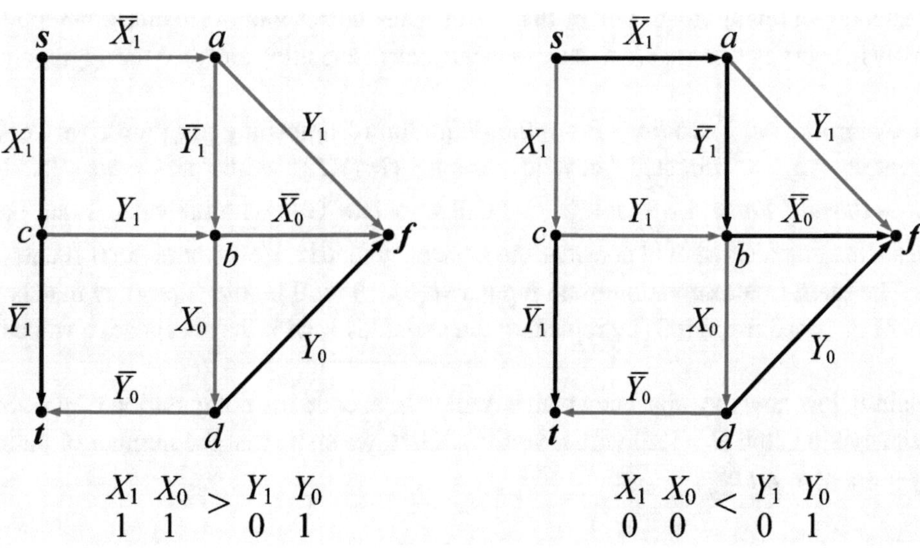

METHODOLOGY

Our proposed system has three phases: pre-computation, cloud computation, and post computation. In the pre-computation phase, input data elements are encrypted under FHE scheme and streamed to the cloud. In the cloud-computation phase, for each data element, the cloud generates a matrix representing the computation and aggregates the values via matrix multiplication. In the post-computation phase, the final matrix, that is the product of all matrices, is downloaded and decrypted at the client. To compute the final outcome of the computation in the post-computation phase, the client simply evaluates the determinant of the decrypted matrix.

Pre-Computation Phase

Recall that the QT and RR values from the ECG signals are computed in the ECG patch. Since encrypting and transmitting is computationally expensive, the data is transferred to a nearby computationally capable device. The values received at the edge device is first encrypted and then transmitted to the cloud. Typically, QT and RR are 16-bit values. Since we will be employing the BGV encryption scheme to manipulate the data in the cloud, these values will be encrypted using the same scheme at the device. Towards this a public-key/private-key is generated for the appropriate level, which in turn depends on the multiplicative depth of the computation performed at the cloud. Only the public-key is stored at the edge device, since it is sufficient to encrypt the data. The private-key is maintained by the doctor and is used only to decrypt the final result of the computation. Using the public-key, the device encrypts the QT and RR values and transmits to the cloud. Since the extended BGV scheme allows multiple slots, we encrypt as many of the values in a single ciphertext. As mentioned before, we will use the scheme with 682 slots it can pack 21(x32) samples of QT and RR with 10 slots of wastage.

Cloud Computation Phase

As the encrypted inputs arrive at the cloud, they will be first encoded into a matrix via the branching program. This matrix will have the property that its determinant will be exactly the output of *f* on that sample. The benefit of this approach will be that the matrices corresponding to different inputs can be aggregated easily in encrypted form. We first explain the matrix encoding and then the aggregation process.

- **Input/Computation Encoding:** From the definition of branching programs, we know that it is represented via a directed acyclic graph $G=(V,E)$ with an edge label function $\varphi : E \rightarrow \{True \,/\, False\} \cup \{x_i, \overline{x_i}\}_{i \in V}$. We will associate True with the value 1 and False with 0. Given such a graph G, we will consider the adjacency matrix $A(G)$ where the (i,j) entry of $A(G)$ is $\varphi(i,j)$. The matrix representation of an input $x=b_1b_2...b_n$ will be the adjacency matrix will be the matrix M obtained from $A(G)$ by replacing the variables x_i with their respective values b_i.

We explain below how the adjacency matrix will help encode the computation of $f(x)$. Suppose we have a direct acyclic graph $G=(V,E)$ with n vertices. First, we show that the number of paths of length t from i to j is equal to $A(G)^t_{i,j}$.

Lemma 2: Let A be the adjacency matrix of a direct acyclic graph $G=(V,E)$. Then for any $t \in N$, and for any vertices $i,j \in V$, the number of paths of length t from i to j is equal to $A(G)^t_{i,j}$.

Proof: We will prove this by induction. As a base case, we note that $A^0=I$ is the matrix of length zero paths, where I is the identity matrix of the appropriate size. There is a path from i to j of length 0 if and only if $i=j$. This is equivalent to saying that there is a path from i to j if and only if $I_{i,j}=1$. As another base case, we note that by definition, $A^1_{i,j} = 1$ if and only if there is a path of length 1 from i to j. We now prove the inductive case. By inductive hypothesis, $A^{t-1}_{i,j}$ is the number of paths from i to j of length$t$-1. Every path of length t from i to j can be decomposed into a path from i to k of length t-1 and a path from k to j of length 1. Therefore the number of paths of length t from i to j is the sum over all k of $A^{t-1}_{i,k} A^1_{k,j}$. We observe that this is equal to $(A^{t-1}A^1)_{i,j} = A^t_{i,j}$. Therefore $A^t_{i,j}$ is the number of paths of length t from i to j.

Now we define the path counting matrix P to be $(I\text{-}A)^{-1}$. We prove that $P_{i,j}$ is the number of paths from i to j.

Corollary 1: For any directed acyclic graph $G=(V,E)$, and for any vertices $i, j \subseteq V$, the total number of paths from i to j in G is $(I - A(G))^{-1}_{i,j}$.

Proof: Applying this lemma, we can see that the total number of paths from i to j is

$$\sum_{t=0}^{n-1} A^t_{i,j}$$

We claim that $I\text{-}A(G)$ is full rank. The matrix $A(G)$ is the adjacency matrix of a directed acyclic graph. Without loss of generality, a DAG never has an edge from i to j if $j<i$. Therefore, $A(G)$ is a strict upper-triangular matrix with zeroes on its diagonal. This means that $I\text{-}A(G)$ has ones all the way along its diagonal, so its determinant is one, proving that $I\text{-}A(G)$ is full rank. By observation,

$$I = (I - A(G))\sum_{t=0}^{n-1} A(G)^t$$

which is equivalent to

$$(I - A(G))^{-1} = \sum_{t=0}^{n-1} A(G)^t$$

Let $P(G) = (I\text{-}A(G))^{-1}$ be the path counting matrix of G. To determine $P(G)_{i,j}$ we have to find a particular element of the inverse of $I\text{-}A$. By applying some elementary linear algebra, we know that solving the linear system $(I\text{-}A)x=I_{\_j}$ gives the column j of P, where $I_{\_j}$ is column j of the identity matrix. Cramer's rule says that if $Bx=b$ and $det(B) \neq 0$ then

$$x_i = \frac{det(B')}{det(B)}$$

where B' is B, except its ith column is replaced with b. Therefore if we replace the ith column of I-A with the jth column of the identity matrix and call the result then

$$P_{i,j} = \frac{det(A')}{det(I - A)}.$$

By inspection, $det(I\text{-}A)=1$ so this simplifies to $P_{i,j} = det(A')$. We observe that this reasoning applies to finite fields as well. If we only want to know whether the number of paths from i to j is a multiple of p, then this expression simplifies to just

$$P_{i,j} = det(A')(mod p).$$

If we know for a fact that there are either zero paths or exactly one path, then it is sufficient to compute this determinant modulo two.

Once we know the branching program we want to evaluate, we can compute $(I\text{-}A(G))^{-1}$ as defined in Corollary 1 to get a matrix such that its determinant is equal to $f(x)$. We compute this matrix symbolically for all x then plug in the values of the bits of x according to the formula to get the "literal" matrix. However, the server only gets the encrypted input bits, i.e. it receives the encryption of each bit of the input. The server can construct the matrix by replacing literal zero and one elements with encryptions of zero and one and replacing elements labeled with input bit indices with the appropriate input ciphertext, negating the ciphertext if the matrix calls for it. Negation of a ciphertext can be performed by adding 1 (modulo 2) and is an efficient homomorphic operation. Hence the matrix in encrypted form can be efficiently computed from the encrypted input using homomorphic operations.

Recall our comparison example from Figure 9. We apply the preceding idea to obtain the corresponding matrix where the rank of the matrix will determine the output of the function. This matrix corresponding to the graph for 2-bit comparison is also displayed in Figure **9**. We remark that this idea is inspired by the work of Ishai and Kushilevitz (Kushilevitz & Ishai, 2000).

Figure 9. Matrix representation of the Comparison Function.

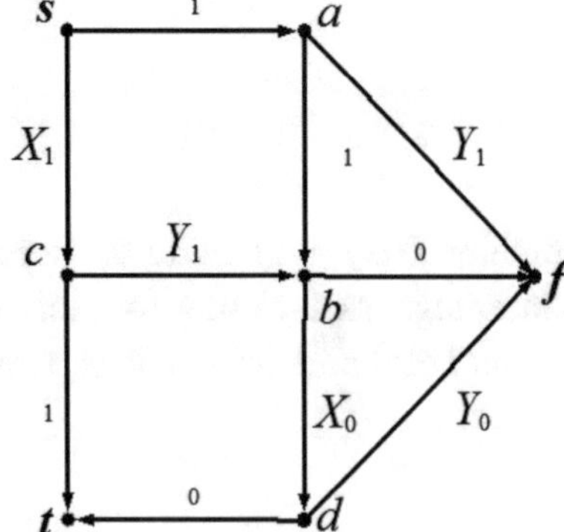

$$\begin{array}{c} \\ f \\ s \\ a \\ c \\ b \\ d \end{array} \begin{array}{c} \begin{array}{cccccc} f & t & a & c & b & d \end{array} \\ \begin{pmatrix} 1 & 0 & 0 & 0 & 0 & 0 \\ 0 & 0 & \overline{X_1} & X_1 & 0 & 0 \\ Y_1 & 0 & 1 & 0 & \overline{Y_1} & 0 \\ 0 & \overline{Y_1} & 0 & 1 & Y_1 & 0 \\ \overline{X_0} & 0 & 0 & 0 & 1 & X_0 \\ Y_0 & \overline{Y_0} & 0 & 0 & 0 & 1 \end{pmatrix} \end{array}$$

Aggregation

Given the matrix representation of two inputs x_1 and x_2, computing the "AND" of $f(x_1)$ and $f(x_2)$ reduces to multiplying the matrices corresponding to the inputs, since

$$\det(AB) = \det(A)\det(B)$$

Recall that multiple data elements can be encrypted in a single ciphertext and SIMD-like operations can be performed homomorphically on the ciphertext. It would be highly desirable to pack multiple elements of the matrix in such a manner that would facilitate matrix multiplication.

A first approach would be to pack the elements of the matrix row-wise or column-wise. Consider the following two 3×3 matrices.

$$A = \begin{pmatrix} a_{1,1} & a_{1,2} & a_{1,3} \\ a_{2,1} & a_{2,2} & a_{2,3} \\ a_{3,1} & a_{3,2} & a_{3,3} \end{pmatrix}, B = \begin{pmatrix} b_{1,1} & b_{1,2} & b_{1,3} \\ b_{2,1} & b_{2,2} & b_{2,3} \\ b_{3,1} & b_{3,2} & b_{3,3} \end{pmatrix}$$

The product of these two matrices will be

$$C = \begin{pmatrix} a_{1,1}b_{1,1} + a_{1,2}b_{2,1} + a_{1,3}b_{3,1} & a_{1,1}b_{1,2} + a_{1,2}b_{2,2} + a_{1,3}b_{3,2} & a_{1,1}b_{1,3} + a_{1,2}b_{2,3} + a_{1,3}b_{3,3} \\ a_{2,1}b_{1,1} + a_{2,2}b_{2,1} + a_{2,3}b_{3,1} & a_{2,1}b_{1,2} + a_{2,2}b_{2,2} + a_{2,3}b_{3,2} & a_{2,1}b_{1,3} + a_{2,2}b_{2,3} + a_{2,3}b_{3,3} \\ a_{3,1}b_{1,1} + a_{3,2}b_{2,1} + a_{3,3}b_{3,1} & a_{3,1}b_{1,2} + a_{3,2}b_{2,2} + a_{3,3}b_{3,2} & a_{3,1}b_{1,3} + a_{3,2}b_{2,3} + a_{3,3}b_{3,3} \end{pmatrix}$$

Suppose we packed the elements of A row-wise and B column-wise in the following manner.

$$\begin{aligned} Row[1] &= (a_{1,1}\, a_{1,2}\, a_{1,3}) & Col[1] &= (b_{1,1}\, b_{2,1}\, b_{3,1}) \\ Row[2] &= (a_{2,1}\, a_{2,2}\, a_{2,3}) & Col[2] &= (b_{1,2}\, b_{2,2}\, b_{3,2}) \\ Row[3] &= (a_{3,1}\, a_{3,2}\, a_{3,3}) & Col[3] &= (b_{1,3}\, b_{2,3}\, b_{3,3}) \end{aligned}$$

Then using a single operation of $Row[1] \times Col[1] = (a_{1,1}b_{1,1}\ a_{1,2}b_{2,1}\ a_{1,3}b_{3,1})$ which looks promising as they are required to compute $C[1,1]$. However HElib does not provide operations to directly sum the elements of a packed ciphertext. It is possible to use rotate and select operations to compute the first entry of the product matrix. However, this still does not give the product matrix in the same form directly as A or B so that we can continue multiplying with C to aggregate the next matrix. More homomorphic operations needs to be performed to bring C to that form. We instead propose a new representation that will allow easy multiplication of matrices and yields the product matrix in the same form.

We represent matrices as a list of vectors representing "diagonals" in the original matrix. More precisely, given a $n \times n$ matrix, we pack the elements into n ciphertexts, where the ith diagonal contains the elements $(1,1 + (i \bmod n))$, $(2,1 + (i + \bmod n))$, …, $(n,1 + (i+n\text{-}1 \bmod n))$. For any matrix A, let $A\{i\}$ denote the ith diagonal. We only consider square matrices, so an $n \times n$ matrix has n diagonals.

In our 3×3 matrix A, the diagonals will be

$$A\{0\} = (a_{1,1}a_{2,2}a_{3,3})$$
$$A\{1\} = (a_{1,2}a_{2,3}a_{3,1})$$
$$A\{2\} = (a_{1,3}a_{2,1}a_{3,2})$$

Given this representation, the matrix product C can be computed as follows

$$C\{1\} = A\{1\}B\{1\}^0 + A\{2\}B\{3\}^1 + A\{3\}B\{2\}^2$$
$$C\{2\} = A\{1\}B\{2\}^0 + A\{2\}B\{1\}^1 + A\{3\}B\{3\}^2$$
$$C\{3\} = A\{1\}B\{3\}^0 + A\{2\}B\{2\}^1 + A\{3\}B\{1\}^2$$

In this notation, concatenation indicates element-by-element multiplication, + indicates element-by-element addition, and v^i indicates the rotation of vector v by i elements, namely the sequence

$[v_i, v_{i+1}, \ldots, v_1, \ldots, v_{i-1}\}$.

We extend this formula to say that when $C=AB$ and A and B are n×n matrices, then

$$C\{i\} = \sum_{j=1}^{n} A\{j\}B\{1+(i-j \bmod n)\}^{j-1}$$

HElib supports all of these operations efficiently, so this algorithm is much more efficient for computing the product of matrices homomorphically. In more detail, each of the diagonals are encrypted into packed ciphertexts. Given two matrices encrypted in diagonal format, we can compute the product in diagonal format using HElib operations. An apparent disadvantage of this method is that while homomorphic matrix multiplication has $\wedge$-depth 1 and its operations can be bundled together efficiently, it still requires many homomorphic multiplications. However, these can be done in parallel. Furthermore, if the matrices are of a special sparse form, we can multiply them more efficiently.

Post-Computation Phase

Recall that at the end of the Cloud Computation phase, after all the encrypted matrices are aggregated, the Cloud possesses a single matrix that contains the value of the aggregated output. This matrix is downloaded by the health provider, such as the doctor. Since the doctor has the private-key associated with the encryption scheme, it can decrypt the matrix. Finally, to compute the answer, the determinant of this matrix needs to be evaluated. The multiplication evaluates an AND operation, while we need the OR. Hence we consider the branching program for the function whose output is the negated output of the function f. This is denoted by $\neg f$. Now we recast the original problem with f using $\neg f$. More precisely,

$$\hat{e}_{i} f(QT_{i}, RR_{i}) = \neg\left(\grave{\imath}_{i} \neg f(QT_{i}, RR_{i})\right)$$

A branching program for $\neg f$ is considered. This means upon receiving the final matrix, the determinant is evaluated and the output is negated to obtain the precise answer to the computation.

OPTIMIZATIONS AND SCALABILITY

Our proposed approach works for any Boolean function that can be represented as a branching program. A branching program can compute any Boolean function by simply branching on all n input bits so that each of $2n$ inputs result in a unique path. The size of this program is exponential in n. However, we are interested in what functions are representable by polynomial-size branching programs. As we have already seen from Lemma 1, any logspace computations can be represented as a branching program and can encompass a wide variety of problems. Therefore, this approach can be used for any logspace computable Boolean functions. The size of the matrix corresponds to the size of the graph. For the equation in our case study, we construct a branching program of size 600.

If A is a band matrix, then there is a small w such that all nonzero entries are within w diagonals of the main diagonal, and we can multiply matrices much more efficiently using operations on bundled plaintexts. This w corresponds to the width of the branching program. By Barrington's theorem, any NC^1 circuit can be converted into an equivalent branching program of polynomial size and width 5. For any such circuit, we can convert it into a band matrix with band width 10. If we pack each entire diagonal into one ciphertext, then we can represent matrices of arbitrary size with just 21 ciphertexts. After multiplying two matrices with band width 10, we get a matrix with band width 11, and after we multiply two matrices with band width 11, we get a matrix with band width 12, and so on. Therefore the resulting matrices remain extremely sparse, even when iteratively multiplying many matrices together. This means that we get the advantage of sparseness for every round of matrix multiplications, not just the first one.

We note that homomorphic evaluation and combining of branching programs can be supported for any branching program using only homomorphic matrix multiplication. It is therefore effective for the server to use highly-optimized software or even special hardware to enhance the efficiency of this operation. The branching program we construct for our case study has width 10, and the corresponding band matrix has width 9.

PERFORMANCE EVALUATION

In this section, we will provide simulated results for our proposed method and will compare them to the circuit-based method, which will be referred to as the "naïve method." Note that, while the circuit method allows a significantly more generalized application domain, we will demonstrate in this section that, once the function to achieve is very well defined (i.e., a Yes/No answer to a pre-determined question), the branching-programs method (which will be referred to as the "matrix method" provides much more improved performance results.

Experimental Setup

In the previous section, we described our methodology. We compare the performance of our method with the naïve method of implementing the circuit that computes the function in entirety. We first describe the naïve method and how the two methods were compared.

Naïve Method

First, we explain how we use the SIMD-like operations in HElib. An example operation is shown in Figure 10, where two 4-bit numbers, A_1=13 and B_1=17 are compared. Simultaneously, two other 4-bit numbers A_0=9 and B_0=11 are compared. These two simultaneous comparisons are an example of how multiple identical operations can be performed in a SIMD environment as a benefit of the "packing" concept introduced previously.

Each individual operation, applied to A_i and B_i is a 4-bit SIMD addition, for which the circuit in Figure 6 can be used. Note that, this circuit is composed of only XOR and AND gates, since the NOT gates (i.e., inverters) can be implemented by XOR gates. The reason for restricting the set of available gates to only these two is previously mentioned: We are only using the GF(2) homomorphic addition and homomorphic multiplication operations, which correspond to bitwise XOR and bitwise AND operations, respectively. Therefore, drawing the circuit for any function we are trying to implement allows us to use two of the four previously mentioned HElib primitives.

A close observation of Figure 6 reveals that, just the bitwise XOR and AND operations will not be sufficient to perform the 4-bit comparison function, which can be denoted as

$$X > Y = \left(x_3 \overline{y_3} \oplus x_2 \overline{y_2} e_3 \oplus x_1 \overline{y_1} e_3 e_2 \oplus x_0 \overline{y_0} e_3 e_2 e_1 \right)$$

In this formulation of the comparison of X and Y (i.e., computation of X>Y), when "slot indices" match for the bits of two numbers (e.g., x_3 and y_3), no rotation is necessary, however, we will use the previously mentioned second set of HElib operations, namely Rotate and Select) to perform alignment operations on the bits. In Figure **6**, the output of the bottom inverter has no connection. The XOR and NOT gates connected to the Y_0 node symbolically depict how SIMD operations actually perform these

Figure 10. An example comparison of two 4-bit numbers.

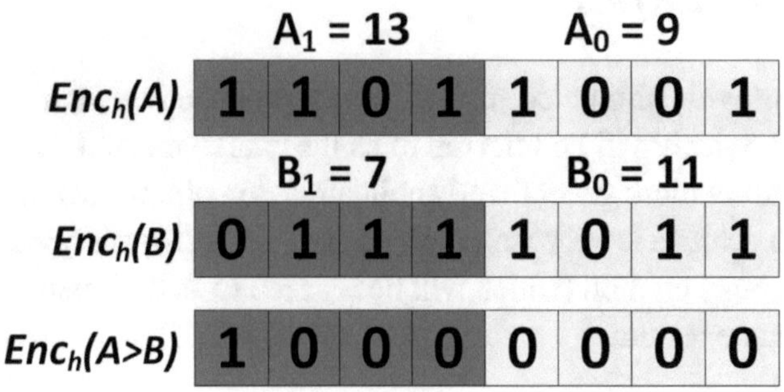

	A_1 = 13				A_0 = 9			
$Enc_h(A)$	1	1	0	1	1	0	0	1
	B_1 = 7				B_0 = 11			
$Enc_h(B)$	0	1	1	1	1	0	1	1
$Enc_h(A>B)$	1	0	0	0	0	0	0	0

Figure 11. Reformulating the X>Y operation in terms of an intermediate variable M

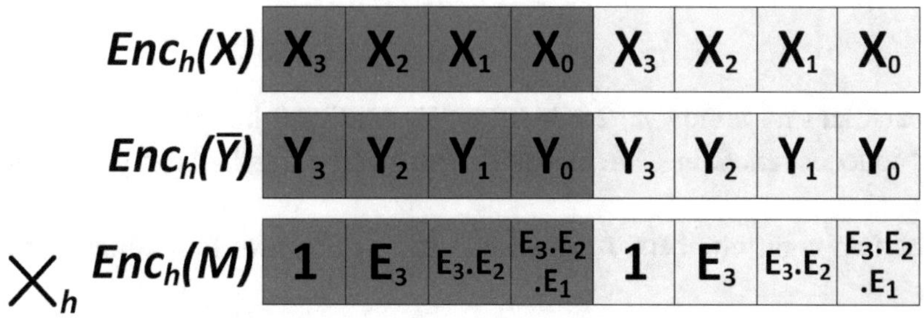

$Enc_h(X)$	X_3	X_2	X_1	X_0	X_3	X_2	X_1	X_0
$Enc_h(\overline{Y})$	Y_3	Y_2	Y_1	Y_0	Y_3	Y_2	Y_1	Y_0
$\times_h$ $Enc_h(M)$	1	E_3	$E_3.E_2$	$E_3.E_2.E_1$	1	E_3	$E_3.E_2$	$E_3.E_2.E_1$

extraneous operations, even though the result will not be used for anything useful. As shown in Figure 11, if we define an intermediate value M as the rotated versions of the E, where E is the equality. Therefore, $E=XNOR(X,Y)$ and $M=(1e_3\ e_3e_2\ e_3e_2e_1)$, where e_i is the ith bit of E.

As can be intuitively visualized from Figure 11, the four operations we are using from HElib will be sufficient to calculate the M and E values, and, therefore the Boolean value of (X>Y).

To compute Equation (1), we need to compute QT^3-RR and check whether it is positive or negative. We evaluate QT^3 as follows. We first compute the n addends in computing QT^2. This can be done by computing

$$Q_i = (QT \times QT_i) \ll i \text{ for } i = 1,\ldots,n$$

where $\ll$ is the left-shift operator. This is the first step in the long-multiplication form of multiplication. Next we multiply each of these n addends by QT to obtain n^2 addends required to compute QT^3. More precisely,

$$A_{j\times n+i} = (Q_j \times Q_i) \ll i \text{ for } i = 1,\ldots,n \text{ and } j = 1,\ldots,n$$

Next we add the value $\neg RR$ and 1 as addends, i.e. A_{n^2+1} is set to the bitwise negation of RR. In two's complement, these two final summands add up to -RR (the additive inverse of RR, not to be confused with the bitwise negation of RR), so it is appropriate to include them as summands in order to subtract RR from QT^3. To sum the n^2+2 addends, we first reduce the number of addends by using a 3-2 compressor. In more detail, this method replaces 3 addends with 2 addends using the following approach. Let a,b,c be three n-bit addends. We replace them by d and e where

$$d = a \oplus b \oplus c$$
$$e = (a \wedge b \oplus b \wedge c \oplus c \wedge a) << 1$$

where each of the operations are done bitwise. The result of this computation reduces the problem of adding three n-bit numbers a,b,c to adding two n+1-bit numbers d and e. Given than we have n^2+2 n-bit addends, we divide them into groups of 3 and perform this operation to get a total of $\left\lceil 2\right\rceil\left(n^2+2\right)/3p$ addends, each n+1-bits long. We now repeat this process to get

$$\lceil 2 \rceil \frac{\lceil 2 \rceil (n^2+2)/3p}{3} p$$

addends where each addend is now n+2-bits long. We continue this process until we only have two $n+O(\log_{3/2} n)$ -bit addends remaining. We then add them using a standard carry-look ahead adder which we describe next.

Let a and b be two m-bit numbers. In the ripple-carry adder, we first compute the propogate and generator bits

$p = a \wedge b$ and $g = a \oplus b$

where the operations are performed bit-wise. Next the carry bits c are computed bitwise

$$c_{i+1} = g_i + p_i \wedge c_i$$

where c_1 is set to 0 and i=1,…,m. Finally the sum is calculated as

$s_i = p_i \oplus c_i$ for i=1,…, m+1

where p_{i+1} is set to 0. Computed this way, will lead to m cascading multiplications. However, by appropriately computing products of p_i efficiently we can bring it down to log$m$ cascading multiplications. In fact, this is what is done in a carry look-ahead adder.

Given this final sum s, to obtain the bit that represents whether QT^3>RR is obtained by selecting the most significant bit of the s.

Matrix Method

For the ith input sample QT_i and RR_i that is provided in encrypted form, we first generate the matrix encoding in encrypted form. Given then matrices for all the samples, the aggregated output is simply the product of these matrices. To generate a matrix encoding, we need a branching program to computeQT^3>R. Towards this we pursue the following approach:

We now describe how to construct the branching program and the ideas behind it. Suppose that the jth bit of QT is 1. Then we know that $QT^3 \geq 2^{3i}$. Therefore if any of the first 2n/3 bits of QT are set then the equation will be true, because the lowest value QT^3 can take will be bigger than the largest value RR can take. By checking through the first 2n/3 bits sequentially we can determine whether this is the case. Now it remains to verify the equation when this is not the case. Here we need to compare the cube of the low order bits of QT with RR. Next we observe in a branching program consider a sequence of vertices reachable from the start vertex through exactly one path. This path can effectively "remember" the path that led up to them and therefore all the bits that were tested along that path in the sequence of vertices. This allows a branching program to simulate a *table lookup*. By branching on each of the $2^{n/3}$ least-significant bits, we get a path for each value of QT below $2^{n/3}$. Once we have this there is a vertex for each possible value which remembers its associated QT value (and therefore know its associated QT^3 value). Next from each such vertex we scan through the bits of RR to determine which is larger. Next we explain how the comparison is performed in the last step.

Before we explain how to compare numbers in a branching program we will briefly recall how to compare numbers in plaintext, such as 254 and 249. Start from the most significant digit and look for the first difference in the digits of the two numbers. The result is determined by the first place where the digits differ, and if the digits never differ then the two numbers are equal. The first digits are the same so we look at the second digit. Five is more than four, so 254 > 249.

The diagram in Figure 12 contains an abbreviated form of the branching program $x^3<y$ for 9-bit inputs x and y. We use x and y to emphasize the fact that this is not the same circuit because we ignore the constant multiplicative factor to the right-hand side of the equation in the original formula. The leftmost vertex is the start vertex and the rightmost vertex is the end vertex. After traversing the edges labelled with x_3=1, x_2=0, and x_1=1 (in that order) we know that x=5, so x^3=125. We compare the bits of y with the bits of 125 from the most significant bit to the least significant bit. At the first difference in the bits of y and 125 we can determine the result, so if we're comparing a particular bit we know that the higher order bits of y were the same as those in 125 (the two bit strings are equal so far). If a bit j is the first bit where y and 216 differ then we can determine which one is bigger: if y_j=1 then $x^3>y$, otherwise $x^3 \leq y$. If the two bits are the same then we continue comparing them until we get to a difference, or until we get to the end. If the last bits are the same and none of the earlier bits are then $x^3=y$, otherwise $x^3>y$.

Similarly, after traversing the edges labeled with x_3=1, x_2=1, and x_1=1 (in that order) we know that x=7, so x^3=343. We can proceed in the same way with the different value of x^3. Each path will compare y with a value of x^3 "known" to that path.

Since we know the symbolic matrix, we can generate the packed ciphertexts homomorphically. This simply uses the rotate and select operations, and we need to generate only 10 packed ciphertexts for our branching program. We evaluate the product of the matrices using Equation. Computing each diagonal of the resulting matrix requires at most 10 rotate and 10 multiply operations and 10 additions.

Figure 12. Diagram of the Branching Program for computing 254 > 249 ?

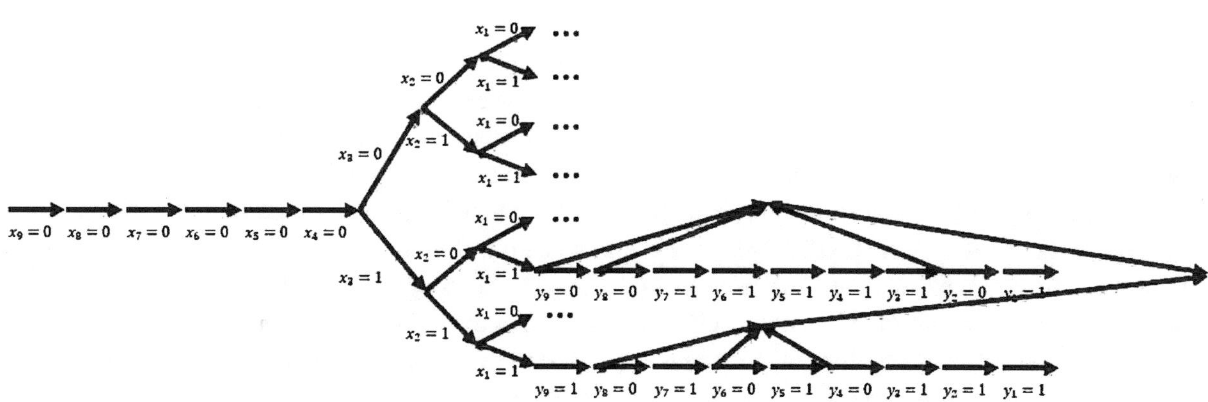

Time Estimation via Simulation

Since the HElib library is not thread-safe, to compare the performance of the two approaches we simulated the computation to estimate the time taken on parallel machines. To accomplish this, we first performed real benchmarks of each individual operation on a single thread, and then used that time to estimate the computational costs for our parallel experiments. We set the length of QT and RR to be 16-bit.

Depth Calculation

In order to use HElib, we need to generate keys for the BGV encryption scheme for a particular level. The level determines the number of sequential multiplications we can perform.

In the naïve method, since we need to both calculate and aggregate the overall depth and for 16-bit inputs, the depth is 44. Aggregation requires $\log T$ multiplications for aggregating T samples. We performed the experiment for T=1, 50, 100, 500, and 1000. Depending on the value of T we instantiated the BGV scheme appropriately.

In the matrix method, there is no multiplication involved in setting up the matrix and only the aggregation involves multiplication. Since every matrix multiplication involves only one sequential multiplication, the overall depth to aggregate and compute is simply $\log T = 12$.

Then we wrote a compiler that took a sequence of operations to be performed on the samples and used a greedy heuristic to assign the computations to the different parallel processors taking into account the dependencies. The greedy heuristic maintains a list of free processors and assigns the next computation to the first available processor in the list. A clock was simulated to determine when the next processor will be available and accordingly the list was updated. In our estimate we assumed that each parallel machine had instantaneous access to the input encryptions and results of computations from other machines. We deliberately ignored the data transfer and sharing costs since it would be hard to assess and incorporate. Nevertheless, we argue that the estimates are conservative in the sense that the naïve method requires a lot of data transfers since it involves more dependencies, while the proposed approach will have significantly less and taking into account the data transfer costs will only improve the relative timing of our approach.

Results

To evaluate our approach we considered processing and aggregating several different numbers of samples. In Figure 13, we provide our results for processing 10 and 10240 samples. We can see that both approaches improve with the number of processors. However, the matrix approach is consistently better than the naïve approach by a factor of 20. The main reason for this is that the cost of computation increases exponentially with the depth of the computation and the depth of the naïve approach is significantly higher than that of the matrix approach. One tradeoff that is not represented in the graph is the amount of network bandwidth used. The communication from the patient's end will be the same for both approaches, but at the doctor's end, an entire matrix (i.e. roughly 20 ciphertexts will have to be downloaded in our approach while only 1 ciphertext will need to be downloaded in the naïve approach. However, in our application, this will only be done once every day (or few hours), so this should not be a significant problem. Another difference with the matrix approach is that the doctor's computer must compute the determinant of the decrypted matrix in order to get the result; in the naïve approach, the result will be directly available (or be a simple "OR" of the decrypted bits).

Figure 13. Simulated computation time for matrix method vs. naïve method of Long QT detection. The matrix method is consistently about 20x faster.

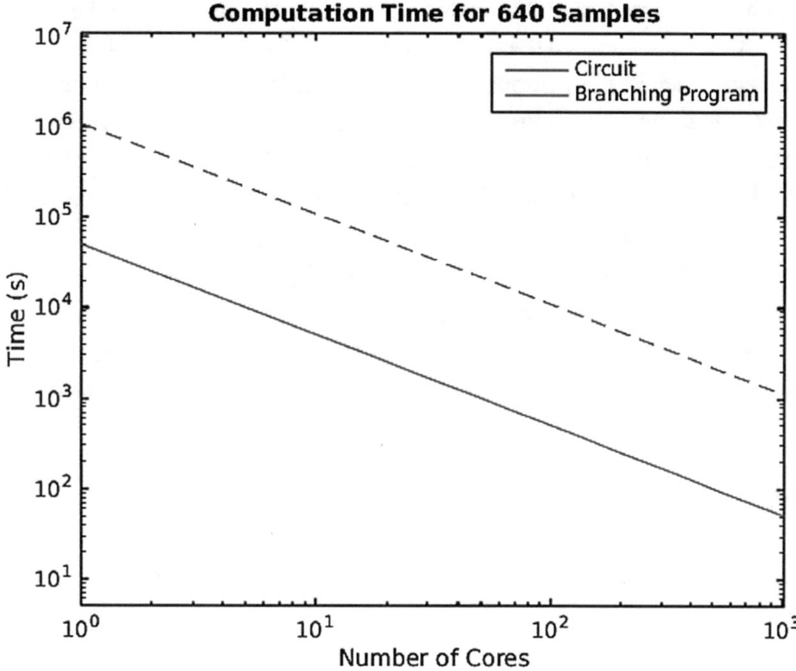

CONCLUSION AND FUTURE WORK

Medical cloud computing is the unstoppable next revolution in healthcare. However, its widespread adoption depends on addressing Protected Health Information (PHI) privacy issues during its acquisition, storage and processing. The system described by the authors before and expanded in this paper provides a way to completely solve data privacy issues while the patient medical data is being stored and processed in the cloud. The enabling component of this system, Fully Homomorphic Encryption (FHE), creates a computational environment, where it is possible to compute on encrypted data. Data privacy issues are automatically eliminated when the only information that is available during transmission and processing is encrypted by a *provably secure* encryption mechanism.

Despite this unparalleled advantage of FHE, its intense computational requirements make it applicable to only a limited set of medical applications. While extensive research is underway to speed up generalized FHE, in this chapter, we focused on a specific cloud computing scenario, where the goal of computation is to detect a set of known cardiac hazard conditions from streamed ECG data. This ECG data, streamed from the patient's house through ECG patches into the cloud, allows long term health monitoring for certain cardiac conditions that are very hard (if not impossible) to detect at a healthcare organization (HCO). Additionally, allowing monitoring outside the HCO has a significant cost-saving and improved diagnosis potential due to the additional information that is being provided to the healthcare professionals.

In this chapter, an extensive analysis and evaluation of the application of FHE into long term healthcare monitoring is presented. Rather than using a circuit-based approach to evaluate the required functions for monitoring, a Branching Programs (BP) based approach is investigated. While the BP approach narrows the application area of FHE, it is shown that it promises a significant speed up for detection applications, where the required result is a Yes/No Boolean value. A Branching Program model is developed in this chapter which detects the Long-QT Syndrome (LQTS) from a set of streamed ECG interval data. A 20x speed-up is observed as compared to the circuit-based methods. This is a promising step towards improving the speed of FHE, which can eventually become a key ingredient of future medical applications.

The solution presented in this chapter detects LQTS by using a formula $QT_c^3 > 2RR$, which is restricted to the QT_c value of 0.5 (i.e., 500 ms). Research is underway to generalize this to a broad set of potential QT_c values that are of clinical relevance, such as 450 ms or 470 ms. Although it looks like a simple extension of the existing work, arbitrarily changing the comparison value requires the re-construction of the Branching Program, and, therefore, is the focus of our future work.

ACKNOWLEDGMENT

This work was supported in part by the National Science Foundation grant CNS-1239423 and a gift from Nvidia Corporation.

REFERENCES

Alling, A., Powers, N., & Soyata, T. (2015). Face Recognition: A Tutorial on Computational Aspects. In *Emerging Research Surrounding Power Consumption and Performance Issues in Utility Computing*. Hershey, PA: IGI.

Badilini, F. (1998). The ISHNE Holter Standard Output File Format. *Annals of Noninvasive Cardiology*, 263-266.

Barrington, D. (1989). Bounded-Width Polynomial Size Brancing Programs Recognized Exactly Those Languages in NC1. *Journal of Computer and System Sciences*, *38*(1), 150–164. doi:10.1016/0022-0000(89)90037-8

Boneh, D., Goh, E.-J., & Nissim, K. (2005). Evaluating 2-DNF Formulas on Ciphertexts. *Proceedings of the 2nd International Conference on Theory of Cryptography*, (pp. 325-341). doi:10.1007/978-3-540-30576-7_18

Brakerski, Z., Gentry, C., & Vaikuntanathan, V. (2012). Leveled Fully Homomorphic Encryption without Bootstrapping. *Proceedings of the 3rd Innovations in Theoretical Computer Science Conference*, (pp. 309-325). doi:10.1145/2090236.2090262

Brakerski, Z., & Vaikuntanathan, V. (2011). Efficient Fully Homomorphic Encryption from Standard LWE. *Foundations of Computer Science*, 97-106.

CR2032. (n.d.). Retrieved from http://en.wikipedia.org/wiki/CR2032_battery

CardioLeaf-Pro. (n.d.). Retrieved from http://www.clearbridgevitalsigns.com/

Couderc, J. (2010). The telemetric and holter ECG warehouse initiative (THEW). A data repository for the design, implementation and validation of ECG-related technologies. *Annual International Conference of the IEEE Engineering in Medicine and Biology Society (EMBC)*, 6252-6255. doi:10.1109/IEMBS.2010.5628067

Damgard, I., Jurik, M., & Nielsen, J. B. (2010). A Generalization of Paillie's Public Key System with Applications to Electronic Voting. *International Journal of Information Security*, *9*(6), 371–385. doi:10.1007/s10207-010-0119-9

DARPA-PROCEED. (n.d.). Retrieved from DARPA-PROCEED: http://www.darpa.mil/Our_Work/I2O/Programs/PROgramming_Computation_on_EncryptEd_Data_(PROCEED).aspx

Diffie, W., & Hellman, M. (1976). New directions in cryptography. *IEEE Transactions on Information Theory*, *22*(6), 644–654. doi:10.1109/TIT.1976.1055638

Dijk, M., Gentry, C., Halevi, S., & Vaikuntanathan, V. (2010). Fully Homomorphic Encryption over the Integers. *Advances in Cryptology (EUROCRYPT)*, 24-43.

El Gamal, T. (1985). A Public Key Cryptosystem and a Signature Scheme based on Discrete Logarithms. *IEEE Transactions on Information Theory*, *31*(4), 469–472. doi:10.1109/TIT.1985.1057074

Fridericia, L. S. (1920). Die Systolendauer im Elektrokardiogramm bei normalen Menschen und bei Herzkranken. *Acta Medica Scandinavica*, *53*(1), 469–486. doi:10.1111/j.0954-6820.1920.tb18266.x

Gentry, C. (2009). *A Fully Homomorphic Encryption Scheme*. Stanford University.

Gentry, C., Halevi, S., & Smart, N. (2012). Homomorphic Evaluation of the AES Circuit. In R. Safavi-Naini & R. Canetti (Eds.), *Advances in Cryptology – CRYPTO 2012* (Vol. 7417, pp. 850–867). Springer Berlin Heidelberg. doi:10.1007/978-3-642-32009-5_49

Goldreich, O. (2008). *Computational complexity - a conceptual perspective*. London: Cambridge University Press. doi:10.1017/CBO9780511804106

Goldwasser, S., & Micali, S. (1982). Probabilistic Encryption - How to Play Mental Poker Keeping Secret all Partial Information. *Proceedings of the 14th Annual ACM Symposium on Theory of Computing*, (pp. 365-377). doi:10.1145/800070.802212

Good, S. (2013). Why Healthcare Must Embrace Cloud Computing. *Forbes*.

Halevi, S., & Shoup, V. (2014). Algorithms in HElib. *Proceedings, Part I, Advanced in Cryptology - CRYPTO 2014 - 34th Annual Cryptology Conference*, (pp. 554-571). Santa Barbara, CA. doi:10.1007/978-3-662-44371-2_31

HElib. (2014). *HElib Fully Homomorphic Encryption Library*. Retrieved from http://www.github.com/shaih/HElib

HIPAA. (2014). Retrieved from http://www.hhs.gov/ocr/privacy/

iPhone5s. (n.d.). Retrieved from http://www.anandtech.com/print/7335/the-iphone5s-review

Ishai, Y., & Paskin, A. (2007). Evaluating Branching Programs on Encrypted Data. *Theory of Cryptography, 4th Theory of Cryptography Conference, (TCC) 2007*, (pp. 575-594). Amsterdam.

Kocabas, O., & Soyata, T. (2014). Medical Data Analytics in the cloud using Homomorphic Encryption. In P. R. Deka (Ed.), *Handbook of Research on Cloud Infrastructures for Big Data Analytics* (pp. 471–488). Hershey, PA: IGI Global; doi:10.4018/978-1-4666-5864-6.ch019

Kocabas, O., Soyata, T., Couderc, J.-P., Aktas, M., Xia, J., & Huang, M. (2013). Assessment of Cloud-based Health Monitoring using Homomorphic Encryption. *Proceedings of the 31st IEEE International Conference on Computer Design (ICCD)*, (pp. 443-446). Ashville, VA, USA. doi:10.1109/ICCD.2013.6657078

Kushilevitz, E., & Ishai, Y. (2000). Randomizing Polynomials: A New Representation with Applications to Round-Efficient Secure Computation. *41st Annual Symposium on Foundations of Computer Science* (pp. 294-304). Redondo Beach: ACM.

Kwon, M. (2015). *A Tutorial on Network Latency and its Measurements*. IGI Global.

Kwon, M., Dou, Z., Heinzelman, W., Soyata, T., Ba, H., & Shi, J. (2014). Use of Network Latency Profiling and Redundancy for Cloud Server Selection. *Proceedings of the 7th IEEE International Conference on Cloud Computing (IEEE CLOUD 2014)*, (pp. 826-832). Alaska. doi:10.1109/CLOUD.2014.114

NIST-AES. (2001). *Advanced encryption standard*. AES.

Page, A., Kocabas, O., Ames, S., Venkitasubramaniam, M., & Soyata, T. (2014). Cloud-based Secure Health Monitoring: Optimizing Fully-Homomorphic Encryption for Streaming Algorithms. *IEEE Globecom 2014 Workshop on Cloud Computing Systems, Networks, and Applications (CCSNA)*. Austin, TX.

Page, A., Kocabas, O., Soyata, T., Aktas, M., & Couderc, J.-P. (2014). Cloud-Based Privacy-Preserving Remote ECG Monitoring and Surveillance. *Annals of Noninvasive Electrocardiology*. doi:10.1111/anec.12204 PMID:25510621

Paillier, P. (1999). *Public Key Cryptosystems Based on Composite Degree Residuosity Classes* (pp. 223–238). Advances in Cryptology. doi:10.1007/3-540-48910-X_16

Patel, C. D., & Shah, A. J. (2005, June). *Cost Model for Planning, Development and Operation of a Data Center.* Retrieved from http://www.hpl.hp.com/techreports/2005/HPL-2005-107R1.pdf

Powers, N., Alling, A., Gyampoh-Vidogah, R., & Soyata, T. (2014, Dec). AXaaS: Case for Acceleration as a Service. *IEEE Globecom 2014 Workshop on Cloud Computing Systems, Networks, and Applications (CCSNA)*. Austin, TX.

Priori, S. G., Bloise, R., & Crotti, L. (2001). The long QT syndrome. *Europace*, *3*(1), 16–27. doi:10.1053/eupc.2000.0141 PMID:11271945

Reichman, A. (2011). *File storage costs less in the cloud than in-house*. Forrester.

Rivest, R., Adleman, L., & Shamir, A. (1978). A method for obtaining digital signatures and public-key cryptosystems. *Communications of the ACM*, *21*(2), 120–126. doi:10.1145/359340.359342

SalesForce.com. (2014). Retrieved from http://www.salesforce.com

Sander, T., Young, A. L., & Yung, M. (1999). Non-Interactive CryptoComputing For NC1. *40th Annual Symposium on Foundations of Computer Science* (pp. 554-567). New York: ACM. doi:10.1109/SFFCS.1999.814630

Shah, R. (2004). Drug-induced QT interval prolongation: Regulatory perspectives and drug development. *Annals of Medicine*, *36*(S1), 47–52. doi:10.1080/17431380410032445 PMID:15176424

Smart, N. P., & Vercauteren, F. (2014). Fully homomorphic SIMD operations. *Designs, Codes and Cryptography*, *71*(1), 57–81. doi:10.1007/s10623-012-9720-4

Soyata, T., Ba, H., Heinzelman, W., Kwon, M., & Shi, J. (2013, Sep). Accelerating Mobile Cloud Computing: A Survey. In H. T. Mouftah & B. Kantarci (Eds.), *Communication Infrastructures for Cloud Computing* (pp. 175–197). Hershey, PA: IGI Global.

Soyata, T., & Friedman, E. G. (1994). Retiming with Non-Zero Clock Skew, Variable Register and Interconnect Delay. *Proceedings of the IEEE Conference on Computer-Aided Design (ICCAD)*, (pp. 234-241).

Soyata, T., Friedman, E. G., & Mulligan, J. H. (1997, January). Incorporating Interconnect, Register, and Clock Distribution Delays into the Retiming Process. *IEEE Transactions on Computer-Aided Design of Integrated Circuits and Systems*, *16*(1), 105–120. doi:10.1109/43.559335

Soyata, T., Muraleedharan, R., Ames, S., Langdon, J. H., Funai, C., Kwon, M., & Heinzelman, W. B. (2012, May). COMBAT: Mobile Cloud-based cOmpute/coMmunications infrastructure for BATtlefield applications. *Proceedings of the Society for Photo-Instrumentation Engineers*, *8403*, 84030K–84030K, 84030K-13. doi:10.1117/12.919146

Soyata, T., Muraleedharan, R., Funai, C., Kwon, M., & Heinzelman, W. (2012, Jul). Cloud-Vision: Real-Time Face Recognition Using a Mobile-Cloudlet-Cloud Acceleration Architecture. *Proceedings of the 17th IEEE Symposium on Computers and Communications (IEEE ISCC 2012)*, (pp. 59-66). Cappadocia, Turkey. doi:10.1109/ISCC.2012.6249269

TI-MSP430. (n.d.). *Overview for MSP430F1x*. Retrieved from http://www.ti.com/lsds/ti/microcontrollers_16-bit_32-bit/msp/ultra-low_power/msp430f1x/overview.page

Wang, H., Liu, W., & Soyata, T. (2014, Mar). Accessing Big Data in the Cloud Using Mobile Devices. In P. R. Chelliah & G. Deka (Eds.), *Handbook of Research on Cloud Infrastructures for Big Data Analytics* (pp. 444–470). Hershey, PA: IGI Global. doi:10.4018/978-1-4666-5864-6.ch018

KEY TERMS AND DEFINITIONS

Additive Homomorphism: A type of homomorphism, where addition operations on unencrypted data correspond to the same addition operations in the encrypted version. There are many encryption mechanisms which are additively homomorphic, but not multiplicatively homomorphic.

Band Matrix: A type of matrix where only the main diagonal and a band of "d" additional diagonals above and below the main diagonal are non-zero. The rest of the matrix is made up of zeros. For example, assume an NxN matrix consisting of N^2 elements, where only the diagonal is non-zero. Then, N elements are non-zero and N^2-N elements are zero. If the "band" extends one diagonal above and below the main diagonal, then, N+2*(N-1) = 3N-2 elements will be non-zero, and N^2-(3N-2) elements will be zero. One can extend the band to the point, where there are N-1 bands, at which point the entire matrix is non-zero (i.e., N^2 elements), and it is no longer a band matrix.

BGV Scheme: An FHE scheme that was introduced by three researchers, Brakerski, Gentry, and Vainkuntanathan, which introduces many optimizations to the original Gentry FHE scheme. One of the most important optimizations is the adoption of a SIMD-like processing structure.

Branching Program: A branching program is a computational model, where the decisions that start from a starting node "s" and end up at a terminal node "t" are modeled as branches.

Ciphertext: The encrypted message. In the case of FHE, a plaintext has multiple slots, corresponding to multiple messages, however, the encrypted message (i.e., the ciphertext) bits or the locations of the encrypted bits are no longer recognizable due to the way FHE encrypts each slot.

Circuit Model: A computational model, where each operation performed on data elements is represented as one of the circuit elements, such as, XOR gates, AND, OR, NOT gates.

Cramer's Rule: This rule can be used to determine the value of a specific a variable X_i in the systems of equations AX=B, where A is an NxN square matrix, and X^T and B are column vectors. To calculate X_i, it suffices to calculate det(A_i)/det(A), where det(A) is the determinant of the entire A matrix, and det(A_i) is the determinant of the same A matrix where the ith column is replaced with the B matrix.

Determinant of a Matrix: Denoted as det(A) which is the determinant of an NxN square matrix A, det(A) contains crucial information about a matrix. For example, if det(A) is zero, this matrix is singular, i.e., it does not represent a solution that is unique for the underlying system of linear equations. Additionally, the determinant can be used to calculate the value of a vector using the Cramer's rule.

Directed Acyclic Graph (DAG): A type of graph which does not contain any cycles (i.e., nodes that start and terminate at the same vertex). Each edge in this graph is directed, i.e., it goes from one specific vertex into another specific vertex.

ECG Patch: A sensor attached to the patient to collect ECG data. This device attaches to the body, typically close to the heart, and provides data to a recorder and/or monitoring device.

Electrocardiogram (ECG): The diagram produced by an ECG machine by turning the voltages in the body, produced by heartbeats, into sketches on an ECG paper. This provides quick visual information for the operation of the patient's heart.

Fully Homomorphic Encryption (FHE): The encryption mechanism that achieve both additive and multiplicative homomorphism. With this type of encryption, it is possible to perform an arbitrary sequence of operations, since addition and multiplication operations are sufficient to represent any form of computation which can be written in terms of these two fundamental operations. Therefore, FHE can be used to perform operations at an arbitrary complexity on encrypted data, without observing the underlying data.

Galois Field 2-GF(2): The field of integer numbers, containing only 2 numbers, 0 and 1. Any operation performed in this field can only produce one of two values, 0 and 1. For more sophisticated computations spanning far beyond a single bit, a careful planning of the operations is necessary to route the carry from one bit to the neighboring bits.

HElib: An FHE library based on the BGV scheme which introduces SIMD type operation on encrypted data. These operations are ADD, MULTIPLY, SHIFT, and BIT SELECT. By using these SIMD operations, a more generalized set of operations can be performed. SIMD nature was introduced to HElib to drastically speed up the FHE execution, since the original version was too slow to be practical.

Homomorphic Encryption (HE): A public key encryption algorithm where addition or multiplication operations in the "unencrypted domain" correspond to the identical addition or multiplication operations in the "encrypted" domain, thereby making it possible to compute on encrypted data. However, in HE, both addition and multiplication operations do not necessarily correspond to the same operations in their encrypted version *simultaneously*.

Log-Space Computation: In computational complexity, Log-space class constitutes a class of problems requiring log(N) space for N entries.

Long QT Syndrome (LQTS): The symptom of prolonged QT interval. This is an indicator of incorrect heart operation. When corrected QTc values are used, the variation among different people should be small. This allows the definition of "safe" QTc values. Typically, values under 500 ms are acceptable, although 440 ms is typically considered a good QTc value. Patients with values over 500 ms are under risk of serious cardiac hazards.

Message: A string of bits constituting a certain amount of information to send. Depending on the type of encryption, bit of this message could have different locations in its encrypted version. A message gets encrypted and decrypted during secure transportation.

Multiplicative Homomorphism: A type of homomorphism, where multiplication operations on unencrypted data correspond to the same multiplication operations in the encrypted version. There are many encryption mechanisms which are multiplicatively homomorphic, but not additively homomorphic.

NC^1 Circuits: In complexity theory, NC class (Nick's class) is a class of problems which can be solved in poly-logarithmic time, $O(\log^c N)$ by using polynomial computational elements, $O(N^k)$. NC^1 specifically implies that, a circuit of depth log(N) can be solved in $O(N^k)$ time.

Plaintext: The bit stream containing the unencrypted message. In the case of FHE, a plaintext has multiple slots, which correspond to multiple messages, not necessarily the same quantity.

Public-Key Encryption: An encryption type, where a public key and private key pair are required for the encryption and decryption to work. Public key is known to everyone, whereas the private key is only known to parties that are receiving secret messages through encryption. While encryption is possible by anyone by using the public key, decryption is only possible when the private key is known.

QT Interval: The QT interval of each heartbeat delineates the ventricular recovery phase of the heart.

QTc Value: A corrected version of the QT interval, which adjusts for heart rate. Bazett suggested almost 100 years ago to use $QTc=QT/\sqrt{RR}$. This is known as Bazett's formula. However, an alternative suggestion from Fridericia proved to be more accurate for a wider range of heart rates. Fridericia's equation has the same form as Bazett's, but replaces the square root of RR with the cube root. These two formulas can be written as: $QTcB = QT/(RR/sec)^{1/2}$ $QTcF = QT/(RR/sec)^{1/3}$. The divisions of RR by 1 second are in place to preserve units between QT and QTc.

RR Interval: The interval between two adjacent R points in an ECG waveform. Since the heart beat is periodic, 60/RR gives the *heart rate* in beats per minute.

Single Instruction Multiple Data (SIMD): A computational mechanism, where a single instruction (e.g., ADD) is applied to a set of data, (e.g., 128). This type of computation requires an underlying computer architecture that is suitable for executing such SIMD instructions. Also, the type of problems that are suitable to this type of computation are limited. Image Processing operations fit perfectly to this model.

Telemetric and Holter ECG Warehouse (THEW): A warehouse of ECG data from healthy patients and patients with various cardiac conditions, such as Long QT Syndrome, LQTS1, LQTS2. This data consists of 24 to 48 hour Holter monitoring. In this chapter, ECG data from THEW is used as simulated patient data.

Torsades de Pointes (TdP): A heart failure (arrhythmia) that can cause death. The risk of TdP increases with LQTS.

Chapter 5
Volunteer Computing on Mobile Devices:
State of the Art and Future Research Directions

Cristiano Tapparello
University of Rochester, USA

Colin Funai
University of Rochester, USA

Shurouq Hijazi
University of Rochester, USA

Abner Aquino
University of Rochester, USA

Bora Karaoglu
The Samraksh Company, USA

He Ba
University of Rochester, USA

Jiye Shi
UCB Pharma, UK

Wendi Heinzelman
University of Rochester, USA

ABSTRACT

Different forms of parallel computing have been proposed to address the high computational requirements of many applications. Building on advances in parallel computing, volunteer computing has been shown to be an efficient way to exploit the computational resources of under utilized devices that are available around the world. The idea of including mobile devices, such as smartphones and tablets, in existing volunteer computing systems has recently been investigated. In this chapter, we present the current state of the art in the mobile volunteer computing research field, where personal mobile devices are the elements that perform the computation. Starting from the motivations and challenges behind the adoption of personal mobile devices as computational resources, we then provide a literature review of the different architectures that have been proposed to support parallel computing on mobile devices. Finally, we present some open issues that need to be investigated in order to extend user participation and improve the overall system performance for mobile volunteer computing.

DOI: 10.4018/978-1-4666-8662-5.ch005

INTRODUCTION

In recent years, the computational requirements of various applications in domains ranging from healthcare to finance have increased dramatically. Several computing infrastructures have been proposed and, among them, parallel computing has been shown to be a viable solution to meeting this increasing computational demand. Following the principle that large computational problems can often be divided into smaller ones, various forms of parallel computing, from hardware dependent solutions such as multi-core and GPU programming, to distributed computing, have been proposed to provide a suitable parallel computing architecture.

Distributed computing is an important class of parallel computing, linking distant high performance computing resources through the Internet. Such systems are essentially cooperative groups of powerful computers that require both an initial investment in hardware and software as well as significant operational costs (e.g., maintenance, direct power consumption and cooling infrastructure) that are mostly energy-related. Increasing operational costs (U.S. Energy Information Administration, 2014), combined with the need to reduce the related carbon footprint, have led researchers to explore energy-efficient alternatives for high performance computing that decrease the overall energy consumption of computation, storage, and communication. Several ideas have been explored, including PowerNap (Meisner, et al., 2009), which relies on the hardware ability to switch to a low power state, and GreenCloud (Liu, et al., 2009), which considers migrating virtual machines between physical machines in order to reduce the total power load of a data center. However, improving energy efficiency in large scale workstations is still considered a major challenge in distributed computing (Zhang, Cheng, & Boutaba, 2010).

Instead of using dedicated hardware for parallel computing, volunteer computing aims to use underutilized personal computational resources. Many computing devices (e.g., personal computers, tablets and mobile devices) under utilize their processing capabilities for the majority of their operational time, during which they could be used for other tasks. Recent studies show that the potential of these resources exceeds any centralized computing system (Anderson D., 2004). Many systems have been proposed with the objective to allow volunteers to dedicate the unused computing cycles on their personal computers, such as the SETI@home project (Anderson, Cobb, Korpela, Lebofsky, & Werthimer, 2002), JXTA (Gong, 2001), XtremeWeb (Fedak, Germain, Neri, & Cappello, 2001), and the Berkeley Open Infrastructure for Network Computing (BOINC) (Anderson D., 2004). BOINC has been one of the most popular volunteer computing platforms, with over 1,000,000 active computers for a large range of application areas throughout the world (Berkeley, 2014).

These solutions attempt to provide a large scale, platform-independent computing infrastructure, but most of them are limited to personal computers. However, the availability of wirelessly connected mobile devices has grown considerably within recent years, creating an enormous collective untapped computational power. The idea of integrating mobile devices into the computational grid was proposed more then a decade ago (Phan, Huang, & Dulan, 2002), when mobile computing devices such as laptops and PDAs were typically restricted by reduced processing power, memory, secondary storage, and bandwidth capabilities. The authors in (Phan, Huang, & Dulan, 2002) recognized that, even if the individual mobile devices have limited resources, considering them as an aggregated sum, they have the potential to play a vital role within distributed computing.

Nowadays, with the recent advances in the area of low powered processors, mobile devices such as smartphones and tablets are able to perform computationally intensive operations, so that they are now considered as alternative computing platforms. For instance, a typical tablet such as the Asus Nexus 7

(Asus, 2013) is equipped with a 1.5 GHz quad-core CPU and 2 GB RAM which, for standard workloads, provides performance comparable to an entry-level laptop processor (CPUBoss, 2015). Although the computing capabilities of mobile processors are not as powerful as the ones of a standard desktop computer, they have been shown to be more energy efficient (Ba, Heinzelman, Janssen, & Shi, 2013).

As a result, many traditional distributed computing platforms have attempted to extend their operation over mobile devices. For example, Hyrax (Marinelli, 2009) provides an Android application to execute jobs for Hadoop Apache on smartphones and, following the same approach, the BOINC project released an Android client (Berkeley, 2014) to include mobile devices in the volunteer computations. More recently, several distributed system architectures and frameworks, such as GEMCloud (Ba, Heinzelman, Janssen, & Shi, 2013), CrowdLab (Cuervo, Gilbert, Wu, & Cox, 2011) and Seattle (Cappos, Beschastnikh, Krishnamurthy, & Anderson, 2009), have been proposed to exploit the computational capabilities of mobile devices, while trying to address the challenges that arise from their integration into a traditional distributed architecture.

In this chapter, we present recent advances in the mobile distributed computing research field, where mobile devices are the elements that perform the computation. This computation is either assigned by a traditional remote server or a local device. In both cases, several studies show that it is feasible and beneficial in terms of both energy and execution time to allow mobile devices to participate in the distributed computation. Moreover, recent research shows promising results toward a distributed computing architecture that opportunistically harvests the computational power of volunteer mobile devices. In the remainder of this chapter, the term mobile device is used to represent a small, handheld computing device, such as a smartphone or a tablet.

The rest of this chapter is organized as follows. In Section CLASSIFICATION OF PARALLEL COMPUTING, we provide a classification of different parallel computing techniques, namely cluster computing, distributed computing and volunteer computing, discussing how mobile devices can provide benefit to the parallel computation. In Section MOTIVATIONS AND CHALLENGES, we discuss the motivations and challenges behind the design of a mobile volunteer computing architecture, while in Section MOBILE DISTRIBUTED COMPUTING ARCHITECTURES, we present a comprehensive review of different frameworks for parallel computing that incorporate mobile devices that are currently proposed in the literature. Section OPEN ISSUES AND FUTURE RESEARCH DIRECTIONS describes the current open issues and future research directions to support mobile volunteer computing. Finally, Section CONCLUSIONS concludes the chapter.

CLASSIFICATION OF PARALLEL COMPUTING

High performance parallel computing has been an approach used to increase the speed of computation by dividing the computational problem into simultaneously computable sections and processing each section on different processing units. Traditionally, these independent processing units reside on the same device (multiprocessor computing), or even on the same chip (multicore computing). On the other hand, researchers have explored new computational architectures where the processors of multiple devices are connected by a communication network and cooperate in the computational job. These architectures can be classified according to the geographical distance between the devices that perform the computation: the parallel execution of computational jobs using a group of co-located computers is typically called *cluster computing*, while the cooperation among distant computers communicating over the Internet is typically referred to as *distributed computing*. While the former relies on a reliable local area network and can be used to solve distributed computing problems that require communication among the devices executing the tasks, the latter, due to the unpredictability of the Internet, typically deals only with what are termed "embarrassingly parallel problems," where there exists no dependency (or communication) between the parallel tasks. Both of these approaches consider that the computation is distributed across dedicated devices that either require direct management or the payment of a fee for accessing the processing power. As a result, the concept of *volunteer computing* has been proposed as an alternate parallel computing system that exploits computing resources donated by general-purpose computer owners.

In what follows, we first briefly describe these three classes of parallel computing, namely cluster computing, distributed computing, and volunteer computing, and then discuss how mobile devices can provide benefit to the distributed computation.

Cluster Computing

Computing clusters are built linking groups of computers through a high-bandwidth low latency local area network. These computers each run their own instance of an operating system, but work together to perform a common task so that they can be viewed as a single system. The computing clusters are developed for a variety of purposes such as load balancing on web servers, computationally intensive scientific calculations, and failure safe operation on critical commercial applications.

Attached Resource Computer (ARCNET) (ARCNET, 2002; Asus, 2013) was the first commercial computing cluster, developed in the late 70s, supporting both parallel computing as well as sharing file systems.

Beowulf clusters utilize standard commodity grade computers with specialized libraries and programs that allow job sharing among them. Beowulf clusters normally run Unix like operating systems, such as BSD, Linux, or Solaris and, potentially, any PC capable of running a Unix like operating system can be used in this configuration. The cluster is organized as multiple computers serving as the worker nodes and one or more computers taking the responsibility of the server. The server controls and coordinates the computing cluster and serves as a gateway between the computing cluster and the outside world. Stone Soupercomputer[1] (Hoffman, Hargrove, & Schultz, 1997) built by Oak Ridge National Laboratory was one of the large scale successful applications of the Beowulf concept.

Due to the dependency of the physical location of the hardware, computing clusters are built to serve a limited set of users located at a particular geographical region. Hence, the demand for computational resources on these systems have a high variance due to the correlation between usage patterns. Combined with the high cost of building computing clusters, this leads to both underutilization and outage of computational resources.

Distributed Computing

Distributed computing overcomes the geographical limitation of cluster computing by allowing distant computers to cooperate in the execution of computational tasks. By integrating geographically diverse multiple computing clusters or individual computers, distributed computing architectures can serve a larger group of consumers with less correlated usage patterns. Although distribution and scheduling of the computing jobs across the distributed computing resources adds another layer of complexity, with the introduction of the Internet, distributed computing systems provide a fairly low cost and high performance solution to large computing problems.

Through distributed computing, computational capabilities can be offered to users as a service. In this new model of computing, also referred to as utility computing, customers can acquire large computing capabilities as needed. The computational tasks are offloaded to the service providers' computing platform, and the results are downloaded back after completion of the tasks. Many commercial instantiations of distributed computing exist today, including Amazon Elastic Compute Cloud (Amazon, 2015). One intrinsic drawback of this approach is that the users' performance is negatively affected by the network delay, since the entire user data and the result of the computation need to be exchanged back and forth with the distributed computing system.

More recently, a new subclass of distributed computing named cloud computing has also been proposed, and it is receiving considerable attention. Distributed computing architectures have evolved into cloud computing systems that not only undertake computational tasks but also serve as data storage systems and provide online access to computer services or resources. These resources are shared by multiple users but are usually dynamically reallocated per demand, thus maximizing the effectiveness of the shared infrastructure. Microsoft's OneDrive (Microsoft, 2015) and IBM Cloud (IBM, 2015) are two of the many commercial examples of this paradigm.

Volunteer Computing

Although distributed computing systems increase the efficiency of parallel computing, they still require a large investment for both hardware and software as well as incurring significant operational costs (i.e., maintenance, direct power consumption and cooling infrastructure). Several studies have shown that many computing devices (i.e., personal computers, tablets and mobile devices) under utilize their processing capabilities for the majority of their operational time. The potential of these resources exceeds any centralized computing system. This is the basis for volunteer computing.

The first volunteer computing project, Great Internet Marsenne Prime Search (Marsenne Research, Inc., 2015), was started in 1996 with the objective of using freely available software on volunteers' computers working in parallel to find prime numbers. Starting from this project, volunteer computing emerged as a result of the wide spread adoption of personal computers and the Internet. With volunteer computing, volunteers can dedicate the unused computer cycles on their personal computers to the distributed computation. This is made possible by middleware systems such as JXTA (Gong, 2001), XtremeWeb (Fedak, Germain, Neri, & Cappello, 2001), and Berkeley Open Infrastructure for Network Computing (BOINC) (Anderson D., 2004). BOINC was originally developed to provide support and increase security for the SETI project (Anderson, Cobb, Korpela, Lebofsky, & Werthimer, 2002) and later extended as a platform for other distributed applications. It is now one of the most popular volunteer computing platforms with over 1,000,000 active participants (Berkeley, 2014).

Parallel Computing on Mobile Devices

The idea of connecting mobile devices into a parallel computing system was proposed in 2002 (Phan, Huang, & Dulan, 2002), when both their computational capabilities and diffusion where still highly limited. With the increase in mobile device computational capabilities, different system architectures have been proposed to exploit their resources for parallel computing. The classification of parallel computing presented in this section can be extended to the case in which the mobile devices are performing the actual computations. In this regard, solutions that group nearby mobile devices using a device to device communication technology such as Bluetooth (Bluetooth Group, 2010) and WiFi Direct (Wi-Fi Alliance, P2P Task Group, 2011), and distributed systems that link together distant devices through an Internet connection have both been investigated. Many traditional distributed computing architectures have recognized the widespread usage, significant computing capabilities and energy efficiency of mobile devices and have attempted to extend their operation over mobile computing platforms. For example, Hyrax (Marinelli, 2009) ports Hadoop Apache, an open-source implementation of MapReduce, to execute jobs on networked Android smartphones. A client version of BOINC was ported to an ARM/Linux platform (Eastlack, 2011) to evaluate the processing power of mobile devices, and an Android client (Berkeley, 2014) to include mobile devices in the distributed computations has also been released by the BOINC project.

MOTIVATIONS AND CHALLENGES

There are several motivating factors that make personal mobile devices suitable for inclusion in a distributed volunteer computing architecture. However, their integration with a traditional system is not straightforward, and some important issues need to be addressed. In what follows, we first describe the motivations behind utilizing personal mobile devices as part of the distributed computing architecture, and then we present the main design challenges.

Motivations

The first motivating factor is the impressive rise in the number of smartphones and tablets across the world. According to a report released by the International Data Corporation (IDC) (IDC, 2015), in 2013 the worldwide smartphone market shipped one billion units in a single year for the first time, representing a 38.4% increase with respect to the 725.3 million units shipped in 2012. Smartphones accounted for 55.1% of all mobile phone shipments in 2013, up from the 41.7% of all mobile phone shipments in 2012. Moreover, IDC recently reported a new single quarter record of 301.3 million shipments for the second quarter of 2014 and forecasts a 23% year increase from the 1.0 billion units shipped in 2013. The progressive increase in worldwide shipments of smartphones, from the first quarter of 2011 to the second quarter of 2014, is presented in Figure 1. A similar trend has been reported for the worldwide tablet market, with a total shipment of 50 million units during the second quarter of 2014, resulting in an 11% year over year increase. These trends in smartphone and tablet sales can be compared with the worldwide PC shipments, that totaled 74.4 million units in the second quarter of 2014, with a year-on-year decline of −1.7% (IDC, 2015). As a result, the global number of smartphones and tablets is continuously growing at a fast pace, and the global number of users outnumbers the users of conventional Laptop and Desktop PCs, reaching almost 30% of the worldwide population (KPCB, 2014). Thus, the computing power offered by mobile devices disseminated across the world is already substantial and is going to increase further in a dramatic fashion in the coming years.

In addition to the large amount of aggregate computing power offered by these personal mobile devices, their intrinsic energy efficient design makes them particularly suitable for the execution of computational tasks. It has been shown that a mobile processor like the Qualcomm Snapdragon S4 that powers the Nexus 7, can be over 20 times more power efficient than a commercial PC CPU such as the Intel Core i3 while, at the same time, achieving half the performance of a desktop processor in standard

Figure 1. Quarterly worldwide shipments of smartphones and operating systems market share from the first quarter of 2011 to the second quarter of 2014. Data source: IDC worldwide quarterly mobile phone tracker (IDC, 2015).

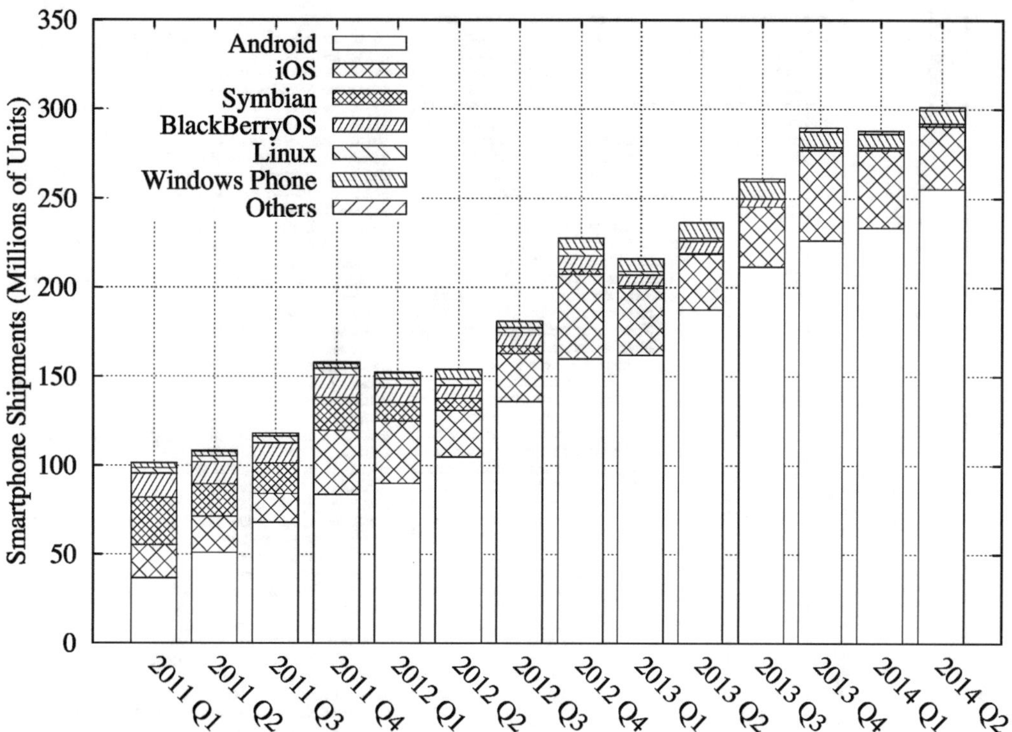

benchmarking tests (CPUBoss, 2015). The computational power evolution of mobile processors from 2010 to 2014 is shown in Figure 2, while a comparison between the energy consumption and the computing time of different mobile devices and workstation configurations is presented in Figure 3. In fact, even if specialized high performance server architectures can provide better performance per consumed power ratios, such servers consume much more power than a mobile device when they are in the idle state (Ba, Heinzelman, Janssen, & Shi, 2013). Moreover, a high performance server requires additional supporting infrastructure for the installation and operational expenses for related equipment (e.g., the cooling system and backup power) and maintenance, thus resulting in a higher total cost of ownership compared to mobile devices. As pointed out in (Schildt, Busching, Jorns, & Wolf, 2013), mobile devices already exist and thus, by using them in a distributed computing system, it is also possible to save the cost, energy and material consumption required for the production and operation of new high performance workstations. Finally, from an environmental point of view, the use of existing mobile devices should be increased. The authors in (Yu, Williams, & Ju, 2010) estimate that only 25% of the total energy budget required for the production and operation of a mobile device is actually attributed to its usage (i.e., energy for charging the battery), while the remaining 75% is used during the manufacturing of the device.

Another motivating factor is the rising costs required for running a distributed computing infrastructure using workstations, which are mainly due to maintenance costs and energy charges. While the energy charges keep increasing (U.S. Energy Information Administration, 2014), for a data-center

Figure 2. Benchmark scores of different mobile processors released between the first quarter of 2010 and the second quarter of 2014.
Data source: Primate Labs Geekbench 3 (Geekbench).

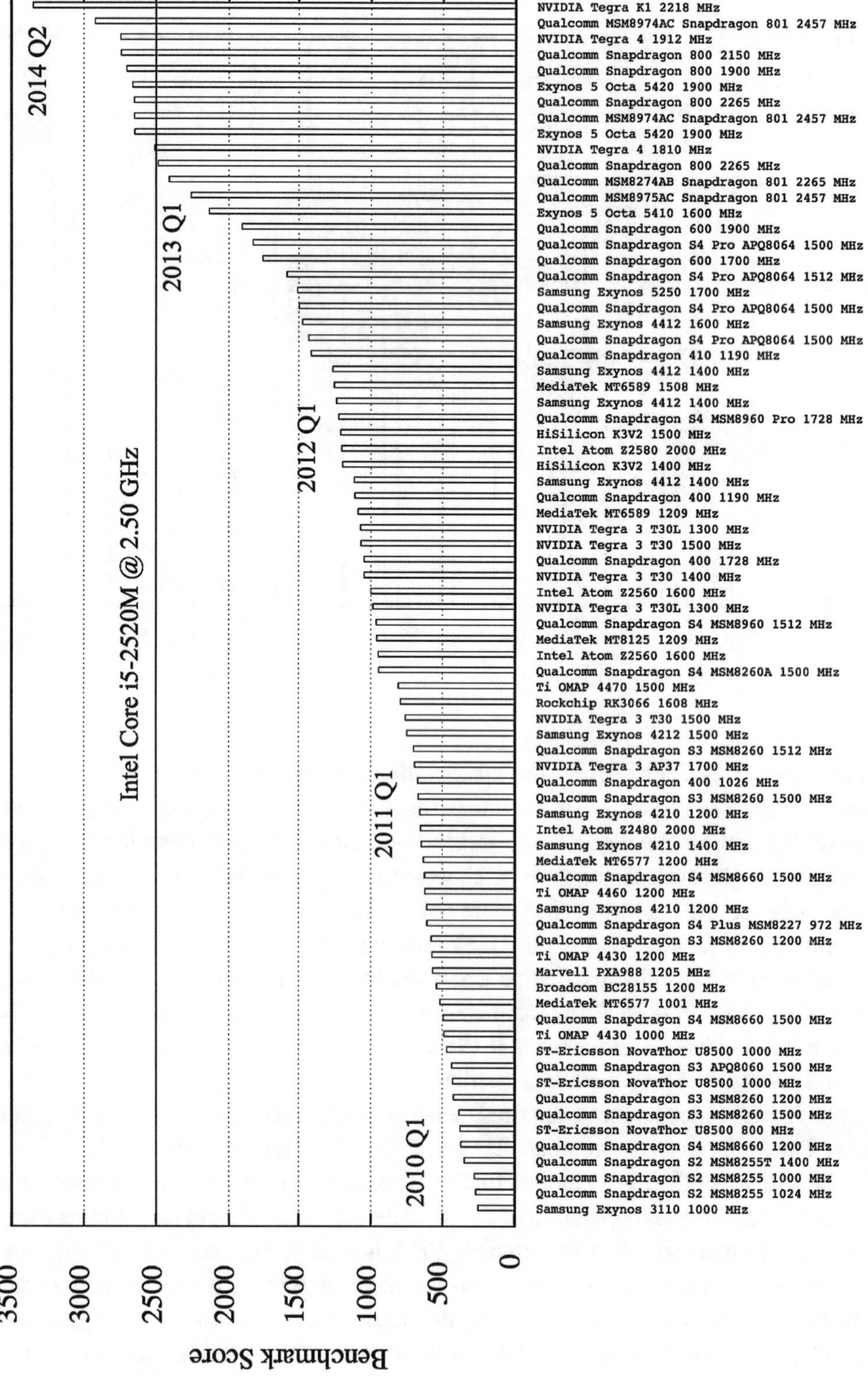

Figure 3. Energy consumption (left) and time to compute (right) as a function of the number of tasks, for 3 mobile devices, namely Xiami Mi-One (MO), Samsung Galaxy S3 (GS3) and Asus Nexus 7 (N7), and 3 workstation configurations (WS1, WS2 and WS3).
Adapted from (Ba, Heinzelman, Janssen, & Shi, 2013).

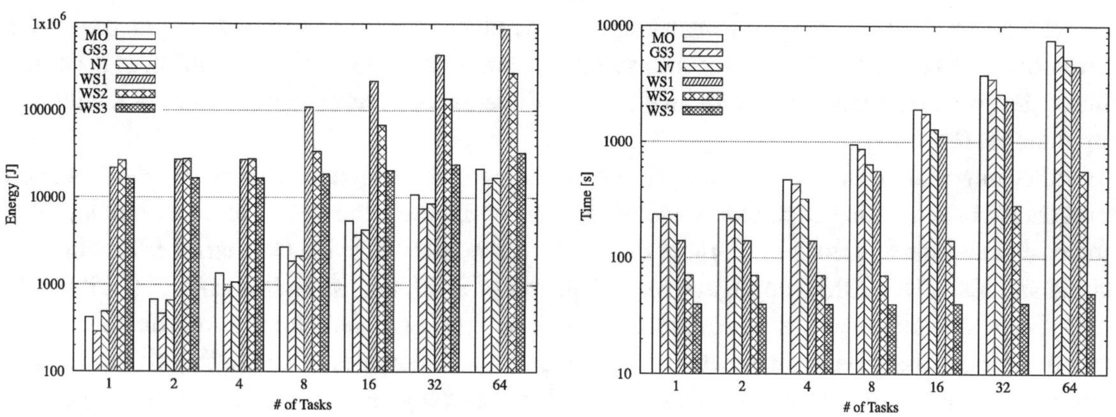

they are based on the industrial rate, which is much higher than the consumer rate at which the mobile devices owned by consumers will operate. In addition, the authors in (Arslan, Singh, Singh, Madhyastha, Sundaresan, & Krishnamurthy, 2012) estimate the cost for powering an Intel Core 2 Duo server to be $74.5/year, compared to $1.33/year for a smartphone with the same computational performance. Thus, using consumer smart devices for distributed computation results in significantly lower energy costs.

Challenges

The first problem to consider when dealing with personal mobile devices is their availability. In particular, smartphones and tablets have mobility as one of their major features, which makes them volatile computing resources. Due to mobility, the devices are not physically available in a specific location, and thus it is possible that most of them will not be available for computing purposes for extended hours. Furthermore, since these devices are battery powered, battery life is also a major concern, which can severely impact the user experience. However, in many cases, mobile devices are unused and do not move for long periods of time during a working day and, especially, at night when most users leave their devices idle while charging the battery. In the idle state, a mobile device typically runs only lightweight background jobs (e.g., email download, data synchronization and application updates) that require only minimal computation and intermittent Internet access. Thus, it is important to devise intelligent algorithms for task scheduling and distribution that take into account the device availability, relative power state (i.e., battery level and charging status) and user utilization patterns in order to maximize computing capacity without negatively impacting the standard mobile device operations.

A second challenge is the need for Internet connectivity, which is necessary for the distribution of the tasks and for the transmission of the computation results. Internet connectivity is a highly limiting factor due to both its cost and its impact on the energy consumption of the device. Moreover, even when the devices are connected to the Internet, the stability and bandwidth of the wireless network are also important elements that need to be considered. This is because channel fluctuations can result in data losses or in reductions of the useful bandwidth, and the bandwidth will then impact the total time required to distribute the computation and receive the results. While it is neither advisable nor feasible for mobile devices to employ conventional wired networking, the current wireless technologies are either limited in speed and require a substantial energy consumption (e.g., 3G and 4G/LTE), or are limited in range (e.g., WiFi). Thus, devising techniques to reduce the cost of communication, preserve the battery power and periodically monitor the availability and relative bandwidth of different networking technologies, is a major requirement for an efficient utilization of personal mobile devices as additional computational resources.

Another important challenge that needs to be considered when dealing with mobile devices is their heterogeneity in processing capabilities and platforms. While the latter seems to be mainly a problem of the past since, starting from 2012, more than 90% of the mobile device OS market is dominated by Android and iOS (IDC, 2015) (during the second quarter of 2014, 84.7% Android and 11.7% iOS (IDC, 2015)), the processing capability varies greatly among devices, especially for the Android market. This makes the design of a general architecture that can leverage advantages of a vast majority of software/hardware platforms very difficult. As an example, when assigning tasks to mobile devices, the computing architecture needs to take into account the hardware resources available at the device and assign computationally intensive tasks to more powerful devices.

MOBILE DISTRIBUTED COMPUTING ARCHITECTURES

Modern mobile devices, such as smartphones and tablets, have become powerful and energy efficient computing architectures, that are both widely available and underutilized for long periods of time. As a result, multiple approaches for integrating mobile devices into a parallel computing infrastructure have been proposed and are currently receiving considerable attention. These studies can be broadly classified in two main categories, depending on the particular entity that is responsible for the management of tasks that need to be executed by the participating devices. This element can either be a remote specialized server that communicates with the mobile devices through an Internet connection, or it can be a mobile device itself, that exploits the presence of other geographically close devices to solve computationally intensive tasks. According to this division, we refer to the first scenario as "Server Driven Mobile Distributed Computing," while we call the latter scenario "User Driven Mobile Distributed Computing." We note that the server driven approach is, in fact, an extension of a traditional distributed computing architecture, where mobile devices can participate in the distributed computation alongside standard PCs. The user driven case, instead, represents a viable way to perform intensive computing when an Internet connection is not available or it is undesirable because of communication delay. For example, many applications in the area of tactical military communications, search and rescue operations, and sensor network operations require computing intensive algorithms, such as image and signal processing, at remote or isolated locations that frequently neither have direct access to the Internet nor are in the vicinity of other devices with Internet access. In both cases, the device that "drives" the computation is considered to be the job coordinator, since it is in charge of the task distribution process and is responsible for the reception and organization of the results of the tasks' execution. An example of such a mobile computing architecture is presented in Figure 4.

Figure 4. Example of a mobile distributed computing architecture where the job coordinator assigns tasks to the participating mobile devices.

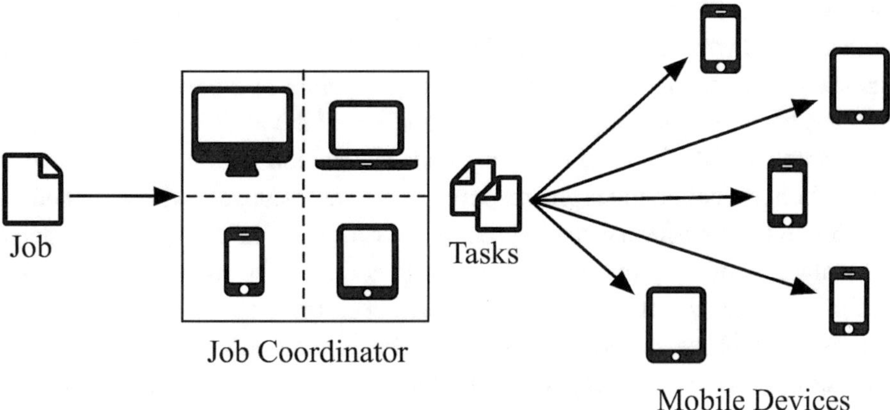

In what follows, we provide a literature review of the different frameworks that have been proposed to use mobile devices for executing tasks in distributed computing. All of these systems follow a similar architecture and communication protocol: a mobile device is connected through a suitable radio communication technology to the job coordinator, it receives the tasks to be computed and, after the execution is completed, the mobile device sends the result of the computation back to the job coordinator. It is important to note that the idea of enabling the execution of rich applications on mobile devices by offloading the computation (or part of it) and storage to a distributed architecture composed of traditional computers has also been proposed. This type of service is typically referred to as mobile cloud computing (Dinh, Lee, Niyato, & Wang, 2013).

Server Driven Mobile Distributed Computing

Mobile OGSI.NET (Chu & Humphrey, 2004)

Mobile OSGI.NET was one of the first attempts to connect mobile devices to a distributed computing architecture. The goal of this framework is to provide a way for mobile and non-mobile devices to collaborate in the execution of resource-demanding applications. The OGSI architecture consists of three components: the Mobile Web Server that handles the message exchanges between the device and the remote server, the Grid Services Module that implements the core processing necessary to execute applications, and the Grid Services, that represent the particular applications that will be executed by the device. In addition, the Grid Services Module monitors the resources of the mobile devices (like, e.g., the battery level) and decides if the mobile device is able to perform the computation, or if it is better to pass the task to another device. Experimental results show that the total time required to compute a set of tasks decreases as the number of devices increases. Moreover, they show that the energy consumption can be efficiently distributed between the devices.

Hyrax (Marinelli, 2009)

Hyrax is a platform derived from Hadoop Apache, an open source implementation of MapReduce, that supports distributed computing on Android devices. The basic idea behind Hyrax is to allow a heterogeneous network of smartphones and servers to cooperate in the execution of computing jobs. The framework has been designed to provide an abstraction of the available resources, thus being able to scale with the number of devices and tolerating node connection and departure. The performance of Hyrax in terms of both execution times and resource usage was evaluated with a testbed of 12 Android smartphones. Although the performance of Hyrax is poor for CPU-intensive tasks, it demonstrates the feasibility and scalability of the proposed framework. In addition, the advantages of using Hyrax as an infrastructure for applications that use mobile data have been investigated through the implementation of a distributed multimedia search and sharing application. The authors of (Marinelli, 2009) stated that Hyrax had not been optimized for battery efficiency, but in several tests it was shown to use significantly less power than a video recording and downloading application.

Computing While Charging (Arslan, Singh, Singh, Madhyastha, Sundaresan, & Krishnamurthy, 2012)

Computing While Charging (CWC) describes and evaluates a scenario in which a company uses the mobile devices provided to its employees for the execution of parallelizable tasks. The main idea behind CWC is that using mobile devices for work-related computing can potentially reduce not only the capital investment in servers but also the cost of energy, since a smartphone can be up to 20x more efficient than a standard server. Thus, the authors of (Arslan, Singh, Singh, Madhyastha, Sundaresan, & Krishnamurthy, 2012) propose a framework where the phones are used for the computation only while being charged, so that the user is not disturbed by the computations. Moreover, while charging the phone has a high probability of being connected to the Internet through a WiFi Access Point. The application monitors the user interactions with the phone and, if a user uses the phone while it is computing a task, the task is interrupted and migrated to a different phone so that the task computation does not have any impact on the user. Moreover, the application incorporates an algorithm that monitors the charging patterns: a test performed on 15 volunteers showed that the users charge their phones predominantly during the night and for an uninterrupted period of several hours. They also ran other experiments to evaluate the impact of the network connectivity on the task completion time, showing that simply accounting for the CPU clock speed results in poor task completion times. CWC also includes an algorithm to predict the time it takes for the tasks to be completed and three task distribution methods with different complexity. The main experiment involved 18 Android phones with different CPU clock speeds and different network connectivity technologies, and it showed that a greedy scheduler is approximately 1.6 times faster than the other tested schedulers.

jUniGrid (Parmar, Jani, Shrivastav, & Patel, 2013)

jUniGrid is a lightweight framework that allows the integration of mobile devices into heterogeneous desktop distributed computing systems to solve high complexity computational problems. jUniGrid introduces two separate applications, that correspond to two functional roles: the Task-Submitter (TS) and the Node-Application (NA). The node application is installed on the devices that execute the tasks, while the task submitter runs on the device that creates the tasks, stores them in a task queue and assigns them to the nodes according to a First In First Out policy. Moreover, jUniGrid works based on a split/merge algorithm. It provides the user with the flexibility to split the job and merge the results according to the requirement of the particular job. This split and merge is accomplished by TS, that also implements all the functionalities for job allocation, monitoring and result aggregation. Thus, the TS is installed on the device that creates task queues and sends them to the nodes in a FIFO fashion, where the first device to be connected receives the first task output, while the node application is installed on the devices that execute the tasks. The paper shows the gains in term of job execution times that can be achieved by allowing mobile devices to participate in the distributed computation. However, the focus of the paper is to provide a basic generalized grid mechanism for cooperative multi-platform processing and does not provide any detail about the specific implementation.

Ocelot (Xu, Bilec, Schaefer, Landis, & Jones, 2013)

Ocelot is a distributed mobile computing platform that leverages mobile devices to execute lightweight computational tasks generated from a Wireless Sensor Network (WSN). Ocelot is modeled after the Berkley Open Infrastructure for Network Computing (BOINC) with the exception of employing smartphones and tablets rather than workstations and server machines, as they reduce the maintenance costs and the power usage. For testing purposes, Ocelot was integrated with a WSN that is deployed to monitor indoor environmental conditions in a building. More specifically, Ocelot was used to monitor and analyze the electrical power consumption and the environmental emissions within the building. In this setting, Ocelot's clients (the mobile devices) are attached to sensors that exchange data through WiFi Direct and/or Bluetooth. Although the clients themselves cannot gather sensory data, they can partition and efficiently process the data through parallel computing. Ocelot's clients serve as nodes that request and receive tasks from a server through XML files. One of Ocelot's main features is having multiple servers to insure an efficient task distribution, as one of the servers is consistently storing the battery status of the nodes to make sure that the scheduling server sends tasks to only those nodes with sufficient power. Once a node receives a task, it will execute the code, which is usually written in Java or C. Currently, Ocelot allows the mobile devices to act only as clients that execute tasks, but allowing the mobile devices to also become servers for the task distribution is considered as future work.

To prove its advantage in reducing energy consumption, Ocelot has been compared against traditional computers. Results show that, while laptops and desktops were 5 times faster than mobile devices, mobile devices consume up to 86% less energy. In addition, adding more devices to the client pool dramatically lowers the total task completion time. As a result, Ocelot proves that it is feasible to distribute tasks among mobile devices and provides considerable energy and cost savings with respect to a system that uses standard computers.

CANDIS (Schildt, Busching, Jorns, & Wolf, 2013)

CANDIS is a framework that distributes computing tasks to mobile devices as well as normal desktop or server hardware and provides an efficient method of reducing costs by taking advantage of the fluctuating energy market prices. The authors in (Schildt, Busching, Jorns, & Wolf, 2013) recognized that distributing computing tasks to mobile devices has been extensively studied. Thus, they focus on devising a computational infrastructure that is able to further reduce the computation costs and energy consumption. CANDIS is a Java-based framework and is thus able to run existing Java code, and desktop, server and Android mobile devices that support Java can be easily connected in the cloud. In such a hybrid cloud, the server compiles the tasks and constructs a scheduler to allocate and distribute the tasks. The paper shows that, while equally dividing the tasks among the available devices might be easier to implement, distributing much smaller tasks results in faster execution times but increases the communication overhead. Thus, CANDIS implements a more efficient allocation method where the server, before assigning the actual tasks, estimates the capability of each client by assigning a benchmarking task and using the results to improve the task allocation scheme. In addition, CANDIS uses information about the price of electricity, which fluctuates dramatically throughout the day (on average, prices are usually much lower late at night and early in the morning). The authors in (Schildt, Busching, Jorns, & Wolf, 2013) conclude that using CANDIS on a large scale not only allow to save money but can also stabilize the electric energy consumptions.

ANGELS (Datta, Dey, Paul, & Mukherjee, 2014)

ANGELS is a framework that allows mobile devices and computers to cooperatively participate in the computation of analytical data. This framework allows the parallel execution of jobs on a set of nodes that can be either mobile devices or standard PCs. For the evaluation of the framework, a "text search" application, in which mobile devices and servers had to find a specific word in a large text file and an algorithm to estimate the value of π have been considered. Experimental results show that the tasks' latency can be substantially reduced when the tasks are distributed among the mobile devices. The framework does not consider the impact of the computation on the user experience. Moreover, the task distribution process considers a simple distribution scheme, in which tasks are assigned as soon as a device becomes available.

Table 1. Server driven mobile distributed computing implementations

Name	Year	Contributions	Task Distribution	Operating System	Applications
Mobile OSGI.NET	2004	Porting of OGSI.NET to mobile devices	Homogeneous tasks. FIFO queue	Microsoft PocketPC 2003	Prime numbers search
Hyrax	2009	Porting of Hadoop to Android devices	Homogeneous tasks. FIFO queue	Android	Distributed multimedia search; Content sharing
Computing While Charging	2012	Profiling charging behaviors, scheduling algorithm, migration of tasks across phones	Heterogeneous tasks. Greedy algorithm based on the Minimum Makespan Scheduling problem with task migration.	Android	Prime numbers search; Word searching; Photo pixels blurring
JUniGrid	2013	Generic framework API for developing grid applications	Homogeneous tasks. FIFO queue	JAVA	DNA sequence matching
Ocelot	2013	Distributed computing system that uses mobile devices as computing resources.	Homogeneous tasks. FIFO queue.	Android, iOS	Dynamic life cycle assessment of a building
CANDIS	2013	Distributed computing system that uses mobile devices and traditional computer as computing resources.	Heterogeneous tasks. Scheduler based on the device computational capability and the energy market prices.	Android	Distributed brute force hash-cracking; XML to JSON conversion
ANGELS	2014	Framework that allows the remote execution of programs within mobile devices. The focus is on the processing of IoT analytical data.	Heterogeneous tasks. Tasks are assigned according to the device computational capability.	Android	Text search; π value estimation

User Driven Mobile Distributed Computing

Serendipity (Shi, Lakafosis, Ammar, & Zegura, 2012)

Serendipity enables a mobile computation initiator to use the computational resources of nearby mobile devices to speed up the computation and preserve some energy. Serendipity improves the mobile device's computational experience by applying optimizing algorithms that minimize local power consumption and/or decrease the computation completion time, while taking into account the constraints of the intermittent communication links such as limited contact duration, limited transfer bandwidth, and completion-time unpredictability. Serendipity follows what is called a "PNP block paradigm": the job is pre-processed and divided into *n* parallel task programs, and the results of the execution of the tasks are finally merged by a post-process algorithm. The goal of this design is to have an initiator disseminate a task (pre-process) to the computational nodes (task programs) it encounters based on the estimated completion time or energy consumption, and finally coalesce the data it receives (post-process).

To do so, three algorithms have been presented: 1) a WaterFilling method where the initiator knows when to contact the nodes and has access to the nodes' profiles in order to predict the number of tasks a node can execute and the time required to process them; 2) a Computing on Dissemination (COD) method, where the initiator does not know the contact time but has access to the nodes' profiles; and 3) the Unpredictable Computing on Dissemination (upCOD), where both the contact time and the nodes' profiles are unknown.

Serendipity has been implemented on Android and showed substantial performance gains when compared to executing tasks locally on the initiator's mobile device. While in all the experiments, the WaterFilling method performed better than COD and upCOD, experimental results show the clear benefit of disseminating tasks on Serendipity rather than executing them locally, especially when the number of tasks exceeds 100. Moreover, Serendipity was able to speed up computation up to 3 times compared to local conventional computing. In addition, Serendipity increases the battery life of mobile devices and allows the saving of a significant amount of energy by distributing the computation between different devices.

Honeybee (Fernando, Loke, & Rahayu, 2013)

Honeybee is a framework that deals with both human and machine computation, where human computation represents a set of operations that require human interaction, like filling out a personal survey form, while machine computation is a generic computer algorithm, like word searching or number sorting. The Honeybee framework distributes a computational intensive task, like a face detection algorithm, among several mobile devices. Honeybee's focus is on keeping the smartphone busy, in the sense that, as soon as one computation is completed, the device is allowed to steal tasks from another slower device. The proposed implementation also focuses more on getting as many tasks done as possible and does not provide a customizable, user friendly interface. Moreover, to each task is assigned a deadline that the mobile device has to satisfy in order to continue getting tasks. If the deadline is not met, the task is passed to another device. Honeybee has been implemented on Android, using Bluetooth as a local communication technology. Experimental results show that managing local connections severely impacts the delegator throughput. As future work, the authors are planning to support different types of D2D communication technologies, e.g., WiFi Direct.

Unity (Jassal, Yadav, Kumar, Naik, Narwal, & Singh, 2013)

Unity represents a system architecture that allows a group of mobile devices to share the workload required to download a data file from the Internet. With this approach, each device downloads small parts of the file and then shares those parts with the other members of the group so that every device will eventually get the complete content. Leveraging short-range technologies such as WiFi and Bluetooth, Unity allows a coordinator to communicate with its peers to split the download as well as restarting it from the point where it stopped in case of a failure.

Unity has been implemented on Android smartphones that have either WiFi or Bluetooth capabilities. Unity employs WiFi HotSpot, an Android utility that uses 802.11 infrastructure mode to allow the coordinator to act as a WiFi AP and all other peers to be connected as clients. As a result, the WiFi HotSpot functionality allows the coordinator to stay awake for the entire duration, while peers are in power saving mode, consuming a negligible amount of energy. After an initial connection phase, where the devices connect to the coordinator, the coordinator determines the size of the file through an HTTP request, divides the load, and then sends a control message containing the file URL to its peers. Subsequently, each peer starts to download its share of the file using its own data connection and sends the data blocks to the coordinator, which collects all the blocks, reconstructs the entire file and distributes it to all the peers. Unity also includes a task distribution scheme that takes into account the variability of the peers' cellular network conditions for better distributing the workload between the mobile devices. Experimental results show an improvement in download speeds up to 27%. In addition, a variations of Unity called Unity-Cloud has also been presented. In Unity-Cloud, a remote server coordinates the formation of the peer to peer group and assigns to each device the part to be downloaded according the relative cellular conditions. As soon as the peers are geographically close, the cloud coordinates the local blocks sharing for reconstructing the original file.

DRAP (Agarwal, 2014)

DRAP proposes a mechanism to group volunteer mobile devices into high performance decentralized computing systems. The idea behind this work is to create an infrastructure where mobile devices in close geographical proximity can form a cloudlet, and share resources with each other and with other nearby devices. The concept of a cloudlet has been introduced in (Satyanarayanan, Bahl, Caceres, & Davies, 2009), and represents a trusted, resource-rich computer or cluster of computers that is well-connected to the Internet and available for use by nearby mobile devices. In DRAP, the cloudlet is represented by a cluster of mobile devices that provides storage capability and computational resources to the other devices in the network. The framework monitors the movement of the participating nodes and implements all the functionalities required to connect the nodes in the network and enable the communications. For routing the communications between the devices, DRAP uses a modified version of the Ad Hoc Distance Vector (AODV) routing protocol. DRAP also includes an algorithm that uses the mobile devices' resources to determine the subset of nodes that should be selected to become part of the cloudlet. Computer simulations prove the feasibility and performance gain of the proposed architecture, for different types of applications. The implementation of DRAP in real life mobile devices is considered as future work.

Table 2. User driven mobile volunteer computing implementations

Name	Year	Contributions	Task Distribution	Operating System	Applications
Serendipity	2012	Distributed computing system that exploits nearby mobile devices	Heterogeneous tasks. Three schemes with different complexity.	Simulations on Emulab	Speech-to-text application
Honeybee	2013	Framework API to support job sharing and crowd-sourcing among mobile devices. Work stealing to achieve load balancing	Heterogeneous tasks. Tasks assigned at random. Scheduler that attempts to minimize the idle time	Android	Face detection; Mandelbrot set generation; Collaborative photography
Unity	2013	System architecture that enables collaborative downloading across co-located mobile devices.	Heterogeneous tasks. Tasks (data to be downloaded) are assigned according to the cellular network conditions	Android	Collaborative file download
DRAP	2014	Cluster formation of volunteer mobile devices for distributed computation. The focus is on how to best group the devices based on their capabilities.	High level description of a Cloudlet Manager that handles task distribution. The details about the task distribution process are not provided	Simulations on ns-3	Testing of the cloudlet formation algorithm

Mobile Volunteer Computing

The architectures presented in the previous sections can all be adapted to allow volunteer users to participate in the parallel computation. However, architectures explicitly designed with the objective of realizing a volunteer computing system by interconnecting personal mobile devices through the Internet have also been developed.

BOINC on Mobile Devices

The first attempt to extend the participation in volunteer computing to mobile devices dates back to 2007 (Eastlack, 2011), with researchers working on getting the application SETI@home (Anderson, Cobb, Korpela, Lebofsky, & Werthimer, 2002) (and other scientific programs) to run efficiently on ARM processors (Berkeley, 2011). Starting from this feasibility study, different Android applications (Berkeley, 2014; Grushko, Aharon, Dov, & Swisz, 2008; AndroBOINC, 2010; Szpakowski, 2013) and a prototype implementation for iOS (Black & Edgar, 2009) have been proposed to extend the participation in BOINC projects to mobile devices. In February 2014, the integration of Android devices into the BOINC system has been extensively promoted with the campaign HTC Power to Give (HTC, 2015), an initiative that aims to create a supercomputer by harnessing the collective processing power of Android smartphones. As of September 2014, the HTC Power to Give application has been installed on 1.7 million devices (Berkeley, 2014).

CrowdLab (Cuervo, Gilbert, Wu, & Cox, 2011)

The idea of creating testbeds by interconnecting volunteer mobile devices has also received considerable attention (Cuervo, Gilbert, Wu, & Cox, 2011; Zayas & Gómez, 2010; Nandugudi, et al., 2013). In particular, CrowdLab (Cuervo, Gilbert, Wu, & Cox, 2011) is a testbed architecture that utilizes volunteer mobile resources to offer features common to infrastructure-based testbeds. CrowdLab allows the execution of guest code on participating mobile devices through hardware virtualization, it supports low-level access to the radio device and the concurrent scheduling of co-located applications. Volunteers contribute resources to CrowdLab in the same way that users contribute spare resources to BOINC. The CrowdLab architecture uses a centralized remote server for tracking the experiments and the current available volunteer resource contributors, and a decentralized local task coordinator that is responsible for the scheduling and task distribution to nearby devices. CrowdLab includes an algorithm to limit the amount of energy that each application can consume in a certain time period. According to this scheduling scheme, a device will not participate in the distributed computation if the owner is actively using it, and it allows the user to set a daily resource budget for running experiments as a percent of battery capacity or as a period of participation.

Seattle (Cappos, Beschastnikh, Krishnamurthy, & Anderson, 2009)

Seattle (Cappos, Beschastnikh, Krishnamurthy, & Anderson, 2009) has been proposed as a distributed computing platform that exploits heterogeneous volunteer devices for educational and research purposes, that supports different operating systems and architectures. Seattle is a general purpose learning platform based on the Python programming language that allows users to develop and test different types of applications ranging from networking to cloud computing. The objective of this platform is to provide researchers and educators the ability to create application prototypes and to evaluate their performance on a wide range of devices distributed around the world. Seattle follows an open source philosophy, and it embraces the heterogeneity of today's end user environment, thus providing a unique environment that is not available on other testbeds. A recent study showed that more than 20,000 devices are currently contributing their resources to Seattle, with more than 500 being mobile devices (Zhuang, Rafetseder, & Cappos, 2013).

GEMCloud (Ba, Heinzelman, Janssen, & Shi, 2013)

More recently, GEMCloud (Green Energy Mobile Cloud) (Ba, Heinzelman, Janssen, & Shi, 2013) has been proposed as a distributed system that utilizes energy efficient personal mobile devices as computing resources instead of desktop computers. Mobile devices are considered to be particularly appealing because of their increasing computing capabilities, great popularity and diffusion as well as for the fact that they can potentially provide energy savings with respect to standard computers. The vision of GEMCloud is to adapt the traditional distributed computing infrastructure by shifting the load of the computation to mobile devices. GEMCloud follows a traditional volunteer computing architecture, where a remote server distributes the tasks to participating devices through an Internet connection. The task distribution is based on the device characteristics and customizable user preferences. In GEMCloud, the user experience is particularly important, and the user is allowed to finely control how much and when to contribute to the distributed computation, including settings on battery level, charging vs. not charging, WiFi vs. 3G/4G communication, and device temperature. Experimental results show a comparison between the completion time and relative energy consumption of different types of tasks and different computing devices. While the mobile devices are always slower than a high performance workstation, GEMCloud shows that some mobile devices have performance comparable to a standard computer, while always consuming much less energy. The GEMCloud application is available for download in the Google Play store.

Starting from the GEMCloud implementation, the authors in (Funai, Tapparello, Ba, Karaouglu, & Heinzelman, 2014) presented a computational infrastructure that extends the ability of mobile devices to participate in volunteer computing through ad hoc networking. The architecture presented in (Funai, Tapparello, Ba, Karaouglu, & Heinzelman, 2014) overcomes the intrinsic requirement of Internet connectivity to participate in volunteer computing by introducing decentralized job coordinators. These job coordinators, referred to as task distribution points, are mobile devices directly connected to the Internet that are able to invite other devices to join the computation via device to device communication. Experimental results show that allowing for additional devices without Internet connectivity to participate in the computation reduces significantly the overall time required for the execution of the tasks, with only minor additional energy consumption at the decentralized job coordinators.

OPEN ISSUES AND FUTURE RESEARCH DIRECTIONS

In Section MOBILE DISTRIBUTED COMPUTING ARCHITECTURES we presented the current state of the art for distributed mobile volunteer computing research. While the different implementations have shown the feasibility and highlighted the substantial performance gains that can be achieved by exploiting personal mobile devices as additional computational elements, there are still several issues that must be considered. The main challenges arise from the intrinsic heterogeneity of resources involved in a distributed mobile system. Addressing these challenges requires the design of an efficient and reliable middleware, tailored to the requirements and challenges of a heterogeneous system. Moreover, for a successful diffusion of volunteer mobile computing, it is necessary to promote the users' participation and to reassure the users that the application will not harm their devices nor compromise their privacy or the performance of their device with regard to its primary purpose. In what follows, we describe some open issues that require additional research in order to improve the overall experience of the different elements of a distributed mobile volunteer computing system.

Table 3. Mobile volunteer computing implementations

Name	Year	Contributions	Task Distribution	Operating System	Applications
Seattle	2009	Distributed computing and general purpose learning platform	Application specific tasks	Maemo Linux	Multiple applications
BOINC	2011	Porting of the BOINC client to Android devices	Project specific tasks	Android	Multiple scientific research projects
CrowdLab	2011	Testbed architecture based on volunteer mobile resources	Application specific tasks	Android	Multiple applications
GEMCloud	2013	Distributed computing system that uses mobile devices as computing resources. Evaluation of computing power and energy efficiency of mobile devices	Heterogeneous tasks assigned at random. FIFO queue subject to user preferences.	Android	Protein structure predictions

Incentive Model

Using mobile devices can provide a substantial gain in terms of both computational power and energy consumption. However, a mobile volunteer computing architecture is based on the assumption that the devices are distributed among different users that donate their spare cycles. While there are philanthropic users that are willing to participate in research projects for major causes in the fields of medicine, science and the environment, it is expected that many participants would not allow the platform to utilize their personal devices without any limitation for free for an extended period of time. Therefore, it is important to consider some form of compensation or economic incentives that will motivate the user to participate in the distributed computation.

Traditional methods for grading and compensating users for their collaboration are based on the absolute computational power of the device, thus preferring devices with high resources over users with limited hardware. Effort-based mechanisms for resource sharing in collaborative applications have also been proposed, and have been shown to increase fairness in heterogeneous systems (Rahman, Meulpolder, Hales, Pouwelse, Epema, & Sips, 2010; Vega, Meseguer, Freitag, & Ochoa, 2013). An analysis of the strategies to pursue in order to improve volunteer participation and retention rates has been presented in (Darch & Carusi, 2010). In particular, based on a qualitative study of users in a volunteer computing project, the authors in (Darch & Carusi, 2010) argued that a volunteer architecture should include a scoring system that is easy to understand by the users and provides an accurate and reliable indication of the user's contribution to the project. Moreover, regular feedback about the distributed computation progress should be made publicly available to reassure the volunteers that the computation in which they are involved is worthwhile and is producing certified scientific results. As an example, positive results for incentives in the form of social contracts for common goals and immediate benefits have been presented in (Jassal, Yadav, Kumar, Naik, Narwal, & Singh, 2013) and (Huerta-Canepa & Lee, 2010).

In order to further enhance participation in the volunteer computing system, researchers have also moved from social mechanisms to monetary based schemes. In this regard, pricing has shown to be effective in encouraging sharing of computing devices, and several solutions have been proposed, such as Flat Rate (Courcoubetis & Weber, 2006), Auction-based (Mondal, Madria, & Kitsuregawa, 2009), Stock-Market and Micropayment approaches (Tan & Jarvis, 2008). The integration of distributed credit-based schemes with the task scheduling policy has also recently been investigated (Rius, Estrada, Cores, & Solsona, 2012). Positive indications on the usefulness of monetary incentives have been provided in (Amazon, 2015).

Several works have been proposed for increasing the participation of users in a traditional volunteer computing system. However, when considering mobile devices, the users not only will incur some cost during their contribution to the distributed computation, such as battery energy and data transmission costs, but their normal use of the mobile devices may be affected when processing tasks. Thus, it is important to revise the existing methods to evaluate the impact of the participation in the distributed computation on the user experience and remunerate the users accordingly. These incentives could form the foundation of a new business model and enhance the efficient use of computational devices.

Device Heterogeneity and Task Distribution

When dealing with devices with different capabilities in terms of power, memory and processing capabilities, it is particularly important to devise algorithms that can explore the available resources and maximize the results that can be achieved through the distributed computation. As different mobile devices have different capabilities and follow different user usage patterns, it is very difficult to group these devices according to their potential contributions to the distributed architecture and, at the same time, devise a task distribution method that is able to classify the mobile devices and distribute the computational workload accordingly.

Moreover, the way in which mobile devices connect to the volunteer distributed architecture creates additional challenges, starting from the availability of an Internet connection itself. Even when available, the heterogeneity of the network services and communication technologies reflect great variations in communication speeds and latencies that negatively affect the performance of both the mobile devices and the distributed computation infrastructure. This is especially problematic when dealing with time sensitive applications that require devices that are not only able to perform the assigned computation in a short amount of time, but that can capitalize on a fast and reliable connection to receive the task and reply with the results. As a result, scheduling tasks on an unpredictable network requires complex rules, which makes it difficult to estimate the availability and the response and transfer time of the mobile devices.

Given the above, identifying and classifying the total available resources are required for devising an efficient task distribution process. As described in (Durrani & Shamsi, 2014), the device attributes can be divided into two categories, namely static and dynamic. The static attributes reflect the intrinsic characteristics of the device and will not change over time like, for example, CPU frequency, number of cores and memory. Dynamic attributes, instead, exhibit dynamic behavior and change over time like, for example, available CPU or number of cores, network connectivity and battery level. We note that the user usage patterns can be seen as a particular dynamic attribute that affects multiple device specific resources. Clearly, static attributes are easy to retrieve because they do not change over time. However, tracking the dynamic changes in resource availability requires a suitable protocol that is able to gather this information with a certain accuracy and, most importantly, limit the impact on the user experience. For an overview of existing resource discovery algorithms for distributed computing systems, we refer the reader to (Ghafarian, Deldari, Javadi, Yaghmaee, & Buyya, 2013) and references therein.

The task distribution policy uses the collected and analyzed mobile device attributes, as well as the user usage patterns and preferences, to efficiently manage all the available resources. This process represents the core of the entire volunteer mobile computing infrastructure. This is because the task distribution dictates the performance of the entire system and can, in fact, determine the success or failure of the adoption of mobile devices as computational devices. The task distribution process is thus fundamental in determining how to divide the job into computational tasks and in finding the best criteria for assigning these tasks to the different clients. Different solutions for a traditional distributed computing system have been proposed, showing promising results in real life testing. An extensive discussion of the existing task distribution policies can be found in (Durrani & Shamsi, 2014).

While all the existing schemes for resource discovery and task distribution can be extended to support the presence of mobile devices, they have been designed focusing on standard computers. Thus, as described earlier, the different characteristics of mobile devices when compared to traditional computing devices can potentially require a substantial revision of the existing policies. Finally, the need for more intelligent algorithms that are able to divide and distribute tasks with different requirements, to predict the task execution times when using devices with different capabilities, to distribute the load accordingly, and to adapt the start and stop of the computation according to the user usage or the resource availability is considered an open problem even for a traditional volunteer computing system (Durrani & Shamsi, 2014).

Result Validation and Aggregation

A volunteer computing system relies on a divide and conquer approach in which the job is divided into several computational tasks that can be processed in parallel, and the results of the distributed computations are then merged to solve the initial problem. These types of algorithms are able to determine the quality and validity of the results only a posteriori, most of the time even after the actual merging of the results of the different tasks, potentially causing the loss of a large amount of computation. Moreover, in a scenario with heterogeneous devices that are potentially executing tasks with different complexity and requirements, it is even more difficult to aggregate and validate the results. Thus, when dividing and assigning the tasks it is important to design a mechanism to verify and, if necessary, discard erroneous intermediate partial results so that the entire computation is not wasted.

Another limitation of the existing systems is that the mobile devices submit their results only at the end of the computation. Most of the implementations presented in Section MOBILE DISTRIBUTED COMPUTING ARCHITECTURES consider the user experience as the most important design constraint, and propose different techniques to stop or migrate the computation to other devices to limit the impact of the task execution on the standard mobile device operations. In situations where the computation is terminated or the migration fails, the partial computation done by the devices is lost. Thus, a framework that exploits partially completed tasks would greatly improve the overall system performance.

Most of the existing volunteer computing systems, as well as the architectures described in Section MOBILE DISTRIBUTED COMPUTING ARCHITECTURES, consider a centralized system, with communication going through a single server or coordinator that fulfills the role of job scheduler and handles the task distribution and result validation. As a result, these systems either do not implement any result aggregation and validation mechanisms or create a considerable overhead on the server and are thus limited to embarrassingly parallel applications (Costa, Veiga, & Ferreira, 2013). Recent solutions tolerate clients' failures by assigning the same task to multiple devices and by replicating the intermediate and final output of the computations across different devices (Costa, Veiga, & Ferreira, 2013; Bruno & Ferreira, 2014). Moreover, the validation of the task results is performed at the server through replication and majority voting. According to this approach, each task has at least two replicas, running on different devices and, upon reception of sufficient results for the same task, the server is able to consider it valid if a strict majority of clients return the same output (Costa, Veiga, & Ferreira, 2013).

Security, Privacy, and Data Confidentiality

Security is an essential factor for the success of the adoption of personal mobile devices as computing elements in a distributed infrastructure. As a matter of fact, creating a secure and trustable environment is an open issue even in traditional volunteer computing systems (Durrani & Shamsi, 2014), both for the tasks coordinator and for the devices that perform the computation. On one hand, the clients need to trust the middleware of the distributed computing framework that it will not harm their devices or compromise their privacy and that it is honest in the description of the credit, processing and storage resources associated with the computation. Moreover, the task distributor needs to implement appropriate security policies so that, for example, hackers may not gain access to the resources of the mobile devices and use them for malicious activities. On the other hand, the task distributor needs to implement some trusting policies in order to discriminate malicious users that are returning false results, as well as mechanisms that prevent the users from gaining access to the content of the assigned tasks and related data. Moreover, dealing with all these problems is complicated by the fact that the devices involved in a distributed system communicate through the Internet, which is intrinsically insecure.

Several security mechanisms have been proposed in the literature in order to reduce the vulnerability of distributed computing systems to malicious attacks. In particular, result validation techniques based on voting (Anderson D., 2004), credibility (Sarmenta, 2001) and spot-checking (Watanabe & Fukushi, 2010) have been proposed and are now included in many architectures. In order to prevent malicious code distribution, many systems integrate code signing techniques. As an example, each BOINC project periodically changes its code signing key, and uses the old private key to generate a signature for the new public key (Berkeley, 2014). Techniques for preventing the intentional or accidental abuse of participating hosts by the volunteer architectures include account based sandboxing (that is, the middleware runs under an unprivileged account and it is not able to access or modify any other data on the computer) and middleware resources monitoring to detect if the resource usage is not in accordance with the application specification (Berkeley, 2014; Cappello, et al., 2005). Most of the available systems still lack solutions to protect against users accessing the content of the assigned tasks and related data, that both typically reside in cleartext in memory (Berkeley, 2014; Durrani & Shamsi, 2014). An extensive presentation of security threats for a distributed computing system has been recently presented in (Subashini & Kavitha, 2011) and (Zissis & Lekkas, 2012).

While different security methods have been proposed for a general volunteer computing system, security is still considered an open issue (Berkeley, 2014; Durrani & Shamsi, 2014; Cappello, et al., 2005). Traditional cluster and distributed computing architectures, instead, represent more controlled systems and implement complex security mechanisms (Cappello, et al., 2005). The possibility of porting some of these methods to volunteer computing systems and, consequently, the development of lightweight mechanisms for securing the communications and to guarantee data integrity over a heterogeneous volunteer system of mobile devices is still under investigation.

CONCLUSION

In this chapter, we presented recent advances in the mobile volunteer computing research field, where mobile devices are the elements that perform the computation. We described the motivations behind the adoption of personal mobile devices as computing resources and the challenges that come from their integration in a distributed system. In addition, we discussed some open issues that arise in the integration of heterogeneous mobile devices into a distributed computing infrastructure, as well as security issues and possible improvements to the task distribution process and the result validation and aggregation.

This chapter provides the research community with a comparison of the existing architectures and a description of the current open problems that will help in the design of future distributed mobile volunteer computing systems.

ACKNOWLEDGMENT

This work was supported in part by Harris Corporation, RF Communications Division, in part by UCB Pharma, and in part by the Center for Emerging and Innovative Sciences (CEIS), an Empire State Development designated Center for Advanced Technology.

REFERENCES

Agarwal, R. (2014). *DRAP: A decentralized public resourced cloudlet for ad-hoc networks.*

Amazon. (2015). *Amazon Elastic Compute Cloud (Amazon EC2).* Retrieved Jan. de 2015 from http://aws.amazon.com/ec2/

Amazon. (2015). *Amazon Mechanical Turk.* Retrieved Jan. de 2015 from https://www.mturk.com/

Anderson, D. (2004). BOINC: A system for public-resource computing and storage. IEEE/ACM GRID. Pittsburgh, PA, USA.

Anderson, D., Cobb, J., Korpela, E., Lebofsky, M., & Werthimer, D. (2002). SETI@home: An experiment in public-resource computing. *Communications of the ACM*, *45*(11), 56–61. doi:10.1145/581571.581573 PMID:12238525

Andro, B. O. I. N. C. (2010). *AndroBOINC - BOINC manager for Android phones.* Retrieved Jan. de 2015 from https://code.google.com/p/androboinc/

ARCNET. (2002). *Attached Resource Computer (ARCNET).* Retrieved Jan. de 2015 from http://www.arcnet.com/

Arslan, M. Y., Singh, I., Singh, S., Madhyastha, H. V., Sundaresan, K., & Krishnamurthy, S. V. (2012). Computing while charging: Building a distributed computing infrastructure using smartphones. ACM CoNEXT. Nice, France.

Asus. (2013). *Asus Nexus 7.* Retrieved Jan. de 2015 from http://www.asus.com/Tablets_Mobile/Nexus_7_2013/

Ba, H., Heinzelman, W., Janssen, C., & Shi, J. (2013). *Mobile computing - A green computing resource.* Shanghai, China: IEEE WCNC. doi:10.1109/WCNC.2013.6555295

Berkeley. (2011). *BOINC on Android.* Retrieved Jan. de 2015 from http://boinc.berkeley.edu/trac/wiki/AndroidBoinc

Berkeley. (2014). *BOINC's Homepage.* Retrieved Jan. de 2015 from http://boinc.berkeley.edu/

Berkeley. (Sep. de 2014). *The 10th BOINC workshop - BOINC/Android status and plans.* Retrieved Jan. de 2015 from http://boinc.berkeley.edu/trac/attachment/wiki/WorkShop14/boinc_on_android_2014.pdf

Black, M., & Edgar, W. (2009). Exploring mobile devices as grid resources: Using an x86 virtual machine to run BOINC on an iPhone. IEEE/ACM Grid Computing. Banff, AB, Canada.

Bluetooth Group. (2010). *Specification of the Bluetooth system.*

Bruno, R., & Ferreira, P. (2014). *Freecycles: Efficient data distribution for volunteer computing.* Amsterdam, The Netherlands: ACM CloudDP. doi:10.1145/2592784.2592788

Cappello, F., Djilali, S., Fedak, G., Herault, T., Magniette, F., Néri, V., & Lodygensky, O. (2005). Computing on large-scale distributed systems: XtremWeb architecture, programming models, security, tests and convergence with grid. *Future Generation Computer Systems*, *21*(3), 417–437. doi:10.1016/j.future.2004.04.011

Cappos, J., Beschastnikh, I., Krishnamurthy, A., & Anderson, T. (2009). *Seattle: A platform for educational cloud computing*. Chattanooga, TN, USA: ACM SIGCSE. doi:10.1145/1508865.1508905

Chu, D. C., & Humphrey, M. (2004). Mobile OGSI.NET: Grid computing on mobile devices. IEEE/ACM GRID. Pittsburgh, PA, USA.

Costa, F., Veiga, L., & Ferreira, P. (2013). Internet-scale support for map-reduce processing. *Journal of Internet Services and Applications*, *4*(1), 1–17. doi:10.1186/1869-0238-4-18

Courcoubetis, C., & Weber, R. (2006). Incentives for large peer-to-peer systems. *IEEE Journal on Selected Areas in Communications*, *24*(5), 1034–1050. doi:10.1109/JSAC.2006.872885

CPUBoss. (2015). *Compare CPU to see which is faster*. Retrieved Jan. de 2015 from http://cpuboss.com

Cuervo, E., Gilbert, P., Wu, B., & Cox, L. (2011). *CrowdLab: An architecture for volunteer mobile testbeds*. Bangalore, India: COMSNETS.

Darch, P., & Carusi, A. (2010). Retaining volunteers in volunteer computing projects,", vol. . *Phil. Trans. R. Soc. A, 368* (1926), 4177–4192.

Datta, P., Dey, S., Paul, H., & Mukherjee, A. (2014). ANGELS: A framework for mobile grids. AIMoC. Kolkata, India.

Dinh, H. T., Lee, C., Niyato, D., & Wang, P. (2013). A survey of mobile cloud computing: Architecture, applications, and approaches. *Wireless Communications and Mobile Computing*, *13*(18), 1587–1611. doi:10.1002/wcm.1203

Durrani, M., & Shamsi, J. A. (2014). Volunteer computing: Requirements, challenges, and solutions. *Journal of Network and Computer Applications*, *39*(C), 369–380. doi:10.1016/j.jnca.2013.07.006

Eastlack, J. R. (2011). *Extending volunteer computing to mobile devices.*

Fedak, G., Germain, C., Neri, V., & Cappello, F. (2001). XtremWeb: a generic global computing system. *IEEE/ACM CCGrid.* Brisbane, Qld.

Fernando, N., Loke, S., & Rahayu, W. (2013). Honeybee: A programming framework for mobile crowd computing. In Mobile and Ubiquitous Systems: Computing, Networking, and Services, ser. Lecture Notes of the Institute for Computer Sciences, Social Informatics and Telecommunications Engineering (Vol. 120, pp. 224-236). Springer Berlin Heidelberg. doi:10.1007/978-3-642-40238-8_19

Funai, C., Tapparello, C., Ba, H., Karaouglu, B., & Heinzelman, W. (2014). *Extending volunteer computing through mobile ad hoc networking*. Austin, TX, USA: IEEE GLOBECOM. doi:10.1109/GLOCOM.2014.7036780

Geekbench. (n.d.). *Geekbench 3: Cross-platform processor benchmark*. Retrieved Jan. de 2015 from http://www.primatelabs.com/geekbench/

Ghafarian, T., Deldari, H., Javadi, B., Yaghmaee, M. H., & Buyya, R. (2013). CycloidGrid: A proximity-aware P2P-based resource discovery architecture in volunteer computing systems. *Future Generation Computer Systems*, *29*(6), 1583–1595. doi:10.1016/j.future.2012.08.010

Gong, L. (2001). JXTA: A network programming environment. *IEEE Internet Computing*, *5*(3), 88–95. doi:10.1109/4236.935182

Grushko, C., Aharon, L., Dov, O. B., & Swisz, K. (2008). *Boincoid*. Retrieved Jan. de 2015 from http://boincoid.sourceforge.net

Hoffman, F. M., Hargrove, W. W., & Schultz, A. J. (1997). *The Stone SouperComputer*. Retrieved Jan. de 2015 from http://www.extremelinux.info/stonesoup/

HTC. (2015). *HTC Power to Give*. Retrieved Jan. de 2015 from http://www.htc.com/us/go/power-to-give/

Huerta-Canepa, G., & Lee, D. (2010). *A virtual cloud computing provider for mobile devices*. San Francisco, CA, USA: ACM MCS. doi:10.1145/1810931.1810937

IBM. (2015). *IBM Cloud*. Retrieved Jan. de 2015 from http://www.ibm.com/cloud-computing/us/en/

IDC. (2015). *International Data Corporation (IDC)*. Retrieved Jan. de 2015 from http://www.idc.com

Jassal, P., Yadav, K., Kumar, A., Naik, V., Narwal, V., & Singh, A. (2013). *Unity: Collaborative downloading content using co-located socially connected peers*. San Diego, CA: IEEE PERCOM.

KPCB. (2014). *Kleiner Perkins Caufield Byers (KPCB) Internet Trends 2014*. Retrieved Jan. de 2015 from http://www.kpcb.com/internet-trends

Liu, L., Wang, H., Liu, X., Jin, X., He, W., & Wang, Q. et al.. (2009). *Greencloud: A new architecture for green data center*. Barcelona, Spain: ICAC-INDST. doi:10.1145/1555312.1555319

Marinelli, E. E. (2009). Hyrax: Cloud computing on mobile devices using mapreduce.

Marsenne Research, Inc. (2015). *Great Internet Mersenne Prime Search*. Retrieved Jan. de 2015 from http://www.mersenne.org

Meisner, D., Gold, B., Wenisch, T., Liu, L., Wang, H., & Liu, X. et al.. (2009). *Powernap: Eliminating server idle power*. Washington, DC: ACM ASPLOS. doi:10.1145/1508244.1508269

Microsoft. (2015). *Microsoft OneDrive*. Retrieved Jan. de 2015 from https://onedrive.live.com/

Mondal, A., Madria, S., & Kitsuregawa, M. (2009). An economic incentive model for encouraging peer collaboration in mobile-p2p networks with support for constraint queries. *Peer-to-Peer Networking and Applications*, *2*(3), 230–251. doi:10.1007/s12083-009-0035-9

Nandugudi, A., Maiti, A., Ki, T., Bulut, F., Demirbas, M., & Kosar, T. et al.. (2013). *Phonelab: A large programmable smartphone testbed*. Roma, Italy: ACM SENSEMINE. doi:10.1145/2536714.2536718

Parmar, K. B., Jani, N. N., Shrivastav, P. S., & Patel, M. H. (2013). jUniGrid: A simplistic framework for integration of mobile devices in heterogeneous grid computing. *International Journal of Multidisciplinary Sciences and Engineering*, *4*(1), 10–15.

Phan, T., Huang, L., & Dulan, C. (2002). *Challenge: Integrating mobile wireless devices into the computational grid*. Atlanta, GA, USA: ACM MobiCom. doi:10.1145/570645.570679

Rahman, R., Meulpolder, M., Hales, D., Pouwelse, J., Epema, D., & Sips, H. (2010). Improving efficiency and fairness in P2P systems with effort-based incentives. IEEE ICC. Cape Town, South Africa.

Rius, J., Estrada, S., Cores, F., & Solsona, F. (2012). Incentive mechanism for scheduling jobs in a peer-to-peer computing system. *Simulation Modelling Practice and Theory*, *25*(0), 36–55. doi:10.1016/j.simpat.2012.02.007

Sarmenta, L. (2001). *Sabotage-tolerance mechanisms for volunteer computing systems. IEEE/ACM CCGrid.* Australia: Brisbane, Qld.

Satyanarayanan, M., Bahl, P., Caceres, R., & Davies, N. (2009). The case for vm-based cloudlets in mobile computing. *IEEE Pervasive Computing / IEEE Computer Society [and] IEEE Communications Society*, *8*(4), 14–23. doi:10.1109/MPRV.2009.82

Schildt, S., Busching, F., Jorns, E., & Wolf, L. (2013). *Candis: Heterogenous mobile cloud framework and energy cost-aware scheduling*. Beijing, China: IEEE GreenCom.

Shi, C., Lakafosis, V., Ammar, M., & Zegura, E. W. (2012). *Serendipity: Enabling remote computing among intermittently connected mobile devices*. Hilton Head, SC, USA: ACM MobiHoc. doi:10.1145/2248371.2248394

Subashini, S., & Kavitha, V. (2011). A survey on security issues in service delivery models of cloud computing. *Journal of Network and Computer Applications*, *34*(1), 1–11. doi:10.1016/j.jnca.2010.07.006

Szpakowski, M. (2013). *NativeBOINC*. Retrieved Jan. de 2015 from http://nativeboinc.org

Tan, G., & Jarvis, S. (2008). A payment-based incentive and service differentiation scheme for peer-to-peer streaming broadcast. *IEEE Transactions on Parallel and Distributed Systems*, *19*(7), 940–953. doi:10.1109/TPDS.2007.70778

U.S. Energy Information Administration. (2014). *Short-term energy outlook*. Retrieved 2015 from http://www.eia.gov/forecasts/steo/pdf/steo_full.pdf

Vega, D., Meseguer, R., Freitag, F., & Ochoa, S. (2013). *Effort-based incentives for resource sharing in collaborative volunteer applications*. Whistler, BC, Canada: IEEE CSCWD. doi:10.1109/CSCWD.2013.6580936

Watanabe, K., & Fukushi, M. (2010). Generalized spot-checking for sabotage-tolerance in volunteer computing systems. IEEE/ACM CCGrid. Melbourne, Australia.

Wi-Fi Alliance, P2P Task Group. (2011). *Wi-Fi Peer-to-Peer (P2P) Technical Specification, Version 1.2*.

Xu, H., Bilec, M., Schaefer, L., Landis, A., & Jones, A. (2013). *Ocelot: A wireless sensor network and computing engine with commodity palmtop computers*. Arlington, VA, USA: IGCC.

Yu, J., Williams, E., & Ju, M. (2010). Analysis of material and energy consumption of mobile phones in China. *Energy Policy*, *38*(8), 4135–4141. doi:10.1016/j.enpol.2010.03.041

Zayas, A. D., & Gómez, P. M. (2010). A testbed for energy profile characterization of ip services in smartphones over live networks. *Mobile Networks and Applications*, *15*(3), 330–343. doi:10.1007/s11036-010-0228-8

Zhang, Q., Cheng, L., & Boutaba, R. (2010). Cloud computing: State-of-the-art and research challenges. *Journal of Internet Services and Applications*, *1*(1), 7–18. doi:10.1007/s13174-010-0007-6

Zhuang, Y., Rafetseder, A., & Cappos, J. (2013). *Experience with Seattle: A community platform for research and education*. Salt Lake City, UT: GREE.

Zissis, D., & Lekkas, D. (2012). Addressing cloud computing security issues. *Future Generation Computer Systems*, *28*(3), 583–592. doi:10.1016/j.future.2010.12.006

KEY TERMS AND DEFINITIONS

Android: Android is a mobile operating system (OS) based on the Linux kernel and currently developed by Google.

Cloud Computing: Internet-based computing in which large groups of remote servers are networked in order to allow sharing of data-processing tasks, centralized data storage, and online access to computer services or resources. The term loosely define any system providing access via the Internet to processing power, storage, software or other computing services, often via a web browser. Typically these services will be rented from an external company that hosts and manages them.

Cluster Computing: Cluster Computing consists of a set of two or more computers connected into a local area network that work together so that, in many respects, they can be viewed as a single system. Usually, computer clusters have each node set to perform the same task, controlled and scheduled by software.

Distributed Computing: The use of multiple computers networked throughout a wide geographical area, or the world via the Internet, in order to solve a single computational problem. In distributed computing, a problem is divided into many tasks, each of which is solved by one or more computers, which communicate with each other by message passing.

Embarrassingly Problems: In parallel computing, an embarrassingly parallel workload, or embarrassingly parallel problem, is one for which little or no effort is required to separate the problem into a number of parallel tasks. This is often the case where there exists no dependency (or communication) between those parallel tasks.

GPU: Graphics processing unit (GPU) is a specialized electronic circuit designed to rapidly manipulate and alter memory to accelerate the creation of images in a frame buffer intended for output to a display. Modern GPUs are very efficient at manipulating computer graphics and image processing, and their highly parallel structure makes them more effective than general-purpose CPUs for algorithms where processing of large blocks of data is done in parallel.

iOS: iOS (previously iPhone OS) is a mobile operating system developed by Apple Inc. and distributed exclusively for Apple hardware. It is the operating system that powers many of the company's iDevices.

Middleware: Software that acts as a bridge between an operating system or database and applications, especially on a network.

Mobile Computing: Mobile Computing refers to the process of performing computation on a mobile device. In addition, mobile computing is used as a generic term describing the ability to use the technology to wirelessly connect to and use centrally located information and/or application software through the application of small, portable, and wireless computing and communication devices.

Mobile Device: A mobile device (also known as a handheld computer or simply handheld) is a small, handheld computing device, typically having a display screen with touch input and/or a miniature keyboard and weighing less than 2 pounds (0.91 kg). Example of mobile devices are ultra-portable computers, smartphones and tablets.

Network Simulator 3 (ns-3): ns-3 is a discrete-event network simulator for Internet systems, targeted primarily for research and educational use. ns-3 is free software, licensed under the GNU GPLv2 license, and is publicly available for research, development, and use.

Parallel Computing: Parallel computing is a form of computation in which many calculations are carried out simultaneously, operating on the principle that large problems can often be divided into smaller ones, which are then solved concurrently ("in parallel"). In the simplest sense, parallel computing is the simultaneous use of multiple computing resources to solve a computational problem.

Smartphone: A smartphone (or smart phone) is a mobile phone that runs an operating system. Smartphones typically combine the features of a phone with those of another popular consumer device, such as a personal digital assistant, a digital camera, a media player or a GPS navigation unit. Later smartphones include all of those plus a touchscreen interface, broadband internet, web browsing, WiFi, 3rd-party apps, motion sensors and mobile payment mechanisms.

Tablet: A tablet is a mobile computer with touch-screen display, circuitry and battery in a single unit. Tablets come equipped with sensors, including cameras, a microphone, an accelerometer and a touchscreen, with finger or stylus gestures substituting for the use of computer mouse and keyboard.

Task Distribution Algorithm: In parallel computing, the task distribution algorithm represents a set of rules that are used to determine how to divide the job into computational tasks, and to find the best criteria for assigning these tasks to the different clients. The task distribution algorithm can collect and analyze different informations and attributes of the clients, as well as the user usage patterns and preferences, to efficiently manage all the available resources.

Volunteer Computing: Volunteer computing is a type of distributed computing in which computer owners donate their computing resources (such as processing power and storage) to one or more scientific computation projects. More recently, volunteer computing has moved to middleware systems that provide a distributed computing infrastructure independent from the scientific computation.

ENDNOTE

1 The Stone Soup is an old folk story in which hungry strangers persuade local people of a town to give them food. It is usually told as a lesson in cooperation, especially in situations of resource scarcity.

Chapter 6
Selling FLOPs:
Telecom Service Providers Can Rent a Cloudlet via Acceleration as a Service (AXaaS)

Nathaniel Powers
University of Rochester, USA

Tolga Soyata
University of Rochester, USA

ABSTRACT

To meet the user demand for an ever-increasing mobile-cloud computing performance for resource-intensive mobile applications, we propose a new service architecture called Acceleration as a Service (AXaaS). We formulate AXaaS based on the observation that most resource-intensive applications, such as real-time face-recognition and augmented reality, have similar resource-demand characteristics: a vast majority of the program execution time is spent on a limited set of library calls, such as Generalized Matrix-Multiply operations (GEMM), or FFT. Our AXaaS model suggests accelerating only these operations by the Telecom Service Providers (TSP). We envision the TSP offering this service through a monthly computational service charge, much like their existing monthly bandwidth charge. We demonstrate the technological and business feasibility of AXaaS on a proof-of-concept real-time face recognition application. We elaborate on the consumer, developer, and the TSP view of this model. Our results confirm AXaaS as a novel and viable business model.

INTRODUCTION

Consumer use of "smart" devices is rapidly increasing due to affordability and increasing wide area network (WAN) performance (Emarketer, 2014). As the capabilities of smart phones expand parallel to the improvement in the WAN performance, so do consumers' expectations for resource-intensive mobile applications. However, mobile devices are ill-suited to execute most these applications due to their hardware limitations. Computational offloading offers a way to augment mobile computation power,

DOI: 10.4018/978-1-4666-8662-5.ch006

but it introduces a communication latency, potentially weakening or negating its advantages. Mobile-cloud computing expands the utility of mobile devices by enhancing the apparent performance of their applications. Offloading data storage and processing from mobile devices to the cloud allows a mobile device to appear more powerful than it really is (Chen, Ogata, & Horikawa, 2012; Soyata, Ba, Heinzelman, Kwon, & Shi, 2013; Cuervo, et al., 2010; Mei, Shimek, Wang, Chandra, & Weissman, 2011; Chun, Ihm, Maniatis, Naik, & Patti, 2011).

Although intensive processes are not actually being handled by the device, the requisite simplicity of the user interface effectively renders the offloading routines as transparent, leading to increasing expectations for performance by consumers, who are by now, quite used to experiencing steady improvements as the norm. An emerging class of mobile applications such as real-time face recognition, linguistic processing/translation and augmented reality (Keller, 2011; Kovachev, D., Cao, Y., & Klamma, R., 2013; Soyata T., Muraleedharan, Funai, Kwon, & Heinzelman, 2012) depend on computationally intensive methods, far surpassing the capabilities of mobile devices. Furthermore, performance improvement potential of these applications due to offloading is limited because of the added communication delays for transporting the code and data during offloading. To enable these applications, solutions based on an intermediary cloudlet device have been proposed to accelerate the computation partially at the source before it reaches the cloud (Kwon, et al., 2014; Verbelen, Simoens, DeTurck, & Dhoedt, 2012; Soyata T., et al., 2012; Satyanarayanan, Bahl, Caceres, & Davies, 2009). These techniques rely on an expensive cloudlet that has substantial computational power. Even if a mobile user makes an investment in such a cloudlet, continuous upgrades will be necessary to keep up with the increasing computational demand from evolving applications.

The commonly employed mobile-cloud model involves connecting to the cloud on a per-user basis. There is no service archetype in place which offers a standardized acceleration of computation for a large number of users. We introduce the AXaaS service model which can potentially connect millions of mobile device users to superior computational resources through the low latency links provided by Telecom Service Providers (TSPs). In our model, TSPs can be thought of as renting a cloudlet to their subscribers. This cloudlet can be orders-of-magnitude faster than one that their users can purchase. Since our target applications demand the use of this cloudlet in a burst form, the accumulated usage is actually very low. This provides an opportunity for the TSPs to aggregate these burst requests from millions of users and service them in powerful datacenters, enabling the aforementioned new class of mobile applications that are currently impossible or impractical to develop. We propose Telecom Service Providers (TSPs) as the most logical provider of AXaaS, due to their existing relationship with their users. By charging a monthly fee (e.g., TFLOPs/month), TSPs may use this revenue to offset the cost of renting computational resources from cloud operators (Amazon EC2, 2013; Azure, 2014). This model absolves the TSP of the burden of building and maintaining proprietary data centers. A variation of this model may also be realized by TSPs that do have existing cloud infrastructures, such as Verizon's Terremark (Verizon-Terremark). The central impetus is enabling universal access to superior computational resources in order to facilitate innovations in the development of mobile applications.

The rest of this chapter is organized as follows: We provide background on existing aaS models and motivate our proposed new aaS offering called Acceleration as a Service (AXaaS). Next, we detail a real-time face recognition application and identify its components that would benefit from acceleration. Based on this brief study, we make a distinctive definition of *acceleration* (which we stylize AX) and consider the types of constituting computations that would be considered AX. An example of the AXaaS model is examined along with an analysis of TSP costs and return on investment (ROI) for the TSP, followed by the implications of the AXaaS offering to end-users. A developer's perspective is discussed in detail, focusing on the development of applications under the AXaaS environment. We explore performance evaluations and make our conclusions at the end of our chapter.

BACKGROUND AND MOTIVATION

"As a service" (aaS) offerings provide convenient, configurable solutions to computational problems by allocating resources over the internet (Dsouza, Kabbedjik, Seo, Jansen, & Brinkkemper, 2012; Costa, Migliavacca, Pietzuch, & Wolf, 2012; Sandikkaya & Harmanci, 2012). To run an exciting new breed of resource-intensive mobile applications such as Real-Time Face Recognition (Powers, Alling, Gyampoh-Vidogah, & Soyata, 2014), Augmented Reality, Real-time Language Translation (Google-Translate; MS-Translator), and Surveillance, it is possible for a user to rent cloud instances. However, the steps required for such a process will discourage even the most willing user. In this section, we will introduce a framework which will enable these applications with nearly zero burden to the user.

Distinguishing AXaaS from Other aaS Services

Our profiling of the aforementioned resource-intensive mobile applications reveal their continuous access to a limited set of highly parallelizable APIs such as, Generalized Matrix-Matrix Multiplication (GEMM) and Fast Fourier Transform (FFT). These applications spend a majority of their time executing these APIs, which can be accelerated through hardware accelerators (e.g., GPUs (Nvidia CUBLAS; Nvidia CUFFT)), thereby significantly improving their performance. This observation lets us conclude that, what our targeted applications need is burst access to extremely high-intensity computation, rather than continuous access to steady, generalized computation. We observe a lack of cloud service offerings for providing generalized burst raw computation to improve the performance of these mobile applications. In this vein, we propose a new service model which shifts its focus from the application to the fundamental APIs, which are very common to many resource-intensive applications. The impact of this shift we are proposing is significant. The only parameter that the service provider has to focus on is providing these APIs in an extremely performance-improved fashion (i.e., "AX amenable"). In other words, while providing the application as a service (i.e., the SaaS model) requires expertise of this software, providing Acceleration as a Service (AXaaS) requires only expertise in optimally trafficking the data-to-be-accelerated over the internet and providing acceleration for these very common APIs. In analyzing the AXaaS model's business viability, we will show that, the acceleration that is offered as a service can dramatically improve user experience, motivating the users to pay for such a new service.

Motivation for Acceleration as a Service

To illustrate the impact of acceleration, we will assume that, a user is running a mobile-based Face Recognition (FR) application on a state-of-the-art mobile phone or tablet over a 4G cellular network. We are particularly interested in performance differences owed to computational offloading. Our assumptions on application parameters are: 1) An image size of 145 KB, 2) result data size of 8 KB for the set of recognized faces, 3) a database size of 5000 faces to be recognized from, 4) Apple iPhone 5S based on the A7 Cyclone with PowerVR G6430 GPU (iPhone-5s) (3.24 double GFLOP/s compute capability),

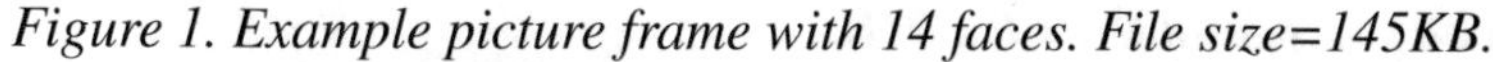

Figure 1. Example picture frame with 14 faces. File size=145KB.

and Nvidia SHIELD tablet, based on the Tegra K1 (Nvidia-Shield, 2014) (15.2 double GFLOP/s) as the mobile platforms running this application, 5) a cloud compute capability of 500 TFLOP/s and 6) WAN speed of 10Mbps (4G Network).

Scenario 1: Assuming that the entirety of the FR application and its data are hosted and executed on the iPhone, our experiments allow us to estimate a single face to be processed and recognized by the iPhone in approximately 4.6 seconds, and by the Nvidia SHIELD in approximately 0.98 seconds. The technical details of the application will be provided in the next section.

Scenario 2: The tablet uploads the captured 145KB image containing 14 faces shown in Figure 1 through a 4G network to some acceleration instance. This instance would rapidly accelerate FR functions and return the result to the mobile back over the 4G. While this approach introduces a communication delay of 249.2 ms, the resultant query time would be only 249.59 ms. Merely 390 μs of rapid computation in the cloud is required to produce a complete set of results.

Scenario 3: While the first two scenarios are based on widely available realistic cell phone network speeds today, if we assume a more futuristic 1Gbps network speed (e.g., 5G, which should be offered within a few years (3GPP-TS23.401, 2008)), the response time to recognize the 80 faces in a single frame shown in Figure 2 would be reduced to 22.84 ms total (20.44 ms is the communication cost).

While a broad array of applications can benefit from AX, the general characteristic of candidate applications for AXaaS involve a significant amount of computation for a small amount of data. For example, in a candidate remote health monitoring application (Kocabas & Soyata, 2014; Kocabas, et al., 2013; Page, Kocabas, Ames, Venkitasubramaniam, & Soyata, 2014; Page, Kocabas, Soyata, Aktas, & Couderc, 2014), Fully Homomorphic Encryption (Gentry, 2009) is used to achieve health data privacy during data transfers as well as computation in the cloud. While FHE-encrypting the data at the acquisition source, such as the patient's house, would imply a high communications overhead, converting the data at the source from AES to FHE via existing algorithms (Gentry, Halevi, & Smart, 2012) completely changes this ratio, thereby making this application AX-amenable. In such a case, the data is only converted to AES, which is a very computationally-light process (NIST:FIPS-197, 2001) by using today's modern mobile devices (iPhone-5s), however, the extremely compute-intensive FHE-based computations can

Figure 2. Example picture frame with 80 faces. File size=1.29MB.

be performed by purchasing AXaaS accelerations. Note that, this conversion also involves a substantial amount of matrix operations (Gentry, Halevi, & Smart, 2012), which we will prove to be true for almost any AXaaS candidate application.

Quantifying the User Experience: The γ

Our key question to formulate a model for AXaaS is: how do these results translate to user experience? Clearly, users will only be willing to pay for services that either enhance their business, daily lives, or for entertainment. Our careful observation of the FR algorithm shows that, it is actually fairly simple to quantify the user experience. Let us define the following metrics:

$$\gamma = K * \lambda \tag{1}$$

where K is the average faces per frame (frame density) and λ is the average frames per second (temporal density). It is clear that, γ (*total faces recognized per second*) is highly related to user experience, but what range of γ values correspond to what type of user experiences ?

In the case of our Scenario 1, when a smart phone or tablet solely recognizes faces, we calculate γ=0.22 and γ=1.02, respectively. In the case of our Scenario 2 and Scenario 3, significantly improved $\gamma \approx 50$ and $\gamma \approx 3500$ are achieved. These simple examples show that, while an advanced mobile device that is available today struggles to recognize even a single face within a second, by augmenting the FR application using AXaaS, the perceived value of the application can be drastically improved, thereby prompting the user to pay for such a service. While most users will happily call γ=10 a *Real-Time Face Recognition*, γ=10-100 will allow the application to be significantly more versatile, allowing the user to run it on highly populated scenes. Finally, γ=100-1000 and beyond will allow *Real-Time Surveillance* over very populated scenes, such as airports and public speeches of government officials.

THE FACE RECOGNITION ALGORITHM

In order to obtain a finer appreciation of the potential benefits of acceleration, we choose Real-Time Mobile-Cloud Face Recognition as our proof-of-concept application, which possesses many representative characteristics of applications that are amenable to AXaaS-based acceleration. In this section, we will study the computational aspects of our Face Recognition (FR) application in detail. The FR algorithm can be divided into three distinct phases: Face Detection, which separates and extracts the actual faces from the source frame, Projection, which converts each detected face into a set of coefficients, and Search, which compares the projection of the detected face with projections of images stored in a database and returns a result with the highest degree of similarity (Alling, Powers, & Soyata, 2015). In this chapter, we will detail each component of the overall face recognition process and will derive its computational requirements.

Detection

To execute detection we have employed the Viola-Jones object detection framework (Viola & Jones, 2001; Viola & Jones, 2001), which provides competitive real-time detection rates. This portion of the algorithm is very well studied (Yang, Kriegman, & Ahuja, 2002) and hardware-based acceleration techniques have been proposed (e.g., FPGA-based acceleration (Cho, Mirzae, Oberg, & Kastner, 2009)). Most modern smart phones have hardware accelerators for this very common function. Today's operating systems, such as Android 4.x, Ice Cream Sandwich or Jelly Bean (Andoid-API) have built-in API functions to take advantage of this hardware acceleration, albeit at a limited capacity of up to a maximum of two faces per frame. We have implemented face detection via GPUs using a frontal face cascade classifier using the open-source computer vision library OpenCV (Bradski & Kaehler, 2008) and Nvidia's CUDA (Nvidia CUDA) programming language. We find that the frame-face density (the K metric introduced in Equation) has a minimal impact on the detection rate for each frame, Table 1 shows detection times for different GPU architectures.

Table 1. Face Detection times for different devices (800×480 frame), with extrapolated estimates marked with (*).

Device	Peak GFLOPS/s	Detection Time (ms)
GTX 480	1345	58
GTX 760	2258	46
GTX 780	3977	35
TESLA K40*	4920	28
GTX Titan Z*	8122	19

Face Detection is highly parallelizable. Typically, a complete detection routine on a single frame involves the application of dozens of classifiers, leading to hundreds of millions of operations. Although we do consider detection to be a process that can significantly benefit from acceleration per se, its implementation outside of mobile devices with a detection capability might be to support extended application functions such as performing FR on scenes with high frame-face density (e.g., K≫5).

Projection

Projection has shown to be the most computation-centric component in our application. The Eigenfaces method (Turk & Pentland, 1991) in the OpenCV FaceRecognizer API (OpenCV-FaceRecognizer) calls for two nearly identical but separable components which are necessary for FR. The first is an off-line initialization which trains a multi-dimensional Eigenspace from database images. Using Principle Component Analysis (PCA) (Kim, Jung, & Kim, 2002), a set of near-orthogonal basis functions called eigenvectors are formed which allow each face in the database to be represented as a unique linear combination thereof. This allows for a significant reduction in data required to represent each face. Finally, a projection vector is generated for each image in the database and stored in a database file, along with the Eigenvectors. Application run-time requires the entirety of the database to be loaded into host memory, the local RAM of the platform running the application.

The second component occurs during FR run-time. The projection of the test face is calculated as a product of the test face (expressed as an array of floating point numbers) and the matrix of eigenvectors formed during the PCA. Since the number of eigenvectors is proportional to the number of images in the training database (equivalent in our case), it clearly follows that the number of operations (FLOPs) necessary to carry out the multiplication will increase with database size, which can be observed in Figure 3.

OpenCV implements matrix multiplication Level-3 BLAS (Basic Linear Algebra Subroutines) GEMM functions (Nvidia CUBLAS). Each call to GEMM involves uploading the test face ($8*n_{pixels}$ bytes in size) and the eigenvector array ($8*n_{pixels}*n_{components}$ bytes) to device memory (i.e., GPU memory).

Figure 3. DB-size dependent Projection times for different architectures.

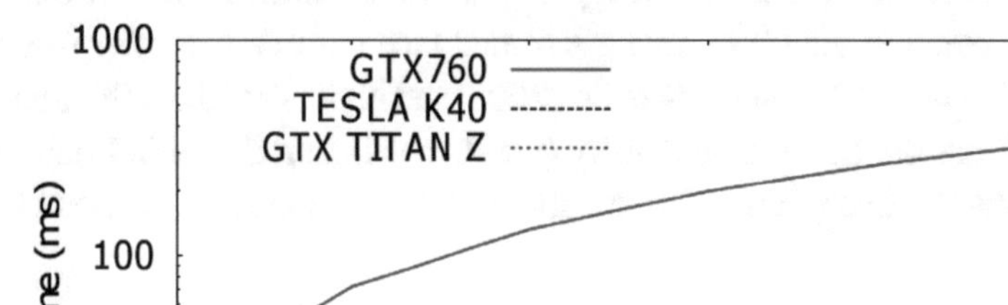

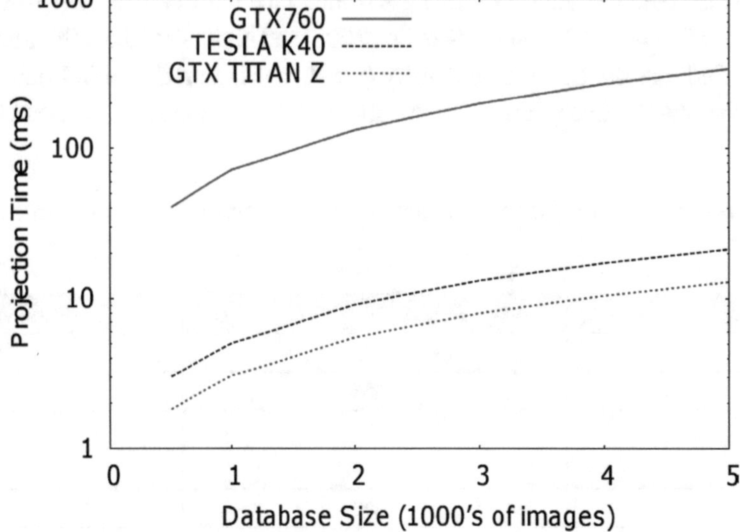

A multi-threaded kernel is then launched which computes the multiplication. Kernel execution of the matrix multiplication consists of billions (i.e., Giga) of both integer and double-precision floating-point operations (denoted as GIOP and GFLOP, respectively).

Search

The final step compares each test face projection to the collection of projections stored in the database compiled during initialization. The prediction result corresponds to the projection in the database with the minimum Euclidean distance to that of the test face. The process time of our routine increases with the square of images in the database since the number of operations scales with the product of image count and number of components (dimensions) of the Eigenspace. The largest database we have tested consisted of 5000 images, each with a resolution of 180×180 pixels, and search times are negligible (<1 ms), since this operation is not compute-intensive.

COMPUTATIONAL ACCELERATION (AX)

In this section, we clearly define the difference between generalized computation vs. computational acceleration. By acceleration (stylized AX), we literally mean a computational impulse; where an extreme number of operations are carried out within an extremely small time interval. Since our target applications spend a vast majority of their execution time in a small set of generalized API calls, such as the generalized Matrix Multiplications (GEMM) as we discussed in the previous section, executing these GEMM calls 100's or 1000's of times faster (i.e., *accelerating* them) will have a dramatic impact on the user's application experience. An example application that may benefit from acceleration is real-time machine translation (MS-Translator; Google-Translate) in which speech is captured by a mobile device, translated into another language and either displayed as text or dictated to the user as audio. Computations used in this application are based on Hidden Markov Models, which rely heavily on processing Discrete Fourier Transforms and can be explicitly expressed as matrix multiplications, or computed directly using high-level libraries such as CUFFT (Nvidia CUFFT), CUBLAS (Nvidia CUBLAS), or CUSPARSE (Nvidia CUSPARSE).

Accelerating Face Recognition

While many other compute-intensive applications can be formulated as candidates for AX, without loss of generality, we will specifically focus on real-time face recognition (FR) in this section. Not all processes that require computation would necessarily benefit from acceleration, though we have shown with our FR application that Projection particularly would, due to the vast number of calls to the GEMM subroutines. This is a highly generalized operation that may be used by an incredibly broad array of applications. There exist other operations at the same abstraction layer which could be used similarly, such as Fast Fourier Transforms (FFTs), sorting and sparse matrix operations. Our key idea in this chapter is to accelerate only such generalized common functions, rather than the application itself, thereby eliminating the necessity to rewrite acceleration routines for every new application.

In the previous section, we introduced a metric to express the user-apparent performance of our FR application (i.e., user experience). γ is the total faces recognized per second, including every frame within that second. We also identified communication and computation as the pivotal deterministic factors for achieving values for γ large enough for the application to be considered useful to users. Providing acceleration (AX) for FR would undoubtedly require the most computationally intensive cloud resources, as well as low-latency communication pipelines between the user and the cloud. Each of these factors are inherently finite in their own regard, thus do present limitations to the amount of acceleration that can be realized. By focusing AX on projection and the underlying GEMM method calls, we will see that application utility lies within the span of possibility. Equation below is an expansion of Equation which clarifies the impact of related parameters on observable performance

$$\gamma^{-1} = \frac{DATA_{up}}{\mathrm{K} * BW_{up}} + \frac{DATA_{down}}{BW_{down}} + \frac{GFLOP_{func}}{GFLOP\,/\,s} + \frac{RTT}{\mathrm{K}} \tag{2}$$

where K represents the frame-face density (in faces per frame), *RTT* (round trip time) represents the network latency, $DATA_{up}$ and $DATA_{down}$ are the uploaded data and downloaded results, along with the bandwidths of the uplink and downlink (BW_{up} and BW_{down}). $GFLOP_{func}$ and *GFLOP/s* represent the total number of GFLOPS required to execute the required functions and the computational speed (in GFLOP per second), respectively.

To maximize γ, we seek the maximization of each term's denominator (upload/download network transfer rates and computation rate). These are the most obvious. Notice that, by increasing the frame-face density K, we can affect an increase in γ by decreasing the ratio of uploaded data to the complexity of summary computation. Maximization of γ may also be sought by minimizing the numerators in each term (upload/download data size as well as contributions from *RTT*). $GFLOP_{func}$ represents the computational cost of a subroutine, for our case, detection, projection, and search, which might be reduced by increasing algorithmic efficiency. Figure 4 shows achievable γ as a function of cloud compute capability, network data rates/latencies as well as frame-face density. Data sizes are as specified previously.

Limitations of AX

The most obvious impediments to real-time performance are the bandwidth limitations and latencies associated with the transport layer. Considerations must be given to radio delays (i.e., 3G/4G/5G), IP Back-haul Transport latencies within the mobile service architecture and the connection between serving gateways (i.e., GGSN/PDNGW) and AX domains. One variant of the AX model places cloud domains in the internet by which they are accessed through a multi-hop connection. While this allows for universal access, it introduces the same IP delays associated with the classical mobile-cloud model (Wang, Liu, & Soyata, 2014; Soyata T., Muraleedharan, Funai, Kwon, & Heinzelman, 2012).

Another possible variant might imagine AX domains as having a direct connection to serving gateways, similar to IMS service provisioning (3GPP-TS23.228). While the 4G LTE Advanced standard claims to offer mobile peak rates up to 100 Mbps, most TSP migrations to the network technology in the U.S. are just beginning. However, we may reasonably assume a gradual increase in network performance and QoS expectations as they evolve.

Figure 4. Relationship between γ *and cloud compute capability on various network generations, for FR application using a 5000-image database. The image in Figure 1 is assumed for WiFi and Figure 2 for all other networks. Network metrics are provided in (BW, RTT), e.g., 100 Mbps bandwidth and 50 ms Round Trip Time.*

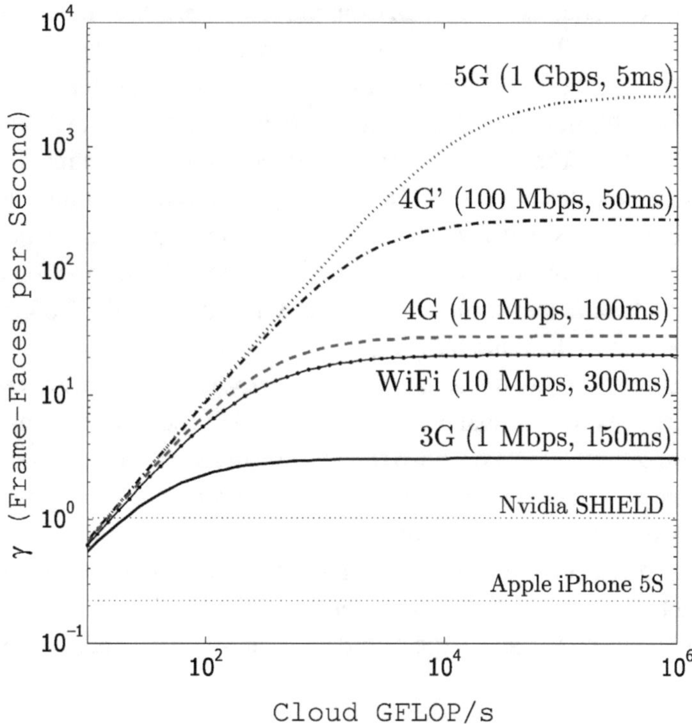

What Figure 4 illustrates clearly is that, 3G network speeds offer little to no acceleration potential for K=1 (one face per frame) in comparison to local execution on a mobile device. Single-face FR requests processed over 3G on a cloud instance even with a PFLOP/s capability barely approach γ=0.5, far from the baseline performance of the Nvidia SHIELD tablet. Each generation of network standards shows dramatic positive contributions to performance for any K, given a reasonably powerful cloud (10–100 TFLOP/s). Furthermore, each subsequent generation approaches a performance limit at much higher cloud compute capability, allowing for future exploitation of advancing computational resources.

Executing and Aggregating AX Requests

We consider a hypothetical cloud architecture of tightly coupled instances whose sole purpose is to execute AX Requests that are coming from *AX-aware* mobile application code. The nature of acceleration requires these computations to occur rapidly and relatively sparsely. We envision a large majority of these requests to execute on GPUs, as they can be utilized in a highly parallel fashion and offer competitive computational capacity for complex processes. Remote access to GPU clusters can be provided by routing traffic from TSP packet data network gateways (PDN-GW) over the internet to AX servers in the cloud. The Head Node in the cluster would be responsible for running the host-side AX requests and delegating requests to devices within the cluster architecture. NVIDIA GPUs are structured in streams, which contain the processes of memory transfers and kernel launches. These streams can be run concurrently in Fermi and Kepler-based GPUs. AX would require the exploitation of this capability to maximize the arithmetic intensity of subroutines and serve multiple users' requests without delays related to process queuing.

The traversal of two AX requests through an example cluster are shown in Figure 5. We see the receipt of a valid AX request for GEMM at the Head Node, including the ID of the requesting device, the function to be performed, and the data on which the function is to be performed (A). Also included is an indication of what database information is required for the computation (*B, which for our purposes represents the FR eigenvector). The function is called into an open CUDA stream on a device, executed and returned to the user (indicated as "Reply" in Figure 5). Also present at the Head Node is a request for an FFT subroutine (denoted as "cufft" (Nvidia CUFFT)) along with all the requisite data. Supposing a higher Computational Quality-of-Service (CQoS) for this device ID, the function is spread over several streams, the graphic of which is meant more to reinforce the concept of CQoS, not the particulars of implementation with respect to the function type.

Multiple AX requests could be aggregated and spread across available resources intelligently by the AX execution *run-time* to ensure minimal response times and fairness for each user. Pushing a request forward to a cloud instance with a device whose streams are already saturated would result in undesired delays. By adding machine instances to the AX pool, or increasing the efficiency of device utilization, the potential for reliable acceleration for any number of subscribers increases. Since we envision a broad range of applications working simultaneously, we grant that resource awareness and allocation is critical in preserving the integrity and performance potential of the service. It may be possible to dedicate portions of the cloud hardware to handle specific data requests (e.g., dedicated GEMM instances or

Figure 5. Example structure of routed AX Requests and Replies.

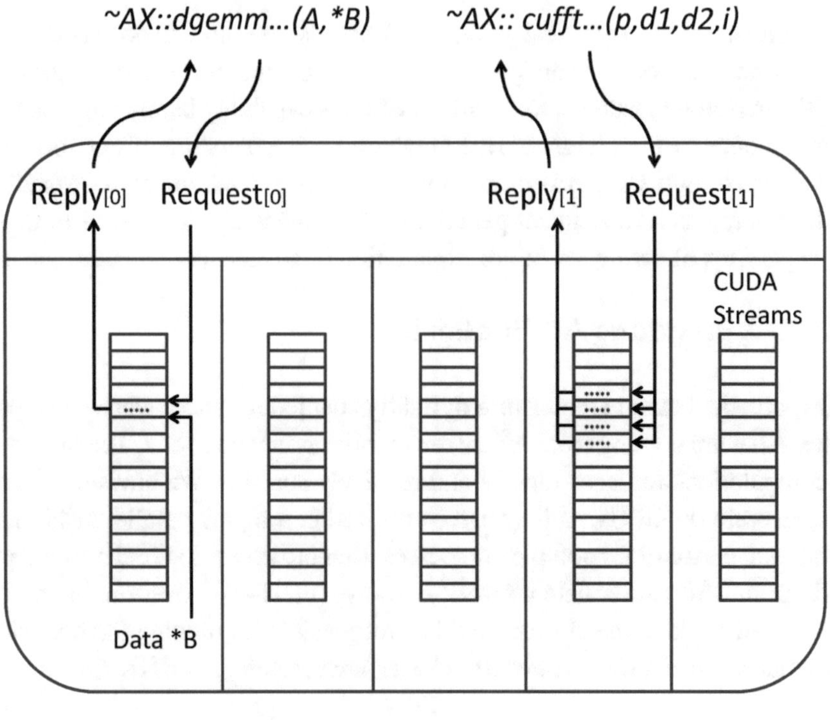

~AX::dgemm...(A,*B)
~AX:: cufft...(p,d1,d2,i)
Reply[0] Request[0]
Reply[1] Request[1]
CUDA Streams
Data *B

dedicated FFT instances). Alternatively, hardware accelerators, instead of computers, may be used to accelerate commonly used AX requests (e.g., FPGA-based (Cho, Mirzae, Oberg, & Kastner, 2009)). As the variety of applications grows, we envision the developers to tailor their code to the accelerated APIs to provide higher-performance applications.

AXaaS: ACCELERATION AS A SERVICE

Our AXaaS model formulates the computational acceleration (AX) for mobile applications (detailed in the previous section) as a billable service (aaS) by the TSP. AXaaS proposes to offer incentives to every participating party: I) TSP, II) consumer, and III) the developer, but begins with a sensitivity to the demands of consumers. Mobile device users simply want better applications and better performance. Developers need an architecture in which these applications and levels of performance can be realized. Cloud operators possess the computational resources to make this happen, however a unified structure does not exist among these entities with a focus on computation. Although this type of support can be implemented on an individual basis, we envision universal availability to enable the widespread adoption of the AXaaS model.

We conceptualize the TSP as the central component necessary for bringing AX to the mainstream. By renting cloud resources on behalf of customers, computational acceleration can be made available to millions of existing TSP customers through a simple augmentation of a monthly service agreement. As developers begin to understand how far the performance boundaries can be pushed, they will flood the market with applications and programming interface extensions and optimizations designed to take advantage of the AX potential. Spurring competition among developers to create and release the "next big thing" would ensure no shortage of options for the consumer. The increasing diversity and utility of applications will attract customers to AXaaS-enabled applications, thereby leading to service subscriptions.

The status of AXaaS today is no different than the introduction of the monthly data-throughput plans, which did not see widespread adoption until the emergence of exciting services that absolutely required more throughput. Movie or music downloads, live-streamed football, baseball, soccer games etc. made these plans a "must" for many users. Such wide adoption prompted TSPs to offer ever-increasing data-throughput levels in their monthly plans to compete with each other. We see the potential of AXaaS being very similar to these services, with the exception of the service focus: *computation*. Existing services only focus on shuttling the data in and out of the mobile device, since the required computation can easily be achieved by the mobile device (e.g., streamed movies). With AXaaS, an additional major constraint is placed on the application: *computation*, which forces portions of the application execution to take place outside the mobile device. AXaaS intelligently decouples two portions of computation: I) general computation, which can easily be achieved on the mobile device, and II) accelerable computation, which is much less data intensive, but substantially more compute-intensive. The AXaaS model is based on the observation that only this second portion needs acceleration and can be obtained from the TSP *as a Service*, while the first part can comfortably take place on the mobile device.

An illustration of the relationship between the consumer, TSP, and cloud operator is given in Figure 6. We see the TSP as a customer to the cloud operator, and as a service broker to its own customers (i.e., the consumer). This model is desirable since the TSP already possesses a vast customer base. It is relatively easy for the TSP to increase mobile device users' awareness of new products and services. Additionally, the TSP already possesses a robust communication network which reaches millions of mobile device users. There already exist cases where 4G is faster than WiFi (Huang, et al., 2012) and with the growth of LTE infrastructure, we expect this disparity to grow. By containing the majority of IP traffic on the TSP network, users are afforded greater connectivity, mobility and speed in comparison to a traditional multi-hop internet connection. Lastly, the TSP has the means to procure the amount of cloud resources necessary to service a large number of users.

TSP VIEW OF AXaaS

The TSP could be considered as the arbiter of resource sharing and task allocation. By purchasing Computing platform instances from cloud operators (e.g., AWS (Amazon EC2, 2013)), or using their own resources (e.g., Terremark (Verizon-Terremark)), a meta-device can be established whose sole purpose is to execute generic Subroutines such as matrix multiplication in support of new compute-intensive applications. AX Requests called through an API layer need only be routed through the existing wireless broadband Network to an instance of AXaaS hardware. When speaking of the TSP, we assume a tier 1 network provider, due to their centrality to the internet backbone, along with their freedom from having to purchase transit services. This does not omit lower tier ISPs as potential AXaaS providers, though they may be faced with additional transit costs and larger communication overheads, thereby limiting their effectiveness in providing AX services.

Resource Acquisition

The Service Level Agreement (SLA) defines a commitment by the cloud providers to provide customers with consistent and reliable accessibility to purchased resources. This is centered on *availability* and *operational up-time*. AXaaS calls for an extension of the SLA to provide consistent and reliable *performance* in the acceleration of processes, which is at the heart of what AXaaS aims to provide. Quality of

Figure 6. The AXaaS model showing the basic AX transport scheme (AX Request and Replies). User Equipment (UE) communicates with LTE nodes (eNodeB) which tether to the IP backbone via Serving and Packet-Data Network Gateways (SGW/PDN-GW). IP traffic is then routed to the nearest AXaaS Head node which delegates resources in the GPU cluster to process AX requests. AX replies are routed via the same path.

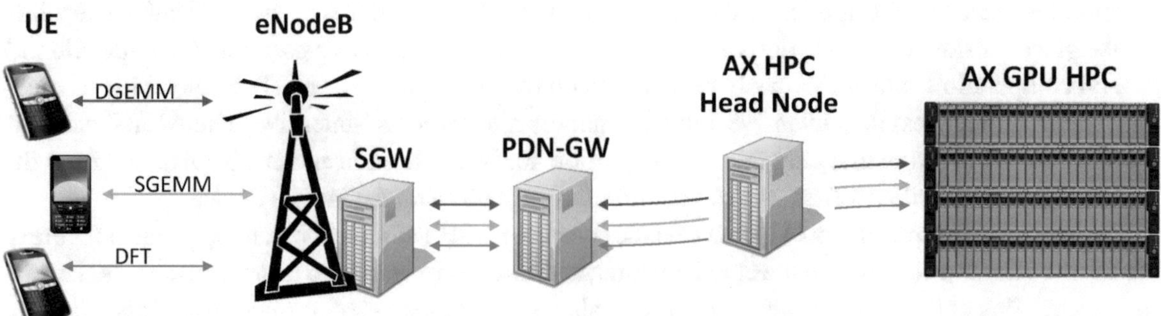

Service (QoS) provisions seek to ensure the efficiency, speed and reliability of communication between entities over networks. Due to the nature of the proposed service model, QoS must also play a crucial role in ensuring maximum performance.

Since we envision the TSP as a broker, the AXaaS model contains two distinct layers: The first is the relationship between the TSP and cloud provider(s) in which resources are allocated, configured, monitored and maintained. Contractual agreements at this level (SLA and QoS) would have to be sufficient for the TSP to satisfy the aggregation of terms set forth on the next level, which is the relationship between the TSP and users. The users' expectations for accessibility and performance must be met in order for subscription and the use of accelerated applications to be advantageous. Separating the service model in this way allows each player to focus on their own area of expertise: cloud providers focus on maintaining their infrastructure on behalf of the TSP, and the TSP focuses on connecting subscribers to resources and handling the communication of data.

As an example formation of an AXaaS cloud, we consider Amazon Web Services who offers flexible, configurable instance types (Amazon-EC2-Pricing; EC2-Instance-Types). AXaaS applications would require high compute-capable instances with GPUs. We suggest a cluster of G2 (GPU compute) instances which can be launched into a common placement group with low latency networking. For our cost analysis we will use instances launched in the U.S. East Region, and specify the instance types as Heavy Utilization Reserved (EC2-Reserved-Instances). These instances have high availability and lower long term costs for the TSP, which can be calculated using the AWS Simple Monthly Calculator. Included are one-time Reserved Instance fees, monthly EC2 instance fees and estimated Data-Out transfer fees for 25 TB. Altogether, this cluster would theoretically allocate a peak 1.3 dEFLOPs (double-precision Exa FLOPs) or 30.1 sEFLOPs (single-precision Exa FLOPs) per month to a subscriber pool at a cost of $3,089.80 to the TSP.

Infrastructure and Personnel Costs

We presume that all cloud-side infrastructure maintenance is handled by the cloud provider in accordance with an SLA. The placement of the instances used for AXaaS must be considered with a perspective on application performance, not just capacity. It would be highly recommended to dedicate all instances within an AXaaS cluster to servicing only AXaaS requests. Programming the clusters for maximum performance requires the employment of various abstraction levels for API subroutines. We have shown previously that the use of these libraries (e.g., CUBLAS) leads to acceleration. Integrating applications with these libraries will be left to the AX developers. TSPs will need to invest in a software team to maintain these libraries and their interfaces for the developers.

Tiered Service Offerings

We conceptualize that the TSP offers AX in tiers using operation counts (FLOPs/mo), bundled with the existing data-throughput plans (GB/mo). Since the plan model graduates in user cost, we assert that it must also graduate in observable performance. We call upon the γ metric we introduced in Equation to assume this function, and frame our tier model around it. We suggest that each higher tier incorporates increasing QoS assurances for network performance (NQoS) and computation performance (CQoS), both of which limit the achievable values for γ. NQoS may be mitigated using various QCI Priorities for AX traffic (3GPP-TS23.401, 2008), via a subscription Tier identifier on the user's mobile device.

Table 2. Subscriber AX plan tiers showing subscriber cost, allocated operation count, Compute-Quality of Service guarantee (CQoS) and Network-Quality of Service guarantee (NQoS).

Tier	I	II	III	IV	V
Monthly Fee (F)	\$10	\$15	\$30	\$50	\$100
TFLOPs Allocation (T)	10	20	40	80	160
GFLOPs/s (CQoS)	80	200	2700	14K	27K
Mbps (NQoS)	5	10	25	50	100

Its function would be to ensure a network transfer rate at least as high as that which is specified. CQoS may be controlled using the same Tier identifier, which would channel AX requests to appropriate GPU instances in the cloud. The quantification of subroutine performance would necessarily be a developmental issue, requiring some testing on the basis of application and platform. An example tiered plan is outlined in Table 2 with an outline of the evolution of advantages.

Tier I: Baseline tier for the casual user offering sufficient acceleration for AX Applications.
Tier II: Same as Tier I, except 2x volume and rate (high-end user).
Tier III: Much higher computational volume and assured network rate, permitting much higher γ values.
Tier IV: Computational volume, and assured network rate, along with γ increase substantially.
Tier V: Maximum computational volume and assured network rates, meant for high profile subscribers with exceptionally demanding applications.

ROI Analysis

To offset the cost of a cluster, the TSP must consider the sum of monthly fees and number of subscribers for each tier. If there are *N* tiers, and each tier *n* has *S* subscribers paying a monthly fee of *F* and the cluster presents a monthly cost of *C*, the gross monthly revenue R generated by the cluster can be calculated using Equation 3. For profitability, *R*>0 must be satisfied.

$$R = \sum_{n=1}^{N} \left(S_n F_n \right) - C \tag{3}$$

As a general principle, we can relate cluster computation allocation similarly. If *T* is the monthly TFLOPs allocation for each tier *n*, and *X* is the maximum theoretical TFLOPs that the cluster can compute monthly, we describe the percent allocation $Alloc_{\%}$ in Equation 4.

$$Alloc_{\%} = \frac{100}{X} \sum_{n=1}^{N} (S_n T_n) \tag{4}$$

To provide an example of the effect of tier distribution we will take four distribution types: *Light*, *Medium*, *Heavy*, and *Balanced*. Refer to Table 3 and Figure 7 which suppose there are 27,000 subscribers to a cluster with a maximum of 1.3M available double-precision TFLOPs per month (i.e., 1.3 dEFLOPs).

Table 3. Allocation and Revenue effects of Tier Distributions.

Distribution	Light	Medium	Balanced	Heavy
Monthly Revenue	$510K	$850K	$996K	$1.4M
Comp. Allocation	56.0%	98.7%	134%	184%
Gross Profit @ 27K	99.4%	99.6%	99.7%	99.8%
Marginal Sub. #	164	99	84	62
Users at 100%	48K	27K	20K	14.6K
Revenue at 100%	$909K	$850K	$737K	$734K
Profit at 100%	99.7%	99.6%	99.6%	99.6%

Taking the *Medium* distribution as an example, we see that the TSP would need at least 99 subscribers to the cluster to break even (Marginal Sub. #). We also see that 27,000 subscribers in a Medium distribution across the tiers allocates 98.7% of the cluster compute capability in TFLOPs per month, and would generate approximately $850K in revenue at a gross margin of 99.64%. Focusing subscribers at the lower-usage level results in less impressive revenues for a given subscriber count, however leaves computational headroom for a greater number of additional subscribers. At 100% allocation, the *Light* distribution offers the best of revenues and profit margins.

Figure 7. Visualization of Tier Distributions in Table 3.

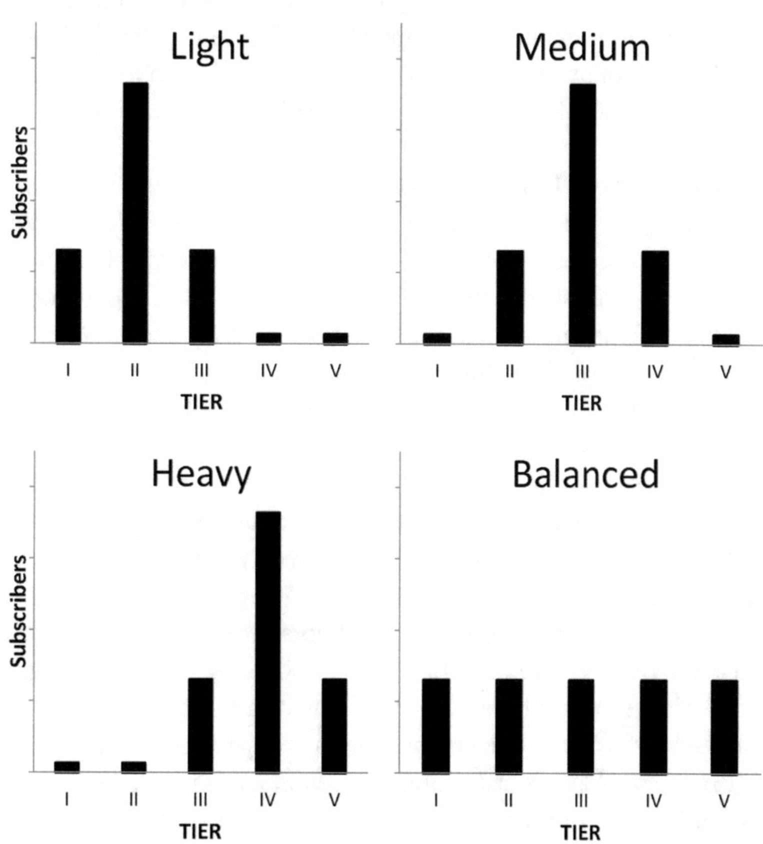

In all cases we are seeing impressive potential revenues and favorable gross margins. It is clear that launching a greater number of clusters to service even more subscribers in multiple regions will result in increased architectural complexity, but also much greater revenues. This section is not meant to be an exhaustive ROI analysis, but rather an initial demonstration of the potential of the AXaaS model. A complete ROI assessment will most definitely include many other considerations, including personnel expenses, which is beyond the scope of this chapter.

END-USER VIEW OF AXaaS

The impetus for a consumer to purchase a product involves its relative utility and cost. If there is an awareness of new significantly useful applications and services, the next question almost invariably is, "how much do they cost ?" The likelihood of a user to continue using a particular product relates to how well it performs and satisfies the user's needs. Useful applications that perform poorly may quickly be relegated to the dust bin. Subscription to AXaaS could be made quite easily by selecting it as an enhancement to an existing data plan. Since each device on the TSP network is identified by its mobile phone number, and is unique and wholly known by the TSP, device registration would be simple. A painless registration experience on the part of the user would enhance overall satisfaction with the service.

Energy Consumption Implications of AXaaS

Users prefer mobile applications with low energy consumption. Since computation requires energy, and our application requires large amounts of computation, we seek a quantifiable understanding of the impact of AX-enabled applications on the energy consumption of a mobile device. We will calculate the power consumption of AX enabled applications in two different scenarios.

- **Mobile-Device-Only Energy Consumption:** We will consider the iPhone 5S, whose battery capacity is approximately 6 Wh (1,570 mAh) (iPhone-5s), or 21,600 Joules. We estimated previously, the iPhone 5s processed a single FR routine in 4.6 seconds (i.e., γ=0.22). Reported by (Moto-X), the Apple A7 processor consumes 520 mA during floating-point operations (1.98 W @ 3.8 V battery voltage). This implies that the device would consume 9.09 Joules of energy in this 4.6 s face recognition interval. Therefore, the 21,600 Joule battery would be sufficient for 3 hours of continuous face recognition at the mere rate of γ=0.22, which will not generate any significant amount of interest for this application.
- **Mobile-AX Energy Consumption:** Let us calculate the energy consumption in the AX-enabled setting. In this scenario, the mobile device would still consume energy to capture an image from its camera, send it to the cloud via the telecom link, and receive the results. We will pick the 4G scenario in Figure 4 (10 Mbps and 100 ms). To process the image in Figure 1 (K=14), the phone would require 250 mJ of energy (116 mJ to send the 145KB image over the 4G link, during which the power consumption is 1W (Zhang, et al., 2010), and 50 mJ for image capture on highly-optimized hardware, and 84 mJ for idle time and to receive the results). This translates to γ=42 at a 0.75 W power consumption, and a battery life of 8 hours for continuous operation. These results show another favorable property of the AX-based acceleration: The *power efficiency* of the application changes from $9.09W/\gamma$ (i.e., Watts per γ) to $18mW/\gamma$, a 500x improvement (i.e., 1.98/0.22 vs. 0.75/42, respectively).

Application Access

Familiarity drives accessibility for a user. We suggest an access method that differs in no part from that which already exists. AX-enabled applications may be listed in their own category and be visible to all users regardless of their AXaaS subscription status. It is important to be able to investigate the range of possibilities before making a decision to subscribe. Non-subscribers who attempt to download an AX application could be redirected to an informational site on the TSP network which describes AXaaS and the ways subscription is necessary to power the application. After subscribing, the entire experience should be absolutely transparent. Besides having the ability to download and execute AXaaS applications, there should be no other indication that anything different has occurred. All application interactions should happen through the usual user interface, and the AXaaS performance guarantee would ensure a seamless experience.

Acceleration in Tiers

Since acceleration is tiered and priced by number of computations per month, the user must consider application use as an exhaustible resource. This way of thinking is quite familiar, as most data plans involve a finite capacity for data transfer. What the user would see in order to evaluate the economy of AXaaS is the number of AX requests they expect to be able to perform per month. This exact unit of measure could differ among TSPs. We suggest that this be a highly visible feature in each application (i.e., an AX-meter), integrated by developers, meant to enable a clear understanding of the application's consumption of billable computation. For users with multiple AX applications, which may not necessarily consume the same amount of computation per request, the client-side API layer must keep track of all usage and report that to the device so all applications may be updated accurately.

DEVELOPER VIEW OF AXaaS

Developers intent on providing state-of-the-art applications must immediately see the benefit of AXaaS. One simplified perspective is that applications reach a point of execution in which a function or group of functions are launched in a computational "black box" that resides in the cloud (AX servers). Since this "black box" consists of CUDA capable GPUs, there exists an array of device API libraries already authored and optimized. Client-side API libraries can be developed in order for mobile applications to remotely invoke function calls in the AX servers. A generalized model is desired for acceleration in which high abstraction subroutines such as CUBLAS (Nvidia CUBLAS) or CUFFT (Nvidia CUFFT) are readily available supporting a broad range of data types and sizes.

Acceleration API (AXAPI)

Considering the acceleration of FR, we begin when a mobile device has performed detection on a source frame from its camera and applied the requisite pre-processing. At this point projection must be offloaded to the cloud. In order for this to occur, the mobile device and the cloud must speak a similar language. In the context of FR, the mobile device must pass the test face data to the cloud, along with instructions specifying the type of process that should be executed on that data.

We suggest the employment of an AX-specific application programming interface (AXAPI) in order for seamless communication and interpretation of data and instructions between devices and the cloud. This would enable the mobile device code in our example to package and upload the test face data, along with an instruction for the cloud to perform GEMM in a single function call. It is obvious that the cloud must be configured and programmed to execute GEMM, and must also be preloaded with the database and Eigenvector. We suppose the Eigenvector is small enough to permanently reside in GPU Global or Constant memory, and is therefore immediately accessible to the GEMM kernel. Supposing the cloud software is ever aware of its resource utilization, it may select the most appropriate device and structure by which a kernel can be launched. The projection vector would then be calculated in a matter of milliseconds. Once a result is determined, it would be formatted and packaged for the return trip to the device which launched the request.

Ranging applications may involve the use of various data types such as single-precision float, complex or integer as well as varying provisional bit depths and decimal resolutions. The implication of the data type and bit depth is the time in which the computing device will take to execute the process. Reducing the bit depth of data by a factor might theoretically reduce the memory bandwidth usage and kernel execution time. Since Nvidia GPUs are inherently optimized for floating point calculations, AX calls with integer data types may in fact be better handled by CPUs, depending on the nature of the problem. General performance may be optimized by having AXAPI route calls to either GPU or CPU hardware such as the Xeon Phi coprocessor (INTEL-XeonPhi), depending on the characteristics of the data to be computed and the nature of the algorithm handling the computation. The use of the AXAPI to enable accelerated applications would simplify exploitation of cloud resources and allow the remaining application functions that do not require acceleration to be executed on mobile devices. We have outlined an example scenario in our background section, in which a mobile device uses acceleration to bypass its computational limitations in order to run a real-time FR application.

Application Framing

Designing applications to take advantage of AXaaS would involve integrating API layer function calls (i.e., AXAPI, as we described previously) at appropriate locations within application code. Having standardized client-side and host-side AX libraries is imperative for ensuring the ease of integration. Wrapping CUDA library functions into a higher abstraction layer would facilitate the entire process. Adapting code to the underlying architecture must be given special attention. Establishing a environment containing tier-controlled delegation of subroutines with varying performance expectations must also be considered in order to reinforce the efficacy of the performance-based tiered plans established by the TSP.

To preserve ease of integration, we imagine the developers to expect minimal modifications of code to enable process offloading. For example, the OpenCV object detection function *detectMultiScale* (OpenCV-FaceRecognizer) could be executed remotely by wrapping the function and its arguments within an AX context. Function *AXdetectMultiScale* in AXAPI might be sufficient by packaging the function arguments along with a function identifier for the AX cloud. The idea is to allow the feel of calling functions locally, with the resulting code executing remotely.

There are some potential third-party GPU cluster development tools readily available to provide a seamless integration of CUDA within a high performance cluster (HPC). While still under development, one possible solution is rCUDA (Duato, Pena, Silla, Mayo, & Quintana-Orti, 2011), which is a middleware aiming to virtualize available CUDA resources in a cluster and offers competitive performance and efficient resource usage over low latency networks. rCUDA seeks to enable the remote exploitation of GPU hardware through the use of an API layer, which is the exact framework we seek for AXaaS. Recent work in the matter by (Sait & Vijayalakshmi, 2014) has shown excellent performance of the virtualized platform with respect to native performance.

Transporting the Application Data

Figure 8 shows the nature of each component of the Projection function of the FR application on the GTX760 GPU. Our current FR projection method involves a large communication overhead across the PCI bus. Nearly 75% of the total projection time is attributed to memory transfer from host to device. In most cases, approximately 99% of all data transferred to device memory is the Eigenvector array. The projection vector generated by the multiplication is also relatively small and contributes minimally to the overall process time. Considerations such as this must be given during the design of applications framed by an acceleration methodology.

Even though the execution time of GEMM is proportional to the database size in our experiments, we do not see execution rate reflecting the intrinsic numerical power of the device until the data set grows large. The theoretical peak of GTX760 is 2258 single-precision GFLOP/s and 86.8 double-precision GFLOP/s. Figure 8 shows that the rate at which computations are performed by GEMM grows rapidly with the number of computations (database size) and appears to approach 86 GFLOP/s, which is 98% of the device's theoretical peak.

None of these results are particularly surprising. What they do provide is a reliable performance benchmark and insights into potential optimizations. Currently, GPU programmers are used to these concepts of 1) shuttling the application data back and forth between the host (CPU) and the device (GPU), 2) the consideration of the compute capability and double vs. single precision computation peaks, 3) GPU memory bandwidth. The AXaaS is a natural expansion of these concepts, where the GPUs reside in the cloud and should be fairly easy to get used to in terms of application development.

Figure 8. Duration and ratio of Projection call components (left), and execution rate of GEMM on the Nvidia GTX 760 (GK104).

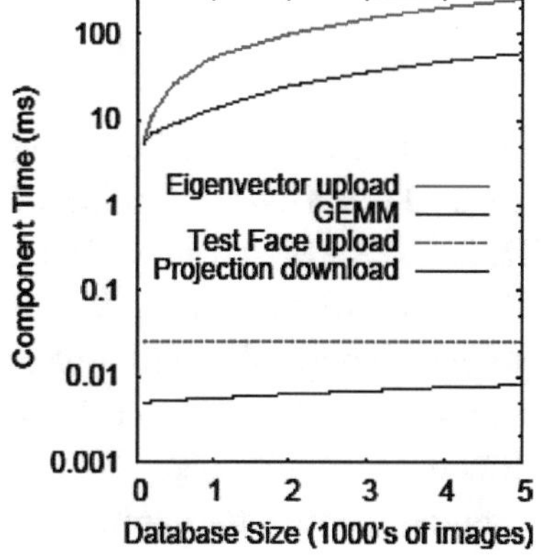

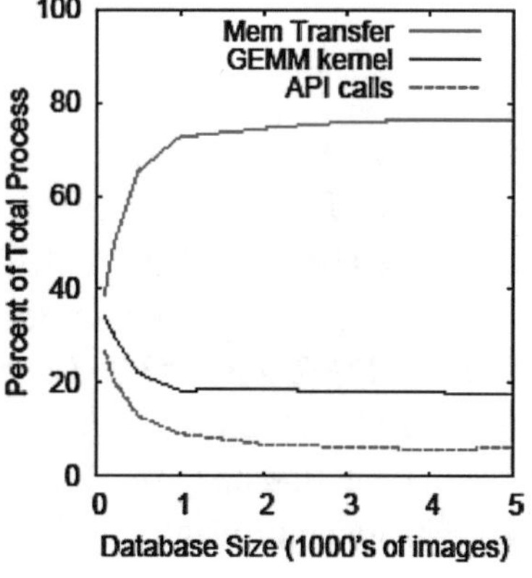

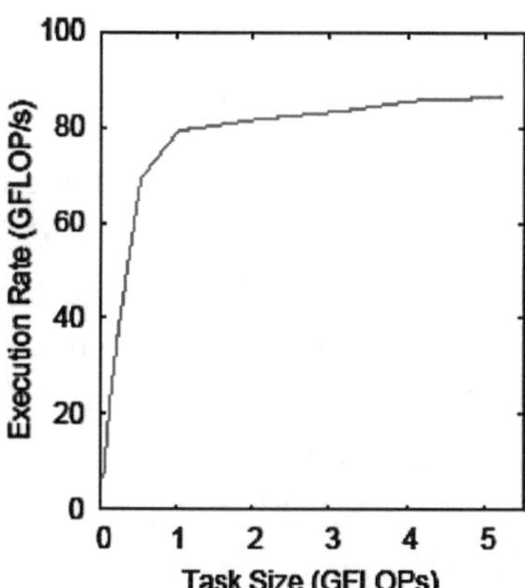

Granularity of AX Requests

The smallest computational quantum in our FR application is the executing GPU kernel (Kirk & Hwu, 2010). Each kernel exists independently of all others and requires no cross-communication as a projection relies on unique data (the test face). We consider acceleration as a multi-user environment involving structured, asynchronous calls to specific acceleration functions. Maximizing performance for multiple users would involve spreading requests across streams and devices in such a way that will avoid queuing. One could consider larger, more complex AX request types that would benefit from finer grained parallelism, in which the process is spread across streams by batching kernels or even across multiple devices, depending on the breadth of the calculation. By applying a heuristic of task and data parallelism, the architecture of the GPU cluster can be efficiently profiled and utilized by the developer in order to provide minimal response times. Data parallelism will affect the occupancy of computing devices on a request basis. Task parallelism may be achieved with a sensitivity to the effects of occupancy and immediate resource availability.

Distribution

The marketplace for AXaaS applications should have visibility to TSP/AX subscribers alone. It would not make sense to advertise architecture-dependent applications to users without front-end access to that architecture. Usual distribution methods such as iTunes, Google Play or the Windows Phone App Store might be integrated with a AX-awareness that filters the list of displayable applications according to the AX subscription status of the browsing device in order to control for illegitimate downloads. Alternatively, applications that are downloaded to a non-subscriber's device could be directed by the API upon launching to the TSP AXaaS subscription domain. Another solution may be that the TSP hosts a proprietary AX application repository in which all TSP subscribers may browse and research applications, but only AX subscribers may purchase and download.

PERFORMANCE EVALUATION

In this section, we will evaluate the performance of AXaaS in a simulated mobile-cloud platform.

Experimental Setup

We identified the performance of individual FR subroutines by profiling our FR application using Nvidia Nsight Visual Studio Edition (Nvidia-VisualStudio). The platform used was a 64-bit Windows 7 Professional workstation with one Intel Core i7-4770K CPU @3.50GHz, 32GB RAM and an NVIDIA GTX 760 (GK104 architecture) GPU. The application was authored in C++ and compiled using Visual Studio 2010, OpenCV Library 2.4.8 and CUDA Toolkit v5.0. To supply the FR application with image data, we used an LG Nexus 4 running Android 4.2 Jelly Bean which can perform face detection using a built-in API, although it is only capable of detecting up to two faces per frame. Meant to support camera focusing, such a capability has uses for FR, but significantly limits the potential scope of the application (i.e., maximum achievable γ). Therefore, the mobile device was mainly used for sourcing frames in our experiments.

Evaluation Criteria

The central focus of our experiments with regard to acceleration was the matrix multiplication (GEMM) component of the Projection routine, since this phase of the FR application dominates the execution time. We had to consider memory bandwidth usage, task size in terms of number of computations and the kernel execution rate. The GTX760 GPU we used in our experiments have nearly identical single- and double-precision floating point performance to the Nvidia GRID K2 units used in the AWS G2 cluster, as shown in Table 4. Therefore, we used the GTX760-based results to estimate the AWS G2 instance performance. We extrapolated our results to the GTX Titan Z GPU in the third column of Table 4 when estimating the performance for tier III, IV, and V operation. We expect the TSP to utilize the lower end GPUs only for acceleration types requiring heavy single-precision due to its lower cost, while GPUs like GTX Titan Z will be necessary for parts of the code that operate on heavy double-precision floating point data, such as the Projection phase of the FR application.

Experimental Results

Table 5 shows measured Projection performance for the GTX760 along with interpolations for the GRID K2, hence leading to our estimations for the AWS HPC (HPC-Servers). Our estimations incorporate optimizations such as: 1) an omission of the eigenvector upload on each kernel launch, since a single upload can be amortized over a vast number of FR requests and 2) a full concurrency, where up to 16 independent streams may be executing simultaneously, which is a realistic assumption for a cloud environment utilizing heavy parallelism. Observe that a fully saturated GRID K2 can theoretically support a computational throughput of 200 FR Projections per second on a 5000-image database. A cluster of five K2 devices augments this to roughly 1000 FR projections per second (last row) for the same database.

Table 4. Comparison of GPU performance and architectures.

GPU	GTX 760	GRID K2	GTX Titan Z
Architecture	GK104	GK104	2 x GK110
CUDA Cores	1,152	1,536	2 x 2,880
GPU Clock	980 MHz	745 MHz	705 MHz
Memory Size	2 GB	4 GB	6+6 GB
GFLOPS (single)	2,258	2,288	8,122
GFLOPS (double)	94	95	2,707

Table 5. GK104 double-precision GEMM performance; Projection times and estimated executable projections per second.

Database Size	1000	2000	3000	4000	5000
760 PJ Time (ms)	71.9	132.3	199.1	269.9	339.9
760 Stream #PJ/s	13.9	7.6	5.0	3.7	2.9
K2 PJ Time (ms)	19.6	33.7	48.1	63.7	80.1
K2 Stream #PJ/s	51.0	29.7	20.8	15.7	12.5
K2 Device #PJ/s	815.8	475.1	332.6	251.4	199.6
(5) K2 Cluster #PJ/s	4079	2376	1663	1257	998.1

Table 6. FR performance for a 5000-image database, for Tiers I, II (K=14), and Tiers III–V (K=80), and predictions for a decade later.

Tier	I	II	III	IV	V	Future
TFLOPs / mo	10	20	40	80	160	400
dGFLOP/s CQoS	80	200	2700	14K	27K	100K
Mbps NQoS	5	10	25	50	100	1000
Nwk Time (ms)	398	199	618	309	154	18.6
Exec Time (ms)	964	386	162	33	16	4.3
Req Time (ms)	1362	585	780	342	170	22.9
K (faces/frame)	14	14	80	80	80	80
FR γ	**10.9**	**25.1**	**103**	**234**	**469**	**3493**

Table 6 provides a list of AXaaS tiers with their network bandwidth and computational limits in the way previously described. This table is an extrapolation of the results provided in Table 5. Tiers I and II are assumed to utilize the Grid K2 GPU devices, and provide a network bandwidth guarantee (NQoS) of 5–10 Mbps, achieving γ values in the 10–20 range, which is perfectly sufficient for the casual user. Tier II allows 2x the allocate-able FLOPs, thereby allowing the user to enjoy 2x more runtime for the month of subscription. The "power tiers" (III–V) achieve much more impressive γ values in the 100–500 range and allow the user 16x more runtime for the month of subscription (i.e., 160 TFLOPs for tier V vs. 10 TFLOPs for tier I).

Our final column looks forward, perhaps a decade into the future. Assuming that LTE-Advanced takes flight, offering full 1 Gbps transfer rates, and considering a cluster of 25 GPU servers, we estimate a potential $\gamma>3000$. Within this time frame, an advanced mobile device such as iPhone is only expected to reach γ values of 1–2 from its current 0.22 based on its past decade's trend. Note that these results are meant to be no more than a back-of-the-envelope analysis to show the long term business viability of AXaaS, rather than a complete business study. Final tier layouts of the product will entirely depend on the resources and business model of the TSP.

CONCLUSION

We proposed a new service architecture called Acceleration as a Service (AXaaS) whose central focus is on accelerating specific portions of advanced mobile application code through cloud-based augmentation. AXaaS is formulated to enable a new generation of resource-intensive mobile applications such as real-time face recognition (FR), real-time language translation and augmented reality. When executed on mobile devices alone, hardware limitations of mobile devices prevent these applications from achieving satisfactory performance levels today. This fact is not expected to change in the foreseeable future considering the mobile architectural improvement trends. Our conceptualization of the AXaaS model is based on our observation that, these resource-intensive mobile applications spend a vast majority of their execution time on a very small set of API functions such as generalized matrix-matrix operations (GEMM) or Fast Fourier Transform (FFT) operations. Therefore, to significantly improve application performance, only these API functions need to be executed much faster (i.e., *accelerated*) instead of the entire application.

We identified Telecom Service Providers (TSPs) as the most logical candidate for providing *acceleration* (abbreviated AX) as a Service (aaS), hence our naming AXaaS. We showed that AXaaS could provide a new lucrative revenue stream for TSPs when offered in different tiers, similar to today's tiered data services. By renting resources from cloud providers, we showed that TSPs could generate favorable gross profit margins from AXaaS subscriptions. We demonstrated that the AXaaS model is scalable: When a large customer base is pooling AX computational resources, they do not experience performance degradations as long as TSPs provision their hardware resources accordingly.

We also provided a study of how AXaaS affects a developers' application programming environment. We showed that the AXaaS programming model (through an interface we termed AXAPI) is very similar to today's GPU programming models with minor modifications, thereby presenting no major barrier for entry to developers. Furthermore, we estimated that, AXaaS-based computation offloading dramatically improves the energy consumption of mobile applications by up to two or three orders-of-magnitude, thereby providing a great avenue for developers to create energy-efficient applications.

Our major focus was the impact of AXaaS on user experience. We defined a metric γ that quantifies user experience, which is the *total number of faces recognized in a second*. While this metric is specific to the real-time FR application, we observed that, such a metric is possible to define for every application that can be augmented by the AXaaS model. For example, real-time language translation can use a similar metric called *sentences translated per second*. It is also clear that the γ metric is directly related to performance, or specifically, the degree of acceleration. User experience will be completely different for different γ values, which we captured through our formulation of "acceleration tiers." In the case of real-time FR, a standalone iPhone 5s can reach γ=0.22, which is barely useful, if not flat out boring. When acceleration is applied, γ=10-20 can be achieved in tiers I and II, which will turn this application into a useful one, while γ=100 in tier III will make the application wholly exciting. On the other hand, γ=200-500 in tiers IV and V will allow the application to be used in demanding organizational scenarios such as real-time surveillance.

While application coding will face minimal changes across different tiers, varying degrees of acceleration in different tiers will completely change the application's relative value and utility. So, from the standpoint of the TSP, different values of γ present different tiers of marketable products which different user groups will be willing to pay for. We showed in our experimental results that, γ=469 is feasible on today's 4G networks, and γ>3000 can be achieved when LTE Advanced becomes commonplace within the next decade. Therefore, we conclude that AXaaS is a novel and viable business model today and will continue to be in the foreseeable future.

ACKNOWLEDGMENT

This work is supported in part by the National Science Foundation grant CNS-1239423 and by Nvidia Corp.

REFERENCES

Alling, A., Powers, N., & Soyata, T. (2015). Face Recognition: A Tutorial on Computational Aspects. In *Emerging Research Surrounding Power Consumption and Performance Issues in Utility Computing*. IGI Global.

Amazon EC2. (2013). Retrieved from Retrieved from: http://aws.amazon.com/ec2/sla/

Amazon-EC2-Pricing. (n.d.). Retrieved from http://aws.amazon.com/ec2/pricing/

Andoid-API. (n.d.). *Android API Reference*. Retrieved from http://developer.android.com/reference/

Microsoft Azure. (2014). Retrieved from Microsoft Azure: http://azure.microsoft.com/en-us/support/legal/sla/

Bradski, G., & Kaehler, A. (2008). *OpenCV Computer Vision with OpenCV Library*. O'Reilly.

Chen, E., Ogata, S., & Horikawa, K. (2012). Offloading android applications to the cloud without customizing android. *Pervasive Computing and Communicatiosn Workshop (PERCOM Workshops)* (pp. 788-793). IEEE. doi:10.1109/PerComW.2012.6197619

Cho, J., Mirzae, S., Oberg, J., & Kastner, R. (2009). FPGA-based face detection system using Haar Classifiers. *Proceedings of the ACM/SIGDA International Symposium on Field Programmable Gate Arrays*, (pp. 103-112). doi:10.1145/1508128.1508144

Chun, B. G., Ihm, S., Maniatis, P., Naik, M., & Patti, A. (2011). Clonecloud: Elastic execution between mobile device and cloud. *Proceedings of the Sixth Conference on Computer Systems*, (pp. 301-314). doi:10.1145/1966445.1966473

Costa, P., Migliavacca, M., Pietzuch, P., & Wolf, A. (2012). NaaS: Network as a Service in the cloud. *2nd USENIX Workshop on Hot Topics in Management of Internet, Cloud, and Enterprise Networks and Services (Hot-ICE '12).*

Cuervo, E., Balasubramaniam, A., Cho, D., Wolman, A., Saroiu, S., Chandra, R., & Bahl, P. (2010). MAUI: Making smartphones last longer with code offload. *Proceedings of the 8th international Conference on Mobile Systems, Applications, and Services* (pp. 49-62). ACM. doi:10.1145/1814433.1814441

Dsouza, A., Kabbedjik, J., Seo, D., Jansen, S., & Brinkkemper, S. (2012). Software-as-a-service: Implications for business and technology in product software companies. *PACIS 2012 Proceedings Pacific Asia Conference on Information.*

Duato, J., Pena, A. J., Silla, F., Mayo, R., & Quintana-Orti, E. S. (2011). Performance of cuda virtualized remote gpus in high performance Clusters. *International Conference on Parallel Processing (ICPP)* (pp. 365-374). IEEE. doi:10.1109/ICPP.2011.58

EC2-Instance-Types. (n.d.). Retrieved from http://aws.amazon.com/ec2/instance-types/

EC2-Reserved-Instances. (n.d.). Retrieved from http://aws.amazon.com/ec2/purchasing-options/reserved-instances/

Emarketer. (2014). *Smartphone Users Worldwide Will Total 175 Billion 2014.* Retrieved from http://www.emarketer.com/Article/Smartphone-Users-Worldwide-Will-Total-175-Billion-2014/1010536/

Gentry, C. (2009). *A Fully Homomorphic Encryption Scheme*. Stanford University.

Gentry, C., Halevi, S., & Smart, N. (2012). *Homomorphic evaluation of the AES circuit* (pp. 850–867). CRYPTO.

Google-Translate. (n.d.). Retrieved from https://translate.google.com/

3GPP-TS23.228. (n.d.). *IP multimedia subsystem (ims); stage 2 (release 9).* Retrieved from 3rd Generation Partnership Project, Tech. Rep., 2010, 3GPP TS 23.228 V9.3.0 (2010-03).

3GPP-TS23.401. (2008). General packet radio service (gprs) enhancements for evolved universal terrestrial radio access network (e-utran) access. Release 8. Retrieved from 3rd Generation Partnership Project, Tech Report 3GPP TS 23.401 V8.1.0.

Halevi, S., & Shoup, V. (2014). Algorithms in HElib. *Proceedings, Part I, Advanced in Cryptology - {CRYPTO} 2014 - 34th Annual Cryptology Conference*, (pp. 554-571). Santa Barbara, CA. doi:10.1007/978-3-662-44371-2_31

HPC-Servers. (n.d.). *High Performance Computing for Servers — Tesla GPUs.* Retrieved from http://www.nvidia.com/object/tesla-servers.html

Huang, J., Qian, F., Gerber, A., Mao, M., Sen, S., & Spatscheck, O. (2012). A close examination of performance and power characteristics of 4G LTE Networks. *Proceedings of the 10th international conference on Mobile systems, applications, and services* (pp. 225-238). ACM. doi:10.1145/2307636.2307658

INTEL-XeonPhi. (n.d.). *INTEL Xeon PHI Family*. Retrieved from http://www.intel.com/content/www/us/en/processors/xeon/xeon-phi-detail.html

iPhone-5s. (n.d.). *The iPhone 5s Specifications*. Retrieved from AnandTech: http://www.anandtech.com/print/7335/the-iphone-5s-review

Keller, J. (2011). *Cloud-Powered Facial Recognition is Terrifying*. Retrieved from http://www.theatlantic.com/technology/archive/2011/09/cloud-powered-facial-recognition-is-terrifying/245867/

Kim, K., Jung, K., & Kim, H. (2002). Face recognition using kernel principal component analysis. *IEEE Signal Processing Letters*, 40–42.

Kirk, D. B., & Hwu, W. M. (2010). *Programming Massively Parallel Processors*. Morgan-Kaufmann.

Kocabas, O., & Soyata, T. (2014). Medical Data Analytics in the cloud using Homomorphic Encryption. In *Handbook of Research on Cloud Infrastructures for Big Data Analytics* (pp. 471–488). US: IGI Global.

Kocabas, O., Soyata, T., Couderc, J.-P., Aktas, M., Xia, J., & Huang, M. (2013). Assessment of Cloud-based Health Monitoring using Homomorphic Encryption. *Proceedings of the 31th IEEE Conference on Computer Design*, (pp. 443-446). Asheville, NC, USA. doi:10.1109/ICCD.2013.6657078

Kovachev, D., Cao, Y., & Klamma, R. (2013). *Mobile Cloud Computing: A Comparison of Application Models*. Retrieved from http://arxiv.org/abs/1107.4940v1

Kwon, M., Dou, Z., Heinzelman, W., Soyata, T., Ba, H., & Shi, J. (2014). Use of Network Latency Profiling and Redundancy for Cloud Server Selection. *Proceedings of the 7th IEEE International Conference on Cloud Computing*, (pp. 826-832). IEEE. doi:10.1109/CLOUD.2014.114

Mei, C., Shimek, J., Wang, C., Chandra, A., & Weissman, J. (2011). *Dynamic outsourcing mobile computation to the cloud*. University of Minnesota.

Moto-X. (n.d.). *Google/Motorola Mobilitys Moto X Outpaces Competition*. Retrieved from https://www.abiresearch.com/press/googlemotorola-mobilitys-moto-x-outpaces-competition

MS-Translator. (n.d.). Retrieved from http://www.microsoft.com/en-us/translator/

NIST. FIPS-197. (2001). Advanced encryption standard (AES). National Institute of Standards and Technology.

Nvidia, C. U. B. L. A. S. (n.d.). Retrieved from https://developer.nvidia.com/cublas

Nvidia, C. U. D. A. (n.d.). *NVIDIA CUDA*. Retrieved from nvidia.com: http://www.nvidia.com/object/cuda_home_new.html

Nvidia, C. U. F. F. T. (n.d.). Retrieved from https://developer.nvidia.com/cufft

Nvidia, C. U. S. P. A. R. S. E. (n.d.). Retrieved from https://developer.nvidia.com/cusparse

Nvidia-Shield. (2014). *The Nvidia Shield Gaming Tablet*. Retrieved from http://shield.nvidia.com/gaming-tablet/

Nvidia-VisualStudio. (n.d.). *NVIDIA Nsight Visual Studio Edition*. Retrieved from https://developer.nvidia.com/nvidia-nsight-visual-studio-edition

OpenCV-FaceRecognizer. (n.d.). *Open CV 3.0.0-dev Documentation*. Retrieved from http://docs.opencv.org/trunk/modules/contrib/doc/facerec/facerec_api.html

Page, A., Kocabas, O., Ames, S., Venkitasubramaniam, M., & Soyata, T. (2014). Cloud-based Secure Health Monitoring: Optimizing Fully-Homomorphic Encryption for Streaming Algorithms. *IEEE Globecom 2014 Workshop on Cloud Computing Systems, Networks, and Applications.*

Page, A., Kocabas, O., Soyata, T., Aktas, M., & Couderc, J.-P. (2014). Cloud-Based Privacy-Preserving Remote ECG Monitoring and Surveillance. *Annals of Noninvasive Electrocardiology*, n/a. doi:10.1111/anec.12204 PMID:25510621

Powers, N., Alling, A., Gyampoh-Vidogah, R., & Soyata, T. (2014). AXaaS: Case for Acceleration as a Service. *IEEE Globecom 2014 Workshop on Cloud Computing Systems, Networks, and Applications.*

Sait, Y., & Vijayalakshmi, R. (2014). Enabling high performance computing in cloud infrastructure using rCUDA.

Sandikkaya, M., & Harmanci, A. (2012). Security problems of Platform as a Service (PaaS) clouds and practical solutions to the problems. *31st International Symposium on Reliable Distributed Systems*. doi:10.1109/SRDS.2012.84

Satyanarayanan, M., Bahl, P., Caceres, R., & Davies, N. (2009). The case for vm-based cloudlets in mobile computing. *Pervasive Computing*, 14-23.

Soyata, T., Ba, H., Heinzelman, W., Kwon, M., & Shi, J. (2013). Accelerating mobile cloud computing: A survey. In *Communication Infrastructures for Cloud Computing* (pp. 175–197). IGI Global.

Soyata, T., Muraleedharan, R., Funai, C., Kwon, M., & Heinzelman, W. (2012). Cloud-Vision: Real-time face recognition using a mobile-cloudlet-cloud acceleration architecture. *Computers and Communications (ISCC), 2012 IEEE Symposium on*, 59-66.

Soyata, T., Muraleedharan, R., Langdon, J., Funai, C., Kwon, M., & Heinzelman, W. (2012). COMBAT: mobile-Cloud-based cOmpute/coMmunications infrastructure for BATtlefield applications. *Proceedings of the Society for Photo-Instrumentation Engineers*, 8403.

Turk, M., & Pentland, A. (1991). Face recognition using eigenfaces. *IEEE Computer Society Conference on Computer Vision and Pattern Recognition, 1991. Proceedings CVPR*, *91*, 568–591.

Verbelen, T., Simoens, P., DeTurck, F., & Dhoedt, B. (2012). Cloudlets: Bringing the cloud to the mobile user. *Proceedings of the third ACM workshop on Mobile cloud computing and services* (pp. 29-36). ACM. doi:10.1145/2307849.2307858

Verizon-Terremark. (n.d.). *Verizon Terremark*. Retrieved from http://www.terremark.com/

Viola, P., & Jones, M. (2001). Rapid object detection using a boosted cascade of simple features. *Proceedings of the 2001 IEEE Computer Society Conference on Computer Vision and Pattern Recognition*, (pp. 511-518). doi:10.1109/CVPR.2001.990517

Viola, P., & Jones, M. J. (2001). Robust real time face detection. *Second International Workshop on Statistical and Computational Theories of Vision - Modeling, Learning, Computing, and Sampling*, (pp. 1-25).

Wang, H., Liu, W., & Soyata, T. (2014). Accessing Big Data in the Cloud Using Mobile Devices. In *Handbook of Research on Cloud Infrastructures for Big Data Anal* (pp. 444–470). IGI Global. doi:10.4018/978-1-4666-5864-6.ch018

Yang, M., Kriegman, D., & Ahuja, N. (2002). Detecting faces in images: A survey. *IEEE Transactions on Pattern Analysis and Machine Intelligence*, *24*(1), 34–58. doi:10.1109/34.982883

Zhang, L., Tiwana, B., Qian, Z., Qang, Z., Dick, R. P., Mao, Z. M., & Yang, L. (2010). Accurate online power estimation and automatic battery behavior based power model generation for smartphones. Intl. Conf. on Hardware-Software Codesign and System Synthesis (CODES+ISSS). Scottsdale, AZ.

KEY TERMS AND DEFINITIONS

3G Network: A set of standards to define the third generation of mobile telecommunications technology. This standard is somehow outdated as of the publication of this book chapter.

4G Network: Fourth generation mobile telecommunications technology offering substantial improvements over the 3G.

5G Network: A telecommunications standard (fifth generation wireless systems) that is not yet available. This technology will offer data rates up to 1 Gbps.

Acceleration (AX): Speeding up an application by intelligently identifying the parts of the code that benefit from faster execution. In the applications introduced in this chapter, these parts of the code that can benefit from AX include FFT, and GEMM routines.

Augmented Reality: A generalized family of applications in which a computer-generated image is super-imposed on an acquired image from a camera. This super-imposed image is intended to provide more information to the user, such as, how a house would look when a refrigerator is placed in it.

AXaaS (Acceleration as a Service): A service offered by a TSP that is based on a monthly service charge. The product to rent is the acceleration of portions of the mobile code that a mobile user is running. In this chapter, it is determined that, the acceleration of a small subset of functions such as GEMM and FFT will be sufficient to drastically improve the performance of certain mobile applications, such as real-time Face Recognition.

Basic Linear Algebra Subroutines (BLAS): A set of API functions that are introduced in three levels. Level 1 BLAS API functions include vector-vector operations. Level 2 BLAS functions include vector-matrix operations, while Level 3 includes matrix-matrix operations.

Cloud Computing: A paradigm where computational and storage services can be purchased on demand from cloud service providers much like gas and electric can be purchased based on usage from utility providers.

Cloud Instance: A server of a storage unit that a cloud user rents from a cloud operator. Each cloud instance comes with a different pricing depending on the time commitment to use this resource, as well as the capability of this resource.

Cloud Operator: The business entity that invests in an infrastructure including multiple datacenters in a broad geographic area. This entity has multiple customers that rents cloud computing services to and has the advantage of pooling resources, thereby taking advantage of economies of scale.

Cloudlet: An intermediate device between a mobile device and the cloud with the purpose of accelerating a mobile application.

Computational Quality of Service (CQoS): Due to the emphasis on the computational intensity, a separate metric, CQoS is defined to quantify a guaranteed level of computational throughput.

Compute-Unified Device Architecture (CUDA): The programming language and the GPU architecture introduced by Nvidia Corp. to provide a complete GPU programming platform for general purpose scientific programmers.

CUFFT, CUSPARSE, CUBLAS: Three Nvidia CUDA based libraries with API functions designed to accelerate FFT, BLAS, and Sparse Matrix operations.

Face Recognition: A computationally-intensive application in which a face that is detected in a picture frame is compared against a set of database faces and a decision is made as to which face it matches with a high probability. This application is a perfect candidate for AXaaS and has been extensively studied in this chapter.

Fast Fourier Transform (FFT): A transformation that turns time-domain data into frequency-domain data, since performing the operations in the frequency domain result in a much lower overall processing time for certain algorithms such as Image Processing.

Generalized Matrix-Matrix Multiplication (GEMM): A family of matrix operations in which each matrix could actually be a vector. A vector could be thought of a matrix with a dimension of 1 in one of the axes.

Graphics Processing Unit (GPU): A device that is capable of processing information in a massively-parallel (MP) fashion. MP processing differs substantially from traditional parallel processing in that, GPUs are actually not good at processing a few threads, but, rather, tens or hundreds of thousands of threads. This makes GPUs suitable computational device for applications that are inherently massively-parallel, such as Image Processing, or general Digital Signal Processing.

IaaS (Infrastructure as a Service): A cloud computing paradigm, where the cloud service provider rents an entire infrastructure which may include servers, storage, and operating software.

Long Term Evolution (LTE): A high speed wireless communication standard that is reasonably widespread. It offers data rates up to 100 Mbps, whereas LTE Advanced promises rates up to 1 Gbps.

Mobile-Cloud Computing: A computing paradigm where the computational and/or storage power of a mobile device is substantially augmented by using cloud resources via a communications link.

Mobile-Cloud Offloading: A process where a part of the mobile application code is executed in the cloud.

Natural Language Processing (NLP): Another computationally-intensive candidate application for AXaaS in which the words that are spoken by a human is being somehow interpreted by a computer.

Network Quality of Service (NQoS): This metric is very close to the traditional QoS in that, a guarantee is defined on the network throughput between the mobile device(s) and the cloud.

PaaS (Platform as a Service): A cloud computing paradigm where the cloud service providers rents a platform, including programming languages, libraries, tools and services. Clients control deploying their applications and cloud providers manage the underlying cloud infrastructure based on demand.

Packet Data Network Gateways (PDN-GW): A Packet Data Network (PDN) Gateway provides connectivity from User Equipment (UE) to external PDNs.

Quality of Service (QoS): A traditional metric defined to quantify a level of *guaranteed* performance, such as bandwidth, computation, and more. In this chapter, this metric is broken down into two inter-related metrics.

Return on Investment (ROI): A metric that is introduced to quantify the amount of time that it would take to receive sufficient profits from an investment to reach overall profitability. After this point, the investment provides profitability going forward.

SaaS (Software as a Service): A cloud computing paradigm where the users run an application directly from the provider's web interface, thereby completely avoiding any investment on the infrastructure to run such software. An example is Microsoft Office 365.

Service Level Agreement (SLA): An agreement signed by the user and the cloud provider with the intent to agree on a set of performance metrics, such as bandwidth and uptime. AXaaS model adds a performance metric to traditional SLAs.

Tegra: A family of processors introduced by Nvidia that contain a CPU and GPU, with multiple cores within each sub-structure.

Telecom Service Provider (TSP): The provider of communication to users, which can offer voice as well as data services through the same exact network by adhering to well-defined standards, such as 3G, 4G, and 5G.

TFLOPS (Tera Floating Point Operations Per Second): A metric that defines how many trillion (Tera) Floating Point operations a computational device is capable of performing per second. Since floating point operations can be single, double, or even quadruple, there is a slight vagueness in this metric. To eliminate this ambiguity, in this chapter two separate metrics have been used. sTFLOPS is the single precision and dTFLOPS is the double-precision floating point operation quantity.

Tiered Pricing: A pricing model where different levels of the same product are offered with varying pricing. In the AXaaS model, this tier structure is based solely on a performance metric γ that quantifies the user experience.

User Experience (γ): A metric that is defined in this chapter to quantify the utility that a consumer is receiving from an AXaaS subscription. A TSP can formulate a pricing structure for the AXaaS based on such a metric. Higher values of γ imply being able to use the same application for much more sophisticated purposes, even if the application itself does not change.

Chapter 7
Towards Privacy-Preserving Medical Cloud Computing Using Homomorphic Encryption

Ovunc Kocabas
University of Rochester, USA

Tolga Soyata
University of Rochester, USA

ABSTRACT

Personal health monitoring tools, such as commercially available wireless ECG patches, can significantly reduce healthcare costs by allowing patient monitoring outside the healthcare organizations. These tools transmit the acquired medical data into the cloud, which could provide an invaluable diagnosis tool for healthcare professionals. Despite the potential of such systems to revolutionize the medical field, the adoption of medical cloud computing in general has been slow due to the strict privacy regulations on patient health information. We present a novel medical cloud computing approach that eliminates privacy concerns associated with the cloud provider. Our approach capitalizes on Fully Homomorphic Encryption (FHE), which enables computations on private health information without actually observing the underlying data. For a feasibility study, we present a working implementation of a long-term cardiac health monitoring application using a well-established open source FHE library.

INTRODUCTION

The Patient Protection and Affordable Care Act (US Government Printing Office) is one of the most significant government efforts to generalize the use of electronic medical records (EMRs) and to incentivize the development of innovative technologies that can help curb rising US healthcare costs. Cloud computing is a viable option to reduce healthcare costs associated with EMRs by outsourcing the storage of medical data to cloud operators (Amazon Web Services; Google Cloud Platform; Microsoft Windows Azure), however, Personal Health Information (PHI) privacy is strictly mandated by the Health Insurance Portability and Accountability Act (HIPAA) (US Department of Health and Human Services, 2014) and

DOI: 10.4018/978-1-4666-8662-5.ch007

the risks associated with a breach of PHI are steep (up to $1.5M depending on the type of violation). Signing a Business Associate Agreement (BAA) (US-HHS) authorizes cloud storage operators (e.g., (CareCloud, 2013) and (Dr Chrono, 2013)) to store PHI data. These offerings are all based on encrypted data storage, however, there is currently no service that offers secure long-term patient monitoring, which would imply computation on encrypted data.

This chapter proposes a novel approach to eliminate privacy concerns. Our proposed Fully Homomorphic Encryption (FHE) based cloud computing solution allows the cloud to perform computations on encrypted data, without actually observing the data (i.e., patient private health information). While this method holds the promise to completely eliminate the cloud-based privacy concerns, it comes at a steep price: FHE-based operations are orders of magnitude slower than regular operations, rendering FHE impractical for generic applications (Bos, Lauter, & Naehrig, 2014; Naehrig, Lauter, & Vaikuntanathan, 2011; Kocabas, Soyata, Couderc, Aktas, Xia, & Huang, 2013; Wang, Hu, Chen, Huang, & Sunar, 2013; Dai, Doroz, & Sunar, 2014). In this chapter, one type of computation is shown to be a promising candidate for FHE-based medical applications: long-term patient monitoring.

Contributions of this chapter are: 1) implementation of a well-known ECG algorithm (Couderc, et al., 2011) using an open source FHE library (Halevi & Shoup, 2014), 2) detailed description of the steps required for such an implementation, which are far from trivial, 3) presentation of a proof-of-concept study on a restricted set of computations for long-term patient health monitoring using real data: specifically, the computation of the average heart rate, minimum and maximum heart rate, and the detection of a cardiac hazard called the drug-induced long QT syndrome (LQTS) (Aktas, Shah, & Akiyama, 2007; Brenyo, Huang, & Aktas, 2011), 4) demonstration of the potential for FHE-based generalized secure medical cloud computing.

Our claims are proven on test data taken from the University of Rochester THEW ECG database (Couderc J.-P., 2010), and it is shown that such operations can be performed homomorphically, thereby guaranteeing information security. Given that cardiac diseases are the #1 cause for deaths in the United States (Hoyert & Xu, 2012), our study is an important and novel step in the development of generalized secure medical cloud computing.

This chapter is organized as follows: We provide background information on FHE, followed by a system- and application-level introduction to our proposed solution. A description of the nature of the acquired medical data and the operations performed on this data are described in the next section and a detailed FHE scheme used for our application development is presented. Our circuit-based computational approach for this development and the details of our implementation are presented. The performance evaluation of our proposed solution details our findings. Conclusions and pointers to future research are provided.

BACKGROUND

Conventional encryption schemes such as AES (NIST-AES, 2001) do not provide a mechanism for computations on encrypted data. When data is encrypted using AES, the only permitted operation on it is *decryption* by using a *secret key*. This implies that AES provides a *secure storage*, but not a *secure computation* mechanism. Cryptographic strength of AES, combined with its ease of its implementation makes AES-based encrypted storage standards the heart of *HIPAA-compliant storage* (Scarfone, Souppaya, & Sexton, 2007), while no current mechanism exists for *HIPAA-compliant computation*. Without this missing component, a system that achieves security in medical data acquisition (Phase I) and storage (Phase II) is possible (Figure **1**), but computation (Phase III) is not.

Fully Homomorphic Encryption (FHE) schemes enable the computation of meaningful operations on encrypted data without observing the actual data. Figure **2** illustrates a conceptual example for adding A = 23 and B = 17 using FHE, where ***A***, ***B*** are the FHE-encrypted ciphertexts of A and B that are sent to the cloud. Homomorphic Addition (denoted as $+_h$) is performed on ***A*** and ***B*** to yield the FHE-encrypted result ***C***, which can be safely transmitted back out of the cloud, where it is decrypted to obtain the intended computation result C.

The idea of FHE was first proposed by Rivest et al. in 1978 (Rivest, Adleman, & Dertouzos, 1978) and remained a puzzle to the researchers over the last three decades until Gentry (Gentry, 2009) proposed the first possible mechanism in 2009. Schemes proposed before (Goldwasser & Micali, 1982; El Gamal, 1985; Cohen & Fischer, 1985; Paillier, 1999; Damgard & Jurik, 2001; Boneh, Goh, & Nissim, 2005) could only perform a limited set of operations (i.e., only addition or only multiplication).

Gentry's FHE scheme can perform arbitrary number of additions and multiplications, allowing a set of generic computations on FHE-encrypted data. Gentry's scheme introduces random noise to ciphertexts during encryption. The amount of noise grows with each homomorphic operation and if it exceeds a threshold, decryption produces an incorrect message. Gentry's novel proposal (Gentry, 2009) uses a method called *bootstrapping* (also known as *recryption*) which resets the noise inside the ciphertexts. However, Gentry's scheme has several inefficiencies related to storage and computation time, which has prevented it from becoming commonplace. Each ciphertext can only encrypt a one-bit message, and to increase the noise threshold, the size of ciphertexts must be large, which results in an expansion of storage space (e.g., the size of a ciphertext encrypting a one-bit message could be multi-million bits). Furthermore, homomorphic operations require a computationally intensive *recryption* operation to periodically reset the noise, making Gentry's FHE scheme impractical (Gentry & Halevi, 2011).

Following Gentry's FHE scheme (Gentry, 2009), several FHE implementations have been proposed to date (Naehrig, Lauter, & Vaikuntanathan, 2011; Dijk, Gentry, Halevi, & Vaikuntanathan, 2010; Brakerski & Vaikuntanathan, 2011; Brakerski & Vaikuntanathan, 2011; Coron, Mandal, Naccache, & Tibouchi, 2011; Gentry & Halevi, 2011; Smart & Vercauteren, 2010) (Stehle & Steinfeld, 2010; Brakerski, Gentry, & Vaikuntanathan, 2012; Gentry, Halevi, & Smart, 2012; Gentry, Halevi, & Smart, 2012). Yet a practical FHE scheme does not exist as of now and improving the performance of FHE remains very active research area (DARPA-PROCEED).

SYSTEM AND APPLICATION MODELING

Figure 2 illustrates our proposed system, which will enable long-term health monitoring of patients securely and automatically. Privacy of the health data is handled in three distinct phases (Kocabas, Soyata, Couderc, Aktas, Xia, & Huang, 2013): Acquisition (Phase I), Storage (Phase II), and Computation (Phase III).

ECG Acquisition Devices

ECG recording technology has advanced to the point where there are personal ECG recording devices that allow patients to record ECG activity at home (e.g., the iPhone attachment from Alivecor (AliveCor), and the ECG patch from Clearbridge VitalSigns CardioLeaf (CardioLeaf, 2013)). Most of today's acquisition devices provide accurate measurements, but do not support long-term trend analysis, which can play a significant role in disease prevention.

Figure 1. Proposed Cloud-based secure long-term patient monitoring system.
Adapted from (Page, Kocabas, Ames, Venkitasubramaniam, & Soyata, 2014).

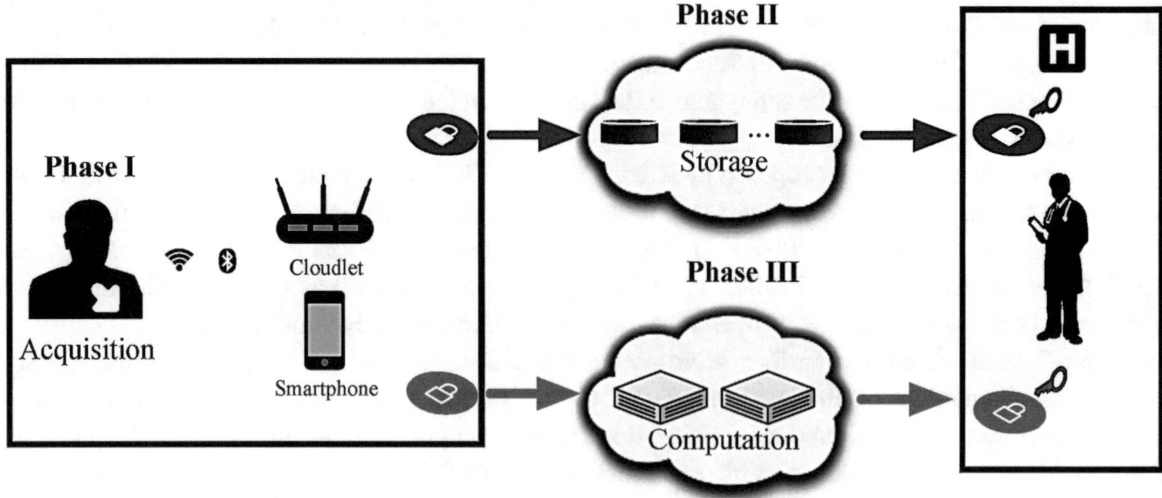

On the left of Figure **1**, Phase I (acquisition) is assumed to be done with such devices, where the data is sampled and converted to digital format. Some computational pre-processing can be performed and the acquired (and partially pre-processed) data is transmitted to the cloud after being encrypted using FHE (Brakerski, Gentry, & Vaikuntanathan, 2012). This encryption step is computationally expensive and necessitates the existence of a nearby computationally capable device such as the patient's smartphone or a cloudlet (Soyata, Ba, Heinzelman, Kwon, & Shi, 2013; Soyata, et al., 2012; Soyata, Muraleedharan, Funai, Kwon, & Heinzelman, 2012). The link between the acquisition device and the computationally capable device can be secured with conventional encryption schemes (NIST-AES, 2001; Rivest, Adleman, & Shamir, 1978).

Storage and Computation of the Patient Data

Two functions of the cloud are outlined in Figure 1: storage (Phase II) and computation (Phase III). Cloud-based monitoring results are transmitted to the doctor's mobile device (on the right) in FHE-encrypted format, where they are decrypted only while the doctor is reviewing the results. Keeping the data in

Figure 2. A conceptual example for Fully Homomorphic Encryption.

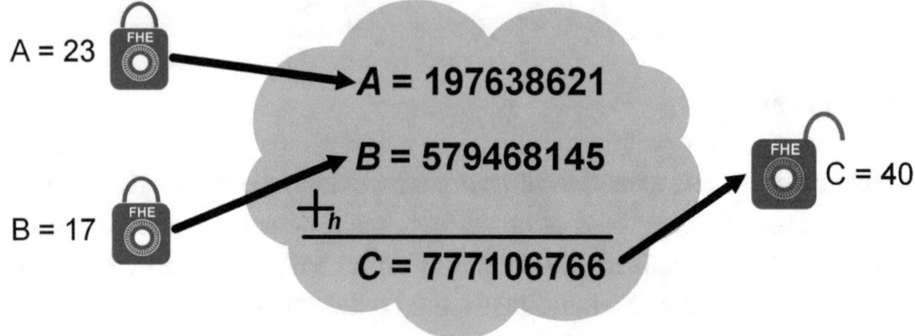

encrypted format from its acquisition point (the ECG patch) to its end point (the doctor's smartphone) enables long-term health monitoring options that didn't exist with storage-only encryption, and will be the focus of this chapter.

Notice that in Figure 1, we propose two alternate paths to transmit the data: Top and bottom paths are storage-only (AES-encrypted) and computation only (FHE-encrypted) data paths, respectively and are synchronized with time-stamp markers. The top path redundantly contains all of the information that the bottom part contains, with one significant distinction: The top (storage-only) version of the data is encrypted with a storage-neutral encryption such as AES (NIST-AES, 2001), whereas, the bottom path is encrypted with a computation-only encryption, such as FHE. While the AES version of the data is meant for long-term storage (e.g., 10 years, mandated by the law), the bottom part is meant for short-term storage, only during the homomorphic computations. This separation is necessary due to the significant bloating of the data up to a million-fold (Wang, Hu, Chen, Huang, & Sunar, 2013; Halevi & Shoup, 2014; Brakerski, Gentry, & Vaikuntanathan, 2012) during homomorphic encryption. This redundancy allows the application to use the bottom path to calculate the time stamp markers for later retrieval from the permanent AES-based storage.

Operations in the Target Medical Application

We have chosen to detect long QT syndrome (LQTS) as our primary medical application because measuring cardiac safety remains one of the most challenging hurdles in the development of new drugs and biotechnological products. The propensity of the drugs to cause potentially fatal arrhythmia, called torsades des pointes (TdP), is a significant public health issue (Woosley, 2001). An estimated 86% of all of the new drugs that are tested in pharmaceutical development show hERG inhibitory activity leading to TdP (Shah R. R., 2005). hERG is a gene that codes a protein subunit of potassium ion channels, and its contribution to the electrical activity of the heart is well known (Fink, Noble, Virag, Varro, & Giles, 2008). Many drugs potentially prolong the heart's ventricular repolarization process (VR), which in some cases trigger TdP, degenerate into ventricular fibrillation, and can cause sudden cardiac death (SCD) (Shah R., 2004).

In addition to LQTS Detection, we will also incorporate functionality into our application to provide vital patient health statistics (Page, Kocabas, Soyata, Aktas, & Couderc, 2014). These are the average, minimum, and maximum heart rates. Although more sophisticated operations are feasible with FHE, we will restrict our focus on these fundamental operations, which form a base that allows the implementation of a more generalized set of operations.

COMPUTATIONAL/FUNCTIONAL MODELING

An observation of the applications mentioned in the previous section reveals distinct patterns for the incoming data and the type of functions applied to this data. In this section, we will describe a computational framework for the proposed system described in the previous section.

Figure 3. QT and RR intervals in ECG.
(Image based on SinusRhythmLabels.png by Anthony Atkielski).

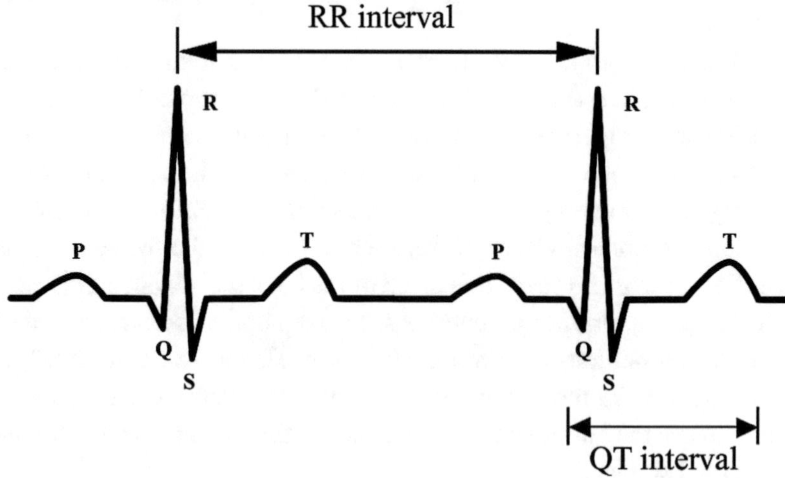

Operations in the Target Medical Application

The input to the LQTS detection is QT and RR intervals (see Figure **3**), computed from raw ECG data by using a set of algorithms validated on a large cohort of subjects (Couderc, et al., 2011). The QT interval represents the ventricular recovery phase of the heart and its prolongation (i.e., long QT) is a marker for a potential Torsades des Pointes (a deadly cardiac hazard, abbreviated as TdP) (Aktas, Shah, & Akiyama, 2007; Brenyo, Huang, & Aktas, 2011; Couderc, et al., 2011; Couderc, Xia, Xu, Kaab, Hinteeser, & Zareba, 2010; Zareba, et al., 1995). The RR interval is the time between QRS complexes, which is used for determining the heart rate.

QT prolongations are detected by first calculating the QT_c (known as the *corrected QT*) as $QT_c = \frac{QT}{\sqrt{RR}}$ from QT and RR intervals using the widely accepted Bazett's formula (Bazzett, 1997). QT_c values are compared to a clinical threshold (e.g., 500 ms) to detect LQTS as shown below

$$QT_c = \frac{QT}{\sqrt{RR}} \Rightarrow \begin{cases} Normal\ QT_c \leq 500 \\ LQTS\ QT_c > 500 \end{cases} \tag{1}$$

which outlines the criteria to distinguish between normal cardiac operation vs. a potential LQTS hazard. Our case study and preliminary results will be derived by computing Equation on the ECG sample dataset obtained from the THEW repository (Couderc J.-P., 2010).

Modeling the Data Stream and Operations

- **Input Data Stream *d*[*i*]:** This is the FHE-encrypted ECG data transmitted from patients' home to the cloud.

- **Computation Functions $f_c(.)$:** These are the functions that are applied to individual data elements $d[i]$. An example function representing the $f_c(.)$ family is

$$f_c(d[i]) = (d[i] > 500)\,|_{i=1,\dots,\psi} \tag{2}$$

which produces ψ individual Boolean results for each of the data elements, denoting whether each data element $d[i]$ is greater than 500 or not. Note that, this function can be used to detect LQTS as shown in Equation .

- **Aggregation Functions $f_a(.)$:** These are the functions that aggregate the results obtained by $f_c(.)$ to provide a summarized result. Let $d_c[i]$ be the results calculated by the computation function $f_c(.)$. Then the aggregation result can be described as

$$d_a[j] = f_a(d_c[i])\,|_{i=1,\dots,\psi,j=1,\dots,\Omega} \tag{3}$$

where $d_a[j]$ are the Ω aggregated results from the ψ element data stream $d[i]$. Note the specific case Ω=1, which denotes the single result obtained from an entire stream of incoming ψ data elements.

An example application of using data elements $d[i]$ and $f_c(.)$, $f_a(.)$ functions is to detect LQTS within a time interval. More specifically, while $d[i]$ could denote ECG samples 10 ms apart, the aggregated result could be the detection of LQTS hazard within a 20 sec interval (i.e., ψ=2000, Ω=1). In this specific example, $f_c(.)$ is chosen to be the comparison function shown in Equation and $f_a(.)$ is chosen to be Logical OR function that aggregates Boolean results generated by the comparison function.

FHE COMPUTATIONAL STRUCTURE

Our proposed system uses one of the most efficient FHE schemes, called the Brakerski-Gentry-Vaikuntanathan (BGV) scheme (Brakerski, Gentry, & Vaikuntanathan, 2012) and its open-source implementation HElib (Halevi & Shoup, 2014). Core of the computations in our implementation resemble Equations and on the incoming FHE-encrypted data stream $d[i]$. Since the operations available in the BGV scheme require an unconventional representation of this data stream $d[i]$ and the evaluation functions $f_c(.)$ and $f_a(.)$, a detailed presentation of the BGV scheme is provided in this section.

Leveled FHE Scheme

Following Gentry (Gentry, 2009), FHE schemes up to date (Dijk, Gentry, Halevi, & Vaikuntanathan, 2010; Brakerski & Vaikuntanathan, 2011; Brakerski & Vaikuntanathan, 2011; Coron, Mandal, Naccache, & Tibouchi, 2011; Gentry & Halevi, 2011; Smart & Vercauteren, 2010; Stehle & Steinfeld, 2010) rely on introducing a small *noise* into a ciphertext during encryption. This noise grows with each operation and can cause decryption errors if it is allowed to exceed a certain threshold. This requires performing the computationally expensive *recrypt* operation to reset the noise after every homomorphic multiplication, which would otherwise increase the noise exponentially.

BGV introduces a *leveled* FHE scheme that avoids the expensive *recrypt* operation. The *leveled* FHE scheme uses a better noise management technique called *modulus-switching* (Brakerski & Vaikuntanathan, 2011), which allows performing cascaded homomorphic multiplications ($\times_h$) without causing decryption errors. A parameter L (the *Level*) is introduced, which must be determined before starting any computation. The level L is predominantly determined by the depth of the $\times_h$ operations for the function to be evaluated and for the rest of the chapter we will use *multiplicative depth* and level L interchangeably. Right after encryption, each ciphertext is set to a level L and L is reduced by one after each $\times_h$ until $L = 1$, at which point further $\times_h$ operations can cause decryption errors.

Leveled FHE improves traditional FHE performance, but introduces an implementation burden: L must be determined *a priori* (before performing any homomorphic operation). During the implementation of our medical application, we will calculate the multiplicative depth of each computation and set the level L accordingly. For the rest of this chapter, we will use the lower case $x_7 \ldots x_0$ notation to denote the plaintext slots, and the upper case bold notation X to denote the ciphertext, i.e., the encrypted version of plaintext $X=(x_7 \ldots x_0)$. Therefore, $X = Enc(X) = Enc(x_7 \ldots x_0)$, where $Enc()$is the homomorphic encryption operation.

Plaintext Space

In the BGV scheme, plaintexts are represented as polynomial rings in the $GF(p^d)$ where p is a prime number that defines the range of polynomial coefficients and d is the degree of the polynomials. Homomorphic addition and multiplication of ciphertexts correspond to addition and multiplication of plaintexts in the specified polynomial ring, respectively. We choose the polynomial ring in $GF(2)$ (i.e., $p = 2$, $d = 1$), where homomorphic addition and multiplication of ciphertexts translate to XOR and AND operations on the plaintexts, respectively. This "functionally complete" set (i.e., XOR and AND) will allow the fundamental operations of our medical application to be represented as a binary circuit using a combination of XOR and AND gates in the following sections.

Message Packing

Representing plaintexts as polynomial rings in $GF(p^d)$ allows the "packing" of multiple messages into a plaintext by partitioning it into independent "slots" (Smart & Vercauteren, 2014), thereby permitting the execution of the same homomorphic operation on multiple slots in a Single Instruction Multiple Data (SIMD) fashion. Figure 4 exemplifies a ciphertext ***X***, encrypting a plaintext that packs two 4-bit messages (X[0] and X[1]), into 8 plaintext slots.

Figure 4. Two 4-bit messages (X[0], X[1]) packed into 8 plaintext slots

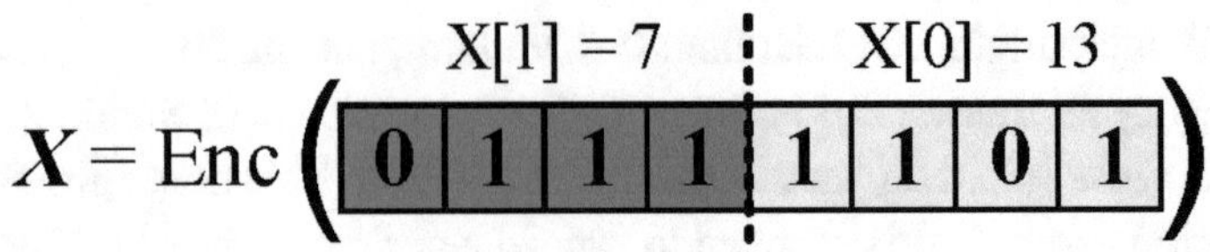

X[1] = 7 | X[0] = 13

X = Enc (0 | 1 | 1 | 1 | 1 | 1 | 0 | 1)

Table 1. Relevant BGV parameters

Term	BGV Definition	Usage in Application
nSlots	Number of slots in plaintext	-
nMsgs	Number of messages	Number of ECG samples
k	Bit-length of a message	ECG sample bit-length
N	Number of ciphertexts	To store all samples

Equation (left) and Table 1 exemplify the relationship among relevant BGV parameters for message packing. In our implementation, which uses 87,896 ECG samples (i.e., "messages," nMsgs = 87,896) packed into plaintexts, containing 682 slots each (nSlots = 682). From Equation (right), 2093 ciphertexts are needed to store these 16-bit ECG samples (i.e., $k = 16$, $N = 2093$).

$$N = \left\lceil \frac{nMsgs}{\left\lfloor \frac{nSlots}{k} \right\rfloor} \right\rceil \Rightarrow \left\lceil \frac{87{,}896}{\left\lfloor \frac{682}{16} \right\rfloor} \right\rceil \Rightarrow N = 2093 \quad (4)$$

Primitive Operations in BGV

Packing allows *nSlots* parallel operations on plaintext slots, but with restricted applicability, as will be detailed in the next section. From a set of existing operations in BGV, we use an orthogonal set of four as shown in Figure 5. Note that, the data contained in a ciphertext (e.g., ciphertext ***A*** in Figure **5**a) does not necessarily have a one-on-one correspondence with the data contained in the unencrypted plaintext slots (1010 0101).

- **Homomorphic Addition ($+_h$):** of two ciphertexts corresponds to a slot-wise XOR of the corresponding plaintext in *GF*(2), as shown in Figure **5**a. $+_h$ does not affect the level *L* of the BGV scheme.
- **Homomorphic Multiplication ($\times_h$):** of two ciphertexts corresponds to a slot-wise AND operation of the corresponding plaintexts, as shown in Figure **5**b. $\times_h$ operation adds one to the level *L* of the ciphertext. Therefore, the depth of multiplications will determine the required level of the BGV scheme.
- **Rotate ($>>>_h$, $<<<_h$):** provides rotation of slots similar to a barrel shifter as shown in Figure 5c. Slots will wrap around based on the rotation direction, thereby potentially garbling the data contained in neighboring slots. This will be corrected using Select operations.
- **Select (sel_{mask}):** chooses between the slots of two plaintexts based on the selection mask as shown in Figure 5d, through an unencrypted binary vector. We will use Select to mask out the bits that are diffused from other messages after a Rotate.

Performance Analysis

Leveled FHE implies an untraditional trade-off scheme: choosing *L* too high slows down the entire chain of homomorphic operations, while small *L* values prohibit evaluating elaborate functions. Figure 6 shows impact of level *L* on ciphertext and public key sizes, which grow substantially with the increased *L*, even

Figure 5. Computational Primitives in BGV

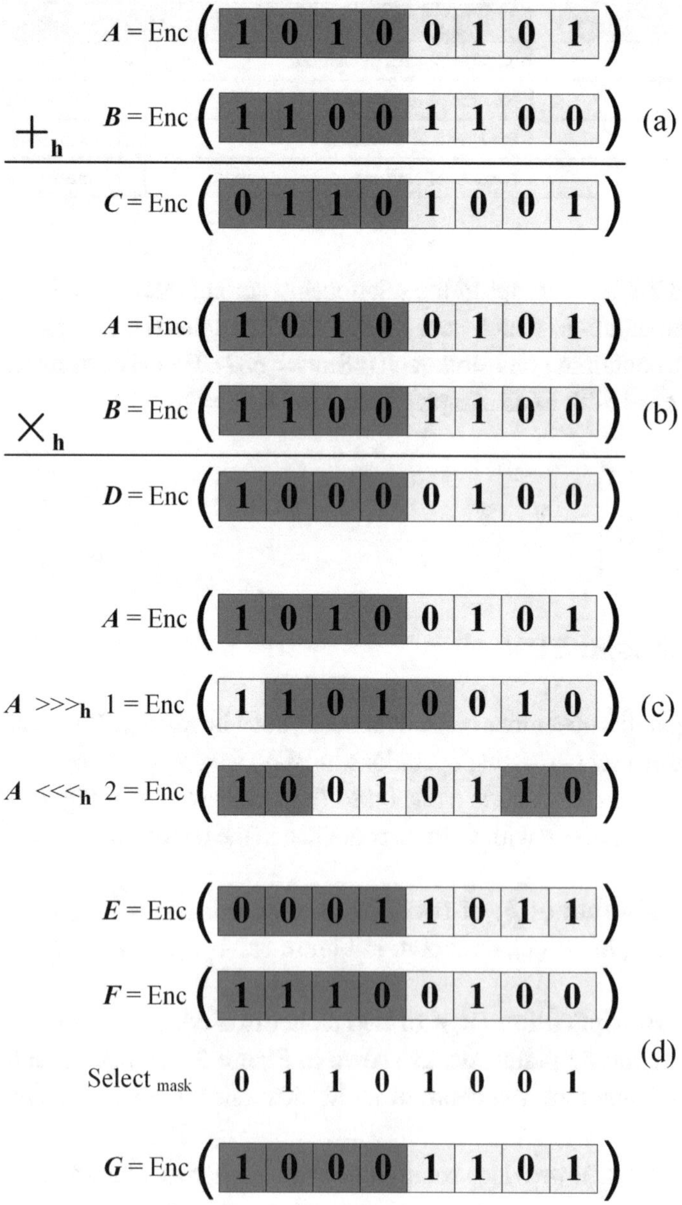

$A = \text{Enc}(1\ 0\ 1\ 0\ 0\ 1\ 0\ 1)$

$+_h \quad B = \text{Enc}(1\ 1\ 0\ 0\ 1\ 1\ 0\ 0)$ (a)

$C = \text{Enc}(0\ 1\ 1\ 0\ 1\ 0\ 0\ 1)$

$A = \text{Enc}(1\ 0\ 1\ 0\ 0\ 1\ 0\ 1)$

$\times_h \quad B = \text{Enc}(1\ 1\ 0\ 0\ 1\ 1\ 0\ 0)$ (b)

$D = \text{Enc}(1\ 0\ 0\ 0\ 0\ 1\ 0\ 0)$

$A = \text{Enc}(1\ 0\ 1\ 0\ 0\ 1\ 0\ 1)$

$A >>>_h 1 = \text{Enc}(1\ 1\ 0\ 1\ 0\ 0\ 1\ 0)$ (c)

$A <<<_h 2 = \text{Enc}(1\ 0\ 0\ 1\ 0\ 1\ 1\ 0)$

$E = \text{Enc}(0\ 0\ 0\ 1\ 1\ 0\ 1\ 1)$

$F = \text{Enc}(1\ 1\ 1\ 0\ 0\ 1\ 0\ 0)$

$\text{Select}_{mask}\ \ 0\ 1\ 1\ 0\ 1\ 0\ 0\ 1$ (d)

$G = \text{Enc}(1\ 0\ 0\ 0\ 1\ 1\ 0\ 1)$

to represent the same data. For example, one bit of plaintext might correspond to a 100KB of storage at $L = 10$, but it might grow to 1MB when the level is $L = 20$, requiring 10× more storage space to perform 20 cascaded homomorphic multiplications instead of 10.

Figure 7 shows a second disadvantage of increased L: Homomorphic operations execute slower with increased L. For example, while a $\times_h$ operation might take one second at $L = 20$, it takes 10 seconds at $L = 40$. Figure 7 presents the performance of individual FHE operations. While addition operation is almost free, rotation and multiplication operations are expensive and will dominate the execution time. This emphasizes the importance of L in formulating our application. When designing our medical application, optimizing the chain of computations to reduce L, multiplications, and rotations will be our priority.

Figure 6. Public Key and Ciphertext Sizes for different BGV level.

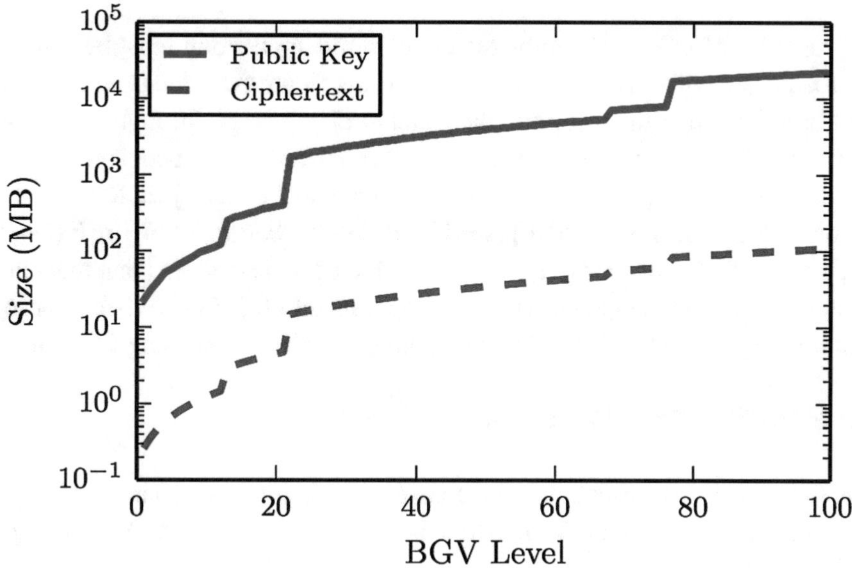

Figure 7. Level-dependent execution times of BGV primitives.

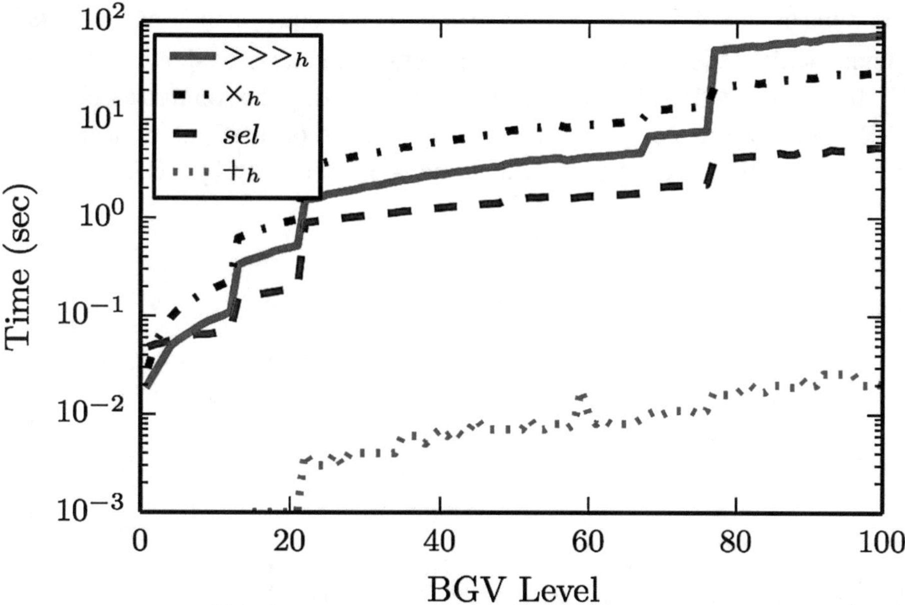

FHE IMPLEMENTATION STEPS

To utilize the properties of BGV efficiently, the entire cloud application must be centered around the computational roadmap shown in Figure 8. The top of this figure (i.e., the *data transformation path*) shows the transformations that the incoming data stream $d[i]$ must go through to produce a properly-formatted ciphertext. This top part is assumed to be performed during data acquisition by a computationally capable device, such as the patient's smartphone or a cloudlet (Wang, Liu, & Soyata, 2014; Powers, Alling, Gyampoh-Vidogah, & Soyata, 2014) (see Figure 1). The bottom of Figure 8 (i.e., the *functional transformation path*) will be the focus of this section, which details the steps that must be taken to convert the computation ($f_c(.)$) and aggregation ($f_a(.)$) functions into BGV primitives. These steps include Function-to-Circuit mapping, Circuit-to-SIMD mapping, and Execution using BGV primitives.

Conversion from Function to Circuit

The first step in functional transformation is the conversion of a function $f(.)$ into a binary circuit. Without loss of generality, this step can be demonstrated on a 4-bit greater-than ($X>Y$) comparator for two numbers X and Y circuit as follows:

$$X > Y = \left(x_3 \overline{y}_3 \oplus x_2 \overline{y}_2 e_3 \oplus x_1 \overline{y}_1 e_3 e_2 \oplus x_0 \overline{y}_0 e_3 e_2 e_1 \right) \tag{5}$$

where x_i is the value of bit i of X, $\overline{y}_i$ is the inverse of bit i of Y, and e_i is their bitwise equality ($x_i = y_i$).

The minimum multiplication depth of a 4-bit comparator circuit is 3 as shown in Figure 9. Each multiplication depth is represented by different shades of gray. Note that, the comparator circuit contains only XOR and AND gates, corresponding to homomorphic addition ($+_h$) and multiplication ($\times_h$) in $GF(2)$, respectively. For clarity we depict inverters, which can be implemented by XORs.

Figure 8. Roadmap for secure cloud computing FHE

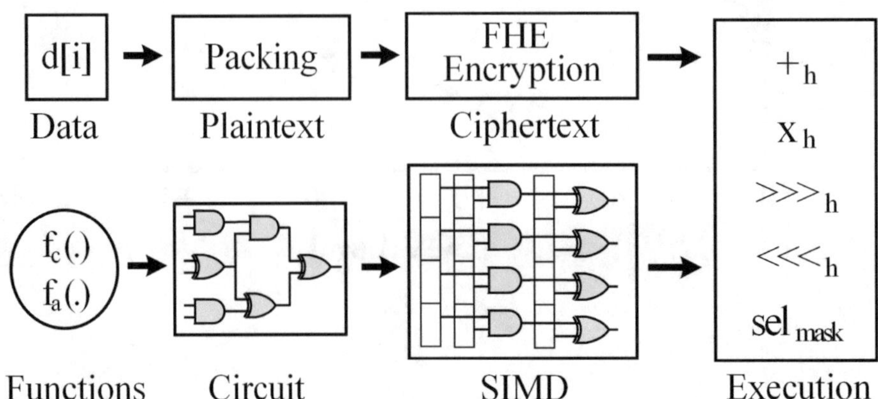

Figure 9. Depth-3 Comparison Circuit for implementing $X > Y = \left(x_3\overline{y}_3 \oplus x_2\overline{y}_2e_3 \oplus x_1\overline{y}_1e_3e_2 \oplus x_0\overline{y}_0e_3e_2e_1\right)$

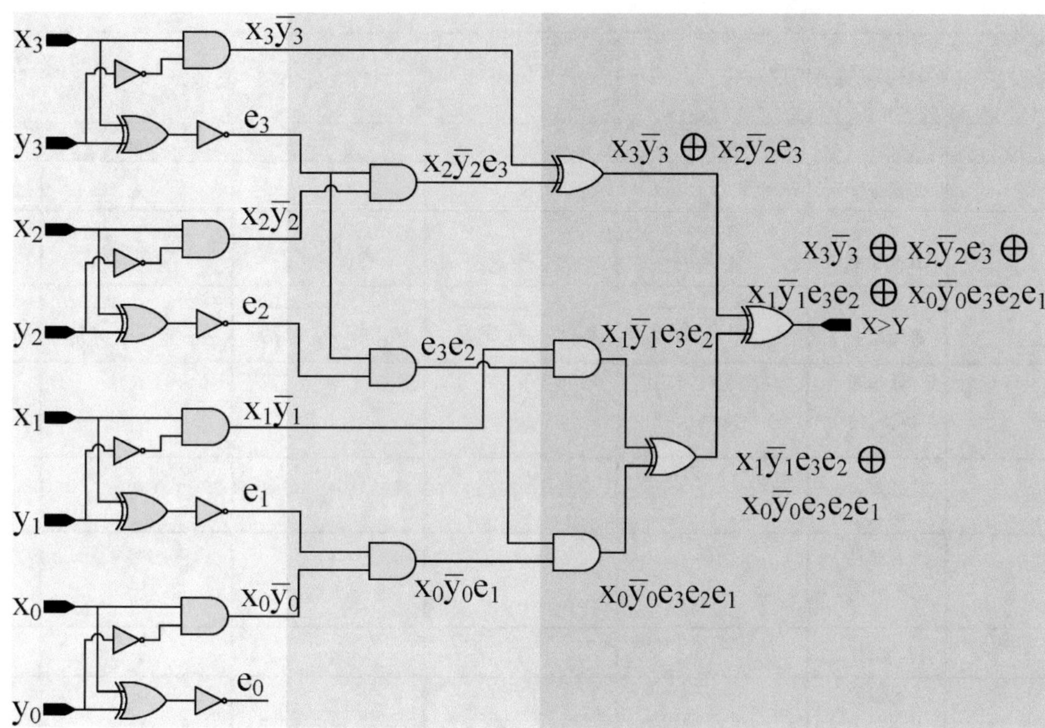

Circuit to SIMD Mapping

This step is necessary to execute homomorphic operations in a SIMD fashion. To gain insight into this concept, remember from the previous sections that each ciphertext encrypts a plaintext that maps the bits of a message into plaintext slots in *GF*(2). Let *X* and *Y* be such ciphertexts that encrypt plaintexts packing *k*-bit messages *X* and *Y*. Further, assume that bit *i* of message *X* is mapped to plaintext slot index *i* (e.g., x_0 is mapped to slot 0) and the plaintext is represented as $(x_{k-1}x_{k-2}\ldots x_1x_0)$. The homomorphic addition operation $X+_hY$ adds (i.e., XOR's) each plaintext bit having the *same slot index*. To state alternatively, a single $+_h$ operation on the ciphertext performs bitwise-XOR operations on *nSlots* plaintext slots in parallel. This has a drawback: No operation can be performed on messages with a *different slot index*, unless proper rotation and selection operations are performed, as detailed previously.

To exemplify these trade-offs, let us focus on the slot index assignments of messages in Equation . Computing terms like $x_3\overline{y}_3, x_2\overline{y}_2, x_1\overline{y}_1, x_0\overline{y}_0$ is equal to performing a single $\times_h$ operation on ciphertexts as

$$X \times_h Y \Leftrightarrow (x_3x_2x_1x_0) \wedge (y_3y_2y_1y_0),$$

where $\Leftrightarrow$ denotes the relationship between the ciphertext and plaintext, and $\wedge$ is slotwise AND. Alternatively, computing terms like $x_2\overline{y}_2e_3$ poses a problem since e_3 is in a different slot index than x_2 and $\overline{y}_2$. This means that we need to rotate ***E*** right to align it with $X \times_h \overline{Y}$. After rotating ***E***, a selection operation is needed to mask out the bits diffusing from neighboring plaintext slots.

Table 2. Sequence of FHE operations for 4-bit comparison. X and Y are 4-bit messages, x_i and y_i's are the bits of the messages at index i.

Step	BGV Operation on Ctxt		Plaintext	Slots		Level of Ctxt
		Slot 3	Slot 2	Slot 1	Slot 0	
1	$E = X$	x_3	x_2	x_1	x_0	L
2	$E = X +_h Y$	$x_3 \oplus y_3$	$x_2 \oplus y_2$	$x_1 \oplus y_1$	$x_0 \oplus y_0$	L
3	$E = X +_h 1$	$e_3 \Leftarrow \overline{x_3 \oplus y_3}$	$e_2 \Leftarrow \overline{x_2 \oplus y_2}$	$e_1 \Leftarrow \overline{x_1 \oplus y_1}$	$e_0 \Leftarrow \overline{x_0 \oplus y_0}$	L
4	$A = E >>>_h 1$	?	e_3	e_2	e_1	L
5	$A = E\ sell_{0111} 1$	1	e_3	e_2	e_1	L
6	$B = E >>>_h 2$	?	?	e_3	e_2	L
7	$B = B\ sel_{0011} 1$	1	1	e_3	e_2	L
8	$C = E >>>_h 3$	?	?	?	e_3	L
9	$C = B\ sel_{0001} 1$	1	1	1	e_3	L
10	$A = A \times_h B$	1	e_3	$e_3 e_2$	$e_2 e_1$	L - 1
11	$M = A \times_h C$	1	e_3	$e_3 e_2$	$e_3 e_2 e_1$	L - 2
12	$Q = Y$	y_3	y_2	y_1	y_0	L
13	$Q = Q +_h 1$	$\overline{y}_3$	$\overline{y}_2$	$\overline{y}_1$	$\overline{y}_0$	L
14	$Q = Q \times_h X$	$x_3\overline{y}_3$	$x_2\overline{y}_2$	$x_1\overline{y}_1$	$x_0\overline{y}_0$	L - 1
15	$M = M \times_h Q$	$x_3\overline{y}_3$	$x_2\overline{y}_2 e_3$	$x_1\overline{y}_1 e_3 e_2$	$x_0\overline{y}_0 e_3 e_2 e_1$	L - 3

Conversion from SIMD to FHE Primitives

To evaluate the circuit in Equation using BGV primitives, we decouple the computation into two separate homomorphic multiplications ($\times_h$) as follows:

$$X >_h Y = (X \times_h Y) \times_h M \Leftrightarrow ((x_3 x_2 x_1 x_0) \wedge (\overline{y}_3 \overline{y}_2 \overline{y}_1 \overline{y}_0)) \wedge (1 e_3 e_3 e_2 e_3 e_2 e_1) \quad (6)$$

M and ***E*** ciphertexts are the encrypted versions of $(1e_3\ e_3e_2\ e_3e_2e_1)$ and $(e_3\ e_2\ e_1\ e_0)$. Table **2** lists the steps for evaluating Equation using BGV primitives, by detailing the intermediate ciphertext levels L and the status of the encrypted plaintext slots. First, we compute ***E*** in Steps 1-3, which requires an XNOR operation to check if the bits of X and Y are equal as follows:

$$e_i = XNOR(x_i, y_i) = \overline{x_i \oplus y_i} = x_i \oplus y_i \oplus 1 \tag{7}$$

- **Naive Computation of *M*:** Calculating ***M*** from ***E*** requires storing rotated versions of ***E*** within temporary ciphertexts ***A***, ***B***, ***C***, which store encrypted values of $(1e_3\ e_2\ e_1)$, $(111e_1)$ and $(11e_2\ e_1)$ in Steps 4-9. Rotation diffuses unwanted bits into ***E*** (represented as "?"), which must be replaced with "1"s via a proper selection mask. ***M*** (encrypted $(1e_3\ e_3e_2\ e_3e_2e_1)$) is computed by multiplying these temporary ciphertexts as $\boldsymbol{M}=\boldsymbol{A}\times_h\boldsymbol{B}\times_h\boldsymbol{C}$ in Steps 10-11. Note that, level L of the ciphertexts is reduced by one after each $\times_h$ (as described previously). In general, computing ***M*** for k-bit messages requires first generating $(k-1)$ rotated versions of ***E*** and then multiplying them by a $\log_2 k$ depth binary-tree circuit.
- **Running Products Method:** The naive method for computing ***M*** requires O(k) of the expensive $>>>_h$ operations which dominate the run-time of $>_h$. A close observation of ***M*** reveals that plaintext slots store running products of the e_i bits. Therefore, computing the running products, as pseudo-coded below, can optimize calculation of M:

  $M \leftarrow M >>>_h 1$
  $\boldsymbol{M} \leftarrow \boldsymbol{M} sel_{mask} \mathbf{1}$, $i \leftarrow 1$
  while $i<k$ **do**
  $\boldsymbol{T} \leftarrow \boldsymbol{M}$
  $T \leftarrow T >>>_h i$
  $\boldsymbol{T} \leftarrow \boldsymbol{T} sel_{mask} 1$
  $\boldsymbol{M} \leftarrow \boldsymbol{M} \times_h \boldsymbol{T}$
  $i \leftarrow i \bullet 2$
  end while

With the optimization, number of $>>>_h$ operations is reduced to $O(\log_2 k)$, resulting in a speedup of $\approx \dfrac{O(k)}{O(\log_2 k)}$ compared to the naive method. We will provide detailed results on this later.

Once ***M*** is computed, the final result of $>_h$ is determined by first computing ***Y*** in Steps 12-13 and then calculating $(\boldsymbol{X} \times_h \boldsymbol{Y} \times_h \boldsymbol{M})$ in Steps 14-15. Note that the resulting ciphertext is at level $L-3$ indicating the cost of $>_h$ as 3 levels, which is same as the multiplicative depth of the comparison circuit in Figure 9. In general, comparison of k-bit messages requires $\log_2 k+1$ levels ($\log_2 k$ levels for computing ***M*** and 1 level for $\times_h$ at the end). Figure 10 shows $>_h$ applied to two 4-bit messages, with a TRUE or FALSE result.

Figure 10. The result of the comparison in Equation 6 is a k-bit integer denoting ZERO (FALSE) or non-zero (TRUE).

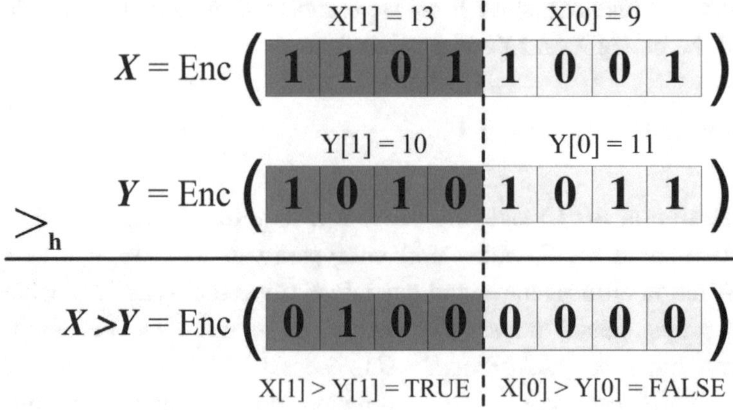

Conversion from SIMD to FHE Primitives

The previous section detailed the implementation of homomorphic comparison ($>_h$), which detects LQTS based on Equation . The result of this comparison is TRUE or FALSE (i.e., LQTS Detected / Not Detected) in the format shown in Figure 10. To detect LQTS in *any sample* within a given interval, a Logical OR aggregation must be performed over multiple comparison results as shown in Equation . Logical OR function can be expressed as a depth-1 circuit using XOR, AND gates as

$$OR(x_i, y_i) = x_i \oplus y_i \oplus x_i y_i \,.$$

The aggregated result will a have similar format shown in Figure 10, in which even a single "1" in any slot means *LQTS Detected.*

The order of applying f_a(.)affects the depth of the circuit required for aggregation. Since our aggregations are associative, they can be performed in two ways (Savage, 1997): sequential (Figure 11a) or as a binary tree (Figure 11b). While both methods require applying the same number of f_a(.)'s for aggregation, binary tree method results in a lower depth circuit. Specifically, if f_a(.) has a multiplicative depth d, then aggregating N results requires $O(N \cdot d)$-depth using the sequential method, while $O(\lceil \log_2 N \rceil \cdot d)$ -depth is sufficient for the binary tree method. Therefore, we will implement aggregation by applying f_a(.) using the binary tree method, which reduces the required level L for BGV.

IMPLEMENTING MEDICAL APPLICATIONS

In this section, we provide details on the FHE-based implementation of medical applications using the computational structure and the implementation steps described in the previous sections. Performance of FHE-based applications depend on two factors: 1) the level L of the FHE scheme, and 2) the number of compute-intensive multiplication and rotation operations. We propose several optimizations to reduce

Figure 11. Aggregation Types: a) Sequential, b) Binary Tree

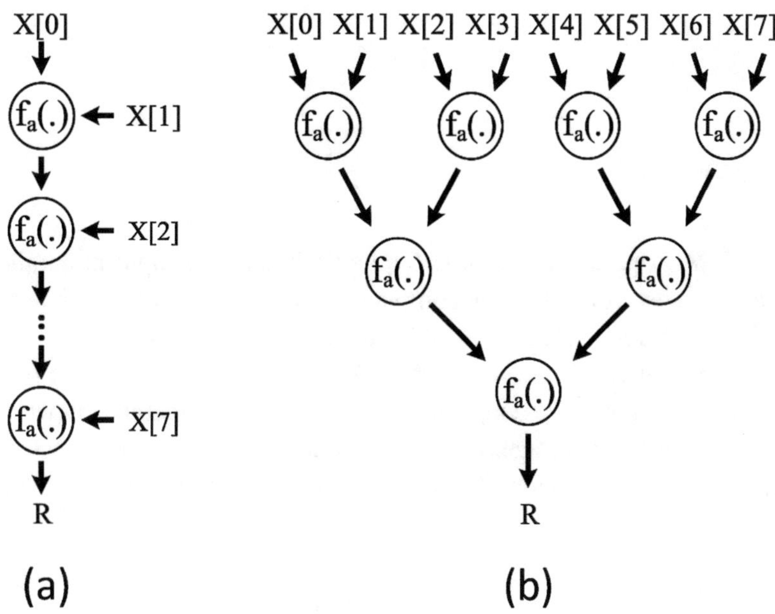

both the level L and the number of expensive FHE operations. We calculate the required level L for each application that operates on N ciphertexts encrypting a vector of k-bit ECG data. Without loss of generality, we specifically focus on three fundamental operations: 1) average heart rate, 2) LQTS detection, and 3) minimum and maximum heart rate calculation. These operations will form a fundamental basis for allowing more sophisticated medical applications.

Conversion from SIMD to FHE Primitives

Finding the average heart rate involves accumulating encrypted values in N ciphertexts. For an efficient implementation of FHE-based accumulation, we use conventional VLSI design techniques similar to Wallace (Wallace, 1964) and Dadda (Dadda, 1965) multipliers that perform high-speed multi-operand additions by reducing both the depth and the number of carry operations. This design approach benefits our FHE-based accumulation in two ways: 1) reducing the number of carry operations avoids compute-intensive $\times_h$ operations, and 2) reducing the depth of computations translates to a reduced L in FHE.

We implement multi-operand additions by using a tree of Carry Save Adders (CSA), which reduces N operands down to 2. Remaining operands are added using a fast parallel-prefix adder with a low-depth carry calculation/propagation to compute the final sum. Both CSA and parallel-prefix adders are amenable to SIMD, which perfectly fits the FHE implementation that we described in the previous section. We will now analyze the implementation details of both CSA and parallel-prefix adders:

- **Carry Save Adder (CSA):** Compresses 3 *k*-bit inputs (*X*, *Y*, *Z*) to 2 outputs (*S*: sum, *C*: carry) as follows:

$$S = X \oplus Y \oplus Z$$

$$C = (XY \vee XZ \vee YZ) << 1 \tag{8}$$

where $\oplus$ and $\vee$ are SIMD operations performed on all *k* bits of the input in parallel. Multiplication depth of the CSA adder is determined by the computation of C, which requires a depth-3 circuit (1 for multiplications and 2 for combining the results of multiplications via $\vee$).

To reduce *N* *k*-bit operands, multiple stages of CSAs can be arranged as a tree by connecting *S* and *C* as inputs to other CSAs. Figure 12 exemplifies the reduction of 8 operands down to 2 by using four levels of CSAs. The number of CSA stages (*nCSAStages*) for reducing *N* operands is lower-bounded by Equation (Savage, 1997) as shown below. The overall multiplication depth required by the CSA compression is equal to *nCSAStages*×3

$$\left\lceil \frac{\log_2(N/2)}{\log_2(3/2)} \right\rceil + 1 \leq nCSAStages \tag{9}$$

- **Further Optimizations to CSA:** The depth of CSA depends on computing *C* which requires OR operations over products of inputs. We show in Table **3** that OR operations can be replaced with XORs for computing *C*, yielding an equivalent result. This wouldn't be a meaningful substitution in a VLSI implementation, since XOR gates typically have a higher delay than OR gates (NCSU, 2014). However, it reduces the depth of CSA from 3 to 1, which results in a ≈3× performance improvement in an FHE implementation. With this optimization, CSA compression requires only *nCSAStages* depth.
- **Parallel-Prefix Adder:** We use the Kogge-Stone adder (Kogge & Stone, 1973) as our parallel-prefix adder, which has a minimum possible multiplication depth, and its implementation is amenable to SIMD as exemplified in Figure 13.

Figure 12. 8:2 compression of the operands using tree of CSAs.

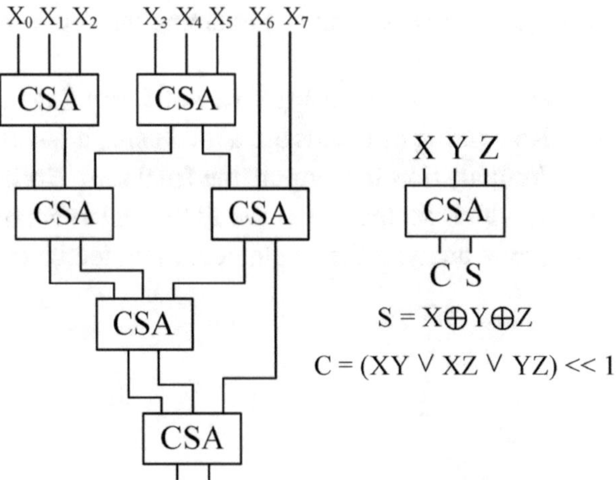

Table 3. Replacing OR with XOR in CSA.

X	Y	Z	XY	XZ	YZ	$XY \perp XZ \perp YZ$	
						$\perp = \vee$	$\perp = \oplus$
0	0	0	0	0	0	0	0
0	0	1	0	0	0	0	0
0	1	0	0	0	0	0	0
0	1	1	0	0	1	1	1
1	0	0	0	0	0	0	0
1	0	1	0	1	0	1	1
1	1	0	1	0	0	1	1
1	1	1	1	1	1	1	1

Figure 13. Kogge-Stone Parallel Prefix Adder

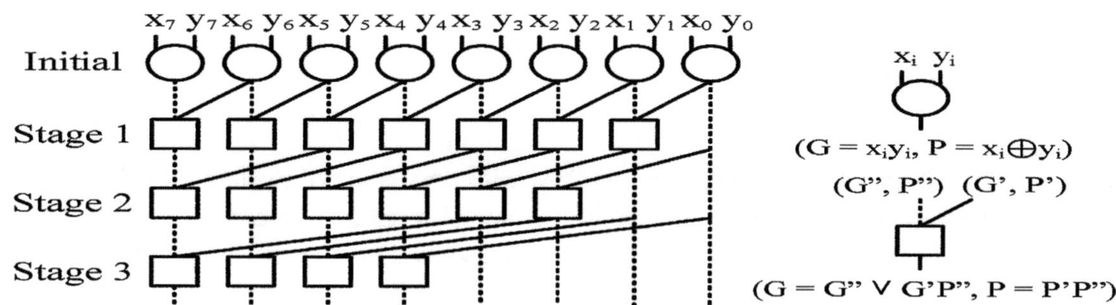

To add two k-bit numbers, Kogge-Stone adder first computes the initial Generate (G) and Propagate (P), which require a single multiplication depth to compute $G = XY$. Then G and P are updated in $\log_2 k$ stages, where each stage requires a depth-2 multiplication for updating G as $G = G'' \vee G'P'$. The final sum (S) is computed as $S = P \oplus (G << 1)$. Therefore, overall multiplication depth of the Kogge-Stone adder is equal to $2\log_2 k+1$.

To compute average heart rate of N ciphertexts encrypting k-bit messages, first we use tree of CSA adders to compress N ciphertexts down to 2 ciphertexts. Then, we add the remaining 2 ciphertexts using a Kogge-Stone adder. We showed that the multiplication depths for tree of CSA and Kogge-Stone adder are $\left\lceil \frac{\log_2(N/2)}{\log_2(3/2)} \right\rceil + 1$ and $2\log_2 k+1$, respectively. Therefore, to compute the average heart rate, the initial level L of BGV should be chosen as

$$L > \left(\left\lceil \frac{\log_2(N/2)}{\log_2(3/2)} \right\rceil + 1 \right) + \left(2\log_2 k + 1 \right).$$

LQTS Detection

LQTS detection requires evaluating Bazett's formula (Bazzett, 1997) homomorphically as described previously. To avoid the expensive square root and division operations, we re-formulate Equation as follows:

$$\frac{QT}{\sqrt{RR}} > 500\ ms \Rightarrow QT^2 > RR \times 250{,}000 \Rightarrow QT_H > RR_H \tag{10}$$

where QT_H=QT^2 and RR_H=RR×250,000 are pre-computed using front-end devices (left side of Figure 1), which transmit the FHE-encrypted versions of QT_H and RR_H into the cloud for LQTS detection. The cloud can perform LQTS detection as outlined in the previous section, by aggregating the result of the individual comparisons using OR operations, as detailed before. To check if an LQTS occurred within a given interval, the back-end device requests the result from the cloud and decrypts it (right side of Figure 1). The back-end device only needs to check presence of a "1" in the decrypted plaintext. If even a single "1" is present, this indicates that during that interval, QT_H was greater than RR_H at least once, i.e., *LQTS condition detected.*

The required depth for LQTS detection is the comparison depth plus the OR-reduction depth, which were shown to have individual depths ($\log_2 k$+1) and $\lceil \log_2 N \rceil$, respectively in the previous section. Therefore, the initial FHE level

$$L > \left(\log_2 k + 1 + \lceil \log_2 N \rceil\right)$$

must be chosen. Figure 14 shows speed-ups obtained with the optimized method for different BGV levels. The parameters are same as that are used in evaluation later in the next section. For each level L, ciphertexts pack 16-bit messages and we observe an average speed-up of ≈3× which close to the best-case theoretical improvement ratio of $\approx \frac{O(k)}{O(\log_2 k)}$.

Figure 14. Normalized run-times (sec) for $>_h$ using Naive (left bars) and Running-products (right bars) method for k=16 (16-bit messages).

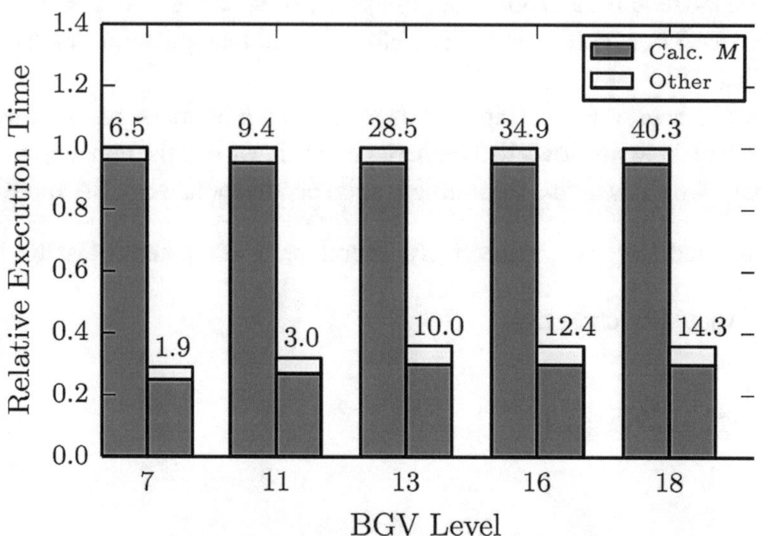

Figure 15. Maximum Computation

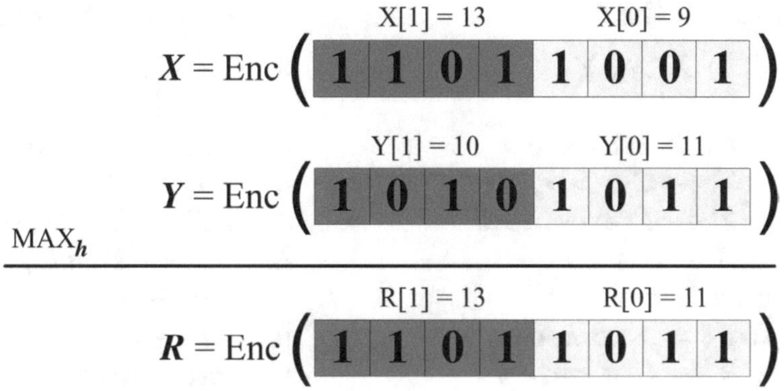

X[1] = 13 X[0] = 9

$\boldsymbol{X} = \text{Enc}(1\ 1\ 0\ 1\ 1\ 0\ 0\ 1)$

Y[1] = 10 Y[0] = 11

$\boldsymbol{Y} = \text{Enc}(1\ 0\ 1\ 0\ 1\ 0\ 1\ 1)$

MAX_h

R[1] = 13 R[0] = 11

$\boldsymbol{R} = \text{Enc}(1\ 1\ 0\ 1\ 1\ 0\ 1\ 1)$

Minimum and Maximum Heart Rate

Minimum and Maximum Heart Rate computations are based on selecting between the same indexed messages packed inside two ciphertexts. Figure 15 presents an example of max $f_c(.)$ function applied to two ciphertexts packing two 4-bit messages.

We model max $f_c(.)$ as a multiplexer circuit as follows:

$$R = \left(X \times_h S\right) +_h \left(Y \times_h \overline{S}\right) \tag{11}$$

where ***S*** acts as the selector of the multiplexer. We use the result of $>_h$ to compute ***S*** as demonstrated in Figure 16.

Figure 16. Generating selector of the multiplexer from comparison.

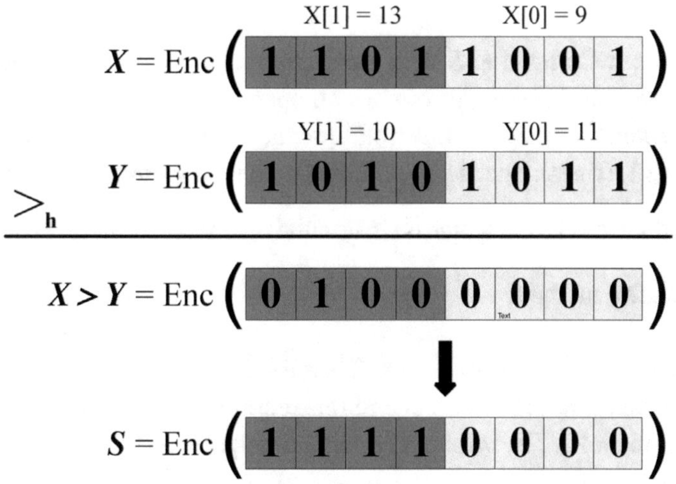

X[1] = 13 X[0] = 9

$\boldsymbol{X} = \text{Enc}(1\ 1\ 0\ 1\ 1\ 0\ 0\ 1)$

Y[1] = 10 Y[0] = 11

$\boldsymbol{Y} = \text{Enc}(1\ 0\ 1\ 0\ 1\ 0\ 1\ 1)$

$>_h$

$\boldsymbol{X} > \boldsymbol{Y} = \text{Enc}(0\ 1\ 0\ 0\ 0\ 0\ 0\ 0)$

$\boldsymbol{S} = \text{Enc}(1\ 1\ 1\ 1\ 0\ 0\ 0\ 0)$

Figure 17. Pseudo-code for computing S using Naive (left) and Total Sums (right) methods

Naïve Method

```
C ← X >_h Y
S ← C
for i = 1 to k do
    T ← C >>>_h i
    T ← T sel_mask 0
    S ← S +_h T
end for
for i = 1 to k do
    T ← C <<<_h i
    T ← T sel_mask 0
    S ← S +_h T
end for
```

Total Sums Method

```
C ← X >_h Y
R ← C, i ← 1
while i < k do
    T ← R
    T ← T >>>_h i
    T ← T sel_mask 0
    R ← R +_h T
    i ← i · 2
end while
L ← C, i ← 1
while i < k do
    T ← L <<<_h i
    T ← T sel_mask 0
    L ← L +_h T
    i ← i · 2
end while
S ← L
S ← S +_h R
```

- **Naive Computation of *S*:** In the previous section, we showed that comparing two *k*-bit numbers will produce a *k*-bit result. If the first number is greater, result will have a single "1" and (k - 1) "0"s. Otherwise the result will contain *k* "0"s. Generating ***S*** requires diffusing the single "1" of the greater than case to all plaintext slots for the corresponding message. We use a combination of rotate and select operations to route the "1" and add the rotated result to generate *k* "1"s. Pseudo-code for generating ***S*** from the comparison result is shown in Figure 17 (left).

- **Total Sums Method:** Computing ***S*** with the naive method requires *2k* rotations, selections and additions. Since we would like to perform a sum operation ($+_h$) on each slot entry, we can use the *Total Sums Algorithm* for vector summation to reduce the number of required rotations to $2\log_2 k$ as shown in Figure 17(right). Speed-ups obtained with this optimized method are plotted in Figure 18. Average speed-up is ≈3.37×, which is close to the theoretical best-case speed-up of $\approx \frac{O(k)}{O(\log_2 k)}$ compared to the naive method.

Generating ***S*** does not involve multiplication. Therefore, the required level is $\log_2 k+1$ (same as $>_h$). Once ***S*** is computed, Minimum, Maximum operations require multiplications in Equation, which adds one more level, totaling $\log_2 k+2$. The Minimum operation requires an additional step: inverting ***S***, which can be formulated as $\bar{S}=S+_h\mathbf{1}$. Using $\bar{S}$ (i.e., inverted ***S***) as the selector in Equation will yield the intended Minimum result.

Figure 18. Normalized run-times (sec) for Maximum using Naive (left bars) and Total-Sums (right bars) methods for k=16 (16-bit messages).

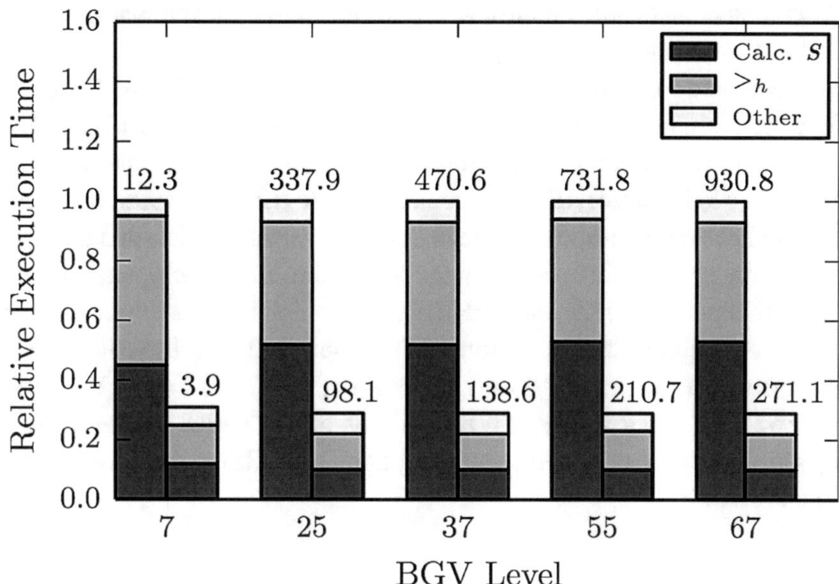

To find the minimum and maximum of N ciphertexts encrypting a vector of k-bit messages, we keep applying min and max $f_c(.)$ in $\log_2 N$ stage binary tree shown in Figure 11b, which has a multiplication depth of

$$\left(\log_2 k + 2\right) \times \left\lceil \log_2 N \right\rceil .$$

Therefore, the initial level L of BGV should be chosen as

$$L > \left(\log_2 k + 2\right) \times \left\lceil \log_2 N \right\rceil .$$

PERFORMANCE EVALUATION

In this section, we will provide the implementation results of the three fundamental operations described in the previous section: 1) average heart rate, 2) LQTS detection, and 3) minimum/maximum heart rate computation.

Experimental Setup

In the previous section, we analyzed the required minimum BGV level (L) for these three fundamental operations, and showed that L depends on two parameters: bit-length of each message inside the plaintext (k) and the total number of ciphertexts (N). Table **4** summarizes the minimum required BGV level L

for each operation for a given pair of k and N values. While 16-bit messages (k = 16) were used for the LQTS detection and the min/max heart rate computations, 32-bit messages (k = 32) were used for the average heart rate computation to provide sufficient space for up to 2^{16} accumulations of 16-bit individual values before an overflow occurs (Kocabas & Soyata, 2014).

To simulate the acquired ECG samples (Phase I in Figure **1**), we used THEW ECG database (Couderc J.-P., 2010), which contains raw ECG data captured from a patient via a 12-lead Holter monitor at a 1000 Hz sampling rate. A 24-hour time period is processed to extract the heart beat information (i.e., the RR interval in Figure **3**) in an ISHNE format annotation file (Badilini, 1998) and can be readily used to simulate our Phase I, where our acquisition devices capture raw ECG data and then pre-process them to extract RR and QT intervals before sending them to cloud in FHE-encrypted format. We encrypted the 87,896 values in this annotation file using FHE, each of which is the temporal distance between two heart beats in number-of-samples acquired from Holter monitor during the RR interval (termed *toc*). Each *toc* value is encoded as a *k*-bit *message* (i.e., *nMsgs*=87,896 and *k*=16). We perform operations over encrypted *toc* values, so our results will be in terms of *toc*, which can be trivially converted to "time" values by multiplying them with the sampling rate (1000 Hz) at the doctor's phone/tablet after decrypting the final result.

Implementation

For implementation, we used the HElib library (Halevi & Shoup, 2014). We ran our simulations on a workstation within the University of Rochester Bluehive cluster (University of Rochester, CIRC), which includes two Intel Xeon E5-2695 Processors and 252GB RAM. Since the HElib library is not thread-safe, we report only single-thread run-time results. We set the parameters of the BGV scheme based on the analysis provided in (Gentry, Halevi, & Smart, 2012). For the fastest execution time, we set the level L of the BGV scheme to the lowest possible value that allows the execution of all homomorphic operations without exceeding the noise threshold.

Table 5 lists the number of messages that one plaintext can pack at different BGV levels (L). From this table, we can calculate L for performing the three fundamental operations on our 24-hour ECG data, containing 87,896 *toc* entries, where we encode each *toc* entry a "message" (*nMsgs* = 87,896), using two different message sizes, 16-bit (k = 16) and 32-bit (k = 32), depending on the operation. For example, for LQTS detection, we use 16-bit message sizes (k = 16) on 87,896 messages (*nMsgs* = 87,896). Therefore, combining Table 4 and Equation, we derive:

$$L > \left(\log_2 k + 1\right) + \lceil \log_2 N \rceil \Rightarrow L > \left(5 + \lceil \log_2 N \rceil\right) \Rightarrow L > \left(5 + \left\lceil \log_2 \left\lceil \frac{87,896}{\left\lfloor \frac{nSlots}{16} \right\rfloor} \right\rceil \right\rceil \right) \Rightarrow L = 18$$

L value can be iteratively computed from equation above. As $L = 18$, which implies packing 42 messages in each ciphertext containing 682 slots. Although $\left(\frac{682}{16}\right) = 42.625$ messages can be packed into 682 slots, partial messages are not utilized in our implementation for simplicity, causing a wasted space

Table 4. BGV Level required for each operation.

Operation Type	Required BGV Level L
Average HR	$\left(\left\lceil \frac{\log_2(N/2)}{\log_2(3/2)} \right\rceil + 1\right) + \left(2\log_2 k + 1\right)$
LQTS	$\left(\log_2 k + 1\right) + \lceil \log_2 N \rceil$
Min, Max HR	$\left(\log_2 k + 2\right) \times \lceil \log_2 N \rceil$

Table 5. Number of packed messages in a plaintext at various BGV levels for different message bit lengths.

BGV Level (L)	*nSlots*	16-bit Messages (k = 16)	32-bit Messages (k = 32)
$1 \leq L < 12$	630	39	19
$12 \leq L < 21$	682	42	21
$22 \leq L < 68$	1285	80	40
$68 \leq L < 77$	1650	103	51
$77 \leq L < 100$	2048	128	64

of 10 slots in each plaintext. Since each plaintext can hold 42 messages, our 24-hour ECG data requires

$$N = \left\lceil \frac{87,896}{42} \right\rceil = 2093 \text{ ciphertexts.}$$

Evaluation Criteria

We evaluate the performance of the proposed system based on three relevant metrics, each quantifying a different operational cost for cloud outsourcing (Amazon Web Services):

- **Computation Rate (Γ):** We define Γ as:

$$\Gamma = \frac{\Gamma_{out}}{\Gamma_{in}}$$

where Γ_{in} is the time interval for the data being transmitted from the patient's house into the cloud, and Γ_{out} is the computation time in the cloud for this data. This "relative" definition allows us to determine whether FHE computations in the cloud can *catch up* with the rate of the incoming data ($\Gamma \leq 1$), or lag behind ($\Gamma > 1$). The significance of the Γ metric is its ability to signal the necessity of additional storage space, and the added computational latency in providing the final result to the doctor. For example, Γ

=2 implies that, 1 hour patient data takes 2 hours to compute, causing a one hour delay in providing the results to the doctor, and additional storage space to buffer the incoming encrypted data (which is not a trivial amount, as we will shortly see).

- **Storage Expansion (Λ):** As shown in Figure 6, FHE significantly expands the amount of storage required to store the encrypted incoming patient data as well as the FHE public keys. This s*torage expansion* becomes worse for increased BGV levels, L. In our definition, Λ=10,000 implies that, to store one byte of plain data in encrypted format, 10,000 bytes of cloud storage is required.
- **Network Throughput (Υ):** FHE-based computations strain the network bandwidth, since large amount of encrypted data must be transmitted over WAN connections (Kwon, Dou, Heinzelman, Soyata, Ba, & Shi, 2014). We define a third metric, Υ, which determines how much data is being transmitted across the WAN during computations. Some cloud operators (e.g., AWS (Amazon Web Services)) only charge for outgoing traffic, not for the incoming traffic. Therefore, we break Υ into two separate parts: Υp_{atient} is the amount of data transferred from front-end devices used by the patient, and Υd_{octor} is the data transferred from cloud to back-end device used by the doctor.

Experimental Results

We present our experimental results in Table 6 for the aforementioned three fundamental operations over 24 hours of ECG data, containing 87,896 *toc* values. Although every row in Table 6 relates to the same 24-hour ECG data described in detail in the previous section, the *partitioning* of the data differs among different rows. For example, for the LQTS detection, the last row indicates $N = 2093$, $L = 18$, $\Gamma = 0.36$. From Table 6, we see that, $\Gamma = 0.36$, translating to a computation time of 24 x 0.36 = 8.64 hours, or, 31,485 seconds, as indicated in the "Run-time" column. Since $\Gamma < 1$, we deduce that, the FHE computations can be done faster than the rate of data arrival, thereby eliminating the necessity to buffer large amounts of data in the cloud. However, the 24-hour ECG data still takes up 52,000× more space than the original raw data, as indicated in the Λ column. Computing LQTS requires shuttling 8.28GB of encrypted data from the patient's house to the cloud (the $\Upsilon_{patient}$ column) and requires transferring 4.1MB of resulting ciphertexts (the Υ_{doctor} column). The significant disparity is due to the substantial amount of aggregation performed during LQTS detection, leaving only the highly summarized results that need to be transferred to the doctor's smartphone. This is good news in the sense that, cloud operators, such as AWS, only charge for outgoing data, which is orders of magnitude lower in this case.

Let us now focus on the remaining rows of Table 6. The specific row we just described was based on 24 hours of accumulated patient data, acquired, transmitted, and computed as a whole (indicated as "24 hr" in the "ECG Data Interval" column). This row assumes that, the LQTS detection does not start until the entire 24-hour dataset arrives. Alternatively, the very first row of the LQTS detection (indicated as "1 min") displays $N = 2$, $L = 7$ and $\Gamma = 0.07$. This can be interpreted as: When the entire 24-hour data is transmitted 1 minute at a time, the amount of each chunk is significantly smaller: 1 minute chunks require only 2 ciphertexts ($N = 2$), each of which is encoded at an FHE level of $L = 7$. The computation time for each chunk is only 3.9 seconds, corresponding to $\Gamma = \frac{3.9s}{60s} = 0.07$. Although this row looks computationally-advantageous based on the computation metric (Γ), we see that, it hurts the Υ_{doctor} metric, since the total amount of data to

Table 6. Operational cost of medical applications based-on: Computation Rate (Γ), Storage Expansion (Λ) and Network Throughput ($\Upsilon_{patient}$ and Υ_{doctor}).

Operation	ECG Data Interval	N	L	Enc. (sec)	Dec. (Sec)	Ctxt (MB)	Ptxt (MB)	Run-time (Sec)	Γ	Λ (K)	$\Upsilon_{patient}$ (GB)	Υ_{doctor} (GB)
	1 min	3	14	0.30	0.24	3.17	274.95	31.2	0.52	41.2	6.5	4564.8
	5 min	15	18	0.41	0.31	4.05	352.23	81.6	0.27	52.6	8.3	1166.4
	15 min	44	21	0.45	0.39	4.72	399.12	215.9	0.24	61.3	9.6	453.1
Average	30 min	46	22	1.88	0.77	14.81	1721.55	677.7	0.38	107.4	15.9	710.9
Heart	60 min	92	23	1.96	0.80	15.49	1783.98	1317.4	0.37	112.2	16.6	371.7
Rate	3 hr	275	26	2.21	0.90	17.55	2038.95	4272.7	0.40	127.2	18.8	140.4
(k=32)	6 hr	550	27	2.30	0.94	18.24	2093.75	8679.8	0.40	132.1	19.6	72.9
	12 hr	1099	29	2.46	1.05	19.63	2247.22	18803.9	0.44	142.1	21.1	39.3
	24 hr	2198	31	2.69	1.15	21.03	2414.25	40997.4	0.47	152.3	22.6	21.1
	1 min	2	7	0.08	0.03	0.90	74.32	3.9	0.07	12.6	1.98	1296.1
	5 min	8	9	0.11	0.05	1.12	96.39	21.6	0.07	15.6	2.47	322.6
	15 min	24	11	0.11	0.05	1.34	110.27	99.9	0.11	18.7	2.95	128.6
LQTS	30 min	44	12	0.13	0.06	1.46	121.73	216.9	0.12	18.9	2.98	70.1
	60 min	88	13	0.28	0.22	2.96	249.03	1362.4	0.38	38.4	6.05	71.1
(k=16)	3 hr	262	15	0.33	0.26	3.39	287.73	3215.2	0.30	44.1	6.93	27.2
	6 hr	524	16	0.39	0.27	3.61	308.25	6741.8	0.31	46.9	7.38	14.5
	12 hr	1047	17	0.40	0.28	3.83	323.87	14393.3	0.33	49.7	7.83	7.7
	24 hr	2093	18	0.41	0.31	4.05	352.23	31485.1	0.36	52.7	8.28	4.1
	1 min	2	7	0.08	0.04	0.90	74.32	3.9	0.07	12.6	1.98	1296.1
	5 min	8	19	0.41	0.32	4.27	36.07	198.1	0.66	15.6	2.47	1229.7
Min	15 min	12	25	2.12	0.86	16.86	1984. 95	1185.4	1.32	18.7	2.95	1618.6
Max	30 min	23	31	2.58	1.06	21.03	2414.25	2852.8	1.58	18.9	2.98	1009.5
	60 min	46	37	3.09	1.27	25.27	2880.37	6946.8	1.93	38.4	6.05	66.5
HR	3 hr	138	49	4.28	1.73	33.86	3850.37	28459.1	2.64	44.1	6.93	270.9
	6 hr	275	55	4.75	1.88	38.21	4372.2	70849	3.28	46.9	7.38	152.8
(k=16)	12 hr	550	61	4.99	2.05	42.57	4918.28	148189.6	3.43	49.7	7.83	85.2
	24 hr	1099	67	5.04	2.29	46.94	5362.7	325331.9	3.77	52.7	8.28	46.9

transfer 24 hours of data in 1 minute chunks ends up being 1296.1 MB. To state alternatively, the smaller the granularity of the results, the worse the Υ_{doctor} becomes, and the better the Γ is. The storage required for these results improves when the chunk size is smaller due to the reduced level, L, to encrypt these chunks. For example, while Λ=12,600 for 1-minute chunks, it increases to Λ52,700 for a single large 24-hour chunk. The trade-offs involving these three parameters become less obvious when the cloud operators' billing is based on availability of the resources. For example, if the application has the flexibility to wait for the results longer, different rows in Table 6 might provide different cost alternatives for the healthcare organization, which is the rationale for our detailed analysis.

CONCLUSION AND FUTURE WORK

In this chapter, we proposed a novel method for privacy- preserving medical cloud computing using Fully Homomorphic Encryption (FHE). Due to the computational complexity of FHE, we provided a detailed analysis of our approach on three fundamental operations: 1) calculation of the average heart rate, 2) calculation of the Minimum and Maximum heart rate, and 3) automated detection of the long-QT Syndrome (LQTS). We demonstrated our results on an FHE-driven program by using a 24-hour set of ECG samples from the THEW database.

Our results show that, a healthcare organization can utilize this program as of today, despite its performance disadvantage. We demonstrated that, the afore- mentioned three fundamental computations could be performed at the same rate of data arrival, eliminating the need to store excessive amounts of data. We defined three performance metrics related to the operation of FHE: Γ, Λ and Υ quantify the computational, storage, and bandwidth requirements of these three fundamental operations. Our results show that, these operations can be performed with reasonable resources, available within cloud computing platforms today. Due to the continuously improving pricing schemes for cloud services and the algorithmic improvements on FHE, the practicality of FHE-based medical cloud computing will improve, and may eventually become commonplace. Therefore, our study is a good step towards making FHE-based medical cloud computing a reality.

ACKNOWLEDGMENT

This work is supported in part by the National Science Foundation grant CNS-1239423 and by Nvidia Corp.

REFERENCES

Aktas, M., Shah, A. H., & Akiyama, T. (2007). Dofetilide-Induced Long QT and Torsades de Pointes. *Annals of Noninvasive Electrocardiology*, *12*(3), 197–202. doi:10.1111/j.1542-474X.2007.00161.x PMID:17617063

AliveCor. (n.d.). *AliveCor Heart Monitor*. Retrieved from http://www.alivecor.com

Amazon Web Services. (n.d.). Retrieved from http://aws.amazon.com

Badilini, F. (1998). The ISHNE Holter Standard Output File Format. *Annals of Noninvasive Cardiology*, 263-266.

Bazzett, H. (1997). An analysis of the time-relations of electrocardiograms. *Annals of Noninvasive Electrocardiology*, *2*(2), 177–194. doi:10.1111/j.1542-474X.1997.tb00325.x

Boneh, D., Goh, E.-J., & Nissim, K. (2005). Evaluating 2-DNF Formulas on Ciphertexts. *Proceedings of the 2nd International Conference on Theory of Cryptography*, (pp. 325-341). doi:10.1007/978-3-540-30576-7_18

Bos, J. W., Lauter, K., & Naehrig, M. (2014). Private predictive analysis on encrypted medical data. *Journal of Biomedical Informatics*, *50*, 234–243. doi:10.1016/j.jbi.2014.04.003 PMID:24835616

Brakerski, Z., Gentry, C., & Vaikuntanathan, V. (2012). Leveled Fully Homomorphic Encryption without Bootstrapping. *Proceedings of the 3rd Innovations in Theoretical Computer Science Conference*, (pp. 309-325). doi:10.1145/2090236.2090262

Brakerski, Z., & Vaikuntanathan, V. (2011). Efficient Fully Homomorphic Encryption from Standard LWE. *Foundations of Computer Science*, 97-106.

Brakerski, Z., & Vaikuntanathan, V. (2011). *Fully homomorphic encryption from ring-LWE and security for key dependent messages* (pp. 505–524). CRYPTO. doi:10.1007/978-3-642-22792-9_29

Brenyo, A. J., Huang, D. T., & Aktas, M. (2011). Congenital long and short qt syndromes. *Cardiology*, *122*(4), 237–247. doi:10.1159/000339537 PMID:22906875

CardioLeaf. (2013). *Clearbridge VitalSigns CardioLeaf PRO*. Retrieved from http://www.clearbridgevitalsigns.com/pro.html

CareCloud. (2013). Retrieved from http://www.carecloud.com/

Cohen, J. D., & Fischer, M. J. (1985). A robust and verifiable cryptographically secure election scheme. *Symposium on Foundations of Computer Science* (pp. 372-382). IEEE. doi:10.1109/SFCS.1985.2

Coron, J.-S., Mandal, A., Naccache, D., & Tibouchi, M. (2011). *Fully homomorphic encryption over the integers with shorter public keys* (pp. 487–504). CRYPTO. doi:10.1007/978-3-642-22792-9_28

Couderc, J., Xia, J., McGrath, M., Zareba, W., Slaton, B., & Kakulavaram, A. et al.. (2011). Increased repolarization heterogeneity is associated with increased mortality in hemodialysis patients. *Computers in Cardiology*, 845–848.

Couderc, J., Xia, J., Xu, X., Kaab, S., Hinteeser, M., & Zareba, W. (2010). Static and dynamic electrocardiographic patterns preceding torsades de pointes in the acquired and congenital long QT syndrome. *Computers in Cardiology*, 357–360. PMID:22068668

Couderc, J.-P. (2010). The Telemetric and Holter ECG Warehouse initiative (THEW): A data repository for the design, implementation and validation of ECG related technologies. *IEEE Engineering in Medicine and Biology Society (EMBC)*, 6252-6255.

Couderc, J.-P., Garnett, C., Li, M., Handzel, R., McNitt, S., Xia, X., & Zareba, W. et al. (2011). Highly automated QT measurement techniques in 7 thorough QT studies implemented under ICH E14 guidelines. *Annals of Noninvasive Electrocardiology*, *16*(1), 13–24. doi:10.1111/j.1542-474X.2010.00402.x PMID:21251129

Dadda, L. (1965). Some schemes for parallel multipliers. *Alta Frequenza*, 349–356.

Dai, W., Doroz, Y., & Sunar, B. (2014). Accelerating ntru based homomorphic encryption using gpus. *High Performance Extreme Computing Conference*.

Damgard, I., & Jurik, M. (2001). *A generalisation, a simplification and some applications of paillier's probabilistic public-key system* (pp. 119–136). Public Key Cryptography.

DARPA-PROCEED. (n.d.). Retrieved from DARPA-PROCEED: http://www.darpa.mil/Our_Work/I2O/Programs/PROgramming_Computation_on_EncryptEd_Data_(PROCEED).aspx

Dijk, M., Gentry, C., Halevi, S., & Vaikuntanathan, V. (2010). Fully Homomorphic Encryption over the Integers. *Advances in Cryptology (EUROCRYPT)*, 24-43.

Dr Chrono. (2013). Retrieved from https://drchrono.com

El Gamal, T. (1985). A Public Key Cryptosystem and a Signature Scheme based on Discrete Logarithms. *IEEE Transactions on Information Theory*, *31*(4), 469–472. doi:10.1109/TIT.1985.1057074

Fink, M., Noble, D., Virag, L., Varro, A., & Giles, W. R. (2008). Contributions of HERG K+ current to repolarization of the human ventricular action potential. *Progress in Biophysics and Molecular Biology*, *96*(1-3), 357–376. doi:10.1016/j.pbiomolbio.2007.07.011 PMID:17919688

Gentry, C. (2009). *A Fully Homomorphic Encryption Scheme*. Stanford University.

Gentry, C., & Halevi, S. (2011). *Fully homomorphic encryption without squashing using depth-3 arithmetic circuits* (pp. 107–109). FOCS. doi:10.1109/FOCS.2011.94

Gentry, C., & Halevi, S. (2011). *Implementing Gentry's fully-homomorphic encryption scheme* (pp. 129–148). EUROCRYPT.

Gentry, C., Halevi, S., & Smart, N. (2012). *Better bootstrapping in fully homomorphic encryption* (pp. 1–16). PKC.

Gentry, C., Halevi, S., & Smart, N. (2012). *Fully homomorphic encryption with polylog overhead* (pp. 465–482). EUROCRYPT.

Gentry, C., Halevi, S., & Smart, N. P. (2012). *Homomorphic evaluation of the AES circuit* (pp. 850–867). CRYPTO.

Goldwasser, S., & Micali, S. (1982). Probabilistic Encryption - How to Play Mental Poker Keeping Secret all Partial Information. *Proceedings of the 14th Annual ACM Symposium on Theory of Computing*, (pp. 365-377). doi:10.1145/800070.802212

Google Cloud Platform. (n.d.). Retrieved from https://cloud.google.com

Halevi, S., & Shoup, V. (2014). *HElib Fully Homomorphic Encryption Library*. Retrieved from http://www.github.com/shaih/HElib

Hoyert, D. L., & Xu, J. (2012). Deaths: Preliminary data for 2011. *National Vital Statistics Reports*, *61*, 1–51. PMID:24984457

Kocabas, O., & Soyata, T. (2014). Medical Data Analytics in the cloud using Homomorphic Encryption. In *Handbook of Research on Cloud Infrastructures for Big Data Analytics* (pp. 471–488). US: IGI Global. doi:10.4018/978-1-4666-5864-6.ch019

Kocabas, O., Soyata, T., Couderc, J.-P., Aktas, M., Xia, J., & Huang, M. (2013). Assessment of Cloud-based Health Monitoring using Homomorphic Encryption. *Proceedings of the 31th IEEE Conference on Computer Design*, (pp. 443-446). Asheville, NC, USA. doi:10.1109/ICCD.2013.6657078

Kogge, P. M., & Stone, H. S. (1973). A parallel algorithm for the efficient solution of a general class of recurrence equations. *Transactions on Computers*, 786-793.

Kwon, M., Dou, Z., Heinzelman, W., Soyata, T., Ba, H., & Shi, J. (2014). Use of Network Latency Profiling and Redundancy for Cloud Server Selection. *Proceedings of the 7th IEEE International Conference on Cloud Computing (IEEE CLOUD 2014)*, (pp. 826-832). Alaska. doi:10.1109/CLOUD.2014.114

Microsoft Windows Azure. (n.d.). Retrieved from http://www.microsoft.com/windowsazure

Naehrig, M., Lauter, K., & Vaikuntanathan, V. (2011). Can homomorphic encryption be practical? *Proceedings of the 3rd ACM workshop on Cloud computing security workshop*. ACM. doi:10.1145/2046660.2046682

NCSU. (2014). *Free PDK 45nm Standard Cell Library*. Retrieved from http://www. eda.ncsu.edu/wiki/FreePDK45

NIST-AES. (2001). *Advanced encryption standard*. AES.

Page, A., Kocabas, O., Ames, S., Venkitasubramaniam, M., & Soyata, T. (2014). Cloud-based Secure Health Monitoring: Optimizing Fully-Homomorphic Encryption for Streaming Algorithms. *IEEE Globecom 2014 Workshop on Cloud Computing Systems, Networks, and Applications (CCSNA)*. Austin, TX.

Page, A., Kocabas, O., Soyata, T., Aktas, M., & Couderc, J.-P. (2014). Cloud-Based Privacy-Preserving Remote ECG Monitoring and Surveillance. *Annals of Noninvasive Electrocardiology*, n/a. doi:10.1111/anec.12204 PMID:25510621

Paillier, P. (1999). *Public Key Cryptosystems Based on Composite Degree Residuosity Classes* (pp. 223–238). Advances in Cryptology. doi:10.1007/3-540-48910-X_16

Powers, N., Alling, A., Gyampoh-Vidogah, R., & Soyata, T. (2014). AXaaS: Case for Acceleration as a Service. *IEEE Globecom 2014 Workshop on Cloud Computing Systems, Networks, and Applications.*

Rivest, R., Adleman, L., & Shamir, A. (1978). A method for obtaining digital signatures and public-key cryptosystems. *Communications of the ACM*, *21*(2), 120–126. doi:10.1145/359340.359342

Rivest, R. L., Adleman, L., & Dertouzos, M. L. (1978). On data banks and privacy homomorphisms . *Foundations of secure computation*, 169-179.

Savage, J. E. (1997). *Models of Computation: Exploring the Power of Computing.*

Scarfone, K., Souppaya, M., & Sexton, M. (2007). Guide to storage encryption technologies for end user devices. *NIST Special Publication*, 111.

Shah, R. (2004). Drug-induced QT interval prolongation: Regulatory perspectives and drug development. *Annals of Medicine*, *36*(s1), 47–52. doi:10.1080/17431380410032445 PMID:15176424

Shah, R. R. (2005). Drug-induced QT interval prolongation regulatory guidance and perspectives on hERG channel studies. *Novartis Foundation Symposium*, (pp. 251-280). doi:10.1002/047002142X.ch19

Smart, N. P., & Vercauteren, F. (2010). *Fully homomorphic encryption with relatively small key and ciphertext sizes* (pp. 420–443). PKC. doi:10.1007/978-3-642-13013-7_25

Smart, N. P., & Vercauteren, F. (2014). Fully homomorphic {SIMD} operations. *Designs, Codes and Cryptography*, *71*(1), 57–81. doi:10.1007/s10623-012-9720-4

Soyata, T., Ba, H., Heinzelman, W., Kwon, M., & Shi, J. (2013). Accelerating mobile cloud computing: A survey. In *Communication Infrastructures for Cloud Computing* (pp. 175–197). IGI Global.

Soyata, T., Muraleedharan, R., Ames, S., Langdon, J., Funai, C., & Kwon, M. et al.. (2012). COMBAT: Mobile Cloud-based cOmpute/coMmunications infrastructure for BATtlefield applications. [Baltimore, MD.]. *Proceedings of the Society for Photo-Instrumentation Engineers*, *8403*, 84030K–84030K, 84030K-13. doi:10.1117/12.919146

Soyata, T., Muraleedharan, R., Funai, C., Kwon, M., & Heinzelman, W. (2012). {Cloud-Vision:} {Real-Time} Face Recognition Using a {Mobile-Cloudlet-Cloud} Acceleration Architecture. *Proceedings of the 17th IEEE Symposium on Computers and Communications (IEEE ISCC 2012)*, (pp. 59-66). Cappadocia, Turkey. doi:10.1109/ISCC.2012.6249269

Stehle, D., & Steinfeld, R. (2010). *Faster fully homomorphic encryption* (pp. 377–394). ASIACRYPT.

University of Rochester. CIRC. (n.d.). *Bluehive Cluster*. Retrieved from http://www.circ.rochester.edu/wiki/ index.php/BlueHive Cluster

US Department of Health and Human Services. (2014). Retrieved from HIPAA: http://www.hhs.gov/ocr/privacy/

US Government Printing Office. (n.d.). *Patient Protection and Affordable Care Act*. Retrieved from http://www.gpo.gov/fdsys/pkg/BILLS-111hr3590enr/pdf/BILLS-111hr3590enr.pdf

US-HHS. (n.d.). *Business Associate Agreement*. Retrieved from http://www.hhs.gov/ocr/privacy/hipaa/understanding/coveredentities/contractprov.html

Wallace, C. S. (1964). A suggestion for a fast multiplier. *Transactions on Electronic Computers*, 14-17.

Wang, H., Liu, W., & Soyata, T. (2014). Accessing Big Data in the Cloud Using Mobile Devices. In P. R. Dek (Ed.), *Handbook of Research on Cloud Infrastructures for Big Data Analytics* (pp. 444–470). Hershey, PA, USA: IGI Global. doi:10.4018/978-1-4666-5864-6.ch018

Wang, W., Hu, Y., Chen, L., Huang, X., & Sunar, B. (2013). *Exploring the feasibility of fully homomorphic encryption*. Transactions on Computers.

Woosley, R. L. (2001). *Drugs That Prolong the QT Interval and/or Induce Torsades de Pointes*. Tech. rep., Torsades.org.

Zareba, W., Moss, A. J., le Cessie, S., Locati, E. H., Robinson, J. L., Hall, W., & Andrews, M. L. (1995). Risk of cardiac events in family members of patients with long QT syndrome. *Journal of the American College of Cardiology*, *26*(7), 1685–1691. doi:10.1016/0735-1097(95)60383-2 PMID:7594104

KEY TERMS AND DEFINITIONS

Additive Homomorphic Encryption: There are two common HE schemes based on the computation that they can perform on ciphertexts: Additive HE and Multiplicative HE. Additive HE schemes can only perform addition of the underlying plaintexts.

Advanced Encryption Standard (AES): A widely used symmetric-key cryptography method based on block ciphers that contain 128-bit message blocks for encryption and decryption.

Bootstrapping: Method that was proposed by Gentry's first FHE scheme, which allows resetting the noise inside ciphertexts without decrypting them. Bootstrapping is achieved by evaluating decryption function homomorphically. This method is also known as recryption and it is widely used in current FHE schemes.

Business Associate Agreement (BAA): An agreement signed by third party service providers to ensure the protection of private health information according to HIPAA rules. In other words, any third party vendor of an entity that is subject to HIPAA rules (e.g., hospitals) must have their third party vendors sign a BAA.

Cloud Computing: A computational paradigm, in which computational, storage, networking and potentially other resources are rented from a Cloud Service provider to avoid excessive infrastructural investments.

ECG Patch: A patch consisting of sensors which are attached to a patient to monitor the electrical activities of patients' heart and record them as ECG signals.

Electrocardiogram (ECG): Recording of the electrical activity of the heart over a period of time. The recording provides useful information to diagnose possible abnormalities related to the heart.

Fully Homomorphic Encryption (FHE): A homomorphic encryption scheme that can perform addition and multiplication operations on ciphertexts. These operations translate to additions and multiplications of the corresponding plaintexts and enable the computation of any function over the ciphertexts.

Health Insurance Portability and Accountability Act (HIPAA): A set of policies to regulate the protection of the privacy of the medical information (PHI) of individuals.

Healthcare Organization (HCO): Organizations that provide health care those are subject to HIPAA rules. These organizations include not only hospitals, but, a chain of their third party vendors that provide services to the hospitals. A breach in this chain could cause any entity inside the chain to involuntarily violate HIPAA.

Holter Monitor: A portable monitoring device used by the patients for continuous monitoring of ECG activities outside the hospital while engaging their daily activities.

Homomorphic Encryption (HE): A special class of public-key cryptography that enables computations on ciphertexts without decrypting them. Computations on ciphertexts translate to meaningful operations on the underlying plaintexts.

Leveled Fully Homomorphic Encryption: A sub-class of fully homomorphic encryption that allows limited number of multiplications on FHE encrypted ciphertexts. The limit of multiplications to be performed is adjusted beforehand and based on multiplication depth, which is also called the *Level.*

Long QT Syndrome (LQTS): A syndrome that causes prolonged QT intervals. It could be inherited through the genes or acquired later and can cause sudden deaths.

Multiplicative Homomorphic Encryption: Multiplicative HE schemes can perform only multiplications of underlying plaintexts.

Protected Health Information (PHI): Information that is linked to an individual's medical condition and contains private content that must be protected. This information includes health records, names, addresses, social security numbers to name a few.

Public-Key Cryptography: A type of cryptography that requires a key pair: public and private key. While the public key is used for encryption and made available to the public, private key is used for decryption and kept secret for the parties that are privately communicating over a public channel.

QT Interval: The interval between Q and T waves of an ECG, which is usually used to diagnose possible problems such as ventricular arrhythmia that can cause sudden deaths.

RR Interval: The interval between the two R waves of an ECG, which is usually used to compute average heart rate of the individuals.

Single Instruction Multiple Data (SIMD): A parallel computation method that relies on executing the same instruction over a set of data. This method is based on parallelism at the data-level.

Symmetric-Key Cryptography: A type of cryptography that uses only a single key for both encrypting and decrypting messages.

Torsades des Pointes (TdP): A heart condition that can cause sudden deaths. It can be diagnosed by measuring QT intervals.

Very Large Scale Integration (VLSI): Design/process technique that embeds millions or even billions of transistors into a single integrated circuit (IC) chip. This allows the VLSI IC to perform highly complex computational tasks.

Chapter 8
Hardware and Software Aspects of VM-Based Mobile-Cloud Offloading

Yang Song
University of Rochester, USA

Haoliang Wang
George Mason University, USA

Tolga Soyata
University of Rochester, USA

ABSTRACT

To allow mobile devices to support resource intensive applications beyond their capabilities, mobile-cloud offloading is introduced to extend the resources of mobile devices by leveraging cloud resources. In this chapter, we will survey the state-of-the-art in VM-based mobile-cloud offloading techniques including their software and architectural aspects in detail. For the software aspects, we will provide the current improvements to different layers of various virtualization systems, particularly focusing on mobile-cloud offloading. Approaches at different offloading granularities will be reviewed and their advantages and disadvantages will be discussed. For the architectural support aspects of the virtualization, three platforms including Intel x86, ARM and NVidia GPUs will be reviewed in terms of their special architectural designs to accommodate virtualization and VM-based offloading.

INTRODUCTION

In the past decade, significant technological advances in the semiconductor technology have dramatically improved the computational and storage capability of handheld mobile devices such as smart phones and tablets. This enabled mobile devices not only to access a vast amount information instantaneously through fast communications networks, but also to perform ever more sophisticated computational tasks such as face and speech recognition, object detection and natural language processing (NLP) pervasively

DOI: 10.4018/978-1-4666-8662-5.ch008

(Wang, Liu, & Soyata, 2014). However, the performance and user experience of these resource-intensive mobile augmented-reality applications are still constrained by the relatively low performance CPU and GPU, as well as limited memory and flash storage of the mobile devices. These resource constraints cannot be easily improved due to the relative size and battery life limitations of mobile devices, as compared to mainstream desktop PCs. Therefore, many applications, which are both latency-sensitive and compute-intensive, such as real-time face recognition, are still beyond the capabilities of today's smartphones and tablets.

To overcome these resource limitations and extend the capabilities of mobile devices to the point, where they can run these resource-intensive applications, mobile-cloud computing (MCC) was introduced to leverage the cloud resources. MCC enables mobile devices to utilize powerful cloud servers to store and access a vast amount of data and process compute-intensive tasks. Mobile-cloud computing has been intensively investigated as an integration of cloud computing into the mobile environment. Utilizing cloud servers for storage is easy and there have already been many popular applications providing data backup and sharing features between the users and the cloud. Unlike storage, utilizing cloud servers for computation acceleration is not trivial. Computation offloading is a solution to alleviate resource limitations on the mobile devices and provide more capabilities for these devices by migrating partial or full computations (code, status and data) to more resourceful computers. The rapid advancement of wireless network connectivity and architectural advancements in mobile devices in recent years have made computation offloading feasible. Currently, offloading computation from mobile devices to cloud servers faces several challenges which is what most of the research in this field focuses on. These challenges are summarized below:

- **What to Offload:** The entire program cannot be offloaded for remote execution. Before offloading, the program needs to be partitioned in one of three ways: 1) manually by the programmer, 2) automatically by the compiler, or 3) at runtime. Manual partitioning will put the burden on the programmers but will potentially result in lower overhead and more flexibility. On the contrary, the automated partitioning can perform offloading on an unmodified program which is more convenient for users, but might result in a higher performance overhead. Different strategies like code tagging and dynamic prediction based on profiling can be applied to increase the performance.
- **When to Offload:** Applications may have different requirements on performance and mobile devices may have different capabilities and energy limitations. Offloading decisions need to be made based on multiple criteria, such as 1) improving performance when the remaining energy is abundant, 2) energy savings when the remaining energy is low, and 3) network conditions at runtime. These decisions can be made by statically and/or dynamically by profiling, which has an impact on the execution overhead.
- **How to Offload:** Emerging cloud computing technologies, combined with virtualization technologies provide a powerful, flexible, manageable and a secure platform for offloading. This attracted a large body of research on VM (Virtual Machine)-based offloading approaches, which study offloading at different granularities such as OS-level, application/thread-level and method-level.

To address these challenges, new schemes have been introduced to achieve seamless offloading between mobile devices and cloud servers. One of the effective approaches is the VM-based approach, where we migrate either an OS-level VM or an application-level VM to remote cloud servers, execute the compute-intensive task there and get the response back to the mobile device through either messages or joining/migrating the thread/VM. To enable VM-based offloading, which significantly differs from traditional mobile cloud computing, we need support from both the software layer (both on mobile devices and the cloud servers) and the cloud hardware layer.

The rest of this chapter is organized as follows: We will start with an introduction to general mobile cloud offloading, VM-based approaches, and the design and implementation challenges in using virtualization technologies to augment mobile-cloud computing by leveraging cloud resources. In the next section, we will provide a detailed discussion of the software support of virtualization. Software aspects of various VM-based mobile cloud offloading systems and frameworks, including OS-level VMs and application-level VMs will reviewed in detail. Architectural support for virtualization will be elaborated on in the following section, where the underlying hardware designs supporting and accelerating virtualization are reviewed. This hardware support section includes specific architectural designs by Intel x86 and ARM CPUs and NVidia GPUs for both desktop computers and mobile devices. We will conclude this chapter and provide pointers to potential future research directions in the final section.

MOBILE CLOUD OFFLOADING

The breakneck pace of the advancement of smartphone technology has turned these devices from mere "phones" to devices that are indispensible in everyday life. Sensory capabilities of mobile devices made an impressive progress with the incorporation of cameras, temperature, humidity, and acceleration sensors among others. Furthermore, a wide range of networking options like USB, WiFi, IR, and 4G made these devices ever more connected with increasing connection speeds. While networking and sensory capabilities of mobile devices are a lot less sensitive to the progress in VLSI technology, the same is not true for their computational and storage capabilities: Every new generation of VLSI (e.g., 32nm vs. 22nm) is expected to improve the performance-per-Watt metric of computational devices, whether mobile or desktop, as prescribed by the Moore's Law.

Since the technological advancement in battery energy densities (i.e., Joules per kg) is significantly slower than the VLSI technology-based energy efficiency of CPUs (i.e., performance per Watt), and the sizes of mobile devices cannot be increased beyond a certain point to improve their battery energy storage capability, the performance-per-Watt metric is expected to dominate the overall performance of mobile devices in the foreseeable future. To continue improving the performance of mobile devices, a possible approach that comes to mind is to take advantage of the improving networking capability of mobile devices by sending the entire or part of the computational task to a mainframe, like a cloud host, and receiving the result via the same network. This method is called *Mobile Cloud Offloading*, in which a mobile device accesses a host machine in cloud to perform all or part of a required computationally-intensive task. Several mechanisms are introduced in the past decades to implement this scheme, among which virtualization stands out as a viable alternative due to its advantages in utilizing and sharing computational resources. Below is a list of considerations when offloading tasks from mobile devices into the cloud.

- **Utilization:** One primary concern for cloud service providers is being able to predict the workload in the cloud at a given point in time. If the mobile tasks that are being initiated by different mobile devices were mapped to pre-determined servers in the cloud, a cloud service provider would have no way to smoothly distribute the workload for optimum efficiency. In other words, while some devices stayed idle, others would be overloaded. Virtualization makes it possible to pool scattered tasks into several servers and leave others idle. This not only allows the cloud operator to run multiple servers at optimum load for a maximum utilization ratio (e.g., 80%) without overloading them, it also allows them to turn off certain servers for maximum power efficiency. These servers could be turned on later when the cumulative load of the datacenter increases, based on an optimum predictive allocation algorithm. When additional servers come online, the workload from other servers could be migrated to them to prepare for additional future demand.

- **Compatibility:** Mobile devices, like smartphones, are of various types running different operating systems (e.g., Linux, Android, iOS). Directly running mobile applications on cloud servers would be severely restrict the device-server compatibility. This would require cloud servers that support pre-determined Operating Systems with no possibility to run applications from mobile devices with different OSs. Virtualization eliminates this compatibility issue by allowing a server to run multiple Operating Systems. Compatibility also refers to the ability to be compatible with different server hardware. To exacerbate the compatibility issue, a typical datacenter contains servers that have many different server models with different hardware. Since virtual machines run on virtual hardware, issues that are introduced by hardware incompatibility are avoided. Furthermore, when datacenter servers are upgraded to better ones, the applications that are running on them can be migrated to these new servers seamlessly.
- **Isolation:** Virtualization permits the isolation of two separate applications that are sharing the same physical resources, thereby preventing any compromise of data and/or code security. Additionally, new tasks can be launched without disturbing tasks that are currently executing. New resources or system extensions can be added without modifying or suspending current resources. Not only are virtual machines are protected from each other, but also an attack on one of the virtual machines can be easily confined by the hypervisor, without spreading to another (or multiple other) VMs.
- **Ease of Deployment:** Virtual machines allow easy and fast installation of new service applications or user machines. Creation of a virtual machine is extremely simple, as it typically just requires copying an existing image and migrating it to a selected server. On the contrary, a non-VM setup of a new system requires purchasing new equipment, new hardware deployment, and OS and application software configuration, which is more time consuming and prevents rapid deployment.

VIRTUALIZATION APPROACHES

The development of modern mobile devices, such as smartphones and tablets, has become the enabling technology for pervasive or ubiquitous computing. While non-resource-intensive applications run on these mobile platforms without a problem, a set of resource-intensive applications, such as augmented reality applications including real-time face recognition, natural language processing, do not achieve satisfactory performance levels due to their computational limitations. These limitations are not expected to improve in the foreseeable future (Satyanarayanan, Bahl, Caceres, & Nigel, 2009) due to the continuous user demand for higher performance and the slow progress in battery technology, placing limitations on the power consumption of the primary computing elements on the mobile device, such as CPU and GPU.

To enable a mobile device to run such resource-intensive applications, the solution is mobile-cloud computing, where the compute-intensive parts of an application are offloaded to a remote server. These remote servers amass much higher computation capability, significantly higher flash storage and local memory and high bandwidth, which imply that, an offloaded mobile application can be substantially accelerated when it can utilize such cloud resources. Furthermore, since the bulk of the execution of the application is being traded-off against potentially higher network traffic to transfer the application data (and application code), energy savings on the mobile device can be achieved when the ratios of network time vs. computation time are in favorable proportions.

Web services provided through XML-RPC and RESTful are commonly used for mobile applications. However, achieving energy savings and/or acceleration when offloading general-purpose computations is not trivial. Several approaches have been proposed to achieve efficient offloading from mobile devices to cloud servers. They can be categorized into two types based on whether the offloading is done transparently or non-transparently.

- **Non-Transparent Offloading:** Requires the developer to re-design the application with explicit mobile-cloud models to benefit from remote servers. To be able to offload, application-specific code has to be properly deployed on the remote server, which may require the user to have full control over the server.
- **Transparent Offloading:** Requires no modification on existing mobile applications. Programmers develop the application as if all of the code is running locally (or at most tag some functions that may be suitable for offloading using directives) and the underlying runtime will automatically transform most of the mobile applications to benefit from seamless offloading to the remote cloud servers.

Virtualization or virtual machine techniques play a key role not only in building cloud computing infrastructures but also in supporting both types of the aforementioned offloading approaches. For the *transparent offloading* approach, it is clear that an application-level virtual machine is essential for the runtime to dynamically analyze and profile the code, make offloading decisions, and partition and transparently migrate the code to the remote servers. For the *non-transparent offloading* approach, code deployment on cloud servers is not trivial due to the co-existence of various platforms, operating systems and libraries. Virtualization is able to hide the low-level details from the executing applications and provide a uniform environment to each application.

Due to the high latency through the internet which significantly hurts the offloading performance, the edge-server or *cloudlet* idea has been proposed as an accelerator in public areas like coffee shops to provide one-hop offloading services to the mobile devices (Soyata T., Muraleedharan, Funai, Kwon, & Heinzelman, 2012; Satyanarayanan, Bahl, Caceres, & Nigel, 2009). To provide offloading services as part of a public network infrastructure, the inherent sharing characteristics of virtualization can be utilized, combined with the ability of isolation and self-management on the cloudlet. To deploy the code, users of the mobile device need to have full control over a remote server. So, for purposes of maintenance, security, and privacy, user actions should be properly limited and isolated. To achieve this goal, a VM-based architecture is the inevitable choice.

Virtualization can be achieved at different levels from the hardware level to the application level. Based on these different virtualization levels, common VM-based approaches can be categorized into OS-level and application-level categories.

- **OS-Level VMs:** Provide better flexibility and ability for the customization of the virtualization environment. However, due to its large overhead, there are challenges in a real deployment using this approach. The large overhead of OS-level VMs are due to the mechanism of deployment which requires one has to transfer the entire VM image over the network before the VM can start. This weakens the acceleration benefit and hurts application responsiveness due to the latency incurred during the transmission of the VM image.
- **Application-Level VM:** Is a process running on top of the operating system of the remote server. It is relatively light-weight and the cost to migrate is relatively low compared to the OS-level VMs. The application, however, has limited flexibility in customizing the VM. For example, an application may not be able to use libraries written in other languages, which may translate to an eventual performance overhead.

VM-BASED OFFLOADING

Virtual Machines have become increasingly more popular in modern cloud computing, since they introduce a new way to run multiple operating systems on a single machine via the decoupling of physical resources. VM-based offloading is one of the most common approaches for offloading computational tasks to cloud server nodes. Compared to a traditional server management framework, the usage of VMs significantly improves certain operational aspects of cloud computing: 1) It enables rational and economical resource partitioning among users, 2) increases resource utilization at the datacenter, 3) lowers the power consumption at the datacenter, 4) it gives administrators higher flexibility for process deployment, and 5) lowers the application programming burden of the programmers.

On the other hand, the virtualization framework for application offloading introduces challenges such as 1) runtime management and data transfer overhead, 2) higher demand for design optimization, 3) new security concerns. Virtualization is usually implemented via the usage of hypervisors. We will now characterize the features of hypervisors and list the strengths and challenges of VM-based offloading.

Hypervisor Layer

Virtualized environments are the foundation of most cloud computing infrastructures. They are usually implemented via the use of a Hypervisor, which is generally a software layer that lies between the Virtual Machines and the physical hardware. Hypervisors can be divided into two major categories (Popek & Goldberg, 1974) .

Type 1 Hypervisors: are directly installed on the physical hardware, and therefore do not require a host operating system (OS) and can have direct access to the underlying physical hardware. QEMU, Xen and Microsoft Hyper-V are Type 1 hypervisors. Kernel-based Virtual Machine (KVM), on the other hand, makes its host OS a Type 1 hypervisor.

Type 2 Hypervisors: are installed above a host OS, and run within the environment provided by the OS. Therefore, the host OS would have direct access to the underlying hardware and is responsible for hardware source and service management. The hypervisor serves as the second layer and simulates virtual machine environments. The widely-adopted VMware Workstation and VirtualBox are two typical Type 2 hypervisors.

We will provide a brief introduction to the three mainstream open-source hypervisors: QEMU, Xen and KVM in terms of their Hypervisor mechanism for virtualization.

- **QEMU:** In its broadest sense, QEMU is a generic hardware emulator. It can be used standalone to create a virtual machine environment, but more often QEMU is executed under Xen or KVM to support device virtualization to the guest. In this case, QEMU provides simulation for peripherals including PCI Bridge, VGA card, mouse/keyboard, hard disk, CD-ROM, network adapters, sound card, etc. (QEMU), using dynamic translation between virtual and physical devices.
- **XEN:** Xen is an open-source Type-1 hypervisor running directly on hardware and is fully responsible for the resource management of the host machine. It utilizes para-virtualization, which permits it to achieve a near-native performance. Since its publication in 2003, Xen has been widely adopted as the basis of many commercial or open-source applications and is in use in the largest cloud environments today (Xen). The most distinguished feature of Xen is that it has a specialized VM with special privileges, named The Control Domain (or Dom0). Dom0 is a customized Linux kernel that can handle resource and I/O access directly, and exposes device control to guest VMs via emulators.
- **KVM:** In the open-source hypervisor projects, the Kernel-based Virtual Machine, or KVM, is a relatively new product which was first introduced in 2006. Soon after its introduction in February 2007, KVM was merged into the Linux kernel (version 2.6.20). KVM provides a complete virtualization environment in which virtual machines appear as normal Linux processes and integrate seamlessly with the rest of the system (Kivity, Kamay, Laor, Lublin, & Liguori, 2007). After this first integration, KVM became the main virtualization package in mainstream Linux OS (e.g. Ubuntu, Fedora).

KVM requires CPU virtualization extensions (Intel VT or AMD-V) and is used together with QEMU. It consists of a loadable kernel module (*kvm.ko*) and a processor-specific module (either *kvm-intel.ko* or *kvm-amd.ko*) at its core. QEMU is also used to provide virtualization for peripherals such as hard disk, CD-ROM and network adapters. KVM is a Type 2 hypervisor while its usage makes the host Linux OS a Type 1 hypervisor. This structure of KVM makes it very different from Xen and QEMU, as shown on Figure 1.

Hypervisor Features

A hypervisor connects the guest VM to the host machine by simulating a near-host environment. To accomplish this task, a hypervisor should incorporate a set of services. We present a brief overview of these services below.

- **CPU Virtualization:** For a completely virtualized CPU, there are a set of requirements that must be met (Popek & Goldberg, 1974). For a CPU architecture that allows virtualization, neither sensitive instructions nor privileged instructions must also be treated as privileged instructions. Since virtual CPUs must behave like real CPUs for more than one VM, the Hypervisor translates and schedules virtual CPU instructions from different guests to the physical CPUs appropriately. This is achieved by allowing a specific guest to have exclusive use of a CPU for a period of time, after which this guest is interrupted and the exclusive use is passed onto another guest. During this

Figure 1. Comparison of Xen, KVM, and QEMU.

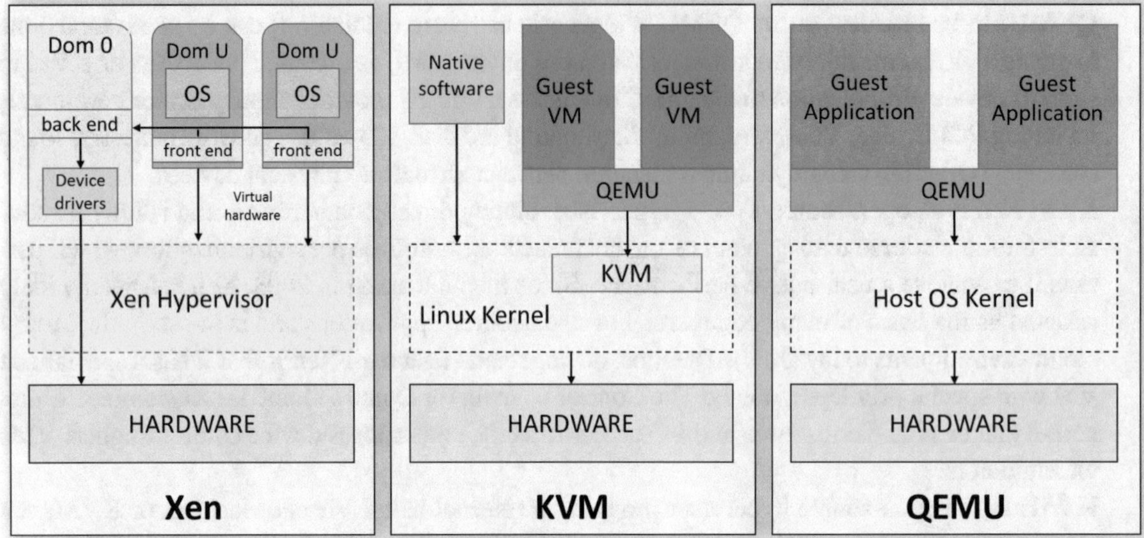

switch, the CPU state of the first guest is saved, and the state of the next guest is loaded before the control is passed onto it. This process is repeated to provide fair and even access to every guest (Chisnall, 2008). This is called Symmetric Multiprocessing (SMP).

- **Memory Virtualization:** Modern CPUs (e.g., x86 and ARM) include a Memory Management Unit (MMU) which performs virtual-to-physical memory address translation. This translation is accelerated by the CPU hardware by providing traps for privileged instructions to map the virtual addresses to corresponding physical addresses. However, Guest VMs cannot directly access the MMU, which would imply that the hypervisor would lose control of the VMs. The hypervisor provides MMU functionality to the guests by utilizing a soft MMU, which utilizes shadow page tables to accomplish its task. Every access to an actual page table invoked by a VM is intercepted by the soft MMU and is replaced by an access to a corresponding shadow page table.
- **Interrupt/Timer Virtualization:** A hypervisor should be able to virtualize and manage the interrupt/timer, the interrupt/timer controller of the guest OS, as well as the access of the guest OS to the controller. At the same time, it must virtualize all interrupts/timers going into the guest OS. Both of these would cause considerable overhead. Modern CPUs also provide hardware extensions for Interrupt/Timer virtualization. For example, ARM defines a Generic Interrupt Controller (GIC) architecture and Generic Timer Architecture. Recent versions of GIC and Generic Timer introduce virtualization extensions that help manage the virtual interrupts/timer from the hypervisor, thereby substantially reducing the overhead caused by the interrupts/timer virtualization. This means that the hypervisor can directly send virtual interrupt/timer without translation (Dall & Nieh, 2014).

- **I/O Virtualization:** I/O virtualization includes two parts of drivers: front-end and back-end. A hypervisor emulates I/O devices by a device emulator running in the host OS or directly on the hardware. KVM and Xen employ QEMU's simulators which have full access to hardware devices by default to implement back-end simulation. On the other hand, front-end drivers are also needed in guest VMs to simulate the usual I/O requests sent by the guest OS. Hypervisor is responsible for the communication between front-end and back-end.

Nevertheless, the case for graphics cards (GPUs) is a lot more complicated. A GPU keeps its own graphics memory, works independently from the motherboard, and involves large data transfers. Meanwhile, most GPUs do not provide state saving/recovery. These features of GPUs make GPU-virtualization a lot more challenging in many aspects, like VM state-switching and multiprocessing management (Chisnall, 2008).

CHALLENGES IN VIRTUALIZATION

Despite many of its advantages, virtualization is not without challenges. We will summarize the primary challenges facing virtualization in this section.

- **Overhead of Deployment and Management:** In Mobile-Cloud computing, offloading can be done via either a VM clone or a VM migration. Additionally, an interactive status transfer is needed for VM management. Both of these require an additional computation and introduce a resource overhead. VM deployment introduces computational resources in several aspects (Shiraz, Abolfazli, Sanaei, & Gani, 2013) including VM creation, VM configuration and VM startup, as well as application deployment.
- **Security Problem:** The security vulnerability of the hypervisor is another challenge that deserves attention. Since hypervisors serve as a new software layer between the guest OS and the physical machine or the host OS, any attack on the hypervisor implies a risk of attack directly to the CPU, memory, I/O, or a combination of these resources. Furthermore, since cloud computing involves big data management, networking and remote control, any vulnerability of the hypervisor translates to service disruptions, data confidentiality breaches, reputation fate-sharing among other issues.
- **GPU Virtualization:** Nowadays, GPUs are receiving widespread adoption in a range of platforms ranging from individual computers to supercomputers. GPU-accelerated computing offers high performance computing (HPC) at a large scale due to its cost-effective, and power-efficient features (e.g., the mobile-cloud face recognition application). However, the use of GPU-acceleration is still at a relatively low level, as compared to CPU-only implementations. Sharing and managing GPU resources in a hypervisor faces several big challenges:

First challenge is to determine how to share GPU resources among several VMs. Historically, most GPUs keep memory outside of OS's main framework, and they do not allow access to multiple concurrent applications. Furthermore, they are unable to save and restore the state of applications. This makes GPU virtualization for cloud computing complex and fragile. As of the preparation of this book chapter, only a few advanced GPUs, like the Nvidia Kepler family, support virtualization to some degree. The new Maxwell family from Nvidia is expected to address this issue much better and full GPU Virtualization is expected to be accomplished within the next upcoming Nvidia generations.

Second challenge is the virtualization overhead, as encountered in CPU virtualization. Although this overhead is unavoidable, some work on GPU virtualization, such as gVirtuS, allows transparent access to the GPU and is independent from the hypervisor, with only a slight overhead introduced relative to actual GPU implementations (Giunta, Montella, Agrillo, & Coviello, 2010). This project is the joint product of the University of Napoli Parthenope and the Open Source Lab initiative and can be accessed at http://osl.uniparthenope.it/projects/gvirtus/.

SOFTWARE SUPPORT FOR VIRTUALIZATION

To leverage virtualization technologies for fast and transparent mobile-cloud offloading, additional modifications need to be made to the traditional virtualization software platforms. Two virtualization approaches are introduced to enable mobile devices to seamlessly offload computation tasks to remote cloud servers. The first one is at the OS-level, which migrates a customized full-fledged virtual machine from the mobile device to the server. The VM image is customized by the developers to accelerate their application on mobile devices. The communication between the mobile and the cloud and the offloading procedure are explicitly defined by application developers. The second approach is at the thread-level, where the underlying application VM (e.g. Java VM) is extended with the ability to profile the program and migrate threads to remote servers. Program partitioning and offloading procedures are transparent to developers and users. The two approaches will be discussed in detail in the following sections.

OS-Level VM

As mentioned in the previous sections, OS-level VMs provide the developers with the flexibility in customizing the VM and offering specific acceleration services to their applications. Additionally VMs offer an isolated environment and good manageability on the remote servers which enables the deployment of self-managing cloudlets. However, one of the greatest challenges with OS-Level VMs in mobile-cloud computing is the high latency to transfer the necessary states to the remote server. In order to provision a customized VM in the cloud, disk images and a VM snapshot (which is typically several gigabytes in total), have to be completely migrated from the mobile device before the VM can be resumed to provide offloading services for the mobile. This migration will take at least five minutes even on a fast 802.11n network at peak network throughput. This time delay is clearly unacceptable for mobile users, especially considering that, one of the advantages of virtualization is application performance acceleration.

To achieve the goal of both high performance and manageability, the VM-based Kimberley architecture was proposed (Satyanarayanan, Bahl, Caceres, & Nigel, 2009) to accelerate the VM migration process. A cloudlet, defined as a self-managed datacenter in a box, was introduced in Kimberley. The cloudlet is able to support a few users at a time and maintains only the soft state, thereby making a loss of connection acceptable. When a mobile client connects to the cloudlet, it notifies the Kimberley Control Manager (KCM) on the cloudlet to download a small VM overlay from either the Internet or the mobile client. A VM overlay is the difference between the memory snapshot and disk of a base VM and the customized VM. Several base VMs are pre-installed on the cloudlet. Application developers will choose one of the base VMs, build their customized VM on top of this base and generate the VM overlay after their customization is complete. When the VM overlay is delivered, a technique called dynamic VM synthesis applies the overlay to the base VM and launches the target VM. Since the size of the overlay is usually much less than the size of the customized VM, the latency of the synthesis is greatly reduced. After the computation is complete, the KCM can simply shutdown the VM and free the resources, providing self-manageability that only needs minimal maintenance.

The Kimberly system was implemented on a Nokia N810 tablet running Maemo 4.0, and the cloudlet infrastructure was implemented on a desktop computer running Ubuntu Linux where VirtualBox was used to provide the VM support. System performance was evaluated by considering the size of VM overlays and the speed of the synthesis operation. According to experimental results, the size of the generated VM overlays is around 100-200 MB for a collection of Linux applications, which is an order of magnitude smaller than a full VM image that can be as large as 8 GB. The processing time for VM synthesis ranged from 60 to 90 seconds and has plenty of potential room for improvement through further optimizations such as parallelized compression and decompression and VM overlay pre-fetching. (Ha, Pillai, Richter, Abe, & Satyanarayanan, 2013) showed that the latency of dynamic VM synthesis can be further optimized by pipelining the transmission and deduplication of the VM overlay. There will be redundant data within and between the memory snapshots and disk images since most of the data in the memory is originally loaded from the disk. The size of overlay can be significantly reduced by exploiting the redundancy and find the minimal set of data that is necessary to build the customized VM launch. The tradeoff between the size of the overlay and the computation complexity can provide significant performance improvement by carefully choosing the delta algorithm and the granularity of the chunks. Additionally, since there are strong boundaries enforced by the hypervisor between the guest and the host systems, it is difficult for the outside layer to accurately interpret higher level abstractions inside a VM, which is called a *semantic gap*. Such a gap prevents a further reduction of the size of the overlay. In (Ha, Pillai, Richter, Abe, & Satyanarayanan, 2013), authors bridge the gap for disks by exploiting the TRIM support and introspecting the file system inside the VM. For memory, since there is no standard (like TRIM for disks), bridging the gap requires the modification of the guest OS and significant effort on maintaining and tracking the memory structure changes.

Another technique used in the paper is pipelining the transmission of VM overlays and *Early Start*. To keep both the network and the CPU busy at the same time to reduce the latency, it is straightforward to divide the large overlay into small chunks and pipeline the chunk transmission and processing so that the transmission latency, as well as computational latency can be partially coalesced. Furthermore, observing that the VM does not really need all of the chunks to be transferred before it can be resumed, we can order the chunk transmission in a way where the earliest needed chunks are transferred first. This way, the VM can be resumed even when a small portion of the overlay is transferred. In the paper, authors use static proofing to obtain the order of the accessed chunks and use on-demand transmissions for the out-of-order chunks. Utilizing all of the previously mentioned techniques, authors evaluated the fully optimized VM synthesis in terms of *first response time* using five software packages. The results show that, except for AR application, the first response time for all other four applications come within ten seconds. They also compare the VM synthesis to the remote installation approach and the fully optimized VM synthesis approach has significant performance advantages in every application except AR.

Application-Level VM

As some VM-based frameworks involve OS-level VM cloning and complete application offloading, others focus on *encapsulating* applications from its operating system. This may exploit application partitioning in which only parts of an application are offloaded. In other words, instead of the physical hardware, the applications themselves are virtualized. This is called an application-level VM. Although this framework has limited usage since every application cannot be virtualized this way, the resource burden is significantly reduced for applications that can take advantage of this form of virtualization.

Application partitioning schemes fall into two main categories: static and dynamic (Chun & Maniatis, 2010). In earlier cloud environments, static partitioning was typically used due to its easier design and reduced resource management burden. However, static partitioning does not provide any optimization for a diverse cloud environment and workload patterns. A dynamic partition algorithm is preferred, since an optimized partial execution between mobile devices and the cloud is not only determined by the application itself but also the mobile platform capability, cloud environment, network speed and specific instantaneous workloads in the cloud.

A typical application-level VM is implemented using software dynamic translation (SDT) (Scott, et al., 2003). The VM keeps sets of byte-code instructions which are physical hardware and operating system independent. Since the translation needs to provide runtime monitoring and function appendix by code modification, based on existing application code, SDT can modify the existing byte-code, injecting additional code and control the code execution. The VM framework lies between applications and the cloud host operating system. The VM operates by decoding, translating and storing the applications' instructions initially. On the host machine, the VM then takes control of application execution by capturing a snapshot and synchronizing the current state, including counters, pointers, PC, condition, registers etc. Instructions for which a context switch is needed are processed next. Applying dynamic translation and offloading, the VM operations are flexible and modular and diverse forms of offloading can be implemented.

CloneCloud (Chun, Ihm, Maniatis, Naik, & Patti, 2011) is an example application-level VM framework which exploits dynamic application partitioning and partition offloading. Mobile-cloud computing under CloneCloud is performed in several steps:

1. Application partitioning is automatically performed according to a partitioning algorithm. The mechanism aims at find a fixed execution point, upon which application is migrated between the mobile devices and the cloud. The algorithm optimizes the partitioning ratio considering network properties (not the network condition), computing capacity of the mobile and the cloud, as well as the estimated energy consumption. Not all of the execution points are valid as there are many constraints for execution availability at every given point. To ensure that a given partitioning is legal, a Static Analyzer is used to identify all possible partitions.
2. The states (e.g. counters, registers, memory, etc.) of the mobile platform and the cloud platform are timely synchronized, during which execution process is suspended.
3. CloneCloud migrates application operations at thread-level, in which way multi-threading is allowed. With the source byte-code transferred, application can perform distributed execution and virtualized computation can be conducted seamlessly.
4. The results of clone execution in the cloud are finally re-integrated back to the mobile platform. When a thread reaches its re-integration point, execution is suspended. It is then packed and merged into the original process.

Networking Virtualization

For a mobile device user performing computation in the cloud via a wireless network and a cloud service, network virtualization is one of the essential and fundamental elements. For a large-scale cloud computing system with large VM image collections and a large data center, networking is important in the following areas: accessing specific VM images, transmitting images between devices and servers, accessing the data center and migrating application offloading. Using traditional networking schema in cloud computing faces several limitations: scalability, flexibility and automatic management.

From the standpoint of the cloud service provider, network congestion is difficult to properly gauge. A cloud service system may start with tens of tenants but suddenly grow to hundreds. Without networking virtualization, physical devices, like routers, must be upgraded to meet incremental requirements. Traditional physical devices are not designed for cloud computing, so the entire networking system must be suspended and wait for device upgrades. Considering a similar case as above, when the cloud system grows and network requirements increase, it is difficult for cloud operators to use heterogeneous networking gear from different vendors, which makes the management and provisioning very difficult. This would result in high management costs, as well as wasted resources and increased overhead.

Using networking virtualization, networking is abstracted from the underlying physical hardware. Operators can manage networking aspects such as specific connection patterns, switching, routing, and security easily. Thus, networking can be organized as a high-level integration and automatically allocated, which helps economic use of resources and reduces energy consumption.

Network performance affects the overall performance of a cloud computing system significantly in terms of both execution speed and resource consumption. Although networking can be virtualized and applied just as in the case of the virtualization of other devices, networking service takes place at different levels in different protocols, depending on the cloud system model. These higher layer models include Infrastructure as a Service (IaaS), Platform as a Service (PaaS), and Software as a Service (SaaS) (Dinh, Lee, Niyato, & Wang, 2013). Generally, IaaS provides more flexible protocol selection to vendors, while PaaS and SaaS usually provide provider-determined network service to customers (Amies, Sluiman, Tong, & Liu, 2012).

When virtual machines are created, IP Addresses are initially allocated. IP Addresses can be generated by the system, reserved as provisioned for VMs, and by using VLANs. Using Internet Protocol Version 6 (IPv6), networks can be created with more available IP addresses and higher security levels. Inside the virtual machines, hypervisors can share a single physical network interface with multiple virtual machines. Hypervisors usually provide virtual networking in three ways: bridging, routing and Network Address Translation (NAT). Under bridge mode, a hypervisor serves as a data transfer interface and the virtual machine is exposed to the Ethernet directly. In routing mode, the hypervisor goes into the network layer and makes the virtual network interface externally visible at the IP level.

Large-scale clouds can emulate more IP addresses than is otherwise physically available by hiding the network of virtual machines from the external network. In this case, NAT is needed as it enables communication with the internet using a hidden virtual machine address. NAT assigns virtual IP addresses, or private local IP addresses which are different from the host IP. As the virtual IP addresses are invisible on the Internet, NAT could create a massive amount of internally-accessible IP addresses for purposes of serving a large numbers of virtual machines. At runtime, NAT software keeps a routing table and changes the IP address information in the data packets based on the table, in which way hypervisors can forward incoming and outgoing data packages.

ARCHITECTURAL SUPPORT FOR VIRTUALIZATION

The x86 and ARM architecture were never designed for virtualization. With the increasing demand for cloud computing inside enterprise data centers, where virtualization has become a standard practice, pure software-based virtualization, without explicit native hardware support, suffered serious performance penalties. Hardware vendors like Intel and AMD have responded to the demand for virtualization with new processor extensions including Intel VT-x and AMD-V. These hardware-assisted virtualization techniques reduce the performance overhead of the traditional approaches such as binary translation and no longer require changes inside the guest operating system. In the following subsections, the architectural support for virtualization in x86, ARM and Nvidia GPU will be discussed in detail.

x86 Virtualization Support

As Popek and Goldberg stated in (Popek & Goldberg, 1974), for a virtualizable CPU architecture, any instruction that is control-sensitive and related to resource configuration must be privileged. However, x86 microprocessor architecture has such features that makes it unable to meet this demand, therefore making it very challenging to support full virtualization on an x86 architecture.

Challenges with X86 Virtualization

In order to implement security in accessing resources, a modern x86 architecture, for example, IA32 (Intel Architecture, 32-bit), provides an instruction segregation mechanism, in which a direct access to pivotal functionality, such as CPU control and memory access, are privileged. To achieve this, x86 CPUs provide four privilege levels, 0, 1, 2 and 3, from most privileged (Ring 0) to least privileged (Ring 3). This model is usually described as a ring structure, named Ring 0 to Ring 3. In practice, Ring 1 and Ring 2 are rarely used by the operating system developers, since for most cases the protection mechanism only has a concept of privileged and unprivileged instructions and the benefits to Ring 1 and 2 are negligible. Therefore, we will just talk about the other two levels in this section: Ring 0, where kernel components of the OS run, and Ring 3, where most user applications run.

The IA32 architecture includes 16 instructions that run in Protected mode which cannot be accessed by user applications. If any code that is running in a Ring greater than 0 attempts to execute one of these instructions, a Protection Fault exception is generated. The list of privileged instructions includes LGDT, LLDT, LTR, LIDT, MOV (control register), MOV (debug register), LMSW, CLTS, INVD, WBINVD, INVLPG, HLT, RDMSR, WRMSR, RDPMC and RDTSC (INTEL-IA-PartGuide, 2010). These instructions are mainly related to loading/writing-to registers that control CPU operation, control/debug, cache state, TLB, model-specific, timestamp etc. For a fully virtualized CPU, the guest OS must be able to run some its components in Ring 0 (highest privileged level). However, hypervisor must have privileged control and occupy Ring 0, and it cannot allow its guest OSs such control. The only solution for the hypervisor is to run the guest OSs in less privileged Ring 1, 2, or 3, which is called ring de-privileging.

The primary task of the hypervisor is to have its guest OS function just like in an non-virtualized CPU environment. However, ring de-privileging introduces plenty of challenges in regard to this requirement (Neiger, Santoni, Leung, Rodgers, & Uhlig, 2006). For example, some registers contained information related to CPU control, which can only be written in Ring 0 but can be read in higher Rings. A guest OS that needs to write to one of these registers could end up not being able to function seamlessly, as in an non-virtualized environment. Furthermore, there are some instructions that operate on segmented memory. If the guest OS executes one of these instructions, hypervisor may not be able to properly rearrange the memory mapping in a virtualized way. To find a solution to these challenges, much effort is made in terms of both software and hardware alternatives. As far as software solutions, there are two alternatives:

- **Binary Translation:** Binary translation is made popular by VMware and is widely used in its products. The general idea of binary translation is that, the hypervisor scans the instruction stream from the guest and re-encodes the privileged instructions into a virtual version. One disadvantage of this approach is the performance penalty for scanning and encoding, especially for I/O intensive applications. On the other hand, some special software like debuggers that require setting breakpoints, makes hypervisor design extremely complicated. This is due to the binary translation changing the actual code, and even the order of the breakpoints and instructions, which makes the debugging process extremely challenging.
- **Paravirtualization:** Unlike binary translation, paravirtualization goes to the root of the problem: the guest operating system. For paravirtualization, the guest OS is modified in a way that privileged instructions are replaced by hypercalls. Thus, the guest OS communicates with the hypervisor via hypercalls and avoids the aforementioned troublesome instructions. However, since the hypervisor is required to handle these interrupts with an extra layer, a performance penalty is introduced.

Despite these software-only solutions, INTEL has made significant effort to facilitate / accelerate virtualization via hardware support, which is called *hardware-assisted virtualization*. Hardware-assisted virtualization can be conceptualized as allowing hypervisors to run in a Ring "-1" which would free the precious Ring 0 for guest VMs. We will talk about the details of Hardware Assisted Virtualization below.

Intel Hardware-Assisted Virtualization

Intel's virtualization extensions for the 32-bit x86 architecture, VT-x, was first introduced in 2005. VT-x refers to a new mode added to the processor, named virtual-machine extensions (VMX) which support virtualization for multiple virtual machines. VMX includes two new CPU operations: VMX root operation and VMX non-root operation. Employing VMX mode, generally a hypervisor runs in VMX root operation and its guest operating systems runs in non-root operation.

- **VMX Root Operation:** Is much the same as an ordinary processor operation from the hypervisor's view when it is operating as a host. What is different is that, it allows a series of VMX instructions. On the other hand, virtual processors for VMs, running in VMX non-root operation, are modified in certain ways to support virtualization. Certain instructions are trapped by the CPU, instead of directly executing on the CPU. This causes transitions between the hypervisor and the VMs, which are called *VM exits*. With VM exits, the access boundary of the guest OSs is limited, therefore the host hypervisor can retain control of the CPU resources. Similarly, when transitioning from hypervisor operation to guest operation, a *VM entry* occurs.
- **VMX Non-Root Operation:** To manage the VMX non-root operation, as well as the two transition operations, namely VM entries and VM exits, VT-x introduces a new data structure called virtual-machine control structure (VMCS). VMCS contains a guest-state area for VMX non-root

operation, and a host-state area for VMX root operation. Upon each transition, VM exits and entries save the current processor state into the corresponding state area in VMCS, and load the next required processor state. VMX mode is implemented by a series of instructions extensions. Table 1 shows a list of the VMX instructions.

VMX operations incorporate all necessary instructions to complete a full lifecycle of a guest virtual machine, by allowing the guest to enter and exit and the host to manage the guest OS and stay in control. Figure 2 shows the lifecycle of VMX operations.

Table 1. Additional instructions introduced by INTEL's VT-x.

Instruction	Description
VMXON	Enter VMX operation
VMCLEAR	Inactive VMCS
VMPTRLD	load the VMCS pointer for an active VM
VMWRITE	Initial/write fields in the current VMCS
VMLAUNCH	Create a VMCS launching
VMCALL	Exit from VMX non-root operation
VMREAD	Read fields in the current VMCS
VMRESUME	Resume VM execution in VMX non-root operation
VMPTRST	Store the pointer to an active VM to memory
VMXOFF	Leave VMX operation

Figure 2. Operation transitions in Intel VT-x.

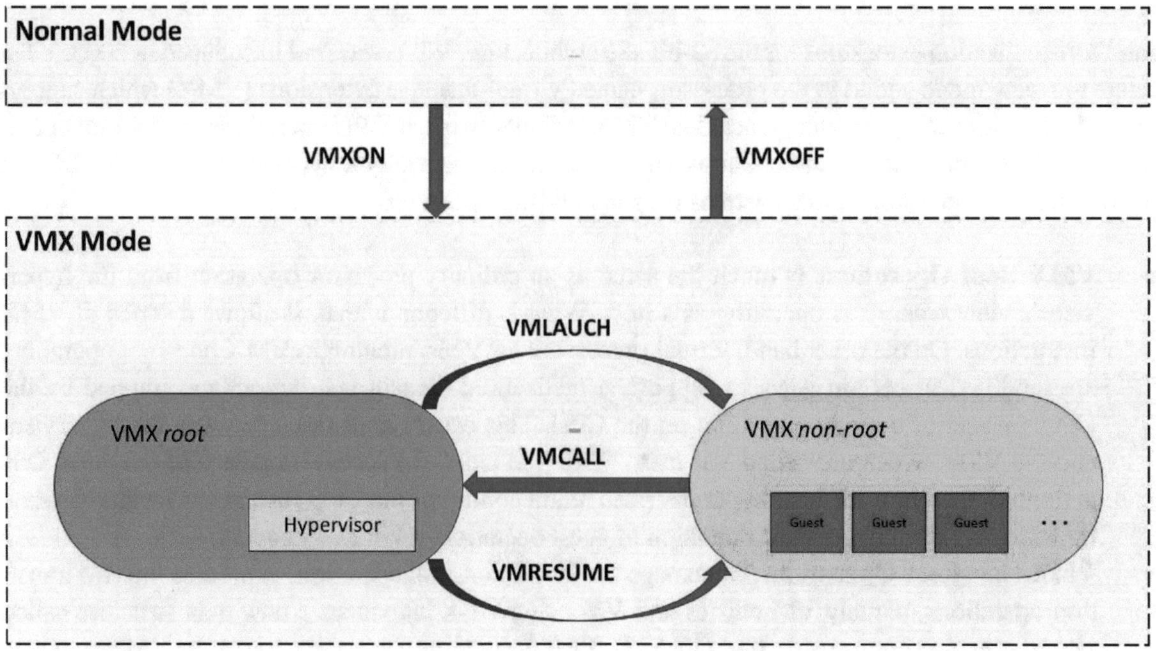

- **VMXON:** The primary entry point to VMX mode is the VMXON instruction. After executing VMXON, the processor would be placed in VMX_ROOT mode.
- **VMCLEAR:** To ensure that the VMCS region is in a pure state before activated, VMCLEAR must be executed before VMPTRLD. VMCLEAR will allocate a new VMCS region in memory and set its state to "clear." Also, the previous VMCS pointer will be invalidated.
- **VMPTRLD:** Executing VMPTRLD initializes a pointer to a new allocated VMCS region for each guest virtual machine.
- **VMWRITE:** After VMPTRLD, the hypervisor will issue a sequence of VMWRITE instructions to create several memory regions in the VMCS. These regions include host-state fields, guest-state fields, VM-exit control fields, VM-entry control fields, and VM-execution control fields.
- **VMLAUNCH:** After the above procedures, VMCS is successfully initialized and is ready to use. The hypervisor will then launch the new created virtual machine by applying VMLAUNCH. Simultaneously, VMCS state will be changed to "launched."
- **VMCALL:** To implement the *VM exit* functionality that is previously mentioned, the VMCALL instruction is used. If the software wants to request a service from host processor, it will VMCALL that service. The hypervisor will implement a VMCALL through one of the hardware-assisted traps.
- **VMREAD:** VMREAD is used to access specific VMCS fields. For example, if a VM exit occurs, the hypervisor uses VMREAD to access the exit-reason field in the VMCS. Depending on different exit reasons, hypervisor might want to access other fields in VMCS.
- **VMRESUME:** VMRESUME can be used to resume a VM execution or launch a guest on the same virtual processor in a "launched" VMCS. For example, after an exception, the hypervisor can resume the state of a virtual machine by VMRESUME.
- **VMXOFF:** If a hypervisor wants to shut down and leave VMX mode, it executes VMXOFF.

In summary, VT-x provides a solution to some of the challenges that exist in pure-software virtualization, by introducing assistance directly from the x86 hardware. Using VT-x, guest operating systems can work at *Ring 0 equivalent* privilege levels. Also, a paravirtualization system can make some use of the hardware-assisted virtualization features to optimize certain operations. For example, a hypervisor can benefit from performing I/O through hardware virtualization extensions rather than software emulated I/O which has higher overhead and is therefore less efficient.

AMD Hardware-Assisted Virtualization

Similar to Intel's VT-x, AMD also provided a set of instruction extensions to assist virtualization, called AMD-v, with the code name "Pacific." The list of the added instructions are shown in Table 2 (AMD64-Virtualization, 2005). The virtual mode of AMD-v is named SVM. AMD-v also provides a mechanism for mode switching and transitioning between the hypervisor to the guest through VMRUN and #VMEXIT instructions. The AMD instruction #VMEXIT is similar to the VT-x instruction VMXOFF which facilitates a VM exit. The guest OS uses VMMCALL which causes the processor to generate an exception and the guest OS requests services from the hypervisor via the use of this instruction, much like the VMCALL in the Intel implementation. AMD-v also introduces a data structure similar to VMCS, called Virtual machine control block (VMCB). A VMCB is also maintained for each guest virtual machine, and contains a set of Control areas and State areas. Control areas contain control and information determine the source of #VMEXIT. The state of virtual processors is stored in the State areas.

Table 2. Additional Instructions introduced by AMD-V.

Instruction	Description
CLGI	Clear Global Interrupt Flag to 0
INVLPGA	Invalidate selective TLB mapping
MOV(CRn)	Move between general registers and control registers
SKINIT	Secure Init, allowing activating of trust software
STGI	Set Global Interrupt Flag to 1
VMLOAD	Load processor state from control block (VMCB)
VMMCALL	Call hypervisor
VMRUN	Run virtual machine
VMSAVE	Save the state of a VM into control block (VMCB)

In addition to these features similar to VT-x, AMD-v provides several extra features related to the x86-64 architecture. Some AMD CPUs contain an integrated memory controller, which allow hypervisors to handle memory management. To achieve memory management, AMD-v includes Shadow Page and Nest Paging mechanisms. Shadow Page mechanism allows a hypervisor to modify the OS's page table and remap memory partitions. Nest Paging allows two levels of memory address translation performed in hardware. Nest Paging keeps a Nest Paging Table to translate guest physical memory addresses to host physical addresses, so that the guest OS can fully control and use its own page tables. Since the translation is done by hardware, it can achieve a near-native performance.

AMD-V also introduces a special Device Exclusion Vector (DEV) interface. Each DEV is kept in an exclusive protection zone. DEV takes charge of upstream accesses for their permission and limit the address zones for devices. This mechanism allows it to protect memory mapped I/O (MMIO) and DRAM from abuse.

ARM Virtualization Support

CPU virtualization for the ARM architecture is a relatively new field of research with slow growth compared to the x86 architecture. ARM brings additional challenges in virtualization (Hwang, et al., 2008) compared to the x86 architecture. In this section, ARM virtualization will be described briefly.

Challenges with ARM Virtualization

As previously mentioned, a typical x86 architecture introduces a four-level privilege system which introduces challenges for virtualization. The case is even worse for ARM which has only one privileged mode and one unprivileged mode. Such a limited scheme forces the guest OS and the applications to run in the same unprivileged mode, and makes the protection of the guest OS more difficult. In the ARM architecture, cache is virtually tagged and therefore there is no ASID attached to the TLB. This feature results in a very high flushing frequency on state switches if we try to distribute memory among guest OSs and applications. To provide support for easier virtualization, starting from ARMv7 in 2010, a new virtualization extension (VE) was introduced as an optional feature on ARM CPUs. VE, along with the previously introduced extension Large Physical Addressing Extensions (LPAE), allow an efficient hardware-assisted implementation of a hypervisor possible in the ARM architecture.

ARM Virtualization Extensions

The principle of virtualization extensions on the ARM architecture is very similar to that of in the x86 architecture, which is, in short, the introduction of a new "-1" privilege ring which is even more privileged than the kernel mode. ARM has two working modes: secure mode and non-secure mode, and VE are only available under the non-secure mode. The newly introduced privileged level is called the *hyp mode*. Similar to the x86 virtual extension operation, certain additional instructions are introduced to facilitate hardware-assisted virtualization in the ARM architecture. For example the "hvc" instruction is used to enter the virtualized operation mode. Without an ASID for TLB, the hyp mode has a register named VMID which keeps a stable mapping to physical memory during state switches. This allows the ARM architecture to eliminate the problems with the aforementioned high flushing rates.

NVidia GPU Virtualization Support

Many compute-intensive applications and games heavily rely on the acceleration attained from Graphics Processing Units (GPUs). Many of the applications in this category are good candidates for a cloud computing environment. Although virtualization of such applications in the cloud would provide all of the previously mentioned benefits of isolation, resource flexibility and security, one of the major drawbacks of virtualization in a cloud computing environment is the lack of support for high-performance GPU virtualization. One primary hurdle for GPU virtualization is the fact that, unlike a CPU which is design to be shared by multiple processes, GPUs usually assumes no multiplexing. Also, the high memory bandwidth demands from a GPU will cause significant overhead in a virtualized environment. Recent advances in virtualization technologies have enabled virtual machines to directly access physical GPUs and exploit their hardware's acceleration using an I/O Pass-through technique. Meanwhile, GPU manufactures like NVidia have also equipped their products with virtualization support assisted by the GPU hardware, similar to the hardware-assisted virtualization that the CPU manufacturers introduced.

Recent advances in hardware have enabled virtualization systems to achieve one-to-one mapping between an I/O device and a VM instance. This allows VMs to use non-virtualization-friendly I/O devices without software emulation (e.g., Network Interface Cards (NIC) and GPUs). One problem with these I/O devices is the use of the traditional Direct Memory Access (DMA) mechanism which will violate the memory isolation enforced by the hypervisor among VMs. A new configurable I/O Memory Management Unit (IOMMU) provided by Intel VT-d and AMD-Vi allows the hypervisor to reconfigure the interrupts and DMA of the physical devices in a way where they are directly mapped into certain guest VMs and the DMA requests will pass through the hypervisor, incurring less overhead while preserving the isolation.

Even with the ability to map one device to one VM, it is still difficult to virtualize devices like GPUs. For these virtualization-unfriendly GPU devices, the hypervisor needs to translate commands from VMs so that it appears to the GPU as if the commands are coming from a single system. Even with such a mapping, multiple GPUs need to be physically installed in a server so that the hypervisor can achieve the mapping, which is not flexible or cost-efficient. To address the problem, NVidia introduced the GRID vGPU technology (Nvidia-Grid-VGPU) in the Kepler architecture to make GPUs more virtualization-friendly. This technology enables multiple VMs to share true GPU hardware acceleration without compromising the graphics experience. With the GRID vGPU technology, each VM has its dedicated memory in the GPU and the native graphics commands of each VM are passed directly onto the GPU, without any translations by the hypervisor.

CONCLUSION AND FUTURE WORK

In this chapter we discussed the state of art in VM-based mobile-cloud offloading techniques in detail both in terms of its software and architectural aspects. We introduced the general structure of multiple widely-adopted virtualization platforms (hypervisors), which are Xen, QEMU, and KVM. We documented the way each one of these hypervisors allow the virtualization of a variety of resources, such as CPU, memory, interrupt/timer, I/O, and network. We listed the challenges of running a hypervisor in a cloud computing environment, since each one of these resources have unique characteristics which cause a different form of a challenge.

We discussed how a guest OS (i.e., a Virtual Machine, or VM) runs CPU instructions as if there is no hypervisor. Kimberley and CloneCloud are the two VMs which run at the OS level and application level, respectively. We discussed these two popular VMs in detail which run without ever leaving the hypervisor's control. We discussed the current improvements to different layers of these two virtualization systems made especially for mobile-cloud offloading purposes. Also, two approaches at different offloading granularities, application and thread-level, were reviewed and their advantages and disadvantages were discussed.

While the virtualization of resources can be achieved using pure software approaches, this typically has a high performance penalty. In 2005 and going forward, almost every CPU manufacturer introduced a form of hardware assistance mechanism for the virtualization of various resources. This is through the introduction of instruction extensions that run on different privilege levels. We detailed the hardware assisted virtualization mechanisms that are introduced by Intel, AMD, ARM, and Nvidia. These platforms are Intel's VMX in the x86 architecture, AMD's AMD-v, ARM's VE (virtualization extensions), and Nvidia's Grid vGPU for GPU virtualization.

As mentioned in this chapter, there still exists challenges yet to be addressed to enable the practical use of VM-based mobile-cloud offloading in daily life, which opens the door to potential directions for future work. One of the challenges is the overhead of the deployment and management of a VM-based offloading system. Offloading via traditional VM clones or VM migration approaches may incur significant communication latency over the Internet and further investigations are required to reduce the transmission and processing overhead of VM-based coarse-grained offloading approaches. Another question that needs to be addressed is the security and privacy for both the offloading service providers and the users. It is important for the service providers that they can detect and prevent malicious code being offloaded to their systems. On the other hand, it is important for the users to assure that their offloaded code and data are secured against other parties including the service providers. Additionally, users also need to be able to verify that their offloaded code is actually executing as expected and is returning the correct results (i.e., functional verification), which requires further investigation in the future.

ACKNOWLEDGMENT

This work was supported in part by the National Science Foundation grant CNS-1239423 and a gift from Nvidia corporation.

REFERENCES

Alling, A., Powers, N., & Soyata, T. (2015). Face Recognition: A Tutorial on Computational Aspects. In *Emerging Research Surrounding Power Consumption and Performance Issues in Utility Computing*. IGI Global.

AMD64-Virtualization. (2005). *Secure virtual machine architecture reference manual*. AMD Publication.

Amies, A., Sluiman, H., Tong, Q. G., & Liu, G. N. (2012). *Infrastructure as a Service Cloud Concepts*. Developing and Hosting Applications on the Cloud.

Chisnall, D. (2008). *The Definitive Guide to the Xen Hypervisor*. Pearson Education.

Chun, B.-G., Ihm, S., Maniatis, P., Naik, M., & Patti, A. (2011). Clonecloud: elastic execution between mobile device and cloud. In *Proceedings of the sixth conference on Computer systems* (pp. 301--314). ACM. doi:10.1145/1966445.1966473

Chun, B.-G., & Maniatis, P. (2010). Dynamically partitioning applications between weak devices and clouds. In *Proceedings of the 1st ACM Workshop on Mobile Cloud Computing \& Services: Social Networks and Beyond* (p. 7). ACM. doi:10.1145/1810931.1810938

Dall, C., & Nieh, J. (2014). KVM/ARM: the design and implementation of the linux ARM hypervisor. In *Proceedings of the 19th international conference on Architectural support for programming languages and operating systems* (pp. 333-348). ACM. doi:10.1145/2541940.2541946

Dinh, H. T., Lee, C., Niyato, D., & Wang, P. (2013). A survey of mobile cloud computing: architecture, applications, and approaches. In *Wireless communications and mobile computing* (pp. 1587–1611). Wiley Online Library. doi:10.1002/wcm.1203

Giunta, G., Montella, R., Agrillo, G., & Coviello, G. (2010). *A GPGPU transparent virtualization component for high performance computing clouds* (pp. 379–391). Springer-Verlag. doi:10.1007/978-3-642-15277-1_37

Ha, K., Pillai, P., Richter, W., Abe, Y., & Satyanarayanan, M. (2013). *Just-in-time provisioning for cyber foraging* (pp. 153–166). MobiSys.

Hwang, J.-Y., Suh, S.-B., Heo, S.-K., Park, C.-J., Ryu, J.-M., Park, S.-Y., & Kim, C.-R. (2008). Xen on ARM: System virtualization using Xen hypervisor for ARM-based secure mobile phones. *Consumer Communications and Networking Conference, 2008. CCNC 2008. 5th IEEE* (pp. 257--161). IEEE. doi:10.1109/ccnc08.2007.64

INTEL-IA-PartGuide. (2010). Intel® 64 and IA-32 Architectures Software Developer's Manual.

Kivity, A., Kamay, Y., Laor, D., Lublin, U., & Liguori, A. (2007). kvm: the Linux virtual machine monitor. *Proceedings of the Linux Symposiu*, pp. 225-230.

Neiger, G., Santoni, A., Leung, F., Rodgers, D., & Uhlig, R. (2006). *Intel Virtualization Technology: Hardware Support for Efficient Processor Virtualization*. Intel Technology Journal.

Nvidia-Grid-VGPU. (n.d.). Retrieved from VIRTUAL GPU TECHNOLOGY: http://www.nvidia.com/object/virtual-gpus.html

Popek, G. J., & Goldberg, R. P. (1974). Formal requirements for virtualizable third generation architectures. In *Communications of the ACM* (pp. 412–421). ACM. doi:10.1145/361011.361073

QEMU. (n.d.). *QEMU Emulator User Documentation*. Retrieved from http://qemu.weilnetz.de/qemu-doc.html

Ravi, V. T., Becchi, M., Agrawal, G., & Chakradhar, S. (2011). Supporting GPU sharing in cloud environments with a transparent runtime consolidation framework. In *Proceedings of the 20th international symposium on High performance distributed computing* (pp. 217--228). ACM. doi:10.1145/1996130.1996160

Satyanarayanan, M., Bahl, P., Caceres, R., & Nigel, D. (2009). The Case for VM-Based Cloudlets in Mobile Computing. *IEEE Transactions on Pervasive Computing*, 14-23.

Scott, K., Kumar, N., Velusamy, S., Childers, B., Davidson, J. W., & Soffa, M. L. (2003). Retargetable and reconfigurable software dynamic translation. In *Proceedings of the international symposium on Code generation and optimization: feedback-directed and runtime optimization* (pp. 36--47). IEEE. doi:10.1109/CGO.2003.1191531

Shiraz, M., Abolfazli, S., Sanaei, Z., & Gani, A. (2013). A study on virtual machine deployment for application outsourcing in mobile cloud computing. *The Journal of Supercomputing*, *63*(3), 946–964. doi:10.1007/s11227-012-0846-y

Soyata, T., Muraleedharan, R., Ames, S., Langdon, J., Funai, C., Kwon, M., & Heinzelman, W. (2012). COMBAT: Mobile Cloud-based cOmpute/coMmunications infrastructure for BATtlefield applications. [Baltimore, MD.]. *Proceedings of the Society for Photo-Instrumentation Engineers*, *8403*, 84030K–84030K, 84030K-13. doi:10.1117/12.919146

Soyata, T., Muraleedharan, R., Funai, C., Kwon, M., & Heinzelman, W. (2012). Cloud-Vision: Real-time face recognition using a mobile-cloudlet-cloud acceleration architecture. *Computers and Communications (ISCC), 2012 IEEE Symposium on*, 59-66.

Wang, H., Liu, W., & Soyata, T. (2014). Accessing Big Data in the Cloud Using Mobile Devices. In P. R. Dek (Ed.), *Handbook of Research on Cloud Infrastructures for Big Data Analytics* (pp. 444–470). Hershey, PA, USA: IGI Global; doi:10.4018/978-1-4666-5864-6.ch018

Xen. (n.d.). *Xen Project Software Overview*. Retrieved from Xen Wiki: http://wiki.xenproject.org/wiki/Xen_Overview#Documentation

KEY TERMS AND DEFINITIONS

AMD-v: AMD's hardware-assisted virtualization technology. AMD-V involves similar features for instructions extension as VT-x. Besides that, AMD-V also provide several modes that help hypervisor to handle memory-partition.

ARM: ARM Holdings is a publicly-traded company that licenses low power-consumption CPU architectures to companies such as Nvidia, Samsung, and many others. This allows the licensees to quickly develop products that require CPU cores. ARM is the dominant architecture for smart-phones and many other low-power devices.

Augmented Reality: A family of emerging applications that supplement computer-generated information with acquired real-time information to augment the information content. An example is an application that super-imposes a dress -from an existing database- on a person without having to actually wear that dress.

Central Processing Unit (CPU): This central piece of hardware controls the movement of the data from the main memory into its cores and executes a program that is written by the developer. It is possible that, multiple Operating Systems (OS) are running on a CPU (i.e., virtualized). Virtualization allows a seamless transition from one OS to another. This is done through hardware support that is built into the CPU hardware (e.g., the x86 architecture).

CloneCloud: A web-based system applied for mobile-cloud offloading. CloneCloud handles the communication and storage tasks in mobile-cloud system and can automatically do partition for a smartphone application and distributed the task between cloud servers and the smartphone via network, in which way help user save energy on smartphones and get better performance.

Cloudlet: An intermediate computationally capable device that has direct WiFi access to a mobile platform and WAN access to the cloud. A cloudlet can be used to perform numerous tasks, such as preprocessing the information received from the mobile device. This could ease the computational burden the mobile device, thereby improving its perceived performance, as well as power consumption.

CPU Cache Memory: Composed of L1, L2 and L3 cache layers (stylized L1$, L2$, and L3$), the purpose of CPU cache memory is to allow quick access to frequently used memory locations by buffering them within the cache hierarchy. The lower the cache memory level is, the smaller (but, faster) the cache is. For example, the Nehalem CPU has a 64KB L1$, which can be accessed in 4 cycles, however, L2$ is 256KB, while it requires 11 cycles for access. L3$ requires 50 cycles and is shared by all cores, however, it is 8MB. In some server CPUs, L4 is available.

CPU Main Memory: Typically in the Gigabyte (GB) range, CPU memory is the highest latency, but high throughput storage medium within the memory hierarchy of the CPU. Access to CPU memory is done through a row buffer, thereby making CPU memory not byte-addressable.

Crowd-Sourcing: Crowdsourcing is to outsource a task which is usually huge to a broad, loosely defined external group of people or devices that are willing to help. In mobile-cloud computing, crowdsourcing is to offload a heavy computation task to the nearby mobile devices through wireless network to accelerate the task or improve the quality of the result.

Face Recognition: A computationally-intensive process that associates the faces in a picture with a known set of faces that exist in a fixed database. Typical implementations consist of three steps for this process: Face Detection identifies the location of the faces in a picture, Projection converts these faces into coordinates in a different vector space called Eigenfaces, and the final Face Recognition step is the search for the closest match in the database.

GPU Main Memory: An example GPU memory type is GDDR5. The biggest difference of GPU memory as compared to CPU memory is its parallelism. GPU memory has 16 banks, and is capable of providing consequent memory locations to 16 threads in parallel. However, if some of the threads cannot make use of these consecutive locations, certain data elements will be wasted, requiring more cycles to feed data to those threads.

GPU Virtualization: Many I/O devices like GPUs are usually not design to be virtualization-friendly. GPU virtualization provides a way for multiple VMs to share a single GPU by adding PCI pass-through support and enabling GPUs to save registers and do context switching.

Graphics Processing Unit (GPU): This device is connected to the CPU through an I/O bus, such as PCIe (PCI Express). GPU code is responsible for explicit data transfers from CPU memory (main memory) and the GPU memory (Global Memory). The GPU code (composed of multiple "kernels") executes inside the GPU cores while using the data within the GPU's Global memory. GPU virtualization is a lot more challenging to implement than CPU virtualization.

gVirtuS: Referring to the GPU Virtualization Service. GVirtuS is an open source project that enables GPU virtualization by giving access of GPU to the virtual machines in a transparent way. GVirtuS currently can only runs on NVidia CUDA based GPUs but is going to be applied on other GPUs in the future. GVirtuS is usually used for remote GPU sharing and can get a relatively satisfactory performance.

Hypervisor: A software or hardware layer lies upon host machine or host OS. Hypervisors provide exclusive virtual runtime environments include CPU, memory and other resources for the virtual machines, and also manage their operation. A hypervior may directly run on the host hardware machine or within a host operating system.

I/O Virtualization: I/O virtualization is to consolidate multiple I/O devices into a single one which is shared by multiple VMs and is dynamically allocated to different entities to achieve better flexibility and overall utilization of the system.

IA32: Intel's third generation x86 architecture. In a broad sense, it also refers to all 32-bits x86 architecture versions (not only Intel's).

IaaS (Infrastructure as a Service): A type of cloud computing model. IaaS denotes the case that a service provider provides a whole physical computer infrastructure, or a virtual machine when applying virtualization technology to the users.

Kimberley: A Virtual machine that is designed to accelerate the virtualization of mobile-cloud application by introducing multiple optimizations for the transfer of the VM image. These optimizations such as VM overlays and VM synthesis aim at reducing the starting latency of a VM due to the long transfer delays required for transferring a VM image.

KVM: A Linux subsystem with full name Kernel-based Virtual Machine, also a type 2 hypervisor which provides virtualization extension to Linux kernel. KVM is only able to work on CPUs with hardware-assisted virtualization extension. When merging into the Linux kernel mainline, KVM turns the Linux operation system into a type 1 hypervisor.

Memory Virtualization: Memory virtualization is to create a distributed memory pool for a cluster by decoupling and gathering the memory from individual systems in the cluster. The pool, which overcomes the physical limitation of traditional memory, can be accessed and managed throughout the entire cluster.

Mobile-Cloud Offloading: Due to the hardware limitations on mobile devices, such as tablets and smart phones, it is feasible to run certain mobile applications in the cloud by outsourcing the application to cloud server. This concept, i.e., mobile-cloud offloading, also saves energy when the cost of communication (i.e., the transfer of data and code) amortizes the cost of computation (i.e., the energy required to execute the program by the CPU and/or GPU).

PaaS (Platform as a Service): As a kind of cloud computing model, PaaS denotes the case that a service provider provides a computation environment including OS, storage device and other servers as a software development platform to the users.

QEMU: A generic device emulator that performs virtualization for kinds of hardware. Working as an independent hypervisor, QEMU can either run a single program (user-mode) or a complete operating system. Besides, QEMU also serves in many other hypervisors, like Xen and KVM, as peripherals emulator.

SaaS (Software as a Service): As a kind of cloud computing model, PaaS denotes the case that a service provider provides a service upon an exact software application, for which users would get access to a certain application without concerning about its maintenance.

Thread: A CPU core could house more than one thread. For example, in the INTEL Nehalem CPU architecture, 4C/8T implies (4 cores, 8 threads). This means that, each core can execute two threads. The ability to execute multiple threads affords each core more "options" for execution. While these two threads share many resources in the core (e.g., fetch and decode units, as well as the L1$ and L2$), this doesn't necessarily hurt the performance, since core-intensive and memory-intensive threads could make a good pair, utilizing the resources much more efficiently than a single thread would.

Virtual Machine (VM): A software that simulates real physical hardware or operating system environment in which programs can execute like in a physical machine. A virtual machine may support the execution form a computing process, an application, a complete operating system to multiple guest operating systems.

VM Clone: A way of virtual machines creation. VM clone means make a copy of an existing virtual machine instead of reinstalling guest OS and/or applications. Creating a VM clone can either fully copy the mother virtual machine and make an independent clone, or just make a clone from snapshot and sharing virtual disk with the mother virtual machine.

VM Image: A copy of the entire state of a virtual machine. A capable virtual machine monitor is able to create and store its VM Images in certain formats (e.g. raw, qcow2, vmdk and vdi) via which the virtual machines can be restored to the same state afterwards.

VM Migration: A way of virtual machines creation. VM Migration, also called Live Migration, means moving a running virtual machine from one host to another with the same virtualized environment. VM migration is done by transferring the full state, including memory, network and other devices to the destination hardware.

VT-x: Intel's hardware-assisted virtualization technology. VT-x involves a set of architectural instructions extension for IA32 CPUs, including VMX root operations and VMX non-root operations. VT-x makes CPU virtualization much simpler in which way reducing the hypervisor complexity and software size.

x86: Introduced by INTEL Corporation in the 80's, x86 is the dominant architecture for server products and Windows-based desktop and laptop computers. Apple also started using x86 CPUs in their laptops and desktops in the late 2000's, which increased the x86 market share even more.

Xen: A wide-used type1 hypervisor that allows multiple operating systems operating as virtual machines on the same host machine. Xen is well-known as its using of paravirtualization, which can run modified paravirtualized guest operating systems in order to get high performance on x86 architecture.

Chapter 9
A Tutorial on Network Latency and Its Measurements

Minseok Kwon
Rochester Institute of Technology, USA

ABSTRACT

Internet latency is crucial in providing reliable and efficient networked services when servers are placed in geographically diverse locations. The trend of mobile, cloud, and distributed computing accelerates the importance of accurate latency measurement due to its nature of rapidly changing locations and interactivity. Accurately measuring latency, however, is not easy due to lack of testing resources, the sheer volume of collected data points, the tedious and repetitive aspect of measurement practice, clock synchronization, and network dynamics. This chapter discusses the techniques that use PlanetLab to measure latency in the Internet, its underlying infrastructure, representative latency results obtained from experiments, and how to use these measure latencies. The chapter covers 1) details of using PlanetLab, 2) the Internet infrastructure that causes the discrepancy between local and global latencies, and 3) measured latency results from our own experiments and analysis on the distributions, averages, and their implications.

INTRODUCTION

Internet latency is crucial in providing reliable and efficient networked services such as online retails (e.g., Amazon), multimedia streaming (e.g., Netflix), and social networking (e.g., Twitter). For example, Netflix runs its servers on the Amazon cloud in geographically diverse locations, and provides video streams from the server that can deliver the content to a client in the shortest time. In order to support this server selection in distributed computing, measuring accurate latency becomes extremely important. The trend of mobile computing like iPhone and Android-based smartphones only accelerates the importance of accurate latency measurement due to its nature of rapidly changing locations and interactivity. Accurately measuring network latency, however, is not an easy task due to lack of testing resources, the sheer volume of collected data points, the tedious and repetitive aspect of measurement practice, and

DOI: 10.4018/978-1-4666-8662-5.ch009

clock synchronization. In addition, the time that latency is measured affects measurement results significantly due to network dynamics, volatile traffic conditions, and network failures. Hence, it is critical to measure latencies over a wide span of time and days to acquire a representative and comprehensive view.

In the literature, latency measurement has been studied extensively. For accurate measurements, end hosts at strategic locations are used (Francis, et al., 2001), latency is estimated based on coordinated using landmark hosts (Ng & Zhang, 2001) or DNS queries (Gummadi, Saroiu, & S., 2002), or routing topology (Dabek, Cox, Kaashoek, & Morris, 2004) (H. Madhyastha, 2006). Measured latencies also help select target servers to achieve specified optimization goals in routing, content distribution networks, and cloud computing (Wendell, Jiang, Freedman, & Rexford, 2010) (Khosla, Fahmy, & Hu, 2012) (Ding, Chen, T., & Fu, 2010). Their objective function is to minimize the total execution time and select best replica servers considering server loads, cost and locations. Recently, mobile-cloud computing has gained considerable attention in which a mobile device offloads its computation to servers in the cloud seamlessly and transparently. Again, choosing right servers is critical to lower execution time, and we can use profiling that estimates execution time as a function of latency, loads, program, and network conditions.

The primary focus of this chapter is to discuss the techniques that use PlanetLab (PlanetLab, 2014) in order to measure latency in the Internet, its underlying infrastructure, representative latency results obtained from experiments, and how to use these measure latencies. As PlanetLab provides a world-scale network testbed, it has become a popular platform for network measurement. Based on our own experience, we discuss details regarding PlanetLab: 1) the fundamentals of PlanetLab, 2) how to establish a PlanetLab site and connect to its network, 3) how to manage an account, nodes, and slices, 4) how to run a server and manage tens or hundreds of servers, and 5) how to collect measurements like latency. Our results imply significant discrepancy between global and local latencies. Here, global latencies refer to latency of a long distance connection like transoceanic network link while local latencies are network delay between regional end-hosts. We look into the causes that make such discrepancy; this helps understand the underlying cause. Additionally, we present measured latency results from our own experiments and analysis on the distributions, averages, and their implications.

This chapter is organized as follows: First, we discuss the basics of PlanetLab and using PlanetLab for network latency measurement purposes. Second, we discuss the underlying network infrastructure that causes different latency measurements for global and local connections. Third, we report measured latencies from our experiments and analyze their causes and effects. Finally, we conclude this chapter with discussion on using measured latencies for applications and systems.

LATENCY VS. THROUGHPUT

What Is Latency?

It would be ideal if data in the Internet services can move from one node to another instantaneously at the speed of light. This is, unfortunately, not possible in reality. As a packet travels from a host (the sender) to subsequent routers or another host (the receiver), the packet experiences different types of delays at hosts, routers, and network links. Those delays include 1) processing delay, 2) queuing delay, 3) transmission delay, and 4) propagation delay. A host or a router needs time to process an incoming packet (processing delay) for packet forwarding such as reading a packet header and searching the routing table to determine the next hop. The packet also often needs to wait in the queue to be transmitted onto the link (queuing delay). Transmission delay (also known as the store-and-forward delay) is the time incurred as a node pushes all the bits of the packet onto the link. Finally, propagation delay is the time required for a bit to propagate over the link from a node (either host or router) to another. End-to-end latency is the sum of such delays incurred either at the end-hosts or in transit. When it comes to end-to-end latency, note that an end-host can impose significant delay as well, e.g., dial-up modems, cable modems, and DSL.

What Is Throughput?

Another important and closely related performance metric is throughput that indicates the rate of file transfer. End-to-end throughput is defined as the amount of data received at the destination per unit time. For instance, when it takes T seconds to transfer all M bits of a file, the average throughput is M/T bps. Throughput is closely related to link bandwidth because higher throughput can be achieved often when larger link bandwidth is available. In most cases, an end-to-end network path consists of multiple hops, and the bottleneck link with the smallest bandwidth among those multiple hops determines the end-to-end throughput. We can also define instantaneous throughput as the rate at which a receiver receives data at any given time.

Relationship between Latency and Throughput

TCP mitigates network congestion by reducing its sending rate, and increases throughput as it sends more data when more network capacity becomes available. One critical component is self-clocking that synchronizes the sending rate and the rate at the bottleneck link. TCP infers the bottleneck link capacity by observing the rate of acknowledgments returned by the receiver (Fahmy & Karwa, 2001). The TCP congestion control mechanism affects end-to-end latency significantly since it changes the sending rate dynamically. There have been attempts to understand the effects of TCP on throughput, latency, and their relationships (Padhye, Firoiu, Towsley, & Kurose, 1998). TCP throughput is computed as a function of round-trip time (*rtt*) and the packet loss rate (*p*):

$$roughput = \frac{\sqrt{1.5}}{rtt\sqrt{p}}.$$

Note that *rtt* is the end-to-end round-trip time computed as the sum of end-to-end latency in both directions, and *p* is the one-way packet loss rate. The throughput function implies that throughput increases in inversely proportion to latency and vice versa.

End-to-End Latency Dynamics

The behaviors, dynamics, and effects of end-to-end latency have been studied from routing and TCP's perspectives. In a comprehensive measurement study (Paxson, 1997), Paxson finds that a significant portion of end-to-end latency suffers from several non-negligible routing pathologies including routing loops, erroneous routing, infrastructure failures, mid-stream altered connectivity, and temporary outages. Another similar study (Savage, Collins, Hoffman, Snell, & Anderson, 1999) discovers that in 30-80% of the cases, end-to-end latency can be shortened if packets follow an alternate path with superior quality. Paxson also finds in another study that variations in end-to-end latency indicate congestion periods that span over a wide range (Paxson, 1996).

TRANSPORTING DATA OVER THE INTERNET

In this section, we will be discussing how data is transported over the Internet. First, a brief description of the TCP/IP (Transmission Control Protocol / Internet Protocol) will be provided, which is the backbone of all Internet communications. We will also provide a discussion on the providers of data transportation: Internet Service Providers (ISPs) and Telephone Service Providers (TSPs). We will elaborate on how these entities affect the aforementioned network latency and network throughout.

TCP/IP Protocol

The Internet uses the TCP/IP protocol for communication between its entities such as hosts on the network edge and routers at the network core. More protocols (other than TCP and IP) are involved in Internet communications, but TCP and IP are considered the most critical ones. The original development of TCP/IP was funded by DARPA, an agency of the United States Department of Defense around 1960-70, e.g., ARPANET was launched in 1966. Now IETE (Internet Engineering Task Force) maintains TCP/IP and related protocols whose details are available in RFCs. The main goal of TCP/IP is to provide internetworking technologies that enable communications between two hosts on different networks. Their design principles include 1) packet switching, 2) autonomy (no internal changes required to interconnect networks), 3) the end-to-end principle, 4) minimalism and a best-effort service model, 5) stateless routers, and 6) decentralized control. The end-to-end principle states that complexity and intelligence should be put at the edges (hosts), not at the network core. This principle is indeed related to minimalism, a best-effort service model, and stateless routers. TCP/IP defines today's Internet architecture, and specifies how data should be addressed, end-to-end connectivity is provided, and packets are routed.

In an effort to tackle the complexity of the network system, the TCP/IP protocol adopts a layering structure with abstraction of services. Each layer is service encapsulation that isolates from other layers (protocols) and hides their details, so that designing and maintenance become significantly simple. From top to bottom, there are application, transport, network, data link, and physical layers. In the application layer, a user runs network applications and application-layer protocols such as Web and HTTP; the transport layer provides end-to-end message (also known as segments) delivery in two modes—reliable (TCP) and unreliable (UDP) data transfers; the network layer is responsible for transmitting packets (also known as datagrams) from one node to another (either hosts or routers), so that a datagram can travel from the source to the destination through a sequence of routers; the link and physical layers help transmit datagrams actually over the link within a same network. As a packet goes through these protocols stacks top to bottom at the sender, each layer prepends additional information (header), and this header is stripped off as the packet arrives and goes through the protocols stack backward at the receiver.

The network layer, specifically the IP protocol, in the Internet protocol suite has two main functions, namely forwarding and routing, which contribute to reducing network latency. In forwarding, a router passes a packet arrives at the input link to the relevant output link toward the next hop (either router or host). To forward the packet, the router needs to search a forwarding table for the target outgoing interface (next hop) using the destination IP address as the keyword. This search must be performed swiftly, ideally faster than the link speed; otherwise, arriving packets will be queued and eventually dropped as the queue becomes full. Since 10-100 Gbps link bandwidth at the backbone networks is not far-fetched, the routers should be able to process and forward packets at least at a comparable speed. Routing algorithms also reduce network latency as they compute the shortest paths from the source to the destination. Popular protocols are OSPF and RIP. In these protocols, each router communicates with neighboring routers, and finds collectively the shortest paths from itself to all the other destinations using Dijkstra's shortest path algorithm or distance-vector routing in graph algorithms. TCP runs on hosts at the network edge only, and helps reduce latency by controlling the sending rate as it predicts incipient network congestions. One challenge is the lack of information and signals from the core network regarding the network conditions (e.g., ICMP source quench packets are no longer in use). With no help from routers, TCP infers the network conditions and congestion by analyzing the pace of returned acknowledgments from the destination. Specifically, the sender aligns its sending rate with the acknowledgment rate (called self-clocking) in order to synchronize its sending rate to the bottleneck link rate. Additionally, TCP changes the amount of data it can send at one time (sliding window) depending on the inferred network congestion—more rapidly initially, and slowly as it nears the full capacity.

Data Transportation over Cable (DOCSIS Standard)

Cable operators, such as Time Warner Cable, transport internet data over the same cable that is used to transport the cable TV signals. The standard that allows this is *Data Over Cable Service Interface Specification (DOCSIS)*. Cable operators already own a high speed HFC (hybrid fiber coaxial) network, which is good enough for transporting internet traffic up to 100 Mbps. The DOCSIS standard went through multiple revisions over the past two decades, starting at DOCSIS 1.0 in 1997. With the introduction of DOC 2.0, internet speeds upto 10 Mbps became available. The newest standard, at the time of the preparation of this document, is DOCSIS 3.0 which allows internet speeds up to 50 or 100 Mbps. With such speeds, users can download movies over the internet without any slowdown and watch them in real-time. DOCSIS3.1 is expected to reach up to Gbps speeds and exceed it.

Data Transportation over Telephone Networks

Today most people purchase a smartphone (e.g., iPhone or Android phones) with a data plan through which a user can send videos, audios, or other kinds of data. Data are transported over wireless phone networks such as 3G, 4G, 5G, and LTE. 3G is the third generation of mobile telecommunications technology whose standards are defined by IMT-2000. The specifications of IMT-2000 are in turn defined by the ITU (International Telecommunication Union). While ITU does not clearly specify the data rate for 3G, its data rates usually range from 200 kbps to 2 Gbps, and the applications span voice over IP, Internet access, video conferencing, and even mobile TV. Successful 3G standards include UMTS in Europe, Japan, an China, CDMA2000 in North America and South Korea, and EDGE (Cingular in the United States). 4G is the next generation mobile telecommunication technology succeeding 3G, and provides ultra-broadband Internet access. The target applications include high-definition mobile TV, 3D TV, cloud computing, and video games. The 4G standards (IMT-Advanced) require the data rates to be 100 Mbps and 1 Gbps for high and low mobility communications, respectively. 4G technologies use MIMO, OFDM, and OFDMA for physical layer transmission, and support Mobile IP and IPv6. Early successful versions are 3GPP LTE, Mobile WiMAX, LTE Advanced.

DSL is arguably the most successful technology that transports data over telephone networks in the wired networks. In the United States, about a half of residential broadband access use DSL, and in some countries in Europe, more than 90% of the residential connections are DSL. By using higher frequency bands, the DSL service can share the telephone line with landline phone service. The data rate of DSL ranges from 256 kbps and can reach even over 100 Mbps downstream. Access networks or technologies including DSL are critical in determining end-to-end latency. Imagine that backbone and regional networks enjoy plenty of available network bandwidth and uncongested network conditions due to the efficiency and correctness of the TCP and IP protocol. Even in this case, if the last mile capacity or network conditions in access networks are not sufficiently large, an application suffers from long end-to-end latency.

Internet Service Providers (ISPs)

Computers (also called end hosts or end systems in networking) are connected to the Internet through Internet Service Providers (ISPs). Examples of ISPs are AT&T, Sprint, Verizon, ComCast, and Time Warner. There are ISPs at several different levels—ISPs that run the backbone networks, corporate ISPs, university ISPs, residential ISPs, and ISPs that provide WiFi hotspots at airports, coffee shops, hotels, and even on the streets. In many cases, these ISPs are cable or telecommunication companies, e.g., in Rochester, NY, residential or small business users can access the Internet via Time Warner Cable or Frontiers (phone). The lower-tier ISPs enable residential broadband network access via DSL or cable modem, high-speed local area network access, wireless access (WiFi), or even relatively slow dial-up modem access to customers. These lower-tier ISPs are connected to upper-tier ISPs that usually is responsible for running the core network in which high-speed fiber optic links (1-10 Gbps) are connected through high-speed routers nationally and internationally.

As indicated earlier, ISPs are organized hierarchically as they provide access to the Internet. A tier-1 ISP runs Internet backbones, a tier-2 ISP is in charge of regional or national coverage and needs a service from a tier-1 ISP, a tier-3 ISP has a smaller area coverage and is a customer of a tier-2 ISP, etc. An ISP is connected to other ISP via a Point of Presence (POP) that is a set of routers to which other ISP's routers can connect. In general, when an ISP wants to access a larger area, the ISP establishes a contract with an upper tier ISP, leases communication links, and connect its routers to the upper tier ISP's routers through POPs. In this contract, the upper tier ISP becomes a provider and the lower tier ISP is a customer. If two ISPs are connected at the same tier level, they are peers with each other.

Telephone Service Providers (TSPs)

A telephone service provider (TSP) provides traditional telecommunication services to users. The examples are Verizon, AT&T, Vonage in the United States, and British Telecom in Britain. Although many of them also provide Internet services, TSPs usually mean only phone-related communication services excluding Internet or TV cable or satellite services. Interestingly, portions of the local wired phone infrastructure are heavily utilized in order to provide access to the Internet. These access technologies include dial-up (mostly in 1990s) and DSL (Digital Subscriber Line, often called broadband access) that use phone lines to access the Internet ISP networks. If a household buys a DSL line, it uses the phone network for both data and voice signals. Today, more popular technologies are wireless communication services like WiFi, 3G/4G, and WiMAX. WiFi (or Wireless LAN or IEEE 802.11) is an inexpensive technology where a user can send and receive data through an access point that is connected to the wired

Internet. One weakness of WiFi is its limited coverage within a few tens of meters of the access point. TSPs also provide wide-area wireless Internet access using 3G/4G cellular technologies and base stations at speeds in excess of 1Mbps.

USE OF PLANETLAB FOR NETWORK LATENCY MEASUREMENT

Network traffic measurement is useful to accurately diagnose the causes of phenomena experienced in the network without clear reasons. The accurate diagnosis is later used for addressing anomalies or improving network performance. The measurement usually includes throughput (or bandwidth), latency (or delay, round-trip time), packet loss rates, network topology, packet jitters, traffic types, link utilization, and energy usage. The analysis of these data sets helps give insights on network behaviors and structures, its causes, and reasons behind perceived phenomena. Discoveries from network measurements can also inspire novel systems and algorithmic techniques that solve current obstacles.

It is, however, not easy to collect real measurement data from a large-scale operational networks. To this end, network researchers should have access to computing resources all over the world that allow experimental systems to run disruptive technologies. ISPs (Internet Service Providers) understandably are not fond of disruptive technologies, and therefore are not supportive of these measurement activities. Motivated by this challenge, PlanetLab (PlanetLab, 2014) was created to provide a worldwide network test-bed to network researchers, so that they can try out their experimental systems and algorithms without disrupting operational networks. We will look into the details of PlanetLab, and how to measure latencies using PlanetLab in this section.

What Is PlanetLab?

PlanetLab consists of over a thousand machines dispersed around the world providing a large-scale network-testing environment to researchers. All the machines are connected to the Internet, and they are hosted by research institutions, universities, and routing centers (a few of them). Researchers use PlanetLab to conduct experiments with new systems and services under real-world conditions. These systems and services include multicast overlays, content distribution networks, network-embedded storage, distributed file sharing, and network measurement. The long-term vision of PlanetLab is beyond a simple network test-bed serving as a deployment platform that enables a seamless transition from early prototype to operational systems. Three benefits are highlighted: 1) a large set of machines distributed in different geographical locations, 2) a realistic network substrate that experiences congestion, failures and link behaviors, and 3) a realistic client workload.

A PlanetLab machine runs a Linux operating system together with mechanisms for remote bootstrapping, distributing software updates, system management, auditing malicious activities, key distribution, and user accounts. The software is bundled as a package called MyPLC. The software supports distributed virtualization, so that an application can run on multiple PlanetLab machines at any given time while other applications are running on the same machines. All of the functions in MyPLC and a PlanetLab machine are controlled remotely. This helps easy management and lowers security risks.

Another goal is to understand how the next generation Internet should be designed to support overlay networks and disruptive technologies. This idea is ironically inspired by the successful Internet that is subject to ossification like other commercially successful systems, e.g., UNIX. The ossified Internet hampers network researchers' new attempts to evolve the underlying protocols and mechanisms in the Internet to solve problems (e.g., security vulnerabilities) and address new challenges (e.g., real-time high-volume data transfer). Overlay networks are flexible enough to try out new protocols and capabilities without modifying the core network functions. If these disruptive technologies turn out to be useful on the PlanetLab overlay, they can be adopted as a new feature at commercial routers; if they are complex despite its usefulness, they can continue to be provided as a part of overlays.

How to Use PlanetLab?

When you have a project that you want to use PlanetLab for, a PI (Principal Investigator) in your institution (either you or someone else) first needs to create a PlanetLab site. A site is a physical location where PlanetLab nodes are located; a node is a dedicated server that runs PlanetLab services. Creating a site requires two actions: 1) signing the consortium membership agreement and 2) connecting two or more nodes to PlanetLab. The PI is responsible for 1) overseeing all slices, 2) account management, and 3) node management at your site where a slice is a set of allocated resources distributed across PlanetLab (a UNIX shell access to many nodes). For example, the PI is responsible for addressing any complaints on malicious activities originated from one of your slices, creating and deleting slices, assigning users to slices, enabling and disabling user accounts, and physical maintenance of the nodes at your site.

Once your site is up and running, you can sign up for an account to start using PlanetLab. In your registration process, you are required to designate which site you belong to. It is important to create an SSH key pair for authentication since remote access to PlanetLab nodes requires SSH login using RSA authentication. After you generate the key pair, you keep your private key file and upload the public key to the PlanetLab website to be populated to other nodes. This SSH key setup helps automate the login process to a group of nodes when you populate your slice to those nodes. Without this setup, you need to login manually each machine, which is practically impossible.

Now you can ask your PI to create a slice for you, or connect your account with an existing slice. After associating with a slice, it takes up to an hour for your slice to be created on all nodes and the public key to propagate to those nodes. Then you can start accessing your slice created on all nodes (of course, except down ones). You log in the node using your slice name as the login name, e.g.,

ssh –l princeton_test1 –I ~/.ssh/id_rsa planetlab-1.cs.princeton.edu.

The machine you will get is a minimal Fedora Core 8 Linux installation with basic software and system libraries installed. You can su to root, add new users, install new packages, and mount directories, but cannot do most privileged administrative operations like network configuration. Note that your slice is set to expire after two months. You will be notified of any upcoming expiration, and can extend the expiration date of your slice by renewing the slice. There are also limits on resources including disk space, memory usage, file descriptors and bandwidth that are assigned on a per-slice basis.

How to Measure Latency with PlanetLab?

When you want to measure latency (or other performance metrics) using PlanetLab, the basic mechanism is to use network programming via sockets at application layers, measure latency between two endpoints, and extend it to a set of nodes in PlanetLab. A major challenge in this process is scalability while extending the experiment to tens to hundreds of machines. One critical preliminary step is to create a list of machines that are alive. To this end, you can utilize the information available on the PlanetLab website that maintains a list of nodes available. Unfortunately, some of these supposedly available nodes do not respond for unknown reasons depending on your locations. Hence, the only way to ensure whether a node is accessible is to manually check the node by using either SSH or ping. This is a tedious but necessary process. After this step, we can login each node using the SSH command discussed earlier with our login name (or slice name). Making use of scripts (e.g., UNIX shell scripts) would help automate the whole process. For instance, we can write a shell script to SSH each node on the list, install packages on each node again using SSH, and then run an application there on each node. Once the experiments are complete, we can collect results by transferring files from each node to the main server. This collection and analyzing the results can all be done automatically again using scripts.

UNDERLYING INFRASTRUCTURE

As we measure latencies, we naturally wonder what network links and points (i.e., routers or switches) packets go through resulting in such measurements. In this section, we briefly discuss the underlying network infrastructure that helps understand the measured latency results. The questions that we will address are: 1) Which network links and components contribute to long latency? 2) What is the bandwidth and latency of a long-distance network link? 3) How is a packet delivered between two continents? and 4) What delay and loss events occur and why?

Why Are Global and Local Latencies Different?

Local area networks (LANs) are connected to the backbone network of its Internet Service Provider (ISP). This connection point is called a Point of Presence (POP). These POPs are then connected to high-level networks via Network Access Points (NAPs), and NAPs are in turn connected to the Internet backbone networks. As local latencies are the sum of link propagation delay and transmission delays at switches, global latencies include relatively long propagation delay at backbone links and delays at other connection points such as POP, routers, and NAPs.

Today, 99% of international traffic travels over submarine communication cables under the sea while only 1% utilizes overseas satellite links. The submarine cables provide considerably more reliable communication with multiple backup paths. The bandwidth of submarine cables is higher than that of satellites, and the propagation delay is smaller. However, laying submarine cables on the seabed costs more than satellites. The bandwidth has increased drastically recently from 100Gbps to a few terabits per second with the advance of fiber optics cable technology. Satellite links are also used as an alternative route when submarine communication cables fail for some reason. Repeaters connect point-to-point submarine cable links and amplify light signals in transit.

As expected, global latencies are significantly larger than local ones simply because of its longer propagation and transmission delays. Here by global latencies, we mean coast-to-coast in the United States or transcontinental connection latencies, and local latencies refer to connection delay within same regions like a same network or a same ISP. For example, round trip time over the transcontinental connections go easily over 100ms while it usually takes less than 30ms for local latencies (Markopoulou, Tobagi, & Manour, 2006). Following is a traceroute result from a computer in Rochester, NY, in the United States to a website in South Korea:

```
1. * * 172.16.0.1 (172.16.0.1)  3.534 ms
2. bundle1.rochnyhly-ubr02.nyroc.rr.com (67.246.240.1)  44.703 ms  26.420 ms  40.392 ms
3. gig9-5.faptnyal-rtr002.wny.northeast.rr.com (24.93.9.78)  11.023 ms  12.773 ms  15.652 ms
4. rdc-72-230-153-12.wny.east.twcable.com (72.230.153.12)  29.129 ms *  18.283 ms
5. rdc-72-230-153-243.wny.east.twcable.com (72.230.153.243)  35.792 ms  31.104 ms *
6. be45.cr0.chi10.tbone.rr.com (107.14.19.106)  37.432 ms *
   ae-3-0.cr0.chi10.tbone.rr.com (66.109.6.72)  34.341 ms
7. ae-6-0.cr0.sjc30.tbone.rr.com (66.109.6.14)  82.626 ms  80.971 ms  83.404 ms
8. ae-0-0.pr0.sjc20.tbone.rr.com (66.109.6.139)  81.536 ms  82.834 ms  88.399 ms
9. 66.109.10.206 (66.109.10.206)  83.414 ms *  82.225 ms
10. 112.174.87.153 (112.174.87.153)  202.003 ms  203.643 ms  206.637 ms
11. 112.174.83.161 (112.174.83.161)  220.072 ms
    112.174.83.73 (112.174.83.73)  406.919 ms
    112.174.83.161 (112.174.83.161)  206.341 ms
12. 112.174.8.221 (112.174.8.221)  260.756 ms
    112.174.48.153 (112.174.48.153)  210.390 ms
    112.174.8.125 (112.174.8.125)  205.498 ms
13. 112.174.63.74 (112.174.63.74)  596.896 ms
    112.174.22.226 (112.174.22.226)  207.012 ms
    112.174.23.14 (112.174.23.14)  610.016 ms
14. 112.188.240.54 (112.188.240.54)  429.317 ms  211.567 ms *
15. 112.175.105.10 (112.175.105.10)  311.066 ms  726.723 ms  226.981 ms
```

In the above example, delay from Hop #9 66.109.10.206 (Virginia, US) to Hop #10 112.174.87.153 (Seoul, Korea) is approximately 120ms, which accounts for the transpacific portion of this connection.

Delay and Loss Events and Their Causes

Prior studies discover that a non-negligible percent of network connections experience on occasion extremely long delay and high loss rates even in the backbone network (Paxson, End-to-End Routing Bahavior in the Internet, 1996) (Savage, Collins, Hoffman, Snell, & Anderson, 1999). Moreover, it is possible to find alternatives shorter than the current routes for a substantial percent of the routes computed by routers. The probable causes are packet drops in the buffer (packet losses), routing anomaly (suboptimal routes), router reconfiguration or errors in router configuration (packet losses or suboptimal routes), and link failures (packet losses or suboptimal routes). These events occur periodically, and in particular are detrimental for real-time traffic and applications like VoIP and video streaming.

LOCAL AND GLOBAL LATENCY

In this section, we discuss communication latency using real measurements in the cloud environment, and study the measurements through statistical analysis. Our goal is to gain insight into the performance of the cloud through these measurements and analysis. This analysis enables us to optimize our algorithms and system design based on the observed latencies and processing times.

In order to measure latencies over wired connections, we ran a simple program that sends ping packets from a client computer to servers in cloud datacenters in January and February 2012. The client computer was located in Rochester, New York, in the United States, and we used the five datacenters available in AWS (AWS, 2012), which are all located in geographically different regions, namely in Virginia and Oregon in the United States, Ireland in Europe, Sao Paolo in South America, and Singapore in Asia. We ran two sets of experiments, one on a weekday and the other over the weekend, to collect data with different network traffic conditions. In each experiment, we measured the round-trip time once every minute for 24 hours (thus the total number of latencies in each experiment is 6×24=1,440.

Table 1 shows the mean and standard deviation of these latencies for the AWS datacenters. The latencies to the Virginia datacenter are the shortest while those to Singapore are the longest, as easily conjectured based on their geographical distances from Rochester. In Figure 1, we show the histograms of latencies for the Oregon AWS datacenter on both the weekend and a weekday, where the x-axis denotes the latencies and the y-axis represents the frequencies of such latencies. The latency distributions for all of the other four datacenters behave similarly to the Oregon data, and they are omitted here due to space limitations (refer to (Project, 2012) for all the measurement data). Note that we limit the range of latencies from 0 to 1000ms. While there were a few latencies over 1000ms, they were negligible. In our measurements, the weekend data show higher variance than the weekday data. While we can surmise a variety of causes for this difference including a local network failure, a high volume of traffic at a certain point of the network, etc., our goal here is obtaining real measurement data to enrich our simulations rather than measuring comprehensive data sets and identifying their causes. All of the histograms show a virtually identical shape, which is similar to a Rayleigh distribution with a peak close to the average and then gradually decreasing as latency increases (Wikipedia, 2012). The figure also shows the x and σ values used for the Rayleigh distribution (refer to Equation 1 for details).

Table 1. Average and standard deviation of latencies over wired connections (in millisecond). Virginia, Oregon, Ireland, Sao Paolo, Singapore

Measured Time	Weekend					Weekday				
Datacenter	VA	OR	IRE	SAO	SING	VA	OR	IRE	SAO	SING
Mean	122	322	294	389	580	42	223	196	389	546
Std Dev	124	525	201	166	242	18	41	25	166	34

Table 2. Average and standard deviation of latencies over wireless connections (in millisecond). Virginia, Oregon, Ireland, Sao Paolo, Singapore

Measured Time	Weekend					Weekday				
Datacenter	VA	OR	IRE	SAO	SING	VA	OR	IRE	SAO	SING
Mean	253	389	293	434	697	930	817	798	872	1061
Std Dev	470	635	520	704	1278	595	710	915	1079	2060

Figure 1. Histograms of latencies at Oregon datacenter on the weekend (a) and a weekday (b).

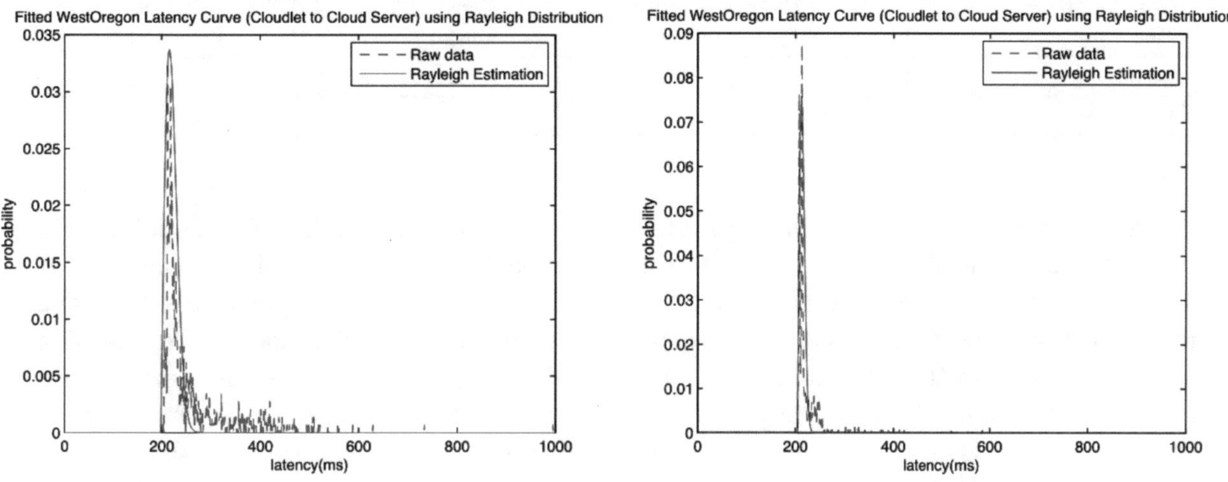

In addition, we measured latencies from a mobile device to servers running at these five different datacenters of AWS. We used an Android phone for the mobile device, and tested over both WiFi and 3G communication links. Similar to the wired connection experiment, the program on the Android phone periodically sent ping packets to the servers (200 times), and recorded their round-trip time. Table II presents the averages and standard deviations of these round-trip times. As expected, the latency to Virginia is the lowest and the one to Singapore is the highest. The latencies of WiFi are smaller than those of 3G, and both are larger than the latencies of wired connections (see Table I). Figure 2 depicts these latency distributions for the AWS Oregon datacenters. These latencies can be approximated by a Rayleigh distribution, as with the latencies over wired connections, although in this case the fit is not as good.

Figure 2. Histograms of latencies at Oregon datacenter via WiFi (a) and 3G (b).

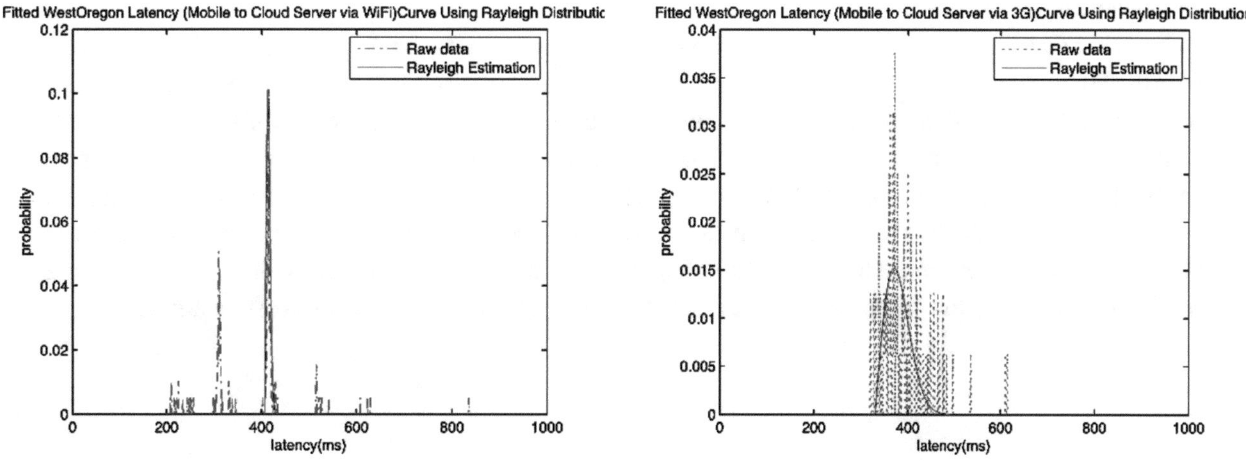

Table 3. Cloud server processing time (in milliseonds)

Instances	Virginia	Oregon	Ireland	Sao Paolo	Singapore
Micro	11,267	4,297	8,166	3,947	3,221
Small	1,565	1,565	1,560	1,557	1,647
Medium	744	751	706	751	712

We also measured the processing times of different AWS instances at these five datacenters. In theory, the same kind of instances at different datacenters should have approximately the same processing power. Of course, the processing time is different for different programs. Our goal here is to measure relative and comparative processing powers of these instances. We executed an odd-even transposition sorting program with $O(n^2)$ time complexity for n=10,000 1,000 times and averaged the measured data (see (Knuth, 1973) for the detailed algorithm). As shown in Table III, the average processing time of the micro instance is much larger than that of the small instance, and the time of the small instance is nearly double that of the large instance regardless of the datacenter. As explained on the AWS web site (AWS, 2012), the micro instance is well-suited for a process in short bursts, but not for long consistent computing. This characteristic contributes to a high standard deviation for the micro instance, e.g., 12,221 at Virginia, and results in high and inconsistent average processing time as well.

In addition to the mean, we study the distributions of the processing times as well. In Figure 3, we show the distributions of processing times for three kinds of AWS instances (micro, small and medium) measured at the Virginia datacenter for a lightweight application. Figure 4 illustrates the processing time distribution for a heavyweight application only for the micro instance at the Virginia datacenter. We use the same sorting application with n=5,000 for the lightweight and n=10,000 for the heavyweight applications. Again, the distributions of the other four datacenters and the rest of the data sets for the heavyweight application are available at (Project, 2012). The results show that the processing times for the micro instance are fairly consistent for the lightweight application while they are varied with a few bursts for the heavyweight application, as explained on the AWS web page (AWS, 2012). The processing times at the small instance closely follow a Gaussian distribution with several anomalies and bursts, and the times for the medium instance concentrate on a small set of data points for both the lightweight and heavyweight applications.

Another distribution depicted in Figure 5 compares the processing times measured with applications with different sizes. We used the same sorting application with n=800, n=3,000, and n=8,000. The figure only shows the processing times measured on the small instance; the data for the micro and medium instances are available at (Project, 2012). All of these data were measured in the Virginia datacenter on a weekday. The figure indicates that the processing times become varied as the size and computing time of the application increases for the small instance (a similar phenomenon was observed for the micro and medium instances). As more computation is required, the performance is more vulnerable to external conditions like available computing resources, the number of other jobs, and network bandwidth.

Figure 3. Histograms of processing time for the micro (a), small (b), and medium (c) instances in Virginia for the lightweight application.

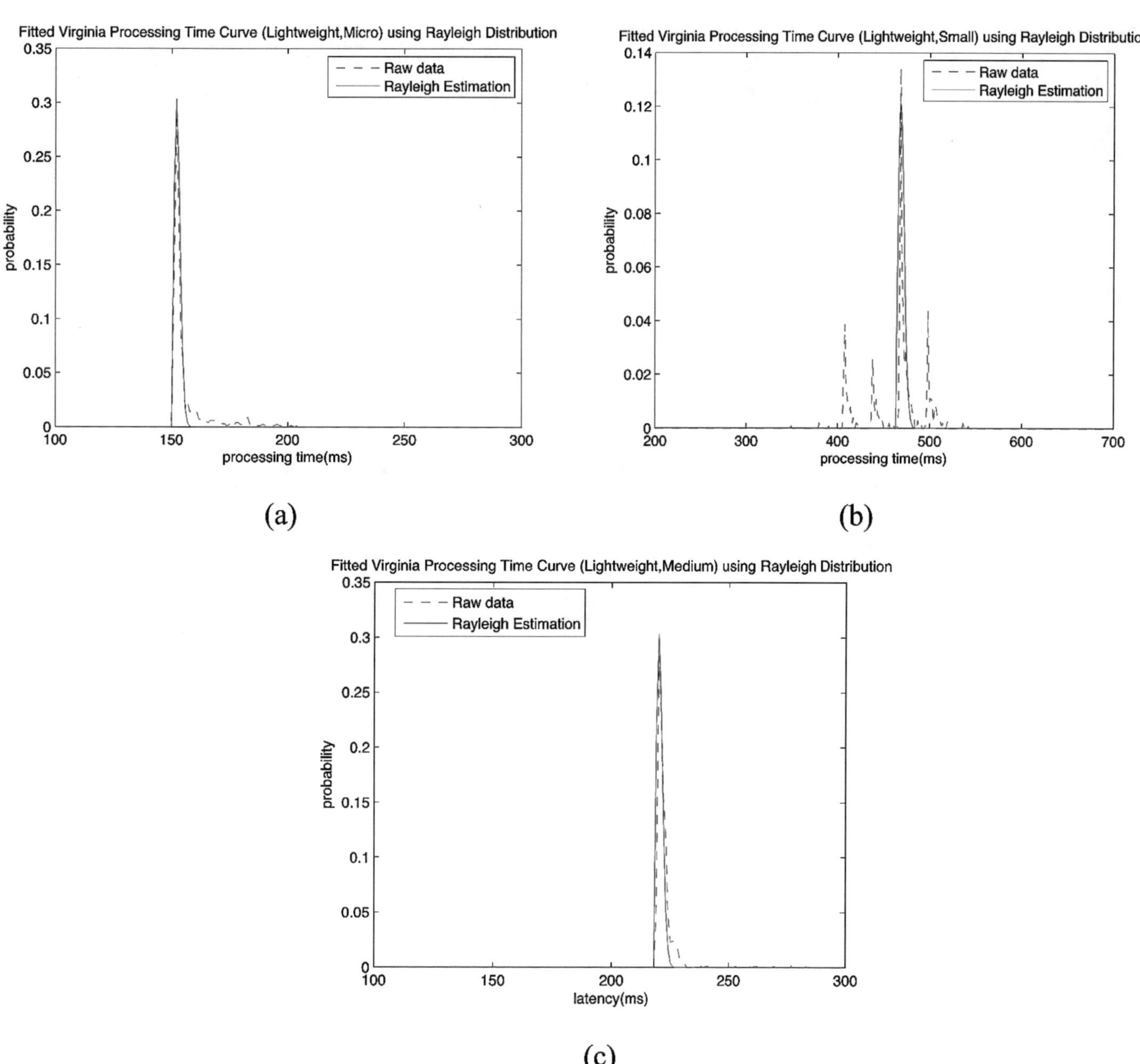

Figure 4. Histograms of processing time for different application sizes on the small instance at the Virginia datacenter.

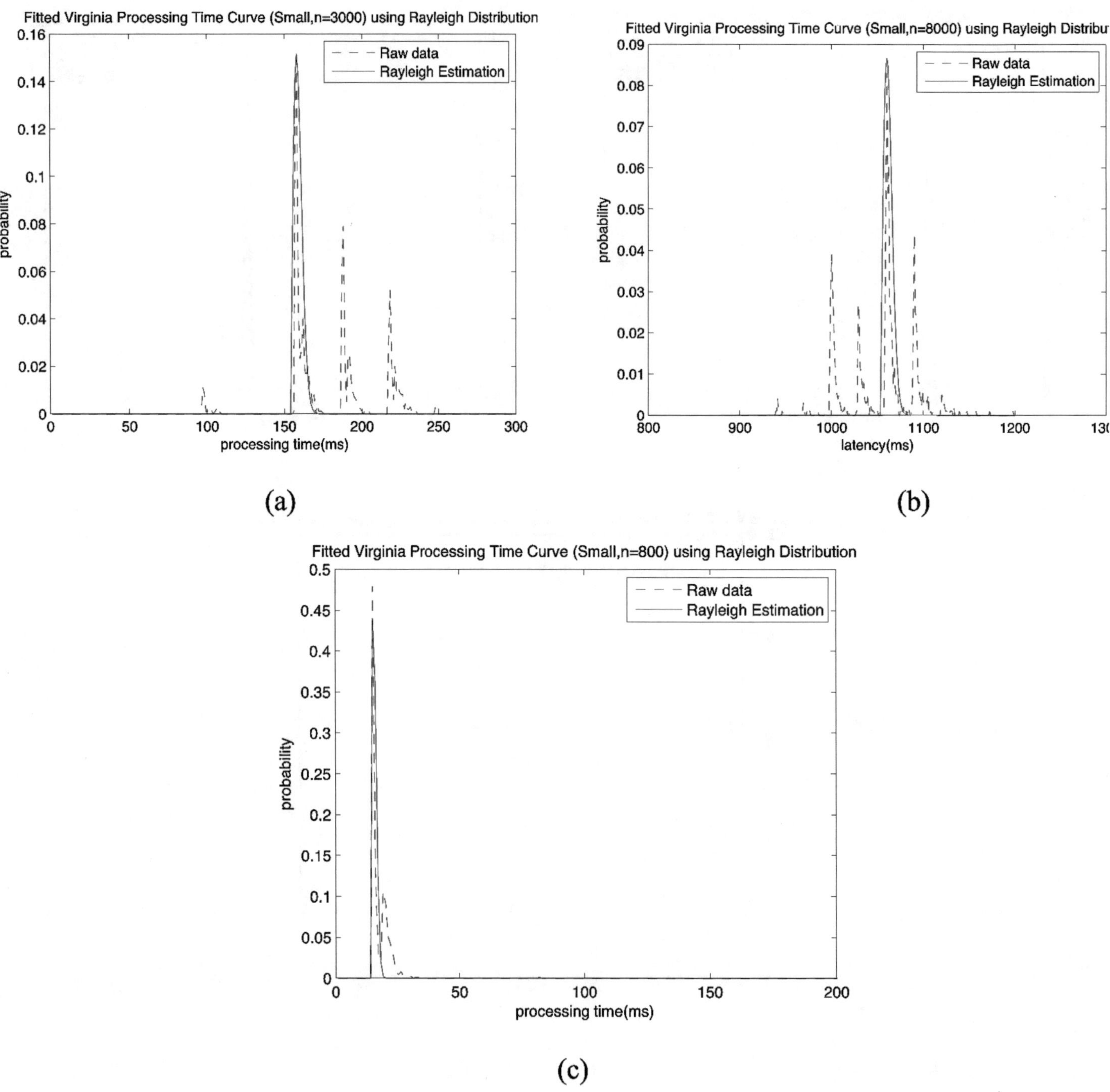

Figure 5. Histograms of processing time for the micro instance at the Virginia datacenter for the heavyweight application.

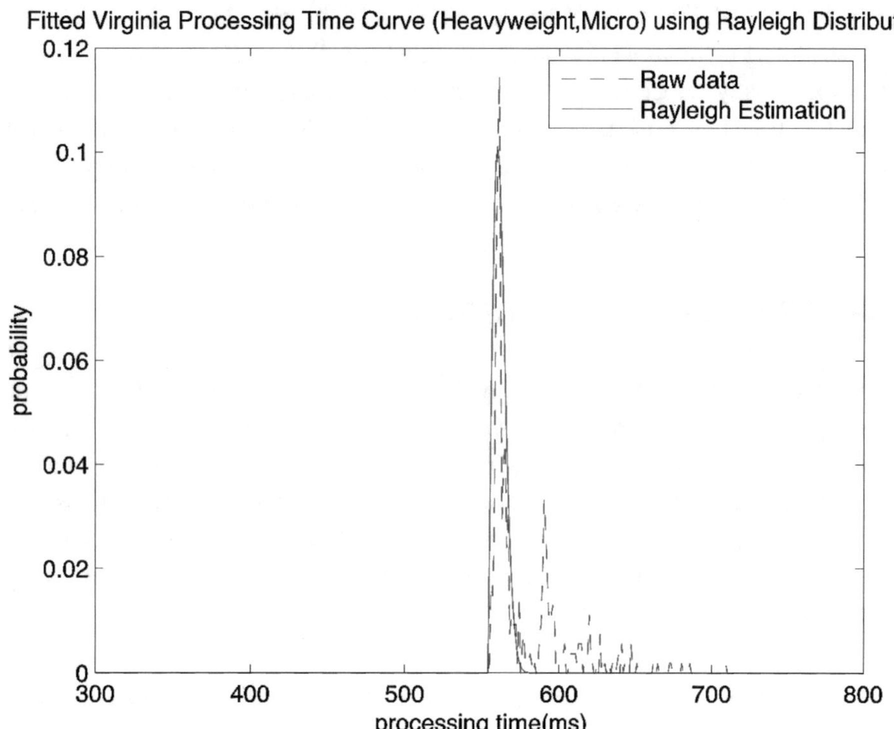

As implied previously, we have found that all of the latency distributions, namely 1) cloudlet to the cloud and 2) mobile to the cloud over either 3G or WiFi, can be approximated (some better than the others) by a Rayleigh distribution with a shifted x-axis. The processing time distributions under different loads are also similar to a Rayleigh distribution. The probability density function of a Rayleigh distribution is

$$\frac{x}{\sigma^2} e^{x^2/2\sigma^2}, x \geq 0 \tag{1}$$

where σ denotes the shape of the distribution (either narrow or wide) and x adjusts the distribution into a different location along the x-axis. We fit curves to the measured data by adjusting the values of σ and x in the Rayleigh distribution to best match the measured data, and we use these models for latency in our simulations in the next section.

Interestingly, we can observe several sub-distributions in some of the probability curves from the measured data, e.g., the mobile to cloud latencies via WiFi for the Oregon datacenter, and some processing time distributions—Figure 3(b), Figures 5(b) and (c). Each sub-distribution is also well-fitted to a Rayleigh distribution. We surmise that locality exists in both latency and processing time due to more than one route in the network and workload locality with the CPUs.

The cloud can be modeled as a graph using the vertices as cloud server locations and the edges as the network latencies (Soyata & Friedman, 1994) (Soyata, Friedman, & Mulligan, 1993) (Soyata & Friedman, 1994) (Soyata, Friedman, & Mulligan, 1995) which will allow sophisticated combinatorial optimization algorithms for task scheduling in the cloud (Soyata & Friedman, 1994) (Soyata, Friedman, & Mulligan, 1997) (Soyata T., 2000). Additionally, rather than pure-software methods, hardware accelerators can be utilized for reducing the computational latency (Li, Ding, Hu, & Soyata, 2014) (Guo, Ipek, & Soyata, 2010) (Soyata & Liobe, 2012). While this will provide a speed-up and mitigate some of the negative impact of the network latencies, the next section focuses on the general effects of the latency on certain latency-sensitive applications.

PERFORMANCE IMPLICATIONS ON APPLICATIONS

To understand the performance implications of network latency, the authors of (Kwon, et al., 2014) compare three data partitioning and server selection algorithms, namely random, fixed, and greedy using estimated latencies. The random algorithm sends tasks to a group of randomly selected servers; the fixed algorithm distributes tasks evenly among servers; and the greedy algorithm selects the server that can finish the task as quickly as possible. In the greedy algorithm, the amount of time to be completed is estimated based on measured latencies in the profile. The results show the clear advantage of using latency profiling to achieve the minimal response time.

Figure 6. Measurement of the response times over actual and simulated links without the cloudlet (left) and with the cloudlet (right).

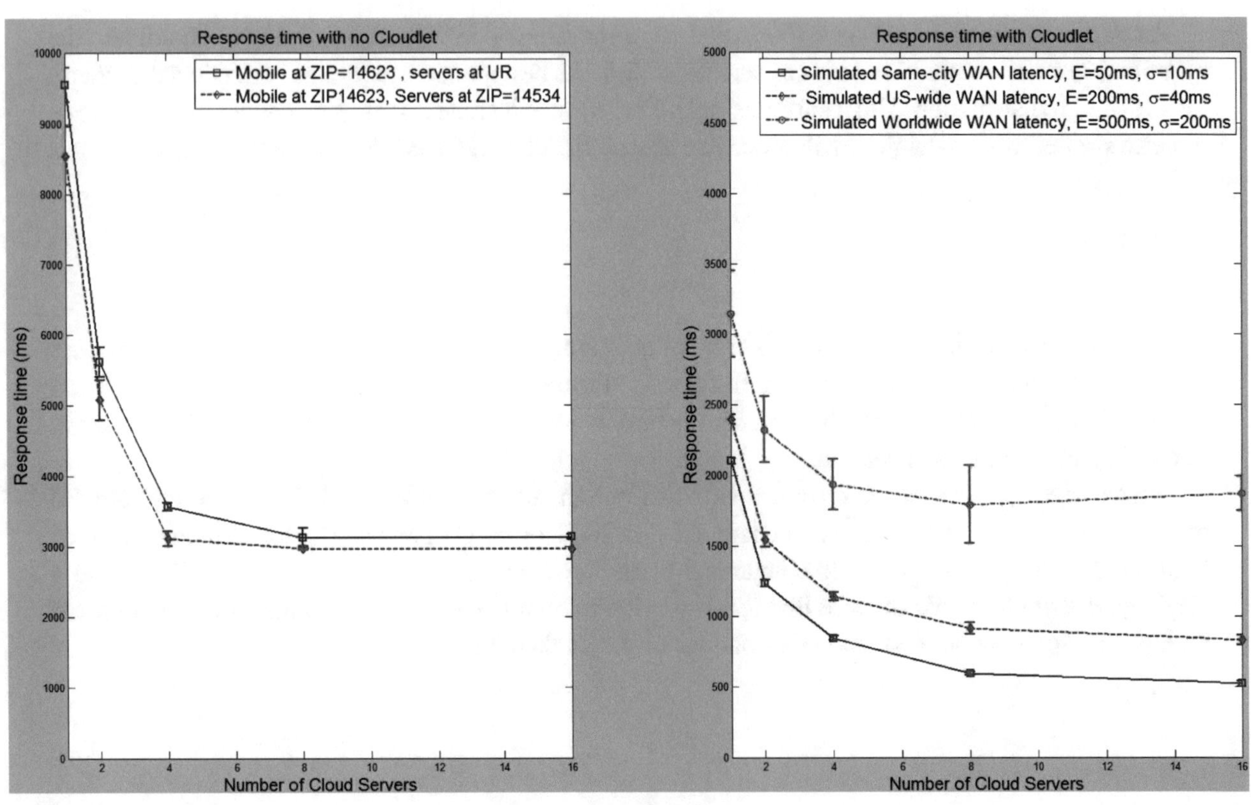

Applications that benefit from latency profiling include bandwidth-hungry or latency-sensitive ones (Page, Kocabas, Soyata, Aktas, & Couderc, 2014), (Wang, Liu, & Soyata, 2014), (Soyata, et al., 2012) (Fahad, et al., 2012), (Hassanalieragh, Soyata, Nadeau, & Sharma, 2014), (Nadeau, Sharma, & Soyata, 2014). An example of a bandwidth-hungry application is a long-term health monitoring system using homomorphic encryption (Kocabas O., et al., 2013), and an example for the latter is face detection or recognition (Soyata, Muraleedharan, Funai, Kwon, & Heinzelman, 2012).

Face detection and recognition applications are tested in a mobile-cloudlet-cloud computing setting in which mobile users can offload applications using virtual resources available on the cloud infrastructure (Kocabas & Soyata, 2014) (Soyata, Ba, Heinzelman, Kwon, & Shi, 2013) (Project, 2012). The cloud servers exhibit diverse latencies and processing times for different instance types and geographical locations, resulting in a wide spectrum of system performance. Figure 6 shows the response times for the Greedy algorithm (Kwon, et al., 2014) run over a narrow-range real cloud environment, when the cloudlet emulator and the cloud servers are located within the same city. To demonstrate the utility of the cloudlet, the results were reported with and without the cloudlet emulator. As evidenced from both plots, the TCP overhead is a significant burden on the mobile. By performing pre-processing on the data received from the mobile and intelligently hiding the TCP overhead partially, the cloudlet is able to provide a 6x speed-up over a naive implementation on the mobile.

The homomorphic encryption application (Kocabas O., et al., 2013) is tested in an Amazon Cloud environment (AWS, 2012) to determine the cost of running this application in a regular outsourced cloud computing scenario. It has been determined that, this application is intensive in incoming traffic, thereby creating an advantage in terms of bandwidth billing. In other words, a significant amount of data is pushed into the cloud, whereas the results are substantially smaller in size, almost by 2-3 orders of magnitude. Operators such as AWS do not charge for the incoming bandwidth, whereas the outgoing traffic is billable. In addition to bandwidth billing, the cost of computation (i.e., GHz/month billing) as well as the cost of storage have also been analyzed in this study.

REFERENCES

AWS. (2012). Retrieved from http://aws.amazon.com

Dabek, F., Cox, R., Kaashoek, F., & Morris, R. (2004). *Vivaldi: A Decentralized Network Coordinate System* (pp. 15–26). ACM SIGCOMM.

Ding, C., Chen, Y. T. X., & Fu, X. (2010). CloudGPS: A Scalable and ISP-friendly Server Selection Scheme in Cloud Computing Environments. IEEE IWQoS, (pp. 1-9).

Fahad, A., Soyata, T., Wang, T., Sharma, G., Heinzelman, W., & Shen, K. (2012). SOLARCAP: Super Capacitor Buffering of Solar Energy for Self-Sustainable Field Systems. *Proceedings of the 25th IEEE International System-On-Chip Conference (SOCC)*, (pp. 236-241). Nigara Falls, NY. doi:10.1109/SOCC.2012.6398354

Fahmy, S., & Karwa, T. (2001). *TCP Congestion Control: Overview and Survey of Ongoing Research.* CSD-TR-01-016, Purdue University. *Computer Science.*

Francis, P., Jamin, S., & Jin, C. (2001, October). IDMaps: A Global Internet Host Distance Estimation Service. *IEEE/ACM Transactions on Networking*, *9*(5), 525–540. doi:10.1109/90.958323

Gummadi, K., Saroiu, S., & S., G. (2002). King: Estimating Latency between Arbitrary Internet End Hosts. *ACM IMW*, (pp. 5-18).

Guo, X., Ipek, E., & Soyata, T. (2010). Resistive Computation: Avoiding the Power Wall with Low-Leakage, {STT-MRAM} Based Computing. *Proceedings of the International Symposium on Computer Architecture (ISCA)*, (pp. 371-382). Saint-Malo, France. doi:10.1145/1815961.1816012

Hassanalieragh, M., Soyata, T., Nadeau, A., & Sharma, G. (2014). Solar-Supercapacitor Harvesting System Design for Energy-Aware Applications. *Proceedings of the 27th IEEE International System-On-Chip Conference*. Las Vegas, NV. doi:10.1109/SOCC.2014.6948941

Kaehler, G., & Bradski, A. (2008). *OpenCV Computer Vision with OpenCV Library*. O'Reilly.

Khosla, R., Fahmy, S., & Hu, Y. (2012). Content Retrieval Using Cloud-based DNS. *IEEE Global Internet Symposium*, (pp. 1-6).

Knuth, D. (1973). *The Art of Computer Programming: Sorting and Searching*. Reading, MA: Addison-Wesley.

Kocabas, O., & Soyata, T. (2014). Medical Data Analytics in the Cloud Using Homomorphic Encryption. In P. Chelliah, & G. Deka, Handbook of Research on Cloud Infrastructures for Big Data Analytics (pp. 471-488). IGI Global. doi:10.4018/978-1-4666-5864-6.ch019

Kocabas, O., Soyata, T., Couderc, J., Aktas, M., Xia, J., & Huang, M. (2013). *Assessment of Cloud-based Health Monitoring Using Homomorphic Encryption* (pp. 443–446). IEEE ICCD. doi:10.1109/ICCD.2013.6657078

Kwon, M., Dou, Z., Heinzelman, W., Soyata, T., Ba, H., & Shi, J. (2014). *Use of Network Latency Profiling and Redundancy for Cloud Server Selection*. IEEE CLOUD. doi:10.1109/CLOUD.2014.114

Li, P., Ding, C., Hu, X., & Soyata, T. (2014). LDetector: A Low Overhead Race Detector for GPU Programs. *5th Workshop on Determinism and Correctness in Parallel Programming (WODET2014)*.

Madhyastha, H. T. A. (2006). A Structural Approach to Latency Prediction. ACM IMC, (pp. 99-104).

Markopoulou, A., Tobagi, F., & Manour, K. (2006, June). Loss and Delay Measurements of Internet Backbones. *Computer Communications*, *29*(10), 1590–1604. doi:10.1016/j.comcom.2005.07.011

Nadeau, A., Sharma, G., & Soyata, T. (2014). State of Charge Estimation for Supercapacitors: A Kalman Filtering Approach. *Proceedings of the 2014 IEEE International Conference on Acoustics, Speech, and Signal Processing (ICASSP)*, (pp. 2213-2217). Florence, Italy.

Ng, E., & Zhang, H. (2001). *Predicting Internet Network Distance with Coordinate-based Approaches* (pp. 170–179). IEEE INFOCOM.

Padhye, J., Firoiu, V., Towsley, D., & Kurose, J. (1998). *Modeling TCP Throughput: A Simple Model and its Empirical Validation* (pp. 303–323). ACM SIGCOMM. doi:10.1145/285237.285291

Page, A., Kocabas, O., Soyata, T., Aktas, M., & Couderc, J. (2014). Cloud-Based Privacy-Preserving Remote ECG Monitoring and Surveillance. *Annals of Noninvasive Electrocardiology*. doi:10.1111/anec.12204 PMID:25510621

Paxson, V. (1996). *End-to-End Routing Bahavior in the Internet*. ACM SIGCOMM.

Paxson, V. (1997). *End-to-End Internet Packet Dynamics*. ACM SIGCOMM.

PlanetLab. (2014). *PlanetLab*. Retrieved from http://www.planet-lab.org

Project, T. M. (2012, February). *AWS Measurements*. Retrieved from http://www.themochaproject.com

Savage, S., Collins, A., Hoffman, E., Snell, J., & Anderson, T. (1999). *The End-to-End Effects of Internet Path Selection* (pp. 289–299). ACM SIGCOMM. doi:10.1145/316188.316233

Soyata, T. (2000). *Incorporating circuit-level information into the retiming process*. University of Rochester.

Soyata, T., Ba, H., Heinzelman, W., Kwon, M., & Shi, J. (2013). Accelerating Mobile-Cloud Computing: A Survey. In H. Mouftah, & B. Kantarci (Eds.), Communication Infrastructures for Cloud Computing (pp. 175-197). IGI Global.

Soyata, T., & Friedman, E. (1994). Retiming with non-zero clock skew, variable register, and interconnect delay. *Proceedings of the IEEE Conference on Computer-Aided Design (ICCAD)*, (pp. 234-241).

Soyata, T., Friedman, E., & Mulligan, J. (1993). Integration of Clock Skew and Register Delays into a Retiming Algorithm. *Proceedings of the IEEE International Symposium on Circuits and Systems*, (pp. 1483-1486).

Soyata, T., & Friedman, E. G. (1994). Synchronous Performance and Reliability Improvements in Pipelined ASICs. *Proceedings of the IEEE ASIC Conference (ASIC)*, (pp. 383-390). doi:10.1109/ASIC.1994.404536

Soyata, T., Friedman, E. G., & Mulligan, J. H. (1995). Monotonicity constraints on path delays for efficient retiming with localized clock skew and variable register delay. *Proceedings of the International Symposium on Circuits and Systems (ISCAS)*, (pp. 1748-1751). Seattle, WA. doi:10.1109/ISCAS.1995.523751

Soyata, T., Friedman, E. G., & Mulligan, J. H. (1997, January). Incorporating Interconnect, Register, and Clock Distribution Delays into the Retiming Process. *IEEE Transactions on Computer-Aided Design of Integrated Circuits and Systems*, *16*(1), 105–120. doi:10.1109/43.559335

Soyata, T., & Liobe, J. (2012). pbCAM: probabilistically-banked Content Addressable Memory. *Proceedings of the 25th IEEE International System-on-Chip Conference (IEEE SOCC)*, (pp. 27-32). Niagara Falls, NY.

Soyata, T., Muraleedharan, R., Ames, S., Langdon, J., Funai, C., Kwon, M., & Heinzelman, W. (2012). COMBAT: mobile-Cloud-based cOmpute/coMmunications infrastructure for BATtlefield applications. *Proceedings of the Society for Photo-Instrumentation Engineers*, 84030K–13, 84030K-13. doi:10.1117/12.919146

Soyata, T., Muraleedharan, R., Funai, C., Kwon, M., & Heinzelman, W. (2012). Cloud-Vision: Real-Time Face Recognition Using a Mobile-Cloudlet-Cloud Acceleration Architecture. *Proceedings of the 17th IEEE Symposium on Computers and Communications (IEEE ISCC)*, (pp. 59-66). Capadoccia, Turkey. doi:10.1109/ISCC.2012.6249269

Wang, H., Liu, W., & Soyata, T. (2014). Accessing Big Data in the Cloud Using Mobile Devices. In P. Chelliah & G. Deka (Eds.), Handbook of Research on Cloud Infrastructures for Big Data Analytics (pp. 444-470). IGI Global. doi:10.4018/978-1-4666-5864-6.ch018

Wendell, P., Jiang, J., Freedman, M., & Rexford, J. (2010). *DONAR: Decentralized Server Selection for Cloud Services.* ACM SIGCOMM. doi:10.1145/1851182.1851211

Wikipedia. (2012). *Rayleigh Distribution.* Retrieved from http://en.wikipedia.org/wiki/Rayleigh_distribution

KEY TERMS AND DEFINITIONS

Application Response Time: The time taken for an application to respond to a user from the user's point of view. While network response time is about how fast the network responds, application response time is end-user perceived time that includes network response time. Application response time is the sum of network response time and transaction response time where transaction response time is the time taken for the server and client to process a request.

Cloud Computing: A type of computing where computing, storage, and networking resources are delivered to users as a utility over the network. The cloud provides an illusion of infinite computing resources, and eliminates an upfront capital expense since users can pay the cost on a need basis. Cloud computing is also used in a pay-as-you-go manner, i.e., elasticity that removes the risks of overprovisioning and underprovisioning.

Cloudlet: A computationally highly capable intermediate device placed between a mobile device and the cloud servers. Mobile-cloud computing benefits from having a cloudlet as the cloudlet can provide far higher computational power with minimal latencies. The cloudlet can also pre-process data sent by a mobile and pass even smaller data to the cloud.

Hop: A part of the route between the source and the destination, specifically a link between two consecutive routers. A hop occurs each time a packet travels from one router to the next one. We can use traceroute or ping to find the number of hops from one host to another.

Internet Service Provider (ISP): A commercial or non-commercial organization that enables users to access the Internet services. ISPs are a multi-tired organization, and pay upstream ISPs with a larger network for Internet access. The Internet services include Internet access, e-mails, domain name registration, web hosting, and Internet transit.

Mobile Computing: Computing and communication activity in which a computer is mobile and transported during its usage. Mobile devices include mobile computers like laptops, mobile phones like smartphones, and wearable computers. The challenges include power consumption, mobile management, communication ranges, security and privacy, and transmission interferences.

Mobile-Cloud Computing: A type of computing in which a mobile client offloads some of its computing to servers in the cloud. As mobiles and cloud computing become more prevalent, mobile-cloud computing becomes popular with high potential for applications. One challenge is how to divide and distribute data from the mobile to servers in the cloud seamlessly and transparently.

Multi-Hop Connection: A network connection that consists of more than one hop. This implies that the connection includes more than one router and links between two routers. Multi-hop connection requires routing decisions at each router to reach the destination.

Network Latency: Time interval measured from the source sending a packet to the destination receiving it. It can be measured either one-way or round-trip time that is the one-way from the source to destination plus the reverse one-way, and measuring round-trip time is more straightforward due to clock synchronization. Ping is a popular service used often for round-trip time measurement.

Network Router: A server that connects more than one network and forwards packets between networks. A router is equipped with specialized hardware and software platforms for fast packet forwarding. Routers also communicate with other routers to compute routes, i.e., the next hop for a specified destination.

Network Switch: A computing device that connects more than one local area network (LAN), and forwards packets between LANs. A switch is a simpler version of a router in the LAN environment, and its main tasks are routing and forwarding.

Network Throughput: The rate of data transmission over a communication channel in the network. It indicates the amount of data received per unit time and usually is measured in bits per second or bps. Note that data loss lowers network throughput because such packets do not arrive successfully at a receiver.

Round-Trip Time (RTT): The time it takes for a packet to travel from a sender to a receiver, and then back to the sender. The rtt time consists of propagation and queuing delays at the core networks, and processing delays at end-hosts.

Telephone Service Provider (TSP): A service provider that allows access to phone and communication services. The examples are AT&T, Verizon, Frontier, and CenturyLink.

Chapter 10
Operational Cost of Running Real-Time Mobile Cloud Applications

Ovunc Kocabas
University of Rochester, USA

Regina Gyampoh-Vidogah
Independent Researcher, UK

Tolga Soyata
University of Rochester, USA

ABSTRACT

This chapter describes the concepts and cost models used for determining the cost of providing cloud services to mobile applications using different pricing models. Two recently implemented mobile-cloud applications are studied in terms of both the cost of providing such services by the cloud operator, and the cost of operating them by the cloud user. Computing resource requirements of both applications are identified and worksheets are presented to demonstrate how businesses can estimate the operational cost of implementing such real-time mobile cloud applications at a large scale, as well as how much cloud operators can profit from providing resources for these applications. In addition, the nature of available service level agreements (SLA) and the importance of quality of service (QoS) specifications within these SLAs are emphasized and explained for mobile cloud application deployment.

INTRODUCTION

Cloud is the platform of multiple servers over a widely disbursed geographic area, connected by the Internet for the purpose of serving data or computation (Bansal, 2013). Mobile Cloud Computing (MCC) can be described as a model for enabling convenient, on-demand network access to a shared pool of configurable computing resources (Shanklin, 2014) from mobile devices. MCC therefore refers to both the applications delivered as services over the Internet and the hardware and system software in data-

DOI: 10.4018/978-1-4666-8662-5.ch010

centers that provide those services. The services themselves have long been referred to as Software as a Service (SaaS). Some vendors use terms such as Infrastructure as a Service (IaaS) and Platform as a Service (PaaS) and others to describe their products, but we abstain from these because accepted definitions for them still differ widely. The datacenter hardware and software is what we will call a *cloud.* When a cloud is made available in paying costs as they occur to the general public, it is called a *public cloud* and the service being sold is *utility computing. Private cloud* on the other hand refers to internal data centers of a business or other organization (Armbrust, et al., 2010).

The point at which these internal data centers are large enough to enable organizations to benefit from the advantages of cloud computing are the subject of much debate. (Kovachev, Cao, & Klamma, 2013) described cloud computing as the sum of SaaS and utility computing, but does not include small or medium-sized datacenters, though some of these rely on virtualization for management. People can be users or providers of SaaS, or utility computing. The focus here is on SaaS providers (cloud users) and cloud providers, who have received less attention than SaaS users. Mobile computing is the delivery of services, software and processing capacity over the Internet, reducing cost, increasing storage, automating systems, decoupling of service delivery from underlying technology, and providing flexibility and mobility of information. However, the actual realization of these benefits is far from being achieved for mobile applications (Kovachev, Cao, & Klamma, 2013).

MCC is introduced as an integration of cloud computing into the mobile environment. It is a model for enabling convenient, on-demand network access to a shared pool of configurable computing resources (Mouftah & Kantarci, 2013). MCC is a model for transparent elastic augmentation of mobile devices via ubiquitous wireless access to cloud storage and computing resources, with context-awareness and dynamic adjusting of offloading in respect to change in operating conditions, while preserving available sensing and interactive capabilities of mobile devices (Fesehaye, Gao, Nahrstedt, & Wang, 2012).

However, there has been some confusion about the mobile cloud computing model about its capabilities and can sometimes be described in general terms that includes almost any kind of outsourcing of hosting and computing resources. In other words, mobile represents a relatively new and fast growing segment of the cloud-computing paradigm (Rimal & Choi, 2012)

In view of the inherent advantages of this technology, enterprises today are looking to cloud computing to help them better deliver existing as well as new, innovative services on demand across network, computing, and storage resources at reduced cost (Chappel, 2013). This is because cloud economics will play a vital role in shaping the mobile cloud industry of the future (IBM, 2013). In a recent (Microsoft, 2010) white paper titled "Economics of the Cloud", it stated that the mobile computing industry is moving towards the cloud driven by three important economies of scale because: 1) large data centers can deploy computational resources at significantly lower costs than smaller ones; 2) demand pooling improves utilization of resources; and 3) multi-tenancy lowers application maintenance and labor costs for large public clouds. The cloud also provides an opportunity for IT professionals to focus more on technological innovation rather than thinking of the budget of "waiting to force things to move." However, many organizations find it difficult to determine the total operating costs of using cloud services (Microsoft, 2010).

The recent survey conducted by (Prasad, Gyani, & Murti, 2012) supports this view and it was revealed that, user and potential users of mobile cloud services would reduce costs and time needed to deploy tools for quicker analysis and planning. 14% somewhat disagreed and in helping to improve planning and performance management in users' organizations, 42% believed they would be helped by use of mobile cloud computing for rapid deployment of specific applications. Respondents also favored cloud usage.

Those with the tendency to use the cloud-based finance applications, 36% had already deployed one or more applications and 23% had deployments in process. Another 28% are considering deployment of one or more cloud-based applications. 13% of all respondents have decided to forgo on-premise to considering cloud-based applications.

These findings suggests that, the key idea revealed concerning mobile cloud computing is to: (1) understand how cloud applications can provide data center operators with greater reach and more rapid deployment; (2) identify and understand how cloud computing can change and reduce current cost; and (3) making sure collaboration with application vendors and enterprises are key to developing applications that fit into each organization's strategic vision for more cost-effective options (Dinh, Lee, Niyato, & Wang, 2013). The chapter briefly describes some of the cost models that have been developed, how this has fed into pricing models of cloud service providers and illustrates how these models can be used to estimate the true operational cost of real-time mobile cloud computing services. The aim is to help decision makers make the business case for specific applications and what services matches the business case.

CLOUD OPERATOR PRICING

In this chapter, a comparison of pricing of major cloud service providers will be provided. We will look at Microsoft Azure, Google Cloud Platform and Amazon Web Services (AWS). For each provider the pricing will be based on the US East region. Operating system is assumed to be Linux.

Microsoft Azure Pricing

Virtual machine lists are based on their properties. Table 1 and Table 2 demonstrate the pricing for basic and standard tiers, which provide all possible machine (instance) configurations. Compute intensive Instances A8 and A9 contain the Intel Xeon E5-2670 CPU @2.6 GHz. Microsoft Azure offers pricing for two tiers: basic and standard. While both tiers are similar in terms of virtual machine configurations, standard tier offers additional capabilities such as load balancing and auto-scaling for performance improvement. These tiers are the data for virtual machines with SSD storage. Storage prices are for persistent storage and billed by GB per month. Table 3 tabulates the storage pricing when the data is stored with 99.9% read/write availability SLA (MS-SLA).

Data transfers are charged based on the direction to Azure data centers. Inbound data transfers, which are the data transfers into the data centers are free of charge. Outbound data transfers are charged based on the data amount shown in Table 4.

Google Cloud Platform Pricing

Google App Engine for PaaS services and Compute Engine for IaaS services are shown in Table 5. Google Compute Engine billing includes a minimum of 10 minutes of usage. After this 10-minute minimum interval, each instance is charged at 1-minute increments (rounded up to the nearest minute). Additionally, Google offers discounts based on sustained (continuous) usage. The f1-micro and g1-small instances are for non resource-intensive tasks that remain active for long periods of time.

Google charges network differently for networking inside the cloud infrastructure and outside communication via the Internet as shown in Table 6. Incoming data into the cloud services and outgoing

Table 1. Basic Tier Pricing for A and D series of virtual machines

Instance Type	Cores	RAM (GB)	Disk Size (GB)	Price (per Hr)
A0	1	0.75	20	$0.018
A1	1	1.75	40	$0.044
A2	2	3.5	60	$0.088
A3	4	7	120	$0.176
A4	8	14	240	$0.352
D1	1	3.5	10	$0.077
D2	2	7	40	$0.154
D3	4	14	100	$0.308
D4	8	28	200	$0.616
D11	2	14	40	$0.195
D12	4	28	100	$0.390
D13	8	56	200	$0.702

Table 2. Microsoft Azure Standard Tier Pricing for A and D series of virtual machines

Instance Type	Cores	RAM (GB)	Disk Size (GB)	Price (per Hr)
A0	1	0.75	20	$0.020
A1	1	1.75	70	$0.060
A2	2	3.5	135	$0.120
A3	4	7	285	$0.240
A4	8	14	605	$0.480
A5	2	14	135	$0.250
A6	4	28	285	$0.500
A7	8	56	605	$1.000
A8	8	56	382	$1.970
A9	16	112	382	$4.470
D1	1	3.5	50	$0.094
D2	2	7	100	$0.188
D3	4	14	250	$0.376
D4	8	28	500	$0.752
D11	2	14	100	$0.238
D12	4	28	200	$0.476
D13	8	56	400	$0.857
D14	16	112	800	$1.542

Table 3. Microsoft Azure Storage Pricing

Storage Capacity (TB per Month)	Price (per GB)
0 – 1	$0.024
1 – 50	$0.0236
50 – 500	$0.0232
500 – 1000	$0.0228
1000 – 5000	$0.0224

Table 4. Microsoft Azure Data Transfer Pricing

Outbound Data Transfers (per Month)	Pricing (per GB)
First 5 GB	Free
5 GB – 10 TB	$0.087
Next 40 TB	$0.083
Next 100 TB	$0.07
Next 350 TB	$0.05

Table 5. Google Compute Engine Pricing

Instance Type	Cores	Memory (GB)	Price	Discounted (25% - 50%)	Discounted (50% - 75%)	Discounted (75% - 100%)
n1-standard-1	1	3.75	$0.063	$0.050	$0.038	$0.025
n1-standard-2	2	7.5	$0.126	$0.101	$0.076	$0.050
n1-standard-4	4	15	$0.252	$0.202	$0.151	$0.101
n1-standard-8	8	30	$0.504	$0.403	$0.302	$0.202
n1-standard-16	16	60	$1.008	$0.806	$0.605	$0.403
n1-highmem-2	2	13	$0.148	$0.118	$0.089	$0.059
n1-highmem-4	4	26	$0.296	$0.237	$0.178	$0.118
n1-highmem-8	8	52	$0.592	$0.474	$0.355	$0.237
n1-highmem-16	16	104	$1.184	$0.947	$0.710	$0.474
n1-highcpu-2	2	1.8	$0.080	$0.064	$0.048	$0.032
n1-highcpu-4	4	3.6	$0.160	$0.128	$0.096	$0.064
n1-highcpu-8	8	7.2	$0.320	$0.256	$0.192	$0.128
n1-highcpu-16	16	14.4	$0.640	$0.512	$0.384	$0.256
f1-micro	1	0.6	$0.012	$0.010	$0.007	$0.005
g1-small	1	1.7	$0.032	$0.026	$0.019	$0.013

Table 6. Google Cloud Platform Network Pricing

Outbound Data Transfers (per GB)	Cost
0 – 1 TB	$0.12
1 – 10 TB	$0.11
> 10 TB	$0.08

data for same zone or to a different cloud service in the same region are free. Alternatively, outgoing data to a different Zone in the same Region or different Region within the US are charged at $0.010 per GB of data movement. Finally storage costs are $0.04 per GB per month for standard disks and $0.325 per GB per month for SSD disks.

Amazon Web Services (AWS) Pricing

The cost of running applications in AWS is determined by three factors: computation, storage and data transfer. We use AWS Elastic Compute Cloud (EC2) instances to calculate computation cost as shown in Table 7. AWS Simple Storage Service (S3) pricing shown in Table 8 is used to calculate the storage costs. Data transfer cost is included for only outgoing data transfers from EC2 and S3 to the Internet as shown in Table 9. Incoming data traffic is free of charge. EC2 instance types and their configurations are detailed in Table 7: EC2 instances are grouped into categories based on their capabilities. t2 and m3 instances are for general purpose applications. c3 instances are optimized for computation with high-performance processors. g2 instances contain GPUs for graphics and general purpose GPU applications. r3 instances are optimized for memory-intensive applications and provide lowest price per GB of RAM. i2 and hs1 instances are optimized for storage and provide lowest price per GB of storage on the instance. The pricing of EC2 instances depends on the usage as shown in Table 7. On demand instances are charged by the hour with no commitments. Reserved instances are charged a one-time upfront fee but in return provide a lower per-hour cost. Reserved instances require a commitment and differ in commitment duration (1 year to 3 years) and utilization (light, medium and heavy). Additionally, EC2 provides Spot Instances, which can be purchased by bidding on unused EC2 instances. Pricing of Spot Instances is set by EC2 and may change based on availability of Spot Instances.

CLOUD OPERATOR SERVICE LEVEL AGREEMENTS

In all instances, with the information provided by service providers, the nature and content of service level agreement can influence the choice of the provider. A Service Level Agreement (SLA) is used as a formal contract between the service provider and a consumer to ensure service quality (Wu, 2014). An SLA should specify the details of the service usually in quantifiable terms. The goal of an SLA is therefore to establish a scalable and automatic management framework that can adapt to dynamic and real time environmental changes using multiple qualities of service (QoS) parameters. The SLA for mobile cloud computing should have terms that include multiple domains with heterogeneous resources. In addition, consumers should be involved in the management process of SLA to a certain extent especially regarding reliability and trust/security. In particular, QoS parameters must be updated dynamically over time due to the continuing changes in the mobile application operating environments (Kwon, et al., 2014).

Table 7. AWS EC2 Instance Pricing

Instance Name	Cores	RAM (GB)	Storage (GB)	Processor Type	On Demand Rate	Reserved Upfront Fee (3 Years)	Hourly Rate (3 Years)
t2.micro	1	1	-	Xeon Family	$0.013	$109	$0.002
t2.small	1	2	-	Xeon Family	$0.026	$218	$0.004
t2.medium	2	4	-	Xeon Family	$0.052	$436	$0.008
m3.medium	1	3.75	1 x 4 SSD	Xeon E5-2670	$0.070	$337	$0.015
m3.large	2	7.5	1 x 32 SSD	Xeon E5-2670	$0.140	$673	$0.030
m3.xlarge	4	15	2 x 40 SSD	Xeon E5-2670	$0.280	$1345	$0.060
m3.2xlarge	8	30	2 x 80 SSD	Xeon E5-2670	$0.560	$2691	$0.120
c3.large	2	3.75	2 x 16 SSD	Xeon E5-2680	$0.105	$508	$0.022
c3.xlarge	4	7.5	2 x 40 SSD	Xeon E5-2680	$0.210	$1016	$0.045
c3.2xlarge	8	15	2 x 80 SSD	Xeon E5-2680	$0.420	$2031	$0.090
c3.4xlarge	16	30	2 x 160 SSD	Xeon E5-2680	$0.840	$4063	$0.180
c3.8xlarge	32	60	2 x 320 SSD	Xeon E5-2680	$1.680	$8126	$0.359
g2.2xlarge	8	15	60 SSD	Xeon E5-2670	$0.650	$6307	$0.060
r3.large	2	15.25	1 x 32 SSD	Xeon E5-2670	$0.175	$1033	$0.026
r3.xlarge	4	30.5	1 x 80 SSD	Xeon E5-2670	$0.350	$2066	$0.052
r3.2xlarge	8	61	1 x 160 SSD	Xeon E5-2670	$0.700	$4132	$0.104
r3.4xlarge	16	122	1 x 320 SSD	Xeon E5-2670	$1.400	$8264	$0.208
r3.8xlarge	32	244	2 x 320 SSD	Xeon E5-2670	$2.800	$16528	$0.416
i2.xlarge	4	30.5	1 x 800 SSD	Xeon E5-2670	$0.853	$2740	$0.121
i2.2xlarge	8	61	2 x 800 SSD	Xeon E5-2670	$1.705	$5480	$0.241
i2.4xlarge	16	122	4 x 800 SSD	Xeon E5-2670	$3.410	$10960	$0.482
i2.8xlarge	32	244	8 x 800 SSD	Xeon E5-2670	$6.820	$21920	$0.964
hs1.8xlarge	16	117	24 x 2048	Xeon Family	$4.600	$16924	$0.76

Table 8. AWS S3 Storage Pricing

Storage Size (TB)	Price (per GB)
0 – 1	$0.03
1 – 50	$0.0295
50 – 500	$0.029
500 – 1000	$0.0285
1000 – 5000	$0.0280
> 5000	$0.0275

Table 9. AWS Data Transfer Pricing

Data Transfer Out Size (TB)	Price (per GB)
0 – 1 (GB)	$0.00
1 TB – 10 TB	$0.12
10 TB – 50 TB	$0.09
50 TB – 150 TB	$0.07
150 TB – 500 TB	$0.05

Amazon and Microsoft Azure offer a tiered service credit plan that gives users credits based on the discrepancy between SLA specifications and the actual service levels delivered. These providers typically offer cloud storage SLA that articulates precise levels of service such as 99.9% uptime and recourse or compensation to the user should the provider fail to provide the service as described. Another normal cloud storage SLA detail is service availability, which specifies the maximum amount of time a read request can take, how many retries are allowed and so on.

Microsoft Azure SLA

Azure Active Directory Premium service is available in the following scenarios such as: Users are able to login to the service, login to access applications on the access panel and reset passwords. IT administrators are able to create, read, write and delete entries in the directory or provision or de-provision users to applications in the directory. Windows Azure has separate SLAs for compute and storage. No SLA is provided for free tier of Azure Active Directory. Availability is calculated over a monthly billing cycle (Azure, 2014).

Google SLA

Google has implemented industry standard systems and procedures for cloud SLA to ensure the security and confidentiality of an application and customer data, protect against anticipated threats or hazards to the security or integrity of an application and customer data, and protect against unauthorized access. Customers have the ability to access, monitor, and use or disclose their data submitted by end users through the service. Customer data and applications can only be used to provide the services to customer and its end users and to help secure and improve the services. For instance, this may include identifying and fixing problems in the services, enhancing the services to better protect against attacks and abuse, and making suggestions aimed at improving performance or reducing costs (Google, 2013).

Amazon EC2 SLA

Amazon AWS SLA policy governs the use of Amazon Elastic Compute Cloud. This SLA applies separately to each account using Amazon EC2 or Amazon EBS. AWS is committed to using commercially reasonable efforts to make Amazon EC2 and Amazon EBS each available with a monthly uptime percentage of at least 99.95%, in each case during any monthly billing cycle. The monthly uptime percentage is less than 99.95% but equal to or greater than 99.0% and service credit of 10% and less than 30% (Amazon EC2, 2013).

SECURITY OF CLOUD OUTSOURCING

Security issues should be considered when computational tasks are being outsourced for mobile cloud applications especially regarding transmission and data receipt (Soyata, Ba, Heinzelman, Kwon, & Shi, 2013). For this reason, placing critical data in the cloud in the hands of a third party to ensure the data remains secured is of paramount importance. This means the data need to be encrypted at all times with clearly defined roles of who manages encryption keys. The data in the cloud needs to be accessible only by authorized users. That is making it restricted and monitoring of who accesses what data through the cloud. This is because protecting clients' data is essential in order to ensure data is not compromised, due to breach or disaster. In this instance the application developers should encrypt the data leaving the backup services to cloud service providers.

CASE STUDY A: CLOUD-BASED HEALTH MONITORING SYSTEM

Automating health monitoring has become significant because of the drive by the US government to modernize the US health system using cloud computing based medical applications. (Kocabas, et al., 2013). (Kocabas & Soyata, 2014) emphasized that, while one motivation for this is to reduce operational costs at the healthcare organization (HCO) by eradicating the datacenters managed by the HCO, an equally important motivation is to improve healthcare by providing the doctors and health professionals with long-term patient data as an auxiliary diagnosis tool (Page, Kocabas, Soyata, Aktas, & Couderc, 2014). This section illustrates how cloud-pricing models can be used to estimate the cost of real-time cloud computing applications conducted in (Kocabas, et al., 2013). To do this, background information on the applications included in the study of long-term patient ECG-data monitoring system are reviewed.

Mobile Cloud Application Description

Despite the undeniable transformation cloud computing made in the application world, medical applications lack the pace of adopting the trend. Due to the Health Insurance Portability and Accountability Act (HIPAA) (HIPAA, n.d.), Personal Health Information (PHI) privacy is treated as the most sensitive information and the penalties associated with its mistreatment are steep. Storage of encrypted PHI through a Business Associate Agreement (BAA) (US-HHS, n.d.) is currently available from cloud operators, such as CareCloud (CareCloud, n.d.). This service is for *storage-only* data and no *medical application* can be executed on this data, as this would require the data to be temporarily transformed into the *unencrypted domain*.

A novel method for running medical cloud applications in the *encrypted domain* has been proposed in (Kocabas, et al., 2013), (Kocabas & Soyata, 2014) that executes applications in a way where the underlying patient PHI is not visible to the cloud during execution, thereby completely eliminating PHI privacy concerns. The method uses Fully Homomorphic Encryption (FHE), which is a type of encryption that allows operations on encrypted data without observing the data itself. While using FHE solves the privacy issues regarding medical cloud computing, one problem prevents its wide adoption: the FHE is still extremely resource-intensive in terms of storage, bandwidth and computational requirements.

The medical application will be used for monitoring patients remotely at their home and providing patient statistical data to the HCO personnel. For the remote monitoring application, detecting Long-QT Syndrome (LQTS) will be used as the target application. Additionally, vital patient health statistics such as average heart rate (HR), minimum and maximum HR will be calculated.

In this section, background information is provided on the cloud application platform and the related outsourcing costs. Figure 1 depicts the conceptualized medical application platform, which is intended to allow patient health monitoring at home through medical data acquisition devices such as ECG patches, or multi-sensory acquisition devices. The acquired patient data is assumed to be encrypted at home (top of Figure 1) and transmitted to the cloud (middle of Figure 1). To ensure PHI privacy, FHE is used, which requires PHI encryption at home. After this encryption, the data is unrecognizable to the cloud. Note that, this information transmission is one-way. On the bottom of Figure 1, the HCO personnel and HCO administrators access the application and transmit their preferences (i.e., two-way). The medical applications run in the cloud, which operate on the encrypted PHI without ever observing the actual medical data. Compared to conventional cloud applications, the significant difference of this application scenario is its resource intensity. A *resource* is defined as one of the three entities that a cloud operator charges for: a) storage, b) computation, and c) communication. Each of these resources will be elaborated on separately and a cost analysis of the medical cloud application will be analyzed based on these resources.

- **Storage:** This most widely utilized resource involves renting a shared storage space from the cloud operator based on the previously provided pricing. The pricing of this resource varies widely based on the allocated space as shown in, for example, Table 3 (Microsoft Azure) and Table 8 (AWS S3 Storage). The most meaningful product to purchase for an HCO is based on per-GB-per-month pricing. As we will describe later, the medical applications have substantial storage requirements to the host the FHE-encrypted PHI.
- **Computation:** The execution of the medical algorithms based on FHE put a substantial strain on cloud computational resources. While it is possible to cut costs by using shared computational instances, it makes a lot more sense to use dedicated *boxes* (i.e., computers) to perform the type of computations. The pricing for these instances is based on per-hour usage of that instance. Examples of computation pricing have been provided in Table 2 (Microsoft Azure), Table 5 (Google Compute Engine), and Table 7 (AWS EC2).

Figure 1. Conceptualized medical application environment and related cloud-pricing metrics. (HCO = Health Care Organization)

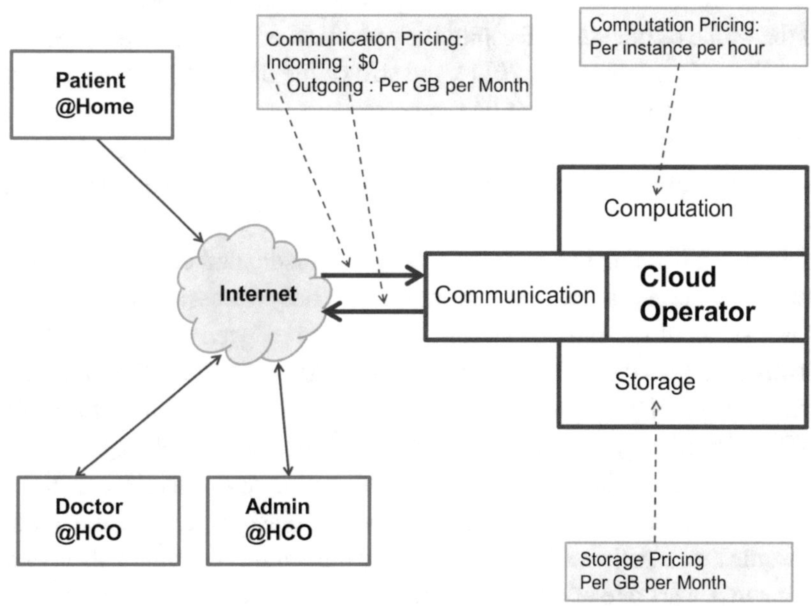

- **Communication:** This resource involves data traffic from and into the cloud operator. Usually cloud providers have no incoming-data costs but, a per-GB-per-month outgoing-data cost, as shown in Figure 1. Examples of pricing are provided previously in Table 4 (Microsoft Azure), Table 6 (Google Cloud Platform), Table 9 (Amazon AWS).

Cloud Outsourcing the Health Monitoring Application

While it is possible to encrypt private health information (PHI) through standard encryption techniques, such as AES (NIST-AES, 2001), such data cannot be used as an input into a medical application without decrypting it. However, decrypting PHI in the cloud even temporarily violates PHI privacy. Therefore, a medical application using a standard encryption such as AES cannot use the cloud for running a medical application. Currently, there exists no offering from any cloud operator that allows running a medical application without violating PHI privacy.

Fully Homomorphic Encryption (FHE) is a type of encryption that allows operations on encrypted data without observing the data itself. While using FHE sounds promising, it puts significant strain on all three types of resources described earlier. We will describe the reasons for this in this section and will evaluate the application in terms of its usage of all three resources:

- **Storage:** The target medical application acquires patient vital information at home for long term monitoring and diagnosis via monitoring devices such as Alivecor iPhone attachment (AliveCor, n.d.). For the FHE-based applications to work, the data has to be homomorphically-encrypted at the source (i.e., patient's home) via a computationally capable device, such as a cloudlet (Soyata, Muraleedharan, Funai, Kwon, & Heinzelman, 2012). Once this is done, the size of the data expands multiple orders of magnitude. To cope with this problem, the data is processed partially before encryption. For example, in the case of a cardiac monitoring, essential values, such as QT and RR intervals, can be extracted from ECG signals through simple algorithms (Couderc, et al., 2011). Note that we focus on the resource requirements of such algorithms, and the algorithms are beyond the scope of our study. Despite the reduction of the data after processing with the described algorithms (Couderc, et al., 2011), the size of the data still places an extreme pressure on the storage resources as will be quantified later.
- **Computation:** In addition to expanding the relevant data significantly, the FHE-based algorithms also require substantial amount of computational resources. One distinction between Storage and Computation, though, is that, while storage must always be occupied, computation resources can be shared within the healthcare organization's (HCO) dedicated computer, thereby allowing significant cost reduction. A patient health monitoring is only necessary during the time-of-monitoring, e.g., 2 weeks out of the entire year, lending itself to reduced costs due to this low duty cycle.
- **Communication:** While the amount of data being transmitted *into* the cloud is substantial (see Figure 1), this transfer is zero cost for cloud operators that do not charge for incoming bandwidth such as AWS as described previously. When the operations are complete, the amount of data being transmitted *out of the cloud* is a lot less than the incoming data, thereby making this resource the least expensive to rent for these types of applications. An insight can be gained into this through an example: Assume that, a patient's ECG data is being transmitted continuously at one beat per second (corresponding to a heart rate of 60). The result of an entire monitoring period (e.g., 5 minutes) is a Yes/No answer, which is, clearly, a lot less data than sum of all of the original ECG samples.

We evaluate the cost of cloud outsourcing of medical applications that use FHE by using an ECG database named THEW (Couderc, 2010). We choose long QT syndrome (LQTS) (Bazzett, 1997) detection as the primary medical application that is widely used for long-term patient monitoring. Additional applications that provide vital patient health information such as Average Heart Rate, Minimum and Maximum Heart Rate are also implemented. All of the medical applications will operate on the same THEW sample data and provide statistics for every 5-minute ECG monitoring period. We implement these applications with the open-source HElib library (Halevi & Shoup) and run our simulations on a cluster node with two Intel Xeon E5-2695 Processors and 63GB RAM. The parameters of HElib are selected based on the analysis provided in (Gentry, Halevi, & Smart, 2012).

Operational Cost Worksheet for Case A

Resource requirements of the aforementioned medical applications (i.e., LQTS detection, average heart rate computation, and min/max heart rate computation) are reported in **Table 10**. We estimate the cost of running these medical applications using Microsoft Azure, Google Compute Engine and Amazon Web Services in the following sections.

Google Compute Engine

We select a Google Compute Engine machine type based on the type of medical computation to be performed. LQTS and Average Heart Rate (HR) are less compute-intensive compared to Minimum and Maximum HR computation. We select an *n1-standard-2* machine type with 2 CPUs to compute LQTS and Average HR. For the Minimum and Maximum HR we select *n1-highcpu-2* machine with 2 CPUs. Based on the duty cycle information provided in Table 10, we use appropriate sustained discount price provided by Google Compute Engine. The total cost of running these computations are reported in Table 11. The sum of the application costs per patient is $81.12 per month for computing all four values (LQTS, average HR, min HR, max HR).

Table 10. Performance of Medical Applications on a Cluster Node over a period of one month.

Medical Application	Run-Time (Hours)	Duty Cycle (%)	Storage (GB)	Data Transfer Out (GB)
LQTS	51.3	7	75.3	322.6
Average HR	197.7	27	252.9	1166.4
Min. & Max. HR	483.2	66	266.5	1229.7

Table 11. Monthly Cost of Running Medical Applications with Google Compute Engine

Medical Application	GCE Instance	GCE Cost	Storage Cost	Transfer Cost	Total Cost
LQTS, Avg. HR	*n1-standard-2*	20.00	13.12	5.32	$38.44
Min. & Max. HR	*n1-highcpu-2*	23.23	10.66	8.79	$42.68

Amazon Web Services (AWS)

For the same computations, to select an EC2 instance type, we look at our application characteristics. LQTS and Average Heart Rate (HR) computation is less compute-intensive compared to Minimum and Maximum HR. A general-purpose instance of *m3.large* with 2 CPU's is enough to compute both LQTS and Average HR in parallel. On the other hand Minimum and Maximum HR are compute-intensive with 67% duty cycle. Therefore a *c3.large* instance optimized for compute-intensive applications could compute both Minimum and Maximum HR in parallel.

Table 12 presents the cost of outsourcing one patient's monitoring to AWS for a month. EC2 costs include both a fixed cost fee and run-time fee. Fixed cost fee is calculated by dividing one-time upfront fee into equal monthly payments. Run-time fee is calculated by multiplying the run-time of the applications with the hourly rate. Since two applications are executed in parallel, we select application run-time as the runtime of the application that takes longer to finish. S3 costs are the storage costs derived from the application storage requirements presented in Table 8. Minimum and Maximum HR computation use same data set, and therefore their storage amount is counted only once. The transfer cost is based on the data transferred out to a doctor at the Health Care Organization from AWS. The overall cost of running all the applications per patient with AWS services is $96 per month.

Microsoft Azure

Based on the application characteristics, we choose *D2* instance for LQTS and Average HR computation and *D11* instance for Minimum and Maximum HR computation. Since LQTS and Average HR is less compute-intensive *D2* instance with 2 cores and 7 GB RAM is enough to compute them in parallel. *D11* instance with 2 cores and 14 GB RAM is chosen for more compute-intensive Minimum and Maximum HR in parallel. Table 13 shows the cost of running the same applications on Microsoft Azure, with a total monthly cost of $148.50 based on the same parameters shown in Table 10.

Table 12. Monthly Cost of Running Medical Applications with AWS Services

Medical Application	EC2 Instance	EC2 Cost	S3 Cost	Transfer Cost	Total Cost
LQTS, Avg. HR	*m3.large*	24.63	9.84	4.20	$38.68
Min. & Max. HR	*c3.large*	43.15	7.86	6.31	$57.32

Table 13. Monthly Cost of Running Medical Applications with Microsoft Azure

Medical Application	Azure VM Type	VM Cost	Storage Cost	Transfer Cost	Total Cost
LQTS, Avg. HR	D2	$30.5	$7.9	$3.4	$41.8
Min. & Max. H	D11	$94.4	$6.4	$5.9	$106.7

CASE STUDY B: REAL-TIME FACE RECOGNITION USING MOCHA

Face recognition is the process of identifying a person by matching the person's facial features to a database that keeps the records of features of many people. This process involves mainly three steps: face detection, projection and search. During the face detection step, the face of a person is detected from an image. Then in the projection step, related features are extracted from the detected face. The related features vary with the methods used for projection. Finally the features are used for matching the face with an entry in the database during the search step. We will explain each step in detail and analyze the complexity and resource requirements in the following sections.

Computational Requirements of Face Recognition

- **Face Detection:** We will use the Viola-Jones method (Viola & Jones, 2001) for face detection, which is one of the fastest and most accurate algorithms for face detection. The Viola-Jones method is the first face detection algorithm that operates in real-time and widely used in mobile devices and cameras. The method detects faces by partitioning the image into rectangular sections and checking the change of intensity between these sections. Each rectangular section, also known as Haar-like feature, contains sum of the pixel intensities covered by the rectangular section. By using the pixel intensities, a face is detected by checking the changes of intensity between the rectangular sections. Complexity of the face detection is depends on the number of pixels in an image. In (Viola & Jones, 2001), it is shown that the number of faces in one image has negligible effect on the complexity of face detection due to nature of classifiers used in Viola-Jones method. The approximate time for face detection is approximated as follows (Alling, Powers, & Soyata, 2015):

$$T_{FD}=n_{pixels}\times 0.01347\times GFLOPS^{-0.622726}$$

where T_{FD} represents the detection time in milliseconds, n_{pixels} is the number of pixels in the image and GFLOPS is the maximum number of floating point operations that a processor can execute per second. Face detection can be performed with the surveillance device (e.g., mobile phone, tablet, surveillance camera) in real-time using Viola-Jones method. Even better performance results can be achieved using a cloudlet that has significant computation power with reasonable cost. For example in (Soyata, Muraleedharan, Funai, Kwon, & Heinzelman, 2012) a cloudlet with Nvidia GT520 GPU card can detect faces from an 800x480 image around 250 ms with a cost less than $100. Therefore we will assume that, face detection will be performed outside the cloud with surveillance devices that could be assisted with a cloudlet. At the end of this step, only face parts of the image are cropped and send to cloud for further processing.

- **Projection:** The projection step uses the image produced from face detection step and projects the image into eigenvalues that represents the weights to reconstruct the image from Eigenfaces stored in the database. The complexity of the projection step thus linearly increases with number of Eigenfaces on the database and image size in terms of pixels. The approximate time for projection step in ms is as follows (Alling, Powers, & Soyata, 2015):

$$T_P = \left(\frac{0.004001 \times p_{db} \times n_{db} \times r_{eigenfaces}}{GFLOPS_{device}} \right)$$

where p_{db} is the pixel count of an image in the database, n_{db} is the number of images in the database and $r_{eigenfaces}$ is the ratio of eigenfaces to images in the database.

- **Search:** This step uses the eigenvectors produced in the projection step and compares them with the eigenvectors in the database for a match. The face is recognized if the similarity of it is close to a database entry. The similarity is calculated by using Euclidean distance between eigenvector of the image and eigenvector for each database entry. Therefore complexity of this step depends on number of images in the database and number of dimensions in the eigenvector. Since the size of eigenvector depends on the number of images in the database, search time in ms can be approximated as follows:

$$T_S = 1000 \times \left(\frac{3.575 \times 10^{-7} \times n_{db}^2 \times 1.018 \times 10^{-4} \times n_{db} + 9.773 \times 10^{-3}}{GFLOPS_{device}} \right)$$

Operational Cost Worksheet for Case B

The computational requirements for face detection are analyzed in detail in (Alling, Powers, & Soyata, 2015) and will not be repeated here. We will use these requirements to calculate the cost of running face recognition in the cloud. First a database needs to be generated that contains Eigenfaces. Complexity of generating an Eigenface database increases exponentially with the number of faces contained in the database. Table 14 shows the computational complexity of building a database on an Nvidia GX760 GPU. Note that database must be loaded into memory during the search step of the face recognition.

We assume that the database has 5000 entries, which requires 5.6 GB storage space. GFLOPS of the CPUs in the cloud instances depend on the type of the processors. We will use the settings for the database with 5,000 images, which requires moderate time to generate a database and provides reason-

Table 14. Resource requirements for generating Eigenface database with an NVIDIA GX760 GPU.

Number of Images in Database	Computation Time	Database Size (GB)
1000	8.5 min	1.1
2000	57 min	2.2
3000	8.7 hr	3.4
4000	49 hr	4.5
5000	182 hr	5.6
10000	342 days	11.4
50000	1115 years	57.9

ably good coverage. Although it requires approximately one week to generate such a database, this step will be performed only once. Therefore we assume that the database is already generated and has a size of 5.6 GB. The cropped images from the face detection are assumed to be 180x180 pixels.

To compute the cost of running face recognition in the cloud, we look at the cost of recognizing a single face on a single virtual instance from cloud providers. This will be used as the unit price of face recognition and can be used for analyzing the cost for different case scenarios. We select virtual instances based on the amount of memory that can store the database, which is around 5.6 GB. Based on the memory requirements, we select the smallest instance that is capable of storing this database in the RAM. We select the high memory machine types from AWS, Microsoft Azure and Google Compute Engine. All high memory machine types have an Intel Xeon 2670 processor and we list the configurations selected from each cloud provider in Table 15.

We use the equations from the previous section to approximate the time for projection and search steps. The computation time of both steps will be based on the GFLOPS of the virtual instances. The virtual instances are assigned to one of the threads of an Intel Xeon processor. GLOPS of a virtual instance (thread) can be calculated as GLOPS = clock frequency (GHz) x (FLOP / cycle). Intel Xeon processors are usually capable of performing 8 floating-point operations per clock cycle, so we assume that GLOPS of a virtual instance is approximately 8 x clock frequency (GHz). Table 16 presents the time for computing each step of recognizing single face on the virtual instances.

The instance configurations have two virtual cores, therefore by using the instance types from Table 15, approximately 1,237K face recognition computations can be done. With these settings the cost of continuous face recognition over the period of a month will depend on two parameters: storage and computation, as shown in Table 17. The network bandwidth cost will be negligible since cloud providers do not charge for incoming data and outgoing data is a simple Yes/No response, which can be neglected. Google Compute Engine charges based on sustained usage discount which reduces the price based on usage. Specifically, for 0-25% usage regular price is charged and price is reduced by 20% with each 25% increase in the usage.

Table 15. Cloud Instance Configurations for Face Recognition.

Cloud Service Provider	Instance Type	Virtual Machines	Memory (GB)	Local Disk (GB)
AWS	r3.large	2	15.25	32
Microsoft Azure	D11	2	14	100
Google Compute	n1-highmem-2	2	13	?

Table 16. Projection and Search times for recognizing one face in the cloud.

CPU Type	GFLOPS	Projection (ms)	Search (ms)	Total (ms)
Intel Xeon 2670	20.8	3895	454	4349

Table 17. Cost of running continuous face recognition for a month in the cloud.

Cloud Service Provider	Compute Cost	Storage Cost	Total Cost
AWS	$48.4	$0.17	$48.57
Microsoft Azure	$161.8	$0.13	$161.93
Google Compute Engine	$75.0	$0.22	$75.22

Service Level Agreements for Cases A and B

SLA management is important for ensuring that QoS is maintained for running real time mobile cloud application for health monitoring and real time face recognition (case A and B). The SLA for health monitoring and real-time face recognition concept should by necessity involve stating the transaction times expected to process the data packets at least at the same rate it receives data management to make sure that patients' data within these systems are accurate and complete, up-to-date with adequate fail safe, secure, backup and archiving process in place that is encrypted. The SLA should ensure storage space of patients being monitored for a 24 hr period is approximately 252 GB per month. Bandwidth requirements are vital and accurate through ECG patches and transmitted via the Internet to be stored on the ECG database.

SURVEY OF CURRENT MOBILE CLOUD OPERATOR COST MODELS

The previous part of this chapter analyzed operational costs strictly in terms of the cloud user, which is generally an organization that outsources these aforementioned applications to one of the existing cloud operators. In the following section, the analysis will be repeated, albeit, from the standpoint of the cloud operators. Cloud operator costs and profit models will be introduced to perform such analysis.

Data centers have evolved dramatically in recent years, due to the advent of social networking services, e-commerce and cloud computing. However, the requirement of services for users can be conflicting in that, there is high availability levels demanded against low sustainability impact and cost values. This means, for cloud service providers, the cost models they have determines their profitability and service levels they can provide. Cost models help business owners and managers of service providers to figure out the cost for cloud services activities and processes. Through the use of financial computations or cost accounting allocation, companies can take basic information relating to resources, energy use, infrastructure development and direct labor and transform data into useful costs for setting the price of services. Companies can put together different cost models based on their needs, whether financial or operational (Markendahl, Makitalo, & Werding, 2008).

Generally, different companies use cost models in their daily operations because the goal is to maximize the economic value for owners and shareholders. Finding ways to lower costs is a crucial step in achieving this goal. Another purpose for cost models is to create a repeatable process that allows owners and managers to apply the model to multiple situations. Through this business process, the company can develop a metric that becomes the standard expected rate of return for projects. This safeguards the company from losing money when engaging in new business opportunities that look profitable but really are not (Slack, Brandon-Jones, & Johnston, 2013).

According to (Fetai & Schuldt, 2012), for many organizations, especially cloud service providers, it is relatively complicated to determine the exact total operational costs incurred by offering own services in the cloud as well as to compare them with the costs incurred by datacenters. For instance, the average cost per year according to (Alford & Morton, 2010), to operate a large datacenter is usually between $10 million to $25 million, while according to an organization with 1,000 file servers faces average costs in the cloud between $22.5 million and $31.1 million. In practice, models exist to help support organizations in analyzing and comparing costs (Alford & Morton, 2010). Some of these cost models identified from literature are explained below.

The methodology adopted for our survey involves reviewing research findings by (Van den Bossche, Vanmechelen, & Broeckhove, 2013) regarding mobile cloud computing topics. This review was undertaken to reveal where there are gaps in the research literature to help contextualize this research in line with best practice approach towards the execution of this real-time research project (Johansson, 2007). This is also to make sure that the research has not already been done. Thus existing literature on this topic was examined to help position this study within the context of existing evidence by (Rickinson & May, 2009) to identify the main components for mobile cloud application cost analysis. For the purpose of this chapter, our scope was to explore (i) current mobile cloud application cost models; (ii) explore the pricing models that have evolved based on these cost models; (iii) illustrate how the operational cost of a mobile application implementation can be calculated and (iv) present a framework for establishing costs. This was based on empirical study in published information of existing work from academia, industrial, marketing and business sites. Secondly, using the various search engines, reading of articles, journals and Government and corporate publications (Rickinson & May, 2009).

Performance and Cost Assessment of Cloud Operations

A performance and cost assessment model has been developed as a modeling technology for modeling the performance and scalability of service oriented applications designed for a variety of platforms. Using a suite of cloud testing applications, (Brebner & Liu, 2011) conducted empirical evaluations of a variety of real cloud infrastructures, including Google App Engine, Amazon EC2, and Microsoft Azure. The insights from these experimental evaluations, and other public/published data, were combined with the modeling technology to predict the resource requirements in terms of cost, application performance, and limitations of a realistic application for different deployment scenarios. Costs in terms of power consumption per year ranges from $7,800 to $13,000 (Australia dollars for Energy business plan). Naturally the real total cost of ownership is substantially more and includes cooling, carbon emission offsets or green power sources, software licensing, maintenance and administration, capital costs and depreciation.

System Utilization Charging Model

(Woitaszek & Tufo, 2010) developed a comprehensive system utilization charging model similar to that used by Amazon EC2 and applied the model to current resources and planned procurements. This is a model for charging computational time, data transfers and storage. The charging rate is between 3 and 5 cents per CPU hour, a rate not competitive with the performance of current commodity processors. System and container ($8M / 5 years) $1,600,000 combined with annual operational staffing of $ 600,000 and annual power and cooling $365,000 and power expenses, the system is estimated to cost $2,565,000 per year. Depending on the number of CPU cores selected, the per-CPUh break-even charge (assuming 100% utilization and including the cost of the attached storage) will be 0.89 cents/CPUh to 1.7 cents/CPUh.

Dynamics of Cost Development

(Kristekova Z. et al, 2012) proposed a simulation model for analyzing cost-benefits between cloud computing and own datacenter, as well as by analyzing different scenarios virtually before transferring them into the real world. This simulation model for cost-benefit analysis of cloud computing versus own datacenter has been proposed with the potential to fill the gap where a cost model that covers dynamic issues of cloud computing is lacking. In their model, to estimate the costs for a server, the initial cost of server, operating system licenses and additional network equipment were taken into account. The costs for server are calculated as product of "number of required server" and "initial costs for server." The costs for operating system licenses consist of "number of required server" and "costs per operating system license." The costs for additional network equipment are calculated as product of "number of server" and "the expenditures of network equipment." The expenditures of network equipment usually consist of 10 to 30% of the costs of server. Additionally, the ongoing maintenance costs for server and network equipment needs to be calculated in order to estimate the costs for infrastructure as sum of "power usage server", "power usage network equipment" multiplied with the costs of the desired tier level. In this way this model includes the power usage of the infrastructure to determine the power usage effectiveness (PUE), which is given by PUE = Total Facility Power/ IT Equipment Power. The PUE value can range from 1.0 to infinity, where 1.0 indicates 100% efficiency. The realistic PUE values are in the 1.3 to 3.0 range.

To calculate the costs for the administration, an estimate of how many servers one administrator can maintain is vital. This in turn depends on the size of datacenter. As such the final administration cost is, the "number of servers" divided by "the number of estimated server maintenance per administrator" multiplied by "the costs for one administrator." For the data transfer costs, many companies rely on the flat rates. After estimating the costs for hardware, software, infrastructure, administration and data transfer, then sum all these costs to obtain the total costs for data center. This particular consideration has fed into pricing component based on for example CPU usage and transactions rate required for processing application requirements (Kristekova Z. et al, 2012).

Inter-Organizational Economic Models for Pricing Cloud Network Services

(Pal & Hui, 2013) developed inter-organizational economic models for pricing cloud network services when several cloud providers co-exist in a market servicing a single application type. The development involved analysis and comparison of models that cloud providers can adopt to provision resources in a manner such that there is *minimum* amount of resources wasted, and at the same time the user service-level/ QoS is maintained. On this basis, the ability to process the number of user requests processed per unit of time on the cloud determines the amount of resources to be provisioned to achieve a required capacity.

View Materialization Cost Model

(Nguyen, Bimonte, d'Orazio, & Darmont, 2012) proposed an approach for decreasing the cost of data management in the cloud, by using a classical database performance optimization technique, such as view materialization. This cost model complements existing materialized view cost models with a monetary cost component that is rudimentary in the cloud. This is the basis of the pricing models incorporated by Amazon to render more versatile service. This model also fits into the 'pay as you go paradigm' of cloud computing and allow providers achieve a multi-criteria optimization of the view materialization versus CPU power consumption problem, under budget constraints.

Nguyen et al, demonstrated the power of the model by introducing a fictitious example, which illustrated the complexity of selecting materialized views in the cloud. In this illustration, the storage cost is say $0.10 per GB per month, and the computing cost is $0.24 per hour and a 500 GB dataset is stored in the cloud for a month. If Q is the monthly query workload, processed in 50 hours then, the storage cost is \$50, computing cost is \$12, for a total of \$62. If some materialized views are used, it was assumed that workload processing time becomes 40 hours. Thus, computing cost becomes \$9.6. However, materialized views use up additional storage space of, 50 GB. Thus, storage cost becomes \$55, for a total cost of \$64.6. This means that overall, performance has improved by 20%, but cost has also increased by 4%.

Cost-Efficient Scheduling of Hybrid Cloud

According to (Van den Bossche, Vanmechelen, & Broeckhove, 2013), MCC has found broad acceptance in both industry and research with public cloud offerings is now often used in conjunction with privately owned infrastructure. Technical aspects such as the impact of network latency, bandwidth constraints, data confidentiality and security, as well as economic aspects such as sunk costs and price uncertainty are key drivers towards the adoption of a hybrid cloud model. This model introduced a hybrid cloud to determine which workloads are to be outsourced and to what cloud provider. The choice of how this is done can minimize the cost of running a partition of the total workload on one or multiple public cloud providers while taking into account the application requirements such as deadline constraints and data requirements according to. This is because, the variety of cost factors, pricing models and cloud provider offerings makes the consideration of the automated scheduling approach in hybrid clouds model worthwhile.

In (Van den Bossche, Vanmechelen, & Broeckhove, 2013) model a set of algorithms were used to cost-efficiently, scheduling the deadline-constrained bag-of-tasks applications on both public cloud providers and private infrastructure was proposed. The algorithms took into account both computational and data transfer costs as well as network bandwidth constraints. Using this model, Bossche et al evaluated and assessed the performance in a realistic setting with respect to cost savings, deadlines met, computational efficiency, and the impact of errors in runtime estimates on these performance metrics. On the basis of this model, some service providers offer mixed public and private options in their price components to maximize the utilization of their computing resources through shared services.

Mercury Cost Model

The Mercury cost model introduced by (Callou, Ferreira, Maciel, Tutsch, & Souza, 2014), is a tool for dependability, performance and energy flow evaluation. The tool supports reliability block diagrams (RBD), stochastic Petri nets (SPNs), continuous-time Markov chains (CTMC) and energy flow models (EFM). The EFM verifies the energy flow on data center architectures, taking into account the energy efficiency and power capacity that each device can provide (assuming power systems) or extract (considering cooling components). The EFM also estimates the sustainability impact and cost issues of data center architectures. The approach of this model is to evaluate and optimize these requirements to support cloud infrastructure solution designers. This offers an integrated approach in order to estimate and optimize high conflicting requirements and the availability levels demanded against the low sustainability impact and cost values.

Cloudlets Model Extending the Utility of Mobile-Cloud Computing

(Soyata, Ba, Heinzelman, Kwon, & Shi, 2013) defined application cost as an objective task that quantifies the fees charged by Cloud operators, such as Amazon Web Services, during the execution of the application. In their example, they stated that, Amazon charges for compute-usage per hour per CPU occurrence. This means increasing the application costs as the required amount of computation increases. According to Soyata et al, cloud operators' charges for Microsoft SQL server, for example, is based on the usage of database occurrences. Hence Soyata et al, proposed the Cloudlet model (Soyata, et al., 2012) of extending the utility of mobile cloud computing without increasing resource use. Soyata et al, illustration shows that, applications requiring higher computational and storage resources might cost more during operation on a Cloud platform such as AWS with variety of options when executing mobile-cloud applications (Wang, Liu, & Soyata, 2014) (Powers, Alling, Gyampoh-Vidogah, & Soyata, 2014) (Page, Kocabas, Ames, & Venkitasubramaniam, 2014).

Table 18 summarizes the cost models identified from literature, what they support and contribution of these models, authors and how they have been used in real life applications. The next section discusses the current application and price components offered by cloud service providers and how they relate to the aspects of the cost models.

On the basis of the cost models, different cloud charging and billing models allow choice of hosting options between and even within cloud platforms. This adds both flexibility and complexity to modeling (Brebner & Liu, 2011). For the purpose of operational costs of mobile computing pricing, operational costs for various resource types and loads such as the cost of CPU, network, data management, security

Table 18. Summary of the Cost Models

Cost Model	Application	Contribution	Author
Service Oriented performance cost model	Modeling the performance and scalability of Service Oriented applications architected for a variety of platforms.	Predict the resource requirements in terms of cost application performance.	(Brebner & Liu, 2011)
System utilisation cost model	Billing model of Computational time, data transfers & storage	Applied to current resources and planned procurements.	(Woitaszek & Tufo, 2010)
Dynamics of cost development	Intended to fill the gap where a cost model that covers dynamic issues for cloud is lacking.	Analysed cost benefits between cloud computing and datacenter.	(Kristekova Z. et al, 2012)
Inter-organizational economic models for pricing cloud network services	Analysis and comparison of models.	The ability to process the number of user requests processed per unit of time on the cloud.	(Pal & Hui, 2013)
View Materialization cost model	For decreasing the cost of data management in the cloud.	Cost model that complement existing materialised view cost model.	(Nguyen, Bimonte, d'Orazio, & Darmont, 2012)
Cost-efficient scheduling of Hybrid Cloud	Determine which workloads are to be outsourced, and to what cloud provide.	Service providers that mixed public and private options in their price components are to maximize the utilization of their computing resources through shared services.	(Van den Bossche, Vanmechelen, & Broeckhove, 2013)
Mercury Model	This model is to evaluate and optimize these requirements to support cloud infrastructure solutions designers.	Offers an integrated approach to estimate and optimize high conflicting requirements and the availability levels demanded against the low sustainability impact and cost values.	(Callou, Ferreira, Maciel, Tutsch, & Souza, 2014)
Cloudlets	For extending the utility of mobile-cloud computing by providing compute and storage resources accessible for end processing of applications	Compared different approaches that enhance application performance via cloud-based execution.	(Soyata, Ba, Heinzelman, Kwon, & Shi, 2013)

operations, transactions and connections are used by providers. These components essentially relate to activity based costing, an accounting concept through which organizations recoup costs incurred throughout normal business activity cycle (Cloudscape, 2013).

The same concept combined with trace analysis, has been applied to resources in the cloud based on the cost models. This emphasizes the fact that a cloud resource, whether it is a system, an application or a service, would have some form of metrics collected either to analyze performance or for the purpose of costing (Mihoob, Molina-Jimenez, & Shrivastava, 2011). Subsequently, providers on the basis of cost models discussed in the previous sections have derived several price components for users which are often not explained but providers have to build into their pricing mechanisms. These are: Transaction, data management, CPU time (resource use), traffic or network capacity and storage space components and the operational expenditures. For the purpose of this chapter, the main pricing components are explained as a basis of working out the operational costs to businesses for implementing real time mobile cloud based systems.

SUMMARY

This chapter provided background on mobile cloud computing in general and described in detail the concepts and cost models that have been used to determine the cost of providing cloud services and running real-time mobile-cloud applications. These cost analyses have been done from two different perspectives: the mobile-cloud user and the cloud operators. From the standpoint of the mobile-cloud user, the cost of running a real-time application involves renting the most suitable cloud resources (computation, storage, network bandwidth) from a cloud operator. On the other hand, the costs of a cloud operator primarily involve datacenter operating expenses such as electricity, equipment depreciation, and the ability to take advantage of economies of scale by sharing resources among multiple customers.

Two case studies are used as the basis of explaining the process of arriving at operational cost:s. First case study is a long-term health monitoring system described by (Kocabas, et al., 2013) that uses Homomorphic encryption to achieve privacy-preserving medical computation in the cloud. The second case study is a real-time mobile-cloud face recognition system described (Soyata, Ba, Heinzelman, Kwon, & Shi, 2013) which uses a cloudlet for acceleration to reduce the computational and network bandwidth burden on cloud instances. This second system is designed primarily as a means to extend the utility of mobile-cloud computing to provide computational and storage resources accessible at the edge of the network, both for end processing of applications and for managing the distribution of applications to other distributed compute resources.

Worksheets which demonstrate how businesses can estimate the operational cost of implementing real-time mobile cloud applications are provided. The starting point of this estimation is first a cost analysis for the mobile cloud operation constructed as the architecture of the system. Then the estimation of each cost component is provided as defined by cloud operators to estimate the actual total operational cost of running the real time mobile application. A simple step has been illustrated to show how the process used in these worksheets can be used to guide in estimating the true real-time mobile cloud application operational costs. The aim is to help decision makers make the business case for specific applications. Steps to establish the application process is to assess current models either to rent or buy. When the analysis of operational costs are established, then construction of real time operational costs should be establish that include the whole process and evaluation of applications.

ACKNOWLEDGMENT

This work was supported in part by the National Science Foundation grant CNS-1239423 and a gift from Nvidia Corporation.

REFERENCES

Alford, T., & Morton, G. (2010). *The Economics of Cloud Computing*. Retrieved from http://www.boozallen.com/media/file/Economics-of-Cloud-Computing.pdf

AliveCor. (n.d.). Retrieved from http://www.alivecor.com/home

Alling, A., Powers, N., & Soyata, T. (2015). Face Recognition: A Tutorial on Computational Aspects. In *Emerging Research Surrounding Power Consumption and Performance Issues in Utility Computing*. Hershey, PA: IGI Global.

Amazon EC2. (2013). Retrieved from Retrieved from: http://aws.amazon.com/ec2/sla/

Armbrust, M., Fox, A., Griffith, R., Joseph, A. D., Katz, R., Konwinski, A., & Stoica, I. et al. (2010). A View of Cloud Computing. *Communications of the ACM*, *53*(4), 50–58. doi:10.1145/1721654.1721672

Microsoft Azure. (2014). Retrieved from Microsoft Azure: http://azure.microsoft.com/en-us/support/legal/sla/

Bansal, N. (2013). Cloud computing technology (with BPOS and Windows Azure). *International Journal of Cloud Computing*, *2*(1), 48–60. doi:10.1504/IJCC.2013.050955

Bazzett, H. (1997). An analysis of the time-relations of electrocardiograms. *Annals of Noninvasive Electrocardiology*, *2*(2), 177–194. doi:10.1111/j.1542-474X.1997.tb00325.x

Brebner, P., & Liu, A. (2011). Performance and Cost Assessment of Cloud Services. *Computer Science*, *6568*, 39–50.

Callou, G., Ferreira, J., Maciel, P., Tutsch, D., & Souza, R. (2014). *Open Access Energies*. Retrieved from An Integrated Modeling Approach to Evaluate and Optimize Data Center Sustainability, Dependability and Cost: http://www.mdpi.com/1996-1073/7/1/238

CareCloud. (n.d.). Retrieved from http://www.carecloud.com/

Chappel, C. (2013, June 22). *Heavy Reading: Unlocking Network value: service Innovation in the Era of SDN, White paper*. Retrieved from http://www.cisco.com/web/solutions/trends/open_network_environment/docs/hr_service_innovation.pdf

Cloudscape. (2013, June 22). *451 Research*. Retrieved from The Cloud Pricing Codex: https://451research.com /report-long?icid=2770

Couderc, J.-P. (2010). The Telemetric and Holter ECG Warehouse initiative (THEW): A data repository for the design, implementation and validation of ECG related technologies. *IEEE Engineering in Medicine and Biology Society (EMBC)*, 6252-6255.

Couderc, J.-P., Garnett, C., Li, M., Handzel, R., McNitt, S., Xia, X., & Zareba, W. et al. (2011). Highly automated QT measurement techniques in 7 thorough QT studies implemented under ICH E14 guidelines. *Annals of Noninvasive Electrocardiology*, *16*(1), 13–24. doi:10.1111/j.1542-474X.2010.00402.x PMID:21251129

Dinh, H. T., Lee, C., Niyato, D., & Wang, P. (2013). Wireless Communications and Mobile Computing. *Wireless communications and mobile computing*, 1587-1611. doi:10.1002/wcm.1203

Fesehaye, D., Gao, Y., Nahrstedt, K., & Wang, G. (2012). Impact of cloudlets on interactive mobile cloud applications. *In Proceedings of Enterprise Distributed Object Computing Conference (EDOC)* (pp. 123-132). Washington DC: IEEE Computer Society, USA. doi:10.1109/EDOC.2012.23

Fetai, I., & Schuldt, H. (2012). Cost-Based Data Consistency in a Data-as-a-Service Cloud Environment. *Cloud 12 Proceedings of the IEEE Fifth International Conference on Cloud Computing* (pp. 526-533). Washington, DC: IEEE.

Gentry, C., Halevi, S., & Smart, N. (2012). *Homomorphic evaluation of the AES circuit* (pp. 850–867). CRYPTO.

Google. (2013, September 1). *Cloud Standards Customer Council.* Retrieved from What to Expect and What to Negotiate: Public Cloud Service Agreements.

Halevi, S., & Shoup, V. (n.d.). *HELib.* Retrieved from HELib: https://github.com.shaih/HElib

HIPAA. (n.d.). *Health Insurance Portability and Accountability Act.* Retrieved from http://www.hhs.gov/ocr/privacy/

IBM. (2013). *Shaping the future of the oil and gas industry with smarter cloud computing. Thought Leadership White Paper.* IBM Corporation. Retrieved from http://www-935.ibm.com/services/multimedia/Shaping_the_future_of_the_oil_and_gas_industry_with_smarter_cloud_computing.pdf

Johansson, K. (2007, June 22). *Cost Effective Deployment Strategies for Heterogeneous Wireless Networks.* Royal Institute of Technology.

Kocabas, O., & Soyata, T. (2014). Medical Data Analytics in the cloud using Homomorphic Encryption. In *Handbook of Research on Cloud Infrastructures for Big Data Analytics* (pp. 471–488). Hershey, PA: IGI Global. doi:10.4018/978-1-4666-5864-6.ch019

Kocabas, O., Soyata, T., Couderc, J.-P., Aktas, M., Xia, J., & Huang, M. (2013). Assessment of Cloud-based Health Monitoring using Homomorphic Encryption. *Proceedings of the 31th IEEE Conference on Computer Design*, (pp. 443-446). Asheville, NC, USA. doi:10.1109/ICCD.2013.6657078

Kovachev, D., Cao, Y., & Klamma, R. (2013). Retrieved from Mobile Cloud Computing: A Comparison of Application Models.: http://arxiv.org/abs/1107.4940v1

Kristekova, Z., ... B. J. (2012, June 15). *Simulation Model for Cost-Benefit Analysis of Cloud Computing versus In-House Datacenters.* Retrieved from http://digisrv-1.biblio.etc.tu-bs.de: 8080/ docportal/servlets/MCRFileNodeServlet

Kwon, M., Dou, Z., Heinzelman, W., Soyata, T., Ba, H., & Shi, J. (2014). Use of Network Latency Profiling and Redundancy for Cloud Server Selection. *Proceedings of the 7th IEEE International Conference on Cloud Computing*, (pp. 826-832). Alaska, USA. doi:10.1109/CLOUD.2014.114

Markendahl, J., Makitalo, O., & Werding, J. (2008). Analysis of Cost Structure and Business Model options for Wireless Access Provisioning using Femtocell solutions. *19th European Regional ITS Conference.*

Microsoft. (2010, May 15). *The Economics of Cloud.* Retrieved from http://www.microsoft.com/en-us/news/presskits/cloud/docs/the-economics-of-the-cloud.pdf

Mihoob, A., Molina-Jimenez, C., & Shrivastava, S. (2011). *Consumer side resource accounting in the cloud.* Berlin, Germany: Springer. doi:10.1007/978-3-642-27260-8_5

Mouftah, H. T., & Kantarci, B. (2013). *Communication Infrastructures for Cloud Computing*. Hershey, PA: IGI Global.

MS-SLA. (n.d.). Retrieved from Microsoft SLA Storage - Introduction: https://azure.microsoft.com/en-us/documentation/articles/storage-introduction/

Nguyen, T.-V.-A., Bimonte, S., d'Orazio, L., & Darmont, J. (2012). Cost models for view materialization in the cloud. *EDBT-ICDT '12 Proceedings of the Joint EDBT/ICDT Workshops*, (pp. 47-54). New York.

NIST-AES. (2001, Nov). *FIPS-197.* Retrieved from Advanced Encryption Standard (AES).

Page, A., Kocabas, O., Ames, S., & Venkitasubramaniam, M. (2014). Cloud-based Secure Health Monitoring: Optimizing Fully-Homomorphic Encryption for Streaming Algorithms. *IEEE Globecom 2014 Workshop on Cloud Computing Systems, Networks, and Applications.*

Page, A., Kocabas, O., Soyata, T., Aktas, M., & Couderc, J.-P. (2014). Cloud-Based Privacy-Preserving Remote ECG Monitoring and Surveillance. *Annals of Noninvasive Electrocardiology*, n/a. doi:10.1111/anec.12204 PMID:25510621

Pal, R., & Hui, P. (2013). Economic Models for Cloud Service Markets: Pricing and Capacity Planning. *Journal of Distributed Computing and Networking*, *496*, 113–124.

Powers, N., Alling, A., Gyampoh-Vidogah, R., & Soyata, T. (2014). AXaaS: Case for Acceleration as a Service. *IEEE Globecom 2014 Workshop on Cloud Computing Systems, Networks, and Applications.*

Prasad, R. M., Gyani, J., & Murti, P. (2012). Mobile Cloud Computing: Implications and Challenges. *Journal of Information Engineering and Applications*, *2*(7), 1–15.

Rickinson, M., & May, H. (2009). *A comparative study of methodological approaches to reviewing literature.* The Higher Education Academy. Retrieved June 15, 2014, from Http://www.heacademy.ac.uk/assets/ documents/ resources/comparativestudy.pdf

Rimal, B., & Choi, E. (2012). A service-oriented taxonomical spectrum, cloudy challenges and opportunities of cloud computing. *International Journal of Communication Systems. Special Issue*, *25*(6), 796–819. doi:10.1002/dac.1279

Shanklin, W. (2014, March 26). *Revisiting Cloud Computing: how has it changed - and changed us?* Retrieved from Gizmag: http://www.gizmag.com/revisiting-cloud-computing/26768/

Slack, N., Brandon-Jones, A., & Johnston, R. (2013). *Operations Management*. Lombarda, Italy: Pearson.

Soyata, T., Ba, H., Heinzelman, W., Kwon, M., & Shi, J. (2013). Accelerating mobile cloud computing: A survey. In *Communication Infrastructures for Cloud Computing* (pp. 175–197). IGI Global.

Soyata, T., Muraleedharan, R., Funai, C., Kwon, M., & Heinzelman, W. (2012). Cloud-Vision: Real-time face recognition using a mobile-cloudlet-cloud acceleration architecture. *Computers and Communications (ISCC), 2012 IEEE Symposium on*, 59-66.

Soyata, T., Muraleedharan, R., Langdon, J., Funai, C., Kwon, M., & Heinzelman, W. (2012). COMBAT: mobile-Cloud-based cOmpute/coMmunications infrastructure for BATtlefield applications. *Proceedings of the Society for Photo-Instrumentation Engineers*, 8403.

US-HHS. (n.d.). *Business Associate Agreement*. Retrieved from http://www.hhs.gov/ocr/privacy/hipaa/understanding/coveredentities/contractprov.html

Van den Bossche, R., Vanmechelen, K., & Broeckhove, J. (2013). Online cost-efficient scheduling of deadline-constrained workloads on hybrid clouds. *Computer Systems*, *29*(4), 973–985. doi:10.1016/j.future.2012.12.012

Viola, P., & Jones, M. (2001). Rapid object detection using a boosted cascade of simple features. *Proceedings of the 2001 IEEE Computer Society Conference on Computer Vision and Pattern Recognition*, (pp. 511-518). doi:10.1109/CVPR.2001.990517

Wang, H., Liu, W., & Soyata, T. (2014). Accessing Big Data in the Cloud Using Mobile Devices. In *Handbook of Research on Cloud Infrastructures for Big Data Analytics* (pp. 444–470). Hershey, PA: IGI Global. doi:10.4018/978-1-4666-5864-6.ch018

Woitaszek, M., & Tufo, H. M. (2010). Developing a Cloud Computing Charging Model for High-Performance Computing. *10th IEEE International Conference on Computer and Information Technology* (pp. 210-217). Bradford: IEEE. doi:10.1109/CIT.2010.72

Wu, L. (2014). *SLA-based Resource Provisioning for Management of Cloud-based Software-as-a-Service Applications* (Doctoral dissertation). Retrieved from University of Melbourne Cloud Laboratory: http://cloudbus.org/students/LinlinPhDThesis2014.pdf

KEY TERMS AND DEFINITIONS

Advanced Encryption Standard (AES): A symmetric-key encryption system used for encrypting/decrypting digital data with the same private key.

Amazon Web Services (AWS): Cloud computing services provided by Amazon.com.

Business Associate Agreement (BAA): An agreement that a vendor of an HCO signs confirming that, they will treat PHI according to HIPAA laws to prevent the HCO itself from violating it.

Cloud Computing: Outsourcing computation and storage to a company that rents these entities at a much lower unit price than is possible to produce by any user. Cloud operators take advantage of economies of scale by aggregating requests from multiple customers to lower the cost of these commodity "utilities."

Cloud Operator: A company that rents computation and storage in a way similar to utility companies (e.g., gas and electric companies) do by adhering to monthly or other types of billing. Most notable cloud operators are Microsoft (Azure), Amazon, and Google.

Datacenter: A facility to store and maintain computer servers, storage devices and networking systems. The high level operating software that runs in the "cloud" allows the cloud operator to channel the computation/storage requests to resources based on cost and availability criteria.

ECG Patch: An external sensor that is attached to a patient's body, typically in multiple body points, that records the ECG signals in a way similar to the ones obtained at the HCO. The advantage of using an ECG patch is the ability to obtain a patient's ECG outside the HCO, for long term health monitoring. This could provide significantly more information to a doctor in terms of the cardiac functionality of a patient over the long term, and potentially allow the doctor to identify cardiac issues that cannot be indentified in short term ECG recordings obtained at the HCO.

Electrocardiogram (ECG): A diagram, typically printed on specialized ECG paper, that contains information about the cardiac functionality of a patient within a short period of time (e.g., less than a minute). The information that is plotted is the voltage levels on each electrode (i.e., "lead"). By looking at such information, multiple cardiac conditions can be readily identified by a healthcare professional.

Face Recognition: A process of identifying a person by comparing facial features of the person with a database of known faces. In this operation, multiple pre-processing steps (such as conversion from faces to Eigenfaces) help substantially reduce the processing necessary to reach the same computational results.

Fully Homomorphic Encryption (FHE): A public key encryption algorithm that can perform addition or multiplication operations on encrypted data. Using FHE, it is possible to do cloud computing, where the cloud cannot observe the data that it is operating on. This allows the introduction of secure medical cloud applications where the medical data privacy concerns are eliminated, since the cloud can never observe the patient data.

Google App Engine: Platform as a Service (PaaS) provided by Google Cloud Platform.

Google Cloud Platform: PaaS and SaaS services provided by Google for deploying and managing applications in the cloud.

Graphics Processing Unit (GPU): A deice that is capable of processing significantly higher amounts of data (typically one or two orders-of-magnitude) as compared to a CPU. Computation using a GPU does not necessarily benefit every application, but, rather, ones that have such massive parallelism. Almost every Image Processing application can benefit from the parallelism of a GPU due to the inherent parallelism in the structure of an image, composed of millions of pixels.

Health Insurance Portability and Accountability Act (HIPAA): A set of rules and regulations to protect the privacy of an individual's medical information, i.e., PHI. An example such rule is covering a computer monitor with a privacy screen to avoid a third party from seeing the individual's information.

Healthcare Organization (HCO): Any organization in the chain of organizations that provides a phase of the healthcare to an individual. These organizations are subject to HIPAA laws.

Hybrid Cloud: A cloud computing deployment model where cloud infrastructure is a combination of private and public cloud resources.

IaaS (Infrastructure as a Service): A cloud computing service model where cloud providers deliver computing infrastructure. These services may include servers, storage, and operating systems. Clients provision resource needed to run their applications and outsource the required resources form cloud providers. Examples of IaaS are Google Compute Engine, Amazon Web Services and Microsoft Azure.

Long QT Syndrome (LQTS): A cardiac condition where the QTc interval is prolonged. The variation among a large population should be small when QTc (corrected) value of the QT interval is used. Safe values of QTc are below 440 ms, though, values under 500 ms are acceptable. Patients with QTc > 500 ms are under risk of serious cardiac hazards.

Microsoft Azure: PaaS and SaaS services provided by Microsoft for deploying and managing applications in the cloud.

Mobile-Cloud Computing: A computing model that combines mobile devices and cloud computing to remedy lack of resources of the mobile devices such as computation power, storage and battery. Mobile devices use cloud resources for data processing and storage.

PaaS (Platform as a Service): A cloud computing service model where cloud providers deliver computing platforms and environments to allow clients to deploy and manage their applications. These services may include programming languages, libraries, tools and services. Clients control deploying applications and cloud providers manage the underlying cloud infrastructure based on demand. Examples of PaaS are Google App Engine, Microsoft Azure, Heroku.com.

Pretty Good Privacy (PGP): A public-key cryptography system to encrypt and sign digital data.

Private Cloud: A cloud computing deployment model where the cloud services is owned and managed by a single organization.

Protected Health Information (PHI): Any information that can be associated with an individual, such has his/her health status. This information must be protected to avoid a privacy violation of the individual.

Public Cloud: A cloud computing deployment model where the cloud services is open to use for general public. The cloud infrastructure may be owned, managed by third party and services are provided to general public.

QT Interval: QT interval is another very common internal obtained from the ECG. This internal on each heartbeat delineates the ventricular recovery phase of the heart.

QTc Value: Since the QT interval varies based on the heart rate, a corrected version of the QT interval is much more meaningful to use in identifying proper cardiac operation. QTc adjusts QT for heart rate, and is, therefore, a lot more steady over a general population. Nearly 100 years ago, Bazzett suggested a correction formula of $QTc=QT/\sqrt{RR}$, which is is known as Bazett's formula, or QTcB. An alternative suggestion followed from Fridericia which proved to be more accurate for a wider range of heart rates, which replaces the square root of RR with the cube root. Bazzett and Frediricia formulas can be written as: $QTcB = QT/(RR/sec)^{1/2}$ $QTcF = QT/(RR/sec)^{1/3}$. The divisions of RR by 1 second (i.e., /sec) are in place to preserve units between QT and QTc.

RR Interval: The most commonly used metric that is obtained from the ECG. Each beat has a similar patterns with readily identifiable Q, R, S, T, and U points. The temporal distance between two R points is called the RR interval, or the heart rate.

SaaS (Software as a Service): A cloud computing service model where cloud providers deliver services as software applications hosted in the cloud. Cloud providers manage the cloud infrastructure that is needed to run application software. Clients access these services from a client interface (e.g, web browser). Examples of SaaS are Gmail, Microsoft Office 365, Saleforce.com.

Service Level Agreement (SLA): An agreement between service providers and clients that establishes the scope, quality and responsibilities of service provider to the client.

Tiered Pricing: A pricing model that sets the price of per unit item based on a range (i.e., tier).

Utility Computing: A service-provisioning model that provides computing resources and infrastructure to clients based on demand. Computing resources might include servers, storage and services. Service providers charge clients based on the usage instead of a flat rate.

Chapter 11
Theoretical Foundation and GPU Implementation of Face Recognition

William Dixon
University of Rochester, USA

Yang Song
University of Rochester, USA

Nathaniel Powers
University of Rochester, USA

Tolga Soyata
University of Rochester, USA

ABSTRACT

Enabling a machine to detect and recognize faces requires significant computational power. This particular system of face recognition makes use of OpenCV (Computer Vision) libraries while leveraging Graphics Processing Units (GPUs) to accelerate the process towards real-time. The processing and recognition algorithms are best sorted into three distinct steps: detection, projection, and search. Each of these steps has unique computational characteristics and requirements driving performance. In particular, the detection and projection processes can be accelerated significantly with GPU usage due to the data types and arithmetic types associated with the algorithms, such as matrix manipulation. This chapter provides a survey of the three main processes and how they contribute to the overarching recognition process.

INTRODUCTION

Humans have the innate skill to continuously gather complex information from another person's face. While it comes naturally to us, it is really quite the feat to be able to do something as simple as recognizing individuals based on a quick gaze over a face. What may differentiate individual faces are inherently subtle variations in features such as skin, skeletal structure, hair and lips. Humans can do this with ease at any angle, most lighting, at a massive scale with a high degree of accuracy.

Computers have a comparatively difficult time with face recognition, even today. At a basic level, in order to recognize faces, a computer must first be able to determine which objects from an image are actual faces. It must then gather enough information by analyzing multiple image fragments to develop patterns associated with a face which may be presented in a variety of aspects and lighting conditions.

DOI: 10.4018/978-1-4666-8662-5.ch011

The computer can then accept new images, detect and analyze faces, then attempt to match these analyzed faces to established representations stored in a database. If a comparison surpasses a particular confidence threshold, the computer will state that it has established a match. If the threshold is not met, the computer can throw the image out or use it to start a new face index, depending on what the developer has programmed the computer to do.

Each of these processes is, by nature of the computational implementation, reducible to a series of steps. Like many computing problems, not every solution utilizes a single method or algorithm. Computer scientists, programmers, mathematicians and others have been making progress on simplifying and solving the problems of computer vision since the 1960's. At first, facial recognition was done partially manually, with people marking locations of features such as the nose and eyes. This information was fed into a computer which sifted through its database of other marked images and returned which match was closest. Over the next two decades, this system was made autonomous and finely-tuned. The parent of many systems used today, including ours, was developed in 1988 by Lawrence Sirovich and Michael Kirby. This system makes use of a broader statistical method called Principal Component Analysis (PCA). PCA essentially parses and manipulates a dataset into uncorrelated sets of correlated data (Kim, Jung, & Kim, 2002). These sets are called principal components, which fall under the more mathematically general term of eigenvectors.

FACE RECOGNITION ALGORITHMIC STRUCTURE

This particular facial recognition algorithm includes three main processes: face detection, projection, and search. Face detection identifies potential faces, projection conducts the bulk of the image processing and obtains quantified data from the faces, and the search compares the face data to the face database, finding the closest match, if one exists. Face detection uses a Viola-Jones algorithm, a lighting-based detector, to find key facial features in an image in rectangular sections compared against one another. The next step in face recognition is projection. Projection reduces each of the detected faces into "Eigenfaces" by removing data of lesser importance from each facial image. PCA is the fundamental tool used in projection and will be given its own section here; however a deep understanding of it is not required to understand most of facial recognition. The database is constructed using the same set of routines employed during real-time operation of projection. This not only simplifies the searching process by reducing it to a comparison of identical data structures, it streamlines the program implementation by relying on the same set of functions for database generation and real-time operation. Searching will then find the most closely matching database face to the newly projected face. If the face is matched with sufficient confidence, the algorithm completes by outputting correlated identification data to the user.

Face Detection (FD)

As humans have eyes, machines have a camera. *Images,* to which we constantly refer, are two-dimensional data constructs consisting of picture elements or *pixels*. In the case of real-time perception, images come and go and persist only for a small interval of time, which we refer to as *frames*. We begin the detection process assuming that an external camera has supplied a frame containing an image that may or may not contain a face or faces (Goldstein, Harmon, & Lesk, 1987). This image resides in the memory of the machine and is accessible to subsequent processes. The Viola-Jones detection algorithm (Viola &

Jones, 2001) uses the brightness of each pixel in the grayscale-converted image to determine what areas of an image are faces by locating general features, and then progressively becoming more specific. The first step in this is representing the relative brightness efficiently, since this algorithm uses this data in a specific way. Each pixel will be represented in terms of the summed pixel intensities above it and to its left, a construct termed *integral image*. Also referred to as *summed area table*, it is a representation that efficiently allows a description of a neighborhood of pixels (Crow, 1984).

With this representation, the total brightness of a rectangular section of the image can be determined by adding and subtracting the summed intensities of the rectangle's corner pixels. For example, the shaded area in Fig. 1 can be evaluated by adding the values at points *A* and *C*, and subtracting the values at *B* and *D* (Yang, Kriegman, & Ahuja, 2002). Additionally, the total intensity of adjacent rectangles can be determined with fewer values, since some of those values are included in the other rectangle representations. More specifically, a single rectangle's intensity sum can be represented with four values, two adjacent rectangles can have each of their sums represented with six values, three rectangles with eight values, and four rectangles with nine values.

Figure 1. Determining the intensity of an image area using only four corner values.

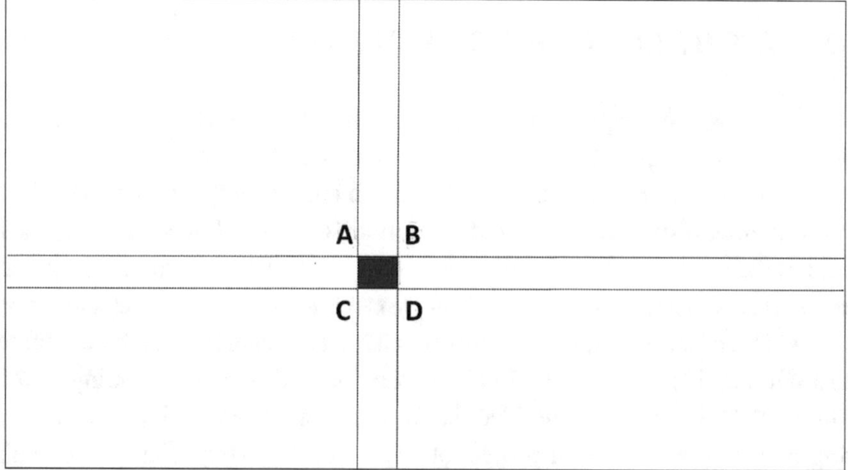

Figure 2. (a) two-rectangle features. (b) three-rectangle features. (c) four-rectangle features.

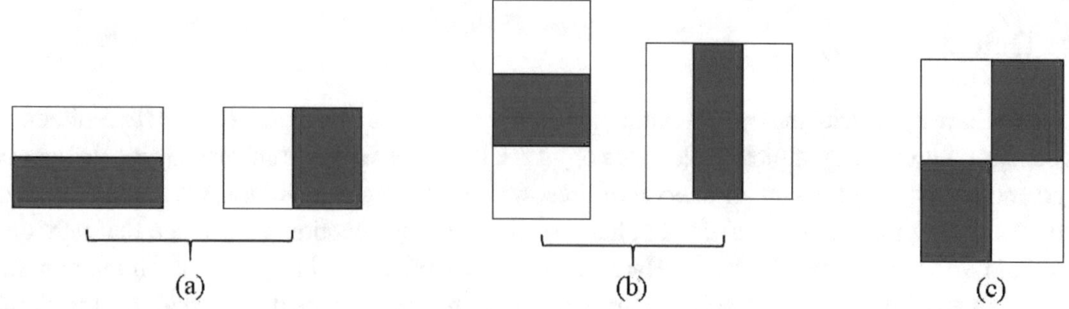

The locating is then accomplished by comparing the total intensities of adjacent rectangular sections of an image, so it is clear why this summed intensity representation of the pixels is useful. There are three main patterns which classify each feature found: two-rectangle features, three-rectangle features, and four-rectangle features, each potentially oriented horizontally, vertically, or diagonally, shown on Fig. 2.

Certain facial features can be recognized as objects in the image based on the way these simple rectangular features are patterned. For example, eyes and the nose are easily recognized with this method because the lighting value of eyes is typically significantly darker than the surrounding areas while the lighting value of the nose is significantly lighter than the surrounding areas. If these recognized features are positioned in a certain way, then that area of the image could potentially include a face. All faces will have those areas, so the algorithm can then throw out the non-face areas and continue processing on the face areas. One might wonder how the algorithm knows how to do this, and it turns out that the algorithm itself must be *trained* to detect faces in this way.

AdaBoost, or *Adaptive Boosting*, was initially introduced by Freund and Schapire in 1995 (Freund, Schapire, & Abe, 1999), and is widely used to solve pattern recognition problems. It is an iterative machine learning algorithm employed in order to form an optimal set of constructs which guide the detection process. The result is to determine features which will most quickly begin to weed out non-face areas. Those features, like the nose and eyes, will be identified first, while other features are progressively added to the detection process. This cascade of identifications maintains the high accuracy of the detection and reduces false positives as much as possible while minimizing fruitless or redundant processing.

Its core idea is to respond to training by different classifiers for the same set of object types, so called *weak classifiers*, and then generate a strong classifier out of those weak classifiers. The algorithm itself is implemented by data reallocation. At each iteration, a new weak classifier is added, for which we assign a weight that indicates the possibility for this classifier being selected for every sample in the training set. Therefore, those well-classified samples would have less possibility to be selected in the next set, and vice versa. In this way, the algorithm tends to concentrate on the information-rich samples that are also harder to classify.

A general description of Adaboost:

1. Begin in sample set $\{x^1, y_1, x^2, y_2, \ldots, x^n, y_n\}$, maximum number of iterations T_{max}, and weight for the samples in each iteration $W_{t,i}$ where t denotes the iteration and i denotes the sample numbering $1,2,\ldots,n$
2. For t=1 to T_{max},
   a. Using $W_{t,i}$ to train the weak classifier for the sample set
   b. Calculate the training error ε_t for this weak classifier
   c. Regarding ε_t, set $\alpha_t = \frac{1}{2}\log\frac{1-\varepsilon_t}{\varepsilon_t}$
   d. Applying a normalization constant, update the weight for next iteration
3. Return weak classifiers and α_t for every t^{th} iteration.

The final adjudication, which we call the strong classifier, can be obtained as a weighted summation of the weak classifiers.

The AdaBoost algorithm offers many advantages. Primarily, the final strong classifier has a relatively high accuracy comparing to other similar method like Bootstrapping and Bagging. As AdaBoost provides a framework instead of particulars, various schemas can be applied to build the weak classifiers, which could be very simple and easy to understand . Finally, AdaBoost doesn't need feature selection, thus developers wouldn't need to worry about over fitting. This customization of feature selection can also be used to train classifiers to detect virtually any application-specific object or set of objects such as vehicles, text patterns or flora/fauna. This face recognition application particularly employs a *frontal face* cascade classifier. The quality of detection with this algorithm is high, such that positive detection rates approach 100% quickly (approximately 10 times faster than a similar non-cascaded algorithm) and false-positive rates stay on the order of 0.1% (Soyata, Muraleedharan, Funai, Kwon, & Heinzelman, 2012).

Once a region in the source frame has been evaluated to contain a face or faces, the OpenCV library function cascade_gpu.detectMultiScale forms an object buffer containing the coordinates of rectangles bounding each face. These 'bounding boxes' are used to define sub-images (containing only a face) which are separated from the source frame and returned to the caller as a list, or vector of image fragments. OpenCV employs the *Mat* datatype, which stands for Matrix. Since we are working so extensively with two dimensional image data, this type is well suited for our application. Each sub-image *Mat* contains a face whose identity remains unknown at this point. In order to complete the recognition process, the machine must have a basis of reference. This requires a training set of images and corresponding identification data. The training set must be used to initialize the Face Recognizer, a process which must be completed before beginning a recognition routine. We bring it up now because computationally, it is nearly identical to the process following detection; projection.

Projection (PJ)

Projection is wholly a data conversion process. Beginning with a two dimensional pixel array (the cropped sub-image of a face), the image ultimately becomes represented as a set of orthogonal coordinates in a multi-dimensional Eigenspace; a single point. The dimensionality of this space can be selected by the developer before runtime and has a large impact on the number of operations (thus time) it takes to perform a complete recognition routine, including projection and searching. The obvious tradeoff is representation accuracy; an external requirement based on the degree of variation between subjects. In typical cases projection significantly reduces the amount of data required to uniquely represent a face. While many details are lost (in comparison with the actual image of the face), the idea is to retain just enough information necessary for a positive identification.

Each dimension of this Eigenspace is represented by something called an "Eigenface". What is being said here, is that a small set of Eigenfaces are sufficient to describe a large data set of unique faces. Using the linear combination of each Eigenface, with each dimension weighted by the test (detected) face projection coefficients (p_k), the expectation is that the result is unique and sufficiently differentiable from any other potential results. This means that the result from any weighted linear combination of Eigenfaces must have a sufficient region of emptiness about it ("headroom") in the Eigenspace in order to preserve the integrity of prediction accuracy. This is achieved by selecting an Eigenspace dimensionality appropriate to the number of objects in the database, as well as a quasi-quantitative degree of variation in their appearances.

The maximum possible number of Eigenfaces for a data set is the number of unique elements, and for Face Recognition this is the number of unique training images. This level of representation can quickly become intractable, as the amount of raw data required can exceed the memory capacity of typical machines. Furthermore, the computational impact of such a large data structure might preclude real-time performance. The following method does allow for an acceptable degree of accuracy while using a relatively small selection of Eigenfaces by assigning an eigenvalue to each Eigenface (Sirovich & Kirby, 1987). This eigenvalue quantifies the corresponding Eigenface's degree of similarity to the *Mean* face; a per-pixel arithmetic average of every training image used to create the initial database. For a database consisting of n images, the percentage of information $P(k)$ covered by the first k Eigenfaces can be calculated as:

$$P\left(k\right)=\frac{\sum_{i=1}^{k}\left(\sum_{j=1}^{n}\varphi_{i,j}\right)^{2}}{\sum_{i=1}^{n}\left(\sum_{j=1}^{n}\varphi_{i,j}\right)^{2}}$$

where the eigenvalue $\varphi_{i,j}$ is the ith component of the eigenvector for the jth image in the database. The precision of the algorithm will increase by retaining a larger number of vectors, which presents an obvious trade-off between accuracy and performance. Resultantly, in order to represent the same amount of information, the necessary ratio of Eigenfaces to training images varies inversely with the size of the database. In Fig. 3, an example is shown where the bottom image is calculated as a linear weighted average of the Eigenfaces on top . Counteracting this assertion is the need for a greater diversity of possible descriptors, i.e., eigenvectors in order to make differentiable representations of unique facial

Figure 3. Specifying a face in terms of weighted averages of Eigenfaces

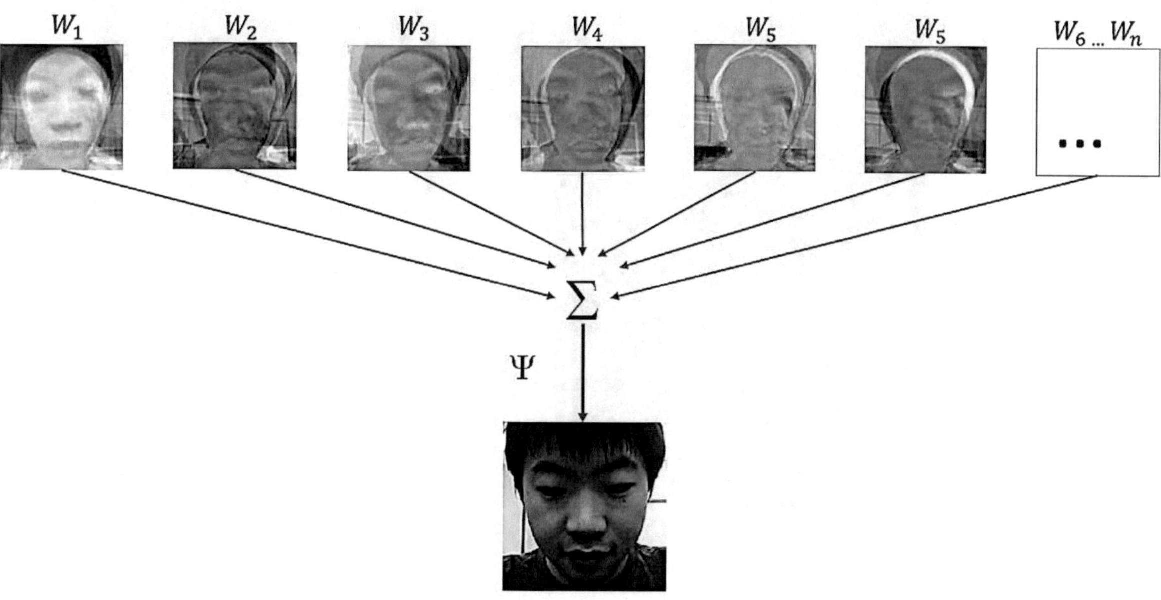

features. Thus the optimal number of eigenvectors used in any application is a point of balance which depends on the number of elements in the database (images) and the degree of variation between them. This variation can be altogether qualitative; optimization might require the application of heuristics, largely by trial and error.

It can be easily inferred that the face can only be perfectly recreated from coordinates in theory, particularly when a face was not part of the initial database. However, complete accuracy is by no means required and is also not practical. Similar to how the application of cascade classifiers makes decisions on what features to use during detection, the projection step uses the statistical method of principal component analysis (PCA) to figure out which information can be discarded with minimal impact on the quality of the representation.

As with eigenvectors in mathematics, Eigenfaces each have an associated eigenvalue. These eigenvalues are used to quantify the quality of data. In terms of each face, the eigenvalues are a measure of how significant the Eigenface information is to the database, and more specifically are a calculation of how different an Eigenface is from the average of the projected faces; the Mean face (a direct result of using PCA). A sum using Eigenface eigenvalues can be used to determine what portion of data that Eigenface covers. From the nature of PCA, the dimensions formed earlier on will contain the largest portion of relevant information. Subsequent dimensions will contribute information in a decreasing order of relevance. If one dimension's contribution is sufficiently small, which is true for many potential Eigenfaces, it should not be included in the set of Eigenfaces. To give an example for how much reduction is typically done while still maintaining accuracy, a set of 500 faces has been reasonably represented with 29 Eigenfaces, shown in Fig. 4.

Figure 4. A set of 29 Eigenfaces is sufficient for a database of 500 training images. Adapted from (Soyata, Muraleedharan, Funai, Kwon, & Heinzelman, 2012).

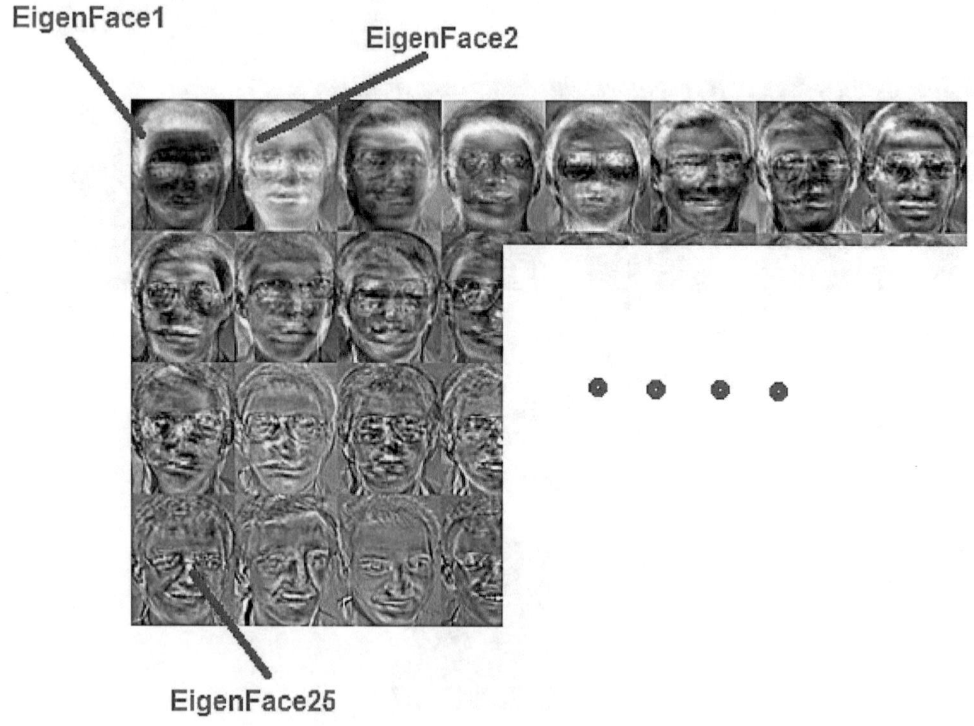

Creating the Eigenspace and database isn't real-time level processing, so both are precompiled and the Eigenfaces are loaded into memory for the actual facial recognition. In order to match a new face with the database, its image must be processed to have the same pixel dimensions as the database images. This process is intermediate and executed immediately after detection on each sub-image that is to be projected. Additionally, the sub-image is made grayscale and histogram equalization is applied in order to enhance the contrast between neighboring pixels and dominant regions. This allows for notably different features to be recognized, since the new face image is then subtracted from the Mean face. This is then projected onto the Eigenspace where the new face is represented as a point in the theoretical multi dimensional space, and within the computer's memory as a linear vector of floating-point numbers. NOTE: implementation with GPUs may require a sensitivity to the floating point precision specified in the source code. The loss of performance when utilizing double precision may not be justified by the level of prediction accuracy gained as a result of a finer-grained Eigenspace. As stated before, the location of all possible projections in the Eigenspace must be given appropriate "headroom" by a prudently configured database compilation. If two neighboring projections in the Eigenspace require the use of double precision floating point variables in order to make a definitive distinction, it is more likely a consequence of a database compilation that used too few dimensions/Eigenfaces. Optimization thus begins with a clear understanding and use of PCA.

Reducing Dimensionality using Principal Component Analysis (PCA)

Principal component analysis is a relatively old but highly successful mathematical technique with many applications. Its primary strength is being able to take related data and parse it into each data point's most significant or unique components when compared with the dataset as a whole. This, in effect, reduces the raw amount of information required in representing each data point, starting with the least impactful removals. Part of this removal results in the reduction of dimensionality of the dataset, or in other words reducing the number of variables that mathematically represent each point. In terms of our facial recognition algorithm, this means that PCA allows the efficient and quantitative representation of a large number of faces in a way that automatically parses similarities and differences between them.

PCA for facial recognition starts off by reframing the two dimensional pre-processed sub-image as a linear vector. Next, an element-wise Mean of all these images is created. Instead of each face image being processed as itself during projection, it is instead processed as its difference from the Mean image. This "normalization" is a step similar to many basic statistical operations, such as the calculation of variance. Similarities such as this are prevalent throughout the details of PCA and should give some intuitive idea as to the nature of the analysis.

Currently each data point that we have represents an image of dimensionality N times M where N and M are the width and height of each normalized image. The value of each of the data point's components is the intensity of the corresponding pixel compared to the intensity of the mean image's corresponding pixel. Therefore, we have a space with N times M axes. Say each image were 50 by 50 pixels – that means we have 2500 axes, even if we have just one image! Compare this to the end result, which is, as in a previous example, a set of 500 images represented on 29 axes.

In order to accomplish such a reduction, PCA creates each axis iteratively with the highest impact axis first. Let us work in a 3 dimensional space for simplicity in explanation. This is a drastic simplification, since that would mean each image would be 3 by 1 or 1 by 3 pixels, however this process is easily generalized to any number of dimensions. The first axis is a line going through the origin (the centroid) of the data and through the line which is as close as possible to every data point in the set. In other words, if you were to sum the Euclidian distances from each data point to the nearest point on the line, this line would be such that every other line would have a greater or equal sum. Yet another way of saying this is that this line goes through the highest variation of the dataset. The next axis is determined the same way, except that it must be orthogonal to the first axis. In this case, we can easily understand the orthogonal requirement as projecting the data points to the plane such that the first line runs directly into or out of it.

We could completely specify the dataset by adding a third axis, however the point of PCA is to reduce the dimensionality of the dataset, so the third axis will be omitted. As stated previously, each new axis is less impactful to the data than the one before. We can quantify how impactful axes are by how small their respective eigenvalues are, and in most datasets, especially those with an initially large dimensionality, omitting some of the later developed axes is a highly reasonable optimization.

Search (S)

The compiled database consists of an ordered set of coordinates. These coordinates are of the dimensionality of the Eigenspace and represent the projections of each image used in its construction. Ideally, the images used are as similar to the manner in which images will be presented to the computer, i.e., faces oriented to the front with a particular aspect ratio and relative zoom level.

Searching essentially calculates the standard Euclidian distance between the test face projection and the projections in the database. This, unfortunately, requires at least a partial comparison with every single element of the database set. The cost of this operation grows super-linearly with the size of the database, so the current method described definitely can stand some optimizations. The test face is finally identified by the correlated information pertaining to the closest projection in the database. If the minimum distance is not within that threshold, the search algorithm may mark this input face as a new face (one that is not already in the database). This face can then potentially be added to the database if desired, or just left as "not a match" and ignored/discarded. Additionally, if the distance is particularly large, the search process may be configured to tag the input image as not a face. This would mean that there was a false positive in the detection algorithm. Particular feedback methods are entirely possible, although retraining the cascade classifiers for detection have not been tried during runtime.

INSTALLATION OF THE FACE RECOGNITION SOFTWARE

This particular implementation of face recognition is a system of a number of pre-existing technologies and algorithms working together. The installation of this face recognition software is therefore somewhat involved and specific, and so this section explains in detail the steps for proper installation.

Required Base Libraries and SDKs

Firstly, a Windows-based PC platform is required for this face recognition software, since much of the required contributing software is Windows-only. Additionally, this software is configured to use an Nvidia GPU, providing a significant performance increase over strict CPU usage. It follows that a compatible Nvidia GPU is necessary for running this software. A list of such GPUs can be found at https://

developer.nvidia.com/cuda-gpus. Additionally, the user should make sure that GPU drivers and other related software are updated to the most recent versions. What follows is a list of prerequisite software technologies used in this face recognition implementation.

- Nvidia CUDA (version 6.5)
- Nvidia Nsight
- Microsoft Visual Studio 2010
- Open CV (version 2.4.9) and the altered source files (OpenCV-WEB; Bradski & Kaehler, 2008).
- CMake (version 3.0.2)

The most recent versions tested at the time this chapter was written are noted, however users are encouraged to attempt to use the most recent versions of the available technologies. One exception to this is Visual Studio. At the time of writing, CMake does not yet support integration of the most recent release of Visual Studio, but does support integration with the 2010 and 2012 releases.

Purpose of Base Libraries and SDKs

OpenCV is the most integral part of this face recognition system. OpenCV provides reliable and recent programs and algorithms directly involved with face recognition, including the detection, projection, and search processes. Additionally, using OpenCV ensures that this package can be used in a widespread and standardized way. The following snippet from the OpenCV about page gives a concise overview of its value and purpose. "OpenCV (Open Source Computer Vision Library) is an open source computer vision and machine learning software library. OpenCV was built to provide a common infrastructure for computer vision applications and to accelerate the use of machine perception in the commercial products."

Nvidia CUDA is the primary software which makes GPU acceleration viable (Nvidia CUBLAS; Nvidia CUFFT). CUDA is a framework built to allow users to easily take advantage of the processing power of modern GPU devices in an optimized way. For many applications, especially those regarding data derived from visual sources, computation with GPUs is much faster than computation with CPUs. Performance increases in this particular application of CUDA will be discussed later. Nvidia also provides toolkit software with CUDA, which contains tools for easy integration with C and C++ development, among other things. Nsight is a software bundled in the toolkit that integrates CUDA development into the Visual Studio environment.

CMake provides an easy method for integrating OpenCV libraries with Visual Studio 2010. CMake will create the proper binaries (ie. executables and dynamic-link libraries) which can then be easily used in the C and C++ code created to implement the algorithms and programs that OpenCV provides. CMake is built with goals in mind which are similar to those cited by OpenCV, and is hence also open source. Therefore, CMake also provides advantages such as availability and standardization for end-users.

Visual Studio is the software which unifies all the other technologies. CMake and the CUDA toolkit provides ways for developers to directly implement face recognition and GPU optimizations in the programs coded with Visual Studio. Additionally, Visual Studio is useful for its primary intended purpose as an IDE (Integrated Development Environment), making coding more user-friendly with built-in debugging, code building and compilation, and other features.

Installation of the Software Components

- **Visual Studio:** Start the installation process off by installing Visual Studio if it is not already installed. Visual Studio can be purchased at http://www.visualstudio.com/downloads/download-visual-studio-vs, but can also be often downloaded for free for academic uses by students at https://www.dreamspark.com with a verified DreamSpark account. Installation for Visual Studio is mostly automated and may depend on your method of acquisition. Microsoft provides general instructions at this webpage http://msdn.microsoft.com/en-us/library/e2h7fzkw.aspx.
- **CUDA:** The proper downloads for CUDA can be found at https://developer.nvidia.com/cuda-downloads. Run the CUDA installation exe and follow the on-screen instructions. For most cases, choose the express installation option. Again, installation here is mostly automated and the on-screen instructions should be sufficient. When installation finishes, verify that some Nsight tools have been installed depending on your installed versions of Visual Studio.
- **OpenCV:** Download OpenCV v2.4.9 from http://sourceforge.net/projects/opencvlibrary/files/opencv-win/. General installation instructions can be found at http://docs.opencv.org/doc/tutorials/introduction/windows_install/windows_install.html#windows-installation, however relevant and more specific material will also be presented here. To begin installation, run the opencv-2.4.9 executable as administrator and extract it to your root hard drive folder (e.g. C:\). Now, open up command prompt (cmd.exe) as administrator and enter the following code, exchanging the directory for where you installed OpenCV. Exclude the –m call if you do not want this installed for all user accounts on the computer.

setx -m OPENCV_DIR C:\OpenCV\Build\x86\vc10 (suggested for Visual Studio 2010 - 32 bit Windows)

setx -m OPENCV_DIR C:\OpenCV\Build\x64\vc10 (suggested for Visual Studio 2010 - 64 bit Windows)

Command prompt should return "SUCCESS: Specified value was saved." after entering the proper code. Next, find the provided modified OpenCV source files (they should include a build and a sources directory). In a separate file explorer window, find the opencv directory. Inside this should also be a build directory and a sources directory. Before copying over the new folders, consider creating backups of the relevant old folders and files, which can be determined by browsing the modified source folder. When ready, copy over the build and sources folders from the modified source files and into the OpenCV directory.

- **CMake:** Go to http://www.cmake.org/download/ and download the CMake Win32 Installer file. Run this installer. Mark the option that says "Add CMake to the system PATH for all users" or "current user" depending on your preference, and click next. The rest of the installation options are user preference.
- **Building with CMake:** Run cmake-gui.exe in the bin folder of the CMake directory. For the "Where is the source code" field, browse and select the "sources" folder found in the opencv directory. For the "Where to build the binaries" field, browse and select the "build" folder found in the opencv directory. Click the Configure button at the bottom of the CMake window and select the proper version of Visual Studio (e.g., Visual Studio 10 2010 Win64). Press finish and wait for the generator to complete. It is okay when red items pop up in the two UI fields. Now go

to Options and check off "Suppress dev warnings." Press configure again. Now there should not be any red text in the lower field. If this is true, continue to press the Generate button. Boot up Visual Studio. Browse to the opencv\build directory and open up opencv.sln in Visual Studio. Wait until Visual Studio has finished processing the initial startup, indicated by saying "Ready" in the bottom left. Next, build the Release and Debug binaries. In Visual Studio 2010, do this by selecting "Release" in the leftmost drop down menu in the top toolbar and press F7. When this completes, repeat the same thing for the Debug selection in the same drop down menu. This may take a while. Each build will be finished when the drop down menu becomes selectable again.

OPENCV-BASED IMPLEMENTATION OF FACE RECOGNITION

OpenCV has built-in implementations for the three main face recognition processes (detection, projection and search). These processes are accomplished sequentially in the order they were presented in this chapter. The specific APIs and algorithms which contribute to Open CV's model of face recognition will be explained in a more code-level scale in the following sections after a brief overview of how Open CV's implementations relate to the general face recognition processes.

OpenCV face detection uses algorithms derived from the Viola-Jones method of face detection and also the machine learning "boosting" system AdaBoost for choosing classifiers used in detection. This set-up requires some input data so that the boosting system can "train" to recognize the probabilistically most useful classifiers, which in turn allows for classifier usage to be effectively cascaded, increasing detection efficiency. This training is done by feeding OpenCV a set of database face images. These images must first be histogram equalized and equally sized before they are loaded into OpenCV.

The rest of the face detection process is essentially identical to the general processes described earlier. OpenCV will apply the feature detection algorithm in a cascade determined by the training algorithm, sorting out faces from non-faces in the input images. The Viola-Jones rectangular features are slightly different in the OpenCV implementation when compared to the general implementation described previously. First, the three types of features are 2-rectangle features, 3-rectangle features, and center-surround features (a rectangle within a rectangle), plus the ability to identify these features diagonally, rather than the 2-, 3-, and 4-rectangle vertical and horizontal features. Furthermore, particularly in the code of OpenCV, these features are referred to as "Haar-like" features or "Haar classifiers" due to their similarity to the mathematics term "Haar wavelet."

Face Detection Algorithm Implementation

OpenCV provides two main classes for object detection: cv::gpu::HOGDescriptor, where HOG stands for Histogram of Gradients and cv::gpu::CascadeClassifier_GPU. Nevertheless, the former one doesn't provide pre-trained module for face features and is thus mainly used in body detection. What we use is the latter one cv::gpu::CascadeClassifier_GPU, which is derived from its CPU version cv::CascadeClassifier. Below are some class APIs we may use.

```
1. gpu::CascadeClassifier_GPU::CascadeClassifier_GPU
Class constructor. Both haar classifier and NVIDIA's nvbin are supported.
2. gpu::CascadeClassifier_GPU::empty
Return a Boolean value to check if the classifier is successfully loaded.
3. gpu::CascadeClassifier_GPU::load
Destroy the old loaded classifier and load a new classifier.
4. gpu::CascadeClassifier_GPU::release
Destroy the current loaded classifier.
5. gpu::CascadeClassifier_GPU:: detectMultiScale
```

This is the core function of the class. The function would return the number of detected objects, and those detected objects are returned as a list of cv::rectangles.

This class is used for detection and can only be used with an existing pre-trained set. OpenCV provides several pre-trained feature sets include eyes, faces and so on. OpenCV also provides a separate class CvCascadeClassifier for classifier training. This class has only one public API:

```
CvCascadeClassifier::train (const std::string _cascadeDirName,
const std::string _posFilename,
const std::string _negFilename,
int _numPos, int _numNeg,
int _precalcValBufSize,
int _precalcIdxBufSize,
int _numStages,
const CvCascadeParams& _cascadeParams,
const CvFeatureParams& _featureParams,
const CvCascadeBoostParams& _stageParams,
bool baseFormatSave = false ;
```

The function needs two types of samples sets: positive and negative, where positive samples includes the objects while negative samples doesn't. An executable program opencv_createsamples can be used to prepare the samples. After the function finished, the trained cascade would be saved in an .xml file.

Eigenvector Projection Algorithm Implementation

In OpenCV, face recognition is performed by a synthetical class cv::FaceRecognizer. cv::FaceRecognizer contains a series of virtual member functions that are implemented by different algorithms. What we are going to use is one of its subclass cv::Eigenfaces corresponding to the Eigenface algorithm.

Considering a set of sample vectors, $S=\{S_1, S_2, \ldots, S_n\}$

1. Firstly, calculate the mean face vector, $\mu = \frac{1}{n}\sum S_i$
2. Let M be the set of mean-subtracted sample vectors. Using the mean face vector to compute Covariance Matrix $\Gamma=MM^T$
3. Covariance Matrix gives the eigenvectors v_i and λ_t as

$$\Gamma v_i = MM^T v_i = \lambda_i$$

OpenCV doesn't provide GPU-accelerated Eigenface algorithm, thus we make some modification of the source code by adding a GPU version projection function. In that way, our cv::Eigenfaces will have the following core member functions.

1. `Eigenfaces::train`

Trains the face recognizer with a vector of images and corresponding labels in C++ STL format. This forms the matrix of basis vectors used in the conversion of image data to Eigenspace coordinates (the projection).

2. `Eigenfaces::update`

Update the face recognizer with an additional vector of images and corresponding labels.

3. `Eigenfaces::search`

Take an input image and return the prediction label as well as the distance. Return -1 and DBL_MAX if no matching found.

4. `Eigenfaces:: project_GPU`

Applying a new added function subspaceProject_GPU to compute the projection in PCA subspace. In the function, we use gpu::gemm instead of gemm to leverage GPU acceleration.

5. `Eigenfaces::save`

Save the current Eigenface model for later use.

6. `Eigenfaces::load`

Load a saved Eigenface model instead of constructing the database from scratch.

Database Search Algorithm Implementation

After the projection is calculated, the Euclidean distance between the test face projection and all database projections are calculated. The nearest point in the Eigenspace is termed the *prediction*, and whether this distance is below a configurable threshold determines its validity. Euclidean distance is simply the line segment between points p and q, for an n-dimensional Eigenspace,

$$D = \sqrt{(p_0 - q_0)^2 + (p_1 - q_1)^2 + \cdots + (p_n - q_n)^2}$$

Database search algorithm is implemented by the API Eigenfaces::search in which it uses cv::norm to calculate the Euclidean distance. Eigenfaces::search is a recursive procedure for traversing the samples and return the minimum distance as well as the corresponding *label*, or the stored data correlating to the image whose projection was nearest to the projection of the test face. This implementation simply uses a string containing the name of the individual, although it would be possible to return data structures containing more detailed information as well. If all distances are larger than threshold, the function returns -1 and DBL_MAX. Note that it is not necessary to calculate the square root of the sum of differences squared in order to find the nearest neighbor. In the spirit of optimization, reducing the number of square root operations by the number of database images for *each frame* might become noticeable for large databases.

EXPERIMENTAL EVALUATION

Figure 5 shows the experimental result of Face Detection on different platforms over several sample sizes. Eleven source frame samples were used containing one to eleven faces, respectively. We use three platforms, a purely CPU (i5 3317U), an entry-level mobile GPU (GT 630M) as well as a powerful desktop GPU (GTX480 SLI). Detection via the GPU shows a remarkable performance increase over pure CPU implementation (Kirk & Hwu, 2010). OpenCV libraries effectively leverage the parallel processing capability of the GPU in order to perform its cascade evaluations and image parsing. Numerous tests over a range of devices showed that even a commercial grade NVIDIA GPU can perform detection of as many as one hundred faces in a single frame, within tens of milliseconds. The number of faces detected per frame, in fact, has a measurable, although negligible effect on the frame-detection rate when using a GPU. The largest impacting factor on the computation rate of each frame would be the pixel density.

Figure 5. Processing time for Face Detection for different processors over several image samples that contain different number of faces.

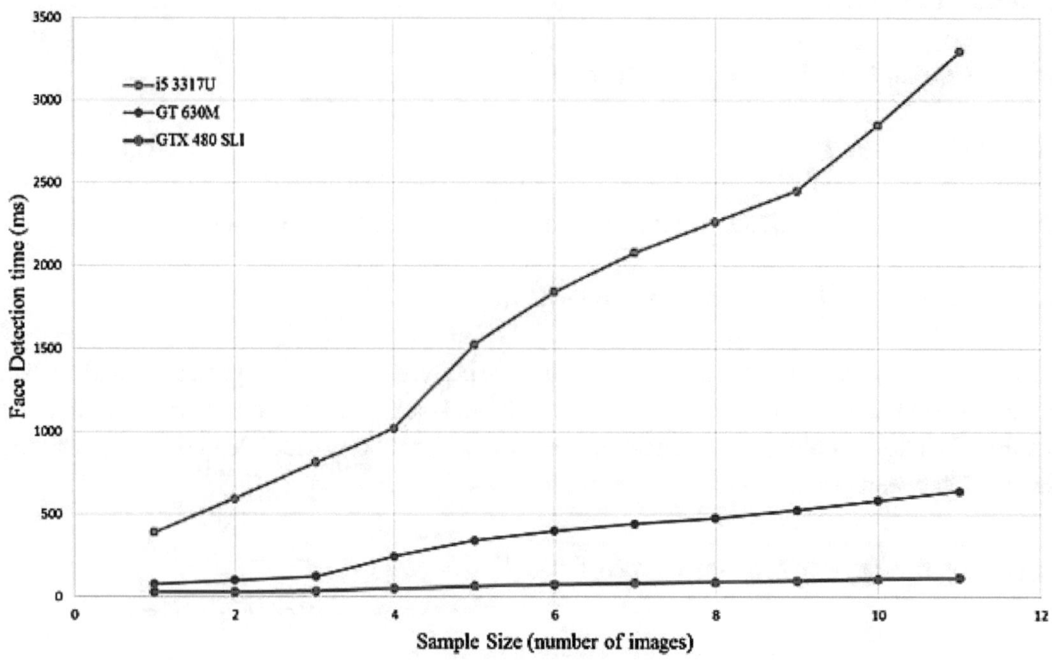

Applications requiring real-time performance ought to consider the expected aspects and scaling of the images being presented to the algorithm and adjust system resolutions accordingly, since detected frames are resized to accommodate the operations of linear algebra in the projection method. For example, applications involving single-object frame detection, such as biometric security, will expect the input data to consist of a detectable object nearly filling the frame. This would not require a high frame resolution upon implementation. Whereas applications involving multiple-object frames such as street-view security would have to operate at higher resolutions to process smaller areas of the frame in order to generate results with an acceptable degree of accuracy. These tradeoffs are entirely testable, and fairly easy to alter in the source code.

Once an indexed list of face-containing rectangle boundaries are generated by the detection process, each sub-image defined by its rectangle is pre-processed to facilitate its conversion to a point in the higher dimensional Eigenspace. The sub-image (or 'test face') is resized to a standard pixel height H and width W as defined in the training and database generation phase. This is to ensure that the mathematical operations carried out during the projection are valid. The test face, while captured as a color image, is converted to grayscale and histogram equalization is applied in order to accentuate differentiable features. At this point, the two-dimensional $H \times W$ Mat structure of the image is reformed as a $1 \times HW$ linear array, preserving the pixel count, but referencing them sequentially as a scan of the test face image: from top-left to bottom-right.

Within the database file residing in Host memory, there are two structures called upon for operations on every test face. The Mean image is a reformed $1 \times HW$ linear array whose entries are corresponding averages of each image used to train the database. That is, the nth pixel in the Mean is the sum of the nth pixel in every training image, divided by the number of training images used. This structure is persistent, either in a file on disk, or maintained in local memory during application runtime. Its values do not change unless the collection of training images changes and a new database compilation occurs. This Mean image is subtracted from the test face. The Eigenvectors' data structure is a two-dimensional $HW \times m$ Mat structure whose columns consist of the linearized Eigenfaces generated by database training. There are exactly HW rows, since there are HW pixels in each training image. There are exactly m columns, where m is the selected dimensionality of the Eigenspace into which faces are projected for comparison.

GPU implementation of projection requires the Mean-adjusted test face array and the Eigenvectors Mat structures to be uploaded to Device (GPU) memory before executing the core operation of projection: matrix multiplication. This operation is handled by gpu::gemm, a member function of the NVIDIA CUDA library CUBLAS. Recall that the eigenvector consists of (HWD) elements, each consisting of 4 Bytes when using single precision floating point. A standard 640×480 image size with a 29-dimensional Eigenspace would result in an Eigenvector sized approximately 35.6MB. 200GB/s memory transfer speed would ideally transfer this particular Eigenvector between Host and Device in 0.18ms, which for real-time applications may not be an acceptable memory transfer overhead. Increasing resolution images and Eigenspace dimensionalities would obviously have a deleterious effect on that overhead, and this becomes an application-dependent concern. One note to developers; if this overhead becomes an issue, it is always possible to upload the Eigenvector structure to Device (GPU) memory at the initiation of the application and store it there permanently during runtime, effectively removing its contribution to memory overhead.

Aside from the issue of memory overhead, there is the issue of computation. The test face projection is finally calculated as the product of the Mean-adjusted test face array and the Eigenvector matrix, as illustrated in Fig. 6. GEMM forces the GPU kernel to undergo a series of multiply-accumulate operations

Figure 6. Core projection operation: the dot-product of mean-adjusted test face and eigenvector matrix, where n is the per-image pixel density and m is the Eigenspace dimensionality.

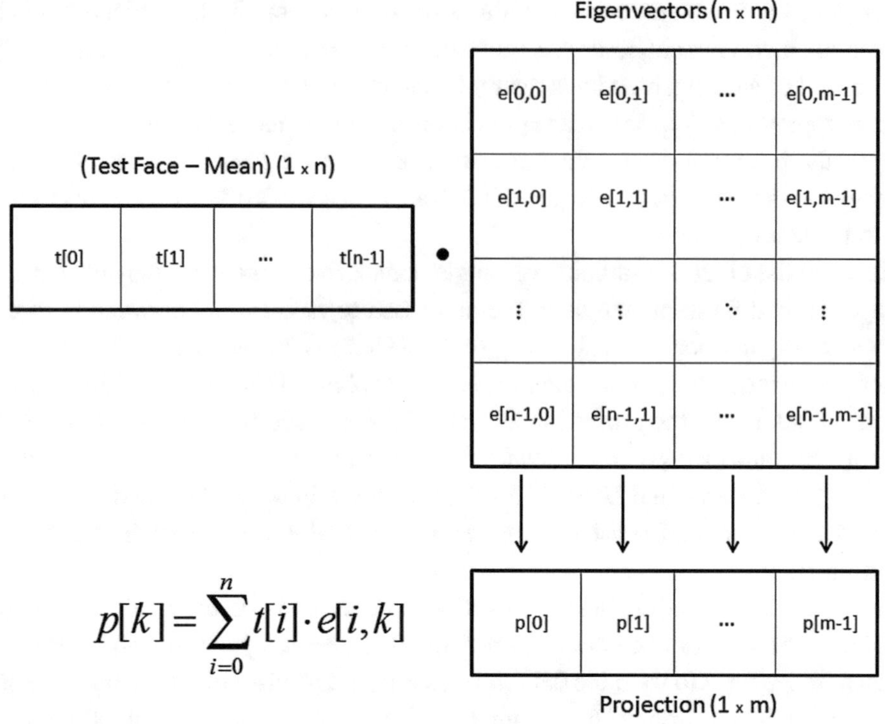

(along with indexing and other memory access operations). OpenCV methods streamline this process and the use of CUBLAS allows the problem to be parallelized in the GPU leading to dramatic acceleration. Parallelization enables all n elements of the projection p_k to be computed concurrently:

$$p_k = \sum_{i=0}^{n} t_i e_{i,k}$$

Hierarchal granularity could permit the concurrent processing of multiple test faces as well, while pipelining the resultant projections back to host memory for Search operations. Mathematically, the most significant impacting factors of the process time are the image pixel density, Eigenspace dimensionality, the source-defined floating-point precision, the core clock speed of the GPU and the manner in which the GEMM kernel is configured to parallelize the process. Our application using gpu::gemm relied on the compiler to make its own decisions about configuring the CUDA device assembly code, thus the register usage and ALU pipelining was completely out of our scope. This did lead to some unexpected results, such as slower GEMM times on theoretically superior devices. Optimizations will most certainly require a greater level of developer control over the lower level workings of the GPU kernel and the manner in which projection computations are to be carried out.

Once there is a 1×*m* projection array, it must be transferred back to Host memory where it can be compared to the database. Note how much smaller the projection is than the test face. Using our previous example, a 640×480 image of size 1.2MB versus a 1×29 projection of size 116 Bytes implies an approximate 10593:1 data ratio, or 99.99% data reduction. This substantiates the earlier claim that the Eigenfaces method requires far less information to represent uniquely identifiable objects.

CONCLUSION AND FUTURE WORK

This chapter has presented the most significant aspects of a modern implementation of a Face recognition application. First, the theoretical aspects of Face recognition are introduced by describing the three-step implementation of the Face recognition. These steps are Face Detection (FD), Projection (P), and Database Search (S). Each of these steps is described in detail and the underlying Principal Component Analysis (PCA) methodology is elaborated on.

To provide a tutorial for installing and implementing Face Recognition, detailed steps are documented which include the installation of the Open Source Computer Vision library (Open CV) and Nvidia CUDA GPU software components. Additionally, a detailed documentation is provided about which functions in the Open CV library are responsible for which one of the functions in the FD, P, and S steps. Experimental results are provided on certain CPU and GPU architectures to allow the readers to compare their results against our experimental results.

ACKNOWLEDGMENT

This work was supported in part by the National Science Foundation grant CNS-1239423 and a gift from Nvidia Corporation.

REFERENCES

Bradski, G., & Kaehler, A. (2008). *Learning OpenCV: Computer vision with the OpenCV library*. O'Reilly Media, Inc.

Crow, F. C. (1984). Summed-area tables for texture mapping. *Computer Graphics*, *18*(3), 207–212. doi:10.1145/964965.808600

Freund, Y., Schapire, R., & Abe, N. (1999). A short introduction to boosting. *Journal-Japanese Society for Artificial Intelligence, 14*(771-780), 1612.

Goldstein, A. J., Harmon, L. D., & Lesk, A. B. (1971). Identification of human faces. *Proceedings of the IEEE, 59*(5), 748–760. doi:10.1109/PROC.1971.8254

Kim, K. I., Jung, K., & Kim, H. J. (2002). Face recognition using kernel principal component analysis. *Signal Processing Letters, IEEE, 9*(2), 40–42. doi:10.1109/97.991133

Kirk, D. B., & Hwu, W. M. W. (2010). *Programming Massively Parallel Processors. Hands-on Approach*. Burlington, MA, USA: Morgan Kaufmann Publishers.

Nvidia, CUBLAS. (n.d.). Retrieved August 18, 2014, from https://developer.nvidia.com/cublas

Nvidia, CUFFT. (n.d.). Retrieved August 18, 2014, from https://developer.nvidia.com/cufft

Open, CV-WEB. (n.d.). *Open CV (Open Source Computer Vision)*. Retrieved August 18, 2014, from http://opencv.org/

Sirovich, L., & Kirby, M. (1987). Low-dimensional procedure for the characterization of human faces. *JOSA A*, *4*(3), 519–524. doi:10.1364/JOSAA.4.000519 PMID:3572578

Soyata, T., Muraleedharan, R., Funai, C., Kwon, M., & Heinzelman, W. (2012, July). Cloud-Vision: Real-time face recognition using a mobile-cloudlet-cloud acceleration architecture. In *Computers and Communications (ISCC), 2012 IEEE Symposium on* (pp. 59-66). IEEE.

Viola, P., & Jones, M. (2001). Rapid object detection using a boosted cascade of simple features. In *Computer Vision and Pattern Recognition, 2001. CVPR 2001. Proceedings of the 2001 IEEE Computer Society Conference on* (*Vol. 1*, pp. 511-518). IEEE. doi:10.1109/CVPR.2001.990517

Yang, M. H., Kriegman, D., & Ahuja, N. (2002). Detecting faces in images: A survey. *IEEE Transactions on Pattern Analysis and Machine Intelligence*, *24*(1), 34–58.

KEY TERMS AND DEFINITIONS

Database Search (S): The final phase of the face recognition algorithm, in which the re-represented face is compared against the database elements' Eigenface values by calculating their Euclidean distances. The distances that are below a specified threshold are candidates for recognized faces.

Eigenface: Used as the backbone of the Face recognition algorithm. For a given set of database images, a set of Eigenfaces are initially calculated, which simply change the coordinate space. Once this step is performed, every image in the database is re-represented in terms of this new coordinate space (e.g., in terms of Eigenfaces).

Face Detection (FR): The first phase of the Face recognition algorithm. In the FR phase, a face (or multiple faces) are cropped from the image that they are in. This "detected" face is then fed into the rest of the algorithm.

Face Recognition: The process of mapping a newly-captured face to one of the faces in a given database. For example, if a database has 500 images, F_1... F_{500}, for a given face F, the Face Recognition algorithm can map it to one of these 500 faces, i.e., recognize it. Alternatively, the algorithm might simply report that, this image is not in the database, or not even a human face.

NVidia CUDA (Computer-Unified Device Architecture): Nvidia's programming language and the hardware architecture. This language was introduced a decade ago to allow programmability for GPUs, with the intent to turn GPUs into general purpose scientific computation devices.

Principal Component Analysis (PCA): A technique for reducing the dimensionality of multi-dimensional data. For example, a 500 image database can be re-represented in terms of 29 Eigenfaces as described in the chapter. This allows a substantial reduction in the database size, while minimally reducing the accuracy of the new representation.

Projection (P): Second phase of the Face recognition algorithm, in which the detected face is re-represented in terms of the Eigenfaces.

Chapter 12
Reach to Mobile Platforms and Availability:
A Planning Tutorial

Rex A Buddenberg
Naval Postgraduate School, USA

ABSTRACT

This chapter is practical system planning tutorial for internetworks that include radio-WANs. Author is retired USCG officer with both operational and program planning experience. In second career, author taught 'plowshares into swords internetworking' at the graduate level. The coaching herein reflects operational, planning, and academic experiences. Considering mobile communications requires adjusting some assumptions and working knowledge from a wholly wired internetwork. The advent of radio – the necessary means to mobile – entails changes in topology, capacity and nature of the media (shared). Further, the extension of the internetwork to mobile usually means rather overt embracing of mission critical applications.

INTRODUCTION

It was a dark, stormy and windy night. The weather service had forecast the 100 knot windstorm correctly and the fishing fleet had all scampered for port and were getting safely tied up. Except for one trawler, with a crew of three, who, as it turned out, pushed luck about an hour too far. As the wind built the Coast Guard established a communications watch, which meant radioing the fishing boat crew every half hour. Further, as the storm built, most of the crews at the lifeboat stations and air station had returned to duty, whether expressly called or not.

As the storm built further, trees started falling and electrical power went out for large swathes of the Oregon coast. The fishing boat was making maddeningly slow progress toward Cape Arago and safety in its lee.

DOI: 10.4018/978-1-4666-8662-5.ch012

As the windstorm peaked, the fishing boat skipper called the Coast Guard and said that he could make no further progress into the wind and had turned around. Heading downwind meant out to sea and in the Pacific that means a really long ways to the next landfall. This electrified the Coast Guard: Coos Bay lifeboat station launched two motor lifeboats and North Bend Air Station launched a helicopter.

The search ended up being fruitless – the fishing vessel was never seen or heard from again. The helicopter only found the two motor lifeboats on scene. After a first search, hampered by darkness and the storm, we decided to recall forces and prepare for a thorough first-light search which was about five hours hence.

On the way back to the air station, the helicopter's engine failed and the pilot auto-rotated into the Pacific Ocean just offshore. The three-man crew exited the aircraft safely but the copilot drowned. The other two crew were washed up on the beach shortly before sunrise.

When the helicopter's engine failed, the pilot radioed a Mayday. Ten miles away, in the operations center (where the author was standing), we did not hear it. The communications system had failed.

Incident Evaluation

As this author unraveled the communications system problems, three stages of events showed.

The third, but immediate observation was that the existing equipment had been maintained properly. Indeed, the immediate failure cause was grid power failure and once electrical power returned, the communications system returned.

The second stage was that the system was inadequately provisioned with backups, especially backup power but also alternate routes. The principles of high availability engineering had not been observed.

But the engineers who deployed the system are not really to blame: the program sponsor had never specified a required level of availability. The first or root problem: the system was never acknowledged as mission critical. The requirements statement simply had no stated availability requirement.

Attending funerals is a graphic and convincing way to learn availability lessons but it's not the recommended approach. This chapter turns the problem around and addresses it in the above logical, albeit not chronological, order.

IMPACTS OF REACH TO MOBILE PLATFORMS

Considering mobile communications requires adjusting some assumptions and working knowledge from a wholly wired internetwork. The advent of radio – the necessary means to mobile – entails changes in topology, capacity and nature of the media (shared). Further, the extension of the internetwork to mobile usually means rather overt embracing of mission critical applications.

- **Topology**. The 'traditional' internet is made up of backbone wide area networks (hereafter terrestrial-WAN) and local area networks (LAN. Both wired and wireless LAN fall in this category). The terrestrial-WAN is largely made up of point-to-point cabling (predominately fiber optic) and can be described as interconnecting a fabric of routers. There are no end systems in this fabric – it's all router-to-router interconnect. The connectionless, stateless nature of Internet Protocol affords this terrestrial-WAN a great deal of modularity – new links can be added transparently and capacity mismatches from one hop to the next are not important to route-ability and hence interoperability. The routing protocols and supporting 'hello' messages find these new links and add them to the routing table. All of this is transparent to the user and allows the terrestrial WAN to grow in capacity and number of links.

Figure 1. Radio Network as LAN at fringe of Internet

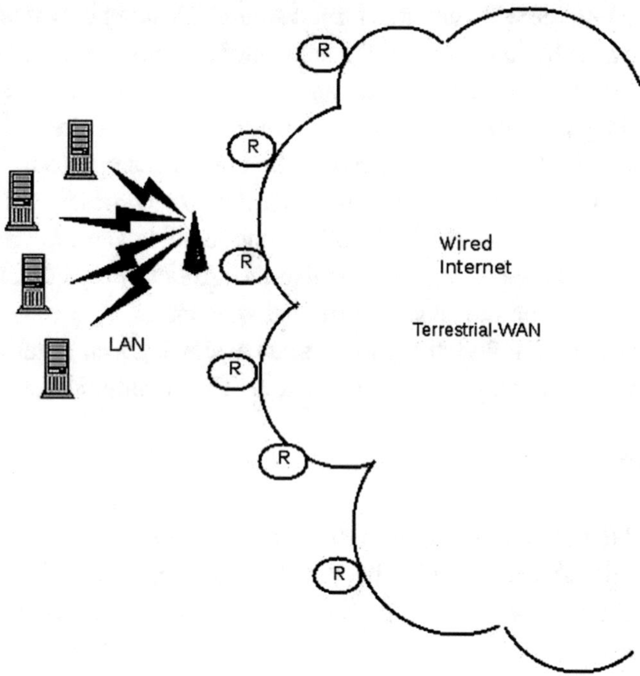

As depicted in Figure 1, LANs are the reach from the last router to end systems and are the part of the infrastructure visible to the user. LANs, of course, come in wired and wireless variations.

This classical topology has been 'stretched' with the advent of WiFi (Brittanica-WiFi). But WiFi remains a LAN technology. WiFi is effective for the LAN task: reach from last router to end system. Topologically, the cellular telephone system is similar – the technology reaching from the tower to the user fits the LAN definition: reach to end system.

But consider the case of a mobile platform such as an ambulance, fire truck, ship, or airplane, and in the foreseeable future the family sedan, where there are many end users in the platform, not just one. An 'instrumented ambulance' provides an excellent representative use case. There may be several end systems attached to a casualty in the ambulance (e.g. monitoring vital signs), an end system for the emergency medical technician wishing to talk with a doctor at the emergency room, a radio-navigation receiver gaining and relaying the vehicle's position, etc. The list can be long and with the internet, it can be open-ended. New applications can be incrementally added as can new instruments (end systems). The topology observation here is that the LAN is within the mobile platform.

The topology difference is that we now need a radio-WAN to interconnect the router in the vehicle and a point on the terrestrial-WAN. See Figure 2. The radio-WAN needs to get the router-router interconnect problem right. (The topology significance does not change if there happen to be multiple routers inside the radio-WAN cloud).

Both WiFi and older (i.e. '3G' and older) cell phone radio technologies can be pressed into this role. But neither will scale well; for example, multiple ambulances. Older cell phone technologies, despite the fact that they use radio, are point-to-point so each mobile platform-to-terrestrial-WAN connection requires a separate channel. And WiFi, while well-suited to the LAN role, is unstable in the radio-WAN role because of its contention-oriented Media Access Controller (MAC). Thus we need the radio-WAN and we need to consider its special constraints, design considerations and characteristics.

Figure 2. Radio-WAN interior of internetwork

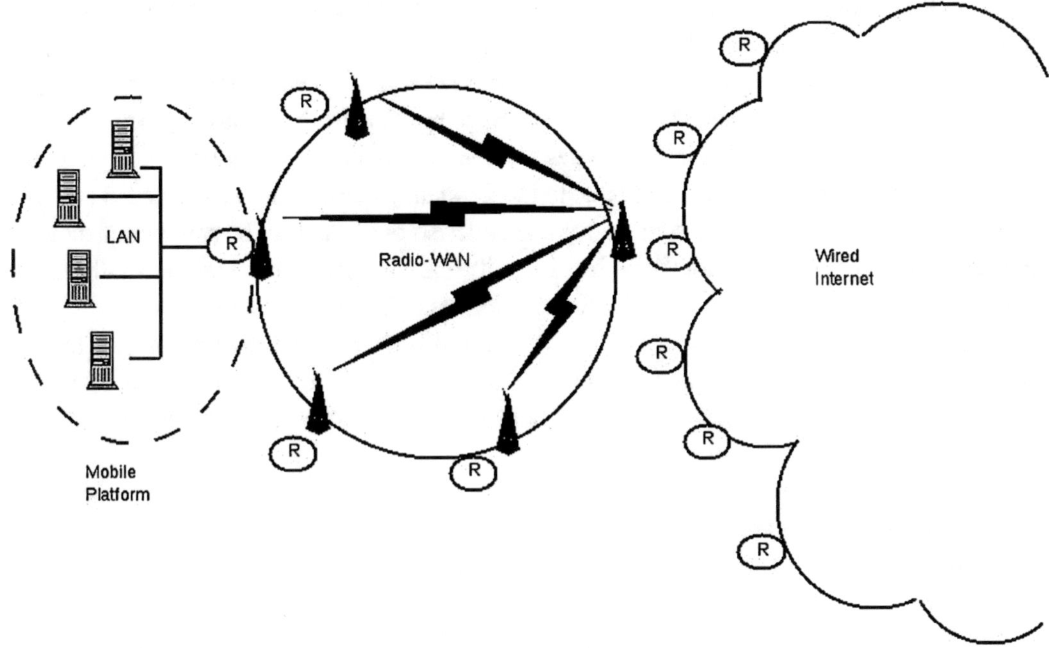

- **Shared Media:** Most of the internet 'plumbing', and almost all of it in the terrestrial-WAN backbone, is point-to-point. But radio is shared. This fact has one important constraint and enables one important concept. The constraint of shared media, is that you must have some way to share it. If every node offering traffic simply shouts it out, the system will jam itself and fail. In naturally point-to-point technologies (like fiber optic) the WAN protocols do not contain a media access protocol (MAC) at all because there are only two parties on the line. But with the radio 'party line' a means for sharing is necessary. Two protocol categories have evolved over the past century (long predating the internet): contention and contention-free. Both have uses – at the fringe of the internet, Figure 1, both are usable – but in the radio-WAN, contention-free is the appropriate choice.

Contention-free protocols (known in pre-internet radio as 'directed network') consist of a net controller (known as the base station or BS in the standards) that controls the network by allocating time slices for each of the subscriber stations (SS) to use. The basic rule is transmit in your time slice but not anyone else's. This means that the BS needs to 'hear' each SS but there is no requirement that the SS's be able to hear each other. A contention-free protocol will not jam – it is stable under overload. This stability under load is critical (as will become obvious when we discuss capacity, below).

There are two secondary benefits of contention-free protocols. One is bandwidth efficiency – most of the communications capacity is used for passing data, not fighting frames onto the network segment. The other major secondary benefit is susceptibility to control. This includes both fault management and configuration management. It is feasible to 'favor' some SS over others, but the basic benefit here is near-determinism – each SS that is recognized in a network segment will get a chance to transmit something every frame.

State of the Technology: During the 1990s, these discussions were largely academic. But starting around 2002, multivendor protocols based on open standards started to appear. The best known of these protocols are IEEE 802.16 (WiMAX) and TIA LTE ('4G').

Frequency Reuse: Many radio systems economize their use of scarce spectrum by building many smaller-footprint spots rather than a single high-site one. Existing Land Mobile Radio systems tend to fall in the second category – a small number of sites serves an entire city or county. But a larger number of smaller sites gets greater total capacity due to the frequency reuse – Cell A and its BS and SSs may be well out of range of Cell F and its associated nodes so both can use the same frequency without interfering. Additionally, more of the high availability and capacity burden is shifted to the terrestrial-WAN by increasing the number of radio base stations and decreasing their radius.

Multicast: The other aspect of the shared media is that multicast has a much larger payoff than it does in an all-wired internet. Definition: multicast is delivery of data to more than one destination for the price of a single transit over the media. There are two reasons worth considering: nature of the data and conservation of (radio-WAN) capacity.

Nature of the Data: Using the instrumented ambulance example use case shows that some of the data from end systems in the ambulance needs to go more than one place. For example, both the doctor in the emergency room and the (911) dispatcher would want to know the ambulance's position. In general, emergency services as a whole has a much higher incidence of data that is multicast in nature than we are used to in the internet to date. Multicast data becomes even more pronounced as applications like those known as Common Operational Picture enter the emergency services world (they've been around in the military since WWII). And as 'self driving' features appear in automobiles, the incidence of multicast data increases here too – the position of my car needs to be transmitted to several other cars in order to keep them from colliding.

Capacity Conservation: As illustrated in next section below, the radio-WAN is very capacity-limited compared to the terrestrial-WAN. Multicast applications that conserve capacity in an over-provisioned internet just don't sound attractive. So while the protocols (multicast IP at the center) for multicast exist and they are implemented in most routers, the industry uptake has been poor simply because there hasn't been much payoff. Few applications use multicast.

- **Capacity:** Both terrestrial-WANs and wired LANs can be provisioned at 10s of gigabits/second of capacity. Indeed, the internet has simply been ignoring Quality of Service issues because it can routinely overprovision by adding more fiber, upgrading the capacity of existing fiber, add more LANs, etc. If there is no congestion, no QoS control mechanism can possibly improve the situation. But the radio-WAN is limited in capacity.

Radio technology of any stripe uses spectrum to communicate. And there is only so much of it. Furthermore, because the radio medium is shared, the spectrum must be pro-rated across all the users of a channel. Some practical numbers should help reader perspective.

- **Narrowband:** Voice radio channels have historically been allocated in slices ranging up to 25KHz is width. Wired telephone (Plain Old Telephone Service (POTS) or POTS in the lingo) allocates 3KHz of bandwidth which allows transmission of human voice from 0-3000 Hz. If this voice is digitized and then compressed, it requires around 2Kbits/sec (with wide variances). If you hook a modem up to a POTS telephone line, you can usually get somewhere between 10 and 30kbits/sec, point-to-point.

- **Broadband:** Uses time slicing rather than frequency division multiplexing to share the medium. So broadband allocations are broader: in the nature of 6MHz (M = mega = million while K = kilo = thousand). In practical terms you will get Mbits of data per subscriber across a radio-WAN. What is important is not whether this is one or two Mbits but the fact that this is four orders of magnitude less than what is available every day in the terrestrial-WAN and the in-platform LANs. Four orders of magnitude may not immediately sound like a lot, but consider it this way: you can get 10,000 radio-WANs worth of capacity through a single terrestrial-WAN link.

In a topology where the wireless LAN is at the fringe of the internet all the reuse tricks (e.g. add more hotspots) are available to us. Typically a single end system is unlikely to use the entire capacity of a network segment. But in the Figure 1 topology, the multitude of end systems on the LAN side of a vehicle's router may very well saturate the capacity of the radio-WAN.

Understanding this capacity limitation does not in any way invalidate internet technology and an extend-the-internet approach. The same constraints would exist with some other technological approach. But the constraints should color both infrastructure design decisions and application development decisions – it makes things a bit different than what we've become used to.

AVAILABILITY

When we extend the internet to mobile platforms, we can expect the incidence of mission critical applications that run over it to increase. Indeed, this is a natural evolution: the tolerance for downtime in the internet tends to decrease over time as its use becomes more important and ubiquitous. The principles outlined below are equally applicable to all parts of the internet, indeed to any system. But internet reach to mobile platforms usually implies some high-availability requirements that need to be faced directly.

Definition of Availability (Ao): Also denoted as Ao for *operational availability* (Wikipedia-Ao) the Availability is defined as the up-time divided by the total-time:

Ao = uptime / total time.

Sin #1: The most important shortcoming in communications acquisition programs is that they fail to state the required availability. At all. This guarantees a single-threaded, low-bidder result that will fail when you need it worst. In a single-threaded system components lack backups so equipment failure equals system failure. In author's experience if the availability requirement is stated, it's usually right, or close enough.

The above equation is simply the expression of the definition; it needs some help to be practically useful. Consider that total time = up time + down time. Or up-time = total-time – down-time. This allows us to substitute for a value that have operational meaning:

Ao = (total-time – down-time) / total-time

By considering how much downtime you can tolerate, you can easily calculate the Ao value required.

Workshop: Usually total time is measured in a calendar quarter or year (Coast Guard radio-navigation systems used calendar quarter but it won't really matter much). So start with 130,000 minutes in a quarter. If you can tolerate a downtime of a half day, then you will get about two nines (0.995). If your tolerance for down time is in minutes rather than hours, you will get four to five nines (0.9997). How much down time can you stand? It is not proper to look at what the vendor advertises – spec-sheet requirements-writing is wrong. Look at your needs.

Effect: Somewhere between Ao = two nines and Ao = four nines, your communications system needs cross a threshold where you must acquire a multiple-threaded system – nobody can repair equipment that fast (the reliability engineering texts refer to this as a 'repairable system'). In a multiply-threaded system, component failure is decoupled from system failure. In addition to increasing the Ao numbers, repairs can be effected on the failed equipment without impairing present operations. So this exercise is critical to capitalization costing – dual threading will double your equipment costs. In author's experience, availability is the easiest requirement to quantify and the easiest to defend in a budget – do it first.

Once we have determined the operational Ao requirement, we can proceed to the systems engineering aspects – how we go about obtaining the Ao requirement needed. There are three principles of high availability engineering; we need only apply them:

1. **Elimination of Single Points of Failure:** This is a slightly more elegant way of saying what most readers will have a gut feel for: add redundancy. When applying this principle to communications systems, this usually boils down to redundant communications paths (alternate routes) and backup power. These redundancies are technologically agnostic – you'd need to have them regardless of the technology choices you make. And these requirements drive your capitalization costs.

Arithmetic tutorial. Availability of a component is an instantaneous probability. So Ao of 0.999 for, say, a router, means that it will be available for all except 0.001 instants. Two routers mounted in parallel have a probability of down time of 0.001*0.001 or 0.000001. This means that the pair of routers have a collective availability of 1 – 0.000001 or Ao = 0.999999. This arithmetic depends of the assumption of independence of mode of failure – whatever causes one component to fail will not also cause the second to also fail. And system failure only occurs when both routers are down.

The common illustration of common-cause failures is in alternate routes – if they both travel through the same conduit then a single backhoe strike can break both of them. You have not eliminated the single points of failure until the alternate routes take diverse paths. In a reach-to-mobile-platforms environment, the need for extensive, distributed coverage tends to make this problem easier – both the terrestrial-WAN segment routes and the interconnecting routers will tend to be diverse anyway. The critical item in such situations is grid electrical power which tends to remain quite centralized.

The qualitative observation here is that as soon as you require dual-threaded infrastructure for Ao reasons, you decouple component failure from system failure. So a specified availability of three or four nines will often be 'good enough'. If it's not, through experience (and fault maintenance logs, see below), you can add more threads later. The side effect to observe here is that meeting the Ao requirements often tends to mean over-provisioning the system – you have more capacity than is needed. This will be true in the terrestrial-WAN (and LAN) portions of the internetwork but not in the radio-WAN.

2. **Reliable Crossover:** This principle is best illustrated by the inverse – a backup comms channel is useless unless you can get to it. The 'gotcha' in redundant systems is that the crossover switch itself becomes a single point of failure. Here internet technology shines: the connectionless, stateless nature of Internet Protocol solves the problem by protocol design. Said in a slightly earthier way, routers do reliable crossover all day, every day.

Observance of this principle shows up a couple of 'don'ts'. Routing does solve the reliable crossover problem. But layer 2 bridging does not – the spanning tree algorithm identifies alternate routes and then refuses to use them to avoid frame ringing. Similarly layer 7 gateways do not demonstrate reliable crossover either; these should only be used for integration of necessary legacy (such as legacy narrow-band voice radio, called Land Mobile Radio in the emergency services world. This solution is properly known as a Voice over IP Layer 7 gateway (Cisco-VOIP)).

3. **Prompt Notification of Failures on Occurrence:** If the first two principles are observed, then the user may never see a failure (exactly what we need). But somebody does need to find failed equipment in order to direct maintenance. For this purpose, all equipment should be equipped with Simple Network Management Protocol (SNMP) agents. The standards language is 'fault management' and fault management is sufficient reason.

SNMP does many useful things beyond fault management. The standards language refers to capacity, accounting, performance and security management as well. But for our purposes these are secondary benefits – fault management is head/shoulders more important.

Comprehensive. Failure notification applies to more than just the internetwork infrastructure. In one direction it applies to end systems – the handset in the EMT's hands and the applications embedded therein should have management agents and be within the management domain. In another direction fault management applies to equipment like air conditioners in the tower huts of a radio system – not normally considered part of the internetwork but critical to its continuing operation.

Ownership of various parts of the infrastructure should be irrelevant to fault management. It's highly likely that applications and the end systems they are installed in will be owned by a different entity than, say, the wired internet foundation. What is important is that one management entity have fault visibility throughout the system. This might be obtained by a contractual agreement to allow a 'look over the shoulder' of an ISPs management database. Early triage of faults is critical to fast restoration.

Compensation: Investment in high availability sounds like a tall order, and it's not trivial. But by the time you have a fully redundant, fault monitored system you can usually relax the maintenance philosophy. Many systems which need high availability but were not engineered as such to start with try to increase availability by implementing 24-hour, on-call maintenance. This ad hoc approach is expensive (whether you use it or not). If you have observed the principles above, you can often relax the maintenance to next-working-day which represents a significant savings.

SECURITY: AUTHENTICITY AND CONFIDENTIALITY

The security concerns in information systems over the internet have existed as long as the internet has. But security over radio has existed for the century that radio existed. There are many examples of insecurities with technologies such as WiFi and cellular telephone – they make the existing internet security problems more acute. Unfortunately the reactions to these insecurities have tended to fall into two categories:

- The security problems are simply ignored at planning time. Then we try to apply duct tape.
- Non-sequiturs. The remedies applied (i.e. the duct tape above) are loosely related to the problem if at all.

This time, before we analyze requirements, it is probably useful to analyze some of the solutions and tools first.

The internet provides a modular differentiation between infrastructure and application that does not exist with the old telephone system or older voice-only radio systems (such as emergency services' Land Mobile Radio). Unrecognized, we will routinely try to provide infrastructure solutions to applications problems. A variant on this theme is the psychological difference between computer centric and network centric world views. Operating system distributions for computers are perfect examples of computer-centric in operation – most of the security measures in the typical distribution are designed to protect the operating system, not the network.

The muddle of security is made worse by other diversions. For example, in the early days of WiFi, the technology came with a rather weak encryption scheme known as Wireless Encryption Protocol. There was much ink spilled in the press about the ability to break the crypto (which was true) but the discussion missed the point that the object protected was not much worth the effort anyway. The real security need – protection of the data – was not addressed at all. Further, if the WiFi network segment is at the fringe of an internetwork that requires public access then you don't want to turn it on anyway!

- **Scope Analysis:** The missing part of the discussion seems to be scope of the security protection. Exactly what is it that we need to be protecting? And over what parts of the information system? The problem is susceptible to easy analysis and the most important tool, the ISO Reference Model, already exists and is well understood – every introductory text on internetworking has an explanation. To analyze scope of security, we need only determine what layer of the ISO Reference Model a security implementation resides. Another way of asking exactly the same question is to determine the object that is being secured (frame, datagram, connection, message). This time, for illustration and sorting purposes, we will look at some existing security tools, then work up to requirements.

For example, layer 2 solutions (like Wireless Encryption Protocol, WEP) secure <u>frames.</u> A frame only surrounds a piece of data for a single hop so frame encryption only provides protection over a single network segment; the protection does not pass through any routers because the frame structure is only valid for that one hop. Protecting frames = layer 2 protection = one hop of scope.

Another example is virtual private network (VPN). A VPN protects IP datagrams from VPN port to VPN port which makes this protection a layer 3 solution. A VPN tunnels out a protected enclave within the internet in the large. A VPN provides no protection beyond that enclave (such as within end systems). VPNs are very useful for their infrastructure protection purposes, but they leave the data unprotected outside their scope.

The third example worth mentioning is transport level security (often recognized by the WWW labeling of 'https:'; labels include Secure Sockets Layer and Transport Level Security). Here the object being secured is a connection. As in TCP connection. Which makes the protection a layer 4/5 one. The scope of this protection is from the TCP 'socket' on one computer to the socket on the other. This provides pretty complete protection over the internet but none at all within the operating systems in each end system beyond the socket. So any malware within either end system's operating system (e.g. key loggers) see the data in unprotected form.

All of these layer 2-5 protections can be classified as infrastructure protection measures. They do have value and the scope analysis indicates what that value is. But they only protect the content – the data – by providing some security to the infrastructure. They do not provide security to the data itself.

The final example is layer 6/7 protections. The best example of layer 6 protection is secure e-mail (S/MIME). Here the data is protected. It is transformed (the definition of layer 6) either by appending a digital signature, encrypting, or both. The scope of the protection can be end-to-end; some secure e-mail implementations can illustrate: outgoing e-mail is secured by encryption and digital signature at origin. This is done before the data ever leaves the end system. It is then communicated to one or more message transfer agents (slang: mail servers) who forward and store data, but are not allowed to change it (if they did, the digital signature would not verify and an encrypted message would not decrypt). Eventually the message is delivered to the receiving end system and is passed through the operating system and into memory (e.g. hard drive) with the protections intact. Only when the message is read are the protections removed, and even then often only for the viewing – they remain intact on the stored copy (some features are implementation-dependent, they're outside the scope of the standard). This greatly limits the exposure of unprotected data: it is never unprotected over the internetwork infrastructure and only under limited conditions in the end systems.

Another implementation example of layer 6 end-to-end security scope is security protections built into SNMP version 3 which allow attachment of digital signatures and (as applicable) encryption to each SNMP message, entirely independent of how it is delivered. The layer 6 protections are vital to security of content, regardless of what other infrastructure protection mechanisms are implemented.

Table 1 organizes the scope observations in tabular form. The important observation of the sort is that layer 6-7 security measures protect the data; layer 2-5 security measures protect the infrastructure.

Table 1. Security scope table

Reference Model Layer	Object Protected	Scope	Example
6-7	Content data	End to end	S/MIME email, XML-sign/-crypt SNMPv3
4-5	Connection (e.g. TCP connection)	TCP socket to TCP socket	SSL, e.g. https connections
3	IP datagram	Network enclave (excluding end systems)	Vendor or company specific VPN
1-2	Frame (ethernet)	Single network segment	WPA

- **Uses and Requirements:** The management requirement discussed above in the third principle of high availability is a perfect example of the need for end-to-end, application layer, security. Consider for a moment the consequences of someone injecting bogus SNMP 'get' message results into the management console. Or, worse, someone injecting bogus SNMP 'set' messages into critical equipment. In this use case, confidentiality is not particularly important, but authenticity is vital.

But this is only a start. Consider the casualty data (e.g. vital signs) in the instrumented ambulance use case: that data must be both authentic and confidential. And the scope requirement is end-to-end. And consider the data from the ambulance's radio-navigation receiver – the consequences of the wrong position showing up on the dispatcher's common operational picture are not good. The ambulance may grow into a case of 'virtual siren' where it is broadcasting it's position to geographical neighbors – here confidentiality is useless and counterproductive but authenticity is again vital. This kind of security agility is easily attainable with layer 6/7 solutions but not by use of lower layer tools.

Another requirements example is an incident commander dealing with a fire. He clearly needs authenticity in his communications with the firefighting team and he needs confidentiality in some of the data (e.g. previously mentioned medical data). But the incident commander needs communications with the general public, for example, to disseminate evacuation orders. This is an example where authenticity is very important but confidentiality is of no value – the evacuation orders must be en claire. In all these variants the security requirements are end-to-end in scope.

- **Security Requirement Generalization:** All applications require authenticity in some form or another, explicit or tacitly assumed. There are no exceptions. And the required scope of this authenticity is always end to end. These two facts enormously simplify the planning problem. Digital signatures are all dependent on Public Key Infrastructures so the obvious requirement is that all end systems need a key pair. But once you have the key pair in hand, addition of encryption to the authenticity capability costs nothing.
- **Applications:** While most of the availability discussion applies to internetwork infrastructure, the requirement for fault monitoring includes end systems and their applications as well. A fireman engaged in fighting a fire cannot stop to diagnose a fault in his handset and voice application, for example.

End-to-end security features are all built into applications that run over the internetwork; they are not part of the infrastructure (terrestrial WANs, radio-WANs, routers, ...).

State of the Industry: Most operating system distributions include an SNMP agent in the distribution (but it's either turned off or not installed). But many applications (like a voice app in your cell phone) do not. If the application is to be considered mission critical, an SNMP agent should be part of it's structure along with end-to-end signatures and encryption option.

There are a variety of e-mail user agents (UA), many of which implement signing and encryption. Most, but not all, implement the S/MIME in a satisfactory way limiting the range of unprotected data within an operating system (hint: check the Sent mail directory for unprotected body parts). Some of these UAs are automated user agents that allow automated insertion of data into e-mail envelopes – it's still e-mail but not necessarily human-to-human (webcams often have such). Once the reader understands all this one can think of lots of applications that can use e-mail for their communications envelope!

Extensible Markup Language (XML) provides -sign and -crypt primitives as part of the language that, if used, have end-to-end scope. An XML statement that has been signed will have authenticity attributes and those attributes remain until the statement is interpreted at destination. The test is easy: is the protection applied before the data leaves origin? And does it remain intact until it reaches destination?

Secure shell (ssh) also provides a layer 6 security means; the scope is end-to-end. Ssh can be programmed into shell scripts and is therefore common in file transfer implementations and file synchronization applications, particularly in the open source world. Some of the history of ssh is germane: the protocol was engineered in the early 1990s, a quarter century after the internet was first invented (about the same time that we started seeing serviceable implementations of S/MIME). The effect is secure communications over an untrusted internetwork, which is a corollary of the original internet ethos: reliable communications over unreliable infrastructure.

Security Planning Observations: Since the internet is made up of one infrastructure and 1001 applications (with new ones appearing regularly), we can observe that end-to-end security can be built into those applications. For mission critical applications, end-to-end scope of security should be a central requirement with authenticity as a ubiquitous, universal requirement. This does not require changes to a pre-existing internetwork infrastructure (other than addition of support services like PKI white pages servers). Infrastructure planning and application development can be on largely separate tracks. This observation should not be used as an excuse to ignore the security problems though.

QUALITY OF SERVICE

Warning to reader: this topic contains more misinformation and mythology than any other. Worse, in requirements discussions, it seems to be the first topic to be thrashed when it should be the last. Never discuss quality of service issues before disposing of the availability issue.

Nomenclature: The quality of service actually experienced by users of an internetwork is normally noted in lower case: qos. Upper case QoS denotes Quality of Service Control or those configuration tweaks that change the defaults in some way. This distinction is crucial, especially for those who enter this discussion from the experience and viewpoint of circuit-switched voice. An example is the behavior of routers: the default behavior is for a router to have a single queue for each outgoing port and datagrams are fed into the queue in FIFO order – first in, first out. The qos experience is what is called 'best effort'. But if the router enables Differential Services, multiple (usually four) queues are set up for each output port. Datagrams are sorted into these queues by examining the Differential Services Code Point in each datagram header. These queues are then drained to the output starting with the highest priority first. The behavior within each queue remains FIFO but the highest marked traffic queue is sent first.

Experienced qos: In circuit-switched telephone systems, qos is simply whether one gets a dial tone or not. In internetworks there are more parameters. For the infrastructure operator, qos generally means bandwidth efficiency – providing the best service to the most users. To an end user, qos can be measured in interactivity, latency and jitter.

Be careful what you ask for. First, in the terrestrial WAN and LAN portions of your internet, over-provisioning is not only possible but usually happens as a side effect of meeting the availability requirements. If there is no congestion, there is no point in QoS controls – they can't possibly improve things and it's quite likely that some measures will degrade qos. For example, in the above example the router is using CPU cycles to sort. This over-provisioning phenomenon is true for servers too – the end systems that are also susceptible to overload. By the time you've met the system replication needs to satisfy availability requirements, the load-sharing will ameliorate congestion problems. The remaining part of our internetwork that needs attention is the radio-WAN.

QoS in the Radio-WAN: As noted above extending the internet to mobile platforms can be assumed to result in some mission-critical applications being implemented on such an internetwork. Which, in qos terms, means that some packets are more urgent than others. In the radio-WAN it is important to be able to distinguish those packets and give them 'head of line' privileges. There are solutions both at layer 2 and layer 3 that need to be considered together.

Layer 3, Differential Services: In the internet, standards exist (RFC 2474) (RFC Base, 1998). The protocol allows an end system to specify an urgency value known as the Differential Services Code Point in IP datagrams. This allows routers to sort these packets to the head of the queues in the router. The effect is that these privileged packets are dispatched first from the router once capacity is available. In a radio-WAN, this means when it is that station's turn to transmit. In protocols like IEEE 802.16 (IEEE 802.16) and TIA LTE (WiMAX) every active station in the radio-WAN gets a turn to transmit every frame, so the urgent traffic will be sent in that time slice.

Layer 2, QoS Control in Radio-WAN: Within the radio-WAN segment, there are QoS Controls that allow a subscriber station to request more capacity (at the expense of other stations) and several other 'knobs'. But before going here, ask whether 1) we have a decent means for controlling and 2) given differential services and the near-deterministic behavior of these radio-WANs whether we can gain any real improvement.

You can't violate the laws of physics. If, for example, one of your radio-WANs is a satellite system using geosynchronous satellites, you have a 300 msec propagation delay that no protocol can improve.

State of the Technology: It should be evident that most of the parts for necessary QoS Control exist (along with a truckload of unnecessary parts). Some thoughts on system and application design:

- Differential services consists of a set of settled standards and hardly any implementation. Routers generally can recognize the DSCP and act accordingly (but have this feature routinely turned off). Some end system operating systems have the latent capability to set the DSCP. But hardly any applications call on these features. Not every application needs to be differential-services capable, but those mission-critical ones in the hands of our emergency services folks do. And not every router needs to have differential services turned on – only those at the border to the radio-WAN do.
- View layer 2 QoS Controls with jaundiced eye. It's not clear that they'll help any, particularly in a near-deterministic MAC environment.

- Some applications are very 'chatty' in that they depend on high interactivity (ironically low round trip latency times) between client and server. These applications are the first to suffer in poor qos environments. Such applications usually do not fail outright, but their performance is likely to be viewed as poor by an end user (a lot of poor-interactivity problems tend to be misdiagnosed as low-capacity problems). In an all-wired internetwork, this is usually not a problem but with the advent of radio-WANs in the topology the issue does become important and it must be solved by adjusting application design and selecting those mission-critical applications that minimize the issue.

CONCLUSION

Investigation of extending the internet to mobile platforms parallels the investigation of 'plowshares into swords': that is, upgrading the office automation internet to meet emergency services' (or military) needs (I particularly like the instructions from Joel, Chapter 3, verse 10). Emergency services require reach to mobile platforms; similarly it's a safe bet that extension of the internet to mobile platforms will require ability to handle mission-critical applications. This chapter illustrates several design characteristics that tend not to need particular emphasis in an all-wired internetwork or an internetwork with wireless LANs at its fringe. But they become critical in an internet that reaches to mobile platforms. The good news is that the sword version retains all the usefulness of the plowshares version of the internet. These observations can be distilled into a few concluding recommendations:

- Build a routed internetwork – extend the internet. Don't be lulled into shortcuts like bridged (layer 2) networks or layer 7 gateways that represent both poor modularization and Ao-defeating single points of failure.
- Pay attention to the availability (Ao) requirement. It is the easiest to quantify and defend in a budget and it will be the capitalization driver. And do it early in the requirements analysis. You need not have every conceivable application in hand, only the one that needs the availability the most (what's commonly referred to as the tall pole in the tent). If the sponsor has not stated an Ao requirement, then the sponsor requirements document is badly flawed. Get that fixed pronto.
- Focus on the radio-WAN often tends to divert attention from the supporting terrestrial WAN. That terrestrial WAN is the foundation, not an afterthought backhaul. The terrestrial WAN design and provisioning is vital to support the availability and reach for the radio-WAN. Further, the trend is to lower power radios meaning that a given level of coverage requires more base stations. This takes advantage of things that the terrestrial internet does best. Out of sight should not man out of mind.
- End systems and applications therein for mission critical jobs should do three things, regardless of the function of a particular application:
    - Secure their content end-to-end (that is, with layer 7 scope). Assume that anyone can both eavesdrop and insert data onto an internetwork – a practical fact given radio-WANs – and protect accordingly. Authenticity is a universal, ubiquitous requirement – get it right first.
    - Multicast. The effectiveness need only be tested in one place: the radio-WAN. The radio-WAN is the place where the bandwidth conservation payoff has value. The rest of the internetwork can be over-provisioned.
    - Implement an SNMP agent that allows remote fault monitoring. As with any other application, authenticity of the SNMP data is vital.

- Implement differential services in applications that require it (non-implementation in an application simply means that it gets routine best-effort service that all other applications do).

Yours to Lose. The internet is a naturally modular technology. It is entirely in accordance with internet ethos to segment the network into terrestrial-WANs, radio-WANs, and LANs. And it is entirely natural to attach end systems only to the LANs. But this natural, by-design, modularity does not pertain to other communications systems, so it is an easy mistake to slip into the mode of implementing internet technology, but using the inherited (non)modularity.

There are two cardinal reasons for good modularity:

- Interoperability
- Life cycle maintainability

Interoperability has to do with interoperation with other infrastructure outside the scope of your own program. Can your corner of the internetwork be routed into the rest of the Internet (constrained only by policy-driven configuration)? Interoperability also has to do with ability to implement applications that are not of your own program or built later. Can your corner of the internetwork implement next year's hot new app (again, constrained by policy not engineering)?

The test of good modularity is a simple life cycle maintenance one: can one component (such as the radio-WAN technology) be changed (or replicated) without requiring cascading changes? In this case, changes on the other side of the routers? If changes are required, the modularity model is inadequate.

If your reach to mobile can be characterized as 'extend the internet to mobile platforms', then the modularity problem is a solved one that requires action on your part to derail.

REFERENCES

Base, R. F. C. (1998). Retrieved from http://www.rfc-base.org/rfc-2474.html

Configuring Voice over IP. (n.d.). Retrieved from http://www.cisco.com/c/en/us/td/docs/ios/12_2/voice/configuration/guide/fvvfax_c/vvfvoip.pdf

IEEE 802.16. (2014). Retrieved from: http://en.wikipedia.org/wiki/IEEE_802.16

Nichols, K., Blake, S., Baker, F., & Black, D. (n.d.). *RFC 2474, Definition of the Differentiated Services Field (DS Field) in the IPv4 and IPv6 Headers*. Academic Press.

Operational Availability. (n.d.). *Operational Availability*. Retrieved from http://en.wikipedia.org/wiki/Operational_availability

POTS, Plain Old Telephone Service. (2014). Retrieved from http://en.wikipedia.org/wiki/Plain_old_telephone_service

Wi-Fi. (n.d.). In *Encyclopedia Brittanica*. Retrieved from http://www.britannica.com/EBchecked/topic/1473553/Wi-Fi

WiMAX. (2014). *WiMAX*. Retrieved from http://en.wikipedia.org/wiki/WiMAX

KEY TERMS AND DEFINITIONS

3G: Third generation cellular telephone. 3G and earlier cellphone technologies are all circuit-switched. 4G cellphone is packet switched.

Availability (Ao): Defined as up-time/total-time. Availability is an instantaneous probability that the system it applies to is functional at any moment in time.

Bridging, Routing, Layer 7 Gatewaying: Bridging means interconnecting multiple network segments by use of layer 2 bridges. Homogeneity (common frame addressing and format) is generally required. Routing means internetworking multiple network segments at layer 3. Frame structure is irrelevant because it's not present at layer 3 so considerable heterogeneity is tolerable, provided each of the network segments is routable. Layer 7 gateways are means of translating non-IP traffic into internet traffic and injecting it into the internetwork infrastructure (and vice versa). Layer 7 gateways are commonly used to interconnect legacy communications systems and applications (such as POTS phone).

LAN: Last network in an internet – reaches from last router to end systems. May be wired (ethernet) or wireless (WiFi, sometimes abbreviated WLAN for wireless LAN). The radio portion of 3G cellphone, despite its circuit-switch nature, is of same topological character – reaches from the pylon to end system.

Multicast: Delivery of data to more than one destination for the price of a single transit over the media.

Network: An overloaded term that means lots of things to different people. Author tends to not use it, preferring 'network segment' for a single segment and 'internetwork' for the larger multiple hop infrastructure.

QoS: Quality of Service Control – those measures applied to the default behavior of the internet to change the quality of service defaults.

qos: Quality of service that is experienced. Components include bandwidth efficiency, latency, jitter, interactivity.

Radio-WAN: Topologically identical to generic WAN but uses radio.

SNMP Get, Set, Trap: Simple Network Management Protocol contains three kinds of messages. Get messages are requests for information by the management console to an agent who replies with a get-response. Set messages set configuration parameters. Trap messages are generated by a management agent in response to some stimulus. For purposes of this paper, traps would be fault indicators.

Terrestrial-WAN: WAN that is made up of wired connectivity.

WAN: Network infrastructure in interior of internetwork. In a pure case, there are no end systems – the WAN is solely performing router-router interconnect.

Compilation of References

3GPP-TS23.228. (n.d.). *IP multimedia subsystem (ims); stage 2 (release 9).* Retrieved from 3rd Generation Partnership Project, Tech. Rep., 2010, 3GPP TS 23.228 V9.3.0 (2010-03).

3GPP-TS23.401. (2008). General packet radio service (gprs) enhancements for evolved universal terrestrial radio access network (e-utran) access. Release 8. Retrieved from 3rd Generation Partnership Project, Tech Report 3GPP TS 23.401 V8.1.0.

Abbas, A., & Khan, S. (2014). A review on the state-of-the-art privacy-preserving approaches in the e-health clouds. *IEEE Journal of Biomedical and Health Informatics*, 1431-1441.

ADI-ReportADC. (2015). *Analog-digital conversion.* Analog Devices, Inc. Retrieved from http://www.analog.com/library/analogDialogue/archives/39-06/Chapter%202%20Sampled%20Data%20Systems%20F.pdf

Adya, A., Bahl, P., Padhye, J., Wolman, A., & Zhou, L. (2004). A multi-radio unification protocol for IEEE 802.11 wireless networks. *BroadNets*, (s. 344-354).

AES. (2012). Retrieved from http://en.wikipedia.org/wiki/Advanced_Encryption_Standard

Agarwal, R. (2014). *DRAP: A decentralized public resourced cloudlet for ad-hoc networks.*

Aggarwal, C., Ashish, N., & Sheth, A. (2013). The Internet of Things: A Survey from the Data-Centric Perspective. In C. Aggarwal, & C. Charu (Eds.), Managing and Mining Sensor Data (pp. 383--428). Springer. doi:10.1007/978-1-4614-6309-2_12

Agu, E., Pedersen, P., Strong, D., Tulu, B., He, Q., Wang, L., & Li, Y. (2013). The smartphone as a medical device.*10th Annual IEEE Communications Society Conference on Sensor, Mesh and Ad Hoc Communications and Networks (SECON)*, (pp. 76-80).

Akbas, M. I., Brust, M. R., Riberio, C. H. C., & Turgut, D. (2011a). fAPEbook - Animal Social life Monitoring with Wireless Sensor and Actor Networks.*IEEE Global Communications Conference (GLOBECOM)*, (pp. 1-5). doi:10.1109/GLOCOM.2011.6134364

Akbas, M. I., Brust, M. R., Riberio, C. H. C., & Turgut, D. (2011b). *Deployment and Mobility for Animal Social Life Monitoring Based on Preferential Attachment* (pp. 488–495). IEEE Local Computer Networks. doi:10.1109/LCN.2011.6115510

Aktas, M., Shah, A. H., & Akiyama, T. (2007). Dofetilide-Induced Long QT and Torsades de Pointes. *Annals of Noninvasive Electrocardiology*, *12*(3), 197–202. doi:10.1111/j.1542-474X.2007.00161.x PMID:17617063

Alam, K. M., Saini, M., Ahmet, D. T., & El-Saddik, A. (2014). *VeDi: A vehicular crowd-sourced video social network for VANETs. IEEE Local Computer Networks (LCN)* (pp. 738–745). Conference Workshops.

Alamri, A., Ansari, W. S., Hassan, M. M., Hossain, M. S., Alelaiwi, A. & Hossain, M. A. (2013). A Survey on Sensor-Cloud: Architecture, Applications, and Approaches. *International Journal of Distributed Sensor Networks*, 917923.1—917923.18.

Al-Fagih, A. E., Al-Turjman, F. M., Alsalih, W. M., & Hassanein, H. S. (2013). A priced public sensing framework for heterogeneous IoT architectures. *IEEE Transactions on Emerging Topics in Computing*, *1*(1), 133–147. doi:10.1109/TETC.2013.2278698

Alford, T., & Morton, G. (2010). *The Economics of Cloud Computing*. Retrieved from http://www.boozallen.com/media/file/Economics-of-Cloud-Computing.pdf

Ali, M. (2009). Green Cloud on the Horizon. *Cloud Computing*, 451-459.

AliveCor. (2014). *AliveCor Heart Monitor*. Retrieved from http://www.alivecor.com/home

AliveCor. (n.d.). Retrieved from http://www.alivecor.com/home

Alkasir, R. S., Ganesana, M., Won, Y. H., Stanciu, L., & Andreescu, S. (2010). Enzyme functionalized nanoparticles for electrochemical biosensors: A comparative study with applications for the detection of bisphenol a. *Biosensors & Bioelectronics*, *26*(1), 43–49. doi:10.1016/j.bios.2010.05.001 PMID:20605712

Alkasir, R. S., Ornatska, M., & Andreescu, S. (2012). Colorimetric paper bioassay for the detection of phenolic compounds. *Analytical Chemistry*, 972909737. PMID:23113670

Alling, A., Powers, N., & Soyata, T. (2015). Face Recognition: A Tutorial on Computational Aspects. In *Emerging Research Surrounding Power Consumption and Performance Issues in Utility Computing*. Hershey, Pennsylvania: IGI Global.

Amazon EC2. (2013). Retrieved from Retrieved from: http://aws.amazon.com/ec2/sla/

Amazon Web Services. (n.d.). Retrieved from http://aws.amazon.com

Amazon. (2015). *Amazon Elastic Compute Cloud (Amazon EC2)*. Retrieved Jan. de 2015 from http://aws.amazon.com/ec2/

Amazon. (2015). *Amazon Mechanical Turk*. Retrieved Jan. de 2015 from https://www.mturk.com/

Amazon-EC2-Pricing. (n.d.). Retrieved from http://aws.amazon.com/ec2/pricing/

AMD64-Virtualization. (2005). *Secure virtual machine architecture reference manual*. AMD Publication.

Amies, A., Sluiman, H., Tong, Q. G., & Liu, G. N. (2012). *Infrastructure as a Service Cloud Concepts*. Developing and Hosting Applications on the Cloud.

Anderson, D. P. (2004). BOINC: A system for public-resource computing and storage. *Grid Computing, 2004. Proceedings. Fifth IEEE/ACM International Workshop on* (s. 4-10). IEEE.

Anderson, D., Cobb, J., Korpela, E., Lebofsky, M., & Werthimer, D. (2002). SETI@home: An experiment in public-resource computing. *Communications of the ACM*, *45*(11), 56–61. doi:10.1145/581571.581573 PMID:12238525

Andoid-API. (n.d.). *Android API Reference*. Retrieved from http://developer.android.com/reference/

Andreescu, S., Barthelmebs, L., & Marty, J. L. (2002). Immobilization of acetylcholinesterase on screen-printed electrodes: Comparative study between three immobilization methods and applications to the detection of organophosphorus insecticides. *Analytica Chimica Acta*, *464*(2), 171–180. doi:10.1016/S0003-2670(02)00518-4

Andreescu, S., Magearu, V., Lougarre, A., Fournier, D., & Marty, J. L. (2001). Immobilization of enzymes on screen-printed sensors via an histidine tail. application to the detection of pesticides using modified cholinesterase. *Analytical Letters*, *34*(4), 529–540. doi:10.1081/AL-100002593

Andro, B. O. I. N. C. (2010). *AndroBOINC - BOINC manager for Android phones*. Retrieved Jan. de 2015 from https://code.google.com/p/androboinc/

Android. (2012). Retrieved from http://www.android.com/

Apple. (2012). Retrieved from http://developer.apple.com/library/mac/#documentation/NetworkingInternet/Conceptual/RemoteNotificationsPG/ApplePushService/ApplePushService.html

ARCNET. (2002). *Attached Resource Computer (ARCNET)*. Retrieved Jan. de 2015 from http://www.arcnet.com/

Armbrust, M., Fox, A., Griffith, R., Joseph, A. D., Katz, R., Konwinski, A., & Stoica, I. et al. (2010). A View of Cloud Computing. *Communications of the ACM*, *53*(4), 50–58. doi:10.1145/1721654.1721672

Arslan, M. Y., Singh, I., Singh, S., Madhyastha, H. V., Sundaresan, K., & Krishnamurthy, S. V. (2012). Computing while charging: Building a distributed computing infrastructure using smartphones. ACM CoNEXT. Nice, France.

Asus. (2013). *Asus Nexus 7*. Retrieved Jan. de 2015 from http://www.asus.com/Tablets_Mobile/Nexus_7_2013/

Atzori, A., Andlera, L., & Morabito, G. (2010). The Internet of Things: A survey. *Computer Networks*, *54*(15), 2787–2805. doi:10.1016/j.comnet.2010.05.010

Atzori, L., Iera, A., & Morabito, G. (2011). SIoT: Giving a social structure to the Internet of Things. *IEEE Communications Letters*, *15*(11), 1193–1195. doi:10.1109/LCOMM.2011.090911.111340

AWS. (2012). Retrieved from http://aws.amazon.com

Ba, H., Heinzelman, W., Janssen, C., & Shi, J. (2013). Mobile computing - a green computing resource. *Wireless Communications and Networking Conference*. IEEE.

Babko, A., & Volkova, A. (1954). The colored peroxide complex of cerium. *Ukrains' kii Khemichnii Zhurna*, 211-215.

Badilini, F. (1998). The ISHNE Holter Standard Output File Format. *Annals of Noninvasive Cardiology*, 263-266.

Ba, H., Heinzelman, W., Janssen, C., & Shi, J. (2013). *Mobile computing - A green computing resource*. Shanghai, China: IEEE WCNC. doi:10.1109/WCNC.2013.6555295

Bansal, N. (2013). Cloud computing technology (with BPOS and Windows Azure). *International Journal of Cloud Computing*, *2*(1), 48–60. doi:10.1504/IJCC.2013.050955

Baqer, M. (2011). Enabling collaboration and coordination of wireless sensor networks via social networks.*Proc. IEEE International Conference on Distributed Computing in Sensor Systems Workshops (DCOSSW)*, (pp. 1--2).

Barrington, D. (1989). Bounded-Width Polynomial Size Brancing Programs Recognized Exactly Those Languages in NC1. *Journal of Computer and System Sciences*, *38*(1), 150–164. doi:10.1016/0022-0000(89)90037-8

Basaleva, L. I., & Weaver, A. C. (2013). Applications of Social Networks and Crowdsourcing for Disaster Management Improvement.*Proc. Int. Conference on Social Computing (SocialCom)*, (pp. 213--219). doi:10.1109/SocialCom.2013.38

Base, R. F. C. (1998). Retrieved from http://www.rfc-base.org/rfc-2474.html

Battiti, R., Bertossi, A., & Bonuccelli, M. (1999). Assigning Codes in Wireless Networks: Bounds and Scaling Properties. *Wireless Networks*, *5*(3), 195–209. doi:10.1023/A:1019146910724

Bayir, M. A., & Demirbas, M. (2014). On the fly learning of mobility profiles for routing in pocket switched networks. *Elsevier Ad Hoc Network*, *16*, 13–27. doi:10.1016/j.adhoc.2013.11.011

Bazett, H. C. (1920). An Analysis of Time Relations of the Electrocardiogram. *Heart (British Cardiac Society)*, 353–370.

Bazzett, H. (1997). An analysis of the time-relations of electrocardiograms. *Annals of Noninvasive Electrocardiology*, *2*(2), 177–194. doi:10.1111/j.1542-474X.1997.tb00325.x

BBN. (2005). Retrieved from http://tools.ietf.org/pdf/rfc4301.pdf

Bergmans, P. (1973). Random coding theorem for broadcast channels with degraded components. *IEEE Transactions on Information Theory*, *19*(2), 197–207. doi:10.1109/TIT.1973.1054980

Berkeley. (2011). *BOINC on Android*. Retrieved Jan. de 2015 from http://boinc.berkeley.edu/trac/wiki/AndroidBoinc

Berkeley. (2014). *BOINC's Homepage*. Retrieved Jan. de 2015 from http://boinc.berkeley.edu/

Berkeley. (Sep. de 2014). *The 10th BOINC workshop - BOINC/Android status and plans*. Retrieved Jan. de 2015 from http://boinc.berkeley.edu/trac/attachment/wiki/WorkShop14/boinc_on_android_2014.pdf

Bhatia, T. S., Khan, S. A., & Bölöni, L. (2013). A modeling framework for inter-cultural social interactions.*Proc. 2nd International Workshop on Human-Agent Interaction Design and Models (HAIDM-13)*, (pp. 16--31).

Black, M., & Edgar, W. (2009). Exploring mobile devices as grid resources: Using an x86 virtual machine to run BOINC on an iPhone. IEEE/ACM Grid Computing. Banff, AB, Canada.

Bluetooth Group. (2010). *Specification of the Bluetooth system.*

BOINC. (2012). Retrieved from http://nativeboinc.org/site/uncat/start

Bölöni, L. (2012). The Spanish Steps flower scam - agent-based modeling of a complex social interaction.*Proc. 11th Int. Conf. on Autonomous Agents and Multiagent Systems (AAMAS)*, (pp. 1345--1346).

Boneh, D., Goh, E.-J., & Nissim, K. (2005). Evaluating 2-DNF Formulas on Ciphertexts.*Proceedings of the 2nd International Conference on Theory of Cryptography*, (pp. 325-341). doi:10.1007/978-3-540-30576-7_18

Bonuccelli, A. A. (1995). Code assignment for hidden terminal interference avoidance in multihop packet radio networks. *IEEE/ACM Transactions on Networking*, 441–449.

Bos, J. W., Lauter, K., & Naehrig, M. (2014). Private predictive analysis on encrypted medical data. *Journal of Biomedical Informatics*, *50*, 234–243. doi:10.1016/j.jbi.2014.04.003 PMID:24835616

Bradski, G., & Kaehler, A. (2008). *Learning OpenCV: Computer vision with the OpenCV library*. O'Reilly Media, Inc.

Bradski, G., & Kaehler, A. (2008). *OpenCV Computer Vision with OpenCV Library*. O'Reilly.

Brakerski, Z., & Vaikuntanathan, V. (2011). Efficient Fully Homomorphic Encryption from Standard LWE. *Foundations of Computer Science*, 97-106.

Brakerski, Z., Gentry, C., & Vaikuntanathan, V. (2012). Leveled Fully Homomorphic Encryption without Bootstrapping.*Proceedings of the 3rd Innovations in Theoretical Computer Science Conference*, (pp. 309-325). doi:10.1145/2090236.2090262

Brakerski, Z., & Vaikuntanathan, V. (2011). *Fully homomorphic encryption from ring-LWE and security for key dependent messages* (pp. 505–524). CRYPTO. doi:10.1007/978-3-642-22792-9_29

Brebner, P., & Liu, A. (2011). Performance and Cost Assessment of Cloud Services. *Computer Science*, *6568*, 39–50.

Brenyo, A. J., Huang, D. T., & Aktas, M. (2011). Congenital long and short qt syndromes. *Cardiology*, *122*(4), 237–247. doi:10.1159/000339537 PMID:22906875

Bruno, R., & Ferreira, P. (2014). *Freecycles: Efficient data distribution for volunteer computing*. Amsterdam, The Netherlands: ACM CloudDP. doi:10.1145/2592784.2592788

Burbank, J. L., Chimento, P. F., Haberman, B. K., & Kasch, W. (2006). Key challenges of military tactical networking and the elusive promise of MANET technology. *IEEE Communications Magazine*, *44*(11), 39–45. doi:10.1109/COM-M.2006.248156

C2DMF. (2012). Retrieved from https://developers.google.com/android/c2dm/

Callou, G., Ferreira, J., Maciel, P., Tutsch, D., & Souza, R. (2014). *Open Access Energies*. Retrieved from An Integrated Modeling Approach to Evaluate and Optimize Data Center Sustainability, Dependability and Cost: http://www.mdpi.com/1996-1073/7/1/238

Cappello, F., Djilali, S., Fedak, G., Herault, T., Magniette, F., Néri, V., & Lodygensky, O. (2005). Computing on large-scale distributed systems: XtremWeb architecture, programming models, security, tests and convergence with grid. *Future Generation Computer Systems*, *21*(3), 417–437. doi:10.1016/j.future.2004.04.011

Cappos, J., Beschastnikh, I., Krishnamurthy, A., & Anderson, T. (2009). *Seattle: A platform for educational cloud computing*. Chattanooga, TN, USA: ACM SIGCSE. doi:10.1145/1508865.1508905

CardioLeaf. (2013). *Clearbridge VitalSigns CardioLeaf PRO*. Retrieved from http://www.clearbridgevitalsigns.com/pro.html

CardioLeaf-Pro. (n.d.). Retrieved from http://www.clearbridgevitalsigns.com/

CareCloud. (2013). Retrieved from http://www.carecloud.com/

Carullo, G., Castiglione, A., Cattaneo, G., Santis, A., Fiore, U., & Palmieri, F. (2013). Feeltrust: Providing trustworthy communications in ubiquitous mobile environment. *IEEE 27th International Conference on Advanced Information Networking and Applications (AINA)*, (pp. 1113-1120).

Chang, C., Ling, S., & Srirama, S. (2014b). Trustworthy Service Discovery for Mobile Social Network in Proximity. *Proc. IEEE Intl Conference on Pervasive Computing and Communications (PERCOM) Workshops*, (pp. 478--483). doi:10.1109/PerComW.2014.6815253

Chang, W., & Wu, J. (2014a). Progressive or Conservative: Rationally Allocate Cooperative Work in Mobile Social Networks. *IEEE Transactions on Parallel and Distributed Systems*. doi:10.1109/TPDS.2014.2330298

Chappel, C. (2013, June 22). *Heavy Reading: Unlocking Network value: service Innovation in the Era of SDN, White paper*. Retrieved from http://www.cisco.com/web/solutions/trends/open_network_environment/docs/hr_service_innovation.pdf

Chen, E. Y., & Itoh, M. (2010). Virtual smartphone over IP. *World of Wireless Mobile and Multimedia Networks (WoWMoM), 2010 IEEE International Symposium on a* (s. 1-6). IEEE.

Chen, E., Ogata, S., & Horikawa, K. (2012). Offloading Android applications to the cloud without customizing Android. *Pervasive Computing and Communications Workshops (PERCOM Workshops), 2012 IEEE International Conference on* (s. 788-793). IEEE.

Chen, E., Ogata, S., & Horikawa, K. (2012). Offloading android applications to the cloud without customizing android. *Pervasive Computing and Communicatiosn Workshop (PERCOM Workshops)* (pp. 788-793). IEEE. doi:10.1109/PerComW.2012.6197619

Chen, S.-Y., Lai, C.-F., Huang, Y.-M., & Jeng, Y.-L. (2013). Intelligent home appliance recognition over IoT cloud network.*Proc. Ninth International Wireless Communications and Mobile Computing Conference (IWCMC)*, (pp. 639--643). doi:10.1109/IWCMC.2013.6583632

Chesnokov, Y., Nerukh, D., & Glen, R. (2006). Individually adaptable automatic QT detector. *Computers in Cardiology*, 337–340.

Chisnall, D. (2008). *The Definitive Guide to the Xen Hypervisor*. Pearson Education.

Cho, J., Mirzae, S., Oberg, J., & Kastner, R. (2009). FPGA-based face detection system using Haar Classifiers. *Proceedings of the ACM/SIGDA International Symposium on Field Programmable Gate Arrays*, (pp. 103-112). doi:10.1145/1508128.1508144

Chowdhury, K., Chanda, P., Agrawal, D., & Zeng, Q.-A. (2005). DCA-a distributed channel allocation scheme for wireless sensor networks. *IEEE PIMRC, 2*, s. 1297-1301.

Chu, D. C., & Humphrey, M. (2004). Mobile OGSI.NET: Grid computing on mobile devices. IEEE/ACM GRID. Pittsburgh, PA, USA.

Chun, B. G., & Maniatis, P. (2009). Augmented smartphone applications through clone cloud execution. *Proceedings of the 8th Workshop on Hot Topics in Operating Systems (HotOS).*

Chun, B. G., Ihm, S., Maniatis, P., Naik, M., & Patti, A. (2011). Clonecloud: Elastic execution between mobile device and cloud.*Proceedings of the Sixth Conference on Computer Systems*, (pp. 301-314). doi:10.1145/1966445.1966473

Chun, B.-G., & Maniatis, P. (2010). Dynamically partitioning applications between weak devices and clouds. In *Proceedings of the 1st ACM Workshop on Mobile Cloud Computing \& Services: Social Networks and Beyond* (p. 7). ACM. doi:10.1145/1810931.1810938

Cidon, I., & Sidi, M. (1989). Distributed assignment algorithms for multi-hop packet-radio networks. *IEEE Transactions on Computers, 38*(10), 1353–1361. doi:10.1109/12.35830

Cloudscape. (2013, June 22). *451 Research.* Retrieved from The Cloud Pricing Codex: https://451research.com /report-long?icid=2770

Cohen, J. D., & Fischer, M. J. (1985). A robust and verifiable cryptographically secure election scheme.*Symposium on Foundations of Computer Science* (pp. 372-382). IEEE. doi:10.1109/SFCS.1985.2

Configuring Voice over IP. (n.d.). Retrieved from http://www.cisco.com/c/en/us/td/docs/ios/12_2/voice/configuration/guide/fvvfax_c/vvfvoip.pdf

Coron, J.-S., Mandal, A., Naccache, D., & Tibouchi, M. (2011). *Fully homomorphic encryption over the integers with shorter public keys* (pp. 487–504). CRYPTO. doi:10.1007/978-3-642-22792-9_28

Corson, M. S., Laroia, R., Li, J., Park, V., Richardson, T., & Tsirtsis, G. (2010). Toward proximity-aware internetworking. *IEEE Wireless Communications, 17*(6), 26-33.

Cortina-Puig, M., Scangas, A. C., Marchese, Z. S., Andreescu, S., Marty, J. L., & Calas-Blanchard, C. (2010). Development of a xanthine oxidase modified amperometric electrode for the determination of the antioxidant capacity. *Electroanalysis, 22*(20), 2429–2433. doi:10.1002/elan.201000248

Costa, F., Veiga, L., & Ferreira, P. (2013). Internet-scale support for map-reduce processing. *Journal of Internet Services and Applications, 4*(1), 1–17. doi:10.1186/1869-0238-4-18

Costa, P., Migliavacca, M., Pietzuch, P., & Wolf, A. (2012). NaaS: Network as a Service in the cloud.*2nd USENIX Workshop on Hot Topics in Management of Internet, Cloud, and Enterprise Networks and Services (Hot-ICE '12).*

Couderc, J.-P. (2010). The Telemetric and Holter ECG Warehouse initiative (THEW): A data repository for the design, implementation and validation of ECG related technologies. *IEEE Engineering in Medicine and Biology Society (EMBC)*, 6252-6255.

Couderc, J. (2010). The telemetric and holter ECG warehouse initiative (THEW). A data repository for the design, implementation and validation of ECG-related technologies.*Annual International Conference of the IEEE Engineering in Medicine and Biology Society (EMBC)*, 6252-6255. doi:10.1109/IEMBS.2010.5628067

Couderc, J.-P., Garnett, C., Li, M., Handzel, R., McNitt, S., Xia, X., & Zareba, W. et al. (2011). Highly automated QT measurement techniques in 7 thorough QT studies implemented under ICH E14 guidelines. *Annals of Noninvasive Electrocardiology*, *16*(1), 13–24. doi:10.1111/j.1542-474X.2010.00402.x PMID:21251129

Couderc, J., Xia, J., McGrath, M., Zareba, W., Slaton, B., & Kakulavaram, A. et al.. (2011). Increased repolarization heterogeneity is associated with increased mortality in hemodialysis patients. *Computers in Cardiology*, 845–848.

Couderc, J., Xia, J., Xu, X., Kaab, S., Hinteeser, M., & Zareba, W. (2010). Static and dynamic electrocardiographic patterns preceding torsades de pointes in the acquired and congenital long QT syndrome. *Computers in Cardiology*, 357–360. PMID:22068668

Courcoubetis, C., & Weber, R. (2006). Incentives for large peer-to-peer systems. *IEEE Journal on Selected Areas in Communications*, *24*(5), 1034–1050. doi:10.1109/JSAC.2006.872885

Cover, T. (1972). Broadcast channels. *IEEE Transactions on Information Theory*, *18*(1), 2–14. doi:10.1109/TIT.1972.1054727

CPUBoss. (2015). *Compare CPU to see which is faster*. Retrieved Jan. de 2015 from http://cpuboss.com

CR2032. (n.d.). Retrieved from http://en.wikipedia.org/wiki/CR2032_battery

Crow, F. C. (1984). Summed-area tables for texture mapping. *Computer Graphics*, *18*(3), 207–212. doi:10.1145/964965.808600

Cuervo, E., Balasubramaniam, A., Cho, D., Wolman, A., Saroiu, S., Chandra, R., & Bahl, P. (2010). MAUI: Making Smartphones last longer with code offload.*Proceedings of the 8th International Conference on Mobile Systems, Applications, and Services*, (pp. 49-62). doi:10.1145/1814433.1814441

Cuervo, E., Gilbert, P., Wu, B., & Cox, L. (2011). *CrowdLab: An architecture for volunteer mobile testbeds*. Bangalore, India: COMSNETS.

Dabek, F., Cox, R., Kaashoek, F., & Morris, R. (2004). *Vivaldi: A Decentralized Network Coordinate System* (pp. 15–26). ACM SIGCOMM.

Dadda, L. (1965). Some schemes for parallel multipliers. *Alta Frequenza*, 349–356.

Dai, W., Doroz, Y., & Sunar, B. (2014). Accelerating ntru based homomorphic encryption using gpus.*High Performance Extreme Computing Conference*.

Dall, C., & Nieh, J. (2014). KVM/ARM: the design and implementation of the linux ARM hypervisor. In *Proceedings of the 19th international conference on Architectural support for programming languages and operating systems* (pp. 333-348). ACM. doi:10.1145/2541940.2541946

Damgard, I., & Jurik, M. (2001). *A generalisation, a simplification and some applications of paillier's probabilistic public-key system* (pp. 119–136). Public Key Cryptography.

Damgard, I., Jurik, M., & Nielsen, J. B. (2010). A Generalization of Paillie's Public Key System with Applications to Electronic Voting. *International Journal of Information Security*, *9*(6), 371–385. doi:10.1007/s10207-010-0119-9

Darch, P., & Carusi, A. (2010). Retaining volunteers in volunteer computing projects,", vol. . *Phil. Trans. R. Soc. A, 368* (1926), 4177–4192.

DARPA-PROCEED. (n.d.). Retrieved from DARPA-PROCEED: http://www.darpa.mil/Our_Work/I2O/Programs/PROgramming_Computation_on_EncryptEd_Data_(PROCEED).aspx

Datta, P., Dey, S., Paul, H., & Mukherjee, A. (2014). ANGELS: A framework for mobile grids. AIMoC. Kolkata, India.

Developers, A. (n.d.). *Tools Help*. Retrieved 2 6, 2015, from Android Developers: http://developer.android.com/tools/help/index.html

DHS-Goals. (2015). *US Department of Homeland Security. Visionary Goals.* Retrieved from http://www.dhs.gov/science-and-technology/visionary-goals

Diffie, W., & Hellman, M. (1976). New directions in cryptography. *IEEE Transactions on Information Theory*, *22*(6), 644–654. doi:10.1109/TIT.1976.1055638

Dijk, M., Gentry, C., Halevi, S., & Vaikuntanathan, V. (2010). Fully Homomorphic Encryption over the Integers. *Advances in Cryptology (EUROCRYPT)*, 24-43.

Dillinger, M., Madani, K., & Alonistioti, N. (2005). *Software defined radio: Architectures, systems and functions*. John Wiley & Sons.

Ding, C., Chen, Y. T. X., & Fu, X. (2010). CloudGPS: A Scalable and ISP-friendly Server Selection Scheme in Cloud Computing Environments. IEEE IWQoS, (pp. 1-9).

Dinh, H. T., Lee, C., Niyato, D., & Wang, P. (2013). A survey of mobile cloud computing: Architecture, applications, and approaches. *Wireless Communications and Mobile Computing*, *13*(18), 1587–1611. doi:10.1002/wcm.1203

Distefano, S., Merlino, G., & Puliafito, A. (2014). A utility paradigm for IoT: The sensing Cloud. *Pervasive and Mobile Computing*. doi:10.1016/j.pmcj.2014.09.006

DOCSIS. (2012). Retrieved from http://en.wikipedia.org/wiki/DOCSIS

Dong, H., & Gibson, J. (2006). Structures for SNR scalable speech coding. *IEEE Transactions on Audio. Speech and Language Processing*, *14*(2), 545–557. doi:10.1109/TSA.2005.857804

Doukas, C., & Maglogiannis, I. (2012). Bringing IoT and cloud computing towards pervasive healthcare.*Sixth International Conference on Innovative Mobile and Internet Services in Ubiquitous Computing (IMIS)*, (pp. 922-926). doi:10.1109/IMIS.2012.26

Dr Chrono. (2013). Retrieved from https://drchrono.com

Dsouza, A., Kabbedjik, J., Seo, D., Jansen, S., & Brinkkemper, S. (2012). Software-as-a-service: Implications for business and technology in product software companies. *PACIS 2012 Proceedings Pacific Asia Conference on Information.*

Duato, J., Pena, A. J., Silla, F., Mayo, R., & Quintana-Orti, E. S. (2011). Performance of cuda virtualized remote gpus in high performance Clusters.*International Conference on Parallel Processing (ICPP)* (pp. 365-374). IEEE. doi:10.1109/ICPP.2011.58

Durrani, M., & Shamsi, J. A. (2014). Volunteer computing: Requirements, challenges, and solutions. *Journal of Network and Computer Applications*, *39*(C), 369–380. doi:10.1016/j.jnca.2013.07.006

Eastlack, J. R. (2011). *Extending volunteer computing to mobile devices.* (Master's thesis). New Mexico State University.

EC2-Instance-Types. (n.d.). Retrieved from http://aws.amazon.com/ec2/instance-types/

EC2-Reserved-Instances. (n.d.). Retrieved from http://aws.amazon.com/ec2/purchasing-options/reserved-instances/

El Gamal, T. (1985). A Public Key Cryptosystem and a Signature Scheme based on Discrete Logarithms. *IEEE Transactions on Information Theory, 31*(4), 469–472. doi:10.1109/TIT.1985.1057074

Emarketer. (2014). *Smartphone Users Worldwide Will Total 175 Billion 2014.* Retrieved from http://www.emarketer.com/Article/Smartphone-Users-Worldwide-Will-Total-175-Billion-2014/1010536/

Ephremides, A., & Truong, T. (1990). Scheduling broadcasts in multihop radio networks. *IEEE Transactions on Communications, 38*(4), 456–460. doi:10.1109/26.52656

Fahad, A., Soyata, T., Wang, T., Sharma, G., Heinzelman, W., & Shen, K. (2012). SOLARCAP: Super Capacitor Buffering of Solar Energy for Self-Sustainable Field Systems.*Proceedings of the 25th IEEE International System-On-Chip Conference (SOCC)*, (pp. 236-241). Nigara Falls, NY. doi:10.1109/SOCC.2012.6398354

Fahmy, S., & Karwa, T. (2001). *TCP Congestion Control: Overview and Survey of Ongoing Research.* CSD-TR-01-016, Purdue University. *Computer Science.*

Fan, Y., Zhu, H., Chen, J., & Shen, X. (2011). Network coding based privacy preservation against traffic analysis in multi-hop wireless networks. *IEEE Transactions on Wireless Communications, 10*(3), 834–843. doi:10.1109/TWC.2011.122010.100087

Fedak, G., Germain, C., Neri, V., & Cappello, F. (2001). XtremWeb: a generic global computing system. *IEEE/ACM CCGrid.* Brisbane, Qld.

Felegyhazi, M., Cagalj, M., Bidokhti, S., & Hubaux, J.-P. (2007). Non-Cooperative Multi-Radio Channel Allocation in Wireless Networks. *IEEE INFOCOM, 1*, s. 1442 -1450.

Fernando, N., Loke, S., & Rahayu, W. (2013). Honeybee: A programming framework for mobile crowd computing. In Mobile and Ubiquitous Systems: Computing, Networking, and Services, ser. Lecture Notes of the Institute for Computer Sciences, Social Informatics and Telecommunications Engineering (Vol. 120, pp. 224-236). Springer Berlin Heidelberg. doi:10.1007/978-3-642-40238-8_19

Fernando, N., Loke, S. W., & Rahayu, W. (2013). Mobile cloud computing: A survey. *Future Generation Computer Systems, 29*(1), 84–106. doi:10.1016/j.future.2012.05.023

Fesehaye, D., Gao, Y., Nahrstedt, K., & Wang, G. (2012). Impact of Cloudlets on Interactive Mobile Cloud Applications.*Enterprise Distributed Object Computing Conference (EDOC)* (s. 123-132). IEEE. doi:10.1109/EDOC.2012.23

Fetai, I., & Schuldt, H. (2012). Cost-Based Data Consistency in a Data-as-a-Service Cloud Environment. *Cloud 12 Proceedings of the IEEE Fifth International Conference on Cloud Computing* (pp. 526-533). Washington, DC: IEEE.

Fink, M., Noble, D., Virag, L., Varro, A., & Giles, W. R. (2008). Contributions of HERG K+ current to repolarization of the human ventricular action potential. *Progress in Biophysics and Molecular Biology, 96*(1-3), 357–376. doi:10.1016/j.pbiomolbio.2007.07.011 PMID:17919688

Flores, H., Srirama, S. N., & Paniagua, C. (2011). A generic middleware framework for handling process intensive hybrid cloud services from mobiles.*Proceedings of the 9th International Conference on Advances in Mobile Computing and Multimedia* (s. 87-94). ACM. doi:10.1145/2095697.2095715

Francis, P., Jamin, S., & Jin, C. (2001, October). IDMaps: A Global Internet Host Distance Estimation Service. *IEEE/ACM Transactions on Networking*, *9*(5), 525–540. doi:10.1109/90.958323

Freund, Y., Schapire, R., & Abe, N. (1999). A short introduction to boosting. *Journal-Japanese Society for Artificial Intelligence, 14*(771-780), 1612.

Fridericia, L. S. (1920). Die Systolendauer im Elektrokardiogramm bei normalen Menschen und bei Herzkranken. *Acta Medica Scandinavica*, 469–486.

Funai, C., Tapparello, C., Ba, H., Karaouglu, B., & Heinzelman, W. (2014). *Extending volunteer computing through mobile ad hoc networking*. Austin, TX, USA: IEEE GLOBECOM. doi:10.1109/GLOCOM.2014.7036780

Ganesana, M., Erlichman, J. S., & Andreescu, S. (2012). Real-time monitoring of superoxide accumulation and antioxidant activity in a brain slice model using an electrochemical cytochrome c biosensor. *Free Radical Biology & Medicine*, *53*(12), 2240–2249. doi:10.1016/j.freeradbiomed.2012.10.540 PMID:23085519

Gao, L., & Wang, X. (2008). A game approach for multi-channel allocation in multi-hop wireless networks. *ACM MOBIHOC*, (s. 303-312).

Gargano, L., & Hammar, M. (2009). A note on submodular set cover on matroids. *Discrete Mathematics*, *309*(18), 5739–5744. doi:10.1016/j.disc.2008.05.019

Ge, B., & Lisdat, F. (2002). Superoxide sensor based on cytochrome c immobilized on mixed-thiol SAM with a new calibration method. *Analytica Chimica Acta*, *454*(1), 53–64. doi:10.1016/S0003-2670(01)01545-8

Geekbench. (n.d.). *Geekbench 3: Cross-platform processor benchmark.* Retrieved Jan. de 2015 from http://www.primatelabs.com/geekbench/

GeForce500. (2011). Retrieved from http://en.wikipedia.org/wiki/GeForce_500_Series

GeForce600. (2012). Retrieved from http://en.wikipedia.org/wiki/GeForce_600_Series

Gekakis, N., Nadeau, A., Hassanalieragh, M., Chen, Y., Liu, Z., Honan, G., & Soyata, T. (2015). Modeling of Supercapacitors as an Energy Buffer for Cyber-Physical Systems. In *Cyber Physical Systems - A Computational Perspective*. Boca Raton, Florida: CRC.

Gentry, C. (2009). *A Fully Homomorphic Encryption Scheme*. Stanford University.

Gentry, C., & Halevi, S. (2011). *Fully homomorphic encryption without squashing using depth-3 arithmetic circuits* (pp. 107–109). FOCS. doi:10.1109/FOCS.2011.94

Gentry, C., & Halevi, S. (2011). *Implementing Gentry's fully-homomorphic encryption scheme* (pp. 129–148). EUROCRYPT.

Gentry, C., Halevi, S., & Smart, N. (2012). *Better bootstrapping in fully homomorphic encryption* (pp. 1–16). PKC.

Gentry, C., Halevi, S., & Smart, N. (2012). *Fully homomorphic encryption with polylog overhead* (pp. 465–482). EUROCRYPT.

Gentry, C., Halevi, S., & Smart, N. (2012). Homomorphic Evaluation of the AES Circuit. In R. Safavi-Naini & R. Canetti (Eds.), *Advances in Cryptology – CRYPTO 2012* (Vol. 7417, pp. 850–867). Springer Berlin Heidelberg. doi:10.1007/978-3-642-32009-5_49

Ghafarian, T., Deldari, H., Javadi, B., Yaghmaee, M. H., & Buyya, R. (2013). CycloidGrid: A proximity-aware P2P-based resource discovery architecture in volunteer computing systems. *Future Generation Computer Systems*, *29*(6), 1583–1595. doi:10.1016/j.future.2012.08.010

Ghose, A., Biswas, P., Bhaumik, C., Sharma, M., Pal, A., & Jha, A. (2012). Road condition monitoring and alert application: Using in-vehicle smartphone as Internet-connected sensor.*Proc. IEEE Intl. Conf. on Pervasive Computing and Communications Workshops (PERCOM Workshops)*, (pp. 489—491). doi:10.1109/PerComW.2012.6197543

Gilbert, P., Cox, L. P., Jung, J., & Wetherall, D. (2010). Toward trustworthy mobile sensing. *ACM Proceedings of the Eleventh Workshop on Mobile Computing Systems and Applications,* (pp. 31-36).

Gilbert, P., Cox, L. P., Jung, J., & Wetherall, D. (2010). Toward Trustworthy Mobile Sensing.*Proc. 11th International Workshop on Mobile Computing Systems and Applicatons (HotMobile)*, (pp. 31--36).

Giunta, G., Montella, R., Agrillo, G., & Coviello, G. (2010). *A GPGPU transparent virtualization component for high performance computing clouds* (pp. 379–391). Springer-Verlag. doi:10.1007/978-3-642-15277-1_37

Gkoulalas-Divannis, A., Loukides, G., & Sun, J. (2014). Toward smarter healthcare: Anonymizing medical data to support research studies. *IBM Journal of Research and Development*, 1–11.

Goldreich, O. (2008). *Computational complexity - a conceptual perspective*. London: Cambridge University Press. doi:10.1017/CBO9780511804106

Goldstein, A. J., Harmon, L. D., & Lesk, A. B. (1971). Identification of human faces. *Proceedings of the IEEE*, *59*(5), 748–760. doi:10.1109/PROC.1971.8254

Goldwasser, S., & Micali, S. (1982). Probabilistic Encryption - How to Play Mental Poker Keeping Secret all Partial Information.*Proceedings of the 14th Annual ACM Symposium on Theory of Computing*, (pp. 365-377). doi:10.1145/800070.802212

Gong, L. (2001). JXTA: A network programming environment. *IEEE Internet Computing*, *5*(3), 88–95. doi:10.1109/4236.935182

Gonzales, S., White, G., & Safranek, T. (2014). Near-realtime assessment of cardiovascular disease risk factors in nebraska by using essence. *Online Journal of Public Health Informatics*, 103–104.

Goodman, D. J., Valenzuela, R., Gayliard, K. T., & Ramamurthi, B. (1989). Packet reservation multiple access for local wireless communications. *IEEE Transactions on Communications*, *37*(8), 885–890. doi:10.1109/26.31190

Good, S. (2013). Why Healthcare Must Embrace Cloud Computing. *Forbes*.

Google Cloud Platform. (n.d.). Retrieved from https://cloud.google.com

Google. (2012). Retrieved from http://code.google.com/appengine

Google. (2013, September 1). *Cloud Standards Customer Council*. Retrieved from What to Expect and What to Negotiate: Public Cloud Service Agreements.

Google-Translate. (n.d.). Retrieved from https://translate.google.com/

Grushko, C., Aharon, L., Dov, O. B., & Swisz, K. (2008). *Boincoid*. Retrieved Jan. de 2015 from http://boincoid.sourceforge.net

Gubbi, J., Buyya, R., Marusic, S., & Palaniswami, M. (2013). Internet of things (iot): A vision, architectural elements. *Future Generation Computer Systems*, *29*(7), 1645–1660. doi:10.1016/j.future.2013.01.010

Gummadi, K., Saroiu, S., & S., G. (2002). King: Estimating Latency between Arbitrary Internet End Hosts. *ACM IMW*, (pp. 5-18).

Guo, X., Ipek, E., & Soyata, T. (2010). Resistive computation: avoiding the power wall with low-leakage, STT-MRAM based computing. ACM SIGARCH Computer Architecture News (s. 371-382). ACM.

Guo, X., Ipek, E., & Soyata, T. (2010). Resistive Computation: Avoiding the Power Wall with Low-Leakage, {STT-MRAM} Based Computing.*Proceedings of the International Symposium on Computer Architecture (ISCA)*, (pp. 371-382). Saint-Malo, France. doi:10.1145/1815961.1816012

Ha, K., Pillai, P., Lewis, G., Simanta, S., Clinch, S., Davies, N., & Satyanarayanan, M. (2012). *The impact of multimedia applications on data center consolidation*. Carnegie Mellon University, School of Computer Seience.

Ha, K., Pillai, P., Richter, W., Abe, Y., & Satyanarayanan, M. (2013). *Just-in-time provisioning for cyber foraging* (pp. 153–166). MobiSys.

Halevi, S., & Shoup, V. (2014). Algorithms in HElib. *Proceedings, Part I, Advanced in Cryptology - CRYPTO 2014 - 34th Annual Cryptology Conference*, (pp. 554-571). Santa Barbara, CA. doi:10.1007/978-3-662-44371-2_31

Halevi, S., & Shoup, V. (2014). *HElib Fully Homomorphic Encryption Library*. Retrieved from http://www.github.com/shaih/HElib

Halevi, S., & Shoup, V. (n.d.). *HELib*. Retrieved from HELib: https://github.com.shaih/HElib

Han, X., Tian, L., Yoon, M., & Lee, M. (2012). A big data model supporting information recommendation in social networks.*Proc. Second International Conference on Cloud and Green Computing (CGC)*, (pp. 810-813). doi:10.1109/CGC.2012.125

Hassanalieragh, M., Soyata, T., Nadeau, A., & Sharma, G. (2014). Solar-Supercapacitor Harvesting System Design for Energy-Aware Applications.*Proceedings of the 27th IEEE International System-on-Chip Conference (IEEE SOCC)*.Las Vegas, NV. doi:10.1109/SOCC.2014.6948941

Hayat, A., Andreescu, D., Bulbul, G., & Andreescu, S. (2014). Redox reactivity of cerium oxide nanoparticles against dopamine. *Journal of Colloid and Interface Science*, *418*, 240–245. doi:10.1016/j.jcis.2013.12.007 PMID:24461841

Hayat, A., & Andreescu, S. (2013). Nanoceria particles as catalytic amplifiers for alkaline phosphatase assays. *Analytical Chemistry*, *85*(21), 10028–10032. doi:10.1021/ac4020963 PMID:24053108

Hayat, A., Bulbul, G., & Andreescu, S. (2014). novel colorimetric approach for the detection of enzyme activity. *Biosensors & Bioelectronics*, *56*, 334–339. doi:10.1016/j.bios.2014.01.003 PMID:24531308

Hayes, S. A., Yu, P., O'Keefe, T. J., O'Keefe, M. J., & Stoffer, J. O. (2002). The phase stability of cerium species in aqueous systems i. e-ph diagram for the ce hclo 4 h 2 o system. *Journal of the Electrochemical Society*, *149*(12), C623–C630. doi:10.1149/1.1516775

Hedley, P. L., Jrgensen, P., Schlamowitz, S., Wangari, R., Moolman-Smook, J., Brink, P. A., & Christiansen, M. et al. (2009). The genetic basis of long qt and short qt syndromes: A mutation update. *Human Mutation*, *30*(11), 1486–1511. doi:10.1002/humu.21106 PMID:19862833

HElib. (2014). *HElib Fully Homomorphic Encryption Library*. Retrieved from http://www.github.com/shaih/HElib

HIPAA. (2014). Retrieved from http://www.hhs.gov/ocr/privacy/

HIPAA. (n.d.). *Health Insurance Portability and Accountability Act*. Retrieved from http://www.hhs.gov/ocr/privacy/

Hoang, D. B., & Chen, L. (2010). Mobile cloud for assistive healthcare (MoCAsH). *Asia-Pacific Services Computing Conference (APSCC)* (s. 325-332). IEEE.

Hoang, D. T., Niyato, D., & Wang, P. (2012). Optimal admission control policy for mobile cloud computing hotspot with cloudlet.*Wireless Communications and Networking Conference (WCNC)* (s. 3145-3149). IEEE. doi:10.1109/WCNC.2012.6214347

Hoffman, F. M., Hargrove, W. W., & Schultz, A. J. (1997). *The Stone SouperComputer*. Retrieved Jan. de 2015 from http://www.extremelinux.info/stonesoup/

Holter, N. (1961). New Method for Heart Studies: Continuous electrocardiography of active subjects over long periods is now practical. *Science*, *134*(3486), 1214–1220. doi:10.1126/science.134.3486.1214 PMID:13908591

Hoyert, D. L., & Xu, J. (2012). Deaths: Preliminary data for 2011. *National Vital Statistics Reports*, *61*, 1–51. PMID:24984457

HPC-Servers. (n.d.). *High Performance Computing for Servers — Tesla GPUs*. Retrieved from http://www.nvidia.com/object/tesla-servers.html

HTC. (2015). *HTC Power to Give*. Retrieved Jan. de 2015 from http://www.htc.com/us/go/power-to-give/

Huang, J., Qian, F., Gerber, A., Mao, M., Sen, S., & Spatscheck, O. (2012). A close examination of performance and power characteristics of 4G LTE Networks.*Proceedings of the 10th international conference on Mobile systems, applications, and services* (pp. 225-238). ACM. doi:10.1145/2307636.2307658

Huerta-Canepa, G., & Lee, D. (2010). *A virtual cloud computing provider for mobile devices*. San Francisco, CA, USA: ACM MCS. doi:10.1145/1810931.1810937

Hu, L. (1993). Distributed code assignments for CDMA packet radio networks. *IEEE/ACM Transactions on Networking*, *1*(6), 668–677. doi:10.1109/90.266055

Hu, X., Du, W., & Spencer, B. (2011). A multi-agent framework for ambient systems development. *Procedia Computer Science*, *5*(1), 82–89. doi:10.1016/j.procs.2011.07.013

Hu, X., Liu, Q., Zhu, C., Leung, V. C. M., Chu, T. H. S., & Chan, H. C. B. (2013). A Mobile Crowdsensing System Enhanced by Cloud-based Social Networking Services.*Proc. First International Workshop on Middleware for Cloud-enabled Sensing*, (pp. 3.1--3.6). doi:10.1145/2541603.2541604

Hu, X., Li, X., Ngai, E.-C.-H., Leung, V., & Kruchten, P. (2014). Multidimensional Context-Aware Social Network Architecture for Mobile Crowdsensing. *IEEE Communications Magazine*, *52*(6), 78–87. doi:10.1109/MCOM.2014.6829948

Hwang, J.-Y., Suh, S.-B., Heo, S.-K., Park, C.-J., Ryu, J.-M., Park, S.-Y., & Kim, C.-R. (2008). Xen on ARM: System virtualization using Xen hypervisor for ARM-based secure mobile phones.*Consumer Communications and Networking Conference, 2008. CCNC 2008. 5th IEEE* (pp. 257--161). IEEE. doi:10.1109/ccnc08.2007.64

I, C.-L., & Chao, P.-H. (1993). Local packing-distributed dynamic channel allocation at cellular base station. *IEEE GLOBECOM*, (s. 293 -301).

I, C.-L., & Chao, P.-H. (1994). Distributed dynamic channel allocation algorithms with adjacent channel constraints. *IEEE PIMRC*, *1*, s. 169 -177.

IBM. (2013). *Shaping the future of the oil and gas industry with smarter cloud computing. Thought Leadership White Paper.* IBM Corporation. Retrieved from http://www-935.ibm.com/services/multimedia/Shaping_the_future_of_the_oil_and_gas_industry_with_smarter_cloud_computing.pdf

IBM. (2015). *IBM Cloud*. Retrieved Jan. de 2015 from http://www.ibm.com/cloud-computing/us/en/

IDC. (2015). *International Data Corporation (IDC)*. Retrieved Jan. de 2015 from http://www.idc.com

IEEE 802.16. (2014). Retrieved from: http://en.wikipedia.org/wiki/IEEE_802.16

Intel. (2012). Retrieved from http://en.wikipedia.org/wiki/Intel_Tick-Tock

INTEL-IA-PartGuide. (2010). Intel® 64 and IA-32 Architectures Software Developer's Manual.

INTEL-XeonPhi. (n.d.). *INTEL Xeon PHI Family*. Retrieved from http://www.intel.com/content/www/us/en/processors/xeon/xeon-phi-detail.html

IOT. (2012). Retrieved from http://en.wikipedia.org/wiki/Internet_of_Things

iPhone5s. (n.d.). Retrieved from http://www.anandtech.com/print/7335/the-iphone5s-review

iPhone-5s. (n.d.). *The iPhone 5s Specifications*. Retrieved from AnandTech: http://www.anandtech.com/print/7335/the-iphone-5s-review

Ishai, Y., & Paskin, A. (2007). Evaluating Branching Programs on Encrypted Data. *Theory of Cryptography, 4th Theory of Cryptography Conference, (TCC) 2007*, (pp. 575-594). Amsterdam.

Ispas, C., Njagi, J., Cates, M., & Andreescu, S. (2008). Electrochemical studies of ceria as electrode material for sensing and biosensing applications. *Journal of the Electrochemical Society*, *155*(8), F169–F176. doi:10.1149/1.2936178

Istamboulie, G., Andreescu, S., Marty, J. L., & Noguer, T. (2007). Highly sensitive detection of organophosphorus insecticides using magnetic microbeads and genetically engineered acetylcholinesterase. *Biosensors & Bioelectronics*, *23*(4), 506–512. doi:10.1016/j.bios.2007.06.022 PMID:17826976

Jain, N., Das, S., & Nasipuri, A. (2001). A multichannel CSMA MAC protocol with receiver-based channel selection for multihop wireless networks. *IEEE ICCCN, 1*, s. 432 -439.

Jararweh, Y., Tabalweh, L., Ababneh, F., & Dosari, F. (2013). Resource efficient mobile computing using cloudlet infrastructure.*IEEE Ninth International Conference on Mobile Ad-hoc and Sensor Networks (MSN)* (pp. 373-377). IEEE. doi:10.1109/MSN.2013.75

Jassal, P., Yadav, K., Kumar, A., Naik, V., Narwal, V., & Singh, A. (2013). *Unity: Collaborative downloading content using co-located socially connected peers*. San Diego, CA: IEEE PERCOM.

Jiang, J. H. (2002). On Distributed Dynamic Channel Allocation in Mobile Cellular Networks. *IEEE Transactions on Parallel and Distributed Systems*, *13*(10), 1024–1037. doi:10.1109/TPDS.2002.1041879

Jiao, F. F., Fung, C. S., Wong, C. K., Wan, Y. F., Dai, D., Kwok, R., & Lam, C. L. (2014). Effects of the multidisciplinary risk assessment and management program for patients with diabetes mellitus (rampdm) on biomedical outcomes, observed cardiovascular events and cardiovascular risks in primary care: A longitudinal comparative study. *Cardiovascular Diabetology*, 1–10. PMID:25142791

Johansson, K. (2007, June 22). *Cost Effective Deployment Strategies for Heterogeneous Wireless Networks*. Royal Institute of Technology.

Juntilla, M. J., Tikkanen, J. T., Kentta, T., Anttonen, O., Aro, A. L., Porthan, K., . . . Huikuri, H. (2014). Early repolarization as a predictor of arrhythmic and nonarrhythmic cardiac events in middle-aged subjects. *Heart rhythm: the official journal of the Heart Rhythm Society*, 1701-1706.

Ju, Y., Lee, Y., Yu, J., Min, C., Shin, I., & Song, J. (2012). SymPhoney: A Coordinated Sensing Flow Execution Engine for Concurrent Mobile Sensing Applications.*Proc. 10th ACM Conference on Embedded Networked Sensor Systems (SenSys)*. doi:10.1145/2426656.2426678

Kantarci, B., & Mouftah, H. (2014). Trustworthy sensing for public safety in cloud-centric internet of things. *IEEE Internet of Things Journal*, 360-368.

Kantarci, B., & Mouftah, H. T. (2014a). Reputation-based Sensing-as-a-Service for Crowd Management Over the Cloud. *Proc. IEEE International Conference on Communications (ICC)*, (pp. 3614--3619). doi:10.1109/ICC.2014.6883882

Kantarci, B., & Mouftah, H. T. (2014b). Trustworthy Sensing for Public Safety in Cloud-Centric Internet of Things. *IEEE Internet of Things Journal*, *1*(4), 360–368. doi:10.1109/JIOT.2014.2337886

Kantarci, B., & Mouftah, H. T. (2014c). Mobility-aware Trustworthy Crowdsourcing in Cloud-Centric Internet of Things. *Proc. IEEE International Symposium on Computers and Communications (ISCC)*. doi:10.1109/ISCC.2014.6912581

Kantarci, B., & Mouftah, H. T. (2014d). Trustworthy Crowdsourcing via Mobile Social Networks.*Proc. IEEE Global Communications Conference (GLOBECOM)*, (pp. 2905--2910).

Kappes, M. (2006). An experimental performance analysis of (MAC) multicast in 802.11b networks for VoIP traffic. *Computer Communications*, *29*(8), 938–948. doi:10.1016/j.comcom.2005.06.014

Karaoglu, B. (2014). *Efficient Use of Resources in Mobile Ad Hoc Networks.* (Ph.D. dissertation). University of Rochester, Rochester, NY.

Karaoglu, B., & Heinzelman, W. (2010). Multicasting vs. Broadcasting: What Are the Trade-Offs? *IEEE GLOBECOM*, (s. 1-5).

Karaoglu, B., & Heinzelman, W. (2012). A Dynamic Channel Allocation Scheme Using Spectrum Sensing for Mobile Ad Hoc Networks. *IEEE GLOBECOM*, (s. 397-402).

Karaoglu, B., & Heinzelman, W. (2014). Cooperative Load Balancing and Dynamic Channel Allocation for Cluster-based Mobile Ad Hoc Networks. *IEEE Transactions on Mobile Computing, PP* (99), 1-1.

Karaoglu, B., Numanoglu, T., & Heinzelman, W. (2011). Analytical performance of soft clustering protocols. *Ad Hoc Networks*, *9*(4), 635–651. doi:10.1016/j.adhoc.2010.08.008

Karn, P. (1990). MACA-a new channel access method for packet radio. *ARRL/CRRL Amateur radio 9th computer networking conference*, (s. 134-140).

Katzela, I., & Naghshineh, M. (1996). Channel assignment schemes for cellular mobile telecommunication systems: A comprehensive survey. *IEEE Personal Communications*, *3*(3), 10–31. doi:10.1109/98.511762

Kavajiri, R., Shimosaka, M., & Kashima, H. (2014). Steered Crowdsensing: Incentive Design towards Quality-Oriented Place-Centric Crowdsensing.*ACM International Joint Conference on Pervasive and Ubiquitous Computing*, (pp. 691--701).

Kavitha, T., & Sridharan, D. (2010). Security vulnerabilities in wireless sensor networks: A survey. *Journal of Information Assurance and Security*, *5*, 31–44.

Kazemi, L., Shahabi, C., & Chen, L. (2013). Geotrucrowd: trustworthy query answering with spatial crowdsourcing. *Proc. 21st ACM SIGSPATIAL International Conference on Advances in Geographic Information Systems*, (pp. 304--313). doi:10.1145/2525314.2525346

Kazemi, L., Shahabi, C., & Chen, L. (2013). Trustworthy query answering with spatial crowdsourcing.*Proceedings of the 21st ACM SIGSPATIAL International Conference on Advances in Geographic Information Systems*, (pp. 314-323).

Keller, J. (2011). *Cloud-Powered Facial Recognition is Terrifying.* Retrieved from http://www.theatlantic.com/technology/archive/2011/09/cloud-powered-facial-recognition-is-terrifying/245867/

Khosla, R., Fahmy, S., & Hu, Y. (2012). Content Retrieval Using Cloud-based DNS.*IEEE Global Internet Symposium*, (pp. 1-6).

Kim, K. I., Jung, K., & Kim, H. J. (2002). Face recognition using kernel principal component analysis. *Signal Processing Letters, IEEE*, *9*(2), 40–42. doi:10.1109/97.991133

Kim, K., Jung, K., & Kim, H. (2002). Face recognition using kernel principal component analysis. *IEEE Signal Processing Letters*, 40–42.

Kim, M., Kotz, D., & Kim, S. (2006). Extracting a Mobility Model from Real User Traces.*Proc. 25th IEEE Intl. Conf. on Computer Communications (INFOCOM)*, (pp. 1--13). doi:10.1109/INFOCOM.2006.173

Kirk, D. B., & Hwu, W. M. W. (2010). *Programming Massively Parallel Processors. Hands-on Approach.* Burlington, MA, USA: Morgan Kaufmann Publishers.

Kivity, A., Kamay, Y., Laor, D., Lublin, U., & Liguori, A. (2007). kvm: the Linux virtual machine monitor.*Proceedings of the Linux Symposiu*, pp. 225-230.

Kleinrock, L., & Tobagi, F. (1975). Packet Switching in Radio Channels: Part I--Carrier Sense Multiple-Access Modes and Their Throughput-Delay Characteristics. *IEEE Transactions on Communications*, *23*(12), 1400–1416. doi:10.1109/TCOM.1975.1092768

Knuth, D. (1973). *The Art of Computer Programming: Sorting and Searching*. Reading, MA: Addison-Wesley.

Kobza, R., Cuculi, F., Abacherli, R., Toggweiler, S., Suter, Y., Frey, F., . . . Erne, P. (2014). Twelve-lead electrocardiography in the young. *Heart rhythm: the official journal of the Heart Rhythm Society*, 2018-2022.

Kocabas, O., & Soyata, T. (2014). Medical Data Analytics in the cloud using Homomorphic Encryption. In *Handbook of Research on Cloud Infrastructures for Big Data Analytics* (pp. 471–488). Hershey, Pennsylvania, US: IGI Global. doi:10.4018/978-1-4666-5864-6.ch019

Kocabas, O., Soyata, T., Couderc, J.-P., Aktas, M., Xia, J., & Huang, M. (2013). Assessment of Cloud-based Health Monitoring using Homomorphic Encryption.*Proceedings of the 31st IEEE International Conference on Computer Design (ICCD)*, (pp. 443-446). Ashville, VA, USA. doi:10.1109/ICCD.2013.6657078

Kogge, P. M., & Stone, H. S. (1973). A parallel algorithm for the efficient solution of a general class of recurrence equations. *Transactions on Computers*, 786-793.

Kovachev, D., Cao, Y., & Klamma, R. (2013). *Mobile Cloud Computing: A Comparison of Application Models*. Retrieved from http://arxiv.org/abs/1107.4940v1

KPCB. (2014). *Kleiner Perkins Caufield Byers (KPCB) Internet Trends 2014*. Retrieved Jan. de 2015 from http://www.kpcb.com/internet-trends

Kristekova, Z., ... B. J. (2012, June 15). *Simulation Model for Cost-Benefit Analysis of Cloud Computing versus In-House Datacenters.* Retrieved from http://digisrv-1.biblio.etc.tu-bs.de: 8080/ docportal/servlets/MCRFileNodeServlet

Kumar, K., Liu, J., Lu, Y.-H., & Bhargava, B. (2013). A Survey of Computation Offloading for Mobile Systems. *Mobile Networks and Applications*, *18*(1), 129–140. doi:10.1007/s11036-012-0368-0

Kundu, E. A., Ghosh, P., Datta, S., Ghosh, A., Chattopadhyay, S., & Chatterjee, M. (2012). Oxidative stress as a potential biomarker for determining disease activity in patients with rheumatoid arthritis. *Free Radical Research, 46*(12), 1482–1489. doi:10.3109/10715762.2012.727991 PMID:22998065

Kushilevitz, E., & Ishai, Y. (2000). Randomizing Polynomials: A New Representation with Applications to Round-Efficient Secure Computation.*41st Annual Symposium on Foundations of Computer Science* (pp. 294-304). Redondo Beach: ACM.

Kwon, M. (2015). *A Tutorial on Network Latency and its Measurements*. Hershey, Pennsylvania: IGI Global.

Kwon, M., Dou, Z., Heinzelman, W., Soyata, T., Ba, H., & Shi, J. (2014). Use of Network Latency Profiling and Redundancy for Cloud Server Selection.*Proceedings of the 7th IEEE International Conference on Cloud Computing (IEEE CLOUD 2014)*, (pp. 826-832). Alaska. doi:10.1109/CLOUD.2014.114

Lane, N. D., Chon, Y., Zhou, L., & Zhang, Y., i, F., Kim, D., Ding, G., Zhao, F. & Cha, H. (2013). Piggyback CrowdSensing (PCS): energy efficient crowdsourcing of mobile sensor data by exploiting smartphone app opportunities. *Proc. 11th ACM Conference on Embedded Networked Sensor Systems*, (pp. 7.1--7.14). doi:10.1145/2517351.2517372

Lauro, R., Lucarelli, F., & Montella, R. (2012). Siaas - sensing instrument as a service using cloud computing to turn physical instrument into ubiquitous service. *IEEE 10th International Symposium on Parallel and Distributed Processing with Applications (ISPA)*, (pp. 861-862).

Lee, S. J., Su, W., & Gerla, M. (2002). On-Demand Multicast Routing Protocol in Multihop Wireless Mobile Networks. *Mobile Networks and Applications, 7*(6), 441–453. doi:10.1023/A:1020756600187

Leiner, B., Nielson, D., & Tobagi, F. (1987). Issues in packet radio network design. *Proceedings of the IEEE, 75*(1), 6–20. doi:10.1109/PROC.1987.13701

Lin, W. H., Zhang, H., & Zhang, Y. T. (2013). Investigation on cardiovascular risk prediction using physiological parameters. *Computational and Mathematical Methods in Medicine*, 1–21. PMID:24489599

Li, P., Ding, C., Hu, X., & Soyata, T. (2014). LDetector: A Low Overhead Race Detector for GPU Programs.*5th Workshop on Determinism and Correctness in Parallel Programming (WODET2014).*

Li, Q., Mark, R. G., & Clifford, G. D. (2008). Robust heart rate estimation from multiple asynchronous noisy sources using signal quality indices and a Kalman filter. *Physiological Measurement, 29*(1), 15–32. doi:10.1088/0967-3334/29/1/002 PMID:18175857

Liu, L., Wang, H., Liu, X., Jin, X., He, W., & Wang, Q. et al.. (2009). *Greencloud: A new architecture for green data center*. Barcelona, Spain: ICAC-INDST. doi:10.1145/1555312.1555319

Liu, R., & Wassel, I. J. (2011). Opportunities and Challenges of Wireless Sensor Networks Using Cloud Services.*Proc. Workshop on Internet of Things and Service Platforms*, (pp. 4.1--4.7). doi:10.1145/2079353.2079357

Li, W., Chao, J., & Ping, Z. (2012). Security structure study of city management platform based on cloud computing under the conception of smart city.*InProc. Fourth International Conference on Multimedia Information Networking and Security (MINES)*, (pp. 91--94). doi:10.1109/MINES.2012.255

Li, Y., & Wang, W. (2013). *The unheralded power of cloudlet computing in the vicinity of mobile devices. IEEE Globecom Workshops* (pp. 4994–4999). GC Wkshps.

Loon, M. S., Eurlings, J. G., Winkens, B., Elwyn, G., Grol, R., Steenkiste, B., & Weijden, T. (2011). Small but important errors in cardiovascular risk calculation by practice nurses: A cross-sectional study in randomised trial setting. *International Journal of Nursing Studies, 48*(3), 285–291. doi:10.1016/j.ijnurstu.2010.03.016 PMID:20439105

Lund, K., Eggen, A., Hadzic, D., Hafsoe, T., & Johnsen, F. T. (2007). Using web services to realize service oriented architecture in military communication networks. *IEEE Communications Magazine*, *45*(10), 47–53. doi:10.1109/MCOM.2007.4342822

MacDonald, V. H. (1979). Advanced mobile phone service: The cellular concept. *The Bell System Technical Journal*, 15–41.

Madhyastha, H. T. A. (2006). A Structural Approach to Latency Prediction. ACM IMC, (pp. 99-104).

Madria, S., Kumar, V., & Dalvi, R. (2014). Sensor Cloud: A Cloud of Virtual Sensors. *IEEE Software*, *31*(2), 70–77. doi:10.1109/MS.2013.141

Maria, D. B. (2015). Retrieved from https://mariadb.org/

Marinelli, E. (2009). *Hyrax: Cloud computing on mobile devices using mapreduce.* (Master's thesis). Carnegie-Mellon University.

Markendahl, J., Makitalo, O., & Werding, J. (2008). Analysis of Cost Structure and Business Model options for Wireless Access Provisioning using Femtocell solutions.*19th European Regional ITS Conference*.

Markopoulou, A., Tobagi, F., & Manour, K. (2006, June). Loss and Delay Measurements of Internet Backbones. *Computer Communications*, *29*(10), 1590–1604. doi:10.1016/j.comcom.2005.07.011

Marsenne Research, Inc. (2015). *Great Internet Mersenne Prime Search*. Retrieved Jan. de 2015 from http://www.mersenne.org

matplotlib. (2015). Retrieved from http://matplotlib.org/

Ma, X., & Chen, X. (2008). Performance Analysis of IEEE 802.11 Broadcast Scheme in Ad Hoc Wireless LANs. *IEEE Transactions on Vehicular Technology*, *57*(6), 3757–3768. doi:10.1109/TVT.2008.918731

MAX4372. (n.d.). *Low-Cost, UCSP/SOT23, Micropower, High-Side Current-Sense Amplifier with Voltage Output*. Retrieved from http://datasheets.maximintegrated.com/en/ds/MAX4372-MAX4372T.pdf

Mei, C., Shimek, J., Wang, C., Chandra, A., & Weissman, J. (2011). *Dynamic outsourcing mobile computation to the cloud*. University of Minnesota.

Meisner, D., Gold, B., Wenisch, T., Liu, L., Wang, H., & Liu, X. et al.. (2009). *Powernap: Eliminating server idle power*. Washington, DC: ACM ASPLOS. doi:10.1145/1508244.1508269

Mezghani, F., Daou, R., Nogueira, M., & Beylot, A.-L. (2014). Content dissemination in vehicular social networks: Taxonomy and user satisfaction. *IEEE Communications Magazine*, *52*(12), 34–40. doi:10.1109/MCOM.2014.6979949

Microsoft Windows Azure. (n.d.). Retrieved from http://www.microsoft.com/windowsazure

Microsoft. (2010, May 15). *The Economics of Cloud.* Retrieved from http://www.microsoft.com/en-us/news/presskits/cloud/docs/the-economics-of-the-cloud.pdf

Microsoft. (2012). Retrieved from http://www.microsoft.com/windowazure

Microsoft. (2015). *Microsoft OneDrive*. Retrieved Jan. de 2015 from https://onedrive.live.com/

Microsoft Azure. (2014). Retrieved from Microsoft Azure: http://azure.microsoft.com/en-us/support/legal/sla/

MicroStrain. (n.d.). *Sensorcloud*. Retrieved Feb 2, 2015, from http://www.sensorcloud.com

Mihoob, A., Molina-Jimenez, C., & Shrivastava, S. (2011). *Consumer side resource accounting in the cloud*. Berlin, Germany: Springer. doi:10.1007/978-3-642-27260-8_5

Miluzzo, E., Lane, N. D., Peterson, K. F. R., Lu, H., Musolesi, M., Eiseman, S. B., & Campbell, A. T. et al. (2008). Sensing meets mobile social networks: The design, implementation and evaluation of the CenceMe application.*Proc. ACM Conf. on Embedded Network Sensor Systems*, (pp. 337--350). doi:10.1145/1460412.1460445

Miorandi, D., Sicari, S., De Pellegrini, F., & Chlamtac, I. (2012). Internet of things: Vision, applications and research challenges. *Ad Hoc Networks*, *10*(7), 1497–1516. doi:10.1016/j.adhoc.2012.02.016

Misra, S., Barthwal, R., & Obaidat, M. S. (2012). Community detection in an integrated Internet of Things and social network architecture.*Proc. IEEE Global Communications Conference (GLOBECOM)*, (pp. 1647--1652). doi:10.1109/GLOCOM.2012.6503350

Misra, S., Chatterjee, S., & Obaidat, M. (2014). *On Theoretical Modeling of Sensor Cloud: A Paradigm Shift From Wireless Sensor Network*. IEEE Systems Journal; doi:10.1109/JSYST.2014.2362617

Mizouni, R., & El Barachi, M. (2013). Mobile Phone Sensing as a Service: Business Model and Use Cases. *Proc. Sevent International Conference on Next Generation Mobile Apps, Services and Technologies (NGMAST)*, (pp. 116--121).

Mondal, A., Madria, S., & Kitsuregawa, M. (2009). An economic incentive model for encouraging peer collaboration in mobile-p2p networks with support for constraint queries. *Peer-to-Peer Networking and Applications*, *2*(3), 230–251. doi:10.1007/s12083-009-0035-9

Montenegro, G., Kushalnagar, N., Hui, J., & Culler, D. (2007). *Transmission of IPv6 Packets over IEEE 802.15.4 Networks*. Internet Engineering Task Force.

Moreno-Vozmediano, R., Montero, R. S., & Llorent, I. M. (2013). Key challenges in cloud computing: Enabling the future internet of services. *IEEE Internet Computing*, *17*(4), 18–25. doi:10.1109/MIC.2012.69

Morris, E. (2011). A new approach for handheld devices in the military. *SEI Blog*. Retrieved from http://blog. sei. cmu. edu/post. cfm/a-new-approach-for-handheld-devices-in-the-military

Moto-X. (n.d.). *Google/Motorola Mobilitys Moto X Outpaces Competition*. Retrieved from https://www.abiresearch.com/press/googlemotorola-mobilitys-moto-x-outpaces-competition

Mouftah, H. T., & Kantarci, B. (2013). *Communication Infrastructures for Cloud Computing*. Hershey, PA: IGI Global.

MS-SLA. (n.d.). Retrieved from Microsoft SLA Storage - Introduction: https://azure.microsoft.com/en-us/documentation/articles/storage-introduction/

MS-Translator. (n.d.). Retrieved from http://www.microsoft.com/en-us/translator/

Musolesi, M., & Mascolo, C. (2007). Designing mobility models based on social network theory. *Mobile Computing and Communications Review*, *11*(3), 59–80. doi:10.1145/1317425.1317433

MySQL. (2015). Retrieved from http://www.mysql.com/

Nadeau, A., Sharma, G., & Soyata, T. (2014). State-of-charge Estimation for Supercapacitors: A Kalman Filtering Formulation.*Proceedings of the 2014 IEEE International Conference on Acoustics, Speech and Signal Processing (ICASSP 2013)*, (pp. 2213-2217). Florence, Italy. doi:10.1109/ICASSP.2014.6853988

Naehrig, M., Lauter, K., & Vaikuntanathan, V. (2011). Can homomorphic encryption be practical?*Proceedings of the 3rd ACM workshop on Cloud computing security workshop*. ACM. doi:10.1145/2046660.2046682

Namboothiri, P., & Sivalingam, K. (2010). Capacity analysis of multi-hop wireless sensor networks using multiple transmission channels: A case study using IEEE 802.15.4 based networks. *IEEE LCN*, (s. 168-171).

Nandugudi, A., Maiti, A., Ki, T., Bulut, F., Demirbas, M., & Kosar, T. et al.. (2013). *Phonelab: A large programmable smartphone testbed*. Roma, Italy: ACM SENSEMINE. doi:10.1145/2536714.2536718

Nasipuri, A., & Das, S. (2000). Multichannel CSMA with signal power-based channel selection for multihop wireless networks. *IEEE VTS Fall, 1*, s. 211 -218.

NCSU. (2014). *Free PDK 45nm Standard Cell Library*. Retrieved from http://www. eda.ncsu.edu/wiki/FreePDK45

Ndumele, C. D., Baer, H. J., Shaykevich, S., Lipsitz, S. R., & Hicks, L. S. (2012). Cardiovascular disease and risk in primary care settings in the united states. *The American Journal of Cardiology*, *109*(4), 521–526. doi:10.1016/j.amjcard.2011.09.047 PMID:22112741

Neiger, G., Santoni, A., Leung, F., Rodgers, D., & Uhlig, R. (2006). *Intel Virtualization Technology: Hardware Support for Efficient Processor Virtualization*. Intel Technology Journal.

Ng, E., & Zhang, H. (2001). *Predicting Internet Network Distance with Coordinate-based Approaches* (pp. 170–179). IEEE INFOCOM.

Nguyen, T.-V.-A., Bimonte, S., d'Orazio, L., & Darmont, J. (2012). Cost models for view materialization in the cloud. *EDBT-ICDT '12 Proceedings of the Joint EDBT/ICDT Workshops*, (pp. 47-54). New York.

Nichols, K., Blake, S., Baker, F., & Black, D. (n.d.). *RFC 2474, Definition of the Differentiated Services Field (DS Field) in the IPv4 and IPv6 Headers*. Academic Press.

NIST. (2001). Retrieved from http://csrc.nist.gov/publications/fips/fips197/fips-197.pdf

NIST. FIPS-197. (2001). Advanced encryption standard (AES). National Institute of Standards and Technology.

NIST-AES. (2001). *Advanced encryption standard*. AES.

Nitti, M., Girau, R., & Atzori, L. (2013). Trustworthiness management in the social internet of things. *IEEE Transactions on Knowledge and Data Engineering*, *26*(5), 1253–1266. doi:10.1109/TKDE.2013.105

Njagi, J., Ball, M., Best, M., Wallace, K. N., & Andreescu, S. (2010). Electrochemical quantification of serotonin in the live embryonic zebrafish intestine. *Analytical Chemistry*, *82*(5), 1822–1830. doi:10.1021/ac902465v PMID:20148518

Njagi, J., Ispas, C., & Andreescu, S. (2008). Mixed ceria-based metal oxides biosensor for operation in oxygen restrictive environments. *Analytical Chemistry*, *80*(19), 7266–7274. doi:10.1021/ac800808a PMID:18720950

Nojiri, H., Shimizu, T., Funakoshi, M., Yamaguchi, O., Zhou, H., Kawakami, S., & Ishikawa, H. et al. (2006). Oxidative stress causes heart failure with impaired mitochondrial respiration. *The Journal of Biological Chemistry*, *281*(44), 33789–33801. doi:10.1074/jbc.M602118200 PMID:16959785

Numanoglu, T. (2009). *Improving the reliability and performance of real-time communications in mobile ad hoc networks*. (Ph.D. dissertation). University of Rochester, Rochester, NY.

Numanoglu, T., & Heinzelman, W. (2008). Improving QoS under lossy channels through adaptive redundancy. *IEEE MASS*, 509-510.

Numanoglu, T., & Heinzelman, W. (2009). Improving QoS in multicasting through adaptive redundancy. *IEEE WCNC*, 1-6.

Numanoglu, T., Heinzelman, W., & Tavli, B. (2007). Multi-rate support for network-wide broadcasting in MANETs. *Networking*, 1140-1144.

Numanoglu, T., Karadeniz, B., Onat, F. A., & Kolagasioglu, A. E. (2012). An embedded radio software emulation platform using OPNET and VxWorks to develop distributed algorithms for military ad-hoc networks. *IEEE MILCOM*, 1-6.

Numanoglu, T., Tavli, B., & Heinzelman, W. B. (2006). Energy efficiency and error resilience in coordinated and non-coordinated medium access control protocols. *Computer Communications*, *29*(17), 3493–3506. doi:10.1016/j.comcom.2006.01.023

NumPy. (2015). Retrieved from http://www.numpy.org/

Nvidia, C. U. D. A. (n.d.). *NVIDIA CUDA*. Retrieved from nvidia.com: http://www.nvidia.com/object/cuda_home_new.html

Nvidia, C. U. S. P. A. R. S. E. (n.d.). Retrieved from https://developer.nvidia.com/cusparse

Nvidia, CUBLAS. (n.d.). Retrieved August 18, 2014, from https://developer.nvidia.com/cublas

Nvidia, CUFFT. (n.d.). Retrieved August 18, 2014, from https://developer.nvidia.com/cufft

Nvidia-Grid-VGPU. (n.d.). Retrieved from VIRTUAL GPU TECHNOLOGY: http://www.nvidia.com/object/virtual-gpus.html

Nvidia-Shield. (2014). *The Nvidia Shield Gaming Tablet*. Retrieved from http://shield.nvidia.com/gaming-tablet/

Nvidia-VisualStudio. (n.d.). *NVIDIA Nsight Visual Studio Edition*. Retrieved from https://developer.nvidia.com/nvidia-nsight-visual-studio-edition

Olteanu, A. C., Oprina, G. D., Tapus, N., & Zeisberg, S. (2013). Enabling mobile devices for home automation using Zigbee.*19th International Conference on Control Systems and Computer Science (CSCS)*, (pp. 189-195). doi:10.1109/CSCS.2013.63

Oommen, B. (2010). Recent advances in learning automata systems.*2nd International Conference on Computer Engineering and Technology (ICCET)*, (pp. 724-735).

Open, CV-WEB. (n.d.). *Open CV (Open Source Computer Vision)*. Retrieved August 18, 2014, from http://opencv.org/

OpenCV-FaceRecognizer. (n.d.). *Open CV 3.0.0-dev Documentation*. Retrieved from http://docs.opencv.org/trunk/modules/contrib/doc/facerec/facerec_api.html

Operational Availability. (n.d.). *Operational Availability*. Retrieved from http://en.wikipedia.org/wiki/Operational_availability

Ornatska, M., Sharpe, E., Andreescu, D., & Andreescu, S. (2011). Paper bioassay based on ceria nanoparticles as colorimetric probes. *Analytical Chemistry*, *83*(11), 4273–4280. doi:10.1021/ac200697y PMID:21524141

OSGi. (2012). Retrieved from http://www.osgi.org/

Otani, H. (2004). Reactive oxygen species as mediators of signal transduction in ischemic preconditioning. *Antioxidants and Redox Signaling*, 449-469.

Ozel, R. E., Ispas, C., Ganesana, M., Leiter, J., & Andreescu, S. (2014). Glutamate oxidase biosensor based on mixed ceria and titania nanoparticles for the detection of glutamate in hypoxic environments. *Biosensors & Bioelectronics*, *52*, 397–402. doi:10.1016/j.bios.2013.08.054 PMID:24090755

Padhye, J., Firoiu, V., Towsley, D., & Kurose, J. (1998). *Modeling TCP Throughput: A Simple Model and its Empirical Validation* (pp. 303–323). ACM SIGCOMM. doi:10.1145/285237.285291

Page, A., Kocabas, O., Ames, S., Venkitasubramaniam, M., & Soyata, T. (2014). Cloud-based Secure Health Monitoring: Optimizing Fully-Homomorphic Encryption for Streaming Algorithms. *IEEE Globecom 2014 Workshop on Cloud Computing Systems, Networks, and Applications.*

Page, A., Kocabas, O., Soyata, T., Aktas, M., & Couderc, J.-P. (2014). Cloud-Based Privacy-Preserving Remote ECG Monitoring and Surveillance. *Annals of Noninvasive Electrocardiology*, n/a. doi:10.1111/anec.12204 PMID:25510621

Paillier, P. (1999). *Public Key Cryptosystems Based on Composite Degree Residuosity Classes* (pp. 223–238). Advances in Cryptology. doi:10.1007/3-540-48910-X_16

Pal, R., & Hui, P. (2013). Economic Models for Cloud Service Markets: Pricing and Capacity Planning. *Journal of Distributed Computing and Networking*, *496*, 113–124.

Parmar, K. B., Jani, N. N., Shrivastav, P. S., & Patel, M. H. (2013). jUniGrid: A simplistic framework for integration of mobile devices in heterogeneous grid computing. *International Journal of Multidisciplinary Sciences and Engineering*, *4*(1), 10–15.

Patel, C. D., & Shah, A. J. (2005, June). *Cost Model for Planning, Development and Operation of a Data Center.* Retrieved from http://www.hpl.hp.com/techreports/2005/HPL-2005-107R1.pdf

Pattichis, C. S., Kyriacou, E., Voskarides, S., Pattichis, M. S., Istepanian, R., & Schizas, C. N. (2002). Wireless telemedicine systems: An overview. *Antennas and Propagation Magazine*, *44*(2), 143–153. doi:10.1109/MAP.2002.1003651

Paxson, V. (1996). *End-to-End Routing Bahavior in the Internet.* ACM SIGCOMM.

Paxson, V. (1997). *End-to-End Internet Packet Dynamics.* ACM SIGCOMM.

Pereira, P. P., Eliasson, J., Kyusakov, R., Delsing, J., Raayetinezhad, A., & Johansson, M. (2013). Enabling Cloud Connectivity for Mobile Internet of Things Applications.*IEEE Seventh International Symposium on Service Oriented System Engineering (SOSE)*, (pp. 518--526). doi:10.1109/SOSE.2013.33

Perera, C., Jayaraman, P., Zaslavsky, A., Christen, P., & Georgapoulos, D. (2013). Dynamic configuration of sensors using mobile sensor hub in Internet of Things paradigm.*Proc. IEEE Eighth Intl. Conf. on Intelligent Sensors, Sensor Networks and Information Processing*, 473--478. doi:10.1109/ISSNIP.2013.6529836

Perera, C., Jayaraman, P., Zaslavsky, A., Christen, P., & Georgapoulos, D. (2014a). Sensing as a service model for smart cities supported by Internet of Things. *Transactions on Emerging Telecommunications Technologies*, *25*(1), 81–93. doi:10.1002/ett.2704

Perera, C., Zaslavsky, A., Liu, C. H., Compton, M., Christen, P., & Georgapoulos, D. (2014b). Sensor Search Techniques for Sensing as a Service Architecture for the Internet of Things. *IEEE Sensors Journal*, *14*(2), 406–420. doi:10.1109/JSEN.2013.2282292

Perrig, A., Stankovic, J., & Wagner, D. (2004). Security in wireless sensor networks. *Communications of the ACM*, *47*(6), 53–57. doi:10.1145/990680.990707

Petr, E. J., Ayers, C. R., Pandey, A., Lemos, J. A., Powell-Wiley, T., Khera, A., & Berry, J. D. et al. (2014). Perceived lifetime risk for cardiovascular disease (from the dallas heart study). *The American Journal of Cardiology*, *114*(1), 53–58. doi:10.1016/j.amjcard.2014.04.006 PMID:24834788

Phan, D. H., Suzuki, J., & Omura, S. & Oba, Katsuya. (2013). Toward Sensor-Cloud Integration as a Service: Optimizing Three-tier Communication in Cloud-integrated Sensor Networks. *Proc. 8th International Conference on Body Area Networks*, (pp. 355-362). doi:10.4108/icst.bodynets.2013.253639

Phan, T., Huang, L., & Dulan, C. (2002). *Challenge: Integrating mobile wireless devices into the computational grid.* Atlanta, GA, USA: ACM MobiCom. doi:10.1145/570645.570679

PIC16F1783. (n.d.). *PIC16F1783 28-Pin 8-Bit Advanced Analog Flash Microcontroller.* Retrieved from http://ww1.microchip.com/downloads/en/DeviceDoc/40001579E.pdf

PIC32. (2012). Retrieved from http://www.microchip.com/pagehandler/en-us/family/32bit/

PlanetLab. (2014). *PlanetLab.* Retrieved from http://www.planet-lab.org

Popek, G. J., & Goldberg, R. P. (1974). Formal requirements for virtualizable third generation architectures. In *Communications of the ACM* (pp. 412–421). ACM. doi:10.1145/361011.361073

POTS, Plain Old Telephone Service. (2014). Retrieved from http://en.wikipedia.org/wiki/Plain_old_telephone_service

Powers, N., Alling, A., Gyampoh-Vidogah, R., & Soyata, T. (2014). AXaaS: Case for Acceleration as a Service. *IEEE Globecom 2014 Workshop on Cloud Computing Systems, Networks, and Applications.*

Prasad, K., Sharma, V., Lackore, S. M., Jenkins, K., Prasad, A., & Sood, A. (2013). Use of Complementary Therapies in Cardiovascular Disease. *The American Journal of Cardiology, 111*(3), 339–345. doi:10.1016/j.amjcard.2012.10.010 PMID:23186602

Prasad, R. M., Gyani, J., & Murti, P. (2012). Mobile Cloud Computing: Implications and Challenges. *Journal of Information Engineering and Applications, 2*(7), 1–15.

Prehofer, C., & Bettstetter, C. (2005). Self-organization in communication networks: Principles and design paradigms. *IEEE Communications Magazine, 43*(7), 78–85. doi:10.1109/MCOM.2005.1470824

Priori, S. G., Bloise, R., & Crotti, L. (2001). The long QT syndrome. *Europace, 3*(1), 16–27. doi:10.1053/eupc.2000.0141 PMID:11271945

Project, T. M. (2012, February). *AWS Measurements.* Retrieved from http://www.themochaproject.com

QEMU. (n.d.). *QEMU Emulator User Documentation.* Retrieved from http://qemu.weilnetz.de/qemu-doc.html

Qualcomm. (2012). Retrieved from http://www.qualcomm.com/snapdragon

Quwaider, M., & Jararweh, Y. (2013). Cloudlet-based for big data collection in body area networks.*International Conference for Internet Technology and Secured Transactions (ICITST),* (pp. 137-141). doi:10.1109/ICITST.2013.6750178

Rahman, R., Meulpolder, M., Hales, D., Pouwelse, J., Epema, D., & Sips, H. (2010). Improving efficiency and fairness in P2P systems with effort-based incentives. IEEE ICC. Cape Town, South Africa.

Rahman, M., El-Saddik, A., & Gueaieb, W. (2011). Augmenting context awareness by combining body sensor networks and social networks. *IEEE Transactions on Instrumentation and Measurement, 60*(2), 345–353. doi:10.1109/TIM.2010.2084190

Ramaswami, R., & Parhi, K. (1989). Distributed scheduling of broadcasts in a radio network. *IEEE INFOCOM,* (s. 497 -504).

Raniwala, A., & Chiueh, T.-c. (2005). Architecture and algorithms for an IEEE 802.11-based multi-channel wireless mesh network. *IEEE INFOCOM, 3,* s. 2223-2234.

Rao, B., Saluia, P., Sharma, N., Mittal, A., & Sharma, S. (2012). Cloud computing for internet of things sensing based applications.*Sixth International Conference on Sensing Technology (ICST),* (pp. 374-380). doi:10.1109/ICSensT.2012.6461705

Ravi, V. T., Becchi, M., Agrawal, G., & Chakradhar, S. (2011). Supporting GPU sharing in cloud environments with a transparent runtime consolidation framework. In *Proceedings of the 20th international symposium on High performance distributed computing* (pp. 217--228). ACM. doi:10.1145/1996130.1996160

Reichman, A. (2011). *File storage costs less in the cloud than in-house*. Forrester.

Rellermeyer, J. S., Alonso, G., & Roscoe, T. (2007). R-OSGi: distributed applications through software modularization. *Proceedings of the ACM/IFIP/USENIX 2007 International Conference on Middleware* (s. 1-20). Springer-Verlag New York, Inc.

Richter, J. (2010). *CLR via c*. Microsoft Press.

Rickinson, M., & May, H. (2009). *A comparative study of methodological approaches to reviewing literature.* The Higher Education Academy. Retrieved June 15, 2014, from Http://www.heacademy.ac.uk/assets/ documents/ resources/ comparativestudy.pdf

Rimal, B., & Choi, E. (2012). A service-oriented taxonomical spectrum, cloudy challenges and opportunities of cloud computing. *International Journal of Communication Systems. Special Issue*, *25*(6), 796–819. doi:10.1002/dac.1279

Rimoldi, B. (1994). Successive refinement of information: Characterization of the achievable rates. *IEEE Transactions on Information Theory*, *40*(1), 253–259. doi:10.1109/18.272493

Rita, T. S. T., Liu, D., Fen, H., & Pau, G. (2011). Bridging vehicle sensor networks with social networks: Applications and challenges.*Proc. IET Intl. Conf. on Communication Technology and Application (ICCTA)*, (pp. 684--688).

Rius, J., Estrada, S., Cores, F., & Solsona, F. (2012). Incentive mechanism for scheduling jobs in a peer-to-peer computing system. *Simulation Modelling Practice and Theory*, *25*(0), 36–55. doi:10.1016/j.simpat.2012.02.007

Rivest, R. L., Adleman, L., & Dertouzos, M. L. (1978). On data banks and privacy homomorphisms . *Foundations of secure computation*, 169-179.

Rivest, R., Adleman, L., & Shamir, A. (1978). A method for obtaining digital signatures and public-key cryptosystems. *Communications of the ACM*, *21*(2), 120–126. doi:10.1145/359340.359342

Sait, Y., & Vijayalakshmi, R. (2014). Enabling high performance computing in cloud infrastructure using rCUDA.

Salamifar, S. E., & Lai, R. Y. (2013). Use of combined scanning electrochemical and fluorescence microscopy for detection of reactive oxygen species in prostate cancer cells. *Analytical Chemistry*, *85*(20), 9417–9421. doi:10.1021/ac402367f PMID:24044675

SalesForce.com. (2014). Retrieved from http://www.salesforce.com

Sander, T., Young, A. L., & Yung, M. (1999). Non-Interactive CryptoComputing For NC1.*40th Annual Symposium on Foundations of Computer Science* (pp. 554-567). New York: ACM. doi:10.1109/SFFCS.1999.814630

Sandikkaya, M., & Harmanci, A. (2012). Security problems of Platform as a Service (PaaS) clouds and practical solutions to the problems.*31st International Symposium on Reliable Distributed Systems*. doi:10.1109/SRDS.2012.84

Sarmenta, L. (2001). *Sabotage-tolerance mechanisms for volunteer computing systems. IEEE/ACM CCGrid*. Australia: Brisbane, Qld.

Sass, P. (1999). Communications networks for the force XXI digitized battlefield. *Mobile Networks and Applications*, *4*(3), 139–155. doi:10.1023/A:1019194714609

Satyanarayanan, M., Bahl, P., Caceres, R., & Nigel, D. (2009). The Case for VM-Based Cloudlets in Mobile Computing. *IEEE Transactions on Pervasive Computing*, 14-23.

Saul, J., Schwartz, P. J., Ackerman, P. J., & Triedman, J. K. (2014). Rationale and objectives for ECG screening in infancy. *Heart rhythm: the official journal of the Heart Rhythm Society*, 2316-2321.

Savage, J. E. (1997). *Models of Computation: Exploring the Power of Computing.*

Savage, S., Collins, A., Hoffman, E., Snell, J., & Anderson, T. (1999). *The End-to-End Effects of Internet Path Selection* (pp. 289–299). ACM SIGCOMM. doi:10.1145/316188.316233

Scarfone, K., Souppaya, M., & Sexton, M. (2007). Guide to storage encryption technologies for end user devices. *NIST Special Publication*, 111.

Schildt, S., Busching, F., Jorns, E., & Wolf, L. (2013). *Candis: Heterogenous mobile cloud framework and energy cost-aware scheduling*. Beijing, China: IEEE GreenCom.

Schurgers, C., Kulkarni, G., & Srivastava, M. (2002). Distributed on-demand address assignment in wireless sensor networks. *IEEE Transactions on Parallel and Distributed Systems*, *13*(10), 1056–1065. doi:10.1109/TPDS.2002.1041881

Scott, K., Kumar, N., Velusamy, S., Childers, B., Davidson, J. W., & Soffa, M. L. (2003). Retargetable and reconfigurable software dynamic translation. In *Proceedings of the international symposium on Code generation and optimization: feedback-directed and runtime optimization* (pp. 36--47). IEEE. doi:10.1109/CGO.2003.1191531

Searles, C. D. (2002). The nitric oxide pathway and oxidative stress in heart failure. *Congestive Heart Failure (Greenwich, Conn.)*, *8*(3), 142–155. doi:10.1111/j.1527-5299.2002.00715.x PMID:12045382

Sen, A., & Huson, M. (1996). A new model for scheduling packet radio networks. *IEEE INFOCOM*, *3*, s. 1116 -1124.

Sensys Medical, I. (n.d.). *Near-Infrared Spectroscopy*. Retrieved from http://www.diabetesnet.com/diabetes-technology/meters-monitors/future-meters-monitors/sensys-medical

Shahabi, C. (2013). Towards a generic framework for trustworthy spatial crowdsourcing.*12th International ACM Workshop on Data Engineering for Wireless and Mobile Access (MobiDE)*, (pp. 1-4). doi:10.1145/2486084.2486085

Shah, R. R. (2005). Drug-induced QT interval prolongation regulatory guidance and perspectives on hERG channel studies.*Novartis Foundation Symposium*, (pp. 251-280). doi:10.1002/047002142X.ch19

Shanklin, W. (2014, March 26). *Revisiting Cloud Computing: how has it changed - and changed us?* Retrieved from Gizmag: http://www.gizmag.com/revisiting-cloud-computing/26768/

Sharpe, E., Bradley, R., Frasco, T., Jayathilaka, D., Marsh, A., & Andreescu, S. (2014). Metal oxide based multisensor array and portable database for field analysis of antioxidants. *Sensors and Actuators. B, Chemical*, *193*, 552–562. doi:10.1016/j.snb.2013.11.088 PMID:24610993

Sharpe, E., Frasco, T., Andreescu, D., & Andreescu, S. (2013). Portable ceria nanoparticle-based assay for rapid detection of food antioxidants (nanocerac). *Analyst (London)*, *138*(1), 249–262. doi:10.1039/C2AN36205H PMID:23139929

Shelby, Z., Hartke, K., & Bormann, C. (2012). *Constrained Application Protocol (CoAP)*. IETF Draft.

Sheng, X., Xiao, X., Tang, J., & Xue, G. (2012a). Sensing as a service: A cloud computing system for mobile phone sensing.*Proc. IEEE Sensors Conference*, (pp. 1--4). doi:10.1109/ICSENS.2012.6411516

Sheng, X., Xiao, X., Tang, J., & Xue, G. (2014). Leveraging GPS-Less Sensing Scheduling for Green Mobile Crowd Sensing. *IEEE Internet of Things Journal*, *1*(4), 328–336. doi:10.1109/JIOT.2014.2334271

Sheu, Y.-C. T.-M.-L.-P. (2002). Dynamic channel allocation with location awareness for multi-hop mobile ad hoc networks. *Computer Communications*, 676–688.

Shi, C., Ammar, M. H., Zegura, E. W., & Naik, M. (2012). Computing in cirrus clouds: the challenge of intermittent connectivity. *Proceedings of the first edition of the MCC workshop on Mobile cloud computing* (s. 23-28). ACM. doi:10.1145/2342509.2342515

Shi, C., Lakafosis, V., Ammar, M., & Zegura, E. W. (2012). *Serendipity: Enabling remote computing among intermittently connected mobile devices*. Hilton Head, SC, USA: ACM MobiHoc. doi:10.1145/2248371.2248394

Shi, J., Mamoulis, N., Wu, D., & Cheung, D. W. (2014). Density-based place clustering in geo-social networks.*Proc. ACM SIGMOD International Conference on Management of Data*, (pp. 99--110).

Shiraz, M., Abolfazli, S., Sanaei, Z., & Gani, A. (2013). A study on virtual machine deployment for application outsourcing in mobile cloud computing. *The Journal of Supercomputing*, *63*(3), 946–964. doi:10.1007/s11227-012-0846-y

Shoukry, Y., Martin, P., Tabuada, P., & Srivastava, M. (2013). Non-invasive spoofing attacks for anti-lock braking systems. In G. Bertoni & J. S. Coron (Eds.), *Cryptographic Hardware and Embedded Systems* (pp. 55–72). Heidelberg, Germany: Springer. doi:10.1007/978-3-642-40349-1_4

Shukla, D., Chandran-Wadia, L., & Iyer, S. (2003). Mitigating the exposed node problem in IEEE 802.11 ad hoc networks. *IEEE ICCCN, 1*, s. 157 - 162.

Singh, N. (1995). Oxidative stress and heart failure. 77-81.

Sirovich, L., & Kirby, M. (1987). Low-dimensional procedure for the characterization of human faces. *JOSA A*, *4*(3), 519–524. doi:10.1364/JOSAA.4.000519 PMID:3572578

Slack, N., Brandon-Jones, A., & Johnston, R. (2013). *Operations Management*. Lombarda, Italy: Pearson.

Smart, N. P., & Vercauteren, F. (2010). *Fully homomorphic encryption with relatively small key and ciphertext sizes* (pp. 420–443). PKC. doi:10.1007/978-3-642-13013-7_25

Smart, N. P., & Vercauteren, F. (2014). Fully homomorphic SIMD operations. *Designs, Codes and Cryptography*, *71*(1), 57–81. doi:10.1007/s10623-012-9720-4

Solmaz, G., & Turgut, D. (2013). Theme Park Mobility in Disaster Scenarios.*Proc. IEEE Global Communications Conference (GLOBECOM)*, (pp. 399-404).

Solmaz, G., & Turgut, D. (2014). Optimizing Event Coverage in Theme Parks. *Wireless Networks (WINET). Journal*, *20*(6), 1445–1459.

Song, W., Zhuang, W., & Cheng, Y. (2007). Load balancing for cellular/WLAN integrated networks. *IEEE Network*, *21*(1), 27–33. doi:10.1109/MNET.2007.314535

Sorenson, H. W. (1970, July). Least-squares estimation: From Gauss to Kalman. *IEEE Spectrum*, *7*(7), 63–68. doi:10.1109/MSPEC.1970.5213471

Soyata, T. (1999). *Incorporating Circuit Level Information into the Retiming Process*. (Ph.D. thesis). University of Rochester.

Soyata, T., Ba, H., Heinzelman, W., Kwon, M., & Shi, J. (2013). Accelerating Mobile-Cloud Computing: A Survey. In H. Mouftah, & B. Kantarci (Eds.), Communication Infrastructures for Cloud Computing (pp. 175-197). IGI Global.

Soyata, T., Friedman, E. G., & Mulligan, J. H., Jr. (1993). Integration of clock skew and register delays into a retiming algorithm. *Circuits and Systems, 1993., ISCAS'93, 1993 IEEE International Symposium on* (s. 1483-1486). IEEE.

Soyata, T., Friedman, E. G., & Mulligan, J. H., Jr. (1995). Monotonicity constraints on path delays for efficient retiming with localized clock skew and variable register delay. *Circuits and Systems, 1995. ISCAS'95., 1995 IEEE International Symposium on* (s. 1748--1751). IEEE.

Soyata, T., Muraleedharan, R., Funai, C., Kwon, M., & Heinzelman, W. (2012). Cloud-Vision: Real-time face recognition using a mobile-cloudlet-cloud acceleration architecture. *Computers and Communications (ISCC), 2012 IEEE Symposium on*, 59-66.

Soyata, T., & Friedman, E. (1994). Retiming with non-zero clock skew, variable register, and interconnect delay.*Proceedings of the IEEE Conference on Computer-Aided Design (ICCAD)*, (pp. 234-241).

Soyata, T., & Friedman, E. G. (1994). Synchronous performance and reliability improvement in pipelined ASICs.*ASIC Conference and Exhibit, 1994. Proceedings., Seventh Annual IEEE International. 3*, s. 383-390. IEEE. doi:10.1109/ASIC.1994.404536

Soyata, T., Friedman, E. G., & Mulligan, J. H. (1997, January). Incorporating Interconnect, Register, and Clock Distribution Delays into the Retiming Process. *IEEE Transactions on Computer-Aided Design of Integrated Circuits and Systems*, *16*(1), 105–120. doi:10.1109/43.559335

Soyata, T., & Liobe, J. (2012). pbCAM: probabilistically-banked Content Addressable Memory.*Proceedings of the 25th IEEE International System-on-Chip Conference (IEEE SOCC)*, (pp. 27-32). Niagara Falls, NY.

Soyata, T., Muraleedharan, R., Ames, S., Langdon, J., Funai, C., Kwon, M., & Heinzelman, W. (2012). COMBAT: Mobile Cloud-based cOmpute/coMmunications infrastructure for BATtlefield applications.[Baltimore, MD.]. *Proceedings of the Society for Photo-Instrumentation Engineers*, *8403*, 84030K–84030K, 84030K-13. doi:10.1117/12.919146

Soyata, T., Muraleedharan, R., Funai, C., Kwon, M., & Heinzelman, W. (2012). Cloud-Vision: Real-time face recognition using a mobile-cloudlet-cloud acceleration architecture.*Symposium on Computers and Communications (ISCC)* (s. 59-66). IEEE. doi:10.1109/ISCC.2012.6249269

SQLite. (2015). Retrieved from https://www.sqlite.org/

Stehle, D., & Steinfeld, R. (2010). *Faster fully homomorphic encryption* (pp. 377–394). ASIACRYPT.

Sterling, C. H. (2008). *Military communications: from ancient times to the 21st century*. Abc-clio.

Stramba-Badiale, M., Priori, S. G., Napolitano, C., Locati, E. H., Vinolas, X., Haverkamp, W., & Schwartz, P. J. et al. (2000). Gene-specific differences in the circadian variation of ventricular repolarization in the long QT syndrome: A key to sudden death during sleep? *Italian Heart Journal*, 323–328. PMID:10832806

Subashini, S., & Kavitha, V. (2011). A survey on security issues in service delivery models of cloud computing. *Journal of Network and Computer Applications*, *34*(1), 1–11. doi:10.1016/j.jnca.2010.07.006

Suciu, G., Vulpe, A., Halunga, S., Fratu, O., Todoran, G., & Suciu, V. (2013). Smart cities built on resilient cloud computing and secure Internet of Things.*Proc. 19th International Conference on Control Systems and Computer Science*, (pp. 513--518). doi:10.1109/CSCS.2013.58

Sun, T. W., Wesel, R. D., Shane, M. R., & Jarett, K. (2004). Superposition turbo TCM for multirate broadcast. *IEEE Transactions on Communications*, *3*(3), 368–371. doi:10.1109/TCOMM.2004.823646

Sun, Y., Luo, H., & Das, S. (2012). A trust-based framework for fault-tolerant data aggregation in wireless multimedia sensor networks. *IEEE Transactions on Dependable and Secure Computing*, *9*(6), 785–797. doi:10.1109/TDSC.2012.68

Szpakowski, M. (2013). *NativeBOINC*. Retrieved Jan. de 2015 from http://nativeboinc.org

Tang, K., & Gerla, M. (2000). MAC layer broadcast support in 802.11 wireless networks. *IEEE MILCOM, 1*, s. 544-548.

Tan, G., & Jarvis, S. (2008). A payment-based incentive and service differentiation scheme for peer-to-peer streaming broadcast. *IEEE Transactions on Parallel and Distributed Systems*, *19*(7), 940–953. doi:10.1109/TPDS.2007.70778

Tan, K., Liu, H., Zhang, J., Zhang, Y., Fang, J., & Voelker, G. M. (2011). Sora: High-performance software radio using general-purpose multi-core processors. *Communications of the ACM*, *54*(1), 99–107. doi:10.1145/1866739.1866760

Tan, W., Blake, M. B., Saleh, I., & Dutdar, S. (2013). Social-network-sourced big data analytics. *IEEE Internet Computing*, *17*(5), 62–69. doi:10.1109/MIC.2013.100

Tavli, B. (2005). *Protocol architectures for energy efficient real-time data communications in mobile ad hoc networks.* (Ph.D. dissertation). University of Rochester, Rochester, NY.

Tavli, B., & Heinzelman, W. B. (2003). TRACE: Time reservation using adaptive control for energy efficiency. *IEEE Journal on Selected Areas in Communications*, *21*(10), 1506–1515. doi:10.1109/JSAC.2003.814897

Tavli, B., & Heinzelman, W. B. (2004). MH-TRACE: Multihop time reservation using adaptive control for energy efficiency. *IEEE Journal on Selected Areas in Communications*, *21*(10), 942–953. doi:10.1109/JSAC.2004.826932

Tavli, B., & Heinzelman, W. B. (2006). Energy and spatial reuse efficient network wide real-time data broadcasting in mobile ad hoc networking. *IEEE Transactions on Mobile Computing*, *5*(10), 1297–1312. doi:10.1109/TMC.2006.151

Tavli, B., & Heinzelman, W. B. (2006). *Mobile ad hoc networks: energy-efficient real-time group communications.* Dordrecht: Springer. doi:10.1007/1-4020-4633-2

Tavli, B., & Heinzelman, W. B. (2007). QoS and energy efficiency in network-wide broadcasting: A MAC layer perspective. *Computer Communications*, *30*(18), 3705–3720. doi:10.1016/j.comcom.2007.07.005

Tavli, B., & Heinzelman, W. B. (2011). Energy-efficient real-time multicast routing in mobile ad hoc networks. *IEEE Transactions on Computers*, *60*(5), 707–722. doi:10.1109/TC.2010.118

Tegra. (2012). Retrieved from http://en.wikipedia.org/wiki/Tegra

Tegra3. (2012). Retrieved from http://www.nvidia.com/object/tegra-3-processor.html

TI-MSP430. (n.d.). *Overview for MSP430F1x.* Retrieved from http://www.ti.com/lsds/ti/microcontrollers_16-bit_32-bit/msp/ultra-low_power/msp430f1x/overview.page

Tobagi, F., & Kleinrock, L. (1975). Packet Switching in Radio Channels: Part II--The Hidden Terminal Problem in Carrier Sense Multiple-Access and the Busy-Tone Solution. *IEEE Transactions on Communications*, *23*(12), 1417–1433. doi:10.1109/TCOM.1975.1092767

Toumpis, S., & Goldsmith, A. (2006). New media access protocols for wireless ad hoc networks based on cross-layer principles. *IEEE Transactions on Wireless Communications*, *5*(8), 2228–2241. doi:10.1109/TWC.2006.1687739

Tsutsui, H. (2001). Oxidative stress in heart failure: The role of mitochondria. *Internal Medicine (Tokyo, Japan)*, *40*(12), 1177–1182. doi:10.2169/internalmedicine.40.1177 PMID:11813840

Turk, M., & Pentland, A. (1991). Face recognition using eigenfaces. *IEEE Computer Society Conference on Computer Vision and Pattern Recognition, 1991. Proceedings CVPR*, *91*, 568–591.

U.S. Energy Information Administration. (2014). *Short-term energy outlook.* Retrieved 2015 from http://www.eia.gov/forecasts/steo/pdf/steo_full.pdf

University of Rochester. CIRC. (n.d.). *Bluehive Cluster*. Retrieved from http://www.circ.rochester.edu/wiki/ index.php/ BlueHive Cluster

US Department of Health and Human Services. (2014). Retrieved from HIPAA: http://www.hhs.gov/ocr/privacy/

US Government Printing Office. (n.d.). *Patient Protection and Affordable Care Act*. Retrieved from http://www.gpo.gov/fdsys/pkg/BILLS-111hr3590enr/pdf/BILLS-111hr3590enr.pdf

US-HHS. (n.d.). *Business Associate Agreement*. Retrieved from http://www.hhs.gov/ocr/privacy/hipaa/understanding/coveredentities/contractprov.html

Van den Bossche, R., Vanmechelen, K., & Broeckhove, J. (2013). Online cost-efficient scheduling of deadline-constrained workloads on hybrid clouds. *Computer Systems*, *29*(4), 973–985. doi:10.1016/j.future.2012.12.012

Varshney, U. (2007). Pervasive healthcare and wireless health monitoring. *Mobile Networks and Applications*, *12*(2-3), 113–127. doi:10.1007/s11036-007-0017-1

Vatta, M. (2009). Intronic variants and splicing errors in cardiovascular diseases. *Heart rhythm: the official journal of the Heart Rhythm Society*, 219-220.

Vazquez, J., & Ipina, D. L. (2008). Social devices: Autonomous artifacts that communicate on the internet. In *The Internet of Things* (pp. 308–324). Berlin, Germany: Springer-Verlag. doi:10.1007/978-3-540-78731-0_20

Vega, D., Meseguer, R., Freitag, F., & Ochoa, S. (2013). *Effort-based incentives for resource sharing in collaborative volunteer applications*. Whistler, BC, Canada: IEEE CSCWD. doi:10.1109/CSCWD.2013.6580936

Verbelen, T., Simoens, P., De Turck, F., & Dhoedt, B. (2012). Cloudlets: Bringing the cloud to the mobile user.*Proceedings of the third ACM workshop on Mobile cloud computing and services* (s. 29-36). ACM. doi:10.1145/2307849.2307858

Verizon-Terremark. (n.d.). *Verizon Terremark*. Retrieved from http://www.terremark.com/

Viola, P., & Jones, M. (2001). Rapid object detection using a boosted cascade of simple features.*Proceedings of the 2001 IEEE Computer Society Conference on Computer Vision and Pattern Recognition*, (pp. 511-518). doi:10.1109/CVPR.2001.990517

Viola, P., & Jones, M. J. (2001). Robust real time face detection.*Second International Workshop on Statistical and Computational Theories of Vision - Modeling, Learning, Computing, and Sampling*, (pp. 1-25).

Wallace, C. S. (1964). A suggestion for a fast multiplier. *Transactions on Electronic Computers*, 14-17.

Wang, H., Liu, W., & Soyata, T. (2014). Accessing Big Data in the Cloud Using Mobile Devices. In P. R. Dek (Ed.), *Handbook of Research on Cloud Infrastructures for Big Data Analytics* (pp. 444–470). Hershey, PA: IGI Global; doi:10.4018/978-1-4666-5864-6.ch018

Wang, L., Xiong, H., & Zhang, D. (2013). effSense: Energy-Efficient and Cost-Effective Data Uploading in Mobile Crowdsensing.*Proc. International Workshop on Pervasive Urban Crowdsensing Architecture and Applications (PUCCA)*, (pp. 1075--1086). doi:10.1145/2494091.2499575

Wang, W., Hu, Y., Chen, L., Huang, X., & Sunar, B. (2013). *Exploring the feasibility of fully homomorphic encryption*. Transactions on Computers.

Watanabe, K., & Fukushi, M. (2010). Generalized spot-checking for sabotage-tolerance in volunteer computing systems. IEEE/ACM CCGrid. Melbourne, Australia.

Wendell, P., Jiang, J., Freedman, M., & Rexford, J. (2010). *DONAR: Decentralized Server Selection for Cloud Services.* ACM SIGCOMM. doi:10.1145/1851182.1851211

Wi-Fi Alliance, P2P Task Group. (2011). *Wi-Fi Peer-to-Peer (P2P) Technical Specification, Version 1.2.*

Wi-Fi. (n.d.). In *Encyclopedia Brittanica.* Retrieved from http://www.britannica.com/EBchecked/topic/1473553/Wi-Fi

WiFiAlliance. (2012). Retrieved from http://www.wi-fi.org/knowledge-center/glossary/wpa2%E2%84%A2

Wikipedia. (2012). *Rayleigh Distribution.* Retrieved from http://en.wikipedia.org/wiki/Rayleigh_distribution

WiMAX. (2014). *WiMAX.* Retrieved from http://en.wikipedia.org/wiki/WiMAX

Winterbourn, C. C. (2008). Reconciling the chemistry and biology of reactive oxygen species. *Nature Chemical Biology, 4*(5), 278–286. doi:10.1038/nchembio.85 PMID:18421291

Woitaszek, M., & Tufo, H. M. (2010). Developing a Cloud Computing Charging Model for High-Performance Computing.*10th IEEE International Conference on Computer and Information Technology* (pp. 210-217). Bradford: IEEE. doi:10.1109/CIT.2010.72

Wojciechowska, C., Romuk, E., Tomasik, A., Skrzep-Poloczek, B., Nowalany-Kozielska, E., Birkner, E., & Jachec, W. (2014). Oxidative stress markers and c-reactive protein are related to severity of heart failure in patients with dilated cardiomyopathy. *Mediators of Inflammation, 2014*, 1–10. doi:10.1155/2014/147040 PMID:25400332

Wood, A., Stankovic, J., Virone, G., Selavo, L., He, Z., Cao, Q., & Stoleru, R. et al. (2008). Context-aware wireless sensor networks for assisted living and residential monitoring. *IEEE Network, 22*(4), 26–33. doi:10.1109/MNET.2008.4579768

Woosley, R. L. (2001). *Drugs That Prolong the QT Interval and/or Induce Torsades de Pointes.* Tech. rep., Torsades.org.

Wozniak, S., Rossberg, M., & Schaefer, G. (2013). *Towards trustworthy mobile social networking services for disaster response* (pp. 528–533). IEEE Pervasive Computing and Communications Workshops. doi:10.1109/PerComW.2013.6529553

Wu, C., Kumekawa, K., & Kato, T. (2009). A MANET protocol considering link stability and bandwidth efficiency. *ICUMT, 1*, s. 1 -8.

Wu, L. (2014). *SLA-based Resource Provisioning for Management of Cloud-based Software-as-a-Service Applications* (Doctoral dissertation). Retrieved from University of Melbourne Cloud Laboratory: http://cloudbus.org/students/LinlinPhDThesis2014.pdf

Xen. (n.d.). *Xen Project Software Overview.* Retrieved from Xen Wiki: http://wiki.xenproject.org/wiki/Xen_Overview#Documentation

Xiao, Y., Simoens, P., Pillai, P., Ha, K., & Satyanarayanan, M. (2013). Lowering the barriers to large-scale mobile crowdsensing.*Proc. 14th Workshop on Mobile Computing Systems and Applications*, (pp. 9.1--9.6). doi:10.1145/2444776.2444789

Xie, J., Das, A., Nandi, S., & Gupta, A. (2005). Improving the reliability of IEEE 802.11 broadcast scheme for multicasting in mobile ad hoc networks. *IEEE WCNC, 1*, s. 126-131.

Xue, J., Yang, Z., Yang, X., Wang, X., Chen, L., & Dai, Y. (2013). VoteTrust: Leveraging friend invitation graph to defend against social network Sybils. *Proceedings - IEEE INFOCOM*, 2400–2408.

Xu, H., Bilec, M., Schaefer, L., Landis, A., & Jones, A. (2013). *Ocelot: A wireless sensor network and computing engine with commodity palmtop computers.* Arlington, VA, USA: IGCC.

Yang, D., Fang, X., & Xue, G. (2011). ESPN: Efficientt server placement in probabilistic networks with budget constraint.*Proc. IEEE Int. Conference on Computer Communications (INFOCOM)*, (pp. 1269--1277). doi:10.1109/INFCOM.2011.5934908

Yang, D., Xue, G., Fan, X., & Tang, J. (2012). Crowdsourcing to smartphones: Incentive mechanism design for mobile phone sensing.*Proc. 18th International Conference on Mobile Computing and Networking (Mobicom)*, (pp. 173--184). doi:10.1145/2348543.2348567

Yang, H., Luo, H., Ye, F., Lu, S., & Zhang, L. (2004). Security in mobile ad hoc networks: Challenges and solutions. *IEEE Wireless Communications*, *11*(1), 38–47. doi:10.1109/MWC.2004.1269716

Yang, M. H., Kriegman, D., & Ahuja, N. (2002). Detecting faces in images: A survey. *IEEE Transactions on Pattern Analysis and Machine Intelligence*, *24*(1), 34–58.

Ye, W., Heidemann, J., & Estrin, D. (2002). An energy-efficient MAC protocol for wireless sensor networks. *IEEE INFOCOM*, (s. 1567-1576).

Yerva, S. R., Saltarin, J., Hoyoung, J., & Aberer, K. (2012). Social and sensor data fusion in the cloud.*Proc. 13th Intl. Conf. on Mobile Data Management (MDM)*, (pp. 276--277). doi:10.1109/MDM.2012.52

Yilmaz, Y. S., Bulut, M. F., Akcora, C. G., Bayir, M. A., & Demirbas, M. (2013). Trend sensing via twitter. *International Journal of Ad Hoc and Ubiquitous Computing*, *14*(1), 16–26. doi:10.1504/IJAHUC.2013.056271

Yu, J., Williams, E., & Ju, M. (2010). Analysis of material and energy consumption of mobile phones in China. *Energy Policy*, *38*(8), 4135–4141. doi:10.1016/j.enpol.2010.03.041

Yu, X., Sun, F., & Cheng, X. (2012). Intelligent urban traffic management system based on cloud computing and Internet of Things.*Proc. International Conference on Computer Science Service System (CSSS)*, (pp. 2169--2172). doi:10.1109/CSSS.2012.539

Zareba, W., Moss, A. J., le Cessie, S., Locati, E. H., Robinson, J. L., Hall, W., & Andrews, M. L. (1995). Risk of cardiac events in family members of patients with long QT syndrome. *Journal of the American College of Cardiology*, *26*(7), 1685–1691. doi:10.1016/0735-1097(95)60383-2 PMID:7594104

Zayas, A. D., & Gómez, P. M. (2010). A testbed for energy profile characterization of ip services in smartphones over live networks. *Mobile Networks and Applications*, *15*(3), 330–343. doi:10.1007/s11036-010-0228-8

Zhang, L., Tiwana, B., Qian, Z., Qang, Z., Dick, R. P., Mao, Z. M., & Yang, L. (2010). Accurate online power estimation and automatic battery behavior based power model generation for smartphones. Intl. Conf. on Hardware-Software Codesign and System Synthesis (CODES+ISSS). Scottsdale, AZ.

Zhang, W., Das, S., & Liu, Y. (2006). A trust based framework for secure data aggregation in wireless sensor networks. 3rd Annual IEEE Communications Society on Sensor and Ad Hoc Communications and Networks, (pp. 60-69).

Zhang, D., Xiong, H., Wang, L., & Chen, G. (2014). CrowdRecruiter: Selecting Participants for Piggyback Crowdsensing under Probabilistic Coverage Constraint.*Proc. ACM International Joint Conference on Pervasive and Ubiquitous Computing*, (pp. 703--714). doi:10.1145/2632048.2632059

Zhang, Q., Cheng, L., & Boutaba, R. (2010). Cloud computing: State-of-the-art and research challenges. *Journal of Internet Services and Applications*, *1*(1), 7–18. doi:10.1007/s13174-010-0007-6

Zhang, X., Kunjithapatham, A., Jeong, S., & Gibbs, S. (2011). Towards an elastic application model for augmenting the computing capabilities of mobile devices with cloud computing. *Mobile Networks and Applications*, *16*(3), 270–284. doi:10.1007/s11036-011-0305-7

Zhang, Y., Meratnia, N., & Havinga, P. (2010). Outlier detection techniques for wireless sensor networks: A Survey. *IEEE Communications Surveys and Tutorials*, *12*(2), 159–170. doi:10.1109/SURV.2010.021510.00088

Zhou, J., Leppanen, T., Harjula, E., Ylianttila, M., Ojala, T., Yu, C., & Yang, L. T. et al. (2013). CloudThings: A common architecture for integrating the Internet of Things with cloud computing.*Proc. IEEE 17th Intl. Conference on Computer Supported Cooperative Work in Design*, (pp. 651--657). doi:10.1109/CSCWD.2013.6581037

Zhuang, Y., Rafetseder, A., & Cappos, J. (2013). *Experience with Seattle: A community platform for research and education*. Salt Lake City, UT: GREE.

Zhu, J., & Roy, S. (2003). MAC for dedicated short range communications in intelligent transport system. *IEEE Communications Magazine*, *41*(12), 60–67. doi:10.1109/MCOM.2003.1252800

Zissis, D., & Lekkas, D. (2012). Addressing cloud computing security issues. *Future Generation Computer Systems*, *28*(3), 583–592. doi:10.1016/j.future.2010.12.006

About the Contributors

Tolga Soyata is an Assistant Professor - Research in the Department of Electrical and Computer Engineering (ECE) at the University of Rochester. Dr. Soyata received a B.S. degree in Electrical and Communications Engineering from Istanbul Technical University in 1988, M.S. degree in ECE from Johns Hopkins University, and Ph.D. in ECE from University of Rochester, in 1992 and 1999, respectively. His current research interests include real-time high-performance computation and energy-aware system design. He teaches four courses on ASIC, FPGA and GPU design and programming.

* * *

Mehmet Aktas grew up in Rochester, New York. He received his BA degree in Biology from the University of Rochester and in 2002 completed his medical school education at SUNY Upstate Medical University. He completed Internal Medicine residency training at the Cleveland Clinic and then proceeded to the University of Rochester Medical Center (URMC) where he completed advanced fellowships in Cardiovascular Diseases and Cardiac Pacing and Electrophysiology. He holds a Masters in Business Administration from the University of Rochester's Simon School. He is on the faculty at URMC as an Assistant Professor of Medicine. He is board certified in Internal Medicine, Cardiovascular Diseases and Cardiac Pacing and Electrophysiology. His clinical work involves the treatment of patients with a variety of complex heart rhythm disorders. His research is focused on improved risk stratification of patients with heart rhythm disorders and development of systems to enable early detection of arrhythmias.

Scott Ames received a B.S. in Computer Science in 2011 from University of Rochester. He is currently pursuing a Ph.D. at University of Rochester, studying Cryptography under Prof. Venkitasubramaniam. His research interests include complexity theory, network and cloud security and secure multiparty computation.

Silvana Andreescu is the Egon Matijević Chair of Chemistry and Professor of Bioanalytical Chemistry in the Department of Chemistry and Biomolecular Science at Clarkson University in Potsdam, NY. She has received a PhD in Chemistry, specializing in biosensors from the University of Perpignan, France, and University of Bucharest, Romania in 2002, and has been a member of the Clarkson faculty since 2005. Between 2003 and 2005 she was a NSF-NATO postdoctoral fellow at the State University of New York at Binghamton. Her research interests are in analytical and bioanalytical chemistry focusing on investigations of basic biochemical mechanisms at bio-interfaces, bio-nanotechnology, biomimetic materials and development of practical biosensors for clinical and environmental monitoring. She is the recipient of a French Government Graduate Fellowship, a NATO-NSF Postdoctoral Fellowship, the NSF-CAREER award, the John W. Graham Faculty Research Award, the Research Excellence Award and a Member of the Million Dollars Club at Clarkson University. She has published more than 80 peer-reviewed journal articles and 18 book chapters, has co-edited two books, has two patents, and has delivered some 100 presentations at professional and academic conferences throughout the world.

Abner Aquino is an Electrical and Computer Engineering student at the University of Rochester. He is a Kearns Scholar, and a Xerox fellow. In the summer of 2014, he worked on the visualization of ad hoc networks in the Wireless Communications and Networking Group (WCNG) at the University of Rochester. He is currently studying abroad in Madrid, Spain.

He Ba is a Ph.D. student in Electrical and Computer Engineering at the University of Rochester. He received his B.S. degree from the Department of Electrical Engineering at the Beijing Institute of Technology in 2008 and his M.S. degree from the Electrical and Computer Engineering department at the University of Rochester in 2011. His research interests lie in the areas of wireless communications, mobile computing and digital signal processing.

Rex Buddenberg has had twenty years in US Coast Guard including several communications jobs. Masters in telecom from Naval Posgtraduate School. Two decades on faculty at NPS teaching 'plowshares into swords internet'.

William Dixon is a student at the University of Rochester expecting a B.S. in Electrical and Computer Engineering and a B.S. in Physics, both in 2016. The bulk of his studies outside of these fields is in Mathematics and Computer Science. Aside from continuing his studies, he tentatively plans to focus on low-level hardware development, especially development which considers quantum regime effects. He also has recent interests in modern chipset implementations and consumer-scale device design and development.

Colin Funai received BS degree (with distinction) and an MS degree in Electrical and Computer Engineering from the University of Rochester in 2012 and 2013 respectively. Since June 2013 he has been a Ph.D. student at the University of Rochester. His current research interests include distributed computing, ad hoc networking, and D2D communications.

Regina Gyampoh-Vidogah is a Consultant in Information Systems and Technology. She received her BSc degree in Information Systems from Birmingham City University in 1997 and her PhD in Information Systems and Information Technology in 2002. Before becoming a consultant, she spent few years lecturing computing, information systems, software development, information technology and project management at postgraduate and undergraduate levels including engineering/construction students at the same University. She went on further to work as a Project Development Manager on a NHS programme for the University of Wolverhampton; Information Systems Manager and Knowledge Management Manager at the Department of Health, National Health Service (delivering race equality national programme); Consultant, IT Knowledge Management Expert with CDKN project in Ethiopia Government's Climate Resilience Green Economy (sectoral reduction mechanism); and Consultant, for contributing to communication strategy and outreach work plan on building and maintaining a project knowledge management platform for Uganda climate change. She is an author of book and book chapters, journal and conference papers. She is a professional member of BCS, Associate member of ASCE and sits on Research Board and Committees and a reviewer of Journal papers.

Moeen Hassanalieragh earned his B.S. degree in Electrical Engineering from Sharif University of Technology in Tehran, Iran in 2012. He is currently a PhD Student at the University of Rochester Electrical and Computer Engineering Department working under the supervision of Dr. Tolga Soyata and Dr. Gaurav Sharma. His research interests include modeling of supercapacitors and supercapacitor-based energy-aware system design.

Wendi Heinzelman is a Professor in the Department of Electrical and Computer Engineering at the University of Rochester, and she holds a secondary appointment in the Computer Science Department at Rochester. She also currently serves as the Dean of Graduate Studies for Arts, Sciences & Engineering. Dr. Heinzelman received a B.S. degree in Electrical Engineering from Cornell University in 1995 and M.S. and Ph.D. degrees in Electrical Engineering and Computer Science from MIT in 1997 and 2000, respectively. Her current research interests lie in the areas of wireless communications and networking, mobile computing, and multimedia communication. She is a member of Networking Networking Women (N^2 Women) and the Society of Women Engineers (SWE), a Distinguished Scientist of ACM Sigmobile, and a Senior Member of the IEEE Communications Society and the IEEE Signal Processing Society.

Shurouq Hijazi is an Electrical and Computer Engineering student at the University of Rochester. She is a Renaissance scholar, and a Xerox fellow. In the summer of 2014, she worked on the GEMCloud project in the Wireless Communications and Networking Group (WCNG) at the University of Rochester, and has continued her work throughout the following semester. She is currently studying abroad in Spain.

Burak Kantarci is an assistant professor at the Department of Electrical & Computer Engineering of Clarkson University. Prior to joining Clarkson, he worked as a research fellow at the School of Electrical Engineering and Computer Science of the University of Ottawa. Dr. Kantarci received the M.Sc. and Ph.D. degrees in Computer Engineering at Istanbul Technical University in 2005 and 2009, respectively. He completed major part of his PhD thesis during his scholarship at the University of Ottawa in 2007 and 2008. He was the recipient of the Siemens Excellence Award in 2005 for his contributions to the optical burst switching research. Dr. Kantarci has co-authored over six-dozen papers in established journals and conferences, and contributed to eight book chapters. He is a co-editor of the book entitled, Communication Infrastructures for Cloud Computing (IGI Global, 2013). He has been serving in the TPCs of Green Communication Systems Track and the Ad Hoc and Sensor Networks Symposium of IEEE GLOBECOM and IEEE ICC conferences. He is a founding member of the IEEE ComSoc-Technical Sub-committee on Green Communications and Computing and the Special Interest Group on Green Data Center and Cloud Computing. He is an editorial board member of IEEE Communications Surveys & Tutorials. Dr. Kantarci is a Senior Member of the IEEE.

Bora Karaoglu received the BS degrees in electrical and electronics engineering (major) and industrial engineering (double major) from the Middle East Technical University, in 2006 and 2007, respectively, and the MS and PhD degrees in electrical and computer engineering from the University of Rochester, in 2008 and in 2014, respectively. He is currently a wireless networking researcher at The Samraksh Company, Virginia, USA. His current research interests include wireless communications and networking, network scalability, and mobile computing.

Ovunc Kocabas received his B.S. degree in Microelectronics Engineering from Sabanci University, Istanbul, Turkey in 2006, and his M.S. degree in Electrical and Computer Engineering from Rice University, Houston, TX in 2011. He is currently working towards his Ph.D degree in Electrical and Computer Engineering at University of Rochester, NY. His research interests include secure cloud computing, computer security, system design, and high performance computer architecture design. He published six conference papers and one book chapter to date in his research areas.

Minseok Kwon is an Associate Professor in the Department of Computer Science at Rochester Institute of Technology. His main research interests are computer networks, mobile computing, cloud computing, and distributed systems. He has co-authored dozens of publications in the areas of peer-to-peer overlay networks, network security, and wireless mobile networks. He also teaches courses in systems, networking, and introductory programming. He received his Ph.D. in Computer Science from Purdue University in 2004.

Hussein T. Mouftah is a Distinguished University Professor and Senior Canada Research Chair in Wireless Sensor Networks at the School of Electrical Engineering and Computer Science of the University of Ottawa, Canada. He has been with the ECE Dept. at Queen's University (1979-2002), where he was prior to his departure a Full Professor and the Department Associate Head. He has six years of industrial experience mainly at Bell Northern Research of Ottawa (then known as Nortel Networks). He served as Editor-in-Chief of the IEEE Communications Magazine (1995-97) and IEEE ComSoc Director of Magazines (1998-99), Chair of the Awards Committee (2002-03), Director of Education (2006-07), and Member of the Board of Governors (1997-99 and 2006-07). He has been a Distinguished Speaker of the IEEE Communications Society (2000-2008). He is the author or coauthor of 10 books, 60 book chapters and more than 1400 technical papers, 14 patents and 143 industrial reports. He is the joint holder of 19 Best Paper and/or Outstanding Paper Awards. He has received numerous prestigious awards, such as the 2007 Royal Society of Canada Thomas W. Eadie Medal, the 2007-2008 University of Ottawa Award for Excellence in Research, the 2008 ORION Leadership Award of Merit, the 2006 IEEE Canada McNaughton Gold Medal, the 2006 EIC Julian Smith Medal, the 2004 IEEE ComSoc Edwin Howard Armstrong Achievement Award, the 2004 George S. Glinski Award for Excellence in Research of the U of O Faculty of Engineering, the 1989 Engineering Medal for Research and Development of the Association of Professional Engineers of Ontario (PEO), and the Ontario Distinguished Researcher Award of the Ontario Innovation Trust. Dr. Mouftah is a Fellow of the IEEE (1990), the Canadian Academy of Engineering (2003), the Engineering Institute of Canada (2005) and the Royal Society of Canada RSC Academy of Science (2008).

Tolga Numanoglu is a senior specialist design engineer at the ASELSAN Inc., Ankara, Turkey. He is currently responsible of designing tactical networking waveforms for software defined military radios. He received his B.S. degree in Electrical and Electronics Engineering from Middle East Technical University in 2003 and M.S. and Ph.D. degrees in Electrical Engineering and Computer Engineering from University of Rochester in 2004 and 2009, respectively. Some of his research and development activities are design of medium access control (MAC) and scheduling, routing layer, interference management and mitigation, adaptive and distributed frequency hopping, distributed network wide localization and synchronization, and adaptive link layer protocols and algorithms.

Alex Page grew up in Maine, and entered the U.S. Navy straight out of high school. After 6 years of service, he moved to Rhode Island to pursue his undergraduate degree, graduating from the University of Rhode Island in 2011 with bachelor's degrees in Computer Engineering, Physics, and Applied Math. In 2012 he was accepted to the University of Rochester's Electrical Engineering PhD program, where he now works in Dr. Soyata's research group. His research is currently focused on computer systems for medical data processing.

Nathaniel Powers served in the United States Marine Corps from 2008 to 2013. Upon discharge from active duty he enrolled at the University of Rochester and is currently a Junior undergraduate with a major in Electrical and Computer Engineering. He is currently engaged in research in facial recognition and alternative cloud computing methodologies under the supervision of Dr. Tolga Soyata.

Jiye Shi is the Director of Computational Structural Biology at UCB Pharma, with more than a decade of experience in drug discovery. He holds a PhD from the University of Cambridge and an MBA from the Simon Business School, University of Rochester, where he received the Hugh H. Whitney award and was elected into ΒΓΣ, the international honor society of AACSB accredited business programs. Dr. Shi's work spans the areas of drug discovery, informatics, structural biology, nanobiotechnology and scientific computing, and his research and subsequent work has been widely recognized for bridging scientific innovation and a broad range of therapeutic applications. Dr. Shi has co-authored more than 50 peer-reviewed scientific publications. In addition, he has led the implementation of large-scale computing platforms for drug discovery, utilizing HPC and cloud infrastructure, as well as crowd-sourced mobile devices. Dr. Shi concurrently holds a visiting fellowship at Kellogg College, University of Oxford, two visiting professorships at the Chinese Academy of Sciences, a visiting research fellowship at the National Institute of Biomedical Innovation in Japan, and a visiting professorship in Shanghai University of Traditional Chinese Medicine. In addition, he serves on the executive management committee of the EPSRC Systems Approaches to Biomedical Sciences Centre for Doctoral Training at the University of Oxford, and co-supervises more than 20 PhD students, postdocs and faculty members in academic institutes throughout the United Kingdom, United States, and China.

Yang Song received his B.S. degree in Electrical and Computer Engineering from Shanghai Jiaotong University in 2009. In 2013, he started to work towards his M.S. degree at the University of Rochester ECE Department, and is expected to be awarded his M.S. degree in 2015. During his M.S. studies, he conducted research in Dr. Tolga Soyata's lab in Mobile Cloud based Hybrid Architecture (MOCHA), Virtualization, and Cloud Computing.

Cristiano Tapparello received the M.Sc. degree (with honors) in Computer Engineering and Ph.D. degree in Information Engineering from the University of Padova, Padova, Italy, in 2008 and 2012, respectively. From January 2012 to October 2013 he has been a Postdoctoral Researcher at the SIGNET group, Department of Information Engineering (DEI) at University of Padova. He is currently a Postdoctoral Research Associate in the Wireless Communications and Networking Group (WCNG) in the Department of Electrical and Computer Engineering at the University of Rochester, Rochester, NY, USA. His current research interests include stochastic modeling and optimization of wireless systems, energy-scavenging solutions for wireless sensor networks, and the design and implementation of mobile computing systems.

Bulent Tavli is an associate professor at the Electrical and Electronics Engineering Department, TOBB University of Economics and Technology, Ankara, Turkey. He received a B.S. degree in Electrical and Electronics Engineering in 1996 from the Middle East Technical University, Ankara, Turkey. He received M.S. and Ph.D. degrees in Electrical and Computer Engineering in 2001 and 2005 from the University of Rochester, Rochester, NY, USA. Telecommunications and embedded systems are his current research areas.

Muthuramakrishnan Venkitasubramaniam is an Assistant Professor in the Computer Science Department at University of Rochester. He received his B.Tech degree in Computer Science from the Indian Institute of Technology, Madras in 2004. He attended Cornell University, where he worked with Rafael Pass receiving his Ph.D. in Computer Science in 2011. Before arriving at University of Rochester, he spent a year at the Courant Institute of Mathematical Sciences (NYU) as a postdoctoral researcher supported by the Computing Innovation Fellowship.

Haoliang Wang is a Ph.D. student in the Department of Computer Science at the George Mason University. He received his B.S degree in Applied Physics from the School of Physics and Optoelectronic Engineering at Dalian University of Technology in 2012 and his M.S. degree from the Department of Electrical and Computer Engineering at the University of Rochester in 2013. His research interests lie in the broad areas of parallel and distributed computing systems and networking.

Index

3G Network 119, 162, 170, 190-191, 210, 212, 276-278, 283, 287, 344, 357
4G Network 185, 210
5G Network 210

A

Acceleration (AX) 189-190, 193, 210
Additive Homomorphic Encryption 245
Additive Homomorphism 149
Ad hoc 36, 41, 45, 64-65, 73, 81, 99, 168, 171
aggregation tasks 13, 15
Amazon Web Services (AWS) 296, 299, 306, 319
AMD-v 253, 260, 263-264, 266, 268
Analog-to-Digital Converter (ADC) 31
Analyte 4, 6, 31
Android 14, 86, 155, 158, 162, 164-165, 167-169, 180, 187, 202, 276, 283
Application Response Time 292
Aptamer 6-7, 31
Aptasensor 31
Augmented Reality 182-184, 204, 210, 250, 269
Availability (Ao) 357
AXaaS (Acceleration as a Service) 210

B

Band Matrix 139, 149-150
bandwidth efficiency 48, 64-66, 70-71, 345, 357
Basic Linear Algebra Subroutines (BLAS) 210
BGV Scheme 124, 128, 134, 144, 150, 219-220, 236
Bioelectrode 6, 31
Biomarker 4, 6, 11-12, 23, 31, 34
Bioprint 11, 31
Biorecognition 6-7, 31
Biosensor 7, 14, 22, 31
bio-sensor circuit 2, 8
Bootstrapping 124, 215, 245, 278, 326
Branching Program 117-118, 123, 129, 132-134, 136, 138-139, 142-143, 146, 150
Business Associate Agreement (BAA) 214, 245, 302, 319

C

calibration curve 4, 8, 12
cardiac hazard 122, 145, 214, 218
Central Processing Unit (CPU) 269
Ciphertext 123-127, 134, 136-137, 139, 144, 150, 215, 219-221, 223-225, 227, 236
Circuit Model 130, 150
CloneCloud 13, 32, 258, 266, 269
Cloud-Centric IoT 84-86, 90, 95-96, 104, 114
Cloud Instance 191-192, 210
Cloudlet 3, 12-15, 17, 22, 32, 86, 119, 168, 182-183, 210, 216, 224, 251, 256-257, 269, 287-289, 292, 307, 314-315
Cloud Operator 193, 210, 294, 296, 299, 303-304, 310, 315, 319-320
Cluster 13, 41, 43-44, 47, 65, 68, 81, 155-156, 168, 175, 180, 191-192, 194-197, 200, 202-204, 236, 270, 305
Cluster Computing 155-156, 180
Coast Guard 342-343
Computation Acceleration 248
Computational Quality of Service (CQoS) 210
Computation Offloading 205, 248
Compute-Unified Device Architecture (CUDA) 210
Concentrator 3, 8, 12-15, 22, 32
Context-Awareness 15, 105, 114, 295
CPU Cache Memory 269
CPU Main Memory 269
Cramer's Rule 135, 150
Crowdsensing 86, 93, 95-96, 99-100, 102-105, 107, 114
Crowd-Sourcing 269
CRP (C-Reactive Protein) 32
cTn (Cardiac Troponin) 32
Current Sense Amplifier 9-10, 32

D

Database Search (S) 339-340
Datacenters 2, 13, 15, 22, 183, 210, 252, 256, 282-284, 286-287, 294-295, 302, 310-312, 315, 320
Determinant of a Matrix 150
Digital-to-Analog Converter (DAC) 32
Directed Acyclic Graph (DAG) 150
Disinformation Probability 98, 114
Distributed Computing 73, 154-159, 162-164, 167, 170-171, 173-175, 180-181, 272
Distributed Networking 81

E

ECG Patch 118-119, 134, 150, 215, 217, 245, 320
Eigenface 308, 326-328, 334-335, 340
ELISA (Enzyme-Linked Immunosorbent Assay) 32
Energy Efficiency 39, 41, 45, 51, 57, 61, 64, 71-73, 92, 154, 158, 249, 313

F

Face Detection 167, 187-188, 202, 269, 289, 307-309, 323, 333, 336, 339-340
Face Recognition 182-184, 187, 189, 204, 210, 248, 250, 269, 307-310, 315, 320, 322-323, 326-327, 330-331, 333-334, 339-341
Fast Fourier Transform (FFT) 184, 204, 211
Fully Homomorphic Encryption (FHE) 15, 116-118, 122, 145, 150, 185, 213-216, 240, 245, 302, 304, 320

G

Galois Field 2-GF(2) 150
Generalized Matrix-Matrix Multiplication (GEMM) 184, 211
Google App Engine 33, 296, 311, 320-321
Google Cloud Platform 213, 296, 320
GPU Main Memory 269
GPU Virtualization 255-256, 265-266, 270
Graphics Processing Unit (GPU) 180, 211, 270, 320
gVirtuS 256, 270

H

Healthcare Organization (HCO) 2, 145, 245, 302, 320
Health Insurance Portability and Accountability Act (HIPAA) 213, 245, 302, 320
HElib 118, 121, 123-124, 128, 137-138, 140-141, 144, 150, 219, 236, 305
histogram equalization 329, 337
Holter Monitor 17, 32, 120, 236, 245
Homomorphic Encryption (HE) 15, 33, 116-118, 121-123, 145, 150-151, 185, 213-217, 220, 240, 245, 289, 302, 304, 315, 320
Hybrid Cloud 166, 313, 320
Hypervisor 15, 32, 252-253, 256-257, 259-261, 263-266, 268, 270-271

I

IA32 260, 270-271
IaaS (Infrastructure as a Service) 32, 211, 270, 320
Internet of Things (IoT) 12-13, 83, 96, 104, 114
Internet Service Provider (ISP) 280, 292
iOS 162, 169, 180

K

Kalman Filter 33
Kimberley 256, 266, 270
KVM 32, 253-254, 266, 270-271

L

LAN 32, 277, 293, 344, 347-348, 354, 357
Language Translation 184, 204-205
Latency Profiling 288-289
Leveled Fully Homomorphic Encryption 245
Lightweight Homomorphic Encryption 15, 33
Log-Space Computation 151
Long QT Syndrome (LQTS) 16, 151, 214, 217, 245, 305, 320
Long Term Evolution (LTE) 33, 211
Long Term Evolution (LTE) Standard 33
low latency 65, 156, 183, 195, 201
LQTS (Long QT Syndrome) 33

M

machine learning 96, 325, 331, 333
Map Reduce 33
Medical Cloud Computing 145, 213-214, 240, 302
Memory Virtualization 270
Microsoft Azure 33, 296, 301, 305-306, 309, 311, 320-321
Middleware 157, 171, 174-175, 180-181, 200
Military Communication Systems 35, 37
Mobile Ad Hoc Networks 36, 73, 81
Mobile Cloud Computing 35, 72-73, 163, 182-183, 211, 248-250, 256, 258, 269, 273, 292-296, 299, 311, 313-315, 321
Mobile Social Network 97, 114

Multicast 35, 41, 51-58, 60-61, 63, 70-71, 81, 278, 357
Multi-Hop Connection 190, 293
Multiplicative Homomorphic Encryption 245
Multiplicative Homomorphism 150-151
MYO (Myoglobin) 33

N

Nanoceria 3-4, 6-7, 33
natural language 211, 247, 250
Natural Language Processing (NLP) 211, 247
NC1 Circuits 133, 151
Network Latency 190, 272-273, 275-276, 278, 288, 293, 313
Network Load 66, 68, 81
Network Protocol 81
Network Quality of Service (NQoS) 211
Network Router 293
Network Simulator 3 (ns-3) 181
Network Switch 293
Network Throughput 211, 256, 293
NVidia CUDA (Computer-Unified Device Architecture) 340

O

Oversampling 33
Oxidative Stress 2-4, 6, 22, 33

P

PaaS (Platform as a Service) 33, 211, 270, 321
Packet Data Network Gateways (PDN-GW) 191, 211
Parallel Computing 153-157, 162, 165, 180-181
Participatory Sensing 87, 92, 101, 114
Plaintext 123-127, 143, 150-151, 220-222, 225, 227, 232, 235-237
PlanetLab 272-273, 278-280
Platform Utility 96, 98, 102-104, 114
Pretty Good Privacy (PGP) 321
Principal Component Analysis (PCA) 323, 328-329, 339, 341
Private Cloud 13, 22-23, 36, 295, 321
Protected Health Information (PHI) 145, 246, 321
Public Cloud 295, 313, 320-321
Public-Key Cryptography 245-246, 321
Public-Key Encryption 151
push-to-talk radios 36

Q

QEMU 253-254, 266, 271
QRS Complex 33
QTc (Corrected QT) Interval 34
QTc Value 16, 117, 121, 125, 146, 151, 321
QT Interval 16, 34, 120, 151, 218, 246, 320-321
Quality of Service (QoS) 15, 41, 45, 63, 72-73, 82, 190, 195, 210-211, 294, 299, 310, 312, 353-354, 357

R

Radio-WAN 344-345, 347-348, 354, 356-357
Reactive Oxygen Species (ROS) 2, 34
Real-time Communication 35, 72
Redox 3-4, 6-7, 34
Remote health monitoring 2, 11, 185
Return on Investment (ROI) 183, 211
Round-Trip Time (rtt) 274, 293
RR Interval 16, 34, 151, 218, 236, 246, 321

S

SaaS (Software as a Service) 34, 211, 271, 321
Sensing-as-a-Service (S2aaS) 83, 86, 104, 115
Sensing Scheduling 90-92, 114
Sensing Service Provider Utility 104, 114
Service Level Agreement (SLA) 194, 211, 299, 321
Single Instruction Multiple Data (SIMD) 151, 220, 246
Social Attractiveness 98, 103, 115
Spatial Channel Reuse 82
superoxide radicals 2-4, 22
Superposition Coding 58, 82
Symmetric-Key Cryptography 245-246

T

Tablet 104, 154-155, 158, 181, 184-186, 191, 236, 257, 307
Task Distribution Algorithm 181
Tegra 185, 211
Telecom Service Provider (TSP) 212
Telemetric and Holter ECG Warehouse (THEW) 152
Telephone Service Provider (TSP) 277, 293
Terrestrial-WAN 344, 347-348, 357
TFLOPS (Tera Floating Point Operations Per Second) 212
therapeutic intervention 2, 4

Tiered Pricing 212, 321
Trustworthiness 14, 83, 94, 100, 103-105, 107, 114-115

U

User Experience (γ) 212
User incentives 94, 104
Utility Computing 157, 295, 321

V

Very Large Scale Integration (VLSI) 246
Virtualization 13, 15, 87, 170, 247, 249-253, 255-256, 258-261, 263-266, 268-271, 278, 295
VM Clone 271
VM Image 13, 256-257, 259, 270-271
VM Migration 256, 266, 271
Voltammogram 4, 34
Volunteer Computing 153-158, 169-175, 181
VT-x 260-264, 268, 271

W

Wide Area Networks 15, 182, 185, 269, 354, 357
WiFi 13-15, 34, 70, 92, 119, 158, 162, 164-165, 167-168, 170, 181, 191, 194, 249, 269, 277-278, 283, 287, 344, 350, 357
Wireless Channel 82

X

x86 247, 249, 260-261, 263-266, 269-271
Xen 32, 253-254, 266, 271

Z

Zigbee 9, 12, 14-15, 22, 34, 119